Unfolding the Deuteronomistic History

Unfolding the Deuteronomistic History

ORIGINS, UPGRADES, PRESENT TEXT

ANTONY F. CAMPBELL and **MARK A. O'BRIEN**

FORTRESS PRESS   **MINNEAPOLIS**

To our religious families
the Order of Preachers
and
the Society of Jesus
with gratitude and joy

Scripture quotations are from the New Revised Standard Version Bible, copyright © 1989 by the Division of Christian Education of the National Council of the Churches of Christ in the USA and used by permission.

Cover art: *David and Saul* (glazed terra-cotta, height 74.8 cm.) by Arthur Boyd (1920–1999), courtesy of the National Gallery of Victoria, Melbourne, Australia, used by permission.

Library of Congress Cataloging-in-Publication Data
Campbell, Antony F.
    Unfolding the Deuteronomistic history : origins, upgrades, present text / Antony F. Campbell and Mark A. O'Brien.
        p. cm.
    Includes bibliographical references and index.
    ISBN 0-8006-2878-0 (alk. paper)
        1. Deuteronomistic history (Biblical criticism) I. O'Brien, Mark A. II. Title.

BS1286.5 .C36 2000
222'.077--dc21

00-041675

The paper used in this publication meets the minimum requirements of American National Standard for Information Sciences—Permanance of Paper for Printed Library Materials, ANSI Z329.48-1984.

Manufactured in the U.S.A.   AF 1-2878
    04   03   02   00   1   2   3   4   5   6   7   8   9   10

Contents

Abbreviations and Sigla

AASF B	Annales Academiae Scientiarum Fennicae, Series B
AB	Anchor Bible
AnBib	Analecta Biblica
ATANT	Abhandlungen zur Theologie des Alten und Neuen Testaments
ATD	Das Alte Testament Deutsch
AusBR	*Australian Biblical Review*
BASOR	*Bulletin of the American Schools of Oriental Research*
BBB	Bonner Biblische Beiträge
BBET	Beiträge zur biblischen Exegese und Theologie
BETL	Bibliotheca Ephemeridum Theologicarum Lovaniensium
Bib	*Biblica*
BibInt	*Biblical Interpretation*
BKAT	Biblischer Kommentar: Altes Testament
BWANT	Beiträge zur Wissenschaft vom Alten und Neuen Testament
BZAW	Beihefte zur ZAW
CBET	Contributions to Biblical Exegesis and Theology
CBQ	*Catholic Biblical Quarterly*
CBQMS	CBQ Monograph Series
ConBOT	Coniectanea biblica, Old Testament
DH	Deuteronomistic History
DH	Martin Noth, *Deuteronomistic History*
dtn	deuteronomic (association with Deuteronomy and/or the reform)
dtr	deuteronomistic (association with the DH)
the Dtr	the individual or group responsible for the composition of the Josianic DH
Dtr¹	1st ed. of the DH (Cross, et al.)
Dtr²	2nd ed. of the DH (Cross, et al.)
DtrG	the basic (exilic) Dtr History (Smend, etc.)
DtrH	Dtr History (alternate abbreviation for Smend, etc., DtrG)
dtrJer	deuteronomistic editing of Jeremiah
DtrN	"nomistic" (law-oriented) editing of DH (Smend, et al.)
DtrP	prophetic editing of DH (Smend, et al.)
E	Elohist
ErFor	Erträge der Forschung
ETL	*Ephemerides Theologicae Lovanienses*
ETS	Erfurter Theologische Studien
FOTL	Forms of Old Testament Literature
FRLANT	Forschungen zur Religion und Literatur des Alten und Neuen Testaments
HAT	Handbuch zum Alten Testament
Heb.	Hebrew Masoretic text
HKL	Hezekian King List
HSM	Harvard Semitic Monographs
HTR	*Harvard Theological Review*
HUCA	*Hebrew Union College Annual*
J	Yahwist
JBL	*Journal of Biblical Literature*
JPSV	Jewish Publication Society Version
JSOT	*Journal for the Study of the Old Testament*
JSOTSup	JSOT Supplement Series
KAT	Kommentar zum Alten Testament
LXX	Septuagint
LXX^A	Septuagint: Codex Alexandrinus
LXX^B	Septuagint: Codex Vaticanus
LXX^L	Septuagint: Lucianic recension
MDB	*Le monde de la Bible*
MT	Masoretic Text
NCB	New Century Bible
NJPSV	New Jewish Publication Society Version
NRSV	New Revised Standard Version
NT	New/Newer Testament
OBO	Orbis biblicus et orientalis
Or	*Orientalia*
OT	Old/Older Testament
OTL	Old Testament Library
OTS	Old Testament Studies
OTS	*Oudtestamentische Studiën*
PR	Prophetic Record
RB	*Revue biblique*
RSV	Revised Standard Version
SBLDS	Society of Biblical Literature Dissertation Series
SBT	Studies in Biblical Theology
SFEG	Schriften der Finnischen Exegetischen Gesellschaft
SJOT	*Scandinavian Journal of the Old Testament*
ThZ	*Theologische Zeitschrift*
VT	*Vetus Testamentum*
VTSup	VT Supplements
Vulg.	Vulgate
WBC	Word Biblical Commentary
WMANT	Wissenschaftliche Monographien zum Alten und Neuen Testament
ZAW	*Zeitschrift für die alttestamentliche Wissenschaft*

Introduction

GENERAL

Unfolding the Deuteronomistic History makes visually accessible to the interested reader the information, insights, and thinking of critical scholarship in Deuteronomy through Second Kings.

The book provides annotations to identify the **text signals** (signals embedded in the text) on which these insights are based. Most annotations include reflection on the **text-history approach** which seeks to account for these signals by development within the text and most provide reflections as to how the **present-text potential** may be exploited in all fidelity to the text to fuel imagination in its use.

Two principles have important implications for the task of analysis. First, one of those self-evident truths which Martin Noth put into words (if not always into practice): because a critical operation is possible does not make it necessary; possibility does not engender necessity.[1] Second, involving reversal of a long-standing scholarly prejudice and emerging from modern acceptance of the skill and intelligence of biblical editors: when an editorial adjustment to the text is identified, interpreters need to explain the value added by such an adjustment; additions require reasons. Alert to the evident ability of ancient editors, critical analysis will be less likely to fragment biblical text and more likely to reveal the value added in the history of the text.[2]

Our interest is not in the very beginnings of traditions but in the coherent texts that have been woven from these beginnings and that have become the source texts for the great narratives of Israel's scriptures. Many works of historical-critical scholarship were interested in such beginnings; this work is not. We can no longer continue the work of the past two centuries as if unlimited vistas of similar opportunity stretched before us—they do not. We cannot honestly return to the innocence of pre-critical study—although some seem to try. We need to continue exploring the many ways of hearing and reading the biblical text both honestly and post-critically, exercising and stretching our cultural imaginations.

---

1. A literary-critical possibility is not a literary-critical necessity. "Eine literarkritische Möglichkeit ist jedoch noch keine literarkritische Notwendigkeit" (Noth, *Könige*, 246).

2. Robert Polzin's characterization of the old approach is classic: tensions in the final text are resolved by appeal to more coherent stages "before those inept redactors got their damned hands on it" (*Samuel and the Deuteronomist*, 2).

1

The Deuteronomistic History

The biblical books of Deuteronomy through Second Kings tell a version of Israel's story from the plains of Moab on the desert fringe just across the Jordan to the exile in Babylon on the far side of the same great desert.[3] The Deuteronomistic History (DH), the story told within these books, is one of the three major narrative texts of Israel's past. Says Martin Noth: "These great compilations are the Pentateuch and the historical works of the Deuteronomist and of the Chronicler." He goes on: "the Deuteronomist's work . . . must first be 'discovered' as a literary entity and unity. . . . We must take the preliminary step of determining its contents, distributed as they are throughout a series of Old Testament 'books'."[4] It was Noth who, in 1943, first identified this work as "a literary entity and unity." He located it in the time of Israel's exile, the work of a single individual.

According to Noth, the history was probably the independent project of a man whom the historical catastrophes he witnessed had inspired with curiosity about the meaning of what had happened, and who tried to answer this question in a comprehensive and self-contained historical account, using those traditions concerning the history of his people to which he had access.[5]

The vision of Noth's work went largely unaltered for a quarter of a century. 1968 saw the beginning of a series of studies that has modified how these Israelite texts are understood.[6] Disappointment with the so-called "historical-critical" study of the Bible and a turning away from approaches found unfruitful and sterile—perhaps, too, a broader malaise—have kept these investigations from generating widespread excitement in biblical fields. Among other factors, attraction to literary approaches diverted energy away from what came to be seen as hair-splitting and verse-splitting techniques. The scholarly energy invested in these studies since 1968 is not unlike the quest for ore-bearing lode in the gold-rush days; unlike those

---

3. Those interested in the implications of "a version" may compare the final views of King Manasseh in Kings and Chronicles, as big-time sinner (cf. 2 Kgs 21:1-18) and as repentant sinner (cf. 2 Chron 33:1-20). Reconcilable? Of course. Different? Markedly.

4. Martin Noth, *The Deuteronomistic History* (henceforth, *DH*) 13, 14–15.

5. Ibid., 145. The catastrophes of World War II may not be far distant from these thoughts.

6. **1968** saw the first publication of Frank Cross's views (drawing attention to features in the text that demanded a Josianic [pre-exilic] date for the DH, with exilic modification), in "The Structure of the Deuteronomic History." **In 1971,** Rudolf Smend drew attention to secondary features in Joshua and Judges (attributed to DtrN), while maintaining an exilic date for the DH, in "Das Gesetz und die Völker." **In 1972,** Walter Dietrich focused on later contributions in 1–2 Kings emphasizing prophetic concerns (attributed to DtrP), again maintaining an exilic date for the DH, in a monograph, *Prophetie und Geschichte.* **In 1973,** Richard Nelson presented a ThD dissertation in which, originally opposing Cross, he was obliged by the evidence to endorse double redaction; later published as *The Double Redaction of the Deuteronomistic History.* **Also in 1973,** Cross's position was made available to a wider public as chap. 10, "The Themes of the Book of Kings and the Structure of the Deuteronomistic History," in *Canaanite Myth and Hebrew Epic.* **In 1975 and 1977,** Timo Veijola developed the contributions of DtrP and DtrN within 1–2 Samuel, again maintaining an exilic date for the DH, in two monographs, *Die ewige Dynastie* and *Das Königtum in der Beurteilung der deuteronomistischen Historiographie.* **In 1983,** Andrew Mayes endorsed the duality of the DH in a study, *The Story of Israel between Settlement and Exile.* **In 1989,** Mark O'Brien brought together insights from both approaches, with a pre-exilic DH from Josiah's time (Cross, et al.), and stages of later (exilic) revision (Smend, et al.), in a monograph, *The Deuteronomistic History Hypothesis.* **In 1994,** much of this was passed in review in a collective volume, *The History of Israel's Traditions: The Heritage of Martin Noth,* edited by Steven L. McKenzie and M. Patrick Graham.

days, the excitement of the old-timers has not been felt on a wider scale.

All of which is a pity, for if the outcome is more complex than the simplicity of Noth's individual thinker in the time of Israel's exile, it is certainly richer. The content canvassed is wide. On the level of the whole, there is both hope and despair; the hope engendered by the promise of reform and the despair that follows when reform is abandoned and political disaster ensues. On the level of the stages of Israel's story (or of its biblical books), there is again a wide canvas: Israel's relationship with its God (Deuteronomy); its occupation of the land (Joshua); its life before kings (Judges); the emergence and establishment of its monarchy (Samuel); and the decline and fall of that monarchy (Kings).

Multiple theological views are expressed within these ancient biblical texts themselves. They hold an ore that is rich and revealing. Deuteronomy is far from a mere lawcode and a potted history of the desert time; there is also what it means to be chosen people, a people loved and a law to be kept, the interplay of divine empowerment and human responsibility. Joshua is no simple story of conquest and allotment; above all, there is the tension between "you will fight for it, with the LORD's help" and "the LORD will fight for it on your behalf, with your help." Judges is no model time of dependence on a protective God; there is God's punishment of Israel's sin, and along with deliverance there is also deterioration. Samuel has all the complexity of the human political situation, and through it the thread traced of God's will; there are prophets for divine guidance and kings for political leadership. The books of Kings should be Israel's high point. But if they were it would be untrue to Israel's experience; fidelity to God, and all that God means, was wanting—so human failure, foreshadowed in Solomon's apostasy, gradually

became reality, first in the exile of the north, finally in the exile of the south.

In all of this, a basic text expressed hope and the promise of reform. The reform failed and experience dashed the hope; revision of the base text attributed this failure to disobedient kings, then included the people in the folly of their kings. What God would do for Israel was spelled out; so was what God required of Israel. The certainty of God's commitment was unalloyed; the impossibility of holding God to the human expression of such commitment was not shirked. The guidance given by prophets was reported; so was the uncertainty of the prophetic word and its encounter with resistance.

For Noth, an exilic date for the DH avoided the need to "ascribe certain passages" to a second dtr author.[7] Naturally, an exilic DH was unlikely to be favorable to Israel's monarchy. For Cross, a pre-exilic Josianic DH allowed for condemnation of northern Israel's behavior (the sin of Jeroboam) and for hope embodied in King Josiah (the choice by God of David and Jerusalem).[8] What *Unfolding the Deuteronomistic History* is able to do is propose a fuller understanding of the text of such a Josianic DH and present how, in the light of subsequent experience, the Josianic text was revised to bring theological theory into line with the lessons of harsh reality.

No one, least of all Noth, thought of the DH springing whole and entire into the midst of Israel's literature. Extensive texts and traditions preceded it and, in many cases, were incorporated into it. Among these, *Unfolding the Deuteronomistic History* gives particular weight to what we term the Conquest Narrative (in Joshua), the

---

7. See the nature of Noth's discussion in *DH*, 20.

8. See Cross's discussion in *Canaanite Myth and Hebrew Epic*, 278–85.

Deliverance Collection (in Judges), and the Prophetic Record (in Samuel–Kings). While some areas of text are scrutinized in close detail, for other extensive blocks this has not seemed appropriate. Where close attention to detail is relevant to the task of unfolding the DH, we have scrutinized the text. For certain other blocks of text, we have focused on the finished product rather than on the raw materials from which the text may have been fashioned.

Today's Task of Reading

Our approach to the biblical text is shown in our notes: text signals, text-history approach, and present-text potential. We seek to identify the signals we see in the text. Particular interpreters will usually see the signals that are of particular interest to them, and we are no different from anyone else in this regard. We are working in the context of unfolding the DH, its origins, its upgrades, and the present text; within our context, we have tried to be thorough and honest. We believe that it is worthwhile pointing out where signals in the text have been or, in our judgment, can be accounted for by hypotheses about the growth of the text—its history. We have discovered, far more than we might have expected from the critical approach, that there is enormous potential in what may be called the "present text" approach. For us, this stems from the conviction that editors and revisers who have worked on the canonical biblical texts have as a rule been intelligent people and that it is always rewarding to ponder the impact of their editing and revising. However, the caution remains that not all editing and revising needs to be aimed at producing a coherent text. There is a place for storage, for variants, for contrast and contradiction.

We hope never to have lost sight of the ultimate significance of text and its interpretation: the communication of meaning or emotion. In working with this sequence of signals, history, and potential, the maxim guiding our operations has been (with acknowledgments to the NRSV committee):

> as faithful as necessary,
> as meaningful as possible.

Two scholarly approaches to reading the Bible are common today. Both are legitimate and both are indeed demanded by the biblical text. Regrettably, some representatives of both approaches have been in the habit of deploring the other. This book advances both, because we believe in the legitimacy of both. The terms most commonly in use are diachronic and synchronic. They serve their purpose well, but they do not get to the heart of the matter. One reading is oriented toward the development of a text. Are there signals in a text suggesting that it has grown into full existence over time rather than been created in a single action? The other reading is oriented toward the interpretation of a text already in existence. Are there signals in the text suggesting how it is to be understood and what meaning we might make of it?

Both readings are demanded by the biblical text. Any text demands to be interpreted—to be read and understood. In the biblical texts of ancient Israel, we assume that changes have been made by editors; some are visible and some are not. We can only identify the visible ones, the ones where aspects of the language or thought have been left unsmoothed so that they jar on a reader. When this happens, two readings are demanded by the text in which it happens. One reading pays attention to what is jarring to discover how the text may have eventuated. The other reading pays attention to what has eventuated—the text that is new, that has changed, that we have as the final text—to discover how it is to be interpreted and what it means.

Development that is devoid of meaning is just that—devoid of meaning. Interpretation that inappropriately ignores development is likely to be fragile and fraudulent. To borrow an image from roadbuilding: development without interpretation is like building a road by preparing the base without adding the final layers of blacktop; and interpretation without development is like laying down blacktop without preparing a base. Nothing says that the same people have to do both jobs, but both jobs have to be done.

Critical analysis in the past all too often treated biblical editors disparagingly. Where their adjustments were felt to intrude upon the text, such adjustments were identified and dismissed.[9] An explanation of why intelligent people might have made these adjustments was not required. Perhaps what is practiced in this volume should be termed New Analysis. Respecting the intelligence and skill of those editors who have given us the biblical text in its later forms, New Analysis adds two further and highly significant stages to the process of historical-critical analysis. When later adjustments to a text have been identified, two questions need to be asked: (i) Assuming intelligent and skillful editors, what reasons can be offered for the presence of this adjustment in precisely this form? (ii) What implications are there for the meaning of the text, now that this adjustment has been made? Too many historical-critical analyses have been exercises in the possible rather than the necessary. When the New Analysis questions are asked, it may become evident that what is possible is not always necessary.

There is a watershed between the analysis of the becoming of a text on the one hand and the interpretation of the text that has become on the other. Long ago, it required insight to realize that texts needed to be compared and conjectures entertained because of possible errors in copying and transmission. It was insight that led to the surprising realization that some biblical texts might result from the combination of sources. Further insight was needed to realize the impact of literary form on the understanding of biblical text. Insight again brought us to realize that the traditions existing before a text's emergence or the editing undertaken after a text's composition often left traces that patient study could identify. The term "methods" is misleading; these are not methods but insights that may be methodically explored and may generate helpful questions. All these insights—underlying text criticism, source criticism, form criticism, tradition history, and redaction criticism—relate to the process by which the final biblical text became what it is.

The interpretation of this text is the crowning achievement that may or may not engage with these insights, but cannot dismiss the reality of what they represent. The fields of archaeology, geography, history, languages, social sciences, and many more have enormous contributions to make to our understanding of an ancient past. These contribute to the understanding of text; they are not the interpretation of text. The interpretation of that final biblical text is too complex and too significant a task to be left to preachers alone. It was von Rad who rightly said: "It would be a great mistake to regard this establishment of the meaning of a text, which is the final stage and crown of exposition, as something simple, a thing which dawns as it were automatically on the expositor's mind."[10] In many ways, von Rad's plea for a

---

9. See the comment from Polzin (above, n. 2).

10. Gerhard von Rad, *Old Testament Theology*, 2.416.

more critical approach to exposition of the text has begun to be answered in the later part of the twentieth century by bringing to bear on the biblical text a diversity of interpretative and literary theoretical approaches. The immense importance of these cannot be overlooked and is too great to be incorporated into a book of this kind. What leads up to a watershed and what leads away from it are usually interconnected, at least for literary texts; at the same time, however, they should not be confused.

For all the arrogance and insensitivity of some historical-critical analysis, "the approach drew attention to the need to take seriously the reality of the human as the context out of which the gospel grew and to which it was addressed."[11] For "gospel" read "Bible" and this aspect of historical-critical study cannot be undervalued nor can its impact be dispensed with in biblical study. This experience of the text must be repeated in each generation; otherwise experience may be replaced by dogma. Without the experience, there is the risk of superstition. The task of "unfolding" is part of the scrutiny of the human in the understanding of biblical text—whether from desire, theological need, or sheer inquisitive passion.

On occasion, historical-critical analysis pursued this scrutiny into atomistic details of the raw material from which the text was crafted. The concern of this present "unfolding" is not to reveal raw materials but to display the texts that have been produced from these materials. In industrial terms, our concern is mainly for the finished product, not the raw material. We seek the value of the product, the stages at which value has been added, and the identification of the value added at each stage.

11. Teresa Okure, "John," in *The International Bible Commentary*, 1438–1505, see p. 1457.

Apart from the importance given to insight, visual presentation, and attention to the text, four aspects of this "unfolding" are significant.

1. Concern for the present biblical text, beginning with attention to the signals in the text and ending with concern for the potential meaning of the present biblical text in the light of these signals.

2. Respect for the intelligence and skill of the biblical editors, who add value at the various stages of the text's development.

3. Acceptance of the possibility that on occasion these biblical editors used the present text as a vehicle to express or preserve other views, variant versions, and contrary or even contradictory traditions.

4. Acceptance that the text is often to be understood as reporting the gist of stories, rather than narrating their performance; the present narrative text is therefore often to be understood as a base for future storytelling. Gaps are left; not all are to be filled. The role of the storyteller is to be taken for granted.

At almost any level, reading the Bible involves three operations. First, where necessary, *making sense of the text*. It may be there are words we do not understand; it may be there is syntax that does not fit the usual rules. If so, we need to make sense of it before our reading can go very far. Second, we need to *make meaning for the text*, to make the best meaning we can today for the sake of the text out of what the text itself is saying in its time. That means our working out to the best of our ability the meaning we believe the text expressed. Third, we need to *make meaning for ourselves*, of our lives and our contexts in dialogue with the text. We need to make choices about the text: do we agree with it or disagree with it; do we dismiss it or treasure it; do we take it at face value or look to its symbolic aspect; do we modify our views to accommodate the text or do we modify the text to accommodate our views?

The Bible, of its very nature, with its richness of diversity and even contrariety, as a rule invites to thought rather than imposes it. For its adherents, aligned with this is the complementary and indispensable role of arousing feeling, firing imagination, and fueling faith.

All these processes involve choices. Choices about the sort of sense we want to make of the text. Choices about the kind of meaning we will look for in the text. Choices about the meaning we want for our lives and our contexts. Genesis 1 says we are made in the image and likeness of God; experience also says we make God in the image and likeness that we choose, whether we accept it as inheritance or shape it for ourselves. With so many choices, no wonder there are so many books.

The aim of this book is primarily to help with the first of these processes: to help make sense of the biblical text. Obviously, the task of making sense of a text flows into the challenge to get at its meaning. Only when these two processes are well advanced do we enter into serious dialogue with the text about meaning for life and context. In this volume, it would be foolish to go far beyond the making of sense into the making of meaning. The book's scope is already large; the approaches and interests of those who read the Bible are too diverse. All readers need to be alert to signals and to accept the painful reality that no reader can be aware of all the signals. What are significant signals for some will be overlooked or ignored by others. When we choose to dismiss certain signals, at best we hope to be aware of our choice. This book has been created to facilitate awareness and choice.

In the book's use, two dogmas must be abandoned or, at the very least, modified. First, the dogma that the present narrative text can be read as presenting a story's performance, the telling of the story. It is our conviction that much of the Bible's narrative text may contain reported stories, sketches of stories, summarized from stories already told and available for the telling of stories again; variants and other views can be noted in such reports. Second, the dogma that the final biblical text must always be able to be read as some form of unitary literary text. It is our conviction that the final text can sometimes function as a repository for traditions that are stored where they can be best used or best retrieved, rather than integrated into their context. Alternatively, conflicting traditions can be juxtaposed or interwoven to preserve the disagreement of past beliefs. And so on.

Texts and Institutions

When we today look at texts in the DH, the Priestly materials, and others, we may well wonder who read these texts, for whose benefit adjustments were made, and what kind of passion generated the energy for changes and revisions. We know very little of the "literary industry" of ancient Israel.[12] Churches did not exist in which sacred texts might be read. Synagogues came on the scene much too late. While festivals were ancient, much of our biblical text is quite unsuitable for proclamation or recital at a sacred festival.

Deuteronomistic and priestly texts may have served as repositories for what motivated the activities of the deuteronomistic and priestly groups. Whatever form of institutionalization gave identity and stability to these groups, their texts and the ideology that drew them or drove them were honed, refined, and regularly updated. A certain parallel can be drawn with the

---

12. See the helpful study by Susan Niditch, *Oral World and Written Word: Ancient Israelite Literature.*

electoral platforms of today's political parties. Enormous energy on the part of a few can be directed into the formulation of the platform. How that text will shape the words and deeds of those belonging to the respective parties will be controlled by factors beyond the text itself. The classic statement of this comes from one American presidential candidate: "I am not bound by the platform; in fact, I have not read it." Such a disclaimer would not have diminished the energy poured into the task of shaping the party platform. Close attention to some of the deuteronomistic, priestly, or similar editorial work suggests comparable activity and commitment may have existed in ancient Israel. Perhaps, secluded in the various groups, those revising the texts gave little attention to the wider concerns of others of their day—let alone to readers a couple of thousand years away. What mattered was that the texts reflected the present urgencies and convictions of the revisers.

The interplay between oral performance and literary text is complicated. We can consider it certain that the function of a text in ancient Israel was unequivocally not the function of a text in our modern society. We today print texts, whether on paper or computer screens, to be disseminated to as wide an audience as possible, for the purpose of being read. The ancients did not. They wrote texts by hand, probably on parchment scrolls (specially prepared skin of sheep or goat), to be preserved rather than disseminated, for the use of what we can assume was a restricted few.[13]

The settings for the composing and keeping of such texts have to be assumed; such assumptions highlight the level of our ignorance. Court, sanctuary, and temple are settings where texts would have been written and kept, especially royal and religious texts. Powerful families are another likely setting, whether priestly families (Aaronide and Zadokite) or political families (descendants of Saul, the northern dynasties, the house of Shaphan or of Hilkiah—whether in Palestine or in exile) or others.[14] We have almost no references to the activities of storytellers; they are veiled in the anonymity of the biblical tradition. Storytelling may have been fostered in prophetic circles; prophetic stories are certainly a major feature of much biblical narrative. At least one wise woman is a skilled storyteller (2 Sam 14:1-20).[15] Our assumption is that there were families or guilds of storytellers in ancient Israel.[16] It is not improbable that the heads of such families or guilds encouraged the writing of reported stories, the preserving of variant traditions, the storage of traditions, and above all the care and conservation of the scrolls and their stories, their copying and upgrading.

---

13. See Niditch, *Oral World and Written Word*; also, but necessarily brief and sketchy for Israel and largely restricted to what the OT text says about itself, Thomas E. Boomershine, "Jesus of Nazareth and the Watershed of Ancient Orality and Literacy."

14. Two articles are particularly important in this regard: Norbert Lohfink, "Gab es eine deuteronomistische Bewegung?" in *Jeremia und die "deuteronomistische Bewegung"* and Rainer Albertz, "Le Milieu des Deutéronomistes," in *Israël construit son histoire*.

When we speak of a dtr movement, we mean those concerned with the dtr reform of Josiah's time and responsible for the dtr texts associated with it. When we speak of a dtr revision, we assume that there were people responsible for articulating the theological impact of the reform's failure, who were associated with the texts produced during the dtr process of revision. More than that would go beyond our brief.

15. See also for women court singers (a term that must include storytellers) 2 Sam 19:35; Qoh 2:8; and 2 Chron 35:25.

16. See Cyrus H. Gordon, *The Common Background of Greek and Hebrew Civilizations*, 37–38.

Evaluating Our Approach

The importance of a book such as this should not be underestimated and should not be overestimated either.

Not to be underestimated. *Unfolding the Deuteronomistic History* presents a possible scenario where the literary and theological activity of Israel was a relatively continuous process in which significant literary achievement was happening in pretty much every century under the monarchy. This is a radically different picture of the origins of the Bible from that being advocated in some circles where, apart from the pre-exilic prophets, the bulk of Israel's literary and theological achievement is located around the time of exile and later. It is equally a radically different picture from that advocating that most biblical texts reported near-contemporary events.

No one should be blind to the influence of fashion or contemporary opinion on even careful scholars or observers. In the world of biblical scholarship, the Babel-Bibel strife of a past generation or the more recent examples of amphictyony and Hittite treaty models provide ample warning. Ideally, conclusions should be reached in response to the perception of the signals in the biblical text. In the realm covered by this book alone, in our judgment, the signals discussed point to limited activity in the tenth century (e.g., the Ark Narrative, the stories of David's Rise, perhaps more), to "preclassical" prophetic activity in the ninth century (i.e., the Prophetic Record), to the extension of the Prophetic Record and the beginnings of the Hezekian movement in the eighth century, to the composition of the DH in the seventh century, to be followed in the sixth century by its exilic revision and reworking. The texts of conquest and deliverance in Joshua and Judges have not been given a chronological placement here.

The pentateuchal narratives and texts, as well as the later work of the Chronicler, etc., have been left aside; they are not part of this book.

It is important to recognize that the signals emphasized here point toward a continuity of theological and literary endeavor within the kingdoms of Israel and Judah. It is equally important to test and evaluate these signals.

Not to be overestimated. When, as we have done here, the biblical text is laid out in specific formats with specific fonts and styles, every verse and every word has to be dealt with. Commentators can skip words and verses here and there. A book of this kind does not allow for that. The danger may be that a false sense of certainty will be engendered—for all the reservations and tentativeness that may be expressed in the relevant notes.

We all know that the biblical authors did not have concordances and computers.[17] They may have had marvelous memories, but they did not always choose to use them. As an example, we have only to look closely at the dtr formulation (1 Kgs 8:15-21) of Solomon's reference to God's promise to David, a promise of major significance in dtr theology (2 Sam 7:4-16). The basic promise that Solomon will build the temple is there, but otherwise the echoes are faint; the dtr name theology is repeated, but little else. Pain-

---

17. Research into the Hebrew Bible has long had the advantages of excellent concordance resources (above all, Mandelkern, Lisowsky, and Even-Shoshan). Now computer applications and tagged texts have come into the field, enabling highly focused studies. Since July 1997, we have been using Accordance 2.1 (with the Hebrew Masoretic text of 1994, based on the Michigan-Claremont-Westminster machine-readable text). The worth of such research is dependent not only on the questions asked and the evaluation of results but also, in terms of reliability, on the quality of the tagging of the Hebrew text; we have tried to steer clear of problems in this area.

staking concordance work or careful computer work reveals the extent of variety as well as the degree of focus in Israel's use of language. More than ever, we must look to the use of language in the service of ideology, and it will often be the ideology rather than the specific language that points to the origins of text. Dtr circles appear to have preached an ideology in a remarkably stereotyped range of language (using "ideology" neutrally for systems of thought and value). Priestly circles were equally concerned with ideological issues and had their own sets of language characteristics.[18] The further we move from identifiable language in the service of identifiable ideology, the further we are from certainty.[19] Clarity of layout in a book like this must not be allowed to lead to an underestimation of the uncertainty involved. Our primary task is to point to signals.

The value of a book like this does not lie in its accurate attribution of all the contributions that have built up the biblical text to its present form. *Unfolding the Deuteronomistic History* points to some of the signals in the text and indicates some ways in which these may be accounted for and the end product interpreted. But it is the overall image of how such texts came to be—how the base text arose to meet a need, how subsequent revisions shaped it to meet changed perceptions of that need, etc.—it is this overall image that

speaks to us of the nature of biblical communication and suggests how we might best make use of that communication for today's needs.

The interpretation of any text is an art. As an art, there is no definitive outcome. Sculpture did not stop with Michelangelo; figure and line were not abandoned after Matisse. We do not attempt the definitive interpretation of a text, even though some interpretations may attain a classic pre-eminence. Definitiveness evokes the categories of right and wrong. We prefer to speak in terms of adequacy and responsibility. By "adequate" we mean an interpretation that accounts for the substantial majority of the signals in the text and is not prejudicially selective. Adequate interpretation pays attention, where appropriate, to the developmental processes of a text and gives full weight to the significance of its final form. By "responsible" we mean making sense of the signals in the text without recourse to explanations that are farfetched or implausible—in the light of the canons of Israelite literature, as best understood in contemporary scholarship. Responsible interpretation is reflective and, within the context of its day, is aware of its strengths and weaknesses.

What we attempt here might once have been called *lineamenta:* offering the outline, features, and contours within which the task of interpretation may be situated and may best go about its business. We are bound by the signals in the biblical text that we must account for. There may be various ways of giving meaning to these signals. Our primary task in this book is to identify the signals as best we can and offer possibilities for interpretation. In outlining a process of development, we claim only that our interpretation of these signals is an adequate and responsible one.

---

18. This is not an issue of what deuteronomistic or priestly figures might have written; it is an issue of what we are able to identify today as theirs.

19. The combination of language and ideology is important. For example, the similarity of language between the DH and the dtr editing of Jeremiah leads Lohfink to conclude to one group, despite differences ("deuteronomistische Bewegung," 359). The difference of ideology between the two (DH and dtrJer) leads Albertz to conclude to two opposed groups, despite similarities of language ("Milieu des Deutéronomistes," 384–85).

The DH in Scholarship:
A Selective Overview

A book of this kind is not the place to situate a review of research; it is neither appropriate nor possible in terms of space and is certainly not desirable in terms of price. We have read widely and carefully, but not exhaustively. We are unwilling to adopt the practice of citing a work peripherally while avoiding discussion of its central issues. Even to make a regular practice of citing agreement or disagreement, with a modicum of discussion, was impossible within the limits of space and price. Wherever we have been indebted to the work of others or debated with such work, we have provided the appropriate references. Beyond that, it has been impossible to engage with much that we do know; it has not always been possible to seek out what we do not know. Where there is fault, we can only ask for understanding and express our regret, our sorrow, and our apology.

Two works need to be singled out. First, the series subtitled *A Literary Study of the Deuteronomic History* (so far: Parts One to Three) by Robert Polzin.[20] We disagree constantly with Polzin on points of interpretation, but we are significantly in his debt for the importance of interpreting the present text. Second, the work of A. Graeme Auld, *Kings Without Privilege*, suggesting "that independent supplementation of a common inherited text may be a better model for understanding the interrelationships of Samuel–Kings and Chronicles."[21] If accepted, the ramifications of Auld's position for the DH are extensive.

The Deuteronomistic History is a hypothesis that was formulated by Noth in 1943. As a hypothesis, it asserted that the traditions of Israel assembled in these books constituted a literary work "which brought together material from highly varied traditions and arranged it according to a carefully conceived plan."[22] The single individual responsible for creating this literary work was under the influence of the theology and the linguistic expression of the book of Deuteronomy. A deuteronomistic presence in Joshua—Kings had long been recognized. Noth's achievement was to argue convincingly that this presence was not the result of occasional editing but reflected a single literary work.

Noth based his hypothesis on four observations. (i) Seven deuteronomistic passages gave a structural organization to the literary work (i.e., Josh 1; 12; 23; Judg 2:11ff.; 1 Sam 12; 1 Kgs 8; 2 Kgs 17:7ff.). (ii) Following on this, Noth believed the divisions of the text did not coincide with the divisions into books; instead the structural divisions were marked by Joshua 23, 1 Samuel 12, and 1 Kings 8. (iii) A chronology that gives the figure of 480 years (1 Kgs 6:1) is based on texts Noth attributes to the history. (iv) The uniformity of the deuteronomistic structural sections pointed to deuteronomistic composition, in marked contrast with the diversity of the older traditions.[23]

Because of numerous references to the exile, Noth located the history's composition in the time of exile. Its message, for Noth, was simple: God was at work in the history of Israel, meeting accelerating moral decline with warning and punishment, and finally "with total annihilation."[24] For Noth, the history bore the mark of

---

20. *Moses and the Deuteronomist*, 1980; *Samuel and the Deuteronomist*, 1989; *David and the Deuteronomist*, 1993.

21. *Kings Without Privilege*, 4.

22. Noth, *DH*, 26.

23. Noth, *DH*, 17–26; see also McKenzie and Graham, *History of Israel's Traditions*; and E. Talstra, *Solomon's Prayer*, esp. pp. 22–33.

24. Noth, *DH*, 134.

"a traditional work, the intention was to be a compilation and explanation of the extant traditions" concerning the history of the people.[25]

Among the mass of studies devoted to the DH after Noth, two areas of focus stand out as particularly significant. One has challenged the unity of Noth's dtr redaction, the other the distinction he drew between dtr and non-dtr material. The challenge to unity has come from two directions. Frank Moore Cross argued that positive signals in the text, such as the promise to David in 2 Samuel 7 of an enduring dynasty and the account of King Josiah's reform in 2 Kings 22–23, point to composition before the exile, in support of Josiah's reform (c. 622). A subsequent edition in the exile completed the history down to that disastrous event.[26] In contrast, Rudolf Smend—followed subsequently by Walter Dietrich and Timo Veijola—placed the original composition in the period of the exile, and saw evidence of two subsequent dtr editors.[27] The first revised some key prophetic speeches in the original history as well as adding a number of traditional prophetic stories, the second emphasized obedience to the law.

The challenge to Noth's understanding of pre-dtr material has also come from two quite different directions. One view argues that the DH contains more conceptually shaped and theologically weighted source material than he supposed. According to Wolfgang Richter, an early "Deliverer Book" in Judges 3–9 underwent two deuteronomic redactions before reaching the hands of Dtr. Contrary to Noth, it was these deuteronomic redactions that were responsible for the theological framework around each of the stories of Israel's "deliverers."[28] More significantly, Antony Campbell has identified a pre-dtr "Prophetic Record" that reaches from 1 Samuel to 2 Kings 10.[29] The implications of Campbell's hypothesis, in particular for the pre-dtr composition of the Books of Kings, go well beyond what Noth proposed—the hypothesis will be outlined in detail below.

A contrary view, by Hans Detlef Hoffmann in Germany and John Van Seters in the USA, argues that one cannot distinguish between dtr and non-dtr material with any certainty.[30] The best that can be said is that the author drew on Israel's traditions in the composition of the history. Whatever these traditions were and whatever form they may have taken—oral or written—they are now an integral part of the whole work and no longer recoverable. In keeping with their elimination of any real distinction between source material and redaction, Hoffmann and Van Seters do not believe one can delineate different levels of dtr redaction. The DH is the work of one exilic author: in this, at least, they are in agreement with Noth.

Frustration at the inability of historical-critical scholarship to agree on the text history of the DH has prompted Robert Polzin to turn to a literary analysis of the text.[31] Polzin's starting

---

25. Noth, *DH*, 133.

26. Cross, *Canaanite Myth and Hebrew Epic*, 274–89.

27. Smend, "Das Gesetz und die Völker," 494–509; Dietrich, *Prophetie und Geschichte*; Veijola, *Ewige Dynastie* and *Königtum*.

28. Wolfgang Richter, *Traditionsgeschichtliche Untersuchungen zum Richterbuch; Die Bearbeitung des "Retterbuches" in der deuteronomischen Epoche;* "Die Überlieferungen um Jephtah. Ri 10, 17–12, 6."

29. Antony F. Campbell, *Of Prophets and Kings*.

30. Hans-Detlef Hoffmann, *Reform und Reformen* and John Van Seters, *In Search of History*. Also "Histories and Historians of the Ancient Near East: The Israelites." Van Seters's approach has been followed by Burke O. Long in his recent commentary on 1 Kings (*1 Kings with an Introduction to Historical Literature*, 14–22).

31. "Not the least embarrassment for historical scholarship is the lack of agreement, after so prolonged an investi-

point is the assumption that the text of Deuteronomy—2 Kings is a unified literary work which he calls "the Deuteronomic History." He employs the term *author* "heuristically to designate that imagined personification of a combination of literary features that seem to constitute the literary composition of the Deuteronomic History."[32] Whether the author was historically one or many is, for Polzin, a question that can only be asked once a close reading of the present text has been undertaken.

Polzin insists that a close reading of the present text must precede any historical-critical analysis. His synchronic reading is at times insightful and helps to drive home the lesson that reading must always begin with and return to the present text. Unfortunately, his reading is not followed by the further refinement of historical analysis, despite his acknowledgment that a literary approach is "operationally prior" and that subsequent historical analysis is necessary "for an adequate understanding."[33] What is "operationally prior" becomes the only operation that Polzin performs and, in the end, it does not do justice to the text.

The understanding of the DH presented here owes a considerable debt to those who have explored the DH hypothesis since Noth's original formulation of it. This is to be expected: we build on the work of those who precede us. We agree with Cross that the first edition of the DH was pre-exilic, culminating in the hope presented by Josiah's reform. However, our analysis goes well beyond Cross's essay-length study, offering a much fuller analysis of the text of the Josianic history, its conceptual plan, and its

structure. While disagreeing with an exilic origin for the history (e.g., Noth and Smend–Dietrich–Veijola), we acknowledge that it was revised during the exilic period.

COMPONENTS

The Present Text and Revised DH

Plenty of minor comments and some major chapters have not been considered part of the DH. They show no characteristics of dtr origin, neither in language or thought; they do not appear to have contributed to the schema identified within the DH. By and large, the major chapters are: Deuteronomy 32 and 33 (the song of Moses and the blessing of Moses); most of Joshua 13–22 and 24; Judges 1, probably 13–16, and most likely 17–21; 2 Samuel 21–24; 1 Kings 20 and most of 22. Whether or not these are regarded by some as part of the DH is not important; what matters is that they do not contribute in the present text to a clarification and identification of what is dtr contribution and dtr theology.

Three options are open to us in reading the DH as present text, prescinding from issues of sources and revisions.

1. Is the present text we are dealing with a revised document—i.e., in this case, an exilic revision of a pre-exilic document?
2. Is the present text we are dealing with an original document—i.e., in this case, an exilic composition (prescinding from subsequent revisions)?
3. Is the present text we are dealing with a document to be read and interpreted, prescinding altogether from whether it is an original or a revised document?

All three options have their advocates in scholarship; all three can be present-text readings.

---

gation, on the basic thematic thrust of the supposed Deuteronomistic History" (*Moses and the Deuteronomist*, 15).

32. Ibid., 18.

33. Ibid., 23.

In our judgment, the text we have is a revision of an earlier document. What signals in the text draw us in this direction? First and foremost, there is the sense that pre-exilic optimism predominates and that exilic pessimism is an add-on rather than being integral to the core of the document.

Optimism is present in Deuteronomy. Of course, Israel must choose between life and death (Deut 30:15-20), but life is within easy reach (Deut 30:11-14). In the book of Joshua, Israel has the whole land, as God had said to Moses (Josh 11:23); nothing failed them of God's good promises (Josh 21:45). In Judges, even when confronted with a deteriorating situation, Israel proclaimed faith in God's power to raise up a deliverer (Judg 3:9, 15; 4:6-7; 6:14). In the books of Samuel, "a trustworthy prophet of the Lord" emerges (1 Sam 3:19) and is instructed by God to anoint Saul as king of Israel (1 Sam 9:1—10:16), later to reject him, and finally to anoint David as future king, a man after God's own heart (1 Sam 13:14). After Samuel, another prophet, Nathan, brings the word of the Lord to David: his house and his kingdom will be made sure forever (2 Sam 7:16). In the books of Kings, there are critical assurances, particularly associated with the division of the kingdom into north and south, of God's unshakable commitment to Jerusalem, the temple, and the Davidic dynasty (for example, 1 Kgs 11:34-36).

There are two areas of shadow. First, the time of the Judges, even at its best, is a period of repeated evil on Israel's part and of general deterioration despite divine deliverance. The remedy is provided by God's gift of kingship, mediated by Samuel. Second, the kings of the north are all judged to have done what was evil in the sight of God; but this is balanced by a majority of southern kings (Davidic dynasty) who are judged to have done what was right in the sight of God.

Israel is called by Moses to obedience, is guided by God or God's prophets, and under King Josiah undertakes a significant reform in obedience to God's word. Despite Israel's fragility under the judges, despite Solomon's apostasy and God's division of the kingdom into north and south, the example of Hezekiah and the promise of Deuteronomy point optimistically to a successful outcome in Josiah's reform. Josiah's unexpected death in battle put an end to all such optimism.

The present text of the DH contains warnings and threats. These can be read as placing Israel constantly before the choice between life and death, between obedience and loyalty on the one hand and disobedience and disloyalty on the other. In one such understanding, God can be seen recognizably at work, "continuously meeting the accelerating moral decline with warnings and punishments and, finally, when these proved fruitless, with total annihilation."[34]

When we subject the text to close scrutiny, it is this "constantly" and "continuously" that breaks down. The warnings and threats do not seem to be integrated into the composition but inserted later at discrete critical points. They read as strategically placed afterthoughts (= revision) rather than integral parts of the composition.

In Deuteronomy, the exhortation to observance of the law (Deut 4:1-40), the warning against apostasy (Deut 29:1-29), and the assurance of hope after the catastrophe of exile (Deut 30:1-10) are clustered outside the core of the book; they are not integral to that core. Of course, a case can be made for a different reading of Deuteronomy. But the uneasiness is there;

---

34. Noth, *DH*, 134.

instinct says revision. In Joshua, there is a sudden shift from the courage needed for conquest to the courage needed for obedience (Josh 1:7-9) and a final discourse from Joshua in similar language, concluding with the explicit threat of exile (Josh 23:1-16, cf. vv. 13, 15-16). In Judges, the faith-shattering doubt is raised whether God's patience is unlimited: "Go and cry to the gods whom you have chosen; let them deliver you in the time of your distress" (Judg 10:10-16, cf. v. 14). In Samuel, a whole new strand of tradition is introduced in which kingship, rather than coming from God's initiative and God's gracious gift, is grudgingly conceded by God in response to the people's demand. It is even depicted as outright rejection of God (1 Sam 8:7-8; 10:18-19). A case can be made—and has been made well—for reading these texts as the balanced portrayal of two differing traditions, reconciled in 1 Samuel 12. But the uneasiness is there; instinct says revision—especially when the idiosyncrasy of 1 Samuel 12 is evaluated. In the books of Kings, there is explicit warning and threat associated with Solomon's apostasy, there is negativity toward Jeroboam's establishment of religion in northern Israel, and there is the long reflection on the fate of the north (2 Kgs 17:7-20, "this occurred because"), which was ultimately to be the fate of Judah. Judah's fate is attributed to the overwhelming influence of Manasseh's sin (2 Kgs 21:1-16; 23:26-27).

"Constantly" and "continuously" are not the adverbs we would choose to describe the place of warning and threat in these texts. Rather, to us they read as strategically situated revisions, coming to terms with an outcome for which the text was unprepared.

This impression is confirmed by assessment of four great pillar passages of the DH: the speeches of Joshua (Josh 23:1-16) and Samuel (1 Sam 12:1-25), the prayer of Solomon (1 Kgs 8:31-53), and the narrative reflection (2 Kgs 17:7-20). None of these fit whole cloth with the DH. The details will have to be left to the body of the book; the instinct that reads these as revisions appended to an earlier document is strengthened.

Close attention to the text confirms this impression in three ways. First, there are texts that could not have originated in an exilic edition. Second, there are texts that in a pre-exilic edition would have closed off options that needed to be kept open. Third, there are texts expressing contrasting views, intelligible as pre-exilic and exilic, but almost irreconcilable otherwise.

As to the first, divine commitment to the temple, the Davidic dynasty, and the city of Jerusalem is clearly expressed and never countermanded. A conditional formulation is given to the dynastic commitment; however questionable such retrospective theology may be, the condition is not applied to temple or city.

The commitment to the temple is clearest following its completion.

> I have put my name there **forever** (1 Kgs 9:3a).
>
> My eyes and my heart will be there **for all time** (1 Kgs 9:3b).

The dynastic commitment has a dynamic all its own. As it is made to Solomon, it is strongly affirmative, but conditional: "I will establish your royal throne over Israel **forever**" (1 Kgs 9:5). The condition is stated in the preceding verse (v. 4) and addressed to Solomon (2nd pers. sing.). The commitment to David is quoted (9:5b) without any mention of a condition. 2 Samuel 7:16 is free of any condition: "Your house and your kingdom shall be made sure **forever** before me; your throne shall be established **forever**." However, the explicitly unconditional emphasis is restricted to Solomon (7:14-15). In the lead-up to the temple consecration, this commitment is twice referred to and twice made conditional for the entire Davidic dynasty (1 Kgs 2:4 and 8:25). The movement across these texts is important: commitment to David's kingdom and throne (2 Sam 7:16); explicitly unconditional for Solomon (2 Sam 7:14-15); conditional for Solomon only (1 Kgs 9:4-5); conditional for the entire Davidic dynasty (1 Kgs 2:4 and 8:25). The last two, at least, would be injurious to God if present unnuanced in a pre-exilic document.

The commitment to the city uses the metaphor of "lamp" (= dominion) and is made in association with David: "that my servant David may **always** have a lamp before me in Jerusalem, the city where I have chosen to put my name" (1 Kgs 11:36). This commitment is reiterated twice more (1 Kgs 15:4, despite Abijam's infidelity; and 2 Kgs 8:19, despite Jehoram's infidelity). Such a commitment first given expression in an exilic document would demean God.

To wrap up what would have seemed intolerable as exilic, it is worth remembering that according to the tenor of the dtr law, obedience to God meant life and length of days (cf. Deut 30:20). Equally, according to Deuteronomy, this obedience was within Israel's reach (Deut 30:11-14). David did it. Hezekiah did it. Josiah did it. According to the text, Josiah's generation did it (2 Kgs 23:3). Such fidelity from significant figures and such commitment from God are hardly to be met with exile and annihilation.

As to the second, texts that speak unequivocally of the fact of exile close off the option of choice between life and death offered by Moses in Deut 30:15-20. Such texts are difficult to imagine in a pre-exilic document. All too early in the DH, the text goes beyond the merely conditional. Deuteronomy 4:25-28 depends on the condition in v. 25. For v. 30, the failure to fulfill the condition is taken for granted: "In your dis-

tress, when all these things have happened to you in time to come, you will return to the LORD your God" (Deut 4:30). The reassertion of this in Deut 30:1-5 is scarcely a prophecy; it speaks of a situation beyond the condition, where the condition has not been met, where the choice has been closed off. "When all these things have happened to you, . . . then the LORD your God will restore your fortunes . . . from there the LORD your God . . . will bring you back" (30:1-4). According to Deut 31:16-18, these things will begin happening once Moses is dead. Israel's options are indeed closed off.

Joshua's warnings in chap. 23 can appear to be entirely conditional. Closer inspection suggests that the utterance is rather more certain. What is said explicitly in v. 15 echoes what is present throughout the discourse: the good that God promised has been fulfilled; apart from vv. 5 and 10, there is scant mention of good for the future. The good is claimed from the past; the action claimed for the future is not good. For example: "until he has destroyed you from this good land" (23:15). V. 16 appears conditional: "if you transgress" (NRSV). When compared with the condition in v. 12 ("For if you turn back"), the different formulation in v. 16 becomes evident; a temporal understanding is more appropriate than a conditional one (cf. JPSV, "When ye transgress.").[35] A pre-exilic writer might have been more sensitive.

As to the third, texts expressing contrasting views, several areas demand consideration. For all of the exegetical endeavor to diminish it, the

---

35. Of course, a conditional understanding is possible, but it is not necessary. Nelson refers to the example of 2 Sam 7:14 as a "conditional sentence" (*Joshua*, 255); 2 Sam 7:14, having been written after Solomon's sin, may well be understood as temporal rather than conditional: "when he commits iniquity," cf. NRSV.

tension between 1 Sam 9:1—10:16 and 1 Sam 7:5—8:22 is palpable. It is relatively intelligible if spread over pre-exilic and exilic documents; it is not so intelligible if claimed for a single document.[36] Without laboring detail, Samuel has delivered Israel from the Philistines (7:13) before YHWH commissions Saul to do so (9:16). God collaborates with Samuel to respond to an initiative of Israel's elders asking for a king because of Samuel's sons, a request that meets with Samuel's disapproval and is twice categorized as the rejection of God (cf. 8:1-22 and 10:17-25; esp. 8:7-8 and 10:19). On the other hand, God takes the initiative of bringing Saul to Samuel for anointing as king-designate (cf. 9:1—10:16; esp. 9:15-16). Even the views about the king are left miles apart. In 8:11-17, the king is a source of suffering, through taxes and similar domestic demands; in 9:16, the king is to deliver from the suffering of Philistine oppression. Not necessarily conflicting in theory; not brought into harmony in the present text. The purported harmonization in 1 Samuel 12 deals with a different situation in which Nahash is a threat and not a defeated enemy (1 Samuel 11).

At the other end of the story, in the account of Josiah's reform, the portrayal of Josiah's generation is deeply conflictual. According to the narrative, "all the people joined in the covenant" (2 Kgs 23:3). According to the prophecy attributed to Huldah, the people were unregenerate apostates, doomed to destruction (22:16-17). Pre-exilic optimism and exilic pessimism could account for such different stances; otherwise they are hard to reconcile.

---

36. Cf. Noth, "Therefore it was not without obvious effort and contrivance that Dtr. supplemented the old account which dealt favorably with the institution of the monarchy by adding long passages reflecting his disapproval of the institution" (*DH*, 83).

In the middle of the story, with Solomon's temple built and consecrated, God's undying commitment is expressed (as we have noted) in immediate proximity to threats of direst destruction (1 Kgs 9:1-9). The former is addressed to Solomon (sing.); the latter to the people (plur.). The former is rich in hope; the latter are close to despair.

Weighing the evidence discussed, we are led to see Deuteronomy through Second Kings as a revised document rather than an original one. Before seeking to identify what was revised, it is desirable to analyze what the revision has achieved, i.e., the shape of the present document.

THE TEXT FROM DEUTERONOMY TO SECOND KINGS

As it stands, the book of Deuteronomy bears ominous overtones. Deuteronomy 4 warns and threatens; the warnings and threats grow worse in Deuteronomy 29–31. Promises of restoration after exile are cold comfort; the exile comes first.

The book of Joshua opens the story of Israel's life in the land. It stands under the instruction given by Moses, itself overshadowed by an emphasis on foreboding and ultimate failure (cf. Deut 31:16-29). The book paints a picture of glowing if brutal success, but ends on an equally ominous note. In the book of Judges, without Joshua's leadership, Israel lapses regularly into apostasy, with concomitant oppression. The deliverer-judges get Israel out of trouble; there is no institutional leadership to keep Israel out of trouble after a deliverer-judge dies. Overall, the situation is portrayed as deteriorating.

The need for stable leadership is evident. The departure of the ark from mainstream Israel makes it urgent. As a first move, the prophet Samuel is approached; his sons have proved unsatisfactory. A king is granted, but not without warnings and threats. In between times, a king has been designated on God's instructions, but the outcome of both procedures is Saul, a tragic and twice-rejected figure. Samuel's discourse of reconciliation portrays Israel as distrustful rather than deserving, points to the possibilities for life, but ends on a note of foreboding.

With the rejection of Saul, the narrative comes to David. David's ascendancy over Israel is secured politically with the capture of Jerusalem and religiously with the coming of the ark there. Despite appalling failures in his personal life, David never abandons either Jerusalem or YHWH. In the terms of 1 Samuel 12, this constitutes obedience and loyalty. Solomon, once his way to the throne had been finagled, is portrayed in similarly successful terms. With the consecration of the temple and the expression of God's commitment, a highpoint is reached in the presentation of Israel's story.

Warning followed the coronation of the king; warning followed the consecration of the temple. Old age found Solomon an active apostate. The nation was divided; loyalties were divided; obedience was lost. Despite God's mandate by Ahijah, the start of the northern kingdom is portrayed pejoratively (esp. 1 Kgs 12:30-33). Responsibility for the end of the northern kingdom is placed directly on the shoulders of the people (2 Kgs 17:7-20). The reign of Manasseh leaves no hope for Jerusalem (2 Kgs 21:12-15; 23:26-27). Even Josiah, the reforming king par excellence, is only rewarded with the clemency of a premature death (22:18-20). The last of David's descendants is released into ambivalence: is there hope or has David's line, like Saul's, reached its end?

Something of this can be caught in the following structure analysis, prescinding from all sorts of detail.

STRUCTURE ANALYSIS

The Revision of the Deuteronomistic History	Deuteronomy—2 Kings
I. Instruction to Israel by Moses	Deuteronomy 1–34
A. Retrospect and prospect (exhortation & warning)	Deut 1–3 and 4
B. Instruction (with introduction & conclusion)	Deut 5–28 + 30:11-20
C. Foreboding: consequences of infidelity	Deut 29–34
II. Story of Israel's life in the land	Joshua—Kings
A. Land occupied	Joshua 1–24
1. Conquest: under Joshua	Josh 1–12
(2. Allocation: under Eleazar, Joshua, and heads	Josh 13–22)
3. Foreboding: consequences of infidelity	Josh 23–(24)
B. Land secured	Judges 1—1 Kings 8
1. Life threatened	Judg 1–12; 13–16; 17–21
(a. Initial failure [disloyalty]	Judg 1:1–2:5)
b. Story of disloyalty and deliverance	Judg 2–12 (13–16)
(c. Final anarchy	Judg 17–21)

2. Life offered	1 Sam 1—2 Sam 5
a. Emergence of prophet at Shiloh	1 Sam 1–3
b. Retreat of ark from Shiloh	1 Sam 4–6
c. Ambivalence of kingship: with warning	1 Sam 7–11 and 12
d. Failure of Saul: disloyalty	1 Sam 13–15
e. Success of David: loyalty	1 Sam 16—2 Sam 5
3. Life secured	2 Sam 6—1 Kgs 11
a. David: ark and kingdom	2 Sam 6–20 (21–24)
b. Solomon: kingdom and temple	1 Kgs 1–8
c. Foreboding: warning and apostasy	1 Kgs 9–11
C. Land lost	1 Kgs 12—2 Kgs 25
1. Division	1 Kgs 12
2. North: **exile—722**	1 Kgs 13—2 Kgs 17
3. South: **exile—587**	1 Kgs 14—2 Kgs 25

COMPONENTS OF THE
DEUTERONOMISTIC HISTORY REVISION

With Josiah's death and the fact that the reform died with him, the process of revision had to be undertaken. An extension was needed to carry the DH down to the sorry end of ancient Israel's independent nationhood. The four kings involved were all of Josiah's family (three sons and a grandson); for whatever reasons—military, political, theological—none of them seems to have embraced his reform. For this extension, see Pattern D among the Tables.

We have no information about the revision of the DH, whether it was done in distinct stages or as a single process over a period of time, etc. What is evident, however, is the existence of text that counters the optimism of the Josianic DH with a pessimism that anticipates the final outcome. Within this negative material, two focuses can be identified. One traces the failure to the very nature of the monarchy; the other places an emphasis on the responsibility of the people, who went along with their kings, and emphasizes also the God-given laws that king and people were to observe. In certain passages (1 Samuel 8 and 2 Kings 21), it can be seen that there was at least a logical sequence in these views with the "royal" aspect focusing on the failure of the monarchy being first.

This ("royal") focus of dtr revision attributed the failure of the reform to the institution of kingship in Israel. The revision was narrow in its extent; radical in its claim. It is found in 1 Samuel and in 1–2 Kings. Its claim is radical and simple: the monarchy in Israel was grudgingly given by God in response to the people's demand. To express this claim, this aspect of the revision draws on Samuel traditions that had not been used for the Josianic DH (cf. within 1 Samuel 7–10). The origin of the monarchy in Israel is presented as a demand from the people, faced with the injustice of Samuel's sons. Those responsible for this "royal" focus expanded the traditional material to introduce a warning against kingship and to spell out something of its burdensome implications. Warned, Israel insists.

The revision draws on a tradition of Saul's selection which relied on the lot and an oracle rather than the direct action of God's prophet. To this tradition is appended a statement of Samuel's having written up the "rights and duties" of the kingship. The upshot of this aspect of editorial revision was to bring to the fore an alternative view of the establishment of the monarchy in ancient Israel, a view in which the people demanded a king, were warned of the consequences, and persisted in their demand. The way was open to relieve God of the responsibility of having passed Israel a poisoned chalice.

There was no need for a revision of David's kingship. The revision that sought to emphasize the responsibility of kings pointed particularly to the shortcomings of Solomon and Jeroboam, of Baasha and Elah, and of course of Ahab; a number of similar points were highlighted in 2 Kings. Instead of an institution set up and guided by God's prophets, this "royal" focus of the dtr revision offered an understanding of the monarchy that was rooted in human failure (Samuel's sons) and in human willfulness (the popular demand). Far from the desired support for the reform, the kingship is consistently cast in a negative light; so failure is hardly surprising. The shadow side of the kingship is brought to the fore.

A further ("national") focus of the dtr revision is far more wide-ranging and is found throughout the DH.[37] This focus is recognizable from two characteristics: first, the responsibility is shared by the people (beyond their demand); second, emphasis is placed on the importance of observing God's law. In its own way, it is a far more radical rethinking of the DH than was involved in the royal focus. It is not a matter of blaming an institution but of sharing this blame with the people. Worse than that, it is the failure to observe the laws promulgated by Moses in Deuteronomy that brought about Israel's failure. Those laws were enjoined on the people; kings were not yet on the scene. The people, and their kings, failed to observe the laws Moses promulgated. Failure was inevitable. This failure is not merely that of an institution and a series of individuals. This is Israel's failure to play its part in the project elaborated by God and promulgated by Moses.

The Josianic Deuteronomistic History

The Josianic DH begins with Moses' address to the people of Israel, presenting to them the law by which they are to live in the promised land. It is the presentation to the people, of God's law, by Moses, the most significant leader figure and lawgiver in Israel's history. But Moses cannot lead Israel into its land; in the DH, a sin of the people has rendered that impossible (Deut 1:37). Joshua led the people into the land, according to the DH, successfully. The continuity of leadership from Moses to Joshua is emphasized by the Dtr at three points: Josh 1:5; 3:7; 4:14 (cf. also Josh 6:27; 11:23).

With Joshua's death, the leadership set up by Moses under God's command was at an end. In the DH, a new period ensues in which God raises up deliverers for a constantly failing people—but not before God had first raised up punishing oppressors. As this deliverance diminishes, the discord in Israel grows. It is not a happy picture. The DH brings a prophet on the scene, Samuel. Under divine command, Samuel

---

37. This national focus understood the deep rightness of Barbara Tuchman's observation: "The *Grosse Politik* approach has been used up. Besides, it is misleading because it allows us to rest on the easy allusion [sic] that it is 'they,' the naughty statesmen, who are always responsible for war while 'we,' the innocent people, are merely led. That impression is a mistake" (*The Proud Tower*, xiv).

anoints Saul and oversees his establishment as Israel's king. Equally under divine command, Samuel dismisses Saul and anoints David. David delivers Israel from the Philistine threat and establishes an enduring kingdom in Israel.

With these moves, a new style of leadership has been introduced by the DH into Israel. A king is established on the throne of Israel by the action of God's prophets; the same prophets claim the right to dismiss such a king for disobedience to God. The prophetic claim is not made for every king; it is made often enough to be critical. Interestingly, the prophetic interventions against kings (Ahijah, Jehu ben Hanani, Elijah, Elisha) are all restricted to the northern kingdom. Samuel anointed David; Nathan confirmed his dynasty. Within the DH, the next prophetic interventions for the southern kings are Isaiah with Hezekiah and Huldah with Josiah. The exception here may be Solomon; he is not addressed by Ahijah, but the prophetic gift of the northern kingdom to Jeroboam involves tearing the kingdom "from the hand of Solomon" (1 Kgs 11:31b)—the accusation of apostasy is not made by the prophet. Before we move to survey these kings, it will help to see the outcome. The Josianic DH culminates in Josiah's reform, following a consultation with the prophetess Huldah. For the Josianic DH, Josiah's reign and reform was to be the climactic moment in Israel's existence. Alas, the DH was wrong. Josiah died in battle, unexpectedly; the reform died with him.

To return to the kings of Israel: Solomon succeeded David; no prophet intervened—Nathan's role was that of courtier. A prophet spoke of the kingdom having been torn from Solomon's power and given to another, Jeroboam (so Ahijah of Shiloh, within vv. 26-40 of 1 Kings 11). The same Ahijah denounced Jeroboam (within vv. 7-16 of 1 Kings 14). No prophet had any role in the

bloody struggles for power that dominated the northern kingdom of Israel after Jeroboam's dynasty.[38] It was a prophet, Elijah, who denounced Ahab for his apostasies and injustice. It was another prophet, Elisha, whose authorization was claimed for the murderous coup by Jehu that wiped out the house of Ahab and the apostasy of Baal worship. As presented by the DH, the role of prophet and king in the leadership of Israel is evident in all of this.

In the Josianic DH, three kings pass unqualified muster to be judged as doing "what was right" in the eyes of God: David, Hezekiah, and Josiah. Two criteria appear to have constituted the test: worship in Jerusalem (the law of centralization) and fidelity to YHWH, God of Israel. The first criterion ruled out all the northern kings; the second ruled out many of the southern ones. The continuation of worship at the high places was a blemish on the record of six southern kings who otherwise were judged to have done what was right.

Within the Josianic DH, it is instructive to observe the interaction of prophet and king in the case of the three good kings, David, Hezekiah, and Josiah. David planned to build the temple in Jerusalem, consulted the prophet Nathan, was rewarded with the promise of a secure dynasty, and was successful in his rule (cf. 2 Samuel 7–8). Hezekiah faced the loss of Jerusalem from Assyrian siege, consulted Isaiah, was rewarded with a favorable prophecy, and Jerusalem was saved (cf. 2 Kings 18–19). Finally, Josiah is portrayed encountering a word from God radically reversing royal policies, consults

---

38. King Baasha is reported to have destroyed the house of Jeroboam (1 Kgs 15:29). While subsequently he is spoken of as exalted out of the dust and made leader over Israel (16:2), beyond this, there is no report in the text of any prophetic designation or authorization.

the prophetess Huldah, and implements the reform.

There can be little doubt that the Josianic DH set its sights on this reform—implementing the laws of Deuteronomy for centralization of worship and the observance of Passover—saw the hand of the prophets guiding Israel's kings in the achievement of Israel's destiny, and expected great things of Josiah: "before him there was no king like him, who turned to the LORD with all his heart, with all his soul, and with all his might, according to all the law of Moses" (2 Kgs 23:25a). Alas, the Josianic DH was mistaken. The reform failed.

Josiah's reaction to "the book of the law," found in the house of the LORD, and the report of the consequent reform and Passover, would need to have been narrated after it had happened, and—in the hypothesis of a Josianic DH—before the shattering event of Josiah's death. Whatever the uncertainties for dating the elements of Josiah's reform, there would have been ample opportunity for compiling the DH's account of the reform (i.e., a decade or so between 622 and 609). It is unlikely Josiah attacked Pharaoh Neco at Megiddo without an army, although there is no reference to it in the text of Kings or Chronicles.[39] The core of 2 Kings 22–23 would have served well as the base for an ideological rallying point in motivating Judah's army.

In its own way, the DH adumbrates what is articulated in the book of Job. Ours is not a world of divine order where right is rewarded and wrong punished. Ours is a world of disorder where expectations and predictions are possible only within a limited sphere—and where good kings get killed.[40] Both the reality of Josiah's death in the DH and the fiction of the book of Job run uncomfortably counter to what has been called "one of the deepest instincts in the civilised mind: the need to establish a principle of causality in human experience."[41]

A structural analysis will again be helpful to outline the fundamental interrelationships of the text. It must be understood as reflecting the Josianic text, again prescinding from all sorts of detail.

---

39. This assumes that Chronicles is right to speak of a military attack (2 Chron 35:20-27); despite Chronicles, the possibility of a diplomatic mission cannot be excluded (cf. 2 Kgs 9:21-28).

40. For readers of the present biblical text, there is a peculiarly cruel irony: Ahab, king of Israel (notorious evildoer) and Josiah, king of Judah (notable reformer) both suffer the same fate: death in battle. According to Chronicles, Josiah disguised himself and nevertheless was shot by Egyptian archers (2 Chron 35:22–23). According to Kings, Ahab disguised himself and nevertheless was shot by a Syrian archer (1 Kgs 22:30-34). Good and bad die alike.

41. Lawrence Langer (*Versions of Survival*, 1982, p. ix) quoted from I. Clendinnen, *Reading the Holocaust*, 45.

STRUCTURE ANALYSIS

The Josianic Deuteronomistic History	Deuteronomy—2 Kings
I. Story of Israel under Moses and Joshua	Deuteronomy 1—Joshua 24
A. Instruction: from Moses	Deut 1–34
B. Occupation: with Joshua	Josh 1–12 and 21:43-45
II. Transition	Joshua 24:29—2 Samuel 5:25
A. Of generations	Josh 24:29-31 and Judg 2:10
B. Of institutions	Judg 2:11—2 Sam 5:25
1. Deliverer-judges: failure	Judg 2:11–13:1
2. Prophets and kings: hope	1 Sam 1:1–16:13
a. Emergence of prophet at Shiloh	1 Sam 1–3
b. Retreat of ark from Shiloh	1 Sam 4–6
c. Coronation of Saul	1 Sam 9–11
d. Rejection of Saul	1 Sam 13–15
e. Designation of David	1 Sam 16:1-13
3. David: success	1 Sam 16:14—2 Sam 5:25
III. Story of Israel under prophets and kings	2 Samuel 6—2 Kings 23
A. Unity: under David and Solomon	2 Sam 6—1 Kgs 8
1. Ark	2 Sam 6
2. Nathan	2 Sam 7
3. Temple	1 Kgs 5–8
B. Disunity	1 Kgs 9—2 Kgs 20
1. Apostasy: Solomon	1 Kgs 9–11
2. Divided kingdom	1 Kgs 12—2 Kgs 20
a. North: to **exile—722** B.C.E.	1 Kgs 12—2 Kgs 17
b. South: to Hezekiah—deliverance	2 Kgs 18–20
C. Reform	2 Kgs 21–23
1. Return to apostasy: Manasseh and Amon	2 Kgs 21
2. **Reform: Josiah—622** B.C.E.	2 Kgs 22–23

CONQUEST NARRATIVE
(PRE-DTR IN THE BOOK OF JOSHUA)

It is well known that Joshua sent spies across the Jordan to search out the land and that a tradition may well have existed in Israel involving military activity in the conquest of Canaan.

Three stories have dominated the understanding of the early part of the book of Joshua in the sacral quality of their power and the attraction exercised on readers or hearers. They are the crossing of the Jordan, the capture of Jericho, and Achan's breach of the ban that led to Israel's defeat before Ai. Trace elements of military presence have been known in the Jordan-crossing narrative, but the all-pervasive emphasis is sacral and liturgical. The king and soldiers of Jericho are mentioned in 6:2 and later (8:2; 10:1), but not again in the story of a great walled city overwhelmed by a shout. Finally, an apparently easy attack on the town of Ai is transformed into shameful defeat by the ritual breach of a single individual.

Beyond these stories, Ai is captured, a deal is struck with Gibeon, and a Jerusalem-based coalition is overcome.

The Conquest Narrative reflects the coherence and continuity of traditions from Joshua 2 to Joshua 10, treating the three sacral stories (Jordan, Jericho, and Achan) as expansions, offering a more God-centered understanding of the conquest of Canaan. In Joshua 11–12, further traditions with this same God-centered understanding extend the conquest to the north and list the conquered kings. The Conquest Narrative itself is set in roman; the expansion is set in italic. Later material, including the fascination with utter destruction, is given a double sideline, indicating its insertion into the text after the completion of the Josianic DH.

No time or setting is suggested for the Conquest Narrative, although a base at Gilgal is prominent.

DELIVERANCE COLLECTION
(PRE-DTR IN THE BOOK OF JUDGES)
The Deliverance Collection is the name we give to three stories of Israel's deliverance by the figures known as deliverer-judges: Ehud, Deborah and Barak, and Gideon.

The three traditional blocks of material vary considerably, from the almost secular portrayal of Ehud's coup to the highly sacral traditions associated with Gideon. The reference to these as a "collection" is justified by the patterned framing elements within which all three are situated.[42] The stories themselves are set in roman

and the framing elements in italic. On rare occasion, framing elements are essential to the story (e.g., Ehud's identification in 3:15); therefore, the terminology of "framing elements" rather than "frame" is used. Richter pointed to a shift in theology from the framing elements of the stories, to the bare account of Othniel (3:7-11), and the initial preface attributed to the Dtr. These moves raise questions for the reader's approach to the text. Even more, they give insight into Israel's distilling of theology from its experience. The combination of effective means and faith-claimed divine action is remarkable.

It is Noth's claim that the stories of the deliverer-judges were associated with the figures of the minor judges by the Dtr, mediated by the presence of Jephthah in both categories.

THE PROPHETIC RECORD
(PRE-DTR IN THE BOOKS OF SAMUEL AND KINGS)
In Noth's view, as we have already seen, the Dtr was "not merely an editor but the author of a history which brought together material from highly varied traditions and arranged it according to a carefully conceived plan."[43] However, "of the approximately 156 chapters in Noth's Deuteronomistic History, he attributed more than two-thirds to prefabricated sources. No wonder that Noth comments: 'In general, then, Dtr. gave his narrative very markedly the character of a traditional work, the intention was to be a compilation and explanation of the extant traditions concerning the history of his people.'"[44]

---

42. The basic studies of these traditions were done by Richter in the early 1960s (cf. *Untersuchungen* and *Bear-*

beitungen). Richter included the Abimelech story (Judges 9) in his collection and suggested the possibility of a ninth-century date. In this area, we have declined to follow.

43. Noth, *DH*, 26.

44. From A. F. Campbell, "Martin Noth and the Deuteronomistic History," in *History of Israel's Traditions*, 31–62. The comment quoted from Noth is in *DH*, 133.

In the book of Deuteronomy, Noth assumed such an "extant tradition": the dtn lawbook, with its introduction and conclusion (cf. 2 Kgs 22:8-10). In the book of Joshua, Noth argued for an earlier source in Joshua 2–11. Noth did not isolate a source collection in the book of Judges; however, such a collection has been claimed by Wolfgang Richter.[45] In the books of Samuel and Kings, Noth's stance was more nuanced. He accepted that the Saul and David traditions formed an adequate base that "absolved Dtr. from the need to organize and construct the narrative himself."[46] Among the sources for the books of Kings, Noth saw "some narrative cycles, each of which accumulated around one prophetic figure."[47] Noth spoke of the Elijah and Elisha cycle, the Isaiah cycle, the story of Ahijah of Shiloh, of Micaiah ben Imlah, and others. As Noth saw these traditions, the prophets "appear chiefly as opponents to the kings."[48] Even with Samuel set apart (by Noth) in the period of the judges, the fact that Ahijah designates Jeroboam as future king and Elisha's disciple anoints Jehu as king did not receive significant attention from Noth—although it may have contributed to his need for the adverb *chiefly* (*vorzugsweise*). In our judgment, the prophetic texts in Kings cannot be dealt with adequately unless they are associated with those in

Samuel.[49] The claim for a Prophetic Record, as a source for the Dtr, emerges out of a closer study of the signals embedded in these traditions in the books of Samuel and Kings.

There are certain clusters of signals in Samuel–Kings that need explaining. They are in passages spread widely across the books and bear remarkable similarities to each other. They are not identical; but they are too similar for the similarity to be coincidental. It matters little whether they are the work of one hand editing the traditions, or result from several generations mulling over the traditions they handed on.[50] What they point to is a striking concern for the understanding of Israel's past, for the role of the prophets in establishing and dismissing kings, and for the remarkable ways in which the prophetic word may be realized in the unfolding of events. They are not deuteronomistic, neither in language nor in concern.

The existence of a Prophetic Record (PR) was first proposed by A. F. Campbell in *Of Prophets and Kings* (1986).

Discovery of the Hypothesis

The observations that suggested the need for this hypothesis can be briefly summarized. A first

---

If anything, the "more than two-thirds" is an underestimate. The avowedly earlier material from Deuteronomy (26 chapters), Joshua (10), Samuel (50), and the prophetic narratives in Kings (23) adds up to 109 chapters. This total does not include the deliverer stories in Judges, or the Book of the Acts of Solomon, or the Chronicles of the Kings of Israel and Judah. The 156 chapters for the History are reckoned as follows: Deuteronomy, 34; Joshua, 13; Judges, 11; 1 Samuel, 31; 2 Samuel, 20; 1 Kings, 22; 2 Kings, 25.

45. Richter, *Untersuchungen* and *Bearbeitung*.

46. Noth, *DH*, 86.

47. Noth, *DH*, 107.

48. Noth, *DH*, 107.

49. Noth refers to the possibility that "the stories of the prophets' interventions in the succession of Israelite kings and dynasties formed a cycle of their own," but the texts he refers to are all exclusively from 1–2 Kings (*DH*, 109). Such intervention, of course, began with Samuel.

50. We need to be cautious about consistently reflecting back on to ancient Israel an obsessive concern for verbal accuracy that was not theirs, since they were not encumbered with our books and computers. It is salutary to note the freedom with which the Deuteronomistic Historians in 1 Kgs 8:16, 18-19 recall the Deuteronomistic Historians in 2 Samuel 7. When the woman of Shunem confronts Elisha and quotes her earlier remark to him, though only a dozen verses apart she is given quite different words to express the thought (2 Kgs 4:16 and 28).

set of observations concerns Saul, David, and Jehu; a second set concerns Jeroboam, Ahab, and Jehu. Jehu is the figure common to both.

Saul, David, and Jehu. Both Saul and David were designated by a prophet in remarkably similar circumstances. Of all Israel's kings, only Jehu received a similar designation from a prophet.

The similar circumstances are:

1. anointing by a prophet
2. done in relative privacy, variously expressed
3. the anointing directly attributed to YHWH
4. the recipient designated as king-designate (*nāgîd*), king-to-be, or simply king
5. having empowering consequences that flow from the anointing.[51]

It needs to be noted that Saul was also dismissed by the same prophet who designated or anointed him. The effective impact of the prophetic word, realized in the unfolding of events, is claimed in 1 Samuel 28 and 2 Samuel 7.

The text is substantially a revision and expansion of the early traditions of David's rise to power in the united kingdom, taking in both the future southern and northern kingdoms.

Jeroboam, Ahab, and Jehu. Speeches of remarkable similarity were spoken by prophets to kings within stories about both Jeroboam and Ahab. Along with these two archetypal figures, of all Israel's kings, again only Jehu was the recipient of a similar speech from a prophet.[52]

Jeroboam was designated and subsequently dismissed—as was Saul. Ahab was dismissed. Jehu was commissioned to destroy the house of Ahab.

The similarities are particularly noteworthy within the three speeches about dismissal (see further below). As in the anointing texts, there is a strong element of direct attribution of the action to YHWH.

The common elements are:

1. the bringing of evil (not in these words in 2 Kings 9)
2. the extirpation of the royal house
3. the cutting off of every male
4. a comparison with the fate of the house of Jeroboam (not in 1 Kings 14 of course)
5. the specific fate of those who die in the city or the country (not in 2 Kgs 9:1-13, but cf. 9:26, 36).

The elements listed here have often been classified as deuteronomistic, because of a bevy of dtr characteristics to be found in the present text of these prophetic speeches.[53] These elements, however, form a core within the speeches that can be read as independent and free-standing. The combined elements themselves are exclusive to these speeches. The possibility has to be envisaged that the core within the speeches is pre-dtr, subject understandably to later dtr expansion. The imagery owes nothing to dtr characteristics.

The ideology, common language, and common reference to the fate of the house of Jeroboam hold this series together. The designation of Jeroboam is bound to the dismissal of Saul by the prophetic action of tearing a cloak and the prophetic speech interpreting that action.[54]

The text is substantially a revision and expansion of the early traditions of Elijah's conflict

---

51. See Campbell, *Of Prophets and Kings*, 17–23.

52. See Campbell, *Of Prophets and Kings*, 23–41. The qualification "within stories" has been added to exclude the case of Baasha (1 Kgs 16:1-4), where a dismissal seems to have been modeled on the earlier stories (ibid., 39–41).

53. For example, Moshe Weinfeld, *Deuteronomy and the Deuteronomic School*, 350–55.

54. On this and other aspects of the wider context, see Campbell, *Of Prophets and Kings*, 41–63.

with Ahab over the worship of Baal and the murder of Naboth. But this is extended back to the prophetic legitimation of Jeroboam and his rejection for apostasy (associated with illegitimate clergy) and concluded with the prophetic legitimation of Jehu, the brutal destruction of Ahab's house, and Jehu's elimination of Baalism from Israel.

Conclusion. These signals in the text constitute a set of similarities that needs to be accounted for. One explanation is the hypothesis of a PR, from the prophetic circles around Elisha, a document extending from 1 Samuel 1 to 2 Kings 10, building on earlier traditions such as the stories of David's rise and the Elijah stories, concluding by bringing Jehu's coup under the legitimation of major prophetic authority (i.e., Samuel in association with Saul and David, Ahijah for Jeroboam, and Elijah for Ahab).

The northern provenance should not surprise. The PR's claim has Samuel (a northerner if anyone was—although he set up his sons in Beersheba!) anoint Saul, a Benjaminite, and David, a Bethlehemite. It has Ahijah (like Samuel associated with Shiloh) transfer the Davidic heritage to Jeroboam for the north. Divisive forces are evident in 2 Samuel 15–20; for all that, David's was a united kingdom of all Israel.

The Recovery of the Text

The observations that lead to the shaping of the hypothesis and the identification of its text can be discussed from the standpoint of Jehu's coup (2 Kings 9–10), the anointing, and the dismissal of the dynasty.

Jehu's coup. The story of Jehu's coup is told in 2 Kings 9–10, a coup that according to the text wiped out the house of Ahab in Israel and with it the worship of the god Baal. It is a story that puts itself under the patronage of the prophet Elijah. What Jehu does, in all its awfulness, is portrayed

as fulfilling the prophecy of Elijah. Three times Elijah's prophecy is explicitly invoked (2 Kgs 9:36; 10:10, 17). An anonymous prophecy is also invoked (2 Kgs 9:25-26). We have no other trace of it, but the reference to the "plot of ground" and the blood of Naboth's children, as well as the circumstances of the divine utterance, suggest the circulation of more versions of the story than the one we have from 1 Kings 21 (cf. 2 Kgs 9:21).

After 2 Kgs 9:1-13, there is no mention in the coup narrative of Jehu's having been anointed or commissioned by Elisha's disciple. It is likely that 9:1-13 was placed before the story of Jehu's coup in order to bring Jehu's action explicitly under the authority and legitimation of the prophetic circles associated with Elisha. The Elisha circles are likely to have been the bearers of the Elijah traditions and probably of many of the earlier prophetic traditions.

The anointing texts. Elisha's disciple anointed Jehu, in private, away from the other army commanders. Samuel's anointing of Saul, also in private (cf. 1 Sam 9:27), shows clear signs of being an overwriting of an older story of a chance meeting with an anonymous prophet, provoked by Saul's search for his father's asses. Samuel's anointing of David, apparently in the relative privacy of his family circle (cf. 1 Sam 16:5), is an account of an event not mentioned in the early traditions about David's rise to power.

If the prophetic circle around Elisha were to claim the legitimate authority to designate kings by anointing in YHWH's name, they could do no better than go back to the figure of Samuel and the establishment of Saul and David. The image of Saul, dismissed from kingly office and replaced by David (1 Sam 15:1—16:13), provides the foundational understanding of the kingship as being in the gift of the prophets, to bestow or withdraw as God wills.

For this portrayal, an account of the emergence of Samuel as a prophet to all Israel would be needed, along with the stories of Samuel's dealings with Saul and David, through to the successful establishment of David as Israel's king, in fulfillment of the word of YHWH through Samuel. Such a narrative can be easily traced within the texts from 1 Sam 1:1 to 2 Sam 8:15.

Samuel dismisses Saul and anoints David. The realization in history of Saul's dismissal is found in the same events that are the realization in history of David's designation by the prophetic anointing. For Saul, the realization in history of his dismissal extends to 1 Samuel 31. For David, the anointing's realization extends at least to 2 Sam 5:3. Elijah condemns Ahab; Elisha's disciple anoints Jehu. The realization in history of Elijah's prophetic words is brought to completion by Jehu's coup, itself presented as the realization in history of his anointing.

The dismissal of dynasties. Elisha's disciple commissioned Jehu to wipe out the house of Ahab, making it like the house of Jeroboam, son of Nebat. There is strong traditional preparation for this. First, in YHWH's name, the prophet Ahijah of Shiloh transfers to Jeroboam what the prophets gave to David: "I will be with you, and will build you an enduring house, as I built for David, and I will give Israel to you" (1 Kgs 11:38b; cf. vv. 29-31, 37). Subsequently, Ahijah predicts that the house of Jeroboam will be wiped out because of Jeroboam's apostasy: "[you] have thrust me behind your back" (1 Kgs 14:9b).

The stereotyped phrases used of the house of Jeroboam are applied to the house of Ahab, patron of the worship in Israel of the god Baal (cf. 1 Kgs 21:17-24). They are spoken to Ahab by the prophet Elijah; as we have noted, the main narrative of Jehu's coup is placed under the patronage of Elijah. They are spoken to Jehu by Elisha's disciple; those responsible for the organization of these traditions can lay claim to the prophetic heritage from Samuel on down for the action of Jehu by which he "wiped out Baal from Israel" (2 Kgs 10:28). Given Elijah's departure before the arrival of Jehu on the scene and the likelihood that the Elijah traditions were preserved in the circles associated with Elisha, it is appropriate that a disciple of Elisha's anoint Jehu—with the figure of Elijah an unmentioned power and presence.[55]

It may help to see these stereotyped phrases without the dtr additions that are part of their present context. They are:

Jeroboam (1 Kings 14)

Crime:

- [You] have thrust me behind your back

Consequences:

- I will bring evil (*rā'â*) upon the house of Jeroboam
- I will cut off from Jeroboam every male (*maštîn bĕqîr*), both bond and free in Israel
- [I] will consume (*bi'artî 'aḥăr'ê*) the house of Jeroboam, just as one burns up dung . . .
- Anyone belonging to Jeroboam who dies in the city, the dogs shall eat; and anyone who dies in the open country, the birds of the air shall eat . . .

Ahab (1 Kings 21)

Crime:

- Have you killed and also taken possession?

Consequences:

- I will bring disaster (*rā'â*) on you
- I will consume (*bi'artî 'aḥăr'ê*) you
- [I] will cut off from Ahab every male (*maštîn bĕqîr*), bond or free, in Israel

---

55. Against Noth, *DH*, 108–9.

- I will make your house like the house of Jeroboam son of Nebat
- Anyone belonging to Ahab who dies in the city the dogs shall eat; and anyone of his who dies in the open country the birds of the air shall eat

Jehu (2 Kings 9)

Commission:
- I anoint you king over the people of the LORD, over Israel

Consequences:
- You shall strike down the house of your master Ahab, . . . the whole house of Ahab shall perish
- I will cut off from Ahab every male (*maštîn bĕqîr*), bond or free, in Israel
- I will make the house of Ahab like the house of Jeroboam son of Nebat

The same language is found in the dtr condemnation of the dynasty of Baasha, attributed to the prophet Jehu ben Hanani (1 Kgs 16:1-4). There is no story as context for this prophetic speech, and there are grounds for seeing it as a dtr construction modeled on the speeches above. 1 Kgs 16:1-4 aside, these phrases are not characteristic of dtr language in any way. Of course it is possible for the dtr editors to employ language in one context that they use nowhere else. The occurrence, however, raises questions. There is an imagistic and figurative quality to the language that is not usually present in dtr passages. The role of the prophet, the anointing, and the language of *nāgîd* (for example, 1 Kgs 14:7) tie these speeches into the realm of prophetic editorial activity and the PR.[56]

The Shape of the Text

The similarities have been too obvious to be overlooked. They have been explained as the result of dtr composition; there has been the appeal to cycles of stories told in prophetic circles.[57] This latter may appear the easy approach, but there are certain features of the texts concerned that sit uncomfortably with the idea of story cycles. While material may, of course, have been drawn extensively from such cycles, an overarching concern has been imprinted on them that extends beyond the individual stories and even the individual cycles.

In the case of the anointing stories, it is clear that the theme of anointing has been superimposed on 1 Sam 9:1–10:16 in a way that demands literary reworking not oral retelling. The treatment of 1 Sam 15:1-35 is similar. In the case of the later prophetic speeches, there is consistent comparison with the house of Jeroboam son of Nebat, thus involving both Ahijah and Elijah. The stories do not have the independence expected within cycles. The stories of prophetic anointing or designation require later stories of

---

56. On *nāgîd*, see the excursus in Campbell, *Of Prophets and Kings*, 47–61. On the Baasha material, see ibid., 39–41.

57. The dtr attribution is best exemplified by Dietrich, *Prophetie und Geschichte*. Noth appeals to prophetic story cycles (*DH*, 107–9). On details, his position is often cautious. For Noth, for example, the phrase "bond or free," adapted by the Deuteronomists in 2 Kgs 14:26, is derived from their sources in the prophetic stories (1 Kgs 14:10; 21:21; 2 Kgs 9:8. See *DH*, 103, n. 1). Similarly, 1 Kgs 14:14–16 for Noth is clearly an addition by the Deuteronomist; "the rest of the Ahijah story can be seen to be pre-Deuteronomistic" (*DH*, 110, n. 3). The language in 1 Kgs 21:21-22, 24 is attributed by Noth to the Deuteronomist, but derived from 1 Kgs 14:10-11 (*DH*, 112). Again, 2 Kgs 9:8b-9 is attributed to the Deuteronomist, but derived from 1 Kings 21, and so ultimately from the prophetic story in 1 Kgs 14:10-11 (*DH*, 113). For Noth, then, there would be no difficulty with all of these phrases being predeuteronomistic. There are no links outside these prophetic speeches to associate this language and imagery with dtn vocabulary.

realization; the stories of prophetic rejection need a wider context and also stand in need of realization. In this, these stories of the PR are quite different from the stories found in 1 Kings 13, 20, and 22.

The stories of the PR are clustered at the start of the united monarchy (Saul and David) and early in the divided monarchy (Jeroboam, Ahab, Jehu). An intervening text is needed between these clusters. It bears marks of concerns common to the stories (e.g., 1 Sam 28:17-19a; 2 Sam 7:4b, 8-10, 11b-12, 14-17). All of this militates against the idea of a cycle of stories, much less of two or more narrative cycles.

Over and above these issues, there is "a movement of narrative logic and a central focus of thematic interest" that binds the whole together from Samuel to Jehu.[58] Samuel is needed to set up and put down Saul, establishing David in his place. God's will, mediated by Samuel, is effective and David succeeds splendidly.[59] Nathan takes up the thread and points back to what God has done and forward to what God will do (2 Samuel 7). Mediated by the prophet Ahijah of Shiloh, the legitimacy given David is transferred to Jeroboam with regard to the ten tribes. Jeroboam is then rejected by the same Ahijah; Ahab emerges and is equally rejected by the prophet Elijah; and finally under Jehu, God's will becomes effective. There is a unity here that escapes the simply cyclical.

There is a clear and coherent text from Samuel to the assertion of David's success (2 Sam 8:15); it is an expanded form of the early David traditions. There is an equally clear and coherent text from Ahab to Jehu; it is an expanded form of the early Elijah traditions. A text can be identified from Jeroboam to Ahab. There is, of course, no question of the Omrides, and especially the Baal-worshipping Ahab, receiving legitimation or designation from the prophets of YHWH. The rejection of Jeroboam's house is concluded in 1 Kgs 15:29; the story leading to the condemnation of Ahab's house is begun in 17:1 with the figure of Elijah. The trace of the PR can be followed across 1 Kings 16, in the wild and turbulent times of Nadab and Baasha, Elah and Zimri, and the triumph of Omri over Tibni. A text exists (within 1 Kgs 16:6-32); prophetic guidance, however, is conspicuously absent.

The text of the PR employs a linear system of reporting the royal succession: X died and Y reigned in his stead. The linear system's exclusive use in the list of the kings of Edom (Gen 36:31-39) is evidence that it could exist independently; a few cases of superfluous repetition provide evidence that this linear system did in fact coexist in Kings alongside the dtr synchronistic system (cf. 1 Kgs 16:28-29; 2 Kgs 8:24-25; 13:9-10; 15:22-23; 15:38—16:1).[60]

Where Solomon's reign is concerned, the situation with regard to prophetic guidance is different. Without naming him, the prophets had already promised David's offspring and successor

---

58. Campbell, *Of Prophets and Kings*, 65.

59. It is important to note that such a figure as Samuel has not been profiled in Israel since Moses and Joshua (cf. 1 Sam 4:1a). Two further observations are important in relation to continuity in the midst of change. In their own way and in their freedom from institutional dependence, these prophets—of whom Samuel is the first—share an affinity with the charisma of the deliverer-judges; in role, they are radically different. The institutional element is introduced by monarchy. Second, in their dismissal of some of the more evil northern kings and their lurid condemnation of the respective royal houses, these prophets set a trend; in the "royal" focus of the revision, blaming the kings will become a paradigm.

60. See Campbell, *Of Prophets and Kings*, 139. It is a reasonable assumption that the linear system was in place before the introduction of the synchronistic system. Each serves different purposes.

(2 Sam 7:12)—who turned out to be Solomon. Already they had prepared the ground for his lack of fidelity (2 Sam 7:14-15). Ahead, secure in the narrative to come, they had his partial replacement waiting in the wings—Jeroboam. Was that enough? Alternatively, was there a gap in substantially a two-part story? Was Solomon well enough known among the many rotten apples in the royal barrel? Was it known only too well that by the end of his time he had rotted to the core? As administrator and temple-builder, Solomon receives extensive treatment from the Deuteronomists; by comparison, he attracts no attention from the prophetic redactors. Was it possible that Solomon was too bad to hire and too big to fire? Or was there no tradition available for the prophetic redactors to build on?

Certainly there is no prophetic designation for Solomon. He was anointed by the priest Zadok although the prophet Nathan was present (1 Kgs 1:38-39; vv. 34 and 45 associate Nathan more closely with the anointing, but v. 39 is explicit about the act: Zadok did it). There is no prophetic condemnation or dismissal either. It would be possible for the PR to be seen in two parts, concluding the first with 2 Sam 8:15 and, in the second, resuming the narrative thread with Jeroboam at 1 Kgs 11:26. There are similar disjunctions in Israel's narratives.

On the other hand, there are the apparently related references to Solomon's building activity in 1 Kgs 3:1 and 9:15a, coupled with the oddly placed references to Pharaoh's daughter so early at 3:1 and correlatively at 9:24, as well as the issue of forced labor in 9:15a and Solomon's apostasy in 11:7. These texts need a setting and the PR as a hypothesis is a strong candidate for the provision of that setting. In which case, it is possible that 1 Kgs 2:10, 12 belonged originally to the PR or have replaced its notice of David's death and Solomon's accession.

The texts of the PR as we have them indicate that it should not be seen as a record of Israel's history. It is a record of the prophetic activity claimed in the guidance of Israel with regard to its kings, from Saul to Jehu. A structure analysis follows. This presentation of the PR is shared with the *1 Samuel* volume (by Campbell) in the FOTL commentary series. Revision of both texts occurred about the same time.

Given the misunderstanding that has occasionally surfaced, it is worth insisting that all of the above is totally independent of any analysis of the royal judgment formulas. The judgment formulas are significant for any consideration of the history of the text after the PR. They are of no significance in the establishment of the hypothesis of a PR.

STRUCTURE ANALYSIS

The Prophetic Record   **1 Samuel 1:1—2 Kings 10:28**

I. Emergence of the prophetic figure in Israel: Samuel   1 Samuel 1:1–4:1a
II. Record of prophetic guidance of Israel's destiny   1 Samuel 9:1—2 Kings 10:28
   A. Concerning SAUL   1 Sam 9:1—
      1. Establishment as king
         a. Designation by prophet: Samuel
         b. Realization in history
      2. Summary of Saul's reign
      3. Rejection as king by prophet: Samuel
   B. Concerning DAVID   1 Sam 16:1—
      1. Establishment as king
         a. Designation by prophet: Samuel
         b. Realization in history
      2. Consummation of David's reign
         a. Promise of a secure dynasty: Nathan
         b. Summary of David's success
      3. Aftermath with Solomon
   C. Concerning JEROBOAM   1 Kgs 11:26—
      1. Establishment as king
         a. Designation by prophet: Ahijah
         b. Realization in history
      2. Summary of Jeroboam's reign
      3. Rejection of house of Jeroboam
         a. Prophetic word of rejection: Ahijah
         b. Realization in history
   D. Concerning AHAB   1 Kgs 16:6—
      1. Anarchic prelude to Ahab's reign
      2. Elijah's triumph over Baalism
      3. Rejection of house of Ahab
         a. Prophetic word of rejection: Elijah
         b. Initial realization in history
   E. Concerning JEHU   2 Kgs 9:1—
      1. Establishment as king
         a. Designation by prophet: Elisha's disciple
         b. Realization in history
      2. Extermination of Baal worship from Israel

JUDGMENT FORMULAS AND PATTERNS

The standard regnal framework provides a structural shape for the narrative of the kings. Nine elements comprise the framework: synchronism (for the two kingdoms), king's age at his accession (Judean kings only), length of reign, capital city, name of queen mother (Judean kings only), judgment formula, source reference, notice of death and burial, succession.

Close analysis of the formulas in which judgment is passed on the kings shows that four patterns exist: A, for the northern kings from Jehu to Hoshea (northern kingdom: middle to end); B, for the southern kings from Rehoboam to Hezekiah (beginning to near-end); C, for the northern kings from Jeroboam to Joram (northern kingdom: beginning to middle); and a fourth pattern, D, for the last four kings of Judah.[61] In the analysis of these patterns, not all elements of the regnal framework have been drawn on; the patterns relate exclusively to the judgment formulas for the kings.

The conclusions can be noted rapidly: pattern A relates to the northern kings after the PR; pattern C relates to the northern kings within the PR; pattern B relates to the southern kings to Hezekiah; and pattern D relates to the last four kings of Judah, all of them of the family of Josiah. Manasseh, Amon, and Josiah are in a class of their own, referred to as pattern B/C.

It has been suggested that the fluctuations within the patterns may be slight enough to allow for a single author or may be appropriate to their context.[62] At issue is less the extent of fluctuation among the patterns and more the regularity with which the particular patterned forms of expression are restricted to defined blocks of kings. The phenomenon must be accounted for. Appropriateness to context is always important. However it is scarcely appropriate to refer to Jehu as "the great reformer" (S. L. McKenzie); no matter the causes endorsed, the man was a murderous thug. On this, Jezebel and Hosea seem agreed.

An extension of the PR is noted, correlated with pattern A. It is suggested that reflection on the fate of the northern kingdom led to a list of its kings, from Jehu to the end, who were infected by the sin of Jeroboam. Despite God's initiative in bringing the kingdom into existence (with Ahijah and Jeroboam), the northern exile was the result of the people's sin, instigated by Jeroboam.

In *Of Prophets and Kings*, Campbell argued reluctantly for the possibility that pattern B might have been associated with a "southern document."[63] A distinctive feature of pattern B is its concern for the high places. This reflects the concerns of reform under Hezekiah. At least three options are possible in relation to the traditions gathered in the judgment formulas of pattern B:

1. Minimal: a King List, drawn up perhaps as a basis for policy;

---

61. See Campbell, *Of Prophets and Kings*, 139–52, esp. 144–51, and the Tables here. Careful study of these patterns is indebted above all to the pioneering work of Helga Weippert, "Die 'deuteronomistischen' Beurteilungen der Könige von Israel und Juda und das Problem der Redaktion der Königsbücher." The most exhaustive work in this area is Baruch Halpern and David S. Vanderhooft, "The Editions of Kings in the 7th–6th Centuries B.C.E." Their study favors DH activity under both Hezekiah and Josiah. Among others favoring a composition from Josiah's time may be noted Steven L. McKenzie, *The Trouble with Kings* and Iain W. Provan, *Hezekiah and the Books of Kings*. For Provan, this Josianic history ends with Hezekiah.

62. Single author: Provan, *Hezekiah*, 54; appropriate: S. L. McKenzie, "The Books of Kings in the Deuteronomistic History," in S. L. McKenzie and M. P. Graham (eds.), *History of Israel's Traditions*, 302–3.

63. *Of Prophets and Kings*, 169–202.

2. Moderate: a document, such as the postulated southern document;

3. Maximal: a history, such as the DH, culminating with Hezekiah.

What we claim here is no more than what is identifiable in the text: simply the list of southern kings who are praised, with the reservation that the high places were not taken away—i.e., reflecting the activity of Hezekiah's time and the concern focused sharply on the high places. We do not want to claim a document such as "the southern document" for this book and reproduce it here. We do not repudiate such a hypothesis; but we do believe it is too speculative to be appropriate in this book. Arguments favoring a Hezekian DH need to offer a coherent horizon, bearing in mind that the dtr concerns for centralization at Jerusalem, for fidelity to YHWH, and observation of the Passover are not the same as a concern for the high places.

TECHNICAL

The formatting of the biblical text (NRSV) is based on two simple principles. First, the contribution of the Josianic Deuteronomist and everything prior to it is flush with the left-hand margin. All contributions after the Josianic Dtr are indented from the LH margin. Second, the former is in a serif font and the latter in a sans serif font.

As far as the pre-dtr traditions are concerned, in each biblical book a pre-existing nucleus has long been taken for granted in scholarship. We have used this nucleus in each case, setting it in roman with expansions etc. in italic. Other pre-dtr contributions have been identified with a single sideline in the margin. So in Deuteronomy, the dtr lawcode is set in roman and its introduction and conclusion are set in italic; in Joshua, the conquest narrative is in roman and its expan-

sion is in italic; in Judges, the deliverance collection is in roman and its framing is in italic; in 1–2 Samuel, the traditions incorporated into the PR are in roman and the prophetic contribution is in italic; in 1 Kings the PR as such is set in italic; and finally, in 2 Kings, the PR and its Extension are in italic. The pre-dtr traditions in Samuel–Kings have long been recognized; their organization as a PR is a more recent hypothesis (see above). What we have identified, for the purposes of this book, as the Hezekian King List (HKL) has been given a single underline, as well as the marginal single sideline.

As for the post-Josianic DH additions (all indented), we have identified certain components of the dtr revision (see above). The extension of the DH has been set in a sans serif font. The "royal" focus of the revision has been set in bold italic in the same sans serif font. The "national" focus of the revision has been set in italic in the same sans serif font. All other contributions added after the Josianic Dtr are set in a sans serif font and marked by a double sideline in the margin.

The basic format is indicated in the footers at the bottom of the pages. The footers on the even-numbered pages note the formatting for the pre-dtr and Josianic dtr traditions. The footers on the odd-numbered pages note the formatting for the material that has been incorporated after the Josianic Dtr. Two rare exceptions have not been placed in the footers. A single-line box has been used in conjunction with a double sideline for 1 Sam 8:11-17; a single-line box has been used in 2 Kings 18–19. It is hoped that these facilitate clarity in the context and are more than adequately explained in the relevant annotations. The use of single-line boxes for options in the sacral traditions of Joshua 3–4 and 6 is also explained where it occurs. A single dotted line has been used in seven places in 1 Kings (1 Kgs

4:29-34 [= Heb., 5:9-14]; 5:13-18 [= Heb., 5:27-32]; 9:16-17a, 23, 26-28; 10:1-29; 16:34; also Josh 6:26) for traditions that are validly argued by some to be pre-dtr and by others to be post-dtr; these are mainly in connection with Solomon and his reputation.

These footers are reproduced below for comparison. To avoid overload, formats are only indicated for the books in which they occur. The material indicated by single and double sidelines needs particular attention. The **single sideline** indicates that the **time of composition** is believed to have been pre-dtr, allowing for *incorporation* into the Josianic DH by the Dtr; the **double sideline** indicates that the **incorporation into the text** is believed to have been after the Dtr, without prejudice to the *time of composition* of the material so marked.

The Josianic DH is the primary punctuated text. Where appropriate, the PR has been punctuated as the secondary text. Other material and editorial additions have been left without initial or final punctuation, or such punctuation has been allotted on an ad hoc basis.

Footers on even-numbered pages:

Deuteronomy

Main pre-DH: dtn lawcode *its introduction and conclusion*		Other pre-DH: single sideline	**Josianic DH:** **from the Dtr**

Joshua

Main pre-DH: Conquest Narrative *and its expansion*		Other pre-DH: single sideline	**Josianic DH:** **from the Dtr**

Judges

Main pre-DH: Deliverance *Collection* its sources *and its framing*		Other pre-DH: single sideline	**Josianic DH:** **from the Dtr**

1 Samuel

Main pre-DH: *Prophetic* Record its sources *and prophetic contribution*		Other pre-DH: single sideline	**Josianic DH:** **from the Dtr**

2 Samuel

Main pre-DH: *Prophetic* Record its sources *and prophetic contribution*		Other pre-DH: single sideline	**Josianic DH:** **from the Dtr**

1 Kings

Main pre-DH: *Prophetic Record*	Other pre-DH: single sideline	HKL: + single underline	**Josianic DH:** **from the Dtr**

2 Kings

Main pre-DH: *Prophetic Record and PR Extension*	Other pre-DH: single sideline	HKL: + single underline	**Josianic DH:** **from the Dtr**

Footers on odd-numbered pages:

Deuteronomy

After the Dtr: indented and sans serif font	*Revision: national focus*	Other: double sideline

Joshua

After the Dtr: indented and sans serif font	*Revision: national focus*	Other: double sideline

Judges

After the Dtr: indented and sans serif font	*Revision: national focus*	Other: double sideline

1 Samuel

After the Dtr: indented and sans serif font	***Revision: royal focus***	*Revision: national focus*	Other: double sideline

2 Samuel

After the Dtr: indented and sans serif font	*Revision: national focus*	Other: double sideline

1 Kings

After the Dtr: indented and sans serif font	***Revision: royal focus***	*Revision: national focus*	Other: double sideline

2 Kings

After the Dtr: indented and sans serif font	DH Extension	***Revision: royal focus***	*Revision: national focus*	Other: double sideline

Certain abbreviations may be noted.

DH is used for the Deuteronomistic History. Where confusion needs to be avoided, Josianic DH is specified as often as possible. The non-DH texts in Deuteronomy to 2 Kings are provided for the sake of completeness. As noted above (at the start of the section "Components"), these texts do not contribute in the present text to a clarification and identification of what is dtr contribution and dtr theology.

dtn = deuteronomic (associated with the book of Deuteronomy and the reform).

dtr = deuteronomistic (associated with the DH).

The Dtr = the "agent" (whether individual or group) responsible for the composition of the Josianic DH. Often, to avoid confusion, the term "the Josianic Dtr" will be used. The usage of other scholars has been respected when quoting or referring to their work.

Abbreviations from the Smend school:

DtrH or DtrG = the basic dtr History (exilic).

DtrN = a level of "nomistic" (law-oriented) editing of DtrH.

DtrP = a level of prophetic editing of DtrH.

The ground-breaking identification of editorial revisions was first done by F. M. Cross, W. Dietrich, and T. Veijola (for references, see note 6 above). Out of respect for the work of these scholars, their text identifications have been noted throughout. It has not seemed appropriate to update these to take account of subsequent publications.[64]

It remains for us to add that, as for *Sources of the Pentateuch*, this book is fully the work of both authors. We have hammered out our part of the text together, to the point where often we are no longer sure who originated what. We are happy to bear joint responsibility for the outcome.

Finally, it gives us pleasure to acknowledge our deep gratitude to K. C. Hanson and his collaborators at Fortress Press for their care and competence.

---

64. An overview of the "Smend school" is provided in R. Smend, *Die Entstehung des Alten Testaments*, 110–25.

The Book of Deuteronomy

INTRODUCTION

The book of Deuteronomy, as it is now, purports to be a speech or speeches of Moses delivered to the people of Israel in the plains of Moab, on the desert fringe to the east of the Jordan, just prior to Israel's crossing into Canaan. If one follows the analysis by Andrew Mayes—a highly respectable one—Deuteronomy had its origins as a lawbook, a book of YHWH's law communicated to Israel by Moses. The law was contained in the core of chaps. 12–26. An exhortatory (or: parenetic) introduction occupies the bulk of chaps. 6–11. Eduard Nielsen distinguishes two major sections in the lawbook: the laws associated in some way with the basic concern for centralization of worship (12:1–19:13); the laws for Israel's life in its new surroundings (19:14–25:19).

At a later stage in its existence, the deuteronomic lawcode was brought into the horizon of Israel's history. Precisely when is not clear, but it was probably in association with the placement of the decalogue in front of the introduction, as what is now chap. 5. Inevitably, this led to a correlation of these laws with those given by God to Moses on Mount Sinai. This deuteronomic lawcode became the "book of the law" that gave guidance and direction to Israel through the course of its history, resumed in the great literary and theological work known to us as the Deuteronomistic History (DH). It is believed to have been some core of Deuteronomy that is reputed to have given impetus to King Josiah's reform (cf. 2 Kings 22–23).

Surprisingly for many, it is with the composition of the DH (or: according to Mayes, with a later exilic stage of the DH) that the concept of covenant and the mindset of treaty were introduced into this area of Israel's literature. It is important, in this context, to reiterate three points that are often neglected in Christian proclamation.

- The affirmation of covenant is a faith statement. No temple vault contains a covenant document signed by God; no liturgical ritual escapes faith.
- A relationship can have existed between God and Israel long before it was widely articulated in terms of covenant (see the discussion in Mayes, and the studies referred to there of McCarthy, Nicholson, and Perlitt).[1]
- The relationship between God and Israel can be expressed in a variety of ways, of which covenant is only one.

Covenant is a theological articulation of the God-Israel relationship. It can be most valuable; it can also be used in ways that are damaging and destructive.

---

1. Mayes, *Deuteronomy*, 64–71. See also D. J. McCarthy, *Treaty and Covenant*, esp. pp. 277–98.

Three options have been put forward to account for the provenance of Deuteronomy and the deuteronomic movement: northern prophetic circles, Jerusalem wisdom circles, and circles associated with the levitical priesthood. Influence from all three areas can be detected; the attribution of Deuteronomy to any one alone has so far found no consensus and an exclusive claim would be difficult to sustain. The influences have been manifold. Preuss lists scholarly positions maintaining origins stretching from Moses to Josiah.[2]

The insistence in the book of Deuteronomy on centralization of sacrificial worship at a single sanctuary points to its origins within circles from Jerusalem. At the same time, the insistence on fidelity to YHWH, God of Israel, over against the seductive aspects of fertility cults and the worship of Baal, has overtones of northern prophetic origin (cf. esp. Hosea; so Nielsen).

Mayes, after quoting Lindblom, leans toward levitical origins, proposing as a probable conclusion "that the authors of Deuteronomy were formerly Levites unconnected with the cult, now attached to the Jerusalem temple."[3] Nielsen appeals respectfully to Aage Bentzen and Gerhard von Rad for the view of the Levites, northern Israelite YHWH priests, as originators of the deuteronomic movement and looks to Deut 33:9-10 as a possible answer to the question of Deuteronomy's origins—"And of Levi he [Moses] said: . . . For they observed your word and kept your covenant. They teach Jacob your ordinances, and Israel your law; they place incense before you, and whole burnt offerings on your altar."[4] Preuss, on the other hand, aligns himself with Moshe Weinfeld, Norbert Lohfink,

Georg Braulik, and Calum Carmichael, to opt for an origin among the scribes and officials of the Jerusalem court.[5] If there is a last word, it has not yet been said.

In another area of Deuteronomy studies, the last word is probably one of plurality. The alternation between singular and plural address in Deuteronomy (German: "der Numeruswechsel") has long been observed. No single explanation appears to suffice. The alternation between source traditions and editing activities accounts for some cases (systematically: Minette de Tillesse).[6] Issues of stylistic emphasis, with the singular appealing to the Israelite as individual and the plural appealing to the Israelite as member of the community, accounts for other cases (systematically: Lohfink).[7] Other cases are not easily explained. It is likely that the original introduction to the lawcode favored the singular address; it is equally likely that the editing associated with the DH favored the plural. It is clear that there are passages where both singular and plural styles must be attributed to a single author (e.g., Deut 4:1-40). The comment from Mayes on this puzzling phenomenon is suitably cautious: "it can by no means be used on its own as the key to the solution to all Deuteronomy's difficulties."[8] It must be observed and given its place within the panoply of observations that influence study of Deuteronomy.

The understanding of law within the book of Deuteronomy is worth reflection. Christian proclamation has all too often drawn its view of OT law from one area of a relatively late stage in biblical Judaism. Both the terms of treaty structure and the biblical portrayal of Israel's history

---

2. Preuss, *Deuteronomium*, 26–29.
3. Mayes, *Deuteronomy*, 107.
4. Neilsen, *Deuteronomium*, 8.

5. Preuss, *Deuteronomium*, 32.
6. "Sections 'tu' et sections 'vous' dans le Deutéronome."
7. *Das Hauptgebot*, 239–58.
8. Mayes, *Deuteronomy*, 35.

with God indicate that the relationship exists before the laws are stipulated. At base, law is not a condition for relationship but a consequence of relationship (cf. Mayes, *Deuteronomy*, 78). On the other hand, treaty structures also invoke blessings and curses that are conditional on obedience. The demands of relationship and the strictures of covenant can cause tension. Mayes is helpful:

> Through introducing the possibility of repentance and forgiveness the tension between the idea that Israel's status as the people of Yahweh precedes and is independent of the covenant, and the idea that disobedience to the covenant demands brings punishment and destruction is to some extent resolved (ibid.).

Given the importance of the book of Deuteronomy in the life and faith of Israel, with its formation spanning at least some 150 years, it is not surprising that it has been the focus of intense editorial and theological activity. Up to the present, consensus in scholarship has been remarkable by its absence.[9] In our judgment, this book is not the place for us to enter these lists. On the other hand, we have not judged it helpful simply to assign the traditions in Deuteronomy 5–11 and 12–26 to the source material incorporated into the DH. Instead, we have appended to each of these chapters a synopsis of the analyses presented in three recent works—two commentaries bracketing a research/review monograph—spanning three decades (1970s, 1980s,

and 1990s) and three countries (Ireland, Denmark, and Germany). With these synopses, the diversity of views will be evident; for insight beyond that, the respective studies need to be consulted.

These books are:

- A. D. H. Mayes, *Deuteronomy*, 1979;
- E. Nielsen, *Deuteronomium*, 1995;
- H. D. Preuss, *Deuteronomium*, 1982.

For Mayes, the analysis has been drawn from his commentary and compared with his introduction. For Nielsen, it has been taken from the typography of his text. For Preuss, it comes from his table of the levels in Deuteronomy; unfortunately, space does not allow a representation of his understanding of the process of growth, which would have lessened the appearance of fragmentation. In the presentation of all three, the verse numbering of the English version provided (NRSV) has been followed and, as far as possible, the divisions within verses have been adjusted to reflect the NRSV.

The uncertainties of any analysis of Deuteronomy are reflected in these studies. Preuss will often put verses in two different layers, with a question mark. The use of "other" under Mayes does not mean that "other" editing is not dtr; rather it reflects the uncertainty of attribution to particular editorial layers and the judgment that the evidence is not there to associate these verses with the layer of editing that Mayes calls a later or second dtr contribution to the book (cf. *Deuteronomy*, 43-46). The categories used by Nielsen are: bold type for pre- and early ("Vor- und Früh-") deuteronomic; roman for deuteronomic; italic for deuteronomistic and post-deuteronomistic. The overlap of categories is evident and indicative. The categories used by Preuss are: in chaps. 5–11, I for the level of the basic (singular) deuteronomic introduction, II for the level (also singular) completing the

---

9. For example, Norbert Lohfink's comment: "Daß das Dtn eine komplizierte Entstehungsgeschichte hat, ist offensichtlich. Doch gibt es darüber keine Theorie, die sich durchgesetzt hätte" (quoted approvingly by Timo Veijola, "Bundestheologische Redaktion im Deuteronomium," in *Das Deuteronomium und seine Querbeziehungen*, 242–76, see p. 242).

deuteronomic introduction, III for the (plural) deuteronomistic editing and associated material, and IV for the mainly later additions; in chaps. 12–26, I is used for the various levels of the old pre-deuteronomic core, II for the deuteronomic activity of collecting and composing, III for the level of deuteronomic editing, IV for the various levels of deuteronomistic editing, and finally V for later material and additions.

The verse divisions "a" and "b" in the analyses of Mayes and Nielsen usually correspond with the masoretic division of the Hebrew text; for Preuss, it is evident that this is not necessarily so. The asterisk (*) is used to denote reference to part of a verse only. Once upon a time, the linguistic distinction between deuteronomic (associated with the book of Deuteronomy and the reform of Josiah) and deuteronomistic (associated with the literary work within Deuteronomy to Kings) was also a distinction in time: deuteronomic referred to the seventh century and deuteronomistic referred to the sixth century B.C.E. With the advocacy of a Josianic DH, this distinction in time has often disappeared. In the present context, it is still useful (and indeed necessary) to distinguish between deuteronomic (= associated with the book of Deuteronomy) and deuteronomistic (= associated with the literary work within Deuteronomy to Kings). In many cases, there may well be a chronological difference present; however, it can no longer be readily assumed.

THE BOOK OF DEUTERONOMY

1 **These are the words that Moses spoke to all Israel beyond the Jordan.**[1]

—in the wilderness, on the plain opposite Suph, between Paran and Tophel, Laban, Hazeroth, and Di-zahab. [2](By the way of Mount Seir it takes eleven days to reach Kadesh-barnea from Horeb.) [3]In the fortieth year, on the first day of the eleventh month, Moses spoke to the Israelites just as the LORD had commanded him to speak to them.[2]

[4]*This was after he had defeated King Sihon of the Amorites, who reigned in Heshbon, and King Og of Bashan, who reigned in Ashtaroth and in Edrei.* [5]*Beyond the Jordan in the land of Moab, Moses undertook to expound this law as follows:*[3]

---

1. The text of the DH was originally identified by Martin Noth (*The Deuteronomistic History;* after this, abbreviated to *DH*). It is unnecessary to rehearse his arguments; it would considerably lengthen our treatment.

2. This material is often regarded as an expansion of the simple introduction in v. 1a. It contains incompatible conflict about the location. V. 2 is out of place in the context, but may explain the place names. V. 3 emphasizes the forty-year stay in the desert, not an eleven-day journey; it does so with the precision of day, month, and year customary in the priestly writing and not found in Deuteronomy. Noth deals with the material differently, in terms of an ancient source and the Dtr's editing of it (*DH*, 46-47; in n. 1 on p. 47, for v. 32 read v. 3a).

3. From the point of view of signals in the text: (i) the reference to expounding the law (v. 5) anticipates chap. 4; both can be attributed to the national focus of the dtr revision. (ii) V. 4 has nothing to tag it to any particular stratum; however, it serves well as an introduction to v. 5. Noth puts the last word of v. 5 with v. 6 (Heb., *lē'mor*; literally, "saying"; NRSV, "as follows"). It is a possible option.

6 The LORD our God spoke to us at Horeb, saying, "You have stayed long enough at this mountain. [7]Resume your journey, and go into the hill country of the Amorites as well as into the neighboring regions—the Arabah, the hill country, the Shephelah, the Negeb, and the seacoast—the land of the Canaanites and the Lebanon, as far as the great river, the river Euphrates. [8]See, I have set the land before you; go in and take possession of the land that I swore to your ancestors, to Abraham, to Isaac, and to Jacob, to give to them and to their descendants after them."[4]

[9] At that time I said to you, "I am unable by myself to bear you. [10]The LORD your God has multiplied you, so that today you are as numerous as the stars of heaven. [11]May the LORD, the God of your ancestors, increase you a thousand times more and bless you, as he has promised you! [12]But how can I bear the heavy burden of your disputes all by myself? [13]Choose for each of your tribes individuals who are wise, discerning, and reputable to be your leaders." [14]You answered me, "The plan you have proposed is a good one." [15]So I took the leaders of your tribes, wise and reputable individuals, and installed them as leaders over you, commanders of thousands, commanders of hundreds, commanders of fifties, commanders of tens, and officials,

---

From the point of view of the present text: the inclusion here lends an emphasis from the outset to the focus on law.

4. The Hebrew text has "the land that the LORD swore to your ancestors" etc; on the ground of this third person reference, Noth attributes the whole clause describing the land to a later addition. The NRSV represents a different text-critical reading.

After the Dtr:	*Revision:*	Other:
indented and sans serif font	*national focus*	double sideline

throughout your tribes. [16]I charged your judges at that time: "Give the members of your community a fair hearing, and judge rightly between one person and another, whether citizen or resident alien. [17]You must not be partial in judging: hear out the small and the great alike; you shall not be intimidated by anyone, for the judgment is God's. Any case that is too hard for you, bring to me, and I will hear it." [18]So I charged you at that time with all the things that you should do.[5]

19 Then, just as the LORD our God had ordered us, we set out from Horeb and went through all that great and terrible wilderness that you saw, on the way to the hill country of the Amorites, until we reached Kadesh-barnea. [20]I said to you, "You have reached the hill country of the Amorites, which the LORD our God is giving us.

[21]See, the LORD your God has given the land to you; go up, take possession, as the LORD, the God of your ancestors, has promised you; do not fear or be dismayed."[6]

22 All of you came to me and said, "Let us send men ahead of us to explore the land for us and bring back a report to us regarding the route by which we should go up and the cities we will come to." [23]The plan seemed good to me, and I selected twelve of you, one from each tribe. [24]They set out and went up into the hill country, and when they reached the Valley of Eshcol they spied it out [25]and gathered some of the land's produce, which they brought down to us. They brought back

---

5. **Text signals** in vv. 9-18. (i) This leadership structure does not feature in the following episode of the spying out of the land (1:22-45); it is not presumed later (cf. 16:18; 29:10). (ii) The appointments are not mentioned in God's order (cf. vv. 6-8; see Nielsen, *Deuteronomium*, 25-26). (iii) The phrase "at that time" (*bāʿēt hahiwʾ*), in vv. 9 and 18, provides a bracket around the passage (see also v. 16). (iv) God's command is given in vv. 6-8; Israel's compliance is noted in vv. 19-20.

Text-history approach. It is possible and, on balance, quite likely that the passage is an insertion; Noth, who nevertheless retains it, comments that it "does not look like a necessary part of the whole" (*DH*, 31; also favoring dtr responsibility, Mayes [*Deuteronomy*, 118] and Preuss [*Deuteronomium*, 80]). If the tradition of Exodus 18 is to be maintained (but cf. Num 11:11-17), these appointments need to be located at Sinai/Horeb. In Exodus, however, the recommendation comes from Jethro just before the formal arrival at Sinai (cf. 18:5; 19:1); here, without reference to Jethro, it is just before the departure from Horeb/Sinai. The traditions involved have been closely interwoven (cf. v. 12).

The phrase "at that time" occurs ten times in the first three chapters of Deuteronomy (1:9, 16, 18; 2:34; 3:4, 8, 12, 18, 21, 23). In all these occurrences, it appears to be indicative of later editing.

Present-text potential. The presence of vv. 9-18 at this early stage in the story is in conformity with the

Exodus tradition. It also portrays Israel from the outset as a great nation, "as numerous as the stars of heaven" (v. 9). The leadership structure is in place that is needed for this people on this critical journey to what will be their home.

6. **Text signals.** (i) Verse 21 is second person singular; its context is second person plural. (ii) It repeats the theme of 1:8.

Text-history approach. Less the repetition than the fact that it is singular in the midst of a plural context suggests that v. 21 is an addition.

Present-text potential. 1:8 is located at the start of Israel's journey; 1:21 here is at the other end of the journey. It is appropriate that God's command (from v. 8) be repeated by Moses (v. 21), with Israel on the southern verge of the promised land and rebelliously unwilling (v. 26) and even afraid (vv. 28-29) to occupy it.

Main pre-DH: dtn lawcode	Other pre-DH:	**Josianic DH:**
its introduction and conclusion	single sideline	**from the Dtr**

a report to us, and said, "It is a good land that the LORD our God is giving us."

26 But you were unwilling to go up. You rebelled against the command of the LORD your God; [27]you grumbled in your tents and said, "It is because the LORD hates us that he has brought us out of the land of Egypt, to hand us over to the Amorites to destroy us. [28]Where are we headed? Our kindred have made our hearts melt by reporting, 'The people are stronger and taller than we; the cities are large and fortified up to heaven! We actually saw there the offspring of the Anakim!' " [29]I said to you, "Have no dread or fear of them. [30]The LORD your God, who goes before you, is the one who will fight for you, just as he did for you in Egypt before your very eyes, [31]and in the wilderness, where you saw how the LORD your God carried you, just as one carries a child, **all the way that you traveled until you reached this place.** [32]But in spite of this, you have no trust in the LORD your God, [33]who goes before you on the way to seek out a place for you to camp, in fire by night, and in the cloud by day, to show you the route you should take."[7]

34 When the LORD heard your words, he was wrathful and swore: [35]"Not one of these—not one of this evil generation—shall see the good land that I swore to give to your ancestors.[8]

[36]except Caleb son of Jephunneh. He shall see it, and to him and to his descendants I will give the land on which he set foot, because of his complete fidelity to the LORD."[9]

[37]Even with me the LORD was angry on your account, saying, "You also shall not enter there. [38]Joshua son of Nun, your assistant, shall enter there; encourage him, for he is the one who will secure Israel's possession of it. [39]And as for your little ones, who you thought would become booty, your children, who today do not yet know right from wrong, they shall enter there; to them I will give it, and they shall take possession of it. [40]But as for you, journey back into the wilderness, in the direction of the Red Sea."[10]

41 You answered me, "We have sinned against the LORD! We are ready to go up and fight, just as the LORD our God commanded us." So all of you strapped on your battle gear, and thought it easy to go up into the hill country. [42]The LORD said to me, "Say to

---

7. The clause set in ordinary type in v. 31a is not only in the singular but also disrupts the sequence portraying the LORD who fights for Israel in Egypt before their eyes (v. 30) and in the desert on their journey (v. 31). An addition is likely.

8. In v. 35, the LXX lacks the qualification, "not one of this evil generation." The phrase makes clear that the LORD's anger affects the entire generation, not just the spies. An addition is possible, but not

necessary (cf. 2:14). The lack in the LXX might have several causes.

9. Verse 36 breaks the narrative movement from the condemned exodus generation to the emerging conquest generation. The verse anticipates Josh 14:6-15 and Judg 1:11-15. Noth retains v. 36, seeing Caleb's "exceptional conduct" as "the crux of the whole story" (*DH*, 50, n. 5). In our view, the crux of the story is the failure of the exodus generation, which had its implications even for Moses. An addition from some later hand is likely.

10. Verse 39 identifies the future generation with "your little ones" and "your children"; the two categories are differentiated from each other in 2 Chron 20:13 and 31:18. LXX (except A) omits the whole reference to "your little ones," either overlooking the differentiation or following a different Hebrew text (cf. παν παιδιον νεον).

| After the Dtr: indented and sans serif font | *Revision: national focus* | Other: double sideline |

them, 'Do not go up and do not fight, for I am not in the midst of you; otherwise you will be defeated by your enemies.'" [43]Although I told you, you would not listen. You rebelled against the command of the LORD and presumptuously went up into the hill country. [44]The Amorites who lived in that hill country then came out against you and chased you as bees do. They beat you down in Seir as far as Hormah. [45]When you returned and wept before the LORD, the LORD would neither heed your voice nor pay you any attention.

[46] After you had stayed at Kadesh as many days as you did

2 we journeyed back into the wilderness, in the direction of the Red Sea, as the LORD had told me and skirted Mount Seir for many days. [2]Then the LORD said to me: [3]"You have been skirting this hill country long enough. Head north, [4]and charge the people as follows: You are about to pass through the territory of your kindred, the descendants of Esau, who live in Seir. They will be afraid of you, so, be very careful [5]not to engage in battle with them, for I will not give you even so much as a foot's length of their land, since I have given Mount Seir to Esau as a possession. [6]You shall purchase food from them for money, so that you may eat; and you shall also buy water from them for money, so that you may drink.

> [7]Surely the LORD your God has blessed you in all your undertakings; he knows your going through this great wilderness. These forty years the LORD your God has been with you; you have lacked nothing."[11]

---

11. The second person singular occurs here in a plural context; the verse looks back on the completed

[8]So we passed by our kin, the descendants of Esau who live in Seir, leaving behind the route of the Arabah, and leaving behind Elath and Ezion-geber.

When we had headed out along the route of the wilderness of Moab, [9]the LORD said to me:[12]

> "Do not harass Moab or engage them in battle, for I will not give you any of its land as a possession, since I have given Ar as a possession to the descendants of Lot." [10](The Emim—a large and numerous people, as tall as the Anakim—had formerly inhabited it. [11]Like the Anakim, they are usually reckoned as Rephaim, though the Moabites call them Emim. [12]Moreover, the Horim had formerly inhabited Seir, but the descendants of Esau dispossessed them, destroying them and settling in their place, as Israel has done in the land that the LORD gave them as a possession.)[13]

---

forty years that in the context are still unfolding. An addition is likely. In relation to the purchase of provisions (v. 6), v. 7 is an emphasis on God's blessing and providence in the wilderness.

12. Our understanding of the DH text in what follows is that Israel's trajectory took them into the wilderness, east of the territory of Moab (cf. v. 8, "the wilderness of Moab"—otherwise unmentioned in biblical text). In this understanding, the reference to Wadi Zered is a way station on the journey, not an entry point into Moab. The approach to the "promised land" (cf. 1:34-35) is signaled by the crossing of the Wadi Arnon (so, basically, Noth, *DH*, 53-54).

13. **Text signals** common to 2:9*-12, 18-23, 24*-25, 30*-31, 37; 3:2, 9-11, 13b-17. (i) One way or another, these passages appear to interrupt a narrative of Israel's journey northward, east of the Dead Sea. In some cases there are divine commands, in others, there are details of antiquarian interest, and so on. (ii) In all these cases, where there is address, it is in the

---

13"Now then, proceed to cross over the Wadi Zered." So we crossed over the Wadi Zered.
    ¹⁴And the length of time we had traveled from Kadesh-barnea until we crossed the Wadi Zered was thirty-eight years, until the entire generation of warriors had perished from the camp, as the LORD had sworn con-

---

singular—in contrast to the plural context. While this alternation between singular and plural cannot be explained by any single phenomenon, in these specific cases later editing seems likely. Suasive evidence could override this perception. (iii) Where divine commands precede narrative report (2:9, 18-19, 24*-25; 3:2), our overall perception is not of a sequence reflecting God's command and Israel's compliance but of commands that have been distilled from the account of Israel's journeying. (iv) The traditions of antiquarian interest (in parentheses in the NRSV) comprise 2:10-12, 20-23; 3:9, 11, and 13b-14.

    Text-history approach. The overall congruence of these factors, some of which will be discussed in more detail in their place, suggests the presence of later additions in these passages. In some cases, the singular might seem appropriate for God's address to Moses; it is difficult to sustain this approach. Of interest is the observation that the antiquarian material appears to have been attached at points where additions were present. .

    Present-text potential. The traditions of vv. 9* and 18-19 explain the absence of conflict with Moab and Ammon in relation to the "descendants of Lot" (cf. Gen 19:30-38). Beyond this, the bulk of this material puts the stamp of prior divine command on the account of Israel's march. The interest of the material we have called "antiquarian" is self-evident.

    After these general comments on what is common to a number of passages, it is appropriate to note some further observations.

    With regard to vv. 9-12. Verse 9 is concerned to prohibit battle against Moab, because Ar has been given to "the descendants of Lot" (cf. Gen 19:30-38; note the contrast in language with Deut 2:29). The verbs

cerning them. ¹⁵Indeed, the LORD's own hand was against them, to root them out from the camp, until all had perished.¹⁴

16 When (Heb.; NRSV, Just as soon as) **all the warriors had died off from among the people, ¹⁷the LORD spoke to me, saying,**
    ¹⁸"Today you are going to cross the boundary of Moab at Ar. ¹⁹When you approach the frontier of the Ammonites, do not harass them or engage them in battle, for I will not give the land of the Ammonites to you as a possession, because I have given it to the descendants of Lot." ²⁰(It also is usually reckoned as a land of Rephaim. Rephaim formerly inhabited it, though the Ammonites call them Zamzummim, ²¹a strong and numerous people, as tall as the Anakim. But the LORD destroyed them from before the Ammonites so that they could dispossess them and settle in their place.

"harass" and "engage" occur as a pair in vv. 9 and 19; the verb "engage" (in battle) is used in vv. 5, 9, 19, and 24. Otherwise, these do not occur in Deuteronomy. The same prohibition and the same reference to Lot recurs with regard to Ammon in vv. 18-19. It would seem that the prohibition concerning the descendants of Esau (2:1-6) has been extended to include Moab and Ammon. This is not the concern of the main narrative, focused on the journey and the battles with Sihon and later Og. For the general context, see the note on 2:9. Verses 10-12 offer information of antiquarian interest on the former inhabitants of the land of Moab.

    14. Verse 14a is in tension with v. 16 and v. 14b duplicates v. 16. V. 15 offers a particular interpretation of v. 14. The tension between vv. 14a and 16 concerns the death of the exodus generation. For v. 14a, this death precedes the crossing of the Wadi Zered; for v. 16, it follows that crossing. A secondary addition is likely, in association with the passage through Moab and Ammon (cf. 2:9*, 18-19). In this understanding, the crossing of the Wadi Zered is an entry into Moab, not just a station along the way.

| After the Dtr:
indented and sans serif font | *Revision:*
national focus | Other:
double sideline |

²²He did the same for the descendants of Esau, who live in Seir, by destroying the Horim before them so that they could dispossess them and settle in their place even to this day. ²³As for the Avvim, who had lived in settlements in the vicinity of Gaza, the Caphtorim, who came from Caphtor, destroyed them and settled in their place.)[15]

²⁴**"Proceed on your journey and cross the Wadi Arnon."**

See, I have handed over to you King Sihon the Amorite of Heshbon, and his land. Begin to take possession by engaging him in battle. ²⁵This day I will begin to put the dread and fear of you upon the peoples everywhere under heaven; when they hear report of you, they will tremble and be in anguish because of you."[16]

26 So I sent messengers from the wilderness of Kedemoth to King Sihon of Heshbon with the following terms of peace: ²⁷"If you let me pass through your land, I will travel only along the road; I will turn aside neither to the right nor to the left. ²⁸You shall sell me food for money, so that I may eat, and supply me water for money, so that I may drink. Only allow me to pass through on foot— ²⁹just as the descendants of Esau who live in Seir have done for me and likewise the Moabites who live in Ar—until I cross the Jordan into the land that the LORD our God is giving us." ³⁰But King Sihon of Heshbon was not willing to let us pass through.[17]

---

15. Verses 18-19 use a different geographical point of reference from their surroundings. The reference in v. 18 is to "the boundary of Moab at Ar"; v. 13 refers to the Wadi Zered and v. 24* to the Wadi Arnon. There is a strong echo of 2:9*, but with reference here to Ammon, not Moab.

Verses 20-23 are similar to vv. 10-12 and offer information on the former inhabitants of the land of Ammon (probably from the same source). The possibility must be kept open that this secondary material may come from several sources. It is noteworthy that in 2:12 the descendants of Esau are reported as dispossessing the Horim, "as Israel has done in the land that the LORD gave them as a possession." In 2:21, it is the LORD who dispossessed the Horim on behalf of the descendants of Esau, as equally the Zamzummim on behalf of the Ammonites (v. 21). Such divine action is not noted for the Caphtorim who dispossessed the Avvim (v. 23).

16. Beyond what has been said at 2:9, we may note that v. 24* speaks of engaging Sihon in battle, whereas in v. 26 Sihon is offered terms of peace. Before the engagement with Sihon, vv. 24*-25 bring to expression the aspect of God's initiative and sovereignty.

17. This passage (vv. 26-30a) has caused interpreters considerable difficulties, which are not insuperable. In our judgment, the primary issue is raised by Noth, who however restricts its impact to characterizing the end of v. 29 as secondary. The issue is larger and concerns not only vv. 26-30a but much of chap. 3. Noth speaks of the issue as: "the false impression that the promised land was originally confined to the region west of the Jordan and extended later only de facto as a result of the behaviour of the Transjordanian kings" (*DH*, 55, n. 1). As Nielsen correctly notes in this connection, such an observation wrongly overlooks the fact that the portrayal of the conquest of Israel's land took place after the death of Moses, under the leadership of Joshua, and following the crossing of the Jordan (p. 40). Passages in the DH confirm this focus on the land west of the Jordan. For example, Deut 1:6-8 includes no reference to east-of-Jordan; our analysis of 2:26—3:28 suggests that the details of eastern conquest are a later embellishment; issues in the book of Joshua will confirm this for the two and a half tribes and the occupation east of Jordan (see esp. the note on Josh 1:12-18). Deuteronomy 11:31 is an example of retained emphasis on the land west of the Jordan.

As a result, we conclude that the role played by Sihon and Og in the DH is not so much historical as theological or ideological. What this might be lies

---

| Main pre-DH: dtn lawcode | Other pre-DH: | **Josianic DH:** |
| *its introduction and conclusion* | single sideline | **from the Dtr** |

for the LORD your God had hardened his spirit and made his heart defiant in order to hand him over to you, as he has now done. [31]The LORD said to me, "See, I have begun to give Sihon and his land over to you. Begin now to take possession of his land."[18]

[32]So when Sihon came out against us, he and all his people for battle at Jahaz,[33]the LORD our God gave him over to us; and we struck him down, along with his offspring and all his people.

[34]At that time we captured all his towns, and in each town we utterly destroyed [= ḥerem] men, women, and children. We left not a single survivor [= hiš'îr śārîd]. [35]Only the livestock we kept as spoil for ourselves, as well as the plunder of the towns that we had captured. [36]From Aroer on the edge of the Wadi Arnon (including the town that is in the wadi itself) as far as Gilead, there was no citadel too high for us. The LORD our God gave everything to us. [37]You did not encroach, however, on the land of the Ammonites, avoiding the whole upper region of the Wadi Jabbok as well as the towns of the hill country, just as the LORD our God had charged.[19]

3 When we headed up the road to Bashan, King Og of Bashan came out against us, he and all his people, for battle at Edrei.[20]

---

outside our present scope. Two aspects are clear. First, the themes of total destruction and the distribution of the land to the two and a half tribes are found together here. In the book of Joshua, both themes are found in apparently late stages of the book's development—but they occur quite separately. Second, the DH's interest in Sihon and Og is limited. They occur together in Deut 1:4; 29:6; 31:4 (all three later stages of revision) and in Josh 2:10 and 9:10. In Deut 1:4 and 29:6, they feature as a matter of record, no more. In Deut 31:4 and Josh 2:10 and 9:10, they function as an example of what awaits the locals west-of-Jordan. The allocation of their land to the two and a half tribes is noted (Deut 3:12*-13; 29:6); its total conquest and clearance is not noted in the DH (outside 2:34-35 and 3:4-8, 13b-17—which in our judgment do not belong within the Josianic DH). What is remarkable in the DH here is the role of human aggression. Sihon's aggression leads to his defeat by Israel. Israel's aggression, advancing north, triggers Og's sortie and his defeat in turn by Israel. In both texts, "the LORD our God gave him over to us" (2:33; 3:3). As will be reiterated in the book of Joshua, certainty is probably out of reach. The possibility has to be entertained that the emphasis on the occupation of territory east of the Jordan by the two and a half tribes is a relatively late concern.

18. As noted, the second person singular occurs here in both verses. V. 30b echoes priestly traditions from the plagues and exodus (but cf. Josh 11:20). On the eve of battle, God's sovereignty, stated in vv. 24b-25, is reaffirmed. In particular, Israel's occupation of land east-of-Jordan is not the result of human obstinacy (i.e., Sihon's refusal, v. 30a), but of divine disposition.

19. Verses 34-37 are introduced by the phrase "at that time" (cf. note on 1:9-18). The language of total destruction in vv. 34-35 is found mainly in late levels of the book of Joshua. It is likely to be secondary here. V. 36 appears associated with this addition (cf. 3:4-6). V. 37 is second person singular in a plural context and returns to the theme of avoiding conflict with the Ammonites, added earlier in v. 19. The present text has the potential for seeing the land east-of-Jordan as belonging within God's promise to Israel.

For the retaining of booty noted here (v. 35) and in 3:7, note the difference in treatment of Jericho (Josh 6:21) and Ai (Josh 8:2, identical with Deut 2:35 and 3:7).

20. The presentation of this tradition has to be differentiated from that concerning Sihon, who blocked Israel's passage to the Jordan crossing. Here the initiative is with Israel, going up north rather than going

---

After the Dtr:	Revision:	Other:
indented and sans serif font	*national focus*	double sideline

²The LORD said to me, "Do not fear him, for I have handed him over to you, along with his people and his land. Do to him as you did to King Sihon of the Amorites, who reigned in Heshbon."²¹

³So the LORD our God also handed over to us King Og of Bashan and all his people.

We struck him down until not a single survivor was left [= *hiš'îr śārîd*]. ⁴At that time we captured all his towns; there was no citadel that we did not take from them—sixty towns, the whole region of Argob, the kingdom of Og in Bashan. ⁵All these were fortress towns with high walls, double gates, and bars, besides a great many villages. ⁶And we utterly destroyed them [= *ḥerem*], as we had done to King Sihon of Heshbon, in each city utterly destroying [= *ḥerem*] men, women, and children. ⁷But all the livestock and the plunder of the towns we kept as spoil for ourselves.²²

8 So at that time we took from the two kings of the Amorites the land beyond the Jordan, from the Wadi Arnon to Mount Hermon ⁹(the Sidonians call Hermon Sirion, while the Amorites call it Senir) ¹⁰all the towns of the tableland, the whole of Gilead, and all of Bashan, as far as Salecah and Edrei, towns of Og's kingdom in Bashan. ¹¹(Now only King Og of Bashan was left of the remnant of the Rephaim. In fact his bed, an iron bed, can still be seen in Rabbah of the Ammonites. By the common cubit it is nine cubits long and four cubits wide.)²³ ¹²As for the land that we took possession of at that time²⁴

The territory north of Aroer, that is on the edge of the Wadi Arnon, as well as half the hill country of Gilead with its towns I gave to the Reubenites and Gadites, ¹³and the rest of Gilead and all of Bashan, Og's kingdom, I gave to the half-tribe of Manasseh (Heb. sentence sequence).²⁵

---

toward the Jordan or toward "the valley opposite Beth-peor" (3:29).

21. In 3:2, we have again the second person singular in a plural context. The verse exhibits the same thinking as 2:24-25*, 30b-31. According to v. 2, God's will controls the action to follow. On the eve of battle, God's sovereignty is reaffirmed.

22. Verses 4-7, introduced by the phrase "at that time," present an image of total conquest, using the language of total destruction. As with 2:34-36, a later addition is likely. For the treatment of booty in v. 7, see above on 2:35. V. 3b is problematic; on the balance of probabilities, we have favored an addition, developing with slight variation the "and we struck" of 2:33. The half-verse here (3:3b) intensifies the fate of "all his people" (2:33b and 3:3a). The emphasis on no survivors would parallel 2:34; on the evidence of the book of Joshua, it is particularly appropriate to a later addition. The possibility, however, that v. 3b was original cannot be denied.

23. Verses 8-11 again involve the phrase "at that time" in their introduction (cf. note on 1:9-18). V. 8 summarizes the traditions concerning Sihon and Og. It sits oddly with v. 12 (esp. in Hebrew); different geographical points of reference are used (e.g., Hermon and Aroer). An addition is probable, supported by the presence of "at that time."

In vv. 9-11, two notices of antiquarian interest bracket the concern in v. 10 for total conquest. It may be derived from the secondary Josh 13:9-11; such issues have to remain uncertain.

24. At the beginning of v. 12, the Hebrew sentence structure is unusual, with the object thrown forward. Again, the phrase "at that time" is involved. Israel's first person plural contrasts with Moses' first person singular in what follows. V. 12a is likely to be an editorial bridge.

25. Verses 12*-13 could well be the Josianic DH's statement of Moses allocation of the land east-of-

---

Main pre-DH: dtn lawcode   Other pre-DH: **Josianic DH:**
its introduction and conclusion   single sideline   **from the Dtr**

(The whole region of Argob: all that portion of Bashan used to be called a land of Rephaim; [14]Jair the Manassite acquired the whole region of Argob as far as the border of the Geshurites and the Maacathites, and he named them—that is, Bashan—after himself, Havvoth-jair, as it is to this day.) [15]To Machir I gave Gilead. [16]And to the Reubenites and the Gadites I gave the territory from Gilead as far as the Wadi Arnon, with the middle of the wadi as a boundary, and up to the Jabbok, the wadi being boundary of the Ammonites; [17]the Arabah also, with the Jordan and its banks, from Chinnereth down to the sea of the Arabah, the Dead Sea, with the lower slopes of Pisgah on the east.[26]

18 At that time, I charged you as follows: "Although the LORD your God has given you this land to occupy, all your troops shall cross over armed as the vanguard of your Israelite kin.[19]Only your wives, your children, and your livestock—I know that you have much livestock—shall stay behind in the towns that I have given to you. [20]When the LORD gives rest to your kindred, as to you, and they too have occupied the land that the LORD your God is giving them beyond the Jordan, then each of you may return to the property that I have given to you."[27]

[21]And I charged Joshua as well at that time, saying: "Your own eyes have seen everything that the LORD your God has done to these two kings; so the LORD will do to all the kingdoms into which you are about to cross. [22]Do not fear them, for it is the LORD your God who fights for you."[28]

23 At that time (*Heb.; NRSV, too*), I entreated the LORD, saying: [24]"O Lord GOD, you have only begun to show your servant your greatness and your might; what god in heaven or on earth can perform deeds and mighty acts like yours! [25]Let me cross over to see the good land beyond the Jordan, that good hill country and the Lebanon."

Jordan to the two and a half tribes. It follows adequately on 3:3a, as distribution follows conquest. It is also possible that these verses (12*-13) belong with the additional material. Certainty is out of reach. But without these verses, there is no allocation of the land east-of-Jordan in the Josianic DH. Retention in the Josianic DH is likely, but Transjordan is far from the central focus of the History; it is certainly not central to the lawcode either (cf. Deut 11:31–12:1).

26. Verses 13b-14 offer another antiquarian note, similar to those in 2:10-12, 20-23; 3:9, 11. Vv. 15-17 contain other traditions about the territory noted in vv. 12b-13a. The traditions about Machir are complex. Alternative traditions are appropriately preserved here, for storage and retrieval.

27. Verses 18-20 concern the participation of the east-of-Jordan tribes in the conquest of the land west of the Jordan. Full discussion is given below with regard to the book of Joshua (cf. the note on Josh 1:12-18). The strategy of leaving wives, children, and livestock unprotected in the east for a considerable period of time is sufficiently improbable that some overwhelming ideal would be needed to override it (see Num 32:16-27, esp. vv. 16-17, for implicit awareness of the problem, avowal of the presence of locals, and silence over strategies for defense of the fortified towns [v. 17]). Certainty is out of reach. It should be said that viewing the texts as later additions is not a statement about the events.

28. Verses 21-22 anticipate Deut 31:7-8, where Moses commissions Joshua to lead the people into the land. The statement of Joshua's future role is noted in 1:37-38; its actualization is not needed until 31:7-8. The repetition of the charge here (3:21-22) has value in relating the fate of Sihon and Og to the future conquest.

After the Dtr:	Revision:	Other:
indented and sans serif font	*national focus*	double sideline

²⁶But the LORD was angry with me on your account and would not heed me. The LORD said to me, "Enough from you! Never speak to me of this matter again! ²⁷Go up to the top of Pisgah and look around you to the west, to the north, to the south, and to the east. Look well, for you shall not cross over this Jordan. ²⁸But charge Joshua, and encourage and strengthen him, because it is he who shall cross over at the head of this people and who shall secure their possession of the land that you will see."²⁹

²⁹**And** (Heb.; NRSV, So) **we remained in the valley opposite Beth-peor.**³⁰

---

29. Verses 23-28, like vv. 21-22, reflect the past (1:37-38) and anticipate the future (34:1, where Moses ascends Mount Pisgah and is shown the whole land). Here, Moses remonstrates with God on his own behalf against the divine disposition of 1:37. This itself is unusual. The language used is also more florid than usual: for "greatness and might," see Deut 11:2; for "deeds and mighty acts," see Ps 145:4; Esth 10:2(!); "good hill country," only here; "west, north, south, and east," only here.

Most probably, the value of these verses lies in their association with the commissioning of Joshua (note both vv. 21-22 and v. 28). They give definitive expression to God's prohibition: "Never speak to me of this matter again!" (3:26). The reference to Mount Pisgah confirms this prohibition; Moses will see the land, not enter it. Joshua's future role is flagged three times (1:38, 3:21-22, 28). Leadership by Moses will give way to leadership by Joshua. The formal commissioning is at 31:7-8.

All three of these passages—vv. 18-20, 21-22, 23-28—are introduced by the phrase "at that time."

30. Verse 29 is an enigma, on more than one count. First, it is in the locality where Israel must arrive, but the narrative never gets there. No matter what is taken out of the text or what is left in, the narrative does not reach Beth-peor (or that locality). The narrative cannot move there from 2:24; some compliance

4 *So now, Israel, give heed to the statutes and ordinances that I am teaching you to observe, so that you may live to enter and occupy the land that the LORD, the God of your ancestors, is giving you. ²You must neither add anything to what I command you nor take away anything from it, but keep the commandments of the LORD your God with which I am charging you. ³You have seen for yourselves what the LORD did with regard to the Baal of Peor—how the LORD your God destroyed from among you everyone who followed the Baal of Peor, ⁴while those of you who held fast to the LORD your God are all alive today.*³¹

---

with God's command in 2:24 is needed. Nor can it move there from 2:33 (or equivalent), because there is no indication of a journey from Jahaz. In 3:1, Israel headed north toward Bashan; the narrative never brings them back—but here they are. Second, while a locality near Mount Pisgah is needed, Beth-peor is not mentioned at either Deut 1:1-5 or 34:1. Third, although the story (Numbers 25) is not in the Josianic DH, Peor is known to Israel as a place of grave apostasy (cf. Deut 4:3; Josh 22:17; Hos 9:10; Ps 106:28). The place of sin remains opposite them as Moses expounds their law. Enigma indeed. The verse is odd but it is the only verse there is.

31. **Text signals** in 4:1-40. (i) There is concern for obedience to the law and the dire consequences of disobedience. (ii) The language in which these concerns are expressed is characteristic of what is found associated with the national focus of the dtr revision. (iii) The theme of God's mercy and Israel's return (vv. 29-31), suggests an exilic or post-exilic setting. (iv) There is a significant shift from Deuteronomy's choice between the alternatives of curse and blessing to an understanding that sees these as sequential, blessing follows curse (Mayes, *Deuteronomy*, 156). (v) 4:1-40 uses both singular and plural address: singular, vv. 3b, 9-10, 19, 21b, 23b* (last phrase)-24, 25* (first and last

---

Main pre-DH: dtn lawcode
its introduction and conclusion

Other pre-DH:
single sideline

Josianic DH:
from the Dtr

*5 See, just as the L*ORD *my God has charged me, I now teach you statutes and ordinances for you to observe in the land that you are about to enter and occupy. ⁶You must observe them diligently, for this will show your wisdom and discernment to the peoples, who, when they hear all these statutes, will say, "Surely this great nation is a wise and discerning people!"⁷For what other great nation has a god so near to it as the L*ORD *our God is whenever we call to him? ⁸And what other great nation has statutes and ordinances as just as this entire law that I am setting before you today?*

*9 But take care and watch yourselves closely, so as neither to forget the things that your eyes have seen nor to let them slip from your mind all the days of your life; make them known to your children and your children's children—¹⁰how you once stood before the L*ORD *your God at Horeb, when the L*ORD *said to me, "Assemble the people for me, and I will let them hear my words, so that they may learn to fear me as*

phrases), 29*-34a, 34b* (last phrase)-40; plural, vv. 1-3a, 5-8, 11-18, 20-21a, 22-23b*, 25*, 26-28, 29a* (first verb), 34b*. Note that not all verses contain address.

Text-history approach. In its focus on the people and its concern for obedience to the law, 4:1-40 falls squarely within the national focus of the dtr revision. Given the alternation of singular and plural address throughout the chapter, a source division on these grounds seems unwise (in agreement with Lohfink and Braulik; for a full discussion, see C. T. Begg, "The Literary Criticism of Deut 4,1-40").

Present-text potential. 4:1-40 spells out how the forthcoming discourse by Moses on the law is to be understood. Aspects of this understanding are emphasized throughout the discourse; here, it is enunciated in full.

*long as they live on the earth, and may teach their children so"; ¹¹you approached and stood at the foot of the mountain while the mountain was blazing up to the very heavens, shrouded in dark clouds.¹²Then the L*ORD *spoke to you out of the fire. You heard the sound of words but saw no form; there was only a voice.¹³He declared to you his covenant, which he charged you to observe, that is, the ten commandments; and he wrote them on two stone tablets. ¹⁴And the L*ORD *charged me at that time to teach you statutes and ordinances for you to observe in the land that you are about to cross into and occupy.*

*15 Since you saw no form when the L*ORD *spoke to you at Horeb out of the fire, take care and watch yourselves closely, ¹⁶so that you do not act corruptly by making an idol for yourselves, in the form of any figure—the likeness of male or female, ¹⁷the likeness of any animal that is on the earth, the likeness of any winged bird that flies in the air, ¹⁸the likeness of anything that creeps on the ground, the likeness of any fish that is in the water under the earth.¹⁹And when you look up to the heavens and see the sun, the moon, and the stars, all the host of heaven, do not be led astray and bow down to them and serve them, things that the L*ORD *your God has allotted to all the peoples everywhere under heaven. ²⁰But the L*ORD *has taken you and brought you out of the iron-smelter, out of Egypt, to become a people of his very own possession, as you are now.*

*21 The L*ORD *was angry with me because of you, and he vowed that I should not cross the Jordan and that I should not enter the good land that the L*ORD *your God is giving for your possession. ²²For I am*

After the Dtr:	Revision:	Other:
indented and sans serif font	*national focus*	double sideline

going to die in this land without crossing over the Jordan, but you are going to cross over to take possession of that good land. 23So be careful not to forget the covenant that the LORD your God made with you, and not to make for yourselves an idol in the form of anything that the LORD your God has forbidden you. 24For the LORD your God is a devouring fire, a jealous God.

25 When you have had children and children's children, and become complacent in the land, if you act corruptly by making an idol in the form of anything, thus doing what is evil in the sight of the LORD your God, and provoking him to anger, 26I call heaven and earth to witness against you today that you will soon utterly perish from the land that you are crossing the Jordan to occupy; you will not live long on it, but will be utterly destroyed. 27The LORD will scatter you among the peoples; only a few of you will be left among the nations where the LORD will lead you. 28There you will serve other gods made by human hands, objects of wood and stone that neither see, nor hear, nor eat, nor smell. 29From there you will seek the LORD your God, and you will find him if you search after him with all your heart and soul. 30In your distress, when all these things have happened to you in time to come, you will return to the LORD your God and heed him. 31Because the LORD your God is a merciful God, he will neither abandon you nor destroy you; he will not forget the covenant with your ancestors that he swore to them.

32 For ask now about former ages, long before your own, ever since the day that God created human beings on the earth; ask from one end of heaven to the other: has anything so great as this ever happened or has its like ever been heard of? 33Has any people ever heard the voice of a god speaking out of a fire, as you have heard, and lived? 34Or has any god ever attempted to go and take a nation for himself from the midst of another nation, by trials, by signs and wonders, by war, by a mighty hand and an outstretched arm, and by terrifying displays of power, as the LORD your God did for you in Egypt before your very eyes? 35To you it was shown so that you would acknowledge that the LORD is God; there is no other besides him. 36From heaven he made you hear his voice to discipline you. On earth he showed you his great fire, while you heard his words coming out of the fire. 37And because he loved your ancestors, he chose their descendants after them. He brought you out of Egypt with his own presence, by his great power, 38driving out before you nations greater and mightier than yourselves, to bring you in, giving you their land for a possession, as it is still today. 39So acknowledge today and take to heart that the LORD is God in heaven above and on the earth beneath; there is no other. 40Keep his statutes and his commandments, which I am commanding you today for your own well-being and that of your descendants after you, so that you may long remain in the land that the LORD your God is giving you for all time.

41 Then Moses set apart on the east side of the Jordan three cities 42to which a homicide could flee, someone who unintentionally kills another person, the two not having been at enmity before; the homicide could flee to one of these cities and live: 43Bezer in the wilderness on the tableland belonging to the Reubenites, Ramoth in

---

Main pre-DH: dtn lawcode
its introduction and conclusion

Other pre-DH:
single sideline

Josianic DH:
from the Dtr

Gilead belonging to the Gadites, and Golan in Bashan belonging to the Manassites.[32]

44 This is the law that Moses set before the Israelites.

[45]These are the decrees and the statutes and ordinances that Moses spoke to the Israelites when they had come out of Egypt, [46]beyond the Jordan in the valley opposite Beth-peor, in the land of King Sihon of the Amorites, who reigned at Heshbon, whom Moses and the Israelites defeated when they came out of Egypt. [47]They occupied his land and the land of King Og of Bashan, the two kings of the Amorites on the eastern side of the Jordan: [48]from Aroer, which is on the edge of the Wadi Arnon, as far as Mount Sirion (that is, Hermon), [49]together with all the Arabah on the east side of the Jordan as far as the Sea of the Arabah, under the slopes of Pisgah.[33]

5 Moses called to (Heb.; NRSV, convened) **all Israel, and said to them:**

Hear, O Israel, the statutes and ordinances that I am addressing to you today; you shall learn them and observe them diligently.[34]

[2]The LORD our God made a covenant with us at Horeb.

[3]Not with our ancestors did the LORD make this covenant, but with us, who are all of us

---

32. The law for the cities of refuge is given in Deut 19:1-3 and 8-10, where there is no mention of these specific cities. Consideration of Num 35:9-15 (towns unspecified) and Josh 20:7-8 (towns specified; cf. also Josh 21:27, 36, 38) suggests a late addition here.

After Moses' account of the conquest of the kingdoms of Sihon and Og on the eastern side of the Jordan (Deut 2:24—3:17*), it is appropriate for him to provide cities of refuge in Transjordan. The location of the narrative report, following 4:1-40, is surprising; it suggests the addition is relatively late.

33. **Text signals.** (i) There are two introductions to the law here—4:44, 45. (ii) V. 44 refers to the law in the singular; 6:1 opens with a singular "commandment." (iii) V. 45 has the plural and the language of 12:1 (with the addition of the normally late ʿēdōt—NRSV, "decrees"; unusual earlier than dtr revision. Note Deut 6:17, 20). (iv) Vv. 46-49 contain information scattered across Deuteronomy 1–3, both original and secondary.

Text-history approach. The location of this material in the history of tradition is both complex and highly controversial; the position suggested here is regarded as no more than one possibility. We suggest that these signals point to a beginning with 4:44, followed by the convocation in 5:1, with 5:2 and the last word (Hebrew) of v. 5 as the Dtr's introduction to the decalogue. Given the complexity of the material and the fact that we are not attempting a new analysis of the book of Deuteronomy, it is appropriate that the bold-type indication of the Dtr's contribution stop before the introduction to the lawcode (i.e., 6:4—11:28).

The statement that Moses "set" the law before Israel is unique. In its own way, it mirrors God's action in "setting" God's name in the Jerusalem temple (above all, 1 Kgs 9:3).

Present-text potential. With the shift from narrative to discourse, it is fitting to have an introduction to Moses' speech—its content (the law, unfolded as decrees, statutes, and ordinances) and its location (specified precisely).

34. **Text signals.** (i) The address is to the people, "O Israel." (ii) Its content is described as "statutes and ordinances." (iii) The task of Israel is to "learn them" and "observe them."

Text-history approach. The concern is with the law and its observance, expressed in a terminology that is closely linked to chap. 4. The sentence fittingly belongs with the national focus of the dtr revision.

Present-text potential. Before the presentation of covenant and decalogue, there is a formal call to attention and an exhortation to diligent observance.

After the Dtr: indented and sans serif font	Revision: national focus	Other: double sideline

*here alive today. [4]The L*ORD *spoke with you face to face at the mountain, out of the fire.* [5](At that time I was standing between the LORD and you to declare to you the words of the LORD; for you were afraid because of the fire and did not go up the mountain.)[35]

And he said:

6 I am the LORD your God, who brought you out of the land of Egypt, out of the house of slavery; [7]you shall have no other gods before me.

8 You shall not make for yourself an idol, whether in the form of anything that is in heaven above, or that is on the earth beneath, or that is in the water under the earth. [9]You shall not bow down to them or worship them; for I the LORD your God am a jealous God, punishing children for the iniquity of parents, to the third and fourth generation of those who reject me, [10]but showing steadfast love to the thousandth generation of those who love me and keep my commandments.

11 You shall not make wrongful use of the name of the LORD your God, for the LORD will not acquit anyone who misuses his name.

12 Observe the sabbath day and keep it holy, as the LORD your God commanded you. [13]Six days you shall labor and do all your work. [14]But the seventh day is a sabbath to the LORD your God; you shall not do any work—you, or your son or your daughter, or your male or female slave, or your ox or your donkey, or any of your livestock, or the resident alien in your towns, so that your male and female slave may rest as well as you. [15]Remember that you were a slave in the land of Egypt, and the LORD your God brought you out from there with a mighty hand and an outstretched arm; therefore the LORD your God commanded you to keep the sabbath day.

16 Honor your father and your mother, as the LORD your God commanded you, so that your days may be long and that it may go well with you in the land that the LORD your God is giving you.

17 You shall not murder.

18 Neither shall you commit adultery.

19 Neither shall you steal.

20 Neither shall you bear false witness against your neighbor.

21 Neither shall you covet your neighbor's wife.

Neither shall you desire your neighbor's house, or field, or male or female slave, or ox, or donkey, or anything that belongs to your neighbor.

22 These words the LORD spoke with a loud voice to your whole assembly at the mountain, out of the fire, the cloud, and the thick darkness, and he added no more. He wrote them on two stone tablets, and gave them to me.[36] [23]When you heard the voice out of the darkness, while the mountain was burning with fire, you approached me

|| all the heads of your tribes and your elders [24]**and you said,**

*Look, the L*ORD *our God has shown us his glory and greatness, and we have heard his voice out of the fire. Today we have seen*

---

35. Verse 5 is in conflict with vv. 4 and 22. The text offers two conflicting views. Vv. 3-4 not only emphasize the validity of the covenant for contemporaries but also make explicit the face-to-face manner of communication. V. 5 expresses a contrary theological position, insisting on Moses' role as intermediary and the people's absence from the mountain.

36. For the rest of chap. 5, we follow the analysis provided by Mayes (*Deuteronomy*, 172-74). The material in italics is associated by Mayes with chap. 4 and his late dtr author; for us, what Mayes identifies in this way is to be located within the national focus of the dtr revision. For chaps. 6-26, see the introduction to the book of Deuteronomy.

Main pre-DH: dtn lawcode   Other pre-DH: **Josianic DH:**
its introduction and conclusion   single sideline   **from the Dtr**

that God may speak to someone and the person may still live.

²⁵"So now why should we die? For this great fire will consume us; if we hear the voice of the LORD our God any longer, we shall die.

²⁶For who is there of all flesh that has heard the voice of the living God speaking out of fire, as we have, and remained alive?

²⁷Go near, you yourself, and hear all that the LORD our God will say. Then tell us everything that the LORD our God tells you, and we will listen and do it."

28 The LORD heard your words when you spoke to me, and the LORD said to me: "I have heard the words of this people, which they have spoken to you; they are right in all that they have spoken.

²⁹If only they had such a mind as this, to fear me and to keep all my commandments always, so that it might go well with them and with their children forever!

³⁰Go say to them, 'Return to your tents.' ³¹But you, stand here by me, and I will tell you all the commandments, the statutes and the ordinances, that you shall teach them, so that they may do them in the land that I am giving them to possess."

³²You must therefore be careful to do as the LORD your God has commanded you; you shall not turn to the right or to the left. ³³You must follow exactly the path that the LORD your God has commanded you, so that you may live, and that it may go well with you, and that you may live long in the land that you are to possess.

6 Now this is the commandment—the statutes and the ordinances—that the LORD your God charged me to teach you to observe in the land that you are about to cross into and occupy.

²so that you and your children and your children's children may fear the LORD your God all the days of your life, and keep all his decrees and his commandments that I am commanding you, so that your days may be long. ³Hear therefore, O Israel, and observe them diligently, so that it may go well with you, and so that you may multiply greatly in a land flowing with milk and honey, as the LORD, the God of your ancestors, has promised you.

4 Hear, O Israel: The LORD is our God, the LORD alone. ⁵You shall love the LORD your God with all your heart, and with all your soul, and with all your might. ⁶Keep these words that I am commanding you today in your heart. ⁷Recite them to your children and talk about them when you are at home and when you are away, when you lie down and when you rise. ⁸Bind them as a sign on your hand, fix them as an emblem on your forehead, ⁹and write them on the doorposts of your house and on your gates.³⁷

---

37. For **6:1-25,** compare the following:

Mayes	**Nielsen**	**Preuss**
i) pre-DH	pre-DH (= bold	i) pre-DH (= I, II)
4-9, 20-25	& roman)	I: 1-3, 20-24
	bold: nil	II: (10-13?)
	roman: 4-9, 10-13	
ii) DH	dtr & post-dtr (italic)	ii) dtr editing
1	1-3, 14-19, 20-25	(= III)
		(10-13?), 14, (15?),
		(16?), 17-18, (19?),
iii) post-DH		iii) post-DH
late dtr		(= additions)
2-3, 10-19		(15?), (16?), 25

No consensus on pre-DH material
Possible consensus on dtr editing: around vv. 14-19

In our judgment, it is appropriate to recognize in the formatting here that 6:1 is likely as a dtr introduction and that vv. 2-3 most probably reflect what we refer to as the national focus of the dtr revision. For the difficulty of attribution regarding "the statutes and the ordinances," note for example Deut 4:1 and 12:1.

After the Dtr:	*Revision:*	Other:
indented and sans serif font	*national focus*	double sideline

10 When the LORD *your God has brought you into the land that he swore to your ancestors, to Abraham, to Isaac, and to Jacob, to give you—a land with fine, large cities that you did not build, [11]houses filled with all sorts of goods that you did not fill, hewn cisterns that you did not hew, vineyards and olive groves that you did not plant—and when you have eaten your fill, [12]take care that you do not forget the* LORD, *who brought you out of the land of Egypt, out of the house of slavery. [13]The* LORD *your God you shall fear; him you shall serve, and by his name alone you shall swear. [14]Do not follow other gods, any of the gods of the peoples who are all around you, [15]because the* LORD *your God, who is present with you, is a jealous God. The anger of the* LORD *your God would be kindled against you and he would destroy you from the face of the earth.*

16 Do not put the LORD *your God to the test, as you tested him at Massah. [17]You must diligently keep the commandments of the* LORD *your God, and his decrees, and his statutes that he has commanded you. [18]Do what is right and good in the sight of the* LORD, *so that it may go well with you, and so that you may go in and occupy the good land that the* LORD *swore to your ancestors to give you, [19]thrusting out all your enemies from before you, as the* LORD *has promised.*

20 When your children ask you in time to come, "What is the meaning of the decrees and the statutes and the ordinances that the LORD *our God has commanded you?" [21]then you shall say to your children, "We were Pharaoh's slaves in Egypt, but the* LORD *brought us out of Egypt with a mighty hand. [22]The* LORD *displayed before our eyes great and awesome signs and wonders against Egypt, against Pharaoh and all his household. [23]He brought us out from there in order to bring us in, to give us the land that he promised on oath to our ancestors. [24]Then the* LORD *commanded us to observe all these statutes, to fear the* LORD *our God, for our lasting good, so as to keep us alive, as is now the case. [25]If we diligently observe this*

entire commandment before the LORD *our God, as he has commanded us, we will be in the right."*

7 *When the* LORD *your God brings you into the land that you are about to enter and occupy, and he clears away many nations before you—the Hittites, the Girgashites, the Amorites, the Canaanites, the Perizzites, the Hivites, and the Jebusites, seven nations mightier and more numerous than you—[2]and when the* LORD *your God gives them over to you and you defeat them, then you must utterly destroy them. Make no covenant with them and show them no mercy. [3]Do not intermarry with them, giving your daughters to their sons or taking their daughters for your sons, [4]for that would turn away your children from following me, to serve other gods. Then the anger of the* LORD *would be kindled against you, and he would destroy you quickly. [5]But this is how you must deal with them: break down their altars, smash their pillars, hew down their sacred poles, and burn their idols with fire. [6]For you are a people holy to the* LORD *your God; the* LORD *your God has chosen you out of all the peoples on earth to be his people, his treasured possession.*[38]

---

38. For **7:1-26,** compare the following:

Mayes	Nielsen	Preuss
i) pre-DH	pre-DH (= bold	i) pre-DH (= I, II)
1-3, 6,	& roman)	I: nil
17-24	bold: nil	II: 1-2, 6*, 17-24,
	roman: 1a, 3, 6	[7-15 (16): insertion
		from various levels]
ii) DH	dtr & post-dtr (italic)	ii) dtr editing (= III)
nil	1b-2, 4-5, 7-11,	(4b?), 5, (6*), 7, 8ab,
	12-16, 17-26	12a, 25a
iii) post-DH		iii) post-DH
late dtr		(= additions)
4-5, 7-15,		3, 4a, (4b?), 22, 25b,
16, 25-26		25c, 26
Other		
22		

Possible consensus on pre-DH material: around v. 1a, 6*
Possible consensus on dtr editing: around vv. 4-5, 7-8, 12a, 25-26

Main pre-DH: dtn lawcode	Other pre-DH:	**Josianic DH:**
its introduction and conclusion	single sideline	**from the Dtr**

7 *It was not because you were more numerous than any other people that the LORD set his heart on you and chose you—for you were the fewest of all peoples.* *8It was because the LORD loved you and kept the oath that he swore to your ancestors, that the LORD has brought you out with a mighty hand, and redeemed you from the house of slavery, from the hand of Pharaoh king of Egypt. 9Know therefore that the LORD your God is God, the faithful God who maintains covenant loyalty with those who love him and keep his commandments, to a thousand generations, 10and who repays in their own person those who reject him. He does not delay but repays in their own person those who reject him. 11Therefore, observe diligently the commandment—the statutes, and the ordinances—that I am commanding you today.*

12 *If you heed these ordinances, by diligently observing them, the LORD your God will maintain with you the covenant loyalty that he swore to your ancestors; 13he will love you, bless you, and multiply you; he will bless the fruit of your womb and the fruit of your ground, your grain and your wine and your oil, the increase of your cattle and the issue of your flock, in the land that he swore to your ancestors to give you. 14You shall be the most blessed of peoples, with neither sterility nor barrenness among you or your livestock. 15The LORD will turn away from you every illness; all the dread diseases of Egypt that you experienced, he will not inflict on you, but he will lay them on all who hate you. 16You shall devour all the peoples that the LORD your God is giving over to you, showing them no pity; you shall not serve their gods, for that would be a snare to you.*

17 *If you say to yourself, "These nations are more numerous than I; how can I dispossess them?" 18do not be afraid of them. Just remember what the LORD your God did to Pharaoh and to all Egypt, 19the great trials that your eyes saw, the signs and wonders, the mighty hand and the outstretched arm by which the LORD your God brought you out. The LORD your God will do the same to all the peoples of whom you are afraid. 20Moreover, the LORD your God will send the pestilence against them, until even the survivors and the fugitives are destroyed. 21Have no dread of them, for the LORD your God, who is present with you, is a great and awesome God. 22The LORD your God will clear away these nations before you little by little; you will not be able to make a quick end of them, otherwise the wild animals would become too numerous for you. 23But the LORD your God will give them over to you, and throw them into great panic, until they are destroyed. 24He will hand their kings over to you and you shall blot out their name from under heaven; no one will be able to stand against you, until you have destroyed them. 25The images of their gods you shall burn with fire. Do not covet the silver or the gold that is on them and take it for yourself, because you could be ensnared by it; for it is abhorrent to the LORD your God. 26Do not bring an abhorrent thing into your house, or you will be set apart for destruction like it. You must utterly detest and abhor it, for it is set apart for destruction.*

8 *This entire commandment that I command you today you must diligently observe, so that you may live and increase, and go in and occupy the land that the LORD promised on oath to your ancestors. 2Remember the long way that the LORD your God has led you these forty years in the wilderness, in order to humble you, testing you to know what was in your heart, whether or not you would keep his commandments. 3He humbled you by letting you hunger, then by feeding you with manna, with which neither you nor your ancestors were acquainted, in order to make you understand that one does not live by bread alone, but by every word that comes from the mouth of the LORD. 4The clothes on your back did not wear out and your feet did not swell these forty years. 5Know then in your heart that as a parent disciplines a child so the LORD your God disciplines you. 6Therefore keep the commandments of the LORD your God, by walking in his ways and by fearing him. 7For the LORD*

After the Dtr:	*Revision:*	Other:
indented and sans serif font	*national focus*	double sideline

your God is bringing you into a good land, a land with flowing streams, with springs and underground waters welling up in valleys and hills, [8]a land of wheat and barley, of vines and fig trees and pomegranates, a land of olive trees and honey, [9]a land where you may eat bread without scarcity, where you will lack nothing, a land whose stones are iron and from whose hills you may mine copper. [10]You shall eat your fill and bless the LORD your God for the good land that he has given you.[39]

11 Take care that you do not forget the LORD your God, by failing to keep his commandments, his ordinances, and his statutes, which I am commanding you today. [12]When you have eaten your fill and have built fine houses and live in them, [13]and when your herds and flocks have multiplied, and your silver and gold is multiplied, and all that you have is multiplied, [14]then do not exalt yourself, forgetting the LORD your God, who brought you out of the land of Egypt, out of the house of slavery, [15]who led you through the great and terrible wilderness, an arid wasteland with poisonous snakes and scorpions. He made water flow for you from flint rock, [16]and fed you in the wilderness with manna that your ancestors did not know, to humble you and to test you, and in the end to do you good. [17]Do not say to yourself, "My power and the

might of my own hand have gotten me this wealth." [18]But remember the LORD your God, for it is he who gives you power to get wealth, so that he may confirm his covenant that he swore to your ancestors, as he is doing today. [19]If you do forget the LORD your God and follow other gods to serve and worship them, I solemnly warn you today that you shall surely perish. [20]Like the nations that the LORD is destroying before you, so shall you perish, because you would not obey the voice of the LORD your God.

9 *Hear, O Israel! You are about to cross the Jordan today, to go in and dispossess nations larger and mightier than you, great cities, fortified to the heavens, [2]a strong and tall people, the offspring of the Anakim, whom you know. You have heard it said of them, "Who can stand up to the Anakim?" [3]Know then today that the LORD your God is the one who crosses over before you as a devouring fire; he will defeat them and subdue them before you, so that you may dispossess and destroy them quickly, as the LORD has promised you.*

4 When the LORD your God thrusts them out before you, do not say to yourself, "It is because of my righteousness that the LORD has brought me in to occupy this land"; it is rather because of the wickedness of these nations that the LORD is dispossessing them before you. [5]It is not because of your righteousness or the uprightness of your heart that you are going in to occupy their land; but because of the wickedness of these nations the LORD your God is dispossessing them before you, in order to fulfill the promise that the LORD made on oath to your ancestors, to Abraham, to Isaac, and to Jacob.

6 Know, then, that the LORD your God is not giving you this good land to occupy because of your righteousness; for you are a stubborn people. [7]Remember and do not forget how you provoked the LORD your God to wrath in the wilderness; you have been rebellious against the LORD from the day you came out of the land of Egypt until you came to this place.

---

39. For **8:1-20,** compare the following:

Mayes	Nielsen	Preuss
i) pre-DH 7-11a, 17-18a	pre-DH (= bold 12-14, & roman) bold: nil roman: 7-11a, 17-18a	i) pre-DH (= I, II) I: nil II: (2-6?), 7-18 [w/o 11b]
ii) DH nil	dtr & post-dtr (italic) 1, 6, 11b-16, 18b-20	ii) dtr editing (= III) 1, (2-6?), 19ab, 20
iii) post-DH late dtr 1-6, 11b, 15-16, 18b-20		iii) post-DH (= additions) 11b

Possible consensus on pre-DH material: around vv. 7-11a, 17-18a
Possible consensus on dtr editing: around vv. 1, 11b, 19-20

Main pre-DH: dtn lawcode *its introduction and conclusion*	Other pre-DH: single sideline	**Josianic DH:** **from the Dtr**

8 Even at Horeb you provoked the LORD to wrath, and the LORD was so angry with you that he was ready to destroy you. ⁹When I went up the mountain to receive the stone tablets, the tablets of the covenant that the LORD made with you, I remained on the mountain forty days and forty nights; I neither ate bread nor drank water. ¹⁰And the LORD gave me the two stone tablets written with the finger of God; on them were all the words that the LORD had spoken to you at the mountain out of the fire on the day of the assembly. ¹¹At the end of forty days and forty nights the LORD gave me the two stone tablets, the tablets of the covenant. ¹²Then the LORD said to me, "Get up, go down quickly from here, for your people whom you have brought from Egypt have acted corruptly. They have been quick to turn from the way that I commanded them; they have cast an image for themselves." ¹³Furthermore the LORD said to me, "I have seen that this people is indeed a stubborn people. ¹⁴Let me alone that I may destroy them and blot out their name from under heaven; and I will make of you a nation mightier and more numerous than they."⁴⁰

15 So I turned and went down from the mountain, while the mountain was ablaze; the two tablets

---

40. For **9:1-29,** compare the following:

Mayes	Nielsen	Preuss
i) pre-DH 1-7a, 13-14, 26-29	pre-DH (= bold & roman) bold: nil roman: nil	i) pre-DH (= I, II) I: nil II: 1-3, (4-6?), (7a?)
ii) DH 9-12, 15-19, 21, 25	dtr & post-dtr (italic) 1-6, 7-29	ii) dtr editing (= III) 8, 9a, 10, 13-14, 15a, 15c, 16-17, 21, 25a, 26-29
iii) post-DH late dtr nil Other 2, 7b-8, 20, 22-24		iii) post-DH (= additions) (7a?), 7b, 9b, 11, 12, 15b, 18-19, 20, 22-24, 25b

No consensus re pre-DH material
Possible consensus re dtr editing: around vv. 7b-8, 20, 22-24

---

of the covenant were in my two hands. ¹⁶Then I saw that you had indeed sinned against the LORD your God, by casting for yourselves an image of a calf; you had been quick to turn from the way that the LORD had commanded you. ¹⁷So I took hold of the two tablets and flung them from my two hands, smashing them before your eyes. ¹⁸Then I lay prostrate before the LORD as before, forty days and forty nights; I neither ate bread nor drank water, because of all the sin you had committed, provoking the LORD by doing what was evil in his sight. ¹⁹For I was afraid that the anger that the LORD bore against you was so fierce that he would destroy you. But the LORD listened to me that time also. ²⁰The LORD was so angry with Aaron that he was ready to destroy him, but I interceded also on behalf of Aaron at that same time. ²¹Then I took the sinful thing you had made, the calf, and burned it with fire and crushed it, grinding it thoroughly, until it was reduced to dust; and I threw the dust of it into the stream that runs down the mountain.

22 At Taberah also, and at Massah, and at Kibroth-hattaavah, you provoked the LORD to wrath. ²³And when the LORD sent you from Kadesh-barnea, saying, "Go up and occupy the land that I have given you," you rebelled against the command of the LORD your God, neither trusting him nor obeying him. ²⁴You have been rebellious against the LORD as long as he has known you.

25 Throughout the forty days and forty nights that I lay prostrate before the LORD when the LORD intended to destroy you. ²⁶I prayed to the LORD and said, "Lord GOD, do not destroy the people who are your very own possession, whom you redeemed in your greatness, whom you brought out of Egypt with a mighty hand. ²⁷Remember your servants, Abraham, Isaac, and Jacob; pay no attention to the stubbornness of this people, their wickedness and their sin, ²⁸otherwise the land from which you have brought us might say, 'Because the LORD was not able to bring them into the land that he promised them, and because he

---

After the Dtr: indented and sans serif font	*Revision:* *national focus*	Other: double sideline

hated them, he has brought them out to let them die in the wilderness.' ²⁹For they are the people of your very own possession, whom you brought out by your great power and by your outstretched arm."

10 *At that time the* LORD *said to me, "Carve out two tablets of stone like the former ones, and come up to me on the mountain, and make an ark of wood. ²I will write on the tablets the words that were on the former tablets, which you smashed, and you shall put them in the ark." ³So I made an ark of acacia wood, cut two tablets of stone like the former ones, and went up the mountain with the two tablets in my hand. ⁴Then he wrote on the tablets the same words as before, the ten commandments that the* LORD *had spoken to you on the mountain out of the fire on the day of the assembly; and the* LORD *gave them to me. ⁵So I turned and came down from the mountain, and put the tablets in the ark that I had made; and there they are, as the* LORD *commanded me.*⁴¹

6 (The Israelites journeyed from Beeroth-bene-jaakan to Moserah. There Aaron died, and there he was buried; his son Eleazar succeeded him as priest.

⁷From there they journeyed to Gudgodah, and from Gudgodah to Jotbathah, a land with flowing streams. ⁸At that time the LORD *set apart the tribe of Levi to carry the ark of the covenant of the* LORD, *to stand before the* LORD *to minister to him, and to bless in his name, to this day. ⁹Therefore Levi has no allotment or inheritance with his kindred; the* LORD *is his inheritance, as the* LORD *your God promised him.)*

10 I stayed on the mountain forty days and forty nights, as I had done the first time. And once again the LORD *listened to me. The* LORD *was unwilling to destroy you. ¹¹The* LORD *said to me, "Get up, go on your journey at the head of the people, that they may go in and occupy the land that I swore to their ancestors to give them."*

12 So now, O Israel, what does the LORD *your God require of you? Only to fear the* LORD *your God, to walk in all his ways, to love him, to serve the* LORD *your God with all your heart and with all your soul, ¹³and to keep the commandments of the* LORD *your God and his decrees that I am commanding you today, for your own well-being. ¹⁴Although heaven and the heaven of heavens belong to the* LORD *your God, the earth with all that is in it, ¹⁵yet the* LORD *set his heart in love on your ancestors alone and chose you, their descendants after them, out of all the peoples, as it is today. ¹⁶Circumcise, then, the foreskin of your heart, and do not be stubborn any longer. ¹⁷For the* LORD *your God is God of gods and* LORD *of lords, the great God, mighty and awesome, who is not partial and takes no bribe, ¹⁸who executes justice for the orphan and the widow, and who loves the strangers, providing them food and clothing. ¹⁹You shall also love the stranger, for you were strangers in the land of Egypt. ²⁰You shall fear the* LORD *your God; him alone you shall worship; to him you shall hold fast, and by his name you shall swear. ²¹He is your praise; he is your God, who has done for you these great and awesome things that your own eyes have seen. ²²Your ancestors went down to Egypt seventy persons; and*

---

41. For **10:1-22,** compare the following:

Mayes	Nielsen	Preuss
i) pre-DH	pre-DH (= bold	i) pre-DH (= I, II)
10-11	& roman)	I: nil
	bold: nil	II: nil
	roman: 12, 20-21a	
ii) DH	dtr & post-dtr (italic)	ii) dtr editing (= III)
1-5	1-5, 8-11, 13-19,	1-5 (?), 10ab, 11
	21b-22	
iii) post-DH		iii) post-DH
late dtr		(= additions)
12-22		6a, 7, //6b//,
Other		(6-7 = P ?), 8-9a,
6-7, 8-9		9b, 10c, 12-13
		14-15b, 15c-19,
		20-22

No consensus re pre-DH material
Possible consensus re dtr editing: around vv. 13-19, 21b-22

Main pre-DH: dtn lawcode	Other pre-DH:	**Josianic DH:**
its introduction and conclusion	single sideline	**from the Dtr**

now the LORD your God has made you as numerous as the stars in heaven.

11 *You shall love the LORD your God, therefore, and keep his charge, his decrees, his ordinances, and his commandments always.* [2]*Remember today that it was not your children (who have not known or seen the discipline of the LORD your God), but it is you who must acknowledge his greatness, his mighty hand and his outstretched arm,* [3]*his signs and his deeds that he did in Egypt to Pharaoh, the king of Egypt, and to all his land;* [4]*what he did to the Egyptian army, to their horses and chariots, how he made the water of the Red Sea flow over them as they pursued you, so that the LORD has destroyed them to this day;* [5]*what he did to you in the wilderness, until you came to this place;* [6]*and what he did to Dathan and Abiram, sons of Eliab son of Reuben, how in the midst of all Israel the earth opened its mouth and swallowed them up, along with their households, their tents, and every living being in their company;* [7]*for it is your own eyes that have seen every great deed that the LORD did.*[42]

---

42. For **11:1-32**, compare the following:

Mayes	Nielsen	Preuss
i) pre-DH	pre-DH (= bold	i) pre-DH (= I, II)
nil	& roman)	I: nil
	bold: 29-30a*	II: nil
	roman: nil	
ii) DH	dtr & post-dtr (italic)	ii) dtr editing (= III)
nil	1, 2-9, 10-21, 22-25,	2-7, 8-9, 10-12,
	26-28, 30a*-32	14b-15, 16-17,
		22-25, 26-28,
		29-32?
		(or: only 31-32?)
iii) post-DH		iii) post-DH
late dtr		(= additions)
1-28, 31-32		1, 13, 14a,
Other		18-21, (29, 30?)
29-30		

No consensus on pre-DH material
Possible consensus on dtr editing: around vv. 1-28, 31-32

---

[8] *Keep, then, this entire commandment that I am commanding you today, so that you may have strength to go in and occupy the land that you are crossing over to occupy,* [9]*and so that you may live long in the land that the LORD swore to your ancestors to give them and to their descendants, a land flowing with milk and honey.* [10]*For the land that you are about to enter to occupy is not like the land of Egypt, from which you have come, where you sow your seed and irrigate by foot like a vegetable garden.* [11]*But the land that you are crossing over to occupy is a land of hills and valleys, watered by rain from the sky,* [12]*a land that the LORD your God looks after. The eyes of the LORD your God are always on it, from the beginning of the year to the end of the year*

[13] *If you will only heed his every commandment that I am commanding you today—loving the LORD your God, and serving him with all your heart and with all your soul—*[14]*then he will give the rain for your land in its season, the early rain and the later rain, and you will gather in your grain, your wine, and your oil;* [15]*and he will give grass in your fields for your livestock, and you will eat your fill.* [16]*Take care, or you will be seduced into turning away, serving other gods and worshiping them,* [17]*for then the anger of the LORD will be kindled against you and he will shut up the heavens, so that there will be no rain and the land will yield no fruit; then you will perish quickly off the good land that the LORD is giving you.*

[18] *You shall put these words of mine in your heart and soul, and you shall bind them as a sign on your hand, and fix them as an emblem on your forehead.* [19]*Teach them to your children, talking about them when you are at home and when you are away, when you lie down and when you rise.* [20]*Write them on the doorposts of your house and on your gates,* [21]*so that your days and the days of your children may be multiplied in the land that the LORD swore to your ancestors to give them, as long as the heavens are above the earth.*

After the Dtr:	Revision:	Other:
indented and sans serif font	*national focus*	double sideline

22 If you will diligently observe this entire commandment that I am commanding you, loving the LORD your God, walking in all his ways, and holding fast to him, 23then the LORD will drive out all these nations before you, and you will dispossess nations larger and mightier than yourselves. 24Every place on which you set foot shall be yours; your territory shall extend from the wilderness to the Lebanon and from the River, the river Euphrates, to the Western Sea. 25No one will be able to stand against you; the LORD your God will put the fear and dread of you on all the land on which you set foot, as he promised you.

26 See, I am setting before you today a blessing and a curse: 27the blessing, if you obey the commandments of the LORD your God that I am commanding you today; 28and the curse, if you do not obey the commandments of the LORD your God, but turn from the way that I am commanding you today, to follow other gods that you have not known.

29 When the LORD your God has brought you into the land that you are entering to occupy, you shall set the blessing on Mount Gerizim and the curse on Mount Ebal. 30As you know, they are beyond the Jordan, some distance to the west, in the land of the Canaanites who live in the Arabah, opposite Gilgal, beside the oak of Moreh.

31 When you cross the Jordan to go in to occupy the land that the LORD your God is giving you, and when you occupy it and live in it, 32you must diligently observe all the statutes and ordinances that I am setting before you today.[43]

---

43. Together with chap. 27, 11:29-32 forms a frame around the dtn code in order to prepare for the ceremony described in Josh 8:30-35. In our judgment, these framing additions are later than the national focus of the dtr revision.

12 These are the statutes and ordinances that you must diligently observe in the land that the LORD, the God of your ancestors, has given you to occupy all the days that you live on the earth.[44]

2 You must demolish completely all the places where the nations whom you are about to dispossess served their gods, on the mountain heights, on the hills, and under every leafy tree. 3Break down their altars, smash their pillars, burn their sacred poles with fire, and hew down the idols of their gods, and thus blot out their name from their places. 4You shall not worship the LORD your God in such ways. 5But you shall seek the place that the LORD your God will choose out of all your tribes as his habitation to put his name there. You shall go there, 6bringing there your burnt offerings and your sacrifices, your tithes and your donations, your votive gifts, your freewill offerings, and the firstlings of your herds and flocks. 7And you shall eat there in the presence of the LORD your God, you and

---

44. For **12:1-32** (= Heb., 12:1-13:1), compare the following:

Mayes	Nielsen	Preuss
i) pre-DH	pre-DH (= bold	i) pre-DH (= I, II, III)
13-19,	& roman)	I: (13-15b, 16-19?),
20-28,	bold: nil	(26-27?)
29-31 (with	roman: 1, 13-19,	II: (13-15b, 16-
13:1-18)	21-25,28, 29-31,	19?), 21a, 21c,
	32b	22, (26-27?),
		(29, 30-31?)
		III: 20, 23-24, (25?)
ii) DH	dtr & post-dtr	ii) dtr editing (= IV)
8-12	(italic) 2-12, 20,	1a, 2-3, (4?), 5*, 6,
	26-27, 32a	7*, 8-12, 21b, (25?),
		28, 29, 30-31,
		32 (= Heb., 13:1)
iii) post-DH		iii) post-DH
late dtr		(= additions)
1-7, 32		1bc, (4?), 5 end,
(Heb., 13:1)		7 end, 15c

Possible consensus re early material: around vv. 13-19, 29-31
Possible consensus re dtr editing: around vv. 2-7, 32a

Main pre-DH: dtn lawcode	Other pre-DH:	**Josianic DH:**
its introduction and conclusion	single sideline	**from the Dtr**

your households together, rejoicing in all the undertakings in which the LORD your God has blessed you.

8 You shall not act as we are acting here today, all of us according to our own desires, ⁹for you have not yet come into the rest and the possession that the LORD your God is giving you. ¹⁰When you cross over the Jordan and live in the land that the LORD your God is allotting to you, and when he gives you rest from your enemies all around so that you live in safety, ¹¹then you shall bring everything that I command you to the place that the LORD your God will choose as a dwelling for his name: your burnt offerings and your sacrifices, your tithes and your donations, and all your choice votive gifts that you vow to the LORD. ¹²And you shall rejoice before the LORD your God, you together with your sons and your daughters, your male and female slaves, and the Levites who reside in your towns (since they have no allotment or inheritance with you).

13 Take care that you do not offer your burnt offerings at any place you happen to see. ¹⁴But only at the place that the LORD will choose in one of your tribes—there you shall offer your burnt offerings and there you shall do everything I command you.

15 Yet whenever you desire you may slaughter and eat meat within any of your towns, according to the blessing that the LORD your God has given you; the unclean and the clean may eat of it, as they would of gazelle or deer. ¹⁶The blood, however, you must not eat; you shall pour it out on the ground like water. ¹⁷Nor may you eat within your towns the tithe of your grain, your wine, and your oil, the firstlings of your herds and your flocks, any of your votive gifts that you vow, your freewill offerings, or your donations; ¹⁸these you shall eat in the presence of the LORD your God at the place that the LORD your God will choose, you together with

your son and your daughter, your male and female slaves, and the Levites resident in your towns, rejoicing in the presence of the LORD your God in all your undertakings. ¹⁹Take care that you do not neglect the Levite as long as you live in your land.

20 When the LORD your God enlarges your territory, as he has promised you, and you say, "I am going to eat some meat," because you wish to eat meat, you may eat meat whenever you have the desire. ²¹If the place where the LORD your God will choose to put his name is too far from you, and you slaughter as I have commanded you any of your herd or flock that the LORD has given you, then you may eat within your towns whenever you desire. ²²Indeed, just as gazelle or deer is eaten, so you may eat it; the unclean and the clean alike may eat it. ²³Only be sure that you do not eat the blood; for the blood is the life, and you shall not eat the life with the meat. ²⁴Do not eat it; you shall pour it out on the ground like water. ²⁵Do not eat it, so that all may go well with you and your children after you, because you do what is right in the sight of the LORD. ²⁶But the sacred donations that are due from you, and your votive gifts, you shall bring to the place that the LORD will choose. ²⁷You shall present your burnt offerings, both the meat and the blood, on the altar of the LORD your God; the blood of your other sacrifices shall be poured out beside the altar of the LORD your God, but the meat you may eat.

28 Be careful to obey all these words that I command you today, so that it may go well with you and with your children after you forever, because you will be doing what is good and right in the sight of the LORD your God.

29 When the LORD your God has cut off before you the nations whom you are about to enter to dispossess them, when you have dispossessed them and live in their land, ³⁰take care

---

that you are not snared into imitating them, after they have been destroyed before you: do not inquire concerning their gods, saying, "How did these nations worship their gods? I also want to do the same." [31]You must not do the same for the LORD your God, because every abhorrent thing that the LORD hates they have done for their gods. They would even burn their sons and their daughters in the fire to their gods. [32]You must diligently observe everything that I command you; do not add to it or take anything from it.

13 If prophets or those who divine by dreams appear among you and promise you omens or portents, [2]and the omens or the portents declared by them take place, and they say, "Let us follow other gods" (whom you have not known) "and let us serve them," [3]you must not heed the words of those prophets or those who divine by dreams; for the LORD your God is testing you, to know whether you indeed love the LORD your God with all your heart and soul. [4]The LORD your God you shall follow, him alone you shall fear, his commandments you shall keep, his voice you shall obey, him you shall serve, and to him you shall hold fast. [5]But those prophets or those who divine by dreams shall be put to death for having spoken treason against the LORD your God—who brought you out of the land of Egypt and redeemed you from the house of slavery—to turn you from the way in which the LORD your God commanded you to walk. So you shall purge the evil from your midst.

6 If anyone secretly entices you—even if it is your brother, your father's son or your mother's son, or your own son or daughter, or the wife you embrace, or your most intimate friend—saying, "Let us go worship other gods," whom neither you nor your ancestors have known, [7]any of the gods of the peoples that are around

you, whether near you or far away from you, from one end of the earth to the other, [8]you must not yield to or heed any such persons. Show them no pity or compassion and do not shield them. [9]But you shall surely kill them; your own hand shall be first against them to execute them, and afterwards the hand of all the people. [10]Stone them to death for trying to turn you away from the LORD your God, who brought you out of the land of Egypt, out of the house of slavery. [11]Then all Israel shall hear and be afraid, and never again do any such wickedness.[45]

12 If you hear it said about one of the towns that the LORD your God is giving you to live in, [13]that scoundrels from among you have gone out and led the inhabitants of the town astray, saying, "Let us go and worship other gods," whom you have not known, [14]then you shall inquire and make a thorough investigation. If the charge is established that such an abhorrent thing has been done among you, [15]you shall put the inhab-

---

45. For **13:1-18** (= Heb., 13:2-19), compare the following:

Mayes	Nielsen	Preuss
i) pre-DH	pre-DH (= bold	i) pre-DH (= I, II, III)
1-3a, 5-15,	& roman)	I: 1a, (1b, 2a?), 3a, 5a,
17-18	bold: nil	6ab, 8, 9, 10ab, 11
	roman: 32b;	II: (1b, 2a?), 12-14
	1-3a, 5a*,	(w/o 13c), 15a
	5b-6, 8-18	III: 15b, 16a
ii) DH	dtr & post-dtr	ii) dtr editing (= IV)
3b-4	(italic)	3b, 4, 5b, 10c,
	32a; 3b-4, 5a*, 7	16b, 17, 18
iii) post-DH		iii) post-DH
late dtr		(= additions)
nil		2b, 6c, 7, 13c, 15c
Other		
1*, 2*, 5*, 6*, 7*,		See also chap. 17
13*, 16, 17*, 18*		

Possible consensus on early material: around vv. 1-2a, 3a, 8-15

Possible consensus on dtr editing: around vv. 3b-4

Main pre-DH: dtn lawcode	Other pre-DH:	**Josianic DH:**
its introduction and conclusion	single sideline	**from the Dtr**

itants of that town to the sword, utterly destroying it and everything in it—even putting its livestock to the sword. [16]All of its spoil you shall gather into its public square; then burn the town and all its spoil with fire, as a whole burnt offering to the LORD your God. It shall remain a perpetual ruin, never to be rebuilt. [17]Do not let anything devoted to destruction stick to your hand, so that the LORD may turn from his fierce anger and show you compassion, and in his compassion multiply you, as he swore to your ancestors, [18]if you obey the voice of the LORD your God by keeping all his commandments that I am commanding you today, doing what is right in the sight of the LORD your God.

14 You are children of the LORD your God. You must not lacerate yourselves or shave your forelocks for the dead. [2]For you are a people holy to the LORD your God; it is you the LORD has chosen out of all the peoples on earth to be his people, his treasured possession.[46]

3 You shall not eat any abhorrent thing. [4]These are the animals you may eat: the ox, the

sheep, the goat, [5]the deer, the gazelle, the roebuck, the wild goat, the ibex, the antelope, and the mountain-sheep. [6]Any animal that divides the hoof and has the hoof cleft in two, and chews the cud, among the animals, you may eat. [7]Yet of those that chew the cud or have the hoof cleft you shall not eat these: the camel, the hare, and the rock badger, because they chew the cud but do not divide the hoof; they are unclean for you. [8]And the pig, because it divides the hoof but does not chew the cud, is unclean for you. You shall not eat their meat, and you shall not touch their carcasses.

9 Of all that live in water you may eat these: whatever has fins and scales you may eat. [10]And whatever does not have fins and scales you shall not eat; it is unclean for you.

11 You may eat any clean birds. [12]But these are the ones that you shall not eat: the eagle, the vulture, the osprey, [13]the buzzard, the kite, of any kind; [14]every raven of any kind; [15]the ostrich, the nighthawk, the sea gull, the hawk, of any kind; [16]the little owl and the great owl, the water hen [17]and the desert owl, the carrion vulture and the cormorant, [18]the stork, the heron, of any kind; the hoopoe and the bat. [19]And all winged insects are unclean for you; they shall not be eaten. [20]You may eat any clean winged creature.

21 You shall not eat anything that dies of itself; you may give it to aliens residing in your towns for them to eat, or you may sell it to a foreigner. For you are a people holy to the LORD your God.

You shall not boil a kid in its mother's milk.

22 Set apart a tithe of all the yield of your seed that is brought in yearly from the field. [23]In the presence of the LORD your God, in the place that he will choose as a dwelling for his name, you shall eat the tithe of your grain, your wine, and your oil, as well as the firstlings of your herd and flock, so that you may learn to fear the LORD

---

46. For **14:1-29,** compare the following:

Mayes	Nielsen	Preuss
i) pre-DH 2-3, 21* 22	pre-DH (= bold & roman) bold: 22 roman: 3-21, 23a*, 24a*, 24b-26a*, 26b-29	i) pre-DH (= I, II, III) I: 1b, (22a?), (28?), (29a?) II: 1a, 2, 22, 28 III: 23*, 29
ii) DH 1, 23-29	dtr & post-dtr (italic) 1-2, 23a*, 23b, 24a*, 26a*	ii) dtr editing (= IV) nil
iii) post-DH late dtr 4-21* Other parts of 12-18		iii) post-DH (= additions) 3-20 (21) [old core =21aα, 21b], 21*, 23aβ, 24-27 (26b)

Possible consensus on early material: around vv. 21*, 22
No consensus re dtr editing

After the Dtr:
indented and sans serif font

Revision:
national focus

Other:
double sideline

your God always. [24]But if, when the LORD your God has blessed you, the distance is so great that you are unable to transport it, because the place where the LORD your God will choose to set his name is too far away from you, [25]then you may turn it into money. With the money secure in hand, go to the place that the LORD your God will choose; [26]spend the money for whatever you wish—oxen, sheep, wine, strong drink, or whatever you desire. And you shall eat there in the presence of the LORD your God, you and your household rejoicing together. [27]As for the Levites resident in your towns, do not neglect them, because they have no allotment or inheritance with you.

28 Every third year you shall bring out the full tithe of your produce for that year, and store it within your towns; [29]the Levites, because they have no allotment or inheritance with you, as well as the resident aliens, the orphans, and the widows in your towns, may come and eat their fill so that the LORD your God may bless you in all the work that you undertake.

15 Every seventh year you shall grant a remission of debts. [2]And this is the manner of the remission: every creditor shall remit the claim that is held against a neighbor, not exacting it of a neighbor who is a member of the community, because the LORD's remission has been proclaimed. [3]Of a foreigner you may exact it, but you must remit your claim on whatever any member of your community owes you. [4]There will, however, be no one in need among you, because the LORD is sure to bless you in the land that the LORD your God is giving you as a possession to occupy, [5]if only you will obey the LORD your God by diligently observing this entire commandment that I command you today. [6]When the LORD your God has blessed you, as he promised you, you will lend to many nations, but you

will not borrow; you will rule over many nations, but they will not rule over you.[47]

7 If there is among you anyone in need, a member of your community in any of your towns within the land that the LORD your God is giving you, do not be hard-hearted or tight-fisted toward your needy neighbor. [8]You should rather open your hand, willingly lending enough to meet the need, whatever it may be. [9]Be careful that you do not entertain a mean thought, thinking, "The seventh year, the year of remission, is near," and therefore view your needy neighbor with hostility and give nothing; your neighbor might cry to the LORD against you, and you would incur guilt. [10]Give liberally and be ungrudging when you do so, for on this account the LORD your God will bless you in all your work and in all that you undertake. [11]Since there will never cease to be some in need on the earth, I therefore command you, "Open your hand to the poor and needy neighbor in your land."

12 If a member of your community, whether a Hebrew man or a Hebrew woman, is sold to you and works for you six years, in the seventh year you shall set that person free. [13]And when you send a male slave out from you a free person,

---

47. For **15:1-23**, compare the following:

Mayes	Nielsen	Preuss
i) pre-DH	pre-DH (= bold & roman) bold:	i) pre-DH (= I, II, III)
1-3, 7-11, 12-18, 19-23	1-2, 19a*, 19b, 21a, 21b*	I: 1, (2a?), (19a? 19b?)
	roman: 3, 7-11, 12-18, 19a*, 20, 21b*, 22-23	II: 19-23 (w/o 21b)
		III: 2(b?), 3, 7-8, 9-11, 12-15, 18
ii) DH	dtr & post-dtr	ii) dtr editing (= IV)
nil	(italic) 4-6	4-6, 16-17
iii) post-DH		iii) post-DH
late dtr		(= additions)
4-6?		21b

Possible consensus on pre-DH material: around vv. 1-3, 7-11, 12-15, 18, 19-23

Possible consensus on dtr editing: around vv. 4-6

Main pre-DH: dtn lawcode	Other pre-DH:	**Josianic DH:**
its introduction and conclusion	single sideline	**from the Dtr**

you shall not send him out empty-handed. [14]Provide liberally out of your flock, your threshing floor, and your wine press, thus giving to him some of the bounty with which the LORD your God has blessed you. [15]Remember that you were a slave in the land of Egypt, and the LORD your God redeemed you; for this reason I lay this command upon you today. [16]But if he says to you, "I will not go out from you," because he loves you and your household, since he is well off with you, [17]then you shall take an awl and thrust it through his earlobe into the door, and he shall be your slave forever.

You shall do the same with regard to your female slave.

18 Do not consider it a hardship when you send them out from you free persons, because for six years they have given you services worth the wages of hired laborers; and the LORD your God will bless you in all that you do.

19 Every firstling male born of your herd and flock you shall consecrate to the LORD your God; you shall not do work with your firstling ox nor shear the firstling of your flock. [20]You shall eat it, you together with your household, in the presence of the LORD your God year by year at the place that the LORD will choose. [21]But if it has any defect—any serious defect, such as lameness or blindness—you shall not sacrifice it to the LORD your God; [22]within your towns you may eat it, the unclean and the clean alike, as you would a gazelle or deer. [23]Its blood, however, you must not eat; you shall pour it out on the ground like water.

16 Observe the month of Abib by keeping the passover for the LORD your God, for in the month of Abib the LORD your God brought you out of Egypt by night. [2]You shall offer the passover sacrifice for the LORD your God, from the flock and the herd, at the place that the LORD will choose as a dwelling for his name. [3]You must not eat with it anything leavened. For seven days you shall eat unleavened bread with it—the bread of affliction—because you came out of the land of Egypt in great haste, so that all the days of your life you may remember the day of your departure from the land of Egypt. [4]No leaven shall be seen with you in all your territory for seven days; and none of the meat of what you slaughter on the evening of the first day shall remain until morning. [5]You are not permitted to offer the passover sacrifice within any of your towns that the LORD your God is giving you. [6]But at the place that the LORD your God will choose as a dwelling for his name, only there shall you offer the passover sacrifice, in the evening at sunset, the time of day when you departed from Egypt. [7]You shall cook it and eat it at the place that the LORD your God will choose; the next morning you may go back to your tents. [8]For six days you shall continue to eat unleavened bread, and on the seventh day there shall be a solemn assembly for the LORD your God, when you shall do no work.

9 You shall count seven weeks; begin to count the seven weeks from the time the sickle is first put to the standing grain. [10]Then you shall keep the festival of weeks for the LORD your God, contributing a freewill offering in proportion to the blessing that you have received from the LORD your God. [11]Rejoice before the LORD your God—you and your sons and your daughters, your male and female slaves, the Levites resident in your towns, as well as the strangers, the orphans, and the widows who are among you— at the place that the LORD your God will choose as a dwelling for his name. [12]Remember that you were a slave in Egypt, and diligently observe these statutes.

13 You shall keep the festival of booths for seven days, when you have gathered in the pro-

| After the Dtr: indented and sans serif font | *Revision: national focus* | Other: double sideline |

duce from your threshing floor and your wine press. [14]Rejoice during your festival, you and your sons and your daughters, your male and female slaves, as well as the Levites, the strangers, the orphans, and the widows resident in your towns. [15]Seven days you shall keep the festival for the LORD your God at the place that the LORD will choose; for the LORD your God will bless you in all your produce and in all your undertakings, and you shall surely celebrate.

16 Three times a year all your males shall appear before the LORD your God at the place that he will choose: at the festival of unleavened bread, at the festival of weeks, and at the festival of booths. They shall not appear before the LORD empty-handed; [17]all shall give as they are able, according to the blessing of the LORD your God that he has given you.[48]

18 You shall appoint judges and officials throughout your tribes, in all your towns that the LORD your God is giving you, and they shall render just decisions for the people. [19]You must not distort justice; you must not show partiality; and you must not accept bribes, for a bribe blinds the eyes of the wise and subverts the cause of those who are in the right. [20]Justice, and only justice, you shall pursue, so that you may live and occupy the land that the LORD your God is giving you.

21 You shall not plant any tree as a sacred pole beside the altar that you make for the LORD your God; [22]nor shall you set up a stone pillar—things that the LORD your God hates.

17 You must not sacrifice to the LORD your God an ox or a sheep that has a defect, anything seriously wrong; for that is abhorrent to the LORD your God.

2 If there is found among you, in one of your towns that the LORD your God is giving you, a man or woman who does what is evil in the sight of the LORD your God, and transgresses his covenant [3]by going to serve other gods and worshiping them—whether the sun or the moon or any of the host of heaven, which I have forbidden—[4]and if it is reported to you or you hear of it, and you make a thorough inquiry, and the charge is proved true that such an abhorrent thing has occurred in Israel, [5]then you shall bring out to your gates that man or that woman who has committed this crime and you shall stone the man or woman to death. [6]On the evidence of two or three witnesses the death sentence shall be executed; a person must not be put to death on the evidence of only one witness. [7]The hands of the witnesses shall be the first raised against the person to execute the death penalty, and afterward the hands of all the

---

48. For **16:1-22**, compare the following:

Mayes	**Nielsen**	**Preuss**
i) pre-DH	pre-DH (= bold	i) pre-DH (= I, II, III)
1-7, 9-17,	& roman) bold:	I: 18, 19, 20a(?),
19, 21-22	1a*, 3a*, 4a, 8a, 8b*,	core of 21, 22a;
	9b, 10a*, 13a*, 13b,	17:1
	16*, 17a, 21*, 22*	II: 21b
	roman: 1a*-2a,	III: 1*-3aα, 3c,
	2b*, 3a*, 4b, 8b*,	4b, 5-7, 9a,
	9a, 10a*, 10b,	10-11, 13-15
	11a*, 11b*, 13a*,	(all of III includes
	14-15, 16*, 17b,	older material)
	18-20, 21*, 22*	
ii) DH	dtr & post-dtr	ii) dtr editing (= IV)
nil	(italic)	22b (note:
	2b*, 5-7, 11a*,	16:18–18:22 have
	11b*-12	dtr final editing)
iii) post-DH		iii) post-DH
late dtr		(= additions)
nil		1* (= by night),
Other		3aβb, 4a, 8a, 8b,
8		9c, 16-17

Possible consensus on pre-DH material: around vv. 1-4, 9-10, 13-15, 19, 21-22
No consensus on dtr editing

Main pre-DH: dtn lawcode
its introduction and conclusion

Other pre-DH:
single sideline

Josianic DH:
from the Dtr

people. So you shall purge the evil from your midst.[49]

8 If a judicial decision is too difficult for you to make between one kind of bloodshed and another, one kind of legal right and another, or one kind of assault and another—any such matters of dispute in your towns—then you shall immediately go up to the place that the Lord your God will choose, [9]where you shall consult with the levitical priests and the judge who is in office in those days; they shall announce to you the decision in the case. [10]Carry out exactly the decision that they announce to you from the place that the Lord will choose, diligently observing everything they instruct you. [11]You must carry out fully the law that they interpret for you or the ruling that they announce to you; do not turn aside from the decision that they announce to you, either to the right or to the left. [12]As for anyone who presumes to disobey the priest appointed to minister there to the Lord your God, or the judge, that person shall

die. So you shall purge the evil from Israel. [13]All the people will hear and be afraid, and will not act presumptuously again.

14 When you have come into the land that the Lord your God is giving you, and have taken possession of it and settled in it, and you say, "I will set a king over me, like all the nations that are around me," [15]you may indeed set over you a king whom the Lord your God will choose. One of your own community you may set as king over you; you are not permitted to put a foreigner over you, who is not of your own community. [16]Even so, he must not acquire many horses for himself, or return the people to Egypt in order to acquire more horses, since the Lord has said to you, "You must never return that way again." [17]And he must not acquire many wives for himself, or else his heart will turn away; also silver and gold he must not acquire in great quantity for himself. [18]When he has taken the throne of his kingdom, he shall have a copy of this law written for him in the presence of the levitical priests. [19]It shall remain with him and he shall read in it all the days of his life, so that he may learn to fear the Lord his God, diligently observing all the words of this law and these statutes, [20]neither exalting himself above other members of the community nor turning aside from the commandment, either to the right or to the left, so that he and his descendants may reign long over his kingdom in Israel.

18 The levitical priests, the whole tribe of Levi, shall have no allotment or inheritance within Israel. They may eat the sacrifices that are the Lord's portion [2]but they shall have no inheritance among the other members of the community; the Lord is their inheritance, as he promised them.

3 This shall be the priests' due from the people, from those offering a sacrifice, whether an

---

49. For **17:1-20,** compare the following:

Mayes	Nielsen	Preuss
i) pre-DH	pre-DH (= bold	i) pre-DH (= I, II, III)
1-7, 8-10a,	& roman) bold: 1a*	For 17:1, see chap. 16.
14-16*,	roman: 1a*, 1b-2a,	I: (Core of 17:2, 4, 5,
17, 20*	2b*, 3a, 4-8a*,	[and end of 7?]
	8b-9a*, 9b-11a*,	belong in chap.
	11b-12a*,	13), [8a, 9]
	12b-16a*,	II: nil
	17a*, 17b, 20	III: 9b, 10, 11
ii) DH	dtr & post-dtr	ii) dtr editing (= IV)
18-19	(italic) 2b*, 3b, 8a*,	2-7 (final form), (12-
	9a*, 11a*, 12a*,	13?), 14-15, 16-20b
	16a*, 16b, 17a*,	
	18-19	
iii) post-DH		iii) post-DH
late dtr		(= additions)
10b-13?,		3b?, 5cβ, (12-13?),
16*? 20*?		20c?

Possible consensus re pre-DH material: around vv. 9b-10a
Possible consensus re dtr editing: around vv. 18-19

After the Dtr:	*Revision:*	Other:
indented and sans serif font	*national focus*	double sideline

ox or a sheep: they shall give to the priest the shoulder, the two jowls, and the stomach. [4]The first fruits of your grain, your wine, and your oil, as well as the first of the fleece of your sheep, you shall give him. [5]For the LORD your God has chosen Levi out of all your tribes, to stand and minister in the name of the LORD, him and his sons for all time. [50]

6 If a Levite leaves any of your towns, from wherever he has been residing in Israel, and comes to the place that the LORD will choose (and he may come whenever he wishes), [7]then he may minister in the name of the LORD his God, like all his fellow-Levites who stand to minister there before the LORD. [8]They shall have equal portions to eat, even though they have income from the sale of family possessions.

9 When you come into the land that the LORD your God is giving you, you must not learn to imitate the abhorrent practices of those nations. [10]No one shall be found among you who makes a son or daughter pass through fire, or who practices divination, or is a soothsayer, or an augur, or a sorcerer, [11]or one who casts spells, or who consults ghosts or spirits, or who seeks oracles from the dead. [12]For whoever does these things is abhorrent to the LORD; it is because of such abhorrent practices that the LORD your God is driving them out before you. [13]You must remain completely loyal to the LORD your God. [14]Although these nations that you are about to dispossess do give heed to soothsayers and diviners, as for you, the LORD your God does not permit you to do so.

15 The LORD your God will raise up for you a prophet like me from among your own people; you shall heed such a prophet. [16]This is what you requested of the LORD your God at Horeb on the day of the assembly when you said: "If I hear the voice of the LORD my God any more, or ever again see this great fire, I will die." [17]Then the LORD replied to me: "They are right in what they have said. [18]I will raise up for them a prophet like you from among their own people; I will put my words in the mouth of the prophet, who shall speak to them everything that I command. [19]Anyone who does not heed the words that the prophet shall speak in my name, I myself will hold accountable. [20]But any prophet who speaks in the name of other gods, or who presumes to speak in my name a word that I have not commanded the prophet to speak—that prophet shall die." [21]You may say to yourself, "How can we recognize a word that the LORD has not spoken?" [22]If a prophet speaks in the name of the LORD but the thing does not take place or prove true, it is a word that the LORD has not spoken. The prophet has spoken it presumptuously; do not be frightened by it.

19 When the LORD your God has cut off the nations whose land the LORD your God is giving you, and you have dispossessed them and settled in their towns and in their houses, [2]you shall set apart three cities in the land that the

---

50. For **18:1-22,** compare the following:

Mayes	Nielsen	Preuss
i) pre-DH	pre-DH (= bold	i) pre-DH (= I, II, III)
1*, 3-4, 6-8,	& roman)	I: (1* + 3 [+ 4?]),
9-12	bold: nil	(6-8?), (10-11, 12a?)
	roman: 1, 3-15,	II: (6-8?)
	21-22	III: 1*, 2, 5, 9-12, 14
ii) DH	dtr & post-dtr	ii) dtr editing (= IV)
1*, 2, 5, 19-22	(italic)	(13?), 15, 16-18,
(or later dtr ?)	2, 16-20	19-22
iii) post-DH		iii) post-DH
late dtr		(= additions)
nil		(10aβ?), (13?)
Other		
13, 14-18		

Possible consensus re pre-DH material: around vv. 1*, 3-4, 6-8, 9-12

Possible consensus re dtr editing: around vv. 15-18, 19-20

Main pre-DH: dtn lawcode	Other pre-DH:	**Josianic DH:**
its introduction and conclusion	single sideline	**from the Dtr**

LORD your God is giving you to possess. ³You shall calculate the distances and divide into three regions the land that the LORD your God gives you as a possession, so that any homicide can flee to one of them.⁵¹

4 Now this is the case of a homicide who might flee there and live, that is, someone who has killed another person unintentionally when the two had not been at enmity before: ⁵Suppose someone goes into the forest with another to cut wood, and when one of them swings the ax to cut down a tree, the head slips from the handle and strikes the other person who then dies; the killer may flee to one of these cities and live. ⁶But if the distance is too great, the avenger of blood in hot anger might pursue and overtake and put the killer to death, although a death sentence was not deserved, since the two had not been at enmity before. ⁷Therefore I command you: You shall set apart three cities.

---

51. For **19:1-21,** compare the following:

Mayes	**Nielsen**	**Preuss**
i) pre-DH	pre-DH (= bold	i) pre-DH (= I, II, III)
1-5, 7,	& roman) bold:	I: 2a, 3b, 4, (5c?), 11,
11-13b*,	14a, 15a*, 16a,	16, 17a, 18bα, 19a
14, 16-21	17a, 18-19a,	II: (5a, 5b?), 6, 7, 8a,
	roman: 1-8,	9b, 10, 12, 15a,
	9b-13, 14b, 15a*,	15c, 17bβ, 18abβ,
	15b, 16b,	19b, (21a?)
	17b, 19b-21	III: 1, 2b, 3a, 17bβ,
		18a, (21a?)
ii) DH	dtr & post-dtr	ii) dtr editing (= IV)
nil	(italic) 9a	8b, 9a, 13, 16-19
iii) post-DH		iii) post-DH
late dtr		(= additions)
nil		14, 15b, 21b(?)
Other		
6, 8-10 (?),		
13b*, 15		

Possible consensus on pre-DH material: around vv. 1-5, 11-12,
Possible consensus on dtr editing: around v. 9a

---

8 If the LORD your God enlarges your territory, as he swore to your ancestors—and he will give you all the land that he promised your ancestors to give you, ⁹provided you diligently observe this entire commandment that I command you today, by loving the LORD your God and walking always in his ways—then you shall add three more cities to these three, ¹⁰so that the blood of an innocent person may not be shed in the land that the LORD your God is giving you as an inheritance, thereby bringing bloodguilt upon you.

11 But if someone at enmity with another lies in wait and attacks and takes the life of that person, and flees into one of these cities, ¹²then the elders of the killer's city shall send to have the culprit taken from there and handed over to the avenger of blood to be put to death. ¹³Show no pity; you shall purge the guilt of innocent blood from Israel, so that it may go well with you.

14 You must not move your neighbor's boundary marker, set up by former generations, on the property that will be allotted to you in the land that the LORD your God is giving you to possess.

15 A single witness shall not suffice to convict a person of any crime or wrongdoing in connection with any offense that may be committed. Only on the evidence of two or three witnesses shall a charge be sustained. ¹⁶If a malicious witness comes forward to accuse someone of wrongdoing, ¹⁷then both parties to the dispute shall appear before the LORD, before the priests and the judges who are in office in those days, ¹⁸and the judges shall make a thorough inquiry. If the witness is a false witness, having testified falsely against another, ¹⁹then you shall do to the false witness just as the false witness had meant to do to the other. So you shall purge the evil from your midst. ²⁰The rest shall hear and be afraid, and a crime such as this shall never again be committed among you. ²¹Show no pity: life

---

After the Dtr:	Revision:	Other:
indented and sans serif font	*national focus*	double sideline

for life, eye for eye, tooth for tooth, hand for hand, foot for foot.

20 When you go out to war against your enemies, and see horses and chariots, an army larger than your own, you shall not be afraid of them; for the Lord your God is with you, who brought you up from the land of Egypt. [2]Before you engage in battle, the priest shall come forward and speak to the troops, [3]and shall say to them: "Hear, O Israel! Today you are drawing near to do battle against your enemies. Do not lose heart, or be afraid, or panic, or be in dread of them; [4]for it is the Lord your God who goes with you, to fight for you against your enemies, to give you victory." [5]Then the officials shall address the troops, saying, "Has anyone built a new house but not dedicated it? He should go back to his house, or he might die in the battle and another dedicate it. [6]Has anyone planted a vineyard but not yet enjoyed its fruit? He should go back to his house, or he might die in the battle and another be first to enjoy its fruit. [7]Has anyone become engaged to a woman but not yet married her? He should go back to his house, or he might die in the battle and another marry her." [8]The officials shall continue to address the troops, saying, "Is anyone afraid or disheartened? He should go back to his house, or he might cause the heart of his comrades to melt like his own." [9]When the officials have finished addressing the troops, then the commanders shall take charge of them.

10 When you draw near to a town to fight against it, offer it terms of peace. [11]If it accepts your terms of peace and surrenders to you, then all the people in it shall serve you at forced labor. [12]If it does not submit to you peacefully, but makes war against you, then you shall besiege it; [13]and when the Lord your God gives it into your hand, you shall put all its males to the sword.

[14]You may, however, take as your booty the women, the children, livestock, and everything else in the town, all its spoil. You may enjoy the spoil of your enemies, which the Lord your God has given you. [15]Thus you shall treat all the towns that are very far from you, which are not towns of the nations here. [16]But as for the towns of these peoples that the Lord your God is giving you as an inheritance, you must not let anything that breathes remain alive. [17]You shall annihilate them—the Hittites and the Amorites, the Canaanites and the Perizzites, the Hivites and the Jebusites—just as the Lord your God has commanded, [18]so that they may not teach you to do all the abhorrent things that they do for their gods, and you thus sin against the Lord your God.[52]

19 If you besiege a town for a long time, making war against it in order to take it, you must not destroy its trees by wielding an ax against them. Although you may take food from them, you must not cut them down. Are trees in the field human beings that they should come under siege from you? [20]You may destroy only

---

52. For **20:1-20,** compare the following:

Mayes	Nielsen	Preuss
i) pre-DH	pre-DH (= bold	i) pre-DH (= I, II, III)
1, 5-9, 10-14,	& roman) bold:	I: 5-7*, 19a, 19b, 20
15-17, 19-20	5a*, 6a, 7a,	II: nil
	roman: 1, 5a*,	III: 1, (2-4a?), 8,
	5b, 6b, 7b, 8-14,	(10-14?), 19c
	19-20	
ii) DH	dtr & post-dtr	ii) dtr editing (= IV)
nil	(italic) 2-4,	2-4, 9, (10-14?),
	15-18	15a, 16, 17a,
		17c, 18
iii) post-DH		iii) post-DH
late dtr		(= additions)
2-4, 18		15b, 17b

Possible consensus on pre-DH material: around vv. 1, 5-7, 10-14, 19-20
Possible consensus on dtr editing: around vv. 2-4, 18

Main pre-DH: dtn lawcode	Other pre-DH:	**Josianic DH:**
its introduction and conclusion	single sideline	**from the Dtr**

the trees that you know do not produce food; you may cut them down for use in building siegeworks against the town that makes war with you, until it falls.

21 If, in the land that the LORD your God is giving you to possess, a body is found lying in open country, and it is not known who struck the person down, [2]then your elders and your judges shall come out to measure the distances to the towns that are near the body. [3]The elders of the town nearest the body shall take a heifer that has never been worked, one that has not pulled in the yoke; [4]the elders of that town shall bring the heifer down to a wadi with running water, which is neither plowed nor sown, and shall break the heifer's neck there in the wadi. [5]Then the priests, the sons of Levi, shall come forward, for the LORD your God has chosen them to minister to him and to pronounce blessings in the name of the LORD, and by their decision all cases of dispute and assault shall be settled. [6]All the elders of that town nearest the body shall wash their hands over the heifer whose neck was broken in the wadi, [7]and they shall declare: "Our hands did not shed this blood, nor were we witnesses to it. [8]Absolve, O LORD, your people Israel, whom you redeemed; do not let the guilt of innocent blood remain in the midst of your people Israel." Then they will be absolved of bloodguilt. [9]So you shall purge the guilt of innocent blood from your midst, because you must do what is right in the sight of the LORD.

[10] When you go out to war against your enemies, and the LORD your God hands them over to you and you take them captive, [11]suppose you see among the captives a beautiful woman whom you desire and want to marry, [12]and so you bring her home to your house: she shall shave her head, pare her nails, [13]discard her captive's garb, and shall remain in your house

a full month, mourning for her father and mother; after that you may go in to her and be her husband, and she shall be your wife. [14]But if you are not satisfied with her, you shall let her go free and not sell her for money. You must not treat her as a slave, since you have dishonored her.[53]

[15] If a man has two wives, one of them loved and the other disliked, and if both the loved and the disliked have borne him sons, the firstborn being the son of the one who is disliked, [16]then on the day when he wills his possessions to his sons, he is not permitted to treat the son of the loved as the firstborn in preference to the son of the disliked, who is the firstborn. [17]He must acknowledge as firstborn the son of the one who is disliked, giving him a double portion of all that he has; since he is the first issue of his virility, the right of the firstborn is his.

[18] If someone has a stubborn and rebellious son who will not obey his father and mother, who does not heed them when they discipline him, [19]then his father and his mother shall take

---

53. For **21:1-23,** compare the following:

Mayes	Nielsen	Preuss
i) pre-DH 1-4, 6-7, 9, 10-14, 15-17, 18-21, 20-23	pre-DH (= bold & roman) bold: 1a*, 1b, 3-4, 6-8, 15-20a, 21a* roman: 1a*, 9-14, 21a*, 21b-23	i) pre-DH (= I, II, III) I: 3-7, 9a, 10(w/o your God)-14, 15- 17, 18-20b, 21a, 22-23a II: 1 (w/o aβ), 2 III: 1aβ, (8?), (9b?), 21b*, 23b
ii) DH nil	dtr & post-dtr (italic) 2, 5, 20b	ii) dtr editing (= IV) 5, (8?), 21b*, 23c
iii) post-DH late dtr 5, 8		iii) post-DH (= additions) (9b?), 20c

Possible consensus on pre-DH material: around vv. 1-4, 6-7, 9-14, 15-17, 18-20a, 21-23
Possible consensus on dtr editing: around v. 5

After the Dtr: indented and sans serif font	*Revision:* *national focus*	Other: double sideline

hold of him and bring him out to the elders of his town at the gate of that place. [20]They shall say to the elders of his town, "This son of ours is stubborn and rebellious. He will not obey us. He is a glutton and a drunkard." [21]Then all the men of the town shall stone him to death. So you shall purge the evil from your midst; and all Israel will hear, and be afraid.

22 When someone is convicted of a crime punishable by death and is executed, and you hang him on a tree, [23]his corpse must not remain all night upon the tree; you shall bury him that same day, for anyone hung on a tree is under God's curse. You must not defile the land that the LORD your God is giving you for possession.

22 You shall not watch your neighbor's ox or sheep straying away and ignore them; you shall take them back to their owner. [2]If the owner does not reside near you or you do not know who the owner is, you shall bring it to your own house, and it shall remain with you until the owner claims it; then you shall return it. [3]You shall do the same with a neighbor's donkey; you shall do the same with a neighbor's garment; and you shall do the same with anything else that your neighbor loses and you find. You may not withhold your help.

4 You shall not see your neighbor's donkey or ox fallen on the road and ignore it; you shall help to lift it up.

5 A woman shall not wear a man's apparel, nor shall a man put on a woman's garment; for whoever does such things is abhorrent to the LORD your God.

6 If you come on a bird's nest, in any tree or on the ground, with fledglings or eggs, with the mother sitting on the fledglings or on the eggs, you shall not take the mother with the young. [7]Let the mother go, taking only the young for

yourself, in order that it may go well with you and you may live long.

8 When you build a new house, you shall make a parapet for your roof; otherwise you might have bloodguilt on your house, if anyone should fall from it.[54]

9 You shall not sow your vineyard with a second kind of seed, or the whole yield will have to be forfeited, both the crop that you have sown and the yield of the vineyard itself.

10 You shall not plow with an ox and a donkey yoked together.

11 You shall not wear clothes made of wool and linen woven together.

12 You shall make tassels on the four corners of the cloak with which you cover yourself.

13 Suppose a man marries a woman, but after going in to her, he dislikes her [14]and makes up charges against her, slandering her by

---

54. For **22:1-30** (= Heb., 22:1–23:1), compare the following:

Mayes	Nielsen	Preuss
i) pre-DH 1-7a, 8-12, 14-19, 22-30 (Heb., 23:1)	pre-DH (= bold & roman) bold: 13-14a*, 14b-19a*, 19b, 22a, 23-24a, 25-30 roman: 1-7a, 8-12, 14a*, 19a*, 20-21, 22b, 24b	i) pre-DH (= I, II, III) I: 1, 4, 5a, (5b?), 6a, 7a, 8a, 9a, 10, 11, 13, 14a, 15, 18, 19a, 19c, 20, 21a, 21b, 22(a?), 23, 24a, 25, 28-29, 30 II: 5c, 6b, 8b, 9b(?), 12, 14b, 16-17, 19b, 21c(?), 24c, 26a, 27 III: 2-3 (+ brother in 1 and 4), (5b?), 24b, 26b?
ii) DH nil	dtr & post-dtr (italic) 7b	ii) dtr editing (= IV) 7b
iii) post-DH late dtr nil Other 7b, 20-21		iii) post-DH (= additions) nil

Possible consensus on pre-DH material: around vv. 1-7a, 8-12, 14-19a, 22-30
Possible consensus on dtr editing: around v. 7b

---

saying, "I married this woman; but when I lay with her, I did not find evidence of her virginity." [15]The father of the young woman and her mother shall then submit the evidence of the young woman's virginity to the elders of the city at the gate. [16]The father of the young woman shall say to the elders: "I gave my daughter in marriage to this man but he dislikes her; [17]now he has made up charges against her, saying, 'I did not find evidence of your daughter's virginity.' But here is the evidence of my daughter's virginity." Then they shall spread out the cloth before the elders of the town. [18]The elders of that town shall take the man and punish him; [19]they shall fine him one hundred shekels of silver (which they shall give to the young woman's father) because he has slandered a virgin of Israel. She shall remain his wife; he shall not be permitted to divorce her as long as he lives.

20 If, however, this charge is true, that evidence of the young woman's virginity was not found, [21]then they shall bring the young woman out to the entrance of her father's house and the men of her town shall stone her to death, because she committed a disgraceful act in Israel by prostituting herself in her father's house. So you shall purge the evil from your midst.

22 If a man is caught lying with the wife of another man, both of them shall die, the man who lay with the woman as well as the woman. So you shall purge the evil from Israel.

23 If there is a young woman, a virgin already engaged to be married, and a man meets her in the town and lies with her, [24]you shall bring both of them to the gate of that town and stone them to death, the young woman because she did not cry for help in the town and the man because he violated his neighbor's wife. So you shall purge the evil from your midst.

25 But if the man meets the engaged woman in the open country, and the man seizes her and lies with her, then only the man who lay with her shall die. [26]You shall do nothing to the young woman; the young woman has not committed an offense punishable by death, because this case is like that of someone who attacks and murders a neighbor. [27]Since he found her in the open country, the engaged woman may have cried for help, but there was no one to rescue her.

28 If a man meets a virgin who is not engaged, and seizes her and lies with her, and they are caught in the act, [29]the man who lay with her shall give fifty shekels of silver to the young woman's father, and she shall become his wife. Because he violated her he shall not be permitted to divorce her as long as he lives.
30 A man shall not marry his father's wife, thereby violating his father's rights.

23 No one whose testicles are crushed or whose penis is cut off shall be admitted to the assembly of the LORD.[55]

---

55. For **23:1-25** (= Heb., 23:2-26), compare the following:

Mayes	Nielsen	Preuss
i) pre-DH	pre-DH (= bold	i) pre-DH (= I, II, III)
1-2a, 3a,	& roman)	I: 10-11, 12-13, 15,
4b-6, 7,	bold: 1-2, 17	18, 19a
9-14, 15-18,	roman: 3a, 3b*,	II: 17, (24-25?)
19-25	6-16, 18-25	III: 9, 14*, 16, 19b,
		20*, (24-25?)
ii) DH	dtr & post-dtr	ii) dtr editing (= IV)
nil	(italic) 3b*-5	14*, 20*
iii) post-DH		iii) post-DH
late dtr		(= additions)
nil		1-8, 21-23a,
Other		23b, 23c
2b, 3b, 4a, 8		

Possible consensus re pre-DH material: around vv. 9-14, 15-18, 19, 20*, 24-25
Possible consensus re dtr editing: around vv. 3b, 4a

After the Dtr:	Revision:	Other:
indented and sans serif font	*national focus*	double sideline

2 Those born of an illicit union shall not be admitted to the assembly of the LORD. Even to the tenth generation, none of their descendants shall be admitted to the assembly of the LORD.

3 No Ammonite or Moabite shall be admitted to the assembly of the LORD. Even to the tenth generation, none of their descendants shall be admitted to the assembly of the LORD, [4]because they did not meet you with food and water on your journey out of Egypt, and because they hired against you Balaam son of Beor, from Pethor of Mesopotamia, to curse you. [5](Yet the LORD your God refused to heed Balaam; the LORD your God turned the curse into a blessing for you, because the LORD your God loved you.) [6]You shall never promote their welfare or their prosperity as long as you live.

7 You shall not abhor any of the Edomites, for they are your kin. You shall not abhor any of the Egyptians, because you were an alien residing in their land. [8]The children of the third generation that are born to them may be admitted to the assembly of the LORD.

9 When you are encamped against your enemies you shall guard against any impropriety.

10 If one of you becomes unclean because of a nocturnal emission, then he shall go outside the camp; he must not come within the camp. [11]When evening comes, he shall wash himself with water, and when the sun has set, he may come back into the camp.

12 You shall have a designated area outside the camp to which you shall go. [13]With your utensils you shall have a trowel; when you relieve yourself outside, you shall dig a hole with it and then cover up your excrement. [14]Because the LORD your God travels along with your camp, to save you and to hand over your enemies to you, therefore your camp must be holy, so that he may not see anything indecent among you and turn away from you.

15 Slaves who have escaped to you from their owners shall not be given back to them. [16]They shall reside with you, in your midst, in any place they choose in any one of your towns, wherever they please; you shall not oppress them.

17 None of the daughters of Israel shall be a temple prostitute; none of the sons of Israel shall be a temple prostitute. [18]You shall not bring the fee of a prostitute or the wages of a male prostitute into the house of the LORD your God in payment for any vow, for both of these are abhorrent to the LORD your God.

19 You shall not charge interest on loans to another Israelite, interest on money, interest on provisions, interest on anything that is lent. [20]On loans to a foreigner you may charge interest, but on loans to another Israelite you may not charge interest, so that the LORD your God may bless you in all your undertakings in the land that you are about to enter and possess.

21 If you make a vow to the LORD your God, do not postpone fulfilling it; for the LORD your God will surely require it of you, and you would incur guilt. [22]But if you refrain from vowing, you will not incur guilt. [23]Whatever your lips utter you must diligently perform, just as you have freely vowed to the LORD your God with your own mouth.

24 If you go into your neighbor's vineyard, you may eat your fill of grapes, as many as you wish, but you shall not put any in a container.

25 If you go into your neighbor's standing grain, you may pluck the ears with your hand, but you shall not put a sickle to your neighbor's standing grain.

24 Suppose a man enters into marriage with a woman, but she does not please him because he finds something objectionable about her, and so he writes her a certificate of divorce, puts it in her hand, and sends her out of his house; she then

---

Main pre-DH: dtn lawcode
its introduction and conclusion

Other pre-DH:
single sideline

Josianic DH:
from the Dtr

leaves his house ²and goes off to become another man's wife. ³Then suppose the second man dislikes her, writes her a bill of divorce, puts it in her hand, and sends her out of his house (or the second man who married her dies); ⁴her first husband, who sent her away, is not permitted to take her again to be his wife after she has been defiled; for that would be abhorrent to the LORD, and you shall not bring guilt on the land that the LORD your God is giving you as a possession.

5 When a man is newly married, he shall not go out with the army or be charged with any related duty. He shall be free at home one year, to be happy with the wife whom he has married.

6 No one shall take a mill or an upper millstone in pledge, for that would be taking a life in pledge.

7 If someone is caught kidnaping another Israelite, enslaving or selling the Israelite, then that kidnaper shall die. So you shall purge the evil from your midst.

8 Guard against an outbreak of a leprous skin disease by being very careful; you shall carefully observe whatever the levitical priests instruct you, just as I have commanded them. ⁹Remember what the LORD your God did to Miriam on your journey out of Egypt.

10 When you make your neighbor a loan of any kind, you shall not go into the house to take the pledge. ¹¹You shall wait outside, while the person to whom you are making the loan brings the pledge out to you. ¹²If the person is poor, you shall not sleep in the garment given you as the pledge. ¹³You shall give the pledge back by sunset, so that your neighbor may sleep in the cloak and bless you; and it will be to your credit before the LORD your God.

14 You shall not withhold the wages of poor and needy laborers, whether other Israelites or aliens who reside in your land in one of your towns ¹⁵You shall pay them their wages daily before sunset, because they are poor and their livelihood depends on them; otherwise they might cry to the LORD against you, and you would incur guilt.⁵⁶

16 Parents shall not be put to death for their children, nor shall children be put to death for their parents; only for their own crimes may persons be put to death.

17 You shall not deprive a resident alien or an orphan of justice; you shall not take a widow's garment in pledge. ¹⁸Remember that you were a slave in Egypt and the LORD your God redeemed you from there; therefore I command you to do this.

19 When you reap your harvest in your field and forget a sheaf in the field, you shall not go back to get it; it shall be left for the alien, the orphan, and the widow, so that the LORD your God may bless you in all your undertakings.

---

56. For **24:1-22,** compare the following:

Mayes	**Nielsen**	**Preuss**
i) pre-DH	pre-DH (= bold	i) pre-DH (= I, II, III)
1-4, 5-8*,	& roman)	I: 1a, 2b, 4a, 4b, 6a,
9*-22	bold: 5-6, 16	7a, 7b*, (8a?),
	roman: 1-4, 7,	14a, 17a, (17b?),
	10-15,17-22	19a, 20a, 21a
		II: 1b, 2a, 3a, 3b(?),
		5a, 5b, 5c, 6b, 7c,
		20b, 21b
		III: (8-9?), 10-11, 12-
		13b, 14b, 15, 18,
		(17-22?), 19b, 19c, 22
ii) DH	dtr & post-dtr	ii) dtr editing (= IV)
nil	(italic) 8-9	4d, 7b*, (8-9?),
		13c, (16?)
iii) post-DH		iii) post-DH
late dtr		(= additions)
nil		4c, 5d, (16?)
Other		
8*, 9*		

Possible consensus on pre-DH material: around vv. 1-4*, 6-7b*, 12-13*, 15, 17-22
Possible consensus on dtr editing: around vv. 8*, 9*

After the Dtr:	*Revision:*	Other:
indented and sans serif font	*national focus*	double sideline

²⁰When you beat your olive trees, do not strip what is left; it shall be for the alien, the orphan, and the widow.

21 When you gather the grapes of your vineyard, do not glean what is left; it shall be for the alien, the orphan, and the widow. ²²Remember that you were a slave in the land of Egypt; therefore I am commanding you to do this.

25 Suppose two persons have a dispute and enter into litigation, and the judges decide between them, declaring one to be in the right and the other to be in the wrong. ²If the one in the wrong deserves to be flogged, the judge shall make that person lie down and be beaten in his presence with the number of lashes proportionate to the offense. ³Forty lashes may be given but not more; if more lashes than these are given, your neighbor will be degraded in your sight.[57]

4 You shall not muzzle an ox while it is treading out the grain.

5 When brothers reside together, and one of them dies and has no son, the wife of the deceased shall not be married outside the family to a stranger. Her husband's brother shall go in to her, taking her in marriage, and performing the duty of a husband's brother to her, ⁶and the firstborn whom she bears shall succeed to the name of the deceased brother, so that his name may not be blotted out of Israel. ⁷But if the man has no desire to marry his brother's widow, then his brother's widow shall go up to the elders at the gate and say, "My husband's brother refuses to perpetuate his brother's name in Israel; he will not perform the duty of a husband's brother to me." ⁸Then the elders of his town shall summon him and speak to him. If he persists, saying, "I have no desire to marry her," ⁹then his brother's wife shall go up to him in the presence of the elders, pull his sandal off his foot, spit in his face, and declare, "This is what is done to the man who does not build up his brother's house." ¹⁰Throughout Israel his family shall be known as "the house of him whose sandal was pulled off."

11 If men get into a fight with one another, and the wife of one intervenes to rescue her husband from the grip of his opponent by reaching out and seizing his genitals, ¹²you shall cut off her hand; show no pity.

13 You shall not have in your bag two kinds of weights, large and small. ¹⁴You shall not have in your house two kinds of measures, large and small. ¹⁵You shall have only a full and honest weight; you shall have only a full and honest measure, so that your days may be long in the land that the LORD your God is giving you. ¹⁶For all who do such things, all who act dishonestly, are abhorrent to the LORD your God.

17 Remember what Amalek did to you on your journey out of Egypt, ¹⁸how he attacked you on the way, when you were faint and weary, and struck down all who lagged behind you; he did not fear God. ¹⁹Therefore when the LORD your God has given you rest from all your enemies on every hand, in the land that the LORD your God is giving you as an inheritance to pos-

---

57. For **25:1-19,** compare the following:

Mayes	Nielsen	Preuss
i) pre-DH	pre-DH (= bold	i) pre-DH (= I, II, III)
1-4, 5-12,	& roman)	I: (1-2?), (4?),
13-16	bold: 1-2, 4-12a,	(in 5-10), 11aα(?),
	13a, 14a	11aβ, 12a(?), 12b,
	roman: 3, 12b,	13a, 13b(?), 14a,
	13b, 14b, 15-16a	14b(?), (15a?), 16a
		II: (1-2?), 3, 5-10
		III: (15a?)
ii) DH	dtr & post-dtr	ii) dtr editing (= IV)
nil	(italic) 16b-19	15b, 16b, 17-19
iii) post-DH		iii) post-DH
late dtr		(= additions)
17-19 (?)		(4?)

Possible consensus on pre-DH material: around vv. 1-4, 5-12, 13-14, 16a
Possible consensus on dtr editing: around vv. 17-19

Main pre-DH: dtn lawcode   Other pre-DH: **Josianic DH:**
its introduction and conclusion   single sideline   **from the Dtr**

sess, you shall blot out the remembrance of Amalek from under heaven; do not forget.

26 *When you have come into the land that the LORD your God is giving you as an inheritance to possess, and you possess it, and settle in it, ²you shall take some of the first of all the fruit of the ground, which you harvest from the land that the LORD your God is giving you, and you shall put it in a basket and go to the place that the LORD your God will choose as a dwelling for his name.*[58]

> ³You shall go to the priest who is in office at that time, and say to him, "Today I declare to the LORD your God that I have come into the land that the LORD swore to our ancestors to give us." ⁴When the priest takes the basket from your hand and sets it down before the altar of the LORD your God

⁵You shall make this response before the LORD your God: "A wandering Aramean was my ancestor; he went down into Egypt and lived there as an alien, few in number, and there he became a great nation, mighty and populous. ⁶When the Egyptians treated us harshly and afflicted us, by imposing hard labor on us, ⁷we cried to the LORD, the God of our ancestors; the LORD heard our voice and saw our affliction, our toil, and our oppression. ⁸The LORD brought us out of Egypt with a mighty hand and an outstretched arm, with a terrifying display of power, and with signs and wonders; and he brought us into this place and gave us this land, a land flowing with milk and honey. ¹⁰So now I bring the first of the fruit of the ground that you, O LORD, have given me." You shall set it down before the LORD your God and bow down before the LORD your God. ¹¹Then you, together with the Levites and the aliens who reside among you, shall celebrate with all the bounty that the LORD your God has given to you and to your house.

12 When you have finished paying all the tithe of your produce in the third year (which is the year of the tithe), giving it to the Levites, the aliens, the orphans, and the widows, so that they may eat their fill within your towns, ¹³then you shall say before the LORD your God: "I have removed the sacred portion from the house, and I have given it to the Levites, the resident aliens, the orphans, and the widows, in accordance with your entire commandment that you commanded me; I have neither transgressed nor forgotten any of your commandments: ¹⁴I have not eaten of it while in mourning; I have not removed any of it while I was unclean; and I have not offered any of it to the dead. I have obeyed the LORD my God, doing just as you commanded me. ¹⁵Look down from your holy habitation, from heaven, and bless your people Israel and the ground that you have given us, as you swore to our ancestors—a land flowing with milk and honey."

16 This very day the LORD your God is commanding you to observe these statutes and ordinances; so observe them diligently with all your heart and with all your soul. ¹⁷Today you have obtained the LORD's agreement: to be your God; and for you to walk in his ways, to keep his statutes, his commandments, and his ordinances, and to obey him. ¹⁸Today

---

58. For **26:1-19,** compare the following:

Mayes	Nielsen	Preuss
i) pre-DH	pre-DH (= bold	i) pre-DH (= I, II, III)
nil	& roman)	I: [5bα(?), 10a(?)], 12a,
	bold: 5a*, 10a,	13a, 14a, (15a?)
	14a	II: 12b, 13b, 14b, (15a?)
	roman: nil	III: 17a*(?), 18a*(?)
ii) DH	dtr & post-dtr	ii) dtr editing (= IV)
nil	(italic) 1-5a*,	1-2, 5b-10a, 10b-11,
	5a*-9, 10b-13,	15b, 16-19*
	14b-19	
iii) post-DH		iii) post-DH
late dtr		(= additions)
1-2, 5-11,		3-4
12-15		
Other		
3-4, 16-19 (?)		

No consensus re pre-DH material
Possible consensus re dtr editing: around vv. 1-2, 5*-9, 10b-11, 15b-19

After the Dtr:	*Revision:*	Other:
indented and sans serif font	*national focus*	double sideline

the LORD has obtained your agreement: to be his treasured people, as he promised you, and to keep his commandments; [19]*for him to set you high above all nations that he has made, in praise and in fame and in honor; and for you to be a people holy to the LORD your God, as he promised.*

27 Then Moses and the elders of Israel charged all the people as follows: Keep the entire commandment that I am commanding you today. [2]On the day that you cross over the Jordan into the land that the LORD your God is giving you, you shall set up large stones and cover them with plaster. [3]You shall write on them all the words of this law when you have crossed over, to enter the land that the LORD your God is giving you, a land flowing with milk and honey, as the LORD, the God of your ancestors, promised you. [4]So when you have crossed over the Jordan, you shall set up these stones, about which I am commanding you today, on Mount Ebal, and you shall cover them with plaster. [5]And you shall build an altar there to the LORD your God, an altar of stones on which you have not used an iron tool. [6]You must build the altar of the LORD your God of unhewn stones. Then offer up burnt offerings on it to the LORD your God, [7]make sacrifices of well-being, and eat them there, rejoicing before the LORD your God. [8]You shall write on the stones all the words of this law very clearly.[59]

9 Then Moses and the levitical priests spoke to all Israel, saying: Keep silence and hear, O Israel! This very day you have become the people of the LORD your God. [10]Therefore obey the LORD your God, observing his commandments and his statutes that I am commanding you today.

11 The same day Moses charged the people as follows: [12]When you have crossed over the Jordan, these shall stand on Mount Gerizim for the blessing of the people: Simeon, Levi, Judah, Issachar, Joseph, and Benjamin. [13]And these shall stand on Mount Ebal for the curse: Reuben, Gad, Asher, Zebulun, Dan, and Naphtali. [14]Then

---

59. **Text signals.** (i) Up to now, the discourse has been exclusively from Moses; but here, it is from "Moses and the elders of Israel" (27:1) and from "Moses and the levitical priests" (27:9). (ii) Concern for the law and the commandment is present in the introduction, with a repeated concern to inculcate

obedience to the law. (iii) This ceremony involving Mounts Ebal and Gerizim (near Shechem) is also mentioned earlier in Deut 11:29-32 and later in Josh 8:30-35. (iv) Singular and plural forms of address are both present; the plural sections are 27:1, 2a*, 4a, 12.

Text-history approach. The focus on Mount Ebal present here (and Deut 11:29-32; Josh 8:30-35) sets these three passages apart from our national focus of the dtr revision, despite some commonalities of language and concern. The passages do not give the impression of addressing the situation of exile and failure. The plural sections might reflect a base for the present text.

Noth briefly reviews the constituent elements of Deuteronomy 27–30, with reference to disconnected additions; nevertheless, they remain within his dtn lawcode (*DH*, 33). For Noth, here, 27:1-8 "is one of the most subsidiary elements in the framework of the Deuteronomic law" and for Noth the Dtr relied on it to introduce Josh 8:30-35 into the DH (ibid., 31-33). We disagree; the same signals can be read differently.

Present-text potential. Following Moses' proclamation of the law beyond the Jordan, provision is now made for its permanence within the land, to be written on stones set up on Mount Ebal. See Josh 8:30-35.

Main pre-DH: dtn lawcode	Other pre-DH:	**Josianic DH:**
its introduction and conclusion	single sideline	**from the Dtr**

the Levites shall declare in a loud voice to all the Israelites:

15 "Cursed be anyone who makes an idol or casts an image, anything abhorrent to the LORD, the work of an artisan, and sets it up in secret." All the people shall respond, saying, "Amen!"

16 "Cursed be anyone who dishonors father or mother." All the people shall say, "Amen!"

17 "Cursed be anyone who moves a neighbor's boundary marker." All the people shall say, "Amen!"

18 "Cursed be anyone who misleads a blind person on the road." All the people shall say, "Amen!"

19 "Cursed be anyone who deprives the alien, the orphan, and the widow of justice." All the people shall say, "Amen!"

20 "Cursed be anyone who lies with his father's wife, because he has violated his father's rights." All the people shall say, "Amen!"

21 "Cursed be anyone who lies with any animal." All the people shall say, "Amen!"

22 "Cursed be anyone who lies with his sister, whether the daughter of his father or the daughter of his mother." All the people shall say, "Amen!"

23 "Cursed be anyone who lies with his mother-in-law." All the people shall say, "Amen!"

24 "Cursed be anyone who strikes down a neighbor in secret." All the people shall say, "Amen!"

25 "Cursed be anyone who takes a bribe to shed innocent blood." All the people shall say, "Amen!"

26 "Cursed be anyone who does not uphold the words of this law by observing them." All the people shall say, "Amen!"

28 *If you will only obey the LORD your God, by diligently observing all his commandments that I am commanding you today, the LORD your God will set you high above all the nations of the earth; ²all these blessings shall come upon you and overtake you, if you obey the LORD your God:*[60]

3 Blessed shall you be in the city, and blessed shall you be in the field.

4 Blessed shall be the fruit of your womb, the fruit of your ground, and the fruit of your livestock, both the increase of your cattle and the issue of your flock.

5 Blessed shall be your basket and your kneading bowl.

6 Blessed shall you be when you come in, and blessed shall you be when you go out.

7 The LORD will cause your enemies who rise against you to be defeated before you; they shall come out against you one way, and flee before you seven ways. ⁸The LORD will command the blessing upon you in your barns, and in all that you undertake; he will bless you in the land that the LORD your God is giving you. ⁹The LORD will establish you as his holy people,

---

60. The analysis of Deuteronomy 28 can become highly complex. It makes good sense to see 28:45-57 and 58-68 as expansions of 28:1-44 (see below). Where 28:1-44 is concerned, Mayes, for example, suggests an original core in vv. 3-6 and 16-19 (*Deuteronomy*, 350). These are matching lists of blessings and curses, almost identical in content, slightly changed in sequence, comprising four vital aspects of life: place, fertility, food, and activity. Mayes notes that these have no contact with other parts of Deuteronomy; this contact is provided by the introductions 28:1-2 and 15 (ibid., 351-52). Expansion is assumed to have taken place in a number of stages, resulting in a preponderance of curses. It is assumed that Deut 28:1-44 belonged in the conclusion to the dtn lawcode. The entire chapter uses singular address (minor exceptions in vv. 14a, 62a, 63*, 68b).

After the Dtr:	Revision:	Other:
indented and sans serif font	*national focus*	double sideline

as he has sworn to you, if you keep the commandments of the Lord your God and walk in his ways. [10]All the peoples of the earth shall see that you are called by the name of the Lord, and they shall be afraid of you. [11]The Lord will make you abound in prosperity, in the fruit of your womb, in the fruit of your livestock, and in the fruit of your ground in the land that the Lord swore to your ancestors to give you. [12]The Lord will open for you his rich storehouse, the heavens, to give the rain of your land in its season and to bless all your undertakings. You will lend to many nations, but you will not borrow. [13]The Lord will make you the head, and not the tail; you shall be only at the top, and not at the bottom—if you obey the commandments of the Lord your God, which I am commanding you today, by diligently observing them, [14]and if you do not turn aside from any of the words that I am commanding you today, either to the right or to the left, following other gods to serve them.

15 But if you will not obey the Lord your God by diligently observing all his commandments and decrees, which I am commanding you today, then all these curses shall come upon you and overtake you:

16 Cursed shall you be in the city, and cursed shall you be in the field.

17 Cursed shall be your basket and your kneading bowl.

18 Cursed shall be the fruit of your womb, the fruit of your ground, the increase of your cattle and the issue of your flock.

19 Cursed shall you be when you come in, and cursed shall you be when you go out.

20 The Lord will send upon you disaster, panic, and frustration in everything you attempt to do, until you are destroyed and perish quickly, on account of the evil of your deeds, because you have forsaken me. [21]The Lord will make the pestilence cling to you until it has consumed you off the land that you are entering to possess. [22]The Lord will afflict you with consumption, fever, inflammation, with fiery heat and drought, and with blight and mildew; they shall pursue you until you perish. [23]The sky over your head shall be bronze, and the earth under you iron. [24]The Lord will change the rain of your land into powder, and only dust shall come down upon you from the sky until you are destroyed.

25 The Lord will cause you to be defeated before your enemies; you shall go out against them one way and flee before them seven ways. You shall become an object of horror to all the kingdoms of the earth. [26]Your corpses shall be food for every bird of the air and animal of the earth, and there shall be no one to frighten them away. [27]The Lord will afflict you with the boils of Egypt, with ulcers, scurvy, and itch, of which you cannot be healed. [28]The Lord will afflict you with madness, blindness, and confusion of mind; [29]you shall grope about at noon as blind people grope in darkness, but you shall be unable to find your way; and you shall be continually abused and robbed, without anyone to help. [30]You shall become engaged to a woman, but another man shall lie with her. You shall build a house, but not live in it. You shall plant a vineyard, but not enjoy its fruit. [31]Your ox shall be butchered before your eyes, but you shall not eat of it. Your donkey shall be stolen in front of you, and shall not be restored to you. Your sheep shall be given to your enemies, without anyone to help you. [32]Your sons and daughters shall be given to another people, while you look on; you will strain your eyes looking for them all day but be powerless to do anything. [33]A people whom you do not know shall eat up the fruit of your ground and of all your labors; you shall be continually abused and crushed, [34]and driven mad by the sight that your eyes shall see. [35]The Lord will strike you on the knees and on the legs with

---

Main pre-DH: dtn lawcode	Other pre-DH:	**Josianic DH:**
its introduction and conclusion	single sideline	**from the Dtr**

grievous boils of which you cannot be healed, from the sole of your foot to the crown of your head. [36]The LORD will bring you, and the king whom you set over you, to a nation that neither you nor your ancestors have known, where you shall serve other gods, of wood and stone. [37]You shall become an object of horror, a proverb, and a byword among all the peoples where the LORD will lead you.

38 You shall carry much seed into the field but shall gather little in, for the locust shall consume it. [39]You shall plant vineyards and dress them, but you shall neither drink the wine nor gather the grapes, for the worm shall eat them. [40]You shall have olive trees throughout all your territory, but you shall not anoint yourself with the oil, for your olives shall drop off. [41]You shall have sons and daughters, but they shall not remain yours, for they shall go into captivity. [42]All your trees and the fruit of your ground the cicada shall take over. [43]Aliens residing among you shall ascend above you higher and higher, while you shall descend lower and lower. [44]They shall lend to you but you shall not lend to them; they shall be the head and you shall be the tail.

45 All these curses shall come upon you, pursuing and overtaking you until you are destroyed, because you did not obey the LORD your God, by observing the commandments and the decrees that he commanded you. [46]They shall be among you and your descendants as a sign and a portent forever.[61]

47 Because you did not serve the LORD your God joyfully and with gladness of heart for the abundance of everything, [48]therefore you shall serve your enemies whom the LORD will send against you, in hunger and thirst, in nakedness and lack of everything. He will put an iron yoke on your neck until he has destroyed you. [49]The LORD will bring a nation from far away, from the end of the earth, to swoop down on you like an eagle, a nation whose language you do not understand, [50]a grim-faced nation showing no respect to the old or favor to the young. [51]It shall consume the fruit of your livestock and the fruit of your ground until you are destroyed, leaving you neither grain, wine, and oil, nor the increase of your cattle and the issue of your flock, until it has made you perish. [52]It shall besiege you in all your towns until your high and fortified walls, in which you trusted, come down throughout your land; it shall besiege you in all your towns throughout the land that the LORD your God has given you. [53]In the desperate straits to which the enemy siege reduces you, you will eat the fruit of your

---

61. **Text signals** for vv. 45-57. (i) A change occurs from the conditional to an outright declaration of failure—"because you did not serve" (v. 47). (ii) Vv. 45-46 are seen as transitional—the proclamation of the law has occurred in the past and Israel is already guilty of disobedience (v. 45, see Mayes [*Deuteronomy*, 356]). (iii) Singular address is used in vv. 45-57.

Text-history approach. The text signals point to vv. 45-57 as an addition to the material in vv. 1-44. The curses of vv. 16-44 are here spoken of as effective among the present and subsequent generations; the possibility of the blessings (vv. 1-15) is no longer seen as an option. Vv. 45-57 focus on siege by a foreign enemy, sent against Israel by God, thus adding an element absent from vv. 15-44 and relevant to Israel's experience of catastrophe.

Present-text potential. The present text goes beyond the blessings and curses as pronounced to the curses as fulfilled. It is worth noting that for all the emphasis on these curses, Israel's theologians never speak of the nation as accursed.

After the Dtr:	Revision:	Other:
indented and sans serif font	*national focus*	double sideline

womb, the flesh of your own sons and daughters whom the LORD your God has given you. [54]Even the most refined and gentle of men among you will begrudge food to his own brother, to the wife whom he embraces, and to the last of his remaining children, [55]giving to none of them any of the flesh of his children whom he is eating, because nothing else remains to him, in the desperate straits to which the enemy siege will reduce you in all your towns. [56]She who is the most refined and gentle among you, so gentle and refined that she does not venture to set the sole of her foot on the ground, will begrudge food to the husband whom she embraces, to her own son, and to her own daughter, [57]begrudging even the afterbirth that comes out from between her thighs, and the children that she bears, because she is eating them in secret for lack of anything else, in the desperate straits to which the enemy siege will reduce you in your towns.

58 If you do not diligently observe all the words of this law that are written in this book, fearing this glorious and awesome name, the LORD your God, [59]then the LORD will overwhelm both you and your offspring with severe and lasting afflictions and grievous and lasting maladies. [60]He will bring back upon you all the diseases of Egypt, of which you were in dread, and they shall cling to you. [61]Every other malady and affliction, even though not recorded in the book of this law, the LORD will inflict on you until you are destroyed. [62]Although once you were as numerous as the stars in heaven, you shall be left few in number, because you did not obey the LORD your God. [63]And just as the LORD took delight in making you prosperous and numerous, so

the LORD will take delight in bringing you to ruin and destruction; you shall be plucked off the land that you are entering to possess. [64]The LORD will scatter you among all peoples, from one end of the earth to the other; and there you shall serve other gods, of wood and stone, which neither you nor your ancestors have known. [65]Among those nations you shall find no ease, no resting place for the sole of your foot. There the LORD will give you a trembling heart, failing eyes, and a languishing spirit. [66]Your life shall hang in doubt before you; night and day you shall be in dread, with no assurance of your life. [67]In the morning you shall say, "If only it were evening!" and at evening you shall say, "If only it were morning!"—because of the dread that your heart shall feel and the sights that your eyes shall see. [68]The LORD will bring you back in ships to Egypt, by a route that I promised you would never see again; and there you shall offer yourselves for sale to your enemies as male and female slaves, but there will be no buyer.[62]

29 *These are the words of the covenant that the LORD commanded Moses to make*

---

62. **Text signals.** (i) Verses 58-68 return to the form of conditional curse ("If you do not … ." v. 58). (ii) A new theme, the concern with Egypt (vv. 60 and 68), envelops the curses of this section. (iii) The address is substantially in the singular (but cf. in vv. 62a, 63*, and 68b).

Text-history approach. A further addition to the curses of vv. 16-44 and 45-57 is the most likely understanding of the text signals.

Present-text potential. The passage brings this chapter of horrors to its ultimate statement: what is at stake is Israel's history—what lies ahead will reverse what has gone before.

Main pre-DH: dtn lawcode
its introduction and conclusion

Other pre-DH:
single sideline

Josianic DH:
from the Dtr

with the Israelites in the land of Moab, in addition to the covenant that he had made with them at Horeb.[63]

2 Moses summoned all Israel and said to them: You have seen all that the LORD did before your eyes in the land of Egypt, to Pharaoh and to all his servants and to all his land, [3]the great trials that your eyes saw, the signs, and those great wonders. [4]But to this day the LORD has not given you a mind to understand, or eyes to see, or ears to hear. [5]I have led you forty years in the wilderness. The clothes on your back have not worn out, and the sandals on your feet have not worn out; [6]you have not eaten bread, and you have not drunk wine or strong drink—so that you may know that I am the LORD your God. [7]When you came to this place, King Sihon of Heshbon and King Og of Bashan came out against us for battle, but we defeated them. [8]We took their land and gave it as an inheritance to the Reubenites, the Gadites, and the half-tribe of Manasseh. [9]Therefore diligently observe the words of this covenant, in order that you may succeed in everything that you do.

10 You stand assembled today, all of you, before the LORD your God—the leaders of your tribes, your elders, and your officials, all the men of Israel, [11]your children, your women, and the aliens who are in your camp, both those who cut your wood and those who draw your water—[12]to enter into the covenant of the LORD your God, sworn by an oath, which the LORD your God is making with you today; [13]in order

---

63. **Text signals** in 29:1-29 (NRSV; Heb., 28:69-29:28). (i) The historical review (29:2-9, NRSV numbering) is a much abbreviated version of the Dtr's own review in chaps. 1–3, with no reference to the issue of rebellion so prominent there. (ii) There is repeated use of *'ālâ*, a term with a restricted range in the DH. In 29:12, 14, 19, it refers to a sworn oath and, in 29:21, it refers to the curses of the covenant (it is not used in chaps. 27–28); it occurs also in Deut 30:7; 1 Kgs 8:31 (2x), all of which are late texts. (iii) The warnings about the consequences of disobedience are similar to those in chap. 4. (iv) The motif of scandalous devastation (of the land), prompting a question and answer, found in vv. 24-25 (Heb., vv. 23-24) recurs in 1 Kgs 9:8-9 (2 Chron 7:21-22) for the temple and in Jer 22:8-9 for the city. (v) The reference to cutting wood and drawing water (v. 11, Heb., v. 10) echoes the story of the Gibeonites in Joshua 9. (vi) The address is plural (exceptions in vv. 3a, 5b, 11-13 [Heb. numbering, vv. 2a, 4b, 10-12]).

Text-history approach. Chap. 29 coheres well with chaps. 4 and 30:1-10, striking the positive note of hope beyond failure—for chap. 4 after the dtr introduction and for 29:1–30:10 before the conclusion (30:11-20). It belongs with these within the national focus of the dtr revision (cf. 1 Kgs 9:6-9). This material, preparing for failure and pointing to hope beyond it, contrasts with the emphasis on past failure in chaps. 9-10. V. 11b appears to include in the covenant even the most menial of the aliens in Israel's midst.

Present-text potential. 29:1 (NRSV numbering) serves as a transitional verse, giving the same status as the decalogue at Horeb to the Mosaic discourse on the commandments, the statutes, and the ordinances delivered in the land of Moab—see Deut 5:28—6:3. The whole section, 29:2—30:20 (NRSV numbering) is cast as a speech of Moses, with a logical order to its parts. For chap. 29, vv. 2-9 set the Moab covenant within a historical context from Egypt to the present; vv. 10-15 emphasize the purpose of this covenant, that is to establish Israel as God's people and the LORD as their God; vv. 16-21 warn against excessive confidence in this covenant; and vv. 22-28 move the focus to the next generation, witnesses to the devastation consequent on abandonment of this covenant (cf. Mayes, *Deuteronomy*, 360-67). V. 29 has the character of a conclusion.

After the Dtr:	Revision:	Other:
indented and sans serif font	national focus	double sideline

that he may establish you today as his people, and that he may be your God, as he promised you and as he swore to your ancestors, to Abraham, to Isaac, and to Jacob. ¹⁴I am making this covenant, sworn by an oath, not only with you who stand here with us today before the LORD our God, ¹⁵but also with those who are not here with us today. ¹⁶You know how we lived in the land of Egypt, and how we came through the midst of the nations through which you passed. ¹⁷You have seen their detestable things, the filthy idols of wood and stone, of silver and gold, that were among them. ¹⁸It may be that there is among you a man or woman, or a family or tribe, whose heart is already turning away from the LORD our God to serve the gods of those nations. It may be that there is among you a root sprouting poisonous and bitter growth. ¹⁹All who hear the words of this oath and bless themselves, thinking in their hearts, "We are safe even though we go our own stubborn ways" (thus bringing disaster on moist and dry alike)—²⁰the LORD will be unwilling to pardon them, for the LORD's anger and passion will smoke against them. All the curses written in this book will descend on them, and the LORD will blot out their names from under heaven. ²¹The LORD will single them out from all the tribes of Israel for calamity, in accordance with all the curses of the covenant written in this book of the law. ²²The next generation, your children who rise up after you, as well as the foreigner who comes from a distant country, will see the devastation of that land and the afflictions with which the LORD has afflicted it— ²³all its soil burned out by sulfur and salt, nothing planted, nothing sprouting, unable to support any vegetation, like the destruction of Sodom and Gomorrah, Admah and Zeboiim, which the LORD destroyed in his fierce anger—²⁴they and indeed all the nations will wonder, "Why has the LORD done thus to this land? What caused this great display of anger?" ²⁵They will conclude, "It is because they abandoned the covenant of the LORD, the God of their ancestors, which he made with them when he brought them out of the land of Egypt. ²⁶They turned and served other gods, worshiping them, gods whom they had not known and whom he had not allotted to them; ²⁷so the anger of the LORD was kindled against that land, bringing on it every curse written in this book. ²⁸The LORD uprooted them from their land in anger, fury, and great wrath, and cast them into another land, as is now the case." ²⁹The secret things belong to the LORD our God, but the revealed things belong to us and to our children forever, to observe all the words of this law.

30 *When all these things have happened to you, the blessings and the curses that I have set before you, if you call them to mind among all the nations where the LORD your God has driven you, ²and return to the LORD your God, and you and your children obey him with all your heart and with all your soul, just as I am commanding you today, ³then the LORD your God will restore your fortunes and have compassion on you, gathering you again from all the peoples among whom the LORD your God has scattered you. ⁴Even if you are exiled to the ends of the world, from there the LORD your God will gather you, and from there he will bring you back. ⁵The LORD your God will*

| Main pre-DH: dtn lawcode | Other pre-DH: | **Josianic DH:** |
| *its introduction and conclusion* | single sideline | **from the Dtr** |

bring you into the land that your ancestors possessed, and you will possess it; he will make you more prosperous and numerous than your ancestors.[64]

*6 Moreover, the L*ord *your God will circumcise your heart and the heart of your descendants, so that you will love the L*ord *your God with all your heart and with all your soul, in order that you may live. [7]The L*ord *your God will put all these curses on your enemies and on the adversaries who*

---

64. **Text signals.** (i) 30:1-10 parallels 4:29-31, giving expression to the theme of return and restoration. (ii) As it stands, 30:1-10 depends on chap. 29 (see 30:1). (iii) 30:1-10 has an emphasis on failure and return that is foreign to the deuteronomic lawcode. (iv) The address in vv. 1-10 is singular.

Text-history approach. Wolff argues for the commonality of 4:29-31 and chap. 28, especially vv. 45-68 with 30:1-10 as late dtr texts (see: links between 30:1 and 28:2, 15, and 45; between 30:9a and 28:11a; and between 30:9b and 28:63; also between 30:10a and 28:45b, rather than 28:1, 15; note the written "book of the law" in 30:10 and 28:58, 61; also links with Jeremiah, etc.—see "The Kerygma of the Deuteronomic Historical Work," 93-97). These associations suggest that 30:1-10 belongs within the national focus of the dtr revision; the concern here is with the individual Israelite, one among the people.

Present-text potential. Two options present themselves for reading vv. 1-10 and 11-14. In the first, the two passages function as cause and effect. Israel will experience failure; the issue of return and the promise of circumcised hearts looks to a situation in which the fulfillment of the law will become possible—as 30:11-14 had put it and still puts it, obedience will then lie within Israel's reach (favored by Campbell). In the second, the two passages speak differently of the same situation, both as future. 30:1-10 anticipates Israel's failure, return, and restoration; 30:11-14 proclaims that fidelity is within Israel's reach and failure can be avoided (favored by O'Brien).

*took advantage of you. [8]Then you shall again obey the L*ord*, observing all his commandments that I am commanding you today, [9]and the L*ord *your God will make you abundantly prosperous in all your undertakings, in the fruit of your body, in the fruit of your livestock, and in the fruit of your soil. For the L*ord *will again take delight in prospering you, just as he delighted in prospering your ancestors, [10]when you obey the L*ord *your God by observing his commandments and decrees that are written in this book of the law, because you turn to the L*ord *your God with all your heart and with all your soul.*

11 Surely, this commandment that I am commanding you today is not too hard for you, nor is it too far away. [12]It is not in heaven, that you should say, "Who will go up to heaven for us, and get it for us so that we may hear it and observe it?" [13]Neither is it beyond the sea, that you should say, "Who will cross to the other side of the sea for us, and get it for us so that we may hear it and observe it?" [14]No, the word is very near to you; it is in your mouth and in your heart for you to observe.[65]

---

65. The entire section, 29:1–30:20, is attributed by Mayes to his second deuteronomistic redaction (*Deuteronomy*, 359). The text layout here expresses our preference for including 30:11-20 with the dtn lawcode. It functions as the conclusion; as such, it follows on 28:44. As opposed to 29:1—30:10, it presents Israel's potential response to the law in a positive light.

At that level, following on 28:44, 30:11-14 forms a bridge from the darkness of the curses in 28:15-44 to the positive light of the choice called for in 30:15-20. The particularity of the blessings and curses (28:1-44) is replaced by a focus on the total presentation; 30:11's "this commandment" (*ḥammiṣwâ hazzo't*) strongly evokes 6:1's "and this is the commandment" (*wĕzo't ḥammiṣwâ*). It is this total presentation that is the

---

After the Dtr:	Revision:	Other:
indented and sans serif font	*national focus*	double sideline

15 See, I have set before you today life and prosperity, death and adversity 16If you obey the commandments of the LORD your God that I am commanding you today, by loving the LORD your God, walking in his ways, and observing his commandments, decrees, and ordinances, then you shall live and become numerous, and the LORD your God will bless you in the land that you are entering to possess. 17But if your heart turns away and you do not hear, but are led astray to bow down to other gods and serve them, 18I declare to you today that you shall perish; you shall not live long in the land that you are crossing the Jordan to enter and possess. 19I call heaven and earth to witness against you today that I have set before you life and death, blessings and curses. Choose life so that you and your descendants may live, 20loving the LORD your God, obeying him, and holding fast to him; for that means life to you and length of days, so that you may live in the land that the LORD swore to give to your ancestors, to Abraham, to Isaac, and to Jacob.66

31 When Moses had finished speaking all these words to all Israel, 2he said to them: "I am now one hundred twenty years old. I am no longer able to get about, and the LORD has told me, 'You shall not cross over this Jordan.' 3The LORD your God himself will cross over before you. He will destroy these nations before you, and you shall dispossess them. Joshua also will cross over before you, as the LORD promised. 4The LORD will do to them as he did to Sihon and Og, the kings of the Amorites, and to their land, when he destroyed them. 5The LORD will give them over to you and you shall deal with them in full accord with the command that I have given to you. 6Be strong and bold; have no fear or dread of them, because it is the LORD your God who goes with you; he will not fail you or forsake you."67

---

object of Israel's choice. It is important that the "commandment" lies within Israel's reach and that obedience is believed possible.

The movement from 28:44 to 30:11 may appear as an awkward sequence; after any presentation of blessings and curses, a reflective gap is needed and may be assumed. Recognition of the transition from specific curses to the general conclusion is facilitated by the awareness that, without 29:1–30:10, the whole is an address by Moses with remarkable coherence (cf. 28:1, 15; 30:11, 15-16).

The address in vv. 11-14 and 15-20 is predominantly singular; the plural is found in v. 18 and in v. 19a.

66. As noted above, 30:15-20 is the conclusion to the presentation of the dtn lawcode. Israel is called on to choose between life and death. Life is equated with fidelity to the commandments of the lawcode and death with disobedience and apostasy. The dtn challenge to Israel is to choose life and to love the LORD their God.

67. **Text signals** in 31:1-6. (i) Old age as the occasion for a final significant gesture by the leader is present in Josh 13:1 and 23:1, also 1 Sam 12:2—all later texts (note the 120 years in Deut 34:7). (ii) The reason given in Deut 3:26 why Moses shall not cross the Jordan is not mentioned, but here two reasons are alleged: Moses' immobility as an old man and God's prohibition. (iii) Vv. 3-6 recapitulate chaps. 2–3 of Deuteronomy in ways that demand scrutiny; first, vv. 3-4 and 6b use the singular where in chaps. 2–3 the Dtr consistently uses the plural and, second, vv. 5-6a, formulated in the plural, clearly depend on vv. 3-4. (iv) The reference to Joshua in v. 3b intrudes abruptly into a series of statements focused exclusively on God; it may reflect an over-scrupulous concern interpreting God's action or protecting Joshua's role.

Text-history approach. These verses could well have been composed in part by the Dtr; however, the signals noted above point rather in a different direction. Both v. 3b and vv. 5-6a give the impression of being subsequent reflections on this later text.

Main pre-DH: dtn lawcode
its introduction and conclusion

Other pre-DH:
single sideline

Josianic DH:
from the Dtr

7 Then Moses summoned Joshua and said to him in the sight of all Israel: "Be strong and bold, for you are the one who will go with this people into the land that the LORD has sworn to their ancestors to give them; and you will put them in possession of it. **8**It is the LORD who goes before you. He will be with you; he will not fail you or forsake you. Do not fear or be dismayed."[68]

9 Then Moses wrote down this law, and gave it to the priests, the sons of Levi, who carried the ark of the covenant of the LORD, and to all the elders of Israel. 10Moses commanded them: "Every seventh year, in the scheduled year of remission, during the festival of booths, 11when all Israel comes to appear before the LORD your God at the place that he will choose, you shall read this law before all Israel in their hearing. 12Assemble the people—men, women, and children, as well as the aliens residing in your towns—so that they may hear and learn to fear the LORD your God and to observe diligently all the words of this law, 13and so that their children, who have not known it, may hear and learn to fear the LORD your God, as long as you live in the land that you are crossing over the Jordan to possess. "69

14 The LORD said to Moses, "Your time to die is near; call Joshua and present yourselves in the tent of meeting, so that I may commission him." So Moses and Joshua went and presented themselves in the tent of meeting, 15and the LORD appeared at the tent in a pillar of cloud; the pillar of cloud stood at the entrance to the tent.[70]

Present-text potential. After the proclamation of the lawcode and before the passing of leadership from Moses to Joshua, 31:1-6 recapitulates the promise of the conquest of the land from the introductory chapters. The familiar word pair ("be strong and bold": Deut 3:28; 31:6, 7, 23; Josh 1:6, 7, 9, 18; 10:25; 1 Chron 22:13; 28:20; 2 Chron 32:7), applied here to the people, leads into the commission to Joshua (cf. Deut 1:38 and 3:28).

68. Here, in vv. 7-8, the Dtr reports Moses' compliance with God's disposition in Deut 1:38 (cf. 3:28); the NRSV's "encourage" (1:38) and "be strong" (here) translate the same Hebrew verb (cf. also 3:28; Josh 1:6, 7, 9, 18).

69. **Text signals** in 31:9-13. (i) Vv. 10-13 make the feast of Succoth an occasion for the reading of the law, rather than a joyous harvest festival (Deut 16:13-15). (ii) There is a particular concern for obedience to the law. This suggests attribution to the national focus of the dtr revision; at this point, there is no emphasis on Israel's inevitable failure. Some verses are in the singular (vv. 11aα and 12a).

Text-history approach. These signals are open to a variety of interpretations. If vv. 9-13 are given to the national focus of the dtr revision, as we suggest, then in the Josianic DH Moses' final act before his death is the charge given to Joshua, in keeping with Deut 1:38. It would be possible, with Noth, to attribute the opening of v. 9 ("Then Moses wrote down this law") and vv. 24-26a to the Dtr; but the sentences do not form a particularly satisfactory sequence. Within the national focus of the dtr revision, the concern for a written law promulgated regularly to all Israel (cf. v. 12) is appropriate. Despite our preference here, it would not be out of the question to give vv. 9-13 to the Dtr.

Present-text potential. Now that Moses has proclaimed the law and as his life is coming to an end, it is appropriate to commit the law to writing and it is fitting to set in place the structures for its regular reading and for its understanding.

70. **Text signals** in 31:14-15. (i) The references to the tent of meeting and pillar of cloud are not found elsewhere in Deuteronomy or the DH; the occurrences of both together are late (e.g., Exod 33:9-10; Num 11:24b-25; 12:5). (ii) YHWH's decision to

---

| After the Dtr: indented and sans serif font | *Revision: national focus* | Other: double sideline |

16 The Lord said to Moses, "Soon you will lie down with your ancestors. Then this people will begin to prostitute themselves to the foreign gods in their midst, the gods of the land into which they are going; they will forsake me, breaking my covenant that I have made with them. [17]My anger will be kindled against them in that day. I will forsake them and hide my face from them; they will become easy prey, and many terrible troubles will come upon them. In that day they will say, 'Have not these troubles come upon us because our God is not in our midst?' [18]On that day I will surely hide my face on account of all the evil they have done by turning to other gods. [19]Now therefore write this song, and teach it to the Israelites; put it in their mouths, in order that this song may be a witness for me against the Israelites. [20]For when I have brought them into the land flowing with milk and honey, which I promised on oath to their ancestors, and they have eaten their fill and grown fat, they will turn to other gods and serve them, despising me and breaking my covenant. [21]And when many

terrible troubles come upon them, this song will confront them as a witness, because it will not be lost from the mouths of their descendants. For I know what they are inclined to do even now, before I have brought them into the land that I promised them on oath." [22]That very day Moses wrote this song and taught it to the Israelites.[71]

23 Then the Lord commissioned Joshua son of Nun and said, "Be strong and bold, for you shall bring the Israelites into the land that I promised them; I will be with you."[72]

24 When Moses had finished writing down in a book the words of this law to the very end, [25]Moses commanded the Levites who carried the ark of the covenant of the

---

commission Joshua is repetitive after having instructed Moses (1:38) and after what Moses has just done (31:7-8).

Text-history approach. An addition from priestly sources is likely, associated with v. 23. It may be that Joshua's responsibility for the establishment of Israel, west of the Jordan, was too important not to be directly commissioned by God (an interpretation that could be favored by aspects of divine discourse, cf. Josh 1:1-6).

Present-text potential. The text presents a cumulative endorsement of Joshua's leadership that, in the present instance, gives concrete expression to the promise of 31:8.

---

71. **Text signals** in 31:16-22. (i) Vv. 16-22 interrupt the sequence from the preparations for Joshua's commissioning by God (vv. 14-15) and the commissioning itself (v. 23); the Lord, as it were, has a distraction standing at the tent. (ii) There is a considerable gap between v. 22 and the text of the song itself. (iii) The language is significant: "to prostitute oneself," referring to worship of a foreign god, while common in the prophets, in the revised DH is found elsewhere only in Judg 2:17; 8:27, 33; "hide my face," again apart from prophets and psalms, is found elsewhere only in Deut 32:20; "many terrible troubles will come upon them," with "troubles" as the subject, is found only here, in Deut 31:17 and 21. (iv) The conquest generation, which in Joshua is remarkably faithful, here is clearly understood as unfaithful.

Text-history approach. An addition is likely, preparing the way for the song of Moses.

Present-text potential. Because it is the song of Moses, its commissioning needs to be completed before the handover to Joshua in v. 23.

72. What was prepared for in vv. 14-15 is now carried out.

Main pre-DH: dtn lawcode	Other pre-DH:	**Josianic DH:**
its introduction and conclusion	single sideline	**from the Dtr**

LORD, saying, *26"Take this book of the law and put it beside the ark of the covenant of the LORD your God; let it remain there as a witness against you. 27For I know well how rebellious and stubborn you are. If you already have been so rebellious toward the LORD while I am still alive among you, how much more after my death! 28Assemble to me all the elders of your tribes and your officials, so that I may recite these words in their hearing and call heaven and earth to witness against them. 29For I know that after my death you will surely act corruptly, turning aside from the way that I have commanded you. In time to come trouble will befall you, because you will do what is evil in the sight of the LORD, provoking him to anger through the work of your hands."73*

30 Then Moses recited the words of this song, to the very end, in the hearing of the whole assembly of Israel:74

32 Give ear, O heavens, and I will speak;
　　let the earth hear the words of
　　　　my mouth.
2May my teaching drop like the rain,
　　my speech condense like the dew;
like gentle rain on grass,
　　like showers on new growth.
3For I will proclaim the name of
　　the LORD;
　　ascribe greatness to our God!

4The Rock, his work is perfect,
　　and all his ways are just.
A faithful God, without deceit,
　　just and upright is he;
5yet his degenerate children have dealt
　　　　falsely with him,
　　a perverse and crooked generation.

---

73. **Text signals** in 31:24-29. (i) Here too, as above (e.g., v. 16), the conquest generation is viewed as unfaithful. (ii) The emphasis on the law relates to future failure (cf. vv. 27, 29). (iii) In vv. 9-13 the law was viewed positively, while here the law is a witness against the people. (iv) In vv. 9-13, the elders were present, while here they need to be assembled. (v) The phrase "the book of the law" (v. 26) is late; the earliest occurrences may be 2 Kgs 22:8 and 11 (cf. note on 2 Kgs 22:10). It occurs in a number of passages attributed to the national focus of the dtr revision (Deut 29:20; 30:10; Josh 1:8; 8:31, 34; 23:6), as well as other late texts. In the context of public reading of the law, note Neh 8:1, 3, 18; 9:3.

Text-history approach. The signals suggest the possibility that, with the introduction of the material on the song (31:16-22 and 31:30—32:44), the need was felt to reemphasize the role of the law. The song is witness against the people (vv. 19, 21) and so too is the law (v. 26). Even though they may be a response to the inclusion of the song, vv. 24-29 are clearly related to vv. 9-13 and so have been kept in the same format.

Present-text potential. There are two witnesses against the Israelites: (i) the song of Moses, taught to the people, to be sung. (ii) the law, written down and entrusted to the priests, to be read publicly. Vv. 9-13 provide for the instruction of the people through the regular reading of the law; vv. 26-29 emphasize a negative function of the law, as witness against the people when they fail.

74. **Text signals** in 31:30—32:44. (i) The song does not feature elsewhere in the DH. (ii) There is evidence for contact with late prophecy and wisdom literature (cf. Mayes, *Deuteronomy*, 380-82).

Text-history approach. A late addition is assumed.

Present-text potential. Here, at the end of Moses' life, the song has God looking down over Israel's history not only to its catastrophic end but beyond to Israel's future restoration. The "end" could have been worse; cf. vv. 26-27.

After the Dtr:	Revision:	Other:
indented and sans serif font	national focus	double sideline

⁶Do you thus repay the LORD,
       O foolish and senseless people?
Is not he your father, who created you,
       who made you and established you?
⁷Remember the days of old,
       consider the years long past;
ask your father, and he will inform you;
       your elders, and they will tell you.
⁸When the Most High apportioned
              the nations,
       when he divided humankind,
he fixed the boundaries of the peoples
       according to the number of the gods;
⁹the LORD's own portion was
              his people,
       Jacob his allotted share.

¹⁰He sustained him in a desert land,
       in a howling wilderness waste;
he shielded him, cared for him,
       guarded him as the apple of his eye.
¹¹As an eagle stirs up its nest,
       and hovers over its young;
as it spreads its wings, takes them up,
       and bears them aloft on its pinions,
¹²the LORD alone guided him;
       no foreign god was with him.
¹³He set him atop the heights of
              the land,
       and fed him with produce of
              the field;
he nursed him with honey from
              the crags,
       with oil from flinty rock;
¹⁴curds from the herd, and milk from
              the flock,
       with fat of lambs and rams;
Bashan bulls and goats,
       together with the choicest wheat—
       you drank fine wine from the blood
              of grapes.

¹⁵Jacob ate his fill;
       Jeshurun grew fat, and kicked.
       You grew fat, bloated, and gorged!
He abandoned God who made him,
       and scoffed at the Rock of his
              salvation.
¹⁶They made him jealous with
              strange gods,
       with abhorrent things they
              provoked him.
¹⁷They sacrificed to demons, not God,
       to deities they had never known,
to new ones recently arrived,
       whom your ancestors had
              not feared.
¹⁸You were unmindful of the Rock that
              bore you;
       you forgot the God who gave
              you birth.

¹⁹The LORD saw it, and was jealous
       he spurned his sons and daughters.
²⁰He said: I will hide my face
              from them,
       I will see what their end will be;
for they are a perverse generation,
       children in whom there is no
              faithfulness.
²¹They made me jealous with what is
              no god,
       provoked me with their idols.
So I will make them jealous with what is
              no people,
       provoke them with a foolish nation.
²²For a fire is kindled by my anger,
       and burns to the depths of Sheol;
it devours the earth and its increase,
       and sets on fire the foundations of
              the mountains.
²³I will heap disasters upon them,
       spend my arrows against them:

Main pre-DH: dtn lawcode   Other pre-DH: **Josianic DH:**
its introduction and conclusion   single sideline   **from the Dtr**

[24]wasting hunger,
> burning consumption,
> bitter pestilence.
The teeth of beasts I will send
> against them,
> with venom of things crawling in
> the dust.
[25]In the street the sword shall bereave,
> and in the chambers terror,
for young man and woman alike,
> nursing child and old gray head.
[26]I thought to scatter them
> and blot out the memory of them
> from humankind;
[27]but I feared provocation by
> the enemy,
> for their adversaries might
> misunderstand
and say, "Our hand is triumphant;
> it was not the LORD who did all this."

[28]They are a nation void of sense;
> there is no understanding in them.
[29]If they were wise, they would
> understand this;
> they would discern what the end
> would be.
[30]How could one have routed
> a thousand,
> and two put a myriad to flight,
unless their Rock had sold them,
> the LORD had given them up?
[31]Indeed their rock is not like our Rock;
> our enemies are fools.
[32]Their vine comes from the vinestock
> of Sodom,
> from the vineyards of Gomorrah;
their grapes are grapes of poison,
> their clusters are bitter;
[33]their wine is the poison of serpents,
> the cruel venom of asps.

[34]Is not this laid up in store with me,
> sealed up in my treasuries?
[35]Vengeance is mine, and recompense,
> for the time when their foot
> shall slip;
because the day of their calamity is
> at hand,
> their doom comes swiftly.

[36]Indeed the LORD will vindicate
> his people,
> have compassion on his servants,
when he sees that their power is gone,
> neither bond nor free remaining.
[37]Then he will say: Where are their gods,
> the rock in which they took refuge,
[38]who ate the fat of their sacrifices,
> and drank the wine of their
> libations?
Let them rise up and help you,
> let them be your protection!

[39]See now that I, even I, am he;
> there is no god besides me.
I kill and I make alive;
> I wound and I heal;
> and no one can deliver from
> my hand.
[40]For I lift up my hand to heaven,
> and swear: As I live forever,
[41]when I whet my flashing sword,
> and my hand takes hold
> on judgment;
I will take vengeance on my adversaries,
> and will repay those who hate me.
[42]I will make my arrows drunk
> with blood,
> and my sword shall devour flesh—
with the blood of the slain and
> the captives,
> from the long-haired enemy.

After the Dtr:	Revision:	Other:
indented and sans serif font	*national focus*	double sideline

⁴³Praise, O heavens, his people,
worship him, all you gods!
For he will avenge the blood of
his children,
and take vengeance on
his adversaries;
he will repay those who hate him,
and cleanse the land for his people.

44 Moses came and recited all the words of this song in the hearing of the people, he and Joshua son of Nun.

45 When Moses had finished reciting all these words to all Israel, ⁴⁶he said to them: "Take to heart all the words that I am giving in witness against you today; give them as a command to your children, so that they may diligently observe all the words of this law. ⁴⁷This is no trifling matter for you, but rather your very life; through it you may live long in the land that you are crossing over the Jordan to possess."⁷⁵

48 On that very day the LORD addressed Moses as follows: ⁴⁹"Ascend this mountain of the Abarim, Mount Nebo, which is in the land of Moab, across from Jericho, and view the land of Canaan, which I am giving to the Israelites for a possession; ⁵⁰you shall die there on the mountain that you ascend and shall be gathered to your kin, as your brother Aaron died on Mount Hor and was gathered to his kin; ⁵¹because both of you broke faith with me among the Israelites at the waters of Meribath-kadesh in the wilderness of Zin, by failing to maintain my holiness among the Israelites. ⁵²Although you may view the land from a distance, you shall not enter it—the land that I am giving to the Israelites."⁷⁶

33 This is the blessing with which Moses, the man of God, blessed the Israelites before his death. ²He said:⁷⁷

---

75. **Text signals** in 32:45-47. "All these words" (v. 45) must refer beyond the song, as v. 46 indicates, so tying vv. 45-47 into the secondary legal emphases earlier in chap. 31.

Text-history approach. An addition belonging in the national focus of the dtr revision is likely.

Present-text potential. On the last day of Moses' life, it is appropriate that his final instruction embraces both the song and the law. It echoes the call to life of 30:15-20.

76. **Text signals** in 32:48-52. (i) Vv. 48-52 are a substantial repetition of the priestly material in Num 27:12-14. (ii) The reason for Moses' death outside the land is different from that given in Deut 3:26, where it is not Moses' fault but the people's, "on your account."

Text-history approach. An addition from priestly sources is likely.

Present-text potential. There has been a steadily rising insistence on the imminence of Moses' death (31:1, 14, 16; 32:48-52). The difficulty of explaining the scandal of his death outside the land warrants the inclusion of a further reason for it (v. 51). The repetition here of Num 27:12-14 also brings to the fore the realization that all of Deuteronomy is portrayed as the final activity of Moses' life.

77. **Text signals** in 33:1-29. The nature of such a collection of blessings makes it difficult to date its composition and its insertion into any given text.

Text-history approach. Though this collection may indeed be early, its insertion here is generally regarded as late.

Present-text potential. The testamentary blessing by an ancestor was a well-known custom (cf. Isaac, Genesis 27; Jacob, Genesis 49). As the leader of the constitutive generation of the people of Israel, it is fitting for Moses to bestow his blessing on the tribes of Israel.

Main pre-DH: dtn lawcode	Other pre-DH:	**Josianic DH:**
its introduction and conclusion	single sideline	**from the Dtr**

The LORD came from Sinai,
   and dawned from Seir upon us;
   he shone forth from Mount Paran.
With him were myriads of holy ones;
   at his right, a host of his own.
³Indeed, O favorite among peoples,
   all his holy ones were in your charge;
they marched at your heels,
   accepted direction from you.
⁴Moses charged us with the law,
   as a possession for the assembly
     of Jacob.
⁵There arose a king in Jeshurun,
   when the leaders of the
     people assembled—
     the united tribes of Israel.

⁶May Reuben live, and not die out,
   even though his numbers are few.

⁷And this he said of Judah:
   O LORD, give heed to Judah,
     and bring him to his people;
   strengthen his hands for him,
     and be a help against his
     adversaries.

⁸And of Levi he said:
   Give to Levi your Thummim,
     and your Urim to your loyal one,
   whom you tested at Massah,
     with whom you contended at
     the waters of Meribah;
⁹who said of his father and mother,
   "I regard them not";
he ignored his kin,
   and did not acknowledge his
     children.
For they observed your word,
   and kept your covenant.
¹⁰They teach Jacob your ordinances,

and Israel your law;
   they place incense before you,
     and whole burnt offerings
     on your altar.
¹¹Bless, O LORD, his substance,
   and accept the work of his hands;
crush the loins of his adversaries,
   of those that hate him, so that they
     do not rise again.

¹²Of Benjamin he said:
   The beloved of the LORD rests in safety—
   the High God surrounds him all
     day long—
     the beloved rests between his
     shoulders.

¹³And of Joseph he said:
   Blessed by the LORD be his land,
     with the choice gifts of
     heaven above,
     and of the deep that lies beneath;
¹⁴with the choice fruits of the sun,
     and the rich yield of the months;
¹⁵with the finest produce of the
     ancient mountains,
     and the abundance of the
     everlasting hills;
¹⁶with the choice gifts of the earth
     and its fullness,
     and the favor of the one who dwells
     on Sinai.
Let these come on the head of Joseph,
   on the brow of the prince among
     his brothers.
¹⁷A firstborn bull—majesty is his!
   His horns are the horns of a
     wild ox;
   with them he gores the peoples,
     driving them to the ends of
     the earth;

After the Dtr:
indented and sans serif font

Revision:
national focus

Other:
double sideline

such are the myriads of Ephraim,
    such the thousands of Manasseh.

[18]And of Zebulun he said:
    Rejoice, Zebulun, in your going out;
        and Issachar, in your tents.
    [19]They call peoples to the mountain;
        there they offer the right sacrifices;
    for they suck the affluence of
        the seas
        and the hidden treasures of the sand.

[20]And of Gad he said:
    Blessed be the enlargement of Gad!
        Gad lives like a lion;
        he tears at arm and scalp.
    [21]He chose the best for himself,
        for there a commander's
            allotment was reserved;
    he came at the head of the people,
        he executed the justice of
            the LORD,
        and his ordinances for Israel.

[22]And of Dan he said:
    Dan is a lion's whelp
        that leaps forth from Bashan.

[23]And of Naphtali he said:
    O Naphtali, sated with favor,
        full of the blessing of the LORD,
        possess the west and the south.

[24]And of Asher he said:
    Most blessed of sons be Asher;
        may he be the favorite of
            his brothers,
        and may he dip his foot in oil.
    [25]Your bars are iron and bronze;
        and as your days, so is
            your strength.

[26]There is none like God, O Jeshurun,
    who rides through the heavens
        to your help,
    majestic through the skies.
[27]He subdues the ancient gods,
    shatters the forces of old;
he drove out the enemy before you,
    and said, "Destroy!"
[28]So Israel lives in safety,
    untroubled is Jacob's abode
in a land of grain and wine,
    where the heavens drop
        down dew.
[29]Happy are you, O Israel! Who is
    like you,
    a people saved by the LORD,
the shield of your help,
    and the sword of your triumph!
Your enemies shall come fawning
    to you,
    and you shall tread on their backs.

34 **Then Moses went up**[78]
|| from the plains of Moab to Mount Nebo

---

78. In Noth's treatment of the DH, only fragments of the report of Moses' death are regarded as surviving; along with vv. 4-6, part of v. 1, especially "the top of Pisgah" (*DH*, 60). It is clear that there is a conflict here between the reports of the DH and P regarding Moses' death. It is assumed that the two accounts have been combined; it is impossible to decide definitively what might have been in one or the other.

A presentation of any DH text will need to reconstruct a report of Moses' death; a presentation of the P text will need to do the same. Two complete reports are not present in 34:1-12. Separate presentations must draw on some common material.

Main pre-DH: dtn lawcode   Other pre-DH: **Josianic DH:**
its introduction and conclusion   single sideline   **from the Dtr**

to the top of Pisgah,
|| which is opposite Jericho[79]
and the LORD showed him the whole land.
|| Gilead as far as Dan, [2]all Naphtali, the land
of Ephraim and Manasseh, all the land of
Judah as far as the Western Sea, [3]the
Negeb, and the Plain—that is, the valley of
Jericho, the city of palm trees—as far as
Zoar.[80]
[4]The LORD said to him, "This is the land of which I swore to Abraham, to Isaac, and to Jacob, saying, 'I will give it to your descendants'; I have let you see it with your eyes, but you shall not cross over there." [5]Then Moses, the servant of the LORD, died there in the land of Moab, at the LORD's command. [6]He was buried in a valley in the land of Moab, opposite Beth-peor, but no one knows his burial place to this day.

[7]Moses was one hundred twenty years old when he died; his sight was unimpaired and his vigor had not abated. [8]The Israelites wept for Moses in the plains of Moab thirty days; then the period of mourning for Moses was ended.

9 Joshua son of Nun was full of the spirit of wisdom, because Moses had laid his hands on him; and the Israelites obeyed him, doing as the LORD had commanded Moses.

10 Never since has there arisen a prophet in Israel like Moses, whom the LORD knew face to face. [11]He was unequaled for all the signs and wonders that the LORD sent him to perform in the land of Egypt, against Pharaoh and all his servants and his entire land, [12]and for all the mighty deeds and all the terrifying displays of power that Moses performed in the sight of all Israel.[81]

---

79. The reference to Mt. Nebo "which is opposite Jericho," echoes 32:49, which is a late secondary verse. So important an event as the death of Moses requires all the geographical precision that can be provided.

80. The description is similar to the geographical detail added in 1:1 and may derive from much the same concern. On the other hand, it is included in his DH by Mayes (*Deuteronomy*, 411). Certainty is out of the question. As with the location of Moses' death, so the extent of the land that he might have been able to see from Mt. Nebo is appropriately described.

81. Verses 7-9 are attributed to the Priestly Writer; vv. 10-12 look back to Exodus–Numbers, giving Moses unique status (in some conflict with Deut 18:18); the assessment of Moses' health contrasts with his enfeebled portrayal in 31:1. The text provides a fitting conclusion to Moses' life and work.

| After the Dtr: indented and sans serif font | *Revision: national focus* | Other: double sideline |

The Book of Joshua

INTRODUCTION

The problem of the book of Joshua is simple to present; it is more complex to resolve. The problem can be expressed by juxtaposing two judgments: no other generation in the biblical history of Israel received the praise that is bestowed on the generation of Joshua; no other book of the Bible has been so widely condemned by so many as a symbol of all that is appalling and inhuman. It is said of Joshua's generation, that "Israel served the Lord all the days of Joshua, and all the days of the elders who outlived Joshua" (Josh 24:31). No other biblical generation received this accolade. It is said of Joshua that he "defeated the whole land, the hill country and the Negeb and the lowland and the slopes, and all their kings; he left no one remaining, but utterly destroyed all that breathed, as the Lord God of Israel commanded" (Josh 10:40). Almost no other biblical action has been so widely condemned. This is the problem of the book of Joshua: a text portraying the generation whose perfect compliance with God's will produced perfectly atrocious behavior.

Any resolution is complex. From the outset, it is worth insisting that Israel's traditions witness to the fact that the local populations were not eliminated but lived on to lead Israel astray; Israel's theologians knew well enough that the utter destruction attributed to Joshua's genera-

tion never occurred. The same can be said of Saul's destruction of the Amalekites (cf. 1 Samuel 15 and 30). But this only intensifies the problem: why should any theologians insist that God commanded such destruction, when they knew that it had not happened?

The elements of the book need to be surveyed; they point toward complexity.

1. Toward the end of the first half is the affirmation that "Joshua took the whole land" (11:23a). It is also noted that "Joshua gave it for an inheritance to Israel according to their tribal allotments" (11:23a). At the beginning of the second half, however, are the Lord's words to Joshua: "very much of the land still remains to be possessed" (13:1).

2. In the second half, the distribution of the land is detailed, until "they finished dividing the land" (19:51). The cities of refuge are established (20:1-9); the Levites are catered for (21:1-42). The process of distribution begins with the tribes east of the Jordan (Reuben, Gad, and the half-tribe of Manasseh; 13:8-32), and a word about the Levites (no inheritance; 13:33). In the basic distribution, various traditions are represented. After the distribution of towns for the Levites (21:1-42), the text returns to issues of the tribes east of the Jordan (22:1-34).

3. A farewell speech by Joshua speaks of the peoples that have been cut off already and

those that remain (23:4); strong warnings are given against marrying their women or worshiping their gods (23:7, 12, 16). The final chapter is the report of Joshua's gathering all Israel at Shechem for the commitment of the people to the LORD, "No, we will serve the LORD!" (24:21).

The complexity can be focused on three issues: possession of the land, extermination of its inhabitants, commitment to YHWH. The first part of the book is affirmative on all three. All the land was possessed; all the inhabitants were exterminated; commitment to YHWH was uncontested. The second part of the book responds differently. Much land remained to be possessed, but the land was distributed to the tribes. The locals remaining would be pushed back by the LORD (23:5) and their land occupied. Commitment to YHWH needed to be encouraged (chap. 23) and at one point was even described by Joshua as impossible (24:19).

All this suggests that the book of Joshua (along with Judges 1) brings together a variety of traditions about Israel's occupation of the promised land. Beyond anything else, the problem remains: why should any theologians insist that God commanded such wholesale destruction of local populations—knowing it had not happened?

No solution known to us is satisfying. The text has at its base a faith conviction that God gave to Israel the land God had promised to Israel. The enormous implications of this faith for living in the land cannot be overlooked. If life and land are God's gift, the giver can attach certain stipulations to the gift. Those who accept the gift accept the stipulations. Even more fundamentally, the recognition that life and land are gifts of God has basic bearing on how life in the land is lived.

For many moderns, God does not have the right to dispose of occupied land. God had nei-

ther the right to promise it to Israel nor the right to give it to Israel. For other moderns, the contrary position is fiercely held; what God promises is promised and what God gives is given. It has been and is expressed in different ways in conflicts around the world. Much too much blood has been shed. This book is no place to explore ethics; but it helps to keep an eye on our modern world, with sorrow and shame, while we cast an eye over this ancient book. A fearful report from the French Revolution may stand witness to the agelessness of such inhuman horror: "There is no more Vendée, citizens, it has perished under our free sword along with its women and children. . . . Following the orders that you gave me I have crushed children under the feet of horses, massacred women who at least . . . will engender no more brigands. I have no prisoners with which to reproach myself."[1]

What unfolding the book of Joshua may do is provide insight about how such a text came into existence, where values are expressed in it that we may want to cherish, the implications for such values of certain sacral transformations, where theological claims are made that we may want to reject. Throughout much of the book, it is possible to see in the present text the interplay of realpolitik and religion. Most recently, realpolitik has been associated with Mao's dictum that "power grows out of the barrel of a gun"; it has always been about the exercise of raw power, whether political or military. The book of Joshua has a different view of the power

---

1. Quoted from S. Schama, *Citizens*, 788. Or there is an early Australian version of Manifest Destiny: "it is in the order of nature that, as civilization advances, savage nations must be exterminated" (quoted from R. Hughes, *The Fatal Shore*, 278).

of religion, the claim to divine action. As the DH unfolds, the interplay of the two in national life—and in the present biblical text—becomes increasingly evident.

In Samuel–Kings, religious power is usually expressed through the prophetic word. More often than not, the fulfillment of that word occurs through what are apparently the normal processes of human history. For example, Saul was rejected and David anointed by the prophet Samuel; but Saul and David were pitted in protracted political and military struggle, and the civil war between David and Saul's heirs was a long one (2 Sam 3:1). On God's behalf, the prophet Ahijah designated Jeroboam as future king; but outwardly it was the politics of taxation that brought him the crown (1 Kings 11–12; cf. the dtr union of both in 12:15b). In Judges, the interplay of religion and realpolitik is present, although more subtly. God raises up deliverers for Israel; reflection brings us to realize that the liberating actions of Ehud, Jael, and Gideon were—all three—daring, courageous, and dangerous.

In Joshua, the interplay is present, but differently again. Surprisingly, for most readers, there are sustained pointers to a narrative in the early part of the book describing an occupation by military force. In a later sacralization, three episodes have dramatically pushed the military aside to bring raw divine power to the fore—the liturgical Jordan crossing, the equally liturgical capture of Jericho, and the role of the ban in the failed assault on Ai. Later reflections are appendages to this. What may be termed the Conquest Narrative (Joshua 2 and similar texts) has almost been lost under the overwhelming impact of the sacralizing stories.

For today's reader, aware of the rhetoric and iconography of ancient religion, it is an important theological challenge to explore in Israel's biblical texts the interplay between the direct exercise of divine power and the cause and effect of the natural world. It is part of the unfolding of the DH.

Other introductory aspects are important and well-known. The stories in the early part of Joshua cover a lot of text and very little land—just some of Benjamin. There are three big Benjaminite stories (the Jordan crossing, the Jericho capture, and the Ai disaster); the leader in these Benjaminite stories is Joshua, an Ephraimite. In the first part of the book, the stories are major and the list-like material is minor; in the second part of the book, the lists are almost everything. What matters in both parts is not *what* happened (the occupation of the land) but *how* it happened (by God's doing). There are stories about how God had Israel triumph marvelously or fail miserably, but nothing pertaining to the details of occupation. There are long lists and minute details of the allocation of the land, by various authorities (after Moses, see Josh 14:1, 6; 17:4; 18:10; 19:49, 51), but almost nothing pertaining to the occupation of the territory allocated.

The first part of the book of Joshua (chaps. 1–12) offers evidence of three theologies; succinctly, we conquered, we possessed, we emptied. According to the Conquest Narrative, we **conquered** our land, with help from God. The evidence for this view remains principally in the story of the Jericho spies (chap. 2), the conquest of Ai (chap. 8) and the victory over the coalition at Gibeon/Makkedah (chaps. 9–10*), with traces in the intervening chapters. The land conquered was substantially that of Benjamin and Judah. The base for the conquest, and presumably for the memories, was Gilgal. According to the "sacral stories," we **possessed** the land, which God gave us when we obeyed. The evidence for this view lies principally in the stories of the Jordan crossing, the fall of Jericho, and the

Achan/Ai debacle (chap. 7), coupled with the similarly conceptualized reach into the north. The land possessed was substantially all Israel. The base for the sacral stories appears to have been, at least in its origins, the sanctuary at Gilgal. Finally, there is what we might term the "extermination level." According to this, they **emptied** the land, in obedience to God's decree. They emptied the whole land, both south and north. Interpretation of the text, its evidence and its theology, probably depended, then as now, on the interpreters: where they stood, what they read, and where their reading stopped. Then as now, what they read and where their reading stopped probably depended on where they stood.

It is worth noting that our attribution of the "extermination" to late passages is controlled by analysis of the language involved. Being late and unrealistic makes it no less appalling, especially as attributed to God's command; precisely, its being late and unrealistic may make it theologically worse. It is not that the term *ḥerem* ("ban") in various forms cannot be early. It can; it is. The fascination with the idea, however, appears to be late. Density of use or breadth of application can be pointers to such fascination.

It is also important to note that the double sideline in our formatting denotes our judgment on the time of the text's *incorporation* into the Josianic DH; it says nothing of the time of its *composition*. A single sideline indicates that the text was incorporated by the Josianic Dtr; therefore it was composed earlier. Any similar conclusion cannot and should not be made about the double sideline. Double sideline material can have been composed early and incorporated late.

The understanding presented here is a more than usually simple view of the growth of the book of Joshua. Encountered piecemeal, it may seem complex. An overview of the main stages may help.

- The initial level identified is the Conquest Narrative, beginning with Joshua 2 and ending in Joshua 10 (10:42-43). It is identified as product; its raw materials are not explored.
- The next level is the expansion of the Conquest Narrative. This has two parts, possibly two stages. Part One is the use of three "sacral" texts—for the Jordan crossing, the fall of Jericho, and the debacle before Ai—in place of the corresponding texts in the Conquest Narrative. Part Two is the extension of the Conquest Narrative to include the north. Parts One and Two may have been part of the same editorial activity; alternatively, Part Two may have been at a stage later than Part One. There is a similar "sacral" quality to the theology in both; 11:6-8 emphasizes YHWH's predominant role.
- These traditions have been incorporated into the Josianic DH. This involved an introduction at the start (Josh 1:1-6), some annotations along the way, and a conclusion at the end (Josh 21:43-45). This conclusion would have followed on the expansion's chap. 12. In this understanding, the end of the main narrative would have been achieved in 11:23, with 12:7-34 as an appendix, and the Dtr's conclusion then in what is now 21:43-45.

So far, so good. The bulk of Joshua 1–12 is relatively simple to discuss. It is when we come to the second half of the book that matters become more problematic. The identification of various traditions, at least broadly, is not so difficult. The timing of their incorporation into the basic text of Joshua is not susceptible of certainty. Hypotheses suggested have to generate a coherent textual sequence. Honesty suggests that the present text as it stands does not give a coherent textual sequence, at least one that respects the signals embedded in the text for our guidance. What contributes to the apparent difficulty is the size of the block that has been added somewhere around this point in the growth of the book—i.e., the core of Joshua 13–21.

Two features are worthy of note: the remarkable distribution of the two terms for "tribe" (*maṭṭeh* and *šēbeṭ*) and the remarkable difficulty of the introduction to chap. 13. First, the terms for tribe. The term *maṭṭeh* is used in Josh 14:1–21:42 (with four exceptions: 18:2, 4, 7; 21:16). The term *šēbeṭ*, which predominates in Joshua 1–12 (two exceptions: 7:1, 18), is used in 13:1-33 (with three exceptions: 13:15, 24, 29) and from 22:7 to the end of the book (with one exception: 22:14). The upshot of these observations is straightforward: Josh 14:1—21:42 bears a linguistic character that marks it off as a block from its surroundings. Any significance beyond this is difficult to interpret. Chronological, editorial, and other factors are all in play; no one factor dominates. (Within the DH, the term *maṭṭeh* is not used in dtr material. Within the DH, the term *šēbeṭ* is used in both source and dtr material; it is not exclusively dtr and has a wide chronological range.) Second, Joshua 13. The introduction to Joshua 13 is problematic. It situates the second half of the book in Joshua's old age which renders highly unlikely the sustained participation of the east-of-Jordan tribes for almost an adult lifetime. The difficulties of its syntax are discussed at 13:1. It does not introduce a distribution of land by Eleazar, Joshua, and the tribal family heads. It does focus on the territories of the east-of-Jordan tribes and on the lack of territory for the Levites, which is not the command of 13:7.

The final three stages may look somewhat as follows.

- The national focus within the process of dtr revision worked over the DH, probably in the time of exile, and among other things composed an exhortation to observance of the law, to go at the start of the book (Josh 1:7-9), and a cautious warning in the form of Joshua's final address (Josh 23:1-16, itself an unfolding of 21:43-45).

- Probably, it was at this stage in the growth of the text, i.e., after the national focus within the dtr revision, that the traditions about the allocation of the land to the nine and a half tribes were introduced (Josh 14:1–19:51) and texts concerning the cities of refuge and the towns allocated to the Levites (Josh 20:1-9 and 21:1-42 respectively). This is situated appropriately between the appendix of 12:7-34 and the dtr conclusion and the dismissal of the east-of-Jordan tribes (now 21:43-45).

- Finally, the story of the great altar by the Jordan was introduced (22:9-34), associated with the return of the east-of-Jordan tribes to their homelands (cf. 22:1-6). Probably in connection with this story, given the linguistic usage in these texts for *šēbeṭ* as "tribe," the traditions of the east-of-Jordan settlement were introduced as chap. 13, along with the list of east-of-Jordan kings (12:1-6). Also among late additions are the assembly at Shechem in Joshua 24, and probably the extermination texts relating to the emptying of the land by the annihilation of the local peoples. This last element is difficult to date. As already noted, it is not so much that the language is late; it is not. Rather, it is that a fascination with this idea appears to be late. Joshua's final exhortation against intermarriage with the locals and worship of their gods (Josh 23:1-16) would make little sense if these texts of annihilation were already in place.

The constituent traditions of the book of Joshua are clear enough: the Conquest Narrative, the sacral texts, the dtr interpretations, the distribution to the tribes, the issues of the east-of-Jordan tribes, the extermination texts, and the assembly at Shechem.[2] What is less clear is the precise points in the growth of the text at which some of these elements were introduced. What is clear, but confusing for dating, is that geographical data for towns and boundaries may be earlier than the composition of the lists in which it is now formulated. It is important that interpreters keep in mind the plausibility of textual sequence at any hypothetical stage. It is equally important that interpretation respects the intelligence of Israel's editors and compilers. It is not always desirable to delve behind the texts produced (the product) to identify the elements from which they have been produced (the raw materials). Where this has not seemed necessary for the purposes of this book, we have refrained.

2. For more extensive treatment of Joshua 1–12, which was the basis for this work, see Campbell, "The Growth of Joshua 1–12 and the Theology of Extermination" in *Reading the Hebrew Bible for a New Millennium*. Edited by Wonil Kim. Vol. 2. Harrisburg, Pa.: Trinity Press International, forthcoming.

THE BOOK OF JOSHUA

1 After the death of Moses[1]
the servant of the LORD, the LORD spoke to Joshua son of Nun, Moses' assistant, saying, [2]**"My servant Moses is dead. Now proceed to cross the Jordan, you and all this people, into the land that I am giving to them, to the Israelites.** [3]**Every place that the sole of your foot will tread upon I have given to you, as I promised to Moses.** [4]**From the wilderness and the Lebanon as far as the great river, the river Euphrates, all the land of the Hittites, to the Great Sea in the west shall be your territory.** [5]**No one shall be able to stand against you all the days of your life. As I was with Moses, so I will be with you; I will not fail you or forsake you.** [6]**Be strong and courageous; for you shall put this people in possession of the land that I swore to their ancestors to give them.**[2]

---

1. This is one of those little introductory phrases that could have been written by just about anybody at just about any time. It is required here as an introduction to Josh 1:1. It is set in roman as a reminder that something of the kind would have once stood as introduction to 2:1.

2. **Text signals** in Josh 1:1-11. Characteristic dtr language is not simply a matter of the words or phrases used but rather of language used in the service of dtr ideology. Dtr ideology is most simply identified as exclusive fidelity to YHWH and centralization of worship (in Jerusalem). At this early stage in the DH, in the wilderness on the eastern fringes of the Jordan, Moses established a program for all Israel in the land west of the Jordan (i.e., the dtn lawcode with its introduction and conclusion). Joshua's job, according to the DH, was to lead the people into the land; this was his charge (Deut 1:38), for this he was commissioned (Deut 31:7-8). This aspect of Joshua's responsibility for executing the program established by Moses will dominate much of the dtr book of Joshua.

[7]*Only be strong and very courageous, being careful to act in accordance with all the law that my servant Moses commanded you; do not turn from it to the right hand or to the left, so that you may be successful wherever you go.* [8]*This book of the law shall not depart out of your mouth; you shall meditate on it day and night, so that you may be careful to act in accordance with all that is written in it. For then you shall make your way prosperous, and then you shall be successful.* [9]*I hereby command you: Be strong and courageous; do not be frightened or dismayed, for the LORD your God is with you wherever you go."*

(i) Joshua is portrayed as "Moses' assistant" and his successor (vv. 1-2). (ii) God speaks to Joshua directly, as with Moses (cf. Num 12:6-8). (iii) The assurance in v. 5 mirrors closely part of Deut 31:8a. (iv) V. 6 mirrors closely Joshua's commission in Deut 31:7. (v) The pair of imperatives in v. 6 ("be strong and courageous"), expressing Joshua's commission, is repeated in vv. 7 and 9; specifically, v. 7 is not in relation to possession of the land but in relation to observance of the law. (vi) Vv. 7-9 find a strong echo in Joshua 23: the encouragement to observe the law (cf. 23:6), the emphasis on the "book of the law" (cf. 23:6), and the assurance of success. (vii) Joshua's order to the officers (vv. 10-11) focuses on action and possession of the land.

Text-history approach. As indicated by the formatting, vv. 1-6 are attributed to the Josianic Dtr. They state in clear terms what has been in view since Deut 1:38 and activated in Deut 31:7-8. The DH is about life in the land west of the Jordan, under Deuteronomy's Mosaic law. With the death of Moses, the time has come for the generation of Joshua. The Dtr is concerned to give appropriate authority to Joshua (cf. Josh 1:5b with Deut 31:8; also 31:6 for Israel). Vv. 1-6 are presented as YHWH's order to Joshua; v. 10 is Joshua's order to the officers for the people.

After the Dtr:	Revision:	Other:
indented and sans serif font	national focus	double sideline

10 Then Joshua commanded the officers of the people, [11]"Pass through the camp, and command the people: 'Prepare your provisions; for in three days you are to cross over the Jordan, to go in to take possession of the land that the LORD your God gives you to possess.' "[3]

12 To the Reubenites, the Gadites, and the half-tribe of Manasseh Joshua said, [13]"Remember the word that Moses the servant of the LORD commanded you, saying, 'The LORD your God is providing you a place of rest, and will give you this land.' [14]Your wives, your little ones, and your livestock shall remain in the land that Moses gave you beyond the Jordan. But all the warriors among you shall cross over armed before your kindred and shall help them, [15]until the LORD gives rest to your kindred as well as to you, and they too take possession of the land that the LORD your God is giving them. Then you shall return to your own land and take possession of it, the land that Moses the servant of the LORD gave you beyond the Jordan to the east."[4]

Verses 7-9 shift from conquest to observance of the law. The signals of vv. 7 and 9 are standard literary pointers to an insertion. The language of v. 6 is taken up in v. 7 and modified; the language of v . 9 allows return to the narrative sequence. The later status of vv. 7-9 was affirmed by Noth (*DH*, 62, n. 1); it was developed by Smend, who follows the issues into Joshua 23 and parts of Judges 1–2 ("Das Gesetz und die Völker"). The strong emphasis on unswerving observance of the law suggests attribution to the national focus identified within the dtr process of revision.

Present-text potential. The movement is from God's endorsement of the Mosaic commissioning of Joshua to Joshua's order for appropriate preparations to be made. Between God's order to proceed and Joshua's order to prepare, there is God's order in vv. 7-9, a reminder that observance of the law requires courage and care. Observance of the law brings success (v. 8). Serious theological thinkers will ponder whether observance is a *condition* (i.e., a right to prosperity and success is earned by observance of the law) or a *consequence* (i.e., an expectation of prosperity and success flows from observance of the law). This is akin to but not identical with the issue of law and the relationship between God and Israel.

3. There is no specifically characteristic dtr language to pin down the attribution of these two verses. Terms like "officers" and "provisions" have appropriately ancient lineage. The "possession of the land" has strong dtr overtones; but the theme is complex and caution is in order (cf. Weinfeld, *Deuteronomy and the Deuteronomic School*, 341-42). What urges attribution to the Dtr here is the leadership role of Joshua. The command is given to Joshua from God in 1:2; it is

appropriate that here Joshua give the command that initiates the move.

4. The status of texts about Reuben, Gad, and the half-tribe of Manasseh needs careful assessment. Certainty is probably out of reach. Questions need to be asked; answers will remain questionable. The major texts are Numbers 32; Deuteronomy 3; Joshua 1, 13, and 22; 1 Chronicles 5 and 12. Also noteworthy is 2 Kgs 10:32-33. The dating for Numbers 32 and Deut 3:18-20 is largely dependent on the overall judgment reached; neither text is a reliable anchor for the tradition.

Pointers toward the need for assessment of the texts in Joshua are as follows. First, in Josh 1:12-18, the stipulation that wives, children, and livestock should remain east of the Jordan while the armed men accompanied the other tribes is unwise in the short term and unrealistic in the long term as military strategy. This is not a question of the needs of the men, sexual or other; it is a question of the security of their families and possessions and the care of their lands and flocks. For a few weeks, the idea would be unwise; until Joshua was "old and advanced in years" (cf. Josh

---

Main pre-DH: Conquest Narrative
and its expansion

Other pre-DH:
single sideline

Josianic DH:
from the Dtr

16 They answered Joshua: "All that you have commanded us we will do, and wherever you send us we will go. 17Just as we obeyed Moses in all things, so we will obey you. Only may the LORD your God be with you, as he was with Moses!" 18Whoever rebels against your orders and disobeys your words, whatever you command, shall be put to death. Only be strong and courageous.

2 And *(Heb.; NRSV, Then)* Joshua son of Nun sent two men secretly from Shittim as spies, saying, "Go, view the land, especially Jericho." So they went, and entered the house of a prostitute whose name was Rahab, and spent the night there. 2The king of Jericho was told, "Some Israelites have come here tonight to search out

---

13:1) would be patently absurd. It might be tolerable as a utopian ideal; as a strategic reality, it would be irresponsible. Divine protection is not mentioned. Families and flocks are not specified at the time of return (Josh 22:4).

Further, it must be said that the placement in the book of Joshua of the traditions concerning these east-of-Jordan tribes is odd. Josh 1:12-18 comes after Joshua's order to the officers to pass through the camp and set preparations in motion. Joshua's address to the eastern tribes would more appropriately precede the officers' activities in preparing to strike camp. The separation from the families has presumably occurred, but has not been mentioned. Joshua 13:8-13, 15-32 and 22:1-34 lie outside the accounts of Joshua's allocation of land to the tribes. This is appropriate, because these tribes received their land from Moses (but cf. the texts in Deuteronomy 2–3). It is also odd; not the mention, but the extensive emphasis if the matter was settled earlier. The Joshua 13 material is repetitive and dispersed; the Joshua 22 material is evidently disparate (see below). No concern for families and flocks is expressed.

In 1 Chronicles 12, there is emphasis on support for David from the tribes east of the Jordan, whether at Ziklag or Hebron. Of the Reubenites, Gadites and the half-tribe of Manasseh, 120,000 came armed for war "to David in Hebron to turn the kingdom of Saul over to him, according to the word of the LORD" (1 Chron 12:23, 37). There is no mention of such support in 2 Samuel 2. East-of-Jordan support for David is evidenced later (see 2 Samuel 15–19, esp. 17:27-29);

no links are specified with the two and a half tribes. Politics is possible (cf. 2 Sam 9:4; 1 Kgs 2:7).

Viewed as integral to what is now the present biblical text, the references to these tribes take for granted the unity of a larger Israel. Viewed as potential additions to an older text, these references may appeal to or insist on the unity of a larger Israel. With certainty out of reach, both possibilities need to be kept open. The appeal to a project without details of its implementation raises the possibility that the texts are in the service of symbol rather than history (cf. the Jubilee). The contribution of the east-of-Jordan tribes to any *events* of occupation may lie out of reach; it is a quite different statement to say that these *texts* are likely to be of symbolic rather than historical worth. Our formatting (here and in Deuteronomy 2–3) favors the later addition of these texts in virtue of their symbolic value. This is a preference, not an assured conclusion. The difficulties of the whole early period are well known. The project of leaving families and flocks is not the same as the issue of tribal participation. Our judgment here expresses a preference about these *texts* and has nothing to say about the *events*.

Text signals in 1:12-18. (i) As noted, the passage follows the order for mobilization (vv. 10-11). (ii) "Be strong and courageous" at the end of v. 18 repeats the imperatives from vv. 6, 7, and 9. (iii) The reference to the LORD's giving rest occurs in both vv. 13 and 15. (iv) V. 18 as a whole would be appropriate to YHWH; it is less appropriate in the mouths of the tribal warriors. In the nine other occurrences of this phrase for rebellion, it is YHWH's command that is rebelled against; tribal warriors are unlikely to have been thought of as giving such authority to Joshua. (v) No

---

After the Dtr:	Revision:	Other:
indented and sans serif font	*national focus*	double sideline

the land." [3]Then the king of Jericho sent orders to Rahab, "Bring out the men who have come to you, who entered your house, for they have come only to search out the whole land." [4]But the woman took the two men and hid them. Then she said, "True, the men came to me, but I did not know where they came from. [5]And when it was time to close the gate at dark, the men went out. Where the men went I do not know. Pursue them quickly, for you can overtake them." [6]She had, however, brought them up to the roof and hidden them with the stalks of flax that she had laid out on the roof. [7]So the men pursued them on the way to the Jordan as far as

---

mention is made here of the separation of the armed men from their families and livestock; nor has it been made earlier.

Text-history approach. In the light of these signals and the general observations above, it is preferable to see vv. 12-18 as later additions—whether or not from the dtr revision is much less certain. The concept of "rest" in v. 13 reflects dtr language; in this context, it could well be later imitation. The addition as a whole makes sense as an appeal to or insistence on the unity of Israel. In our judgment, the attribution of this order to Moses (cf. Deut 3:18-20) is equally secondary.

Verse 18a is puzzling, its puzzle unresolved. If the disobedience is to Joshua's command, the occurrence is unique. The authority given Joshua would seem more appropriate coming from YHWH (cf. v. 6). As the text stands, the two and a half tribes concede supreme authority to Joshua—an authority not exercised by Moses. The final sentence echoes vv. 6, 7, and 9.

Present-text potential. Joshua's command to the officers concerns the whole camp (1:10-11). Joshua then addresses the smaller group of two and a half tribes, underscoring their participation in the campaign ahead. The unified involvement of all Israel under Joshua is emphasized.

---

the fords. As soon as the pursuers had gone out, the gate was shut.[5]

---

5. Joshua 2 has been widely recognized as a story that does not prepare the way for the Jordan crossing and the capture of Jericho as found in the present text. It is dismissed by some (e.g., Van Seters, "not the beginning of the earliest conquest account but a later addition" ["Joshua's Campaign," 3]), given due weight by others (e.g., Nelson, "the Rahab narrative can be thought of as functioning in at least three systems of meaning: on its own as a tale told in Israel, as the first episode in the pre-deuteronomistic book, and as part of the larger sweep of DH" [*Joshua*, 41]). Our presentation is based on the belief that significant elements of a pre-dtr Conquest Narrative can be identified in the text, beginning with the Rahab story (and ending with 10:42-43). We do not discuss the raw materials that may have gone into such a product.

Text signals in Josh 2:1-24. (i) With an introductory phrase such as "After the death of Moses" (cf. 1:1), this could be the beginning of an independent narrative. (ii) The initiative is with Joshua; there is no order from God. (iii) The mission has "the land" in view, more than just Jericho (vv. 1-3, 9, 14, 18, 24). (iv) The king of Jericho plays a role in the story (vv. 2-3); the kings do not have active roles in the "sacral" stories. (v) The Jordan can be crossed normally (vv. 7, 23). (vi) Rahab's words, "I know that the LORD has given you the land … and that all the inhabitants of the land melt in fear before you" (v. 9) are compatible with a military campaign (cf. v. 24). (vii) A military campaign also appears to be envisaged in vv. 17-21, with possible street fighting and a need for signs and secrecy.

Text-history approach. The text signals point to a narrative that extends beyond the Rahab story, that will involve territory referred to as "the land," and that will involve a military campaign under God's aegis. As such, we believe that Joshua 2 functions as an introduction to a pre-dtr Conquest Narrative, just as Joshua 1 functions as an introduction to the dtr Conquest Narrative.

Main pre-DH: Conquest Narrative
and its expansion

Other pre-DH:
single sideline

Josianic DH:
from the Dtr

8 Before they went to sleep, she came up to them on the roof [9]and said to the men: "I know that the Lord has given you the land, and that dread of you has fallen on us, and that all the inhabitants of the land melt in fear before you. **[10]For we have heard how the Lord dried up the water of the Red Sea before you when you came out of Egypt, and what you did to the two kings of the Amorites that were beyond the Jordan, to Sihon and Og, whom you utterly destroyed. [11]As soon as we heard it, our hearts melted, and there was no courage left in any of us because of you.**[6]

Present-text potential. The three days of Joshua 2 can be correlated with the three days of Josh 1:11 on the broad level of storytelling rather than with detailed chronological precision. The faith professed by Rahab is fully coherent with God's actions in the "sacral" stories to come. Joshua's action in sending out spies is not a failure of trust but a matter of normal preparations, preparations that in due course will be unnecessary. Further more detailed possibilities can be found in Nelson, *Joshua*, 40-47.

6. **Text signals** in 2:10-11. (i) Sihon and Og are mentioned together, probably an indication of dtr origin (cf. their mention in Deuteronomy 2–3 and later dtr: Deut 1:4; 29:7 [Heb., v. 6]; 31:4; also 1 Kgs 4:19). (ii) The confessional statement of v. 11b is almost identical with the secondary dtr text, Deut 4:39 (cf. also 1 Kgs 8:23). (iii) If vv. 10-11 are dtr, it is possible that v. 10a could be dependent on Josh 4:23b.

Text-history approach. The insertion of vv. 10-11 ties Rahab's confessional statement into Israel's experience of deliverance at the Sea and of God's recent action on Israel's behalf, preparing the way for the stories to come.

Present-text potential. The verses expand Rahab's confession and enhance the articulation of her faith, with a view both to the Jordan crossing and to the fall of Jericho.

The Lord your God is indeed God in heaven above and on earth below.[7]
[12]Now then, since I have dealt kindly with you, swear to me by the Lord that you in turn will deal kindly with my family. Give me a sign of good faith [13]that you will spare my father and mother, my brothers and sisters, and all who belong to them, and deliver our lives from death." [14]The men said to her, "Our life for yours! If you do not tell this business of ours, then we will deal kindly and faithfully with you when the Lord gives us the land."

15 Then she let them down by a rope through the window, for her house was on the outer side of the city wall and she resided within the wall itself. [16]She said to them, "Go toward the hill country, so that the pursuers may not come upon you. Hide yourselves there three days, until the pursuers have returned; then afterward you may go your way." [17]The men said to her, "We will be released from this oath that you have made us swear to you [18]if we invade the land and you do not tie this crimson cord in the window through which you let us down, and you do not gather into your house your father and mother, your brothers, and all your family. [19]If any of you go out of the doors of your house into the street, they shall be responsible for their own death, and we shall be innocent; but if a hand is laid upon any who are with you in the house, we shall bear the responsibility for their death. [20]But if you tell this business of ours, then we shall be released from this oath that you made us swear to you." [21]She said, "According to your words, so be it." She sent them away and they departed. Then she tied the crimson cord in the window.

---

7. As noted in the text signals of the preceding note, this confessional statement is almost identical with Deut 4:39 (also 1 Kgs 8:23), attributed to the national focus within the dtr revision process.

| After the Dtr:
indented and sans serif font | *Revision:*
national focus | Other:
double sideline |

22 They departed and went into the hill country and stayed there three days, until the pursuers returned. The pursuers had searched all along the way and found nothing. ²³Then the two men came down again from the hill country. They crossed over, came to Joshua son of Nun, and told him all that had happened to them. ²⁴They said to Joshua, "Truly the LORD has given all the land into our hands; moreover all the inhabitants of the land melt in fear before us."

3 Early in the morning Joshua rose and set out from Shittim with all the Israelites, and they came to the Jordan. They lodged (*Heb. and* RSV; NRSV, *camped*) there before crossing over.[8]

---

8. Joshua's early morning rise makes better sense following on the report of the spies in 2:24 than it does following the officers' orders in 1:10-11. On the other hand, the second set of orders from the officers, at the end of three days (3:2), makes good sense following on 1:10-11. The emphasis on following the ark may suggest more of a journey than simply from the Jordan bank of 3:1 to Gilgal of 4:19—e.g., from Shittim (according to 3:1, roughly a day's journey).

At this point, the thread of what we have been calling the Conquest Narrative is replaced by three passages that can best be described as "sacral" texts. The primary characteristic of these texts that qualifies them as sacral is clear: Israel's successful penetration into the territory west of the Jordan is not due to force of arms or strategy but solely to the exercise of divine power. The waters of the Jordan are extensively dried up at the presence of the ark. The walls of Jericho fall at Israel's shout. A battle for Ai is lost because a single individual has breached God's ban.

Around these passages or stories are traces of a "conquest account" that demonstrates different concerns. Already in Joshua 2, spies have been sent in and have made arrangements with Rahab to spare her life and the lives of her family in the street fighting that is anticipated. Before the siege of Jericho, there is an interest in its king and soldiers (6:2) that does not

²*At the end of three days the officers went through the camp* ³*and commanded the people, "When you see the ark of the covenant of the LORD your God being carried by the levitical priests, then you shall set out from your place. Follow it—*⁴*yet there shall be a space between you and it, a distance of about two thousand cubits, do not come any nearer to it—*(Heb. order and our punctuation)[9] *so that you may know the way you should go, for you have not passed this way before."*[10]

---

recur; instead, the account finishes with a return to Rahab and her family. The king of Jericho features again in connection with Ai and its king (8:1-2); there is no reference there to a failed first attempt on Ai. In the story of chap. 8, the two references to an earlier attempt ("as before," vv. 5 and 6) appear to be secondary (see below). The agreement with the Gibeonites brings Joshua into conflict with a coalition of five kings. Successful against them, Joshua and all Israel returned to Gilgal (cf. 10:15 or 42-43).

The sacral texts are important. They do not add anything to the territory taken. They make a faith statement about what was happening in the taking of territory: God was at work. Many a modern will not like this theology. That is beside the point. The point is the claim of the texts that God was wonderfully at work in the achievements of Israel. Israel also emphasized what it did not achieve (cf. Josh 13:13; 15:63; 16:10; and 17:12; also Judges 1); later texts sought to explain why in God's wisdom this was so (i.e., Judg 2:1-5 and in 2:20—3:6).

9. The NRSV understandably places this section of v. 4 as a separate sentence at the end of the verse. The caution against coming too close to the ark is appropriate. Surprisingly far from the command to "follow it" is the reason: because you do not know the way. The NRSV's order makes sense, but does not explain how the caution came to be where it is. It is likely to be a liturgical annotation; see the following note.

10. This is as good a point as any to discuss the nature of this Jordan crossing text. It is clearly sacral; the role of the military is minimal. It is a scene of

---

Main pre-DH: Conquest Narrative
and its expansion

Other pre-DH:
single sideline

**Josianic DH:
from the Dtr**

unsurpassed liturgical imagination, with a clear space of a kilometer or so surrounding the ark. As a military operation, it would have been a nightmare. The whole procedure has the aura of total divine control and power.

It is also a nightmare as a source-critical operation (cf. Soggin, *Joshua*, 50-54; "extreme complexity," 52). For example, Vogt needs four documents and half a dozen additions to cope with the text, in what is an economical analysis (see Soggin; Campbell, *Study Companion*, 173-77). It is not clear what sort of life situation such documents came from, nor what life situation they addressed; above all, coherent completeness is not achieved. A change to a genre-critical approach may generate insight. Joshua 3–4 and 6 are clearly associated with sanctuary liturgies, presumably from Gilgal. If the genre is recognized as "the script for a liturgy," the core of chaps. 3–4 gives the text for a liturgy while a number of liturgical annotations point to options or cautions.

It helps to be aware that in the background of both the Jordan-crossing text and the Jericho-capture text three factors are probably at play: the telling of stories, the celebrating of liturgies, and the composing of documentary texts (e.g., the DH). The texts cannot be neatly analyzed across these processes; instead the processes leave their traces in the text. They complicate the lives of most interpreters. Story and liturgy are not to be rigidly separated. What is told in story can be celebrated in liturgy and vice versa; liturgical annotations can provide detail for storytellers.

It is important to be aware that liturgy works through symbol. A liturgical procession might stop at the Jordan banks; presumably the Jordan's flow would not stop. The liturgical celebration is not repetition of what once happened, but the use of symbol to remember that this unstoppable Jordan was once witness to the power of the God who alone could and once did stop these waters.

It is important, too, to be aware of the function of many narrative texts. They may report on the gist of past performances; they may function as the base for future performances. They are not the record of a performance; for that they are much too short.

[Liturgical annotation: sanctification option]
⁵Then Joshua said to the people, "Sanctify yourselves; for tomorrow the LORD will do wonders among you."[11]

⁶To the priests Joshua said, "Take up the ark of the covenant, and pass on in front of the people." So they took up the ark of the covenant and went in front of the people.[12]

7 The LORD said to Joshua, "This day I will begin to exalt you in the sight of all Israel, so that they may know that I will be with you as I was with Moses. ⁸You are the one who shall command the priests who bear the ark of the covenant, 'When you come to the edge of the waters of the Jordan, you shall stand still in the Jordan.' "[13]

To keep our formatting simple, the liturgical annotations that follow are identified by subheads, within square brackets and in small print. The subheads and the accompanying annotations are enclosed within single-line boxes for ease of reading. In our judgment, a simple present-text reading is out of the question.

11. A liturgical annotation pointing to the option of an extended liturgy, having a rite of sanctification for participants on the eve of the great procession. As an option, it is to be exercised the day before the officers issued their command (in the preceding verse).

12. If the option offered in 3:5 has been exercised, 3:6 here is speaking of the morrow, the following day. Without 3:5, it follows on the officers' command. Two meanings are possible. Theologically, Joshua has the leadership role in the liturgy. Prosaically, Joshua is giving the signal to start proceedings. Liturgists learn not to leave ceremonies without clear signals and appropriate directives.

13. This assurance echoes the dtr understanding from 1:2-5 that Joshua has taken over the leadership

After the Dtr:	Revision:	Other:
indented and sans serif font	*national focus*	double sideline

[Liturgical annotation:

optional divine speech]

⁹Joshua then said to the Israelites, "Draw near and hear the words of the LORD your God."[14]

¹⁰And *(Heb.)* Joshua said, "By this you shall know that among you is the living God who without fail will drive out from before you the Canaanites, Hittites, Hivites, Perizzites, Girgashites, Amorites, and Jebusites."[15]

[Liturgical annotation]

¹¹"See (Heb.), the ark of the covenant of the Lord of all the earth is going to pass before you into the Jordan."[16]

[Option 1: choice-of-carriers]

¹²"So now select twelve men from the tribes of Israel, one from each tribe."[17]

[Option 2: preparatory announcement]

¹³"When the soles of the feet of the priests who bear the ark of the LORD, the Lord of all the earth, rest in the waters of the Jordan, the waters of the Jordan flowing from above shall be cut off; they shall stand in a single heap."[18]

role of Moses. The Josianic Dtr is insistent that Joshua is to function as the president of the proceedings. However, the precise compliance with the command of v. 8 (the order Joshua is to give) is not found in what follows.

14. In what follows, there is no report of a compliance with Joshua's command here and nothing that passes satisfactorily for "the words of the LORD." Understood as a liturgical annotation, this verse can be read on its own or in relation to vv. 11-13. On its own, it offers the option for a divine speech, a speech that is not included in the text. Alternatively, the verse can be read in relation to vv. 11-13 as their introduction—but not very satisfactorily. If, as we judge preferable, vv. 11-13 are better attributed to Joshua, then v. 9 needs to be read on its own.

15. Verse 10 does not offer the "words of the LORD" but a speech of Joshua. It provides the full seven-item list of local peoples, found elsewhere only at Deut 7:1 and Josh 24:11; neither of these suggests an early attribution. For the six-item list, without the Girgashites, see below (9:1; 11:3; 12:8). V. 10's "And Joshua said" is identical with v. 9's introduction, despite the minor NRSV variation. As it stands in the text, the addition offers an overarching perspective within which to situate the Jordan crossing. The marvel of the crossing is evidence that God will drive out the locals before Israel.

16. The words in this verse and the two that follow can be attributed either to Joshua (cf. v. 9a) or to "the LORD your God" (cf. v. 9b). However, vv. 11-13 are not what would be expected as "the words of the LORD" (v. 9). Attribution to Joshua is more likely. The phrase "Lord of all the earth" (*ʾădôn kōl hāʾāreṣ*) is rare and most probably late (cf. Josh 3:11, 13; Mic 4:13; Zech 4:14; 6:5; Ps 97:5). If late, v. 12 may have been Joshua's original command. It is appropriate that Joshua, presides and directs proceedings. V. 11 is a preparatory statement for either (or both) of the options that follow.

17. Liturgically, it would be appropriate to select suitable carriers of the stones ahead of time. V. 12 prepares for the river sanctuary option; the follow-up comes in 4:4-7. Note that the selection of carriers for the Gilgal sanctuary stones is ordered in 4:2-3. For discussion of the two options, see note on 4:4-7.

18. Verse 13 precedes the procession's departure in v. 14. As a preparatory announcement, it signals the sequence of the ceremony and prepares for what is to come.

Main pre-DH: Conquest Narrative
and its expansion

Other pre-DH:
single sideline

**Josianic DH:
from the Dtr**

14 When the people set out from their tents to cross over the Jordan, the priests bearing the ark of the covenant were in front of the people. ¹⁵Now the Jordan overflows all its banks throughout the time of harvest. So when those who bore the ark had come to the Jordan, and the feet of the priests bearing the ark were dipped in the edge of the water, ¹⁶the waters flowing from above stood still, rising up in a single heap far off at Adam, the city that is beside Zarethan, while those flowing toward the sea of the Arabah, the Dead Sea, were wholly cut off. Then the people crossed over opposite Jericho. ¹⁷While all Israel were crossing over on dry ground, the priests who bore the ark of the covenant of the LORD stood on dry ground in the middle of the Jordan, until the entire nation finished crossing over the Jordan.¹⁹

4 *When the entire nation had finished crossing over the Jordan, the LORD said to Joshua: ²"Select twelve men from the people, one from each tribe, ³and command them, 'Take twelve stones from here out of the middle of the Jordan, from the place where the priests' feet stood, carry them over with you, and lay them down in the place where you camp tonight.' "*

[Liturgical annotation:
mid-river memorial option, part 1]
⁴Then Joshua summoned the twelve men from the Israelites, whom he had appointed, one from each tribe. ⁵Joshua said to them, "Pass on before the ark of the LORD your God into the middle of the Jordan, and each of you take up a stone on his shoulder, one for each of the tribes of the Israelites,

---

19. With the liturgical preliminaries out of the way, the core of the narrative takes up from 3:2-4 and proceeds with v. 14. At vv. 15-16, the narrative tells of what had happened once in times past; the liturgical representation is a celebration of that happening, a wonder that would not happen again.

---

⁶so that this may be a sign among you. When your children ask in time to come, 'What do those stones mean to you?' ⁷then you shall tell them that the waters of the Jordan were cut off in front of the ark of the covenant of the LORD. When it crossed over the Jordan, the waters of the Jordan were cut off. So these stones shall be to the Israelites a memorial forever."²⁰

---

20. The text of Joshua 3–4 refers to establishing memorials at two sites, one in the middle of the Jordan (4:9) and the other in Gilgal (4:8, 20). Two readings are possible. One is a present-text reading, with two actions corresponding to the two sites. The other has two options: either one site in mid-Jordan or one site at Gilgal. A present-text reading has an almost rhythmic structure: instructions are given relating to site one (Gilgal), then instructions relating to site two (Jordan); execution by the Israelites is reported for site one (4:8), then by Joshua for site two (4:9). Joshua's role, in establishing site one at Gilgal, is reported at 4:20. The catechesis for site two is given with the instructions (4:6-7); the catechesis for site one is given with Joshua's action (4:21-24). The catecheses are different. For the mid-river memorial, the focus is on the *ark's* crossing ("the waters of the Jordan were cut off in front of the ark of the covenant of the LORD"); for the Gilgal memorial, the focus is on *Israel's* crossing ("Israel crossed over the Jordan here on dry ground"), paralleled with the Red Sea episode.

Dtr attribution for these two catecheses is possible, with Noth (*Das Buch Josua*, 37) and Nelson (*Joshua*, 66); however, it is not necessary and is problematic. Such formulas, attached to memorial sites or actions, can be long-lasting; the text base is small and does not extend beyond this into the DH (cf. Exod 12:26; 13:14; Deut 6:20); the two theologies are different and show no identification with dtr levels. Attribution here is uncertain.

In a two-options reading (as formatted), both options were presumably not actualized in one and the

---

8 The Israelites did as Joshua commanded. They took up twelve stones out of the middle of the Jordan, according to the number of the tribes of the Israelites, as the LORD told Joshua, carried them over with them to the place where they camped, and laid them down there.

[Liturgical annotation: mid-river memorial option, part 2]
⁹Joshua set up twelve stones in the middle of the Jordan, in the place where the feet of the priests bearing the ark of the covenant had stood; and they are there to this day.

---

10 The priests who bore the ark remained standing in the middle of the Jordan, until everything was finished that the LORD commanded Joshua to tell the people.

‖ according to all that Moses had commanded Joshua.[21]

| 10b The people crossed over in haste.
¹¹As soon as all the people had finished crossing over, the ark of the LORD, and the priests, crossed over in front of the people.

‖‖ ¹²The Reubenites, the Gadites, and the half-tribe of Manasseh crossed over armed before the Israelites, as Moses had ordered them.[22]

| ¹³About forty thousand armed for war crossed over before the LORD to the plains of Jericho for battle.[23]

---

same liturgical ceremony. Our formatting has opted for the Gilgal site, with the mid-river site as an option. This can be reversed, but the mid-river option does not have an account of compliance by the twelve men (by contrast with 4:8). 4:5, with its "take up a stone on his shoulder," verges on the cryptic. The action required is for each of the twelve to find a suitable stone, hoist it onto his shoulder, and bring it to Joshua, who would put it "in the place where the feet of the priests . . . stood" (4:9). Note that for the Gilgal memorial, the stones were taken "from the place where the priests' feet stood" (4:3).

From a practical point of view, reenacting the establishment of the mid-river memorial would not have been possible unless the waters of the Jordan were at a low level. Otherwise, observation from the bank would have had to suffice.

21. The phrase appears to contradict the preceding "that the LORD commanded Joshua"; it can be understood as interpreting—the LORD, through Moses, commanded Joshua. It is missing from the earliest Greek versions. It is probably an addition and could have been added at almost any time.

22. The position of 4:12 immediately before the note of military presence in v. 13 points to a possible addition; it takes very literally the "before the Israelites" here and in 1:14. The Hebrew used for "armed" (*ḥāmūšîm*) is the same as in 1:14; it is not the same in the following v. 13, which has *ḥălûṣîm*. See the discussion at 1:12-18.

23. 4:10b and 13 reflect a warlike context; the reference to crossing "in haste" is at odds with the solemn liturgical style of the procession across the Jordan. Two questions are evident: Where does this material come from? What does it mean in its present place? The answer to the first is that the material probably comes from the Conquest Narrative account replaced by the sacral text of Joshua 3–4. However the material (a verse and a half) is too fragmentary and there is not enough context preserved to suggest that we have here the remains of a military source. The verse and a half may have been taken from such a source (the Conquest Narrative); it is not a remnant that allows the source to be recovered. Hence a single sideline rather than the formatting of the Conquest Narrative.

The answer to the second question can be claimed for today's readers; it may well have been the same for ancient Israel's compilers. The presence of the warriors is a reminder that the sacral overthrow of the Canaanites and the great city of Jericho could not be taken for granted by Israel. Israel was ready to take military means to secure its territory; God's action made military means unnecessary. Israel could and did

---

Main pre-DH: Conquest Narrative
and its expansion

Other pre-DH:
single sideline

**Josianic DH:
from the Dtr**

14 On that day the LORD exalted Joshua in the sight of all Israel; and they stood in awe of him, as they had stood in awe of Moses, all the days of his life.[24]

[Liturgical annotation: signal option]

15 The LORD said to Joshua, [16]"Command the priests who bear the ark of the covenant, to come up out of the Jordan." [17]Joshua therefore commanded the priests, "Come up out of the Jordan."[25]

---

[18]*When the priests bearing the ark of the covenant of the LORD came up from the middle of the Jordan, and the soles of the priests' feet touched dry ground, the waters of the Jordan returned to their place and overflowed all its banks, as before.*

19 The people came up out of the Jordan on the tenth day of the first month, and they camped in Gilgal on the east border of Jericho. [20]Those twelve stones, which they had taken out of the Jordan, Joshua set up in Gilgal, [21]saying to the Israelites, "When your children ask their parents in time to

come, 'What do these stones mean?' [22]then you shall let your children know, 'Israel crossed over the Jordan here on dry ground.' [23]For the LORD your God dried up the waters of the Jordan for you until you crossed over, as the LORD your God did to the Red Sea, which he dried up for us until we crossed over, [24]so that all the peoples of the earth may know that the hand of the LORD is mighty, and so that you may fear the LORD your God forever."[26]

5 When all the kings of the Amorites beyond the Jordan to the west, and all the kings of the Canaanites by the sea, heard that the LORD had dried up the waters of the Jordan for the Israelites until they had crossed over, their hearts melted, and there was no longer any spirit in them, because of the Israelites.[27]

2 At that time the LORD said to Joshua, "Make flint knives and circumcise the Israelites a second time." [3]So Joshua made flint knives, and circumcised the Israelites at Gibeath-haaraloth. [4]This is the reason why

---

lose battles. In Israel's texts, God's word needed usually to be followed by Israel's action. The military here function as a reminder of the need for that action as a rule. The Hebrew used here for "armed" (*ḥālûṣ*) recurs in Josh 6:7, 9, 13. A sacral text does not exclude a military presence.

24. This is the appropriate dtr follow-up to the LORD's assurance of exaltation, emphasized by the Josianic Dtr in 3:7.

25. Verse 11 already has the priests crossing over and therefore emerging from the Jordan. V. 18 is concerned with the return of the Jordan to its normal flow. Vv. 15-16, therefore, note a liturgical option that the signal to come up from the Jordan might well be given by Joshua. In this, it is coherent with both 3:6 and 3:8.

26. The Gilgal memorial, commemorating the Jordan crossing, is brought into association with the drying up of the Reed Sea (*yam sûp*) at the exodus. As Israel crossed the Reed Sea (i.e., came out from Egypt), so they crossed this Jordan (i.e., entered the land). The comment by Childs is important: "It seems highly probable that the language of the Reed Sea was influenced by the Jordan tradition of the river's crossing which introduced the language of a path through the sea and the river's stoppage" (*Exodus*, 223).

27. In Noth's view, the "collector" who had shaped and introduced Joshua 2 could be identified in 5:1, as later in 6:27; 9:3-4aα; 10:2, 5, 40-42; 11:1-2, and 16-20 (*Das Buch Josua*, 12, also p. 29). The collector was identified for Noth by the concern to draw the individual stories into a picture of wider conquest. With the acceptance of a Conquest Narrative this role for a collector is no longer necessary.

| After the Dtr: indented and sans serif font | *Revision: national focus* | Other: double sideline |

Joshua circumcised them: all the males of the people who came out of Egypt, all the warriors, had died during the journey through the wilderness after they had come out of Egypt. ⁵Although all the people who came out had been circumcised, yet all the people born on the journey through the wilderness after they had come out of Egypt had not been circumcised. ⁶For the Israelites traveled forty years in the wilderness, until all the nation, the warriors who came out of Egypt, perished, not having listened to the voice of the LORD. To them the LORD swore

that he would not let them see the land that he had sworn to their ancestors to give us, a land flowing with milk and honey. ⁷So it was their children, whom he raised up in their place, that Joshua circumcised; for they were uncircumcised, because they had not been circumcised on the way.

8 When the circumcising of all the nation was done, they remained in their places in the camp until they were healed. ⁹The LORD said to Joshua, "Today I have rolled away from you the disgrace of Egypt." And so that place is called Gilgal to this day.²⁸

10 While the Israelites were camped in Gilgal they kept the passover in the evening on the fourteenth day of the month in the plains of Jericho. ¹¹On the day after the passover, on that very day, they ate the produce of the land, unleavened cakes and parched grain. ¹²The manna ceased on the day they ate the produce of the land, and

---

5:1 itself echoes 2:10-11a; there is the reference to hearing, the description of YHWH's wonder, the identification of the Amorites as western, the melting of hearts, and the lack of courage/spirit. 2:10-11a were attributed to the Josianic Dtr; a similar attribution is appropriate for 5:1. A comparison of the two passages brings out the force of the comment in 4:23. 2:10 refers to the drying up of the waters of the Reed Sea; 5:1 refers to the drying up of the waters of the Jordan. Together they delicately underline the dtr ability to conceptualize the movements of Israel's history; the wilderness period is encapsulated between the two crossings.

These kings of the Amorites feature in the Conquest Narrative at 10:5. The distinction between Amorites (in the hill country) and Canaanites (elsewhere) is found in the DH as early as Deut 1:7. The lists of peoples, usually containing both names, are of uncertain origin.

The text of Joshua 5 gathers together three traditions that belong to the transition between the wilderness and the land: the circumcision after the wilderness sojourn (vv. 2-9), the observance of Passover and the end of the manna (vv. 10-12), and Joshua's encounter with the "commander of the army of the LORD" (vv. 13-15). In the present state of our knowledge, attribution of any of these three would be imprudent. The double sideline is no more than an acknowledgment of this.

---

28. Two issues are central to an understanding of these verses and their place in Israel's thought: first, the concern for circumcision as essential in Israel (cf. Genesis 17); second, the idea that circumcision was impossible in the wilderness. For the textual revisions in this material, see Nelson, *Joshua*, 72-73. It may be that the national circumcision not only signals the end of the wilderness period, but that it was also understood as a requirement for the celebration of Passover (cf. Exod 12:48). References to circumcising are rare. Genesis 17 has ten, Genesis 34 has four, and Josh 5:2-9 has six; that is twenty of the thirty-one verses involved (on the uncertainties of Genesis 34, see Campbell and O'Brien, *Sources of the Pentateuch*, 118-20). The "disgrace of Egypt" is mentioned only here. For Noth, vv. 4, 6-7 are additions in dtr style (*Das Buch Josua*, 39). In isolated or fragmentary passages such as these, imitation is always possible.

| Main pre-DH: Conquest Narrative
and its expansion | Other pre-DH:
single sideline | **Josianic DH:**
from the Dtr |

the Israelites no longer had manna; they ate the crops of the land of Canaan that year.[29]

13 Once when Joshua was by Jericho, he looked up and saw a man standing before him with a drawn sword in his hand. Joshua went to him and said to him, "Are you one of us, or one of our adversaries?" [14]He replied, "Neither; but as commander of the army of the LORD I have now come." And Joshua fell on his face to the earth and worshiped, and he said to him, "What do you command your servant, my lord?" [15]The commander of the army of the LORD said to Joshua, "Remove the sandals from your feet, for the place where you stand is holy." And Joshua did so.[30]

6 Now Jericho was shut up inside and out because of the Israelites; no one came out and no one went in. [2]The LORD said to Joshua, "See, I have handed Jericho over to you, along with its king and soldiers.[31]

[3]*You shall march around the city, all the warriors circling the city once. Thus you shall do for six days.*[32]

> [Option]
> [4]*with seven priests bearing seven trumpets of rams' horns before the ark*

Joshua is to embark; but it is unmentioned. The command to "remove the sandals from your feet" echoes Exod 3:5; but the parallel with Moses is not pursued. With no context to control its interpretation, the fragment's impact remains open.

29. The observance of Passover here closes off the wilderness period in chiastic fashion. At the exodus, Passover was celebrated before the Reed Sea crossing; here, Passover is celebrated after the Jordan crossing. The sequence of events in the text requires it; nevertheless, the encapsulating symbolism is powerful. This Passover has been associated with the Passover celebrated by Josiah, of which it is said that "no such Passover had been kept since the days of the judges who judged Israel" (2 Kgs 23:22). Joshua's generation was reputed to have served the LORD; in the dtr understanding, Israel's behavior was equally reputable during the lifetime of each of the judges. Such exemplary Passover observance could have been credited to the time of the Judges. The conjunction of the celebration of the Passover and the cessation of the manna are further pointers to the sacral nature of Israel's entry into the land.

30. This fragment cries out for a context to enable its interpretation. The "drawn sword" recalls the angel blocking Balaam (Num 22:23, 31); while the angel blocked Balaam's way, the point of the story was God's authorization given to Balaam (Num 22:35). No authorization is given to Joshua. The "commander of the army" fits in with the campaign on which

31. At one level the siege is not surprising; the collapse of the walls is not immediate. At another level, the marching around the city is presented in what follows without any note of threat from the inhabitants of Jericho. More significantly, the text refers to Jericho's "king and soldiers"; there is no mention of either in the rest of the chapter. However, "Jericho and its king" features twice more in the Conquest Narrative (8:2; 10:1)—but not in the sacral texts. 9:3 puts Jericho and Ai together as though their experience was the same; in the present text, it is not the same. With 10:28 and 30, we are in the list-like text rather than story; yet even there, the king of Jericho features. An earlier Conquest Narrative is to be assumed. Such a tradition is assumed in Josh 24:11 with its claim that "the citizens of Jericho fought against you." Following 6:2, military capture has been replaced by sacral intervention.

32. **Text signals** in 6:3-20. (i) The march of the ark around the city is structured sacrally rather than strategically. It will last for six days and a seventh (cf. Gen 1:1—2:4a). In the same vein, one circuit on each of six days; seven circuits on the seventh day. At the end, the cry is "Shout! For the LORD has given you the city" (v. 16). As a result, "they raised a great

---

shout, and the wall fell down flat" (v. 20). Sacral or psychological warfare might petrify the defenders; it does not affect the walls. That a shout brings the walls down is God's doing. (ii) There is potential conflict in the portrayal of trumpet-blowing priests and the portrayal of people commanded to be utterly silent (v. 10). (iii) In v. 5, the people's shout will follow a long blast with the ram's horn/trumpet. In v. 10, the people's shout will follow an order from Joshua. In vv. 16 and 20, both procedures are reported: Joshua gives the order (v. 16); the trumpets are sounded (v. 20). After both, the people shout (v. 20a and 20b). (iv) Joshua is formally identified in v. 6 as "Joshua son of Nun"; the previous mention was as "Joshua" in 6:2. (v) In the overall context, the term "the people" (hā'ām) needs to be understood as the "people" in general rather than the more specific "army." But the order of march, specified in vv. 9 and 13, is warriors, trumpet-blowing priests, priests bearing the ark, and the rearguard (ham'assēp, rare, otherwise only Num 10:25 [Dan]; Isa 52:12 [God]); the people are not mentioned. Presumably the people follow or constitute the rearguard, but it is not said. The presence of the people (hā'ām) is needed in the procession for their shout, which is decisive in the collapse of the walls. (vi) A series of four instructions—destruction of Jericho, sparing of Rahab, observance of the ban, items for the treasury—intervenes between Joshua's order to shout (v. 16) and the people's response (v. 20).

Text-history approach. The heart of the matter is that a complex history has resulted in a complex text. The precise unraveling of its past is probably out of reach. The issue confronting us is how best to represent what is visible in the text we have. Silence may conflict with trumpet blowing, but silence can be restricted to the people and trumpet blowing to the priests. A silent people offers one focus; trumpet-blowing priests, with their escort, offer a different focus. In vv. 16 and 20, duplication appears unavoidable.

As was noted under Joshua 3–4, these texts have in their backgrounds three complicating factors: the telling of stories, the celebrating of liturgies, and the composing of documentary texts (e.g., the DH). The texts cannot be neatly divided across these three activ-

ities; but the activities tend to have left their traces in the texts.

The text of vv. 3-20 has been formatted to highlight the focus on the silent people and the (optional) focus on the trumpet-blowing priests. The names of two legendary movie makers might be associated with these focuses. Alfred Hitchcock is renowned for taut suspense; Cecil B. de Mille for opulent spectacle. The suspense of silence would make for great storytelling: wandering tribes fresh out of the wilderness, confronted by a massively walled Canaanite city, and their devastating weapon—seven days silence. On the other hand, the opulent spectacle would make for great liturgy: the clash and color of armed guards and robed priests, the fanfare of trumpets, the ritual splendor of the ark.

It would be too easy to point to the text of a story and the script of a liturgy. Either focus would serve for storytelling; either focus would serve for liturgy. The nature of the text does not make such decisions for us. The elements are merely combined and available. No more. As noted already, liturgy works through symbol. Armed masses are not needed; a few symbolic figures would suffice. Circuits of the ancient city ruins are not needed; any suitable circuit would do. And so on. What is clear from the versions and the texts is that these traditions were given much reflection and were preserved in several forms (see Nelson, *Joshua*, 83-93). Our role is to understand as best we can what we have before us. The text may report from past performances; it may provide the base for future performances. We are entitled to believe that it is not the record of any specific performance.

Difficulties remain. The analysis offered here does not answer all the questions that can be asked; it may point to the processes at work in generating the text.

Present-text potential. Joshua 6 can be read, as it usually is, as a report of the wonder of Jericho's capture, its city walls falling flat at Israel's shout. The tradition is in the text. It functions as symbol for the conquest, a symbolism that is not extended to the great cities of Jerusalem, Gezer, Beth-shean, Taanach, Dor, Ibleam, and Megiddo, among others. A broad reading of Joshua 6 ably presents that tradition for Jericho.

| Main pre-DH: Conquest Narrative *and its expansion* | Other pre-DH: single sideline | **Josianic DH: from the Dtr** |

On the seventh day you shall march around the city seven times.

> [Option]
>
> *the priests blowing the trumpets. ⁵When there is (Heb.; NRSV, they make) a long blast with the ram's horn, as soon as you hear the sound of the trumpet*³³

Then all the people shall shout with a great shout; and the wall of the city will fall down flat, and all the people shall charge straight ahead.

⁶So Joshua son of Nun summoned the priests and said to them, "Take up the ark of the covenant."

> [Option]
>
> *and have seven priests carry seven trumpets of rams' horns in front of the ark of the LORD*

A close reading is more difficult insofar as the text does not sustain a unified presentation. Read closely, Joshua 6 is best understood as a base for performance. It contains pointers for flair in the use of suspense (the tension of a silent march), for variety in spectacle (the splendor of a trumpet-blowing procession), and for integration into the broader narrative (vv. 17-19). At this level, instead of completeness the text offers possibilities; it needs to be used with selective care.

33. There are signals in v. 5 that need special attention. First, the general Hebrew word for "horn" (*qeren*) is used (only here in Joshua) rather than the more specific forms for trumpet. Second, v. 5 begins with an unusual and probably stative verbal construction. Third, the Hebrew verb represented by the NRSV's "shall shout" lacks the expected conjunction "and" (see also *tāqʻû*, v. 16). These signals suggest the possibility of an earlier text in some form, probably beyond recovery. In the present text, the blast of the horn (*qeren*) has been integrated with the sound of the trumpet as part of the optional expansion. Equally in the present text, the signal for the people's shout is specified in v. 10 as Joshua's command.

⁷To the people he said, "Go forward and march around the city; have the armed men pass on before the ark of the LORD."

8 And it happened (Heb.) as Joshua had commanded the people.

> [Option]
>
> *The seven priests carrying the seven trumpets of rams' horns before the LORD went forward, blowing the trumpets, with the ark of the covenant of the LORD following them. ⁹And the armed men went before the priests who blew the trumpets; the rear guard came after the ark, while the trumpets blew continually.*

¹⁰And (Heb.) to the people Joshua gave this command: "You shall not shout or let your voice be heard, nor shall you utter a word, until the day I tell you to shout. Then you shall shout." ¹¹So the ark of the LORD went around the city, circling it once; and they came into the camp, and spent the night in the camp.

12 Then Joshua rose early in the morning, and the priests took up the ark of the LORD.

> [Option]
>
> *¹³The seven priests carrying the seven trumpets of rams' horns before the ark of the LORD passed on, blowing the trumpets continually. The armed men went before them, and the rear guard came after the ark of the LORD, while the trumpets blew continually.*

¹⁴And they marched around the city on the second day (Heb. order) once and then returned to the camp. They did this for six days.

15 On the seventh day they rose early, at dawn, and marched around the city in the same manner seven times. It was only on that day that they marched around the city seven times. ¹⁶And at the seventh time,

After the Dtr:	Revision:	Other:
indented and sans serif font	*national focus*	double sideline

> [Option]
> *when the priests had blown the trumpets*

Joshua said to the people, "Shout! For the LORD has given you the city."

> [Compositional adaptation]
> - *[17]The city and all that is in it shall be devoted to the LORD for destruction.*
> - *Only Rahab the prostitute and all who are with her in her house shall live because she hid the messengers we sent.*
> - *[18]As for you, keep away from the things devoted to destruction, so as not to covet and take any of the devoted things and make the camp of Israel an object for destruction, bringing trouble upon it.*
> - *[19]But all silver and gold, and vessels of bronze and iron, are sacred to the LORD; they shall go into the treasury of the LORD.[34]*

[20]So the people shouted[35]

> [Option]
> *and the trumpets were blown. As soon as the people heard the sound of the trumpets, and the people shouted* (Heb.; NRSV, they raised)

a great shout, and the wall fell down flat; so the people charged straight ahead into the city and captured it.

---

34. Verses 17-19 come between Joshua's command to shout (v. 16b) and the people's shout (v. 20). In storytelling, this would make for an intolerable interruption in the unfolding of the story. In liturgy, it would be confusing at least and disastrous at worst. It is important to take into account here the nature of the texts. We have argued that the biblical narrative texts are often a report of the rehearsal of a tradition or a base for future performance. The narrator or storyteller (or liturgical planner) had the text available to expand or rearrange, a text that made suggestions and demanded selections. In this case, interruptions such as vv. 17-19 are not so surprising or so intolerable. They are, on the other hand, more likely to derive from subsequent expansion of the written text than from the initial writing itself, where a more cohesive sequence might have been expected.

All four verses are most economically attributed to the editorial activity associated with the insertion of the sacral texts. V. 17 has the noun *ḥerem* ("ban") associated with YHWH ("to the LORD"), unique in the DH (cf. Lev 27:28; Mic 4:13); these two verses (6:17-18) and chap. 7 account for twelve of the eighteen occurrences of the noun in the DH. "Rahab the prostitute" occurs only here and in v. 25. The spies are referred to as messengers only here and in v. 25. In Hebrew, the "spared" of v. 25 echoes the "shall live" of v. 17. V. 18 prepares for the Achan story (chap. 7); it presupposes v. 17a. V. 19 is anachronistic if the Jerusalem temple is meant (as later). A reference to Gilgal or Gibeon is not impossible (cf. Josh 9:23, 27). The fear of being ensnared by the gold and silver of idols is in Deut 7:25 and the noun *ḥerem* in Deut 7:26; some association is possible. The verse claims that Joshua's generation did the right thing with the silver and gold of Jericho—with the exception, of course, of Achan who stole some (Josh 7:21).

35. This clause in Hebrew is most problematic. The verb is anomalous (unique in the MT) and is singular. It is not represented in the LXX (but on LXX and Vulg. see Barthélemy, *Critique textuelle*, 5–6). To retain it seems willful; but corruption is possible, and (despite suggestions) we do not have a satisfactory explanation for the introduction of the clause. Its presence or absence makes no difference to the analysis of the text. As it stands, it is the people's response to Joshua's command in v. 16. If it were omitted, the second occurrence of "and the people shouted," later in the same verse, would move from the optional expansion box to the core material and take over the same function—response to Joshua's command. This second

---

Main pre-DH: Conquest Narrative
and its expansion

Other pre-DH:
single sideline

Josianic DH:
from the Dtr

²¹Then they devoted to destruction by the edge of the sword all in the city, both men and women, young and old, oxen, sheep, and donkeys. ²²Joshua said to the two men who had spied out the land, "Go into the prostitute's house, and bring the woman out of it and all who belong to her, as you swore to her." ²³So the young men who had been spies went in and brought Rahab out, along with her father, her mother, her brothers, and all who belonged to her—they brought all her kindred out—and set them outside the camp of Israel. ²⁴They burned down the city, and everything in it.³⁶

Only the silver and gold, and the vessels of bronze and iron, they put into the treasury of the house of the LORD. ²⁵But Rahab the prostitute, with her family and all who belonged to her, Joshua spared. Her family has lived in Israel ever since. For she hid the messengers whom Joshua sent to spy out Jericho.³⁷

    26 Joshua then pronounced this oath, saying,

"Cursed before the LORD be anyone
    who tries
      to build this city—this Jericho!
At the cost of his firstborn he shall lay its
    foundation,
    and at the cost of his youngest he shall
      set up its gates!"³⁸

27 So the LORD was with Joshua; and his fame was in all the land.³⁹

7 But the Israelites broke faith in regard to the devoted things: Achan son of Carmi son of Zabdi son of Zerah, of the tribe of Judah, took some of the devoted things; and the anger of the LORD burned against the Israelites.⁴⁰

---

clause is formally irreproachable and as the text stands is resumptive in function.

36. Verses 21-24 are more expansive than v. 17, with some shifts of language. As part of the Conquest Narrative, the destruction level is remembered as a model in Josh 8:2; 9:3; 10:1.

37. Here we have a report of the compliance of Israel with the commands of Joshua in vv. 17-19, with discreet avoidance of any specifics about the destruction (*ḥerem*) and Achan's breach of it—the subject of chap. 7.

The precious items that were "put into the treasury of the house of the LORD" constitute an embarrassment (see above on v. 19). The reference to Rahab echoes the language of v. 17b. It is difficult to give a reason for the repetition after vv. 22-23. Possibly, a need was felt to insist on the compliance with Joshua's command (using its language); possibly, the reasons lie in the circumstances of the texts which now escape us.

38. The curse could have been recorded at any time and in almost any context. See the comment on 1 Kgs 16:34; a dotted sideline appropriately expresses this uncertainty. Its attribution is immaterial to the present concerns.

39. Attribution to the Dtr is appropriate; it fits the horizon of dtr concern for Joshua's leadership role (cf. Josh 1:2-5; 3:7-8; 4:14).

40. 7:1 reads like a summary, anticipating the story to come. "The Israelites broke faith": the breach of faith is not raised in the story until the LORD's speech (vv. 10-15). The verb here is *māʿal*, not used in vv. 10-15, in fact not used elsewhere in Joshua except for 22:16, 20, 31. It is a late verb (cf. Fritz, *Das Buch Josua*, 79); apart from Joshua 22, its principal occurrences are in Leviticus (3x), Numbers (3x), Ezekiel (7x), and Chronicles (11x).

"Achan son of Carmi son of Zabdi son of Serah, of the tribe of Judah": Achan is not identified in the story as the wrongdoer until vv. 18-19; his tribal and familial ties are rehearsed in vv. 17-18. The identification of the tribe of Judah here and in v. 18 uses the term *maṭṭeh* (regarded generally as exilic/post-exilic), not the term *šebeṭ* used in vv. 14-16 and elsewhere in Joshua 1–12 (for the distribution of these two terms

---

2 Joshua sent men from Jericho to Ai, which is near Beth-aven, east of Bethel, and said to them, "Go up and spy out the land." And the men went up and spied out Ai. ³They returned to Joshua and said to him, "Not all the people need go up; about two or three thousand men should go up and attack Ai. Since they are so few, do not make the whole people toil up there." ⁴So about three thousand of the people went up there; and they fled before the men of Ai. ⁵The men of Ai killed about thirty-six of them, chasing them from outside the gate as far as Shebarim and killing them on the slope. The hearts of the people melted and turned to water.[41]

6 Then Joshua tore his clothes, and fell to the ground on his face before the ark of the LORD until the evening, he and the elders of Israel; and they put dust on their heads. ⁷Joshua said, "Ah, Lord GOD! Why have you brought this people across the Jordan at all, to hand us over to the Amorites so as to destroy us? Would that we had been content to settle beyond the Jordan! ⁸O Lord, what can I say, now that Israel has turned their backs to their enemies! ⁹The Canaanites and all the inhabitants of the land will hear of it, and surround us, and cut off our name from the earth. Then what will you do for your great name?"[42]

10 The LORD said to Joshua, "Stand up! Why have you fallen upon your face? ¹¹Israel has sinned. they have transgressed my covenant that I imposed on them.[43]

---

here, see the introduction to the book of Joshua). The emphasis on Achan as belonging to Judah may well be late. An interest associated with the story of Josh 22:9-34 seems highly likely (cf. *maṭṭeh* in 22:14 and Achan in 22:20).

The anger of the LORD is first referred to after 7:1 at the end of the story (v. 26). "Anger" (*'ap*) is used in Joshua only at 7:1, 26; 23:16. While reference to YHWH's anger is common in dtr texts, it is neither late nor exclusive to dtr (e.g., Num 25:3; 2 Sam 6:7; 24:20; Isa 5:25; 9:12, 17, 21; 10:4; Hos 8:5; 11:9; 13:11; 14:4). The use here may not be significant.

41. The story of chap. 7 is different from both the crossing of the Jordan and the capture of Jericho; it is, nevertheless, just as much a sacral story as these. In all three, the sacral is central. As in the case of the Jordan crossing and the Jericho capture, there is an apparent disparity between the cause and its effect. The attack is expected to be a pushover (7:3). It was not superior force or superior strategy that repulsed the attackers; according to the text, it was Israel's sin (v. 11). The fate of a people in battle is decided by one individual's breach of sacral law. The chapter is then devoted to the righting of this sacral wrong. It is hardly a story of battle. Vv. 6-15 are concerned with the cause of the disaster; vv. 16-26 are concerned with the identification and punishment of Achan. In contrast to the other two sacral stories, Achan's breach of the ban did not need to replace the story of the conquest of Ai.

Instead, it precedes the conquest account. Note how the geographical location of Ai is given in v. 2, not in v. 1.

42. In vv. 7-9, v. 7 has echoes of Deut 1:27. The major difference is that in Deuteronomy it is Israel that grumbles; here it is Joshua and all the elders who lament and Joshua who speaks. In Hebrew, only the clause "to hand us over to the Amorites" is identical in both passages. There is no evidence to support an addition. The cutting off of Israel's name is otherwise found only in Isa 48:19. Concern for YHWH's "great name" (v. 9b) is not in Deuteronomy; it is not found in Exod 32:7-14 or Num 14:11-25 . Although the text base is limited, the clause (v. 9b) could be late (cf. 1 Sam 12:22; 1 Kgs 8:42; Jer 10:6; 44:26; Ezek 36:23; Mal 1:11; Pss 76:2; 99:3; 2 Chron 6:32).

The sacral aspect is emphasized by vv. 7-9. They locate responsibility with YHWH. This is not military action in which YHWH supports Joshua and Israel; it is action where the responsibility is YHWH's, not Joshua's, and where Israel is mentioned only as "turning their backs to their enemies" (v. 8; only here).

43. The concern with the transgression of YHWH's covenant (*'ābar bĕrît*) in vv. 11a and 15b is found in

---

They have taken some of the devoted things; they have stolen, they have acted deceitfully, and they have put them among their own belongings. [12]*Therefore the Israelites are unable to stand before their enemies; they turn their backs to their enemies, because they have become a thing devoted for destruction themselves. I will be with you no more, unless you destroy the devoted things from among you.* [13]*Proceed to sanctify the people, and say, 'Sanctify yourselves for tomorrow; for thus says the* LORD, *the God of Israel, "There are devoted things among you, O Israel; you will be unable to stand before your enemies until you take away the devoted things from among you."* [14]*In the morning therefore you shall come forward tribe by tribe. The tribe that the* LORD *takes shall come near by clans, the clan that the* LORD *takes shall come near by households, and the household that the* LORD *takes shall come near one by one.* [15]*And the one who is taken as having the devoted things shall be burned with fire, together with all that he has,*

> for having transgressed the covenant of the LORD, and [44]

for having done an outrageous thing in Israel.' "

[16] *So Joshua rose early in the morning, and brought Israel near tribe by tribe, and the tribe of Judah was taken.* [17]*He brought near the clans of Judah, and the clan of the Zerahites was taken; and he brought near the clan of the Zerahites, family by family, and Zabdi was taken.* [18]*And he brought near*

his household one by one, and Achan son of Carmi son of Zabdi son of Zerah, [of the tribe of Judah,][45] *was taken.* [19]*Then Joshua said to Achan, "My son, give glory to the* LORD *God of Israel and make confession to him. Tell me now what you have done; do not hide it from me."* [20]*And Achan answered Joshua, "It is true; I am the one who sinned against the* LORD *God of Israel. This is what I did:* [21]*when I saw among the spoil a beautiful mantle from Shinar, and two hundred shekels of silver, and a bar of gold weighing fifty shekels, then I coveted them and took them. They now lie hidden in the ground inside my tent, with the silver underneath."*

[22] *So Joshua sent messengers, and they ran to the tent; and there it was, hidden in his tent with the silver underneath.* [23]*They took them out of the tent and brought them to Joshua and all the Israelites; and they spread them out before the* LORD. [24]*Then Joshua and all Israel with him took Achan son of Zerah, with the silver, the mantle, and the bar of gold, with his sons and daughters, with his oxen, donkeys, and sheep, and his tent and all that he had; and they brought them up to the Valley of Achor.* [25]*Joshua said, "Why did you bring trouble on us? The* LORD *is bringing trouble on you today." And all Israel stoned him to death; they burned them with fire, cast stones on them,* [26]*and raised over him a great heap of stones that remains to this day. Then the* LORD *turned from his burning anger. Therefore that place to this day is called the Valley of Achor.*[46]

Josh 23:16. As indicated, it is likely that these references come from the national focus within the dtr revising (in the DH, cf. also Deut 17:2; 29:12; Judg 2:20; 2 Kgs 18:12; elsewhere, note Hos 6:7; 8:1; also Isa 24:5; 33:8; Jer 34:18). The Hebrew of v. 11 has five "and also" (*wĕgam*) clauses after "Israel has sinned" (so: transgressed; taken; stolen; acted deceitfully; put among their own). The sentence structure allows for additions—and also conceals them.

44. See the preceding note on v. 11. V. 15b, as a whole, may be an addition.

45. Unnecessary after v. 16; absent from LXX.

46. With this story, the overlay of the "sacral stories" is complete; their influence on the understanding of the narrative continues and the narrative itself is extended into the north (ending with 11:23; 12:7-8a, and the list of kings). The Jordan has been crossed, Jericho captured, and human greed denied in favor of divine intervention. The theology can be simplified as: God worked wonders for us and we reaped the benefits; but, when we disobeyed, we failed. A parallel

---

After the Dtr: indented and sans serif font	Revision: national focus	Other: double sideline

8 Then the LORD said to Joshua, "Do not fear or be dismayed; take all the fighting men with you, and go up now to Ai. See, I have handed over to you the king of Ai with his people, his city, and his land. [2]You shall do to Ai and its king as you did to Jericho and its king; only its spoil and its livestock you may take as booty for yourselves. Set an ambush against the city, behind it."[47]

3 So Joshua and all the fighting men set out to go up against Ai. Joshua chose thirty thousand warriors and sent them out by night [4]with the command, "You shall lie in ambush against the city, behind it; do not go very far from the city, but all of you stay alert. [5]I and all the people who are with me will approach the city. When they come out against us, *as before*, we shall flee from them. [6]They will come out after us until we have drawn them away from the city; for they will say, 'They are fleeing from us, *as before*.' While we flee from them, [7]you shall rise up from the ambush and seize the city; for the LORD your God will give it into your hand. [8]And when you

have taken the city, you shall set the city on fire, doing as the LORD has ordered; see, I have commanded you." [9]So Joshua sent them out; and they went to the place of ambush, and lay between Bethel and Ai, to the west of Ai; but Joshua spent that night in the camp.

10 In the morning Joshua rose early and mustered the people, and went up, with the elders of Israel, before the people to Ai. [11]All the fighting men who were with him went up, and drew near before the city, and camped on the north side of Ai, with a ravine between them and Ai. [12]Taking about five thousand men, he set them in ambush between Bethel and Ai, to the west of the city. [13]So they stationed the forces, the main encampment that was north of the city and its rear guard west of the city. But Joshua spent that night in the valley. [14]When the king of Ai saw this, he and all his people, the inhabitants of the city, hurried out early in the morning to the meeting place facing the Arabah to meet Israel in battle; but he did not know that there

---

can be seen in Joshua's victory over Amalek at Rephidim, where the victory is correlated with equally mismatched means—Moses' upheld hands (Exod 17:8-13). An explicit parallel is drawn in Josh 4:23 with the Reed Sea crossing where Israel's journey began.

47. With the attack on Ai, the Conquest Narrative moves out of the Jordan valley and into the hill country of Benjamin. As in the Conquest Narrative at Jericho (6:1-2) and with echoes of the language there, the king of Ai is to be handed over to Joshua, along with his people, city, and land. Ai is to be treated as Jericho was (with repeated emphasis on the king)—with the difference that spoil and livestock might be taken as booty (v. 2). The ambush tactics are pure military strategy. Note the difference from the sacral story of the preceding chapter; here "all the fighting men" are to go (8:1), while there "not all the people need go up" (7:3).

In 8:3-9 the detailed strategy is planned and preparations set in train; in vv. 10-23 the successful execution of the strategy is narrated; in vv. 24-29 the fate of Ai and its inhabitants is reported. By contrast with the minimal mention of battle in chap. 7, this is a fully military account. It is a story of battle under Joshua's leadership, with some support from the LORD. Twice there is reference to the previous battle, "as before" (vv. 5 and 6); both are likely to derive from the editor inserting the sacral story of chap. 7. They occur in the plotting of strategy, which was not plotted in chap. 7; the tactic of luring the enemy from their city is described as mimicking the previous defeat. The "previous defeat" is not mentioned before or after. There is no hint in 8:1 that this is a second battle. The exhortation not to fear or be dismayed offers an excellent opportunity for some such reference; there is none. Both elements of the exhortation recur in 10:25; the first element alone is found in 10:8 and also 11:6.

| Main pre-DH: Conquest Narrative *and its expansion* | Other pre-DH: single sideline | **Josianic DH: from the Dtr** |

was an ambush against him behind the city. [15]And Joshua and all Israel made a pretense of being beaten before them, and fled in the direction of the wilderness. [16]So all the people who were in the city were called together to pursue them, and as they pursued Joshua they were drawn away from the city. [17]There was not a man left in Ai or Bethel who did not go out after Israel; they left the city open, and pursued Israel.

18 Then the LORD said to Joshua, "Stretch out the sword that is in your hand toward Ai; for I will give it into your hand." And Joshua stretched out the sword that was in his hand toward the city. [19]As soon as he stretched out his hand, the troops in ambush rose quickly out of their place and rushed forward. They entered the city, took it, and at once set the city on fire. [20]So when the men of Ai looked back, the smoke of the city was rising to the sky. They had no power to flee this way or that, for the people who fled to the wilderness turned back against the pursuers. [21]When Joshua and all Israel saw that the ambush had taken the city and that the smoke of the city was rising, then they turned back and struck down the men of Ai. [22]And the others came out from the city against them; so they were surrounded by Israelites, some on one side, and some on the other; and Israel struck them down until no one was left who survived or escaped. [23]But the king of Ai was taken alive and brought to Joshua.

24 When Israel had finished slaughtering all the inhabitants of Ai in the open wilderness where they pursued them, and when all of them to the very last had fallen by the edge of the sword, all Israel returned to Ai, and attacked it with the edge of the sword. [25]The total of those who fell that day, both men and women, was twelve thousand—all the people of Ai. [26]For Joshua did not draw back his hand, with which he stretched out the sword, until he had utterly destroyed all the inhabitants of Ai. [27]Only the livestock and the spoil of that city Israel took as their booty, according to the word of the LORD that he had issued to Joshua. [28]So Joshua burned Ai, and made it forever a heap of ruins, as it is to this day. [29]And he hanged the king of Ai on a tree until evening; and at sunset Joshua commanded, and they took his body down from the tree, threw it down at the entrance of the gate of the city, and raised over it a great heap of stones, which stands there to this day.

30 Then Joshua built on Mount Ebal an altar to the LORD, the God of Israel, [31]just as Moses the servant of the LORD had commanded the Israelites, as it is written in the book of the law of Moses, "an altar of unhewn stones, on which no iron tool has been used"; and they offered on it burnt offerings to the LORD, and sacrificed offerings of well-being. [32]And there, in the presence of the Israelites, Joshua wrote on the stones a copy of the law of Moses, which he had written. [33]All Israel, alien as well as citizen, with their elders and officers and their judges, stood on opposite sides of the ark in front of the levitical priests who carried the ark of the covenant of the LORD, half of them in front of Mount Gerizim and half of them in front of Mount Ebal, as Moses the servant of the LORD had commanded at the first, that they should bless the people of Israel. [34]And afterward he read all the words of the law, blessings and curses, according to all that is written in the book of the law. [35]There was not a word of all that Moses commanded that Joshua did not read before all the assembly of Israel, and the women, and the little ones, and the aliens who resided among them.[48]

---

48. 8:30-35 is associated with Deut 11:29-32 and 27:1-26. See the notes above on Deut 11:32 and 27:8.

| After the Dtr: | *Revision:* | Other: |
| indented and sans serif font | *national focus* | double sideline |

9 *Now when all the kings who were beyond the Jordan in the hill country and in the lowland all along the coast of the Great Sea toward Lebanon*

|| the Hittites, the Amorites, the Canaanites, the Perizzites, the Hivites, and the Jebusites[49]

heard (Heb.; NRSV, of this), *²they gathered together with one accord to fight Joshua and Israel.*[50]

It is best understood as later than the national focus within the dtr revision. In the course of a careful and detailed analysis, J. L'Hour concludes that, although old traditions are reflected, the present form and position of these three passages is due to a post-dtr redactor ("L'Alliance de Sichem," 182).

What Moses did on the plains of Moab is in these verses reported for Joshua in the hill country of Ephraim (in compliance with Deuteronomy 27). The placement invites explanation. Was the trio of crossing the Jordan, capturing Jericho, and conquering Ai seen as the core of the conquest? Was Ai symbolic, as the first town in the hill country? Was acknowledgment of the law of primary urgency? Does the debacle of Ai elicit this rite of commitment to the law?

49. This six-item list of local peoples is found here and in Deut 20:17; Josh 11:3; 12:8; and Judg 3:5 (also Exod 3:8, 17; 23:23; 33:2; 34:11—considered secondary). As at 11:3 and 12:8, the context concerns kings not peoples. The six peoples listed are not correlated with the three geographical locations of 9:1a. Attribution remains uncertain. The list functions to correlate the coalition of kings in the land with Israel's traditional enemies in the land.

50. As with 7:1, 9:1-2 is a summary of what is to come. It reaches well beyond the immediate Gibeon story of chap. 9; it is not present in the narrative beginning with 9:3. It should be noted that 9:1; 10:1; and 11:1 have the same Hebrew construction (as does 5:1); 9:3 does not. The concern with kings tallies with 12:7-24. Attribution to the expansion of the Conquest Narrative is probable, bringing into view the full sweep of a narrative that extends beyond the localized conquest ending with 10:42-43. It is possible that the

3 But when the inhabitants of Gibeon heard what Joshua had done to Jericho and to Ai, ⁴they on their part acted with cunning. They went and prepared provisions, and took worn-out sacks for their donkeys, and wineskins, worn-out and torn and mended, ⁵with worn-out, patched sandals on their feet, and worn-out clothes; and all their provisions were dry and moldy. ⁶They went to Joshua in the camp at Gilgal, and said to him and to the Israelites, "We have come from a far country; so now make a treaty with us." ⁷But the Israelites said to the Hivites, "Perhaps you live among us; then how can we make a treaty with you?" ⁸They said to Joshua, "We are your servants." And Joshua said to them, "Who are you? And where do you come from?" ⁹They said to him, "Your servants have come from a very far country, because of the name of the LORD your God; for we have heard a report of him, of all that he did in Egypt,[51] **¹⁰and of all that he did**

---

opening phrase of 9:1 and 11:1 was modeled on the original in 10:1.

51. The Conquest Narrative has brought Israel over the Jordan and acquired both Jericho, in the Jordan valley, and Ai, in the Benjamin hill country. This Gibeon tradition adds another major city to the "conquest," while remaining within the territory of Benjamin. Certain elements of the narrative will be noted as of later origin, but our concern is to identify a text that may have been part of the Conquest Narrative, rather than to identify the raw materials that can be sighted in that text.

As with the story of Rahab and her family, this story of Gibeon and its inhabitants is inextricably woven into the Conquest Narrative. Their place in the tradition invites reflection. For the Gibeon story, vv. 15b and 18-21 point to an ongoing engagement in later Israel. We do not have the original Jericho story, but we may surmise that for Jericho, Ai, and Gibeon all three stories were dissimilar. Three types are present: Jericho, the walled city that was taken when so

---

| Main pre-DH: Conquest Narrative *and its expansion* | Other pre-DH: single sideline | **Josianic DH: from the Dtr** |

to the two kings of the Amorites who were beyond the Jordan, King Sihon of Heshbon, and King Og of Bashan who lived in Ashtaroth.[52]

[11]So our elders and all the inhabitants of our country said to us, 'Take provisions in your hand for the journey; go to meet them, and say to them, "We are your servants; come now, make a treaty with us." ' [12]Here is our bread; it was still warm when we took it from our houses as our food for the journey, on the day we set out to come to you, but now, see, it is dry and moldy; [13]these wineskins were new when we filled them, and see, they are burst; and these garments and sandals of ours are worn out from the very long journey." [14]So the leaders partook of their provisions, and did not ask direction from the LORD. [15]And Joshua made peace with them, guaranteeing their lives by a treaty.

‖ and the leaders of the congregation swore
‖ an oath to them[53]

---

many were not; Ai, captured in battle; Gibeon, spared by covenant (9:15a; cf. Judg 2:2). Is the Gibeon tradition preserved as a type of the cities that remained in Israel and labored for Israel (cf. Judg 1:28, 30, 33, 35)? Is the labor category among the most menial (cf. Deut 29:11 [Heb., 29:10]; "you are cursed," Josh 9:23)—and even so, within the covenant? Is the Gibeon story associated with the tradition of the locals as a snare for Israel, given expression later (cf. Judg 2:1-5, 20-23; 3:4-6)? The text is silent; the echoes remain.

52. The concern for both Sihon and Og is a pointer to dtr origin (see above at 2:10).

53. The phrase "leaders of the congregation" is late and almost exclusively priestly (cf. Exod 16:22; 34:31; Num 4:34; 16:2; 31:13; 32:2; and Josh 9:15, 18; 22:30). The text associated with this term (9:15b, 18-21) is almost certainly late. What the added text offers is a version justifying Israel's response when the double-cross was discovered.

16 But when three days had passed after they had made a treaty with them, they heard that they were their neighbors and were living among them. [17]So the Israelites set out and reached their cities on the third day. Now their cities were Gibeon, Chephirah, Beeroth, and Kiriath-jearim.

‖ [18]But the Israelites did not attack them, because the leaders of the congregation had sworn to them by the LORD, the God of Israel. Then all the congregation murmured against the leaders. [19]But all the leaders said to all the congregation, "We have sworn to them by the LORD, the God of Israel, and now we must not touch them. [20]This is what we will do to them: We will let them live, so that wrath may not come upon us, because of the oath that we swore to them." [21]The leaders said to them, "Let them live." So they became hewers of wood and drawers of water for all the congregation, as the leaders had decided concerning them.[54]

22 Joshua summoned them, and said to them, "Why did you deceive us, saying, 'We are very far from you,' while in fact you are living among us? [23]Now therefore you are cursed, and some of you shall always be slaves, hewers of wood and drawers of water for the house of my God." [24]They answered Joshua,

because it was told to your servants for a certainty that the LORD your God had commanded his servant Moses to give you all the land, and to destroy all the inhabitants of the land before you; so we were in great fear for our lives because of you, and did this thing. [25]And now[55]

---

54. See the preceding note on 9:15b.

55. In the DH, both the description of Moses as YHWH's servant (16 occurrences in Joshua) and the

---

After the Dtr:	Revision:	Other:
indented and sans serif font	*national focus*	double sideline

"We are in your hand: do as it seems good and right in your sight to do to us." ²⁶This is what he did for them: He saved them from the Israelites; and they did not kill them. ²⁷But on that day Joshua made them hewers of wood and drawers of water for the congregation and for the altar of the Lord, to continue to this day, **in the place that he should choose.**[56]

10 When King Adoni-zedek of Jerusalem heard how Joshua had taken Ai, and had utterly destroyed it, doing to Ai and its king as he had done to Jericho and its king, and how the inhabitants of Gibeon had made peace with Israel and were among them, ²he became greatly frightened, because Gibeon was a large city, like one of the royal cities, and was larger than Ai, and all its men were warriors. ³So King Adoni-zedek of Jerusalem sent a message to King Hoham of Hebron, to King Piram of Jarmuth, to King Japhia of Lachish, and to King Debir of Eglon, saying, ⁴"Come up and help me, and let us attack Gibeon; for it has made peace with Joshua and with the Israelites." ⁵Then the five kings of the Amorites—the king of Jerusalem, the king of Hebron, the king of Jarmuth, the king of Lachish, and the king of Eglon—gathered their forces, and went up with all their armies and camped against Gibeon, and made war against it.[57]

6 And the Gibeonites sent to Joshua at the camp in Gilgal, saying, "Do not abandon your servants; come up to us quickly, and save us, and help us; for all the kings of the Amorites who live in the hill country are gathered against us." ⁷So Joshua went up from Gilgal, he and all the fighting force with him, all the mighty warriors. ⁸The Lord said to Joshua, "Do not fear them, for I have handed them over to you; not one of them shall stand before you." ⁹So Joshua came upon them suddenly, having marched up all night from Gilgal. ¹⁰And the Lord threw them into a panic before Israel, who inflicted a great

---

emphasis on destruction are favorites of late dtr editing. This apparent insertion is most probably from the national focus within the process of dtr revision, but the Josianic Dtr cannot be excluded (cf. 1:2; 2:10-11; 5:1).

56. The reference at the end of v. 27, "in the place that he should choose," is attributed to the Dtr (cf. Noth, *DH*, 64: "the stereotyped Deuteronomic formula for the site of the legitimate sanctuary"). Attribution to the national focus within the dtr revision process is statistically unlikely, but possible.

57. The contribution of 10:1-27, 42-43 to the Conquest Narrative is summed up in v. 42. Joshua took the land of five kings in one action, because God fought for Israel. The protagonist is Joshua; the supporting role is God's. The formulation is prudent; it refers to "these kings" and "their land" (v. 42). The occupation of Jerusalem will be achieved under David (cf. Judg 1:8, 21).

The story is an appropriate follow-up to the preceding conquests; it opens with reference to Jericho, Ai, and Gibeon. The territory of the coalition of five kings would extend the land acquired further south: Jerusalem, Hebron, Jarmuth, Lachish, and Eglon. Joshua, and Israel with him, is portrayed as based at Gilgal (10:6, 9, 15, 43).

The text appears to offer two versions of the story. One version was restricted to reporting Israel's massive success in battle; it ends with Joshua's return to Gilgal (v. 15). The other version embellished the story with details of the pursuit, of Israel's return to Joshua at Makkedah, and of the gruesome treatment of the five kings there. The return to Gilgal is again noted (v. 43).

With the completion of these actions, the Conquest Narrative has accounted for the fundamentals of the territory of Benjamin and Judah.

Main pre-DH: Conquest Narrative
and its expansion

Other pre-DH:
single sideline

Josianic DH:
from the Dtr

slaughter on them at Gibeon, chased them by the way of the ascent of Beth-horon, and struck them down as far as Azekah and Makkedah. [11]As they fled before Israel, while they were going down the slope of Beth-horon, the LORD threw down huge stones from heaven on them as far as Azekah, and they died; there were more who died because of the hailstones than the Israelites killed with the sword.

12 On the day when the LORD gave the Amorites over to the Israelites, Joshua spoke to the LORD; and he said in the sight of Israel,

"Sun, stand still at Gibeon,
and Moon, in the valley of Aijalon."
[13]And the sun stood still, and the moon stopped,
until the nation took vengeance on their enemies.

Is this not written in the Book of Jashar? The sun stopped in midheaven, and did not hurry to set for about a whole day. [14]There has been no day like it before or since, when the LORD heeded a human voice; for the LORD fought for Israel.

15 Then Joshua returned, and all Israel with him, to the camp at Gilgal.

16 Meanwhile, these five kings fled and hid themselves in the cave at Makkedah. [17]And it was told Joshua, "The five kings have been found, hidden in the cave at Makkedah." [18]Joshua said, "Roll large stones against the mouth of the cave, and set men by it to guard them; [19]but do not stay there yourselves; pursue your enemies, and attack them from the rear. Do not let them enter their towns, for the LORD your God has given them into your hand." [20]When Joshua and the Israelites had finished inflicting a very great slaughter on them, until they were wiped out, and when the survivors had entered into the fortified towns, [21]all the people returned safe to Joshua in the camp at Makkedah; no one dared to speak against any of the Israelites.

22 Then Joshua said, "Open the mouth of the cave, and bring those five kings out to me from the cave." [23]They did so, and brought the five kings out to him from the cave, the king of Jerusalem, the king of Hebron, the king of Jarmuth, the king of Lachish, and the king of Eglon. [24]When they brought the kings out to Joshua, Joshua summoned all the Israelites, and said to the chiefs of the warriors who had gone with him, "Come near, put your feet on the necks of these kings." Then they came near and put their feet on their necks. [25]And Joshua said to them, "Do not be afraid or dismayed; be strong and courageous; for thus the LORD will do to all the enemies against whom you fight." [26]Afterward Joshua struck them down and put them to death, and he hung them on five trees. And they hung on the trees until evening. [27]At sunset Joshua commanded, and they took them down from the trees and threw them into the cave where they had hidden themselves; they set large stones against the mouth of the cave, which remain to this very day.

28 Joshua took Makkedah on that day, and struck it and its king with the edge of the sword; he utterly destroyed every person in it; he left no one remaining. And he did to the king of Makkedah as he had done to the king of Jericho.[58]

---

58. **Text signals** in vv. 28-39 (40-41). (i) The verses are list-like in quality. They treat six southern towns: Makkedah, Libnah, Lachish, Eglon, Hebron, and Debir. Of these, three figured in the Jerusalem coalition. Four of the six kings are specifically mentioned as being killed in the capture of their town: the kings of Makkedah, Libnah, Hebron, and Debir. The same fate may be assumed for the kings of Lachish and Eglon, but it is not made explicit. In the Conquest Narrative, five kings were put to death (10:26). Only the king of Hebron is specifically mentioned in

---

After the Dtr:
indented and sans serif font

Revision:
national focus

Other:
double sideline

29 Then Joshua passed on from Makkedah, and all Israel with him, to Libnah, and fought against Libnah. ³⁰The LORD gave it also and its king into the hand of Israel; and he struck it with the edge of the sword, and every person in it; he left no one remaining in it; and he did to its king as he had done to the king of Jericho.

31 Next Joshua passed on from Libnah, and all Israel with him, to Lachish, and laid siege to it, and assaulted it. ³²The LORD gave Lachish into the hand of Israel, and he took it on the second day, and struck it with the edge of the sword, and every person in it, as he had done to Libnah.

both (vv. 23 and 37); the other two (the kings of Lachish and Eglon) are passed over in silence (vv. 31-32, 34-35). There is a mixture of intrusion (one death twice) and collusion (two deaths in silence).

(ii) *Ḥerem* language (= the ban, utter destruction) is used for four of the six towns (vv. 28, 35, 37, 39) as well as in the final summary (v. 40). The *ḥerem* is extended effectively to the other two towns, Lachish and Libnah, by association with Eglon (v. 35) and Debir (v. 39). In the Conquest Narrative, *ḥerem* language was used once for Jericho (6:21), once for Ai (8:26), and once in relation to both (10:1); otherwise, it is used in 2:10 (dtr), the Achan story (6:17, 18; 7:1, 11, 12, 13, 15), and in secondary additions (11:11, 12, 20, 21).

(iii) Under the concern for extermination, we may include the phrase *hiš'îr śārîd*, which the NRSV translates as "left no one remaining." It is used, as with *ḥerem*, for four of the six towns (vv. 28, 30, 37, 39) as well as in the final summary (v. 40); it is also used for King Horam of Gezer (v. 33). It is absent for Lachish and Eglon; as with *ḥerem*, it is extended effectively to them by association with Libnah (v. 32 and indirectly in v. 35). In the conquest narrative, this language is used once for Ai (8:22) and once in a secondary addition (11:8).

(iv) Equally under the concern for extermination, we may include the language of √*nkh lĕpî ḥereb*, which the NRSV translates as striking with the edge of the sword. It is used for all six towns. In the conquest narrative, it occurs once for Jericho (6:21) and once in association with Ai (8:24); it occurs three times in a secondary addition (11:11, 12, 14) and also in 19:47.

(v) Verses 40-41, in contrast with vv. 42-43, have a wide vision ("the whole land" v. 40, with details); they

have an emphasis on extermination and destruction, attributed to God's command. V. 41, syntactically bound to v. 40, embraces the territory of the south.

Text-history approach. There is an overlap between this list and the preceding narrative. At least one king (Hebron) is noted in both as being executed; implicitly, this happens also for two others (Lachish and Eglon). The concern for *ḥerem* and extermination is denser and more marked in these verses than anywhere else. What these observations record in detail is what the reader knows instinctively: the list of towns in vv. 28-39 is quite different from the stories earlier in the book. Unpleasantly evident in these verses is a massive emphasis on destruction and extermination. So evident a difference may point to a separate origin. Sandwiched between the end of the Makkedah account (vv. 22-27) and the return of Joshua and all Israel to their camp at Gilgal (vv. 42-43), these verses are situated exactly where a later addition makes best sense. As an addition, it is appropriate that the summary verses (vv. 40-41), with their emphasis on extensive territory and "all **their** kings" (but in the text, only three kings explicitly), precede the conquest narrative's conclusion, with its emphasis rather on "all **these** kings" (five) and their land (vv. 42-43).

In the light of the comment in the introduction, it may be noted that in the Conquest Narrative the language of destruction is used sparingly for Jericho, Ai, and the coalition. Two items are used for Jericho (destruction and sword, 6:21), three for Ai (survivor, sword, and destruction, 8:22, 24, 26), and one for the coalition (destruction, 10:1). By contrast, the density of use in 10:28-41 suggests a fascination with the issue. The different densities can be accounted for by the

| Main pre-DH: Conquest Narrative *and its expansion* | Other pre-DH: single sideline | **Josianic DH: from the Dtr** |

33 Then King Horam of Gezer came up to help Lachish; and Joshua struck him and his people, leaving him no survivors.

34 From Lachish Joshua passed on with all Israel to Eglon; and they laid siege to it, and assaulted it; [35]and they took it that day, and struck it with the edge of the sword; and every person in it he utterly destroyed that day, as he had done to Lachish.

36 Then Joshua went up with all Israel from Eglon to Hebron; they assaulted it, [37]and took it, and struck it with the edge of the sword, and its king and its towns, and every person in it; he left no one remaining,

just as he had done to Eglon, and utterly destroyed it with every person in it.[59]

38 Then Joshua, with all Israel, turned back to Debir and assaulted it, [39]and he took it with its king and all its towns; they struck them with the edge of the sword, and utterly destroyed every person in it; he left no one remaining; just as he had done to Hebron, and, as he had done to Libnah and its king, so he did to Debir and its king.

40 So Joshua defeated the whole land, the hill country and the Negeb and the lowland and the slopes, and all their kings; he left no one remaining, but utterly destroyed all that breathed, as the LORD God of Israel commanded. [41]And Joshua defeated them from Kadesh-barnea to Gaza, and all the country of Goshen, as far as Gibeon.

[42]Joshua took all these kings and their land at one time, because the LORD God of Israel fought for Israel. [43]Then Joshua returned, and all Israel with him, to the camp at Gilgal.[60]

11 *When King Jabin of Hazor heard* (Heb.; NRSV, *of this*), *he sent to King Jobab of Madon, to the king of Shimron, to the king of Achshaph, [2]and to the kings who were in the northern hill country, and in*

---

different genres of narrative and list. An explanation is still needed for this difference in genres and for the list's focus on extermination—as though nothing else mattered. A stark contrast is provided by the immediately preceding 10:22-27 where all five kings are killed and none of the extermination language is used.

Joshua's move from Gilgal to Gibeon, in response to the appeal for help (10:6-7), and the return from Makkedah to Gilgal after the pursuit and the killing of the kings (either 10:15 or 10:43) makes acceptable sense. On the other hand, Joshua's return from Debir to Gilgal, after the extensive campaign and conquest of the south, makes little or no sense. A return from Debir to Gilgal, from deep in the south of the territory to its northeastern periphery, is perplexing both from a narrative and a strategic point of view.

Present-text potential. In their present situation, these verses fill in details of the southern operation, before the report of Joshua's return to Gilgal (vv. 42-43). They detail an intensity of annihilation that was not previously insisted on. They do not provide total coverage of the southern campaign; there is no mention of Ai, Gibeon, Jerusalem, or Jarmuth for example. Vv. 40-41, however, allow the reader to realize that what is specified for some is symbolic of all.

---

59. This passage on Hebron sits uncomfortably with, to say the least, or is in strong contrast to the tradition in Josh 14:6-15. See the note there.

60. With the return of Joshua and all Israel to Gilgal, the Conquest Narrative is at an end. The theology can be simplified as: Israel conquered the land, with some remarkable help from God. The stories of how Israel crossed the Jordan and how Israel captured Jericho have been replaced by the sacral stories of how God wonderfully acted on Israel's behalf. Help from God is visible in the capture of Ai and obvious in the victory at Gibeon/Makkedah. The conquest covers the power centers of the territory of Benjamin and Judah.

After the Dtr:	Revision:	Other:
indented and sans serif font	national focus	double sideline

the Arabah south of Chinneroth, and in the lowland, and in Naphoth-dor on the west.[61]

> [3]the *(Heb.; NRSV, to the)* Canaanites in the east and the west, the Amorites, the Hittites, the Perizzites, and the Jebusites in the

hill country, and the Hivites under Hermon in the land of Mizpah.[62]

[4]*They came out, with all their troops, a great army, in number like the sand on the seashore, with very many horses and chariots.* [5]*All these kings joined their forces, and came and camped together at the waters of Merom, to fight with Israel.*

[6] *And the* LORD *said to Joshua, "Do not be afraid of them, for tomorrow at this time I will hand over all of them, slain, to Israel; you shall hamstring their horses, and burn their chariots with fire."* [7]*So Joshua came suddenly upon them with all his fighting force, by the waters of Merom, and fell upon them.* [8]*And the* LORD *handed them over to Israel, who attacked them and chased them as far as Great Sidon and Misrephoth-maim, and eastward as far as the valley of Mizpeh.*

> They struck them down, until they had left no one remaining. 9 Joshua did to them as the LORD commanded him; he hamstrung their horses, and burned their chariots with fire.[63]

---

61. **Text signals.** 11:1-2, 4-8a, 16-19, 23. Three "pointers" are relevant here; they are no more than pointers. (i) There is no reference to Joshua's whereabouts. The LORD addresses him in 11:6; he and his troops launch a sudden attack at Merom (11:7). Merom is in the north of Galilee; Joshua was last based at Gilgal in the south. (ii) The introduction at v. 1 is disconnected and vague. The Hebrew reads: "When Jabin, king of Hazor, heard"; the NRSV adds "of this." As the text flows, Jabin may have heard of Joshua's return to Gilgal (10:43), or of his campaign through the south (10:28-41), or of the slaughter of five kings near Makkedah (10:16-27). None of these explain why Jabin of Hazor (in northern Galilee) should have rallied allies and prepared for battle at Merom. The introduction assumes a strategic intention far wider than that of the Conquest Narrative. (iii) In line with the sacral stories, YHWH is the effective protagonist rather than Joshua and the army of Israel. Hamstringing horses and burning chariots (11:6b) are good guerrilla tactics. Nevertheless, the emphasis is on YHWH's action: before, "I will hand over all of them, slain, to Israel" (v. 6a); after, "and the LORD handed them over to Israel" (v. 8). (iv) Beyond these pointers, vv. 16-19 describe an extensive territory, from the south into the valley of Lebanon. The war lasted a long time (v. 18). We have no details of this long war, not even a list like 10:28-39. There is a commingling of territorial details embracing the whole land and combat with kings that is apparently northern.

Text-history approach. When all three "pointers" are taken together, especially in association with the extensive summary in vv. 16-19, it seems likely that a concern to cover the conquest of all Israel's land has led to an expansion of the sacralized conquest account.

Potential of this expansion (11:1-2, 4-8a, 16-19, 23). For the present text of the entire chapter, see the

note on 11:23. The text signals discussed can be overlooked and the point is then to bring the conquest of the north into association with the stories of God's action in the south. Alternatively, the signals can become the focus of attention, in which case the text is a good example of how narratives are constructed to confirm faith. Faith is expressed in the stories of the south; the text extends that faith to the north.

62. As at 9:1 and 12:8b, the list of peoples sits uncomfortably with the appeal in vv. 1-2 that is sent out to kings not peoples. Again, the list functions to correlate Israel's foes, the kings of the north, with Israel's traditional enemies in the land. Given the different sets of kings involved, it is not surprising that, in the main, geographical correlation is lacking.

63. Verses 8b-15 have the same emphases and linguistic features that were characteristic of 10:28-41; no one was left remaining, they were struck down with the sword, utter destruction was in force. It is

---

Main pre-DH: Conquest Narrative
and its expansion

Other pre-DH:
single sideline

Josianic DH:
from the Dtr

10 Joshua turned back at that time, and took Hazor, and struck its king down with the sword. Before that time Hazor was the head of all those kingdoms. [11]And they put to the sword all who were in it, utterly destroying them; there was no one left who breathed, and he burned Hazor with fire. [12]And all the towns of those kings, and all their kings, Joshua took, and struck them with the edge of the sword, utterly destroying them, as Moses the servant of the LORD had commanded. [13]But Israel burned none of the towns that stood on mounds except Hazor, which Joshua did burn. [14]All the spoil of these towns, and the livestock, the Israelites took for their booty; but all the people they struck down with the edge of the sword, until they had destroyed them, and they did not leave any who breathed. [15]As the LORD had commanded his servant Moses, so Moses commanded Joshua, and so Joshua did; he left nothing undone of all that the LORD had commanded Moses.

16 So Joshua took all that land: the hill country and all the Negeb and all the land of Goshen and the low-land and the Arabah and the hill country of Israel and its lowland, [17]from Mount Halak, which rises toward Seir, as far as Baal-gad in the valley of Lebanon below Mount Hermon. He took all their kings, struck them down, and put them to death. [18]Joshua made war a long time with all those kings. [19]There was not a town that made peace with the Israelites, except the Hivites, the inhabitants of Gibeon; all were taken in battle.

[20]For it was the LORD's doing to harden their hearts so that they would come against Israel in battle, in order that they might be utterly destroyed, and might receive no mercy, but be exterminated, just as the LORD had commanded Moses.[64]

21 At that time Joshua came and wiped out the Anakim from the hill country, from Hebron, from Debir, from Anab, and from all the hill country of Judah, and from all the hill country of Israel; Joshua utterly destroyed them with their towns. [22]None of the Anakim was left in the land of the Israelites; some remained only in Gaza, in Gath, and in Ashdod.[65]

[23]So Joshua took the whole land, **according to all that the LORD had spoken to Moses;** *and Joshua gave it for an inheritance to Israel according*

---

64. Verse 20 is unlikely to have belonged with the surrounding levels of text. The hardening of hearts by God occurs only here in Joshua and, of course, in Exodus (see esp. Exod 4:21; 9:12; 10:20, 27; 11:10; 14:4, 8, 17; contrast the language of Isa 6:10). The language of utter destruction and extermination occurs, but not the language of leaving none remaining. The use of *tĕḥinnâ* for "mercy" or "favor" has only one parallel, which is late (Ezra 9:8); otherwise, it means "plea" or "supplication." These signals point to the verse as a later and separate addition.

65. The note on the Anakim (vv. 21-22) is one of those little traditions that is difficult to identify with precision. It could have been associated with the Joshua text at almost any time. Concern with the Anakim (not the "descendants of the giants") is restricted to the books of Deuteronomy and Joshua. It is possible that the note was added along with 10:28-41 and 11:8b-15. The concern for utter destruction and for none remaining is present. The general temporal note, "at that time" (*bāʿēt hahî'*) occurs also in 11:10; elsewhere in Joshua, only at 5:2 and 6:26 (both secondary).

---

probable that 11:8b-15 comes from the same level as 10:28-41. Vv. 8b-9 in their own way repeat and expand v. 7. The emphasis on YHWH's command (v. 9) forms an envelope with v. 15 and its emphasis on the pattern of command from YHWH to Moses to Joshua (cf. Deut 31:14; Josh 11:23).

After the Dtr:	*Revision:*	Other:
indented and sans serif font	*national focus*	double sideline

to their tribal allotments. *And the land was undisturbed, without war* (Heb.; NRSV, had rest from war).[66]

---

66. The Conquest Narrative took the story of Israel's move into the land first across the Jordan, next up to Ai and Gibeon, and then deep into the south (if the defeat of the five-king coalition—Hebron, Lachish, Eglon, south of Jarmuth—was followed up). With the expansion of the Conquest Narrative, the north is included in sketchy fashion. The expansion may well be part of the same activity that introduced the sacral stories, although this is not absolutely necessary. The expansion shares the theological horizon of the sacral stories; it is unlikely to have preceded their incorporation into the text. With the summary verse of 11:23, not only is the "whole land" claimed, but also Joshua's distribution of the land by tribal allotments is reported. The final comment that the land was at peace (*wĕhāʾāreṣ šāqṭâ mimilḥāmâ*) is akin to the comments in Judges (3:11, 30; 5:31; 8:28); it is not to be confused with the dtr concept of "rest" (√*NWḤ*). See also Josh 14:15b and the note on Josh 21:45.

Noth comments concerning the Caleb and Hebron tradition: "Note that Josh. 14.6aβb-15a in its present setting is not related to the introduction 14.6aα and does not fit the context if read with the final sentence (Josh. 14:15b); its original place was before Josh. 11:23b, as is shown by the fact that Josh. 14.15b is the same as Josh. 11.23b" (*DH*, 65). Respectfully, we disagree. The three Hebrew words of Josh. 14:15b and 11:23b are identical; that is undisputed. There is also the association with the Anakim in both texts. First and foremost, however, it would be thoroughly out of place to have a passage on an individual's capture of a particular town at this point in the Joshua narrative. The context of Joshua 14 is not particularly suitable; with due respect to Noth's judgment, the context of Joshua 11 is thoroughly unsuitable. Second, it is to be noted that according to the tradition attested to in Josh 11:21, the extermination of the Anakim was attributed to Joshua. Third, the tentative formulation of the Caleb tradition, "it may

12 Now these are the kings of the land, whom the Israelites defeated, whose land they occupied beyond the Jordan toward the east, from the Wadi Arnon to Mount Hermon, with all the Arabah eastward: ²King Sihon of the Amorites who lived at Heshbon, and ruled from Aroer, which is on the edge of the Wadi Arnon, and from the middle of the valley as far as the river Jabbok, the boundary of the Ammonites, that is, half of Gilead, ³and the Arabah to the Sea of Chinneroth eastward, and in the direction of Beth-jeshimoth, to the sea of the Arabah, the Dead Sea, southward to the foot of the slopes of Pisgah; ⁴and King Og of Bashan, one of the last of the Rephaim, who lived at Ashtaroth and at Edrei. ⁵and ruled over Mount Hermon and Salecah and all Bashan to the boundary of the Geshurites and the Maacathites, and over half of Gilead to the boundary of King Sihon of Heshbon. ⁶Moses, the servant of the LORD, and the Israelites defeated them; and Moses the servant of the LORD gave their land for a possession to the Reubenites and the Gadites and the half-tribe of Manasseh.[67]

---

be that the LORD will be with me" (Josh 14:12), is contrary to the tenor of Joshua 1–12, to say nothing of 10:36-37. For further discussion, see the note on Josh 14:12.

The insistence that this conquest was in accordance with God's commands to Moses is probably to be attributed to the Dtr. What was emphasized at the beginning (1:1-6) is recalled at the end.

67. 12:1-6 is concerned with the kings and territories east of the Jordan. The concern for Reuben, Gad, and the half-tribe of Manasseh surfaces in the book of Joshua at 1:12-18; 4:12; 12:1-6; 13:8-13, 15-32; (14:3-4; 18:7); 22:1-6 (7-8), 9-34. It is discussed at length in the note on 1:12-18. Our judgment there on these

---

| Main pre-DH: Conquest Narrative *and its expansion* | Other pre-DH: single sideline | **Josianic DH: from the Dtr** |

7 *The following are the kings of the land whom Joshua and the Israelites defeated on the west side of the Jordan, from Baal-gad in the valley of Lebanon to Mount Halak, that rises toward Seir (and Joshua gave their land to the tribes of Israel as a possession according to their allotments, ⁸in the hill country, in the lowland, in the Arabah, in the slopes, in the wilderness, and in the Negeb):*⁶⁸

the Hittites, (Heb.; NRSV, the land of the Hittites,) Amorites, Canaanites, Perizzites, Hivites, and Jebusites⁶⁹

⁹*the king of Jericho*	*one*
the king of Ai, which is next to Bethel	*one*
¹⁰*the king of Jerusalem*	*one*
the king of Hebron	*one*
¹¹*the king of Jarmuth*	*one*
the king of Lachish	*one*
¹²*the king of Eglon*	*one*
the king of Gezer	*one*
¹³*the king of Debir*	*one*
the king of Geder	*one*
¹⁴*the king of Hormah*	*one*
the king of Arad	*one*
¹⁵*the king of Libnah*	*one*
the king of Adullam	*one*
¹⁶*the king of Makkedah*	*one*
the king of Bethel	*one*
¹⁷*the king of Tappuah*	*one*
the king of Hepher	*one*
¹⁸*the king of Aphek*	*one*
the king of Lasharon	*one*
¹⁹*the king of Madon*	*one*
the king of Hazor	*one*
²⁰*the king of Shimron-meron*	*one*
the king of Achshaph	*one*
²¹*the king of Taanach*	*one*
the king of Megiddo	*one*
²²*the king of Kedesh*	*one*
the king of Jokneam in Carmel	*one*
²³*the king of Dor in Naphath-dor*	*one*
the king of Goiim in Galilee,	*one*
²⁴*the king of Tirzah*	*one*

thirty-one kings in all.

texts (as text) favored their treatment as later additions; it should be noted that this was expressed as a preference, not as an assured conclusion. 1:12-18 and 4:12 and 22:1-6 have been formatted as additions, later than the Josianic DH. It is equally possible that the similar concerns for issues of territory—these east-of-Jordan kings (12:1-6) and the lists of tribal territories east of the Jordan (13:8-13, 15-32)—were inserted in front of the text-block 14:1—21:42, in association with the addition of the story in 22:9-34, inserted after the block. The existence of 14:3-4 is a pointer, although not probative, to the probable absence of 13:8-33 at the time 14:3-4 was formulated.

68. The list of kings in 12:7-24 was attributed by Noth to his Dtr (*DH*, 65-66). This does not hold up well when we note that the major roles for the kings are in the Conquest Narrative and its expansion. Vv. 7-24 (with the exception of v. 8b) are centered on the kings and show an interest in the total conquest, including the kings of the northern coalition. In this, it goes beyond the Conquest Narrative and so is attributed to the expansion, in association with 11:1-8a, 16-19, and 23.

69. This is the list of six nations we have encountered twice before (9:1; 11:3). Attribution remains uncertain; but, as before, the peoples are not correlated with the kings or the territories. The list serves to associate these defeated kings with the traditional enemies of Israel in the land.

13 Now Joshua was old and advanced in years; and the LORD said to him, "You are old and advanced in years.
And very much of the land still remains to be possessed.⁷⁰

70. It is important to note here and for all of Joshua 13–24 that our double sideline refers to the time of

incorporation into the DH (i.e., after the Josianic Dtr) and not to the time of composition—some texts existed that, for whatever reason, were not incorporated by the Josianic Dtr. The single sideline, denoting material incorporated into the DH by the Josianic Dtr, naturally has implications for the time of composition—to have been incorporated by the Josianic Dtr, material must have been composed before the Josianic Dtr. Detailed proposals in certain areas are not appropriate to this book; we note the nature of the texts and must leave many problems and their solution to others.

Text signals in 13:1-33. (i) V. 1 introduces a speech from YHWH to Joshua concerning possession of the land. It is the second and last such speech in the book; the first was 1:1-9. (ii) V. 1 concerns land as yet unpossessed; v. 7 concerns division of land as an inheritance for the nine and a half tribes. (iii) Joshua is presented as "old and advanced in years," not apparently the case in the earlier part of the book. The phrase is identical with Josh 23:1b, where it is introduced as "a long time" after the earlier part of the book (cf. the dtr "rest" in 23:1a). (iv) This description of Joshua expressed here by YHWH is repeated in 23:1-2, where it is expressed by Joshua himself. (v) The reference to the extensive land remaining to be possessed (v. 1b) is in some tension with 11:16-19, 23. The remaining nations recur as a theme in Joshua 23. (vi) The land described in vv. 2-6 is not that allocated in the following chapters. Instead, it consists of the Philistine territory (SW), the land of Geshur (NE), and territory associated with biblical Lebanon (N). (vii) V. 7 refers to the division of "this land" to the nine and a half tribes. The allotment of the land by Joshua to the nine and a half tribes is begun in chap. 14. (viii) Vv. 8-33 describe the allotment and other dispositions made not by Joshua but by Moses: for the territories east of the Jordan (the two and a half tribes) and for the Levites (who have no inheritance of land). (ix) Vv. 8-33 have a diptych-like structure. In a first panel, vv. 8-14 deal with the east-of-Jordan tribes as a whole (vv. 8-13) and then with the Levites (v. 14); in a second panel, vv. 15-33 deal with the same tribes singly (vv. 15-32) and then with the Levites again (v. 33).

Text-history approach. Where Joshua 13–24 is concerned, there is considerable controversy on the issues of origins and upgrades; there is also uncertainty in relation to the DH. The issues of origins and upgrades, dates of composition and questions of reliability will not be pursued here. Our principal concern has to be with the different issue of incorporation into the Josianic DH.

The correlation of 13:1-33 with what follows requires careful evaluation. Experienced exegetes of the caliber of Noth, Soggin, Fritz, and most recently Nelson have read vv. 1 and 7 together; therefore they can be read that way. It must be admitted, however, that no ancient Israelite who wanted to say that the land needed to be occupied and so must now be divided among the nine and a half tribes would have written vv. 1 and 7 the way they are. There are much clearer expressions for the settlement of conquered land. Verse 1 has the language of land remaining to be possessed—not of conquered land waiting to be allocated. By contrast, v. 7 has the language of land to be allocated—possession is assumed.

Joshua 14 opens with a solemn statement about the distribution. It is done by Eleazar, Joshua, and the heads; it is done as the LORD commanded Moses (14:2). There is no mention of the LORD's command to Joshua (13:1, 7). While there is undoubted complexity in chaps. 14–19, there is also an overarching unity. Joshua's advanced age is not mentioned.

If Joshua 13 is regarded as a later preface to Joshua 14–19, a number of advances are made. First, the signals in the text can be fundamentally accounted for. Second, Joshua's allocation of the land is placed under YHWH's direction, just as its conquest was (1:1-6). Third, the account of the Mosaic allocation of land to the east-of-Jordan tribes fills a lacuna in chaps. 14–19. Fourth, the claim of the Levites to a substitute for land (13:14, 33) signals a lacuna that will not be filled formally until chap. 21 (cf. similar signals in 14:3-4 and 18:7).

Despite these advances, significant problems remain. First, only the early part of v. 1 (including the LORD's saying: "You are old and advanced in years") is coherent with v. 7. Second, the latter part of v. 1

Main pre-DH: Conquest Narrative
and its expansion

Other pre-DH:
single sideline

Josianic DH:
from the Dtr

(from: "and very much of the land") belongs solely with vv. 2-6 (cf. Smend, "Das Gesetz und die Völker," 497-500). Third, v. 8 (beginning literally "With it") does not follow coherently on v. 7; the half-tribes involved are different. Fourth, the combination of vv. 1* and 7 cannot coherently introduce chap. 14.

Something of the following needs to be envisaged. (i) At the level of the Josianic DH, 12:7-24 was followed by 21:43-45. (ii) The dtr revision, in its national focus, added the exhortation in 1:7-9 and gave Joshua a farewell discourse (chap. 23). (iii) Next, 14:1–21:42 was added, following immediately on 12:24. This insertion was necessarily placed in front of the Josianic conclusion (now 21:43-45). (iv) As part of a following stage, YHWH's command to take possession of the land (Josh 1:1-6) was balanced by a similar command to divide the land among the tribes (Josh 13:1*, 7; note: "this land"). (v) Finally—and given the messiness of the text the complexity is inescapable—13:2-6 with their lead-in from v. 1 were added to stake a claim to a broader expanse of territory and 13:8-33 brought in the interests of the east-of-Jordan tribes (to be correlated with 1:12-18 and later 22:1-6 [7-8]; 22:9-34) and also of the Levites. At some point, Joshua 24 was introduced.

Present-text potential. With exploitable ambiguity, YHWH's address to Joshua gives divine authorization for the distribution of the land by lot, as divine authorization was given for its conquest in 1:1-6. It has a side effect that is seldom emphasized: it denies a historical understanding to the book of Joshua. If Joshua is "old and advanced in years" (13:1), a historian must ask where Israel has been in the long time since the completion of Joshua 1–12 (cf. 23:1). Because it provides no answer, the text demands that it not be held to historical account. Both occupation and distribution by lot are theological structures.

Coupled with v. 1, vv. 2-6 delicately indicate that this divine mandate extends beyond the lands of Joshua 1–12. The distribution by Moses of land to the two and a half tribes east of the Jordan is reported, together (vv. 8-13) and singly (vv. 15-31 [32]). The needs of the Levites are foreshadowed. The way is clear for undivided attention to be focused on the allocation of land to the nine and a half tribes.

71. Verses 2-6 pick up on the anomaly of the "remaining land" and identify territories beyond those featured in Joshua 1–12. The detail is difficult. V. 6 modulates with restrained ambiguity into the allotment commanded by God. The verb for "allot" (in v. 6) is used in this sense in Joshua only at 17:5 and 23:4.

72. Divide "this land" is ordered here; the object, "this land," is not explicit in v. 6 (Heb.; NRSV makes it explicit). The discontinuity between vv. 2-6 and vv. 1 and 7 has been widely noted. The reference to the nine and a half tribes sits oddly with a broad understanding of "this land" (cf. Geshur here and in 13:11, 13).

After the Dtr:	Revision:	Other:
indented and sans serif font	*national focus*	double sideline

them: [9]from Aroer, which is on the edge of the Wadi Arnon, and the town that is in the middle of the valley, and all the tableland from Medeba as far as Dibon; [10]and all the cities of King Sihon of the Amorites, who reigned in Heshbon, as far as the boundary of the Ammonites; [11]and Gilead, and the region of the Geshurites and Maacathites, and all Mount Hermon, and all Bashan to Salecah; [12]all the kingdom of Og in Bashan, who reigned in Ashtaroth and in Edrei (he alone was left of the survivors of the Rephaim); these Moses had defeated and driven out. [13]Yet the Israelites did not drive out the Geshurites or the Maacathites; but Geshur and Maacath live within Israel to this day.[73]

14 To the tribe of Levi alone Moses gave no inheritance; the offerings by fire to the LORD God of Israel are their inheritance, as he said to them.[74]

15 Moses gave an inheritance to the tribe of the Reubenites according to their clans. [16]Their territory was from Aroer, which is on the edge of the Wadi Arnon, and the town that is in the middle of the valley, and all the tableland by Medeba; [17]with Heshbon, and all its towns that are in the tableland; Dibon, and Bamoth-baal, and Beth-baal-meon, [18]and Jahaz, and Kedemoth, and Mephaath, [19]and Kiriathaim, and Sibmah, and Zereth-shahar on the hill of the valley, [20]and Beth-peor, and the slopes of Pisgah, and Beth-jeshimoth, [21]that is, all the towns of the tableland, and all the kingdom of King Sihon of the Amorites, who reigned in Heshbon, whom Moses defeated with the leaders of Midian, Evi and Rekem and Zur and Hur and Reba, as princes of Sihon, who lived in the land. [22]Along with the rest of those they put to death, the Israelites also put to the sword Balaam son of Beor, who practiced divination. [23]And the border of the Reubenites was the Jordan and its banks. This was the inheritance of the Reubenites,

---

73. We have pointed out the possibility that, from the beginning in 1:12-18, the references to the tribes east of the Jordan (Reuben, Gad, and half Manasseh) may be later insertions. As has been noted, the insertion of these traditions here is most probably to be associated with the interest that spurred inclusion of the story in 22:9-34. The allocation of the east-of-Jordan land is appropriately attributed to Moses. As the Hebrew stands, the "with it" of v. 8 depends on the reference to the half-tribe of Manasseh in v. 7. The territory is described globally for all three groups; each group will be dealt with individually in vv. 15-31.

Verse 13 is the first of four notes in Joshua about peoples that the Israelites did not drive out (cf. 15:63; 16:10; and 17:11-13); here the Geshurites and Maacathites. In Judges 1, there is no mention of the east-of-Jordan tribes. Otherwise, these failures are mentioned there: Jerusalem (1:21), Gezer (1:29), and Beth-shean, Taanach, Dor, Ibleam, and Megiddo (1:27-28). Judges 1 mentions others as well (cf. 1:19, 30, 31-32, 33).

74. Towns are allocated to the Levites in 21:1-42. Before this, it is insisted several times that the Levites have no inheritance in Israel (13:14, 33; 14:3, 4; 18:7). Different reasons are given: offerings by fire instead (13:14; cf. LXX); the God of Israel is their inheritance (13:33; omitted from LXX); no reason given (14:3); no portion, but towns and pasture lands instead (14:4); priesthood is their heritage (18:7). The identity and history of the Levites is bedeviled with uncertainty. J. L. McKenzie comments: "the preexilic history of the Levites includes a complex historical process which thus far has defied analysis" (*Dictionary of the Bible*, 505).

Main pre-DH: Conquest Narrative
and its expansion

Other pre-DH:
single sideline

**Josianic DH:
from the Dtr**

according to their families with their towns and villages.[75]

24 Moses gave an inheritance also to the tribe of the Gadites, according to their families. [25]Their territory was Jazer, and all the towns of Gilead, and half the land of the Ammonites, to Aroer, which is east of Rabbah, [26]and from Heshbon to Ramath-mizpeh and Betonim, and from Mahanaim to the territory of Debir, [27]and in the valley Beth-haram, Beth-nimrah, Succoth, and Zaphon, the rest of the kingdom of King Sihon of Heshbon, the Jordan and its banks, as far as the lower end of the Sea of Chinnereth, eastward beyond the Jordan. [28]This is the inheritance of the Gadites according to their clans, with their towns and villages.

29 Moses gave an inheritance to the half-tribe of Manasseh; it was allotted to the half-tribe of the Manassites according to their families. [30]Their territory extended from Mahanaim, through all Bashan, the whole kingdom of King Og of Bashan, and all the settlements of Jair, which are in Bashan, sixty towns, [31]and half of Gilead, and Ashtaroth, and Edrei, the towns of the kingdom of Og in Bashan; these were allotted to the people of Machir son of Manasseh according to their clans—for half the Machirites.

32 These are the inheritances that Moses distributed in the plains of Moab, beyond the Jordan east of Jericho. [33]But to the tribe of Levi Moses gave no inheritance; the LORD God of Israel is their inheritance, as he said to them.[76]

14 These are the inheritances that the Israelites received in the land of Canaan, which the priest Eleazar, and Joshua son of Nun, and the heads of the families of the tribes of the Israelites distributed to them.[77]

---

75. Verses 15-32 provide a detailed identification of the territory of the Reubenites (vv. 15-23), Gadites (vv. 24-28), and the half-tribe of Manasseh (vv. 29-31). It is specified that all three allocations are done by Moses. A summary verse wraps up the issue of inheritances distributed by Moses east of the Jordan (v. 32).

76. Verse 33 provides a repeated comment on the non-inheritance of the Levites. It attributes their lack of an inheritance to Moses, who said that the LORD God of Israel is their inheritance.

77. **Text signals** for Joshua 14–19 in general. (i) A distribution of the land by lot (*gôral*) under the aegis of Eleazar the priest, Joshua son of Nun, and "the heads of the families of the tribes" begins here and is concluded in 19:51. (ii) A new element is introduced at 18:1 with the assembling of the congregation of Israel at Shiloh, with the tent of meeting there and with a note that "the land lay subdued before them." (iii) Shiloh and the tent of meeting are included in 19:51, where the task was "finished." (iv) The language of "subdued" for the land and "finished" for the task echoes Gen 1:28 and 2:1-2 respectively. (v) A new beginning is suggested at 18:1 not only by the assembling of the congregation but also by the beginning of a process of seven lots for the seven remaining tribes. (vi) The lists in chaps. 14–17 are considerably more detailed than those for chaps. 18–19. (vii) For Judah (15:1-63) a clear distinction is made between the tribal boundaries (vv. 1-13) and the names of the towns within them (vv. 20-63). For the other tribes, the two categories tend to be mingled. (viii) While Joshua has the leading role in chaps. 1–12, emphasized by the Dtr, in chaps. 14–19 the priest Eleazar is mentioned before Joshua. (ix) The phrase "heads of the families of the tribes" is rare (Num 32:28; Josh 14:1; 19:51; 21:1), but probably late; its more frequent equivalent, "heads of the ancestral houses"/"heads of families," is a predominantly priestly and late designation. (x) The distribution of the two terms for "tribe" is note-

---

worthy: *šēbeṭ* in chap. 13 (with the exception of 13:15, 24, 29) and *maṭṭeh* in chaps. 14–19 (with the exception of 18:2, 4, 7).

Text-history approach. Several factors are important to a consideration of this block of text (chaps. 14–19). The idea of the tribes gathered at the central sanctuary was favored in the context of an amphictyony. The amphictyony hypothesis was proposed cautiously by Noth, embraced eagerly by followers, and abandoned under the weight of contrary evidence. The location at Shiloh is attractive at first sight; on closer inspection it is problematic. References to the town have a limited distribution; nothing associates them with particularly priestly concerns. Joshua references apart (chaps. 18–22), there are four in Judges (18:31; 21:12, 19, 21), those associated with the ark narrative (1 Sam 4:3, 4, 12), with the disgraced Elide priesthood and the emergence of the prophet Samuel (1 Sam 1–3; 14:3; 1 Kgs 2:27), with the prophet Ahijah (1 Kgs 14:2, 4), with dtr passages in Jeremiah (7:12, 14; 26:6, 9) as well as Ps 78:60 and Jer 41:5. An old tradition about Shiloh as the place of God's dwelling cannot be ruled out (cf. Judg 18:31; Ps 78:60). Respectful use of the name is unlikely after the Jeremiah passages made it a symbol of rejection and destruction. On the other hand, the "tent of meeting," the role of Eleazar the priest, the use of the lot (*gôral*), and the role of the family heads (even if the phrase here is rare—4 occurrences) are clearly priestly concerns. Bethel, Jericho, and Ophrah have been raised by some in relation to a potentially late dating for the chapters; a conquest narrative based on Gilgal and including Jericho, Ai, and Gibeon has to cast an uncertain light over such evidence.

Chaps. 18–19 seem to constitute a separate text within the larger block, accounting for seven allotments, even if the three elements added at 18:1 were later—i.e., the congregation, at Shiloh, and the tent of meeting. It must be said, however, that considerable restructuring of chaps. 14–19 is required, if most of these elements are judged to be additions (i.e., Eleazar, the lot, the heads, the congregation, the tent, Shiloh). The overall emphasis of the block, with detailed attention to Judah, minimal detail for

the far north, and no detail at all for the near north (e.g., Ephraim), adds complexity to the question of date.

These considerations lead toward uncertainty. Alt, in two studies, argued for the use of both premonarchic boundary lists ("System der Stammesgrenzen," 1927) and administrative town lists from the time of Josiah ("Judas Gaue," 1925). Some later studies have argued for periods earlier in the monarchy (cf. Soggin, *Joshua*, 11-12; Nelson, *Joshua*, 185-91). The interplay of the real with the ideal and of the parts with the whole—only some among the factors involved— point to an almost impossibly complex situation. For example: elements complicating the situation are noted by Na'aman, "it is only by combining the tribal reality, the political situation in the time of the United Monarchy and the historiographic objectives of the writers, that the tribal allotments of Joshua 13–19 can be fully understood and historically exploited" (*Borders and Districts*, 117); factors underlying the uncertainty are articulated by Kallai, "the historical period that is found to be reflected in a given description does not necessarily imply the time of its composition or the phases of its formulation" (*Historical Geography of the Bible*, 17); the complexity itself is described by Auld, reflecting on the influence of Alt and Noth, "And nowhere have detailed successor studies evidenced more striking contrariety in their results. Many of these studies testify to the extraordinary literary complexity of Jos. 13–21" (*Joshua, Moses and the Land*, 104).

Our concern is for the textual product rather than the raw material that went into its making. Were the distribution accounts incorporated into the Josianic DH or added afterwards? This can only be determined, insofar as it can be determined at all, by investigation of the text itself and of the context within the Josianic DH. There are no signals within the text of the distribution accounts that suggest attribution to dtr circles and no signals within the Josianic DH that require a distribution account beyond Josh 11:23 (matters not attended to by Auld [*Joshua, Moses and the Land*] and Fritz [*Das Buch Josua*]). Furthermore, of course, there is no preparation in the Josianic DH for

---

Main pre-DH: Conquest Narrative
and its expansion

Other pre-DH:
single sideline

Josianic DH:
from the Dtr

²Their inheritance was by lot, as the LORD had commanded Moses for the nine and one-half tribes. ³For Moses had given an inheritance to the two and one-half tribes beyond the Jordan; but to the Levites he gave no inheritance among them. ⁴For the people of Joseph were two tribes, Manasseh and Ephraim; and no portion was given to the Levites in the land, but only towns to live in, with their pasture lands for

their flocks and herds. ⁵The Israelites did as the LORD commanded Moses; they allotted the land.⁷⁸

---

the presence of either Eleazar or the family heads. Eleazar has no particular standing in the DH; Deut 10:6, widely regarded as late, merely mentions his succession to Aaron. Interestingly, Joshua 1–12 (at the Josianic DH or any level) is notably less systematic than Joshua 14–19, for all of its unevenness.

All things considered, we have opted for a double sideline, indicating incorporation after the Josianic DH, without prejudice to the time of composition. Josh 11:23a* (pre-dtr) has a general statement of Joshua's giving the whole land by tribal allotment. The Josianic Dtr's 21:43-45 speaks of YHWH's gift of the whole land, its possession and settlement, without reference to tribal allotments. Space for chaps. 14–19 is clearly created by Josh 11:23a; it need not be filled by the Josianic Dtr. In fact, at the level of the Josianic DH, chaps. 14–19 seem improbable, given their unequal weighting in favor of Judah to the detriment of the dtr concern for "the whole land."

Present-text potential. The chapters describe the distribution of the whole land to the whole people (with the east-of-Jordan tribes in chap. 13). The distribution is by YHWH's allotment, under the aegis of the priestly, political, and family authority—and with a significant priority given to Judah. For a detailed "literal-structural" reading of Joshua 14–21, see J. Svensson, *Towns and Toponyms*.

14:1-5 gives a general overview of distribution of the land west of the Jordan. Note: it is described as "distribution" not "occupation." The occupation is presumed; it hardly merits a verse (cf. 21:43b, dtr!).

78. **Text signals** in 14:1-5. It needs to be said that 14:1-5 is disappointing as an introduction to a major block of text such as Josh 14:1–19:51 or 21:42. It is not much more coherent than 13:1-7. (i) Lists are usually begun with the demonstrative adjective (this/these) and the appropriate noun (see, for example, Num 1:5; 33:1; Josh 12:1, 7; 15:20; 19:51; 1 Kgs 4:2, 8). Instead, here the demonstrative adjective is followed by a relative clause, as in 13:32 (elsewhere: Num 34:29; 1 Chron 6:16 [NRSV, 6:31]; cf. Zech 1:10; 8:17). (ii) The people of Israel are named first, but as recipients of the inheritances rather than those conducting the distribution. In v. 5, the people of Israel are again to the fore, this time as the agents. (iii) The distribution is carried out by Eleazar the priest, Joshua son of Nun, and the heads of the tribal families (as noted, this precise formula occurs here and in Num 32:28; Josh 19:51; 21:1—i.e., it is used in this context only). (iv) Distribution by the "lot" is mentioned. (v) The tribes are specified as "nine and one-half"; the focus therefore extends to 19:51. (vi) The east-of-Jordan tribes and the Levites are mentioned as having been provided for by Moses (vv. 3-4). (vii) There is no indication of where this distribution is happening.

Text-history approach. The unusual introduction is symbolic of the unusual character of this little passage. Where the participants have come from traditionally is not disclosed; where they are geographically is not mentioned. Their responsibility is extended to the nine and one-half tribes. There is a tension with the introduction in 18:1-10. There is an integration of both introductions in 19:51. The presence of vv. 3-4 favors an understanding in which 13:8-33 is not yet present; it cannot be said to require such an understanding.

Present-text potential. The strange and unsatisfactory aspects noted hardly bring illumination to the meaning of the text. As present text, it is best taken as what it purports to be: an introduction to the distribution of land among the nine and a half tribes.

| After the Dtr: indented and sans serif font | Revision: national focus | Other: double sideline |

6 Then the people of Judah came to Joshua at Gilgal; and Caleb son of Jephunneh the Kenizzite said to him, "You know what the LORD said to Moses the man of God in Kadesh-barnea concerning you and me. [7]I was forty years old when Moses the servant of the LORD sent me from Kadesh-barnea to spy out the land; and I brought him an honest report. [8]But my companions who went up with me made the heart of the people melt; yet I wholeheartedly followed the LORD my God. [9]And Moses swore on that day, saying, 'Surely the land on which your foot has trodden shall be an inheritance for you and your children forever, because you have wholeheartedly followed the LORD my God.' [10]And now, as you see, the LORD has kept me alive, as he said, these forty-five years since the time that the LORD spoke this word to Moses, while Israel was journeying through the wilderness; and here I am today, eighty-five years old. [11]I am still as strong today as I was on the day that Moses sent me; my strength now is as my strength was then, for war, and for going and coming. [12]So now give me this hill country of which the LORD spoke on that day; for you heard on that day how the Anakim were there, with great fortified cities; it may be that the LORD will be with me, and I shall drive them out, as the LORD said."[79]

---

79. **Text signals** in 14:6-15. (i) The people of Judah come to Joshua at Gilgal, but it is Caleb who speaks on behalf of his own interests. (ii) There is no mention of the "lot" until 15:1. (iii) The reference in vv. 6b-9 is to Deut 1:19-39. V. 36, the key verse relating to Caleb, is classified as a later addition there (cf. Num 14:24 which is formulated differently; note also 14:30). (iv) The tentative nature of v. 12 (e.g., "it may

13 Then Joshua blessed him, and gave Hebron to Caleb son of Jephunneh for an inheritance. [14]So Hebron became the inheritance of Caleb son of Jephunneh the Kenizzite to this day, because he wholeheartedly followed the LORD, the God of Israel. [15]Now the name of Hebron formerly

---

be" (*'ûlay*) in regard to the LORD's being with Caleb and driving out the Anakim is inappropriate following (the secondary) Deut 1:36 and the general context of Joshua (cf. chaps. 1–12), to say nothing of Josh 10:36-37. (v) In Josh 11:21, victory over the Anakim is credited to Joshua; in 14:11-12, the victory lies in the future and will be credited to Caleb. (vi) 14:13 places the allocation of Hebron within the gift of Joshua. (vii) 14:15b is identical with 11:23b.

Text-history approach. The capture of Hebron is variously attested in the tradition. According to Josh 10:36-37, Joshua and all Israel took it, wiping out its king and population; also, in Josh 11:21, Joshua wiped out the Anakim there. According to Josh 14:13, Caleb received Hebron with Joshua's blessing (after having asked for the "hill country," v. 12). According to Josh 14:13-14, Caleb received Hebron from Joshua, within the general allocation of land to the tribe of Judah. According to Judg 1:10, Judah "went against" the inhabitants of Hebron (cf. Josh 15:14 for the names). According to Judg 1:20, Hebron was given to Caleb. The substance of these traditions can be reconciled easily enough; the differences of formulation are unsettling. Note that this allocation to Caleb is attributed to Joshua at Gilgal, with no mention of Eleazar, the priest. Caleb volunteers to drive out the enemy from the hill country, implying that this land has not yet been conquered.

It is likely that the Caleb tradition in Josh 14:6-15 is one of those fragments of tradition that survived and needed to be preserved somewhere in the texts of ancient Israel. Its insertion here, before the major allocation to the tribes, would appear to be the least troublesome place to locate it (in our judgment, more

---

Main pre-DH: Conquest Narrative
and its expansion

Other pre-DH:
single sideline

Josianic DH:
from the Dtr

was Kiriath-arba; this Arba was the greatest man among the Anakim. And the land was undisturbed, without war *(Heb.; NRSV, had rest from war)*.[80]

15 The lot for the tribe of the people of Judah according to their families reached southward to the boundary of Edom, to the wilderness of Zin at the farthest south. [2]And their south boundary ran from the end of the Dead Sea, from the bay that faces southward; [3]it goes out southward of the ascent of Akrabbim, passes along to Zin, and goes up south of Kadesh-barnea, along by Hezron, up to Addar, makes a turn

to Karka, [4]passes along to Azmon, goes out by the Wadi of Egypt, and comes to its end at the sea. This shall be your south boundary. [5]And the east boundary is the Dead Sea, to the mouth of the Jordan. And the boundary on the north side runs from the bay of the sea at the mouth of the Jordan; [6]and the boundary goes up to Beth-hoglah, and passes along north of Beth-arabah; and the boundary goes up to the Stone of Bohan, Reuben's son; [7]and the boundary goes up to Debir from the Valley of Achor, and so northward, turning toward Gilgal, which is opposite the ascent of Adummim, which is on the south side of the valley; and the boundary passes along to the waters of En-shemesh, and ends at En-rogel; [8]then the boundary goes up by the valley of the son of Hinnom at the southern slope of the Jebusites (that is, Jerusalem); and the boundary goes up to the top of the mountain that lies over against the valley of Hinnom, on the west, at the northern end of the valley of Rephaim; [9]then the boundary extends from the top of the mountain to the spring of the Waters of Nephtoah, and from there to the towns of Mount Ephron; then the boundary bends around to Baalah (that is, Kiriath-jearim); [10]and the boundary circles west of Baalah to Mount Seir, passes along to the northern slope of Mount Jearim (that is, Chesalon), and goes down to Beth-shemesh, and passes along by Timnah; [11]the boundary goes out to the slope of the hill north of Ekron, then the boundary bends around to Shikkeron, and passes along to Mount Baalah, and goes out to Jabneel; then the boundary comes to an end at the sea. [12]And the west boundary was the Mediterranean with its coast. This

suitable than with 11:23a—against Noth, *DH*, 65, 67). A fairly late insertion is likely (cf. Deut 1:36).

Nelson identifies five passages in Joshua—that he terms "land grant narrative"—for Caleb, here; for Achsah, Josh 15:18-19; for the daughters of Zelophe-had, Josh 17:3-6; for the tribe of Joseph, Josh 17:14-18; and for the tribe of Levi, Josh 21:1-3 (see *Joshua*, 177). The similarity of pattern suggests preserved fragments of tradition, as does the almost verbatim repetition of the Achsah material (from Josh 15:18-19) in Judg 1:14-15.

Present-text potential. Following the prepara-tions for a general distribution of the land to the tribes, the particular situation of Caleb and Hebron is narrated, within the holding to be allocated shortly to Judah. The usual movement of Hebrew narrative is from the general to the particular. In this case, an exception is being made; the move is from the partic-ular (Caleb and Hebron) to the general (the land of the tribe of Judah).

80. As at 11:23b, 14:15b's comment that the land was at peace (*wĕhāʾāreṣ šāqṭâ mimilḥāmâ*) is akin to the comments in Judges (3:11, 30; 5:31; 8:28); it is not to be confused with the dtr concept of "rest" (√*NWḤ*).

| After the Dtr: indented and sans serif font | *Revision: national focus* | Other: double sideline |

is the boundary surrounding the people of Judah according to their families.[81]

13 According to the commandment of the LORD to Joshua, he gave to Caleb son of Jephunneh a portion among the people of Judah, Kiriath-arba, that is, Hebron (Arba was the father of Anak). [14]And Caleb drove out from there the three sons of Anak: Sheshai, Ahiman, and Talmai, the descendants of Anak. [15]From there he went up against the inhabitants of Debir; now the name of Debir formerly was Kiriath-sepher. [16]And Caleb said, "Whoever attacks Kiriath-sepher and takes it, to him I will give my daughter Achsah as wife." [17]Othniel son of Kenaz, the brother of Caleb, took it; and he gave him his daughter Achsah as wife. [18]When she came to him, she urged him to ask her father for a field. As she dismounted from her donkey, Caleb said to her, "What do you wish?" [19]She said to him, "Give me a present; since you have set me in the land of the Negeb, give me springs of water as well." So Caleb gave her the upper springs and the lower springs.[82]

20 This is the inheritance of the tribe of the people of Judah according to their families. [21]The towns belonging to the tribe of the people of Judah in the extreme South, toward the boundary of Edom, were Kabzeel, Eder, Jagur, [22]Kinah, Dimonah, Adadah, [23]Kedesh, Hazor, Ithnan, [24]Ziph, Telem, Bealoth, [25]Hazor-hadattah, Kerioth-hezron (that is, Hazor), [26]Amam, Shema, Moladah, [27]Hazar-gaddah, Heshmon, Beth-pelet, [28]Hazar-shual, Beer-sheba, Biziothiah, [29]Baalah, Iim, Ezem, [30]Eltolad, Chesil, Hormah, [31]Ziklag, Madmannah, Sansannah, [32]Lebaoth, Shilhim, Ain, and Rimmon: in all, twenty-nine towns, with their villages.[83]

33 And in the Lowland, Eshtaol, Zorah, Ashnah, [34]Zanoah, En-gannim, Tappuah, Enam, [35]Jarmuth, Adullam, Socoh, Azekah, [36]Shaaraim, Adithaim, Gederah, Gederothaim: fourteen towns with their villages.

37 Zenan, Hadashah, Migdal-gad, [38]Dilan, Mizpeh, Jokthe-el, [39]Lachish, Bozkath, Eglon, [40]Cabbon, Lahmam, Chitlish, [41]Gederoth, Beth-dagon, Naamah, and Makkedah: sixteen towns with their villages.

42 Libnah, Ether, Ashan, [43]Iphtah, Ashnah, Nezib, [44]Keilah, Achzib, and Mareshah: nine towns with their villages.

45 Ekron, with its dependencies and its villages; [46]from Ekron to the sea, all that were near Ashdod, with their villages.

47 Ashdod, its towns and its villages; Gaza, its towns and its villages; to the Wadi of Egypt, and the Great Sea with its coast.

48 And in the hill country, Shamir, Jattir, Socoh, [49]Dannah, Kiriath-sannah (that is, Debir), [50]Anab, Eshtemoh, Anim, [51]Goshen, Holon, and Giloh: eleven towns with their villages.

52 Arab, Dumah, Eshan, [53]Janim, Beth-tappuah, Aphekah, [54]Humtah, Kiriath-arba (that is, Hebron), and Zior: nine towns with their villages.

---

81. 15:1-12 describes the territory of the tribe of Judah. For the southern boundary of Judah, note the parallel with the description of the southern boundary of Israel (Num 34:3-5).

82. 15:13-19 describes that part of the territory of Judah allocated to Caleb and includes a note about Othniel and Achsah, his wife. With minor variations in the Hebrew, the passage is repeated in Judg 1:11-15.

83. 15:20-62 gives the details of the towns within the allocation of Judah.

Main pre-DH: Conquest Narrative
and its expansion

Other pre-DH:
single sideline

Josianic DH:
from the Dtr

55 Maon, Carmel, Ziph, Juttah, [56]Jezreel, Jokdeam, Zanoah, [57]Kain, Gibeah, and Timnah: ten towns with their villages.

58 Halhul, Beth-zur, Gedor, [59]Maarath, Beth-anoth, and Eltekon: six towns with their villages.

60 Kiriath-baal (that is, Kiriath-jearim), and Rabbah: two towns with their villages.

61 In the wilderness, Beth-arabah, Middin, Secacah, [62]Nibshan, the City of Salt, and En-gedi: six towns with their villages.

63 But the people of Judah could not drive out the Jebusites, the inhabitants of Jerusalem; so the Jebusites live with the people of Judah in Jerusalem to this day.[84]

16 The allotment of the Josephites went from the Jordan by Jericho, east of the waters of Jericho, into the wilderness, going up from Jericho into the hill country to Bethel; [2]then going from Bethel to Luz, it passes along to Ataroth, the territory of the Archites; [3]then it goes down westward to the territory of the Japhletites, as far as the territory of Lower Beth-horon, then to Gezer, and it ends at the sea.[85]

4 The Josephites—Manasseh and Ephraim—received their inheritance.

5 The territory of the Ephraimites by their families was as follows: the boundary of their inheritance on the east was Ataroth-addar as far as Upper Beth-horon, [6]and the boundary goes from there to the sea; on the north is Michmethath; then on the east the boundary makes a turn toward Taanath-shiloh, and passes along beyond it on the east to Janoah, [7]then it goes down from Janoah to Ataroth and to Naarah, and touches Jericho, ending at the Jordan. [8]From Tappuah the boundary goes westward to the Wadi Kanah, and ends at the sea. Such is the inheritance of the tribe of the Ephraimites by their families, [9]with the towns that were set apart for the Ephraimites within the inheritance of the Manassites, all those towns with their villages. [10]They did not, however, drive out the Canaanites who lived in Gezer: so the Canaanites have lived within Ephraim to this day but have been made to do forced labor.[86]

17 Then allotment was made to the tribe of Manasseh, for he was the firstborn of Joseph. To Machir the firstborn of Manasseh, the father of Gilead, were allotted Gilead and Bashan, because he was a warrior. [2]And allotments were made to the rest of the tribe of Manasseh, by their families, Abiezer, Helek, Asriel, Shechem, Hepher, and Shemida; these were the male descendants of Manasseh son of Joseph, by their families.[87]

---

84. 15:63 notes that the people of Judah were unable to capture Jerusalem. This is repeated in Judg 1:21, but replacing Judah with Benjamin. See the note above on 13:13.

85. 16:1—17:18 concerns the tribe of Joseph, subdivided into Ephraim and Manasseh. 16:1-3 gives a global description of the territory, with an introduction in v. 4 to the tribes of Ephraim and Manasseh.

86. 16:5-10 spells out the details for the tribe of Ephraim. V. 10 notes their failure with regard to Gezer (cf. Judg 1:29, and the note above on 13:13).

87. 17:1-13 gives the details for the tribe of Manasseh. Vv. 1-2 duplicate some matters relating to the east-of-Jordan tribes (cf. 13:29-31). Vv. 3-6 treat the case of the daughters of Zelophehad; the issue of their marriages and inheritance is regulated by Moses in Num 36:1-12. Vv. 7-10 provide details with regard to Manasseh.

| After the Dtr: indented and sans serif font | *Revision: national focus* | Other: double sideline |

3 Now Zelophehad son of Hepher son of Gilead son of Machir son of Manasseh had no sons, but only daughters; and these are the names of his daughters: Mahlah, Noah, Hoglah, Milcah, and Tirzah. [4]They came before the priest Eleazar and Joshua son of Nun and the leaders, and said, "The LORD commanded Moses to give us an inheritance along with our male kin." So according to the commandment of the LORD he gave them an inheritance among the kinsmen of their father. [5]Thus there fell to Manasseh ten portions, besides the land of Gilead and Bashan, which is on the other side of the Jordan, [6]because the daughters of Manasseh received an inheritance along with his sons. The land of Gilead was allotted to the rest of the Manassites.

7 The territory of Manasseh reached from Asher to Michmethath, which is east of Shechem; then the boundary goes along southward to the inhabitants of En-tappuah. [8]The land of Tappuah belonged to Manasseh, but the town of Tappuah on the boundary of Manasseh belonged to the Ephraimites. [9]Then the boundary went down to the Wadi Kanah. The towns here, to the south of the wadi, among the towns of Manasseh, belong to Ephraim. Then the boundary of Manasseh goes along the north side of the wadi and ends at the sea. [10]The land to the south is Ephraim's and that to the north is Manasseh's, with the sea forming its boundary; on the north Asher is reached, and on the east Issachar. [11]Within Issachar and Asher, Manasseh had Beth-shean and its villages, Ibleam and its villages, the inhabitants of Dor and its villages, the inhabitants of En-dor and its villages, the inhabitants of Taanach and its villages, and the inhabitants of Megiddo and its vil-

lages (the third is Naphath). [12]Yet the Manassites could not take possession of those towns; but the Canaanites continued to live in that land. [13]But when the Israelites grew strong, they put the Canaanites to forced labor, but did not utterly drive them out.[88]

14 The tribe of Joseph spoke to Joshua, saying, "Why have you given me but one lot and one portion as an inheritance, since we are a numerous people, whom all along the LORD has blessed?" [15]And Joshua said to them, "If you are a numerous people, go up to the forest, and clear ground there for yourselves in the land of the Perizzites and the Rephaim, since the hill country of Ephraim is too narrow for you." [16]The tribe of Joseph said, "The hill country is not enough for us; yet all the Canaanites who live in the plain have chariots of iron, both those in Beth-shean and its villages and those in the Valley of Jezreel." [17]Then Joshua said to the house of Joseph, to Ephraim and Manasseh, "You are indeed a numerous people, and have great power; you shall not have one lot only, [18]but the hill country shall be yours, for though it is a forest, you shall clear it and possess it to its farthest borders; for you shall drive out the Canaanites, though they have chariots of iron, and though they are strong."[89]

---

88. 17:11-13 points to the difficulty the Israelites had with the city-dwellers in the plains; here the tribe of Manasseh could not take the five major towns in their territory (Beth-shean, Ibleam, Dor, Taanach, and Megiddo; cf. Judg 1:27-28, and the note above on 13:13).

89. 17:14-18 deals with the claim of the tribe of Joseph to an extra allocation. V. 18 specifies that the people themselves shall clear and occupy the land militarily.

Main pre-DH: Conquest Narrative
and its expansion   Other pre-DH:
single sideline   **Josianic DH:
from the Dtr**

18 Then the whole congregation of the Israelites assembled at Shiloh, and set up the tent of meeting there. The land lay subdued before them.[90]

2 There remained among the Israelites seven tribes whose inheritance had not yet been apportioned. [3]So Joshua said to the Israelites, "How long will you be slack about going in and taking possession of the land that the LORD, the God of your ancestors, has given you? [4]Provide three men from each tribe, and I will send them out that they may begin to go throughout the land, writing a description of it with a view to their inheritances. Then come back to me.

[5]They shall divide it into seven portions, Judah continuing in its territory on the south, and the house of Joseph in their territory on the north. [6]You shall describe the land in seven divisions and bring the description here to me; and I will cast lots for you here before the LORD our God. [7]The Levites have no portion among you, for the priesthood of the LORD is their heritage; and Gad and Reuben and the half-tribe of Manasseh have received their inheritance beyond the Jordan eastward, which Moses the servant of the LORD gave them."[91]

8 So the men started on their way; and Joshua charged those who went to write the description of the land, saying, "Go throughout the land and write a description of it, and come back to me; and I will cast lots for you here before the LORD in Shiloh." [9]So the men went and traversed the land and set down in a book a description of it by towns in seven divisions; then they came back to Joshua in the camp at Shiloh, [10]and Joshua cast lots for them in Shiloh before the LORD; and there Joshua apportioned the land to the Israelites, to each a portion.

11 The lot of the tribe of Benjamin according to its families came up, and the territory allotted to it fell between the tribe of Judah and the tribe of Joseph. [12]On the

---

90. There is a change of gear in the text's reporting here. 14:1 introduced Eleazar, Joshua, and the heads of the families as distributors of the land; no place was specified. In that session, the territories of Judah and Joseph (Ephraim and Manasseh) were determined, using a variety of traditions.

18:1, in language strongly reminiscent of the Priestly tradition, has a congregation of Israelites assemble at Shiloh. The land is described as "subdued" (*nikběšâ*; cf. Gen 1:28). There will be no further reference to the failure to drive others out (not until the national focus within the dtr revision in 23:13). 19:51 will indicate that the distributors in this session are the same Eleazar, Joshua, and the heads of the families. However, they are said to have allocated the inheritances by lot (applicable only after 18:1) at the tent of meeting (a Priestly term). After 18:1, the pattern changes markedly: the lot (*gôrāl*) is regularly used in conjunction with a verb (come out or come up; cf. 18:11; 19:1, 10, 17, 24, 32, 40; otherwise only 16:1); the information on territory and towns is usually sketchier; the pattern is more regular.

What we may refer to as the Shiloh session, is marked by reference to the lot. Allocations by lot are made for seven tribes: Benjamin, Simeon, Zebulun, Issachar, Asher, Naphtali, and Dan.

91. 18:2-10 gives a general description of the preliminaries involved: a survey of the land, its division into seven, and the allocation of these seven parts by lot. The accusation of Israel's being "slack about going in and taking possession of the land" (18:3) suggests a military and not a sacral understanding. The territories are supposed to lie between Judah in the south and Joseph in the north (v. 5)—scarcely the case. V. 7 refers again to the Levites and the two and one-half tribes.

After the Dtr:
indented and sans serif font

Revision:
national focus

Other:
double sideline

north side their boundary began at the Jordan; then the boundary goes up to the slope of Jericho on the north, then up through the hill country westward; and it ends at the wilderness of Beth-aven. [13]From there the boundary passes along southward in the direction of Luz, to the slope of Luz (that is, Bethel), then the boundary goes down to Ataroth-addar, on the mountain that lies south of Lower Beth-horon. [14]Then the boundary goes in another direction, turning on the western side southward from the mountain that lies to the south, opposite Beth-horon, and it ends at Kiriath-baal (that is, Kiriath-jearim), a town belonging to the tribe of Judah. This forms the western side. [15]The southern side begins at the outskirts of Kiriath-jearim; and the boundary goes from there to Ephron, to the spring of the Waters of Nephtoah; [16]then the boundary goes down to the border of the mountain that overlooks the valley of the son of Hinnom, which is at the north end of the valley of Rephaim; and it then goes down the valley of Hinnom, south of the slope of the Jebusites, and downward to En-rogel; [17]then it bends in a northerly direction going on to En-shemesh, and from there goes to Geliloth, which is opposite the ascent of Adummim; then it goes down to the Stone of Bohan, Reuben's son; [18]and passing on to the north of the slope of Beth-arabah it goes down to the Arabah; [19]then the boundary passes on to the north of the slope of Beth-hoglah; and the boundary ends at the northern bay of the Dead Sea, at the south end of the Jordan: this is the southern border. [20]The Jordan forms its boundary on the eastern side. This is the inheritance of the tribe of Benjamin, according to its families, boundary by boundary all around.[92]

21 Now the towns of the tribe of Benjamin according to their families were Jericho, Beth-hoglah, Emek-keziz, [22]Beth-arabah, Zemaraim, Bethel, [23]Avvim, Parah, Ophrah, [24]Chephar-ammoni, Ophni, and Geba—twelve towns with their villages: [25]Gibeon, Ramah, Beeroth, [26]Mizpeh, Chephirah, Mozah, [27]Rekem, Irpeel, Taralah, [28]Zela, Haeleph, Jebus (that is, Jerusalem), Gibeah and Kiriath-jearim—fourteen towns with their villages. This is the inheritance of the tribe of Benjamin according to its families.

19 The second lot came out for Simeon, for the tribe of Simeon, according to its families; its inheritance lay within the inheritance of the tribe of Judah. [2]It had for its inheritance Beer-sheba, Sheba, Moladah, [3]Hazar-shual, Balah, Ezem, [4]Eltolad, Bethul, Hormah, [5]Ziklag, Beth-marcaboth, Hazar-susah, [6]Beth-lebaoth, and Sharuhen—thirteen towns with their villages; [7]Ain, Rimmon, Ether, and Ashan—four towns with their villages; [8]together with all the villages all around these towns as far as Baalath-beer, Ramah of the Negeb. This was the inheritance of the tribe of Simeon according to its families. [9]The inheritance of the tribe of Simeon formed part of the territory of Judah; because the portion of the tribe of Judah was too large for them, the tribe of

---

92. 18:11-28 reports the first lot being for the tribe of Benjamin; the details of its towns are given in vv. 21-28.

Main pre-DH: Conquest Narrative
and its expansion

Other pre-DH:
single sideline

Josianic DH:
from the Dtr

Simeon obtained an inheritance within their inheritance.[93]

10 The third lot came up for the tribe of Zebulun, according to its families. The boundary of its inheritance reached as far as Sarid; [11]then its boundary goes up westward, and on to Maralah, and touches Dabbesheth, then the wadi that is east of Jokneam; [12]from Sarid it goes in the other direction eastward toward the sunrise to the boundary of Chisloth-tabor; from there it goes to Daberath, then up to Japhia; [13]from there it passes along on the east toward the sunrise to Gath-hepher, to Eth-kazin, and going on to Rimmon it bends toward Neah; [14]then on the north the boundary makes a turn to Hannathon, and it ends at the valley of Iphtah-el; [15]and Kattath, Nahalal, Shimron, Idalah, and Bethlehem—twelve towns with their villages. [16]This is the inheritance of the tribe of Zebulun, according to its families—these towns with their villages.[94]

17 The fourth lot came out for Issachar, for the tribe of Issachar, according to its families. [18]Its territory included Jezreel, Chesulloth, Shunem, [19]Hapharaim, Shion, Anaharath, [20]Rabbith, Kishion, Ebez, [21]Remeth, En-gannim, En-haddah, Beth-pazzez; [22]the boundary also touches Tabor, Shahazumah, and Beth-shemesh, and its boundary ends at the Jordan—sixteen towns with their villages. [23]This is the inher-

itance of the tribe of Issachar, according to its families—the towns with their villages.[95]

24 The fifth lot came out for the tribe of Asher according to its families. [25]Its boundary included Helkath, Hali, Beten, Achshaph, [26]Allammelech, Amad, and Mishal; on the west it touches Carmel and Shihor-libnath, [27]then it turns eastward, goes to Beth-dagon, and touches Zebulun and the valley of Iphtah-el northward to Beth-emek and Neiel; then it continues in the north to Cabul, [28]Ebron, Rehob, Hammon, Kanah, as far as Sidon the Great; [29]then the boundary turns to Ramah, reaching to the fortified city of Tyre; then the boundary turns to Hosah, and it ends at the sea; Mahalab, Achzib, [30]Ummah, Aphek, and Rehob—twenty-two towns with their villages. [31]This is the inheritance of the tribe of Asher according to its families—these towns with their villages.[96]

32 The sixth lot came out for the tribe of Naphtali, for the tribe of Naphtali, according to its families. [33]And its boundary ran from Heleph, from the oak in Zaanannim, and Adami-nekeb, and Jabneel, as far as Lakkum; and it ended at the Jordan; [34]then the boundary turns westward to Aznoth-tabor, and goes from there to Hukkok, touching Zebulun at the south, and Asher on the west, and Judah on the east at the Jordan. [35]The fortified towns are Ziddim, Zer, Hammath, Rakkath, Chinnereth, [36]Adamah, Ramah, Hazor, [37]Kedesh, Edrei, En-hazor, [38]Iron, Migdal-el, Horem, Beth-anath, and Beth-shemesh—

---

93. 19:1-9 reports the second lot being for the tribe of Simeon. Its territory is simply described as being within Judah (vv. 1 and 9), sandwiching the details of its towns.

94. 19:10-16 reports the third lot being for the tribe of Zebulun, territory and towns.

95. 19:17-23 reports the fourth lot being for the tribe of Issachar, its territory and towns.

96. 19:24-31 reports the fifth lot being for the tribe of Asher, its territory and towns.

After the Dtr:	Revision:	Other:
indented and sans serif font	*national focus*	double sideline

nineteen towns with their villages. [39]This is the inheritance of the tribe of Naphtali according to its families—the towns with their villages.[97]

40 The seventh lot came out for the tribe of Dan, according to its families. [41]The territory of its inheritance included Zorah, Eshtaol, Ir-shemesh, [42]Shaalabbin, Aijalon, Ithlah, [43]Elon, Timnah, Ekron, [44]Eltekeh, Gibbethon, Baalath, [45]Jehud, Bene-berak, Gath-rimmon, [46]Me-jarkon, and Rakkon at the border opposite Joppa. [47]When the territory of the Danites was lost to them, the Danites went up and fought against Leshem, and after capturing it and putting it to the sword, they took possession of it and settled in it, calling Leshem, Dan, after their ancestor Dan. [48]This is the inheritance of the tribe of Dan, according to their families—these towns with their villages.[98]

49 When they had finished distributing the several territories of the land as inheritances, the Israelites gave an inheritance among them to Joshua son of Nun. [50]By command of the LORD they gave him the town that he asked for, Timnath-serah in the hill country of Ephraim; he rebuilt the town, and settled in it.[99]

51 These are the inheritances that the priest Eleazar and Joshua son of Nun and the heads of the families of the tribes of the Israelites distributed by lot at Shiloh before the LORD, at the entrance of the tent of meeting. So they finished dividing the land.[100]

20 Then the LORD spoke to Joshua, saying, [2]"Say to the Israelites, 'Appoint the cities of refuge, of which I spoke to you through Moses, [3]so that anyone who kills a person without intent or by mistake may flee there; they shall be for you a refuge from the avenger of blood. [4]The slayer shall flee to one of these cities and shall stand at the entrance of the gate of the city, and explain the case to the elders of that city; then the fugitive shall be taken into the city, and given a place, and shall remain with them. [5]And if the avenger of blood is in pursuit, they shall not give up the slayer, because the neighbor was killed by mistake, there having been no enmity between them before. [6]The slayer shall remain in that city until there is a trial before the congregation, until the death of the one who is high priest at the time: then the slayer may return home, to the town in which the deed was done.'"[100]

---

97. 19:32-39 reports the sixth lot being for the tribe of Naphtali, its territory and towns.

98. 19:40-48 reports the seventh lot being for the tribe of Dan, its territory and towns.

99. 19:49-50 reports the gift by the Israelites of a particular inheritance for Joshua, "the town that he asked for, Timnath-serah" (v. 50). The lot has been replaced by the "command of the LORD" (v. 50).

100. 19:51 is a notice concluding the allocation by lot at Shiloh, presided over by Eleazar, Joshua, and the heads of the families "at the entrance of the tent of meeting" (v. 51).

101. 20:1-9 attends to a further geographical issue: the establishment of the cities of refuge. In a vengeance system of law, where it is the avenger's duty to kill a killer, there is little opportunity for adjudication between intentional and unintentional killing, between murder and manslaughter. The theory of the cities of refuge is to create such an opportunity; a killer can flee to the nearest city of refuge and be safe there until adjudication takes place (cf. Exod 21:12-14; Deut 19:1-7 [8-10]; Num 35:9-15).

Main pre-DH: Conquest Narrative
and its expansion

Other pre-DH:
single sideline

Josianic DH:
from the Dtr

7 So they set apart Kedesh in Galilee in the hill country of Naphtali, and Shechem in the hill country of Ephraim, and Kiriath-arba (that is, Hebron) in the hill country of Judah. [8]And beyond the Jordan east of Jericho, they appointed Bezer in the wilderness on the tableland, from the tribe of Reuben, and Ramoth in Gilead, from the tribe of Gad, and Golan in Bashan, from the tribe of Manasseh. [9]These were the cities designated for all the Israelites, and for the aliens residing among them, that anyone who killed a person without intent could flee there, so as not to die by the hand of the avenger of blood, until there was a trial before the congregation.

21 Then the heads of the families of the Levites came to the priest Eleazar and to Joshua son of Nun and to the heads of the families of the tribes of the Israelites; [2]they said to them at Shiloh in the land of Canaan, "The LORD commanded through Moses that we be given towns to live in, along with their pasture lands for our livestock." [3]So by command of the LORD the Israelites gave to the Levites the following

towns and pasture lands out of their inheritance.[102]

4 The lot came out for the families of the Kohathites. So those Levites who were descendants of Aaron the priest received by lot thirteen towns from the tribes of Judah, Simeon, and Benjamin.

5 The rest of the Kohathites received by lot ten towns from the families of the tribe of Ephraim, from the tribe of Dan, and the half-tribe of Manasseh.

6 The Gershonites received by lot thirteen towns from the families of the tribe of Issachar, from the tribe of Asher, from the tribe of Naphtali, and from the half-tribe of Manasseh in Bashan.

7 The Merarites according to their families received twelve towns from the tribe of Reuben, the tribe of Gad, and the tribe of Zebulun.

8 These towns and their pasture lands the Israelites gave by lot to the Levites, as the LORD had commanded through Moses.

According to vv. 1-6, an initial examination is made by the elders of the city (v. 4), followed by either a trial before the congregation (cf. Num 35:12) or an amnesty on the death of the high priest (post-exilic). For the textual revisions in this material, see Nelson, *Joshua*, 226-31. Vv. 7-8 name six such cities, three east of the Jordan (cf. Deut 4:41-43) and three west of it. As noted at Deut 4:43, the dtr law is in Deut 19:1-3, 8-10 and while mentioning six cities gives no names or geographical specifics. A late addition here is likely.

102. 21:1-42 deals with a further issue associated with the allocation of tribal territory: the allocation of towns for the Levites. As has been repeated several times (Josh 13:14, 33; 14:3-4; 18:7), the Levites are not restricted to a tribal territory in Israel. Here they are appointed towns throughout the territory of Israel (as promised in 14:4b).

An association with the previous list of cities of refuge is noted; "the city of refuge was a kind of chief city of the district" (cf. vv. 13, 21, 27, 32, and 38; Soggin, *Joshua*, 204). Attribution to the second half of the tenth century has been argued (Albright, Cazelles, Haran, de Vaux, and Mazar); others suggest the time of Josiah's reform (Alt, Noth). Soggin advocates the desire for restoration by a reforming king (*Joshua*, 203-4). Nelson, on the other hand, describes the text as having "the earmarks of a scholarly imitation rather than an actual archival source" (*Joshua*, 237).

After the Dtr:	Revision:	Other:
indented and sans serif font	*national focus*	double sideline

9 Out of the tribe of Judah and the tribe of Simeon they gave the following towns mentioned by name, [10]which went to the descendants of Aaron, one of the families of the Kohathites who belonged to the Levites, since the lot fell to them first. [11]They gave them Kiriath-arba (Arba being the father of Anak), that is Hebron, in the hill country of Judah, along with the pasture lands around it. [12]But the fields of the town and its villages had been given to Caleb son of Jephunneh as his holding.

13 To the descendants of Aaron the priest they gave Hebron, the city of refuge for the slayer, with its pasture lands, Libnah with its pasture lands, [14]Jattir with its pasture lands, Eshtemoa with its pasture lands, [15]Holon with its pasture lands, Debir with its pasture lands, [16]Ain with its pasture lands, Juttah with its pasture lands, and Beth-shemesh with its pasture lands—nine towns out of these two tribes. [17]Out of the tribe of Benjamin: Gibeon with its pasture lands, Geba with its pasture lands, [18]Anathoth with its pasture lands, and Almon with its pasture lands—four towns. [19]The towns of the descendants of Aaron—the priests— were thirteen in all, with their pasture lands.

20 As to the rest of the Kohathites belonging to the Kohathite families of the Levites, the towns allotted to them were out of the tribe of Ephraim. [21]To them were given Shechem, the city of refuge for the slayer, with its pasture lands in the hill country of Ephraim, Gezer with its pasture lands, [22]Kibzaim with its pasture lands, and Beth-horon with its pasture lands—four towns. [23]Out of the tribe of Dan: Elteke with its pasture lands, Gibbethon with its pasture lands, [24]Aijalon with its pasture lands, Gath-rimmon with its pasture lands—four towns.

[25]Out of the half-tribe of Manasseh: Taanach with its pasture lands, and Gath-rimmon with its pasture lands—two towns. [26]The towns of the families of the rest of the Kohathites were ten in all, with their pasture lands.

27 To the Gershonites, one of the families of the Levites, were given out of the half-tribe of Manasseh, Golan in Bashan with its pasture lands, the city of refuge for the slayer, and Beeshterah with its pasture lands—two towns. [28]Out of the tribe of Issachar: Kishion with its pasture lands, Daberath with its pasture lands, [29]Jarmuth with its pasture lands, En-gannim with its pasture lands—four towns. [30]Out of the tribe of Asher: Mishal with its pasture lands, Abdon with its pasture lands, [31]Helkath with its pasture lands, and Rehob with its pasture lands—four towns. [32]Out of the tribe of Naphtali: Kedesh in Galilee with its pasture lands, the city of refuge for the slayer, Hammoth-dor with its pasture lands, and Kartan with its pasture lands—three towns. [33]The towns of the several families of the Gershonites were in all thirteen, with their pasture lands.

34 To the rest of the Levites—the Merarite families—were given out of the tribe of Zebulun: Jokneam with its pasture lands, Kartah with its pasture lands, [35]Dimnah with its pasture lands, Nahalal with its pasture lands—four towns. [36]Out of the tribe of Reuben: Bezer with its pasture lands, Jahzah with its pasture lands, [37]Kedemoth with its pasture lands, and Mephaath with its pasture lands—four towns. [38]Out of the tribe of Gad: Ramoth in Gilead with its pasture lands, the city of refuge for the slayer, Mahanaim with its pasture lands, [39]Heshbon with its pasture lands, Jazer with its

---

pasture lands—four towns in all. ⁴⁰As for the towns of the several Merarite families, that is, the remainder of the families of the Levites, those allotted to them were twelve in all.

41 The towns of the Levites within the holdings of the Israelites were in all forty-eight towns with their pasture lands. ⁴²Each of these towns had its pasture lands around it; so it was with all these towns.

43 Thus the LORD gave to Israel all the land that he swore to their ancestors that he would give them; and having taken possession of it, they settled there. ⁴⁴And the LORD gave them rest on every side just as he had sworn to their ancestors; not one of all their enemies had withstood them, for the LORD had given all their enemies into their hands. ⁴⁵Not one of all the good promises that the LORD had made to the house of Israel had failed; all came to pass.[103]

---

103. 21:43-45 is, in our judgment, the Josianic Dtr's conclusion. At the level of the Josianic DH there was no assembly, therefore no dismissal. As can be seen from the formatting, we regard 22:1-34; 23:1-13; and 24:1-28, 32-33 as later additions to the book. We attribute 24:29-31 to the Josianic Dtr, closing off the life of Joshua and his generation.

Text signals in 21:43-45. (i) The land is described as what the LORD swore to give. It is a characteristically dtr phrase. (ii) The language of "rest on every side" is also characteristically dtr (cf. Deut 12:10; Josh 23:1; 2 Sam 7:1; 1 Kgs 5:4 [Heb., v. 18]; note also Deut 25:19; and Judg 2:14; 8:34; 1 Sam 12:11; and 2 Sam 7:11). (iii) The language of God's swearing to the ancestors is overwhelmingly dtr. (iv) The theme of the LORD giving Israel's enemies into their hands is rare and mainly dtr (cf. Deut 21:10; also Deut 20:14; 28:7, 25; and Judg 3:28; 1 Sam 24:4 [Heb., v. 5]). (v) The language of not one thing/promise/word failing/falling is

22 Then Joshua summoned the Reubenites, the Gadites, and the half-tribe of Manasseh, ²and said to them, "You have observed all that Moses the servant of the

---

mainly dtr (cf. Josh 23:14; 1 Kgs 8:56; 2 Kgs 10:10; also 1 Sam 3:19).

Text-history approach. The text signals in 21:43-45 point to dtr origin. The question is: where do the verses come from in the range of dtr activity? The Josianic Dtr? The later dtr revisers? Even later dtr imitators? Noth himself comments of 21:43–22:6 that it is "so close to Dtr. in style that one could attribute it to Dtr. himself" except that it comes after Josh 11:23aβ and anticipates passages like Josh 23:9b, 14b (*DH*, 67).

Josh 11:23aβ says: "and Joshua gave it for an inheritance to Israel according to their tribal allotments." We have attributed this to the expansion of the Conquest Narrative, therefore pre-dtr. For Noth, it was the work of the Dtr. Noth is well aware of its brevity: "Dtr. has already (Josh. 11:23aβ) mentioned the distribution of the conquered area among the tribes—briefly, to be sure, but in terms suggesting that he has finished with the topic" (*DH*, 66). The suggestion that the Dtr has "finished with the topic" comes from Noth, not the text; we do not share it with him.

Even in Noth's attribution of the text, where the whole of 11:23 goes to the Dtr, the verse can be understood as a general statement, allowing of some unfolding. This is a common technique in Hebrew narrative. It is what allows for the insertion of most of chaps. 13–21. In our attribution of the text, where only a qualifying clause in 11:23a is attributed to the Dtr, the sequence from 11:23 to 21:43-45 is fully acceptable. In 11:23, it is reported that Joshua took the whole land, according to all that the LORD had spoken to Moses, and he distributed the land to Israel by allotment. In 21:43-45, the report is raised to a higher level. No longer is it Joshua who took the land; it is YHWH who gave to Israel the land, qualified as the land YHWH had sworn to give them. Further, possession and settlement are specified, together with rest

---

| After the Dtr: indented and sans serif font | Revision: national focus | Other: double sideline |

LORD commanded you, and have obeyed me in all that I have commanded you; ³you have not forsaken your kindred these many days, down to this day, but have been careful to keep the charge of the LORD your God. ⁴And now the LORD your God has given rest to your kindred, as he promised them; therefore turn and go to your tents in the land where your possession lies, which Moses the servant of the LORD gave you on the other side of the Jordan." ⁵Take good care to observe the commandment and instruction that Moses the servant of the

LORD commanded you, to love the LORD your God, to walk in all his ways, to keep his commandments, and to hold fast to him, and to serve him with all your heart and with all your soul. ⁶So Joshua blessed them and sent them away, and they went to their tents.¹⁰⁴

---

from surrounding enemies. This last clause is in dtr terminology; at 11:23b, it is not. The reference to the fulfillment of God's promises is made in 21:45. It is absent from 11:23. Of course for Noth it is present in 23:14b, for example. Since Smend's study ("Das Gesetz und die Völker"), we accept that Josh 23:1-16 is from a later dtr revision (our national focus).

At the level of the Josianic DH, 21:43-45 is the final statement about the task that YHWH commissioned Joshua to undertake in Josh 1:1-6. Joshua was to bring the people into the land (1:2). YHWH would give them the land, as promised to Moses, in its full extent, with no one able to withstand them (1:3-6). Here, 21:43-45 reports the fulfillment of these promises. What YHWH said YHWH would do YHWH has done. "All came to pass" (21:45b; cf. 23:14b).

Present-text potential. What Josh 21:43-45 achieves is to bring to an appropriate close a task that began as far back as Deut 1:34-39. There God spoke of a future generation, at that time still little children (1:39), who would enter and take possession of the land. Here the great narrative sweep of that journey is drawn to a close. Joshua's generation has entered the land; they have taken possession and settled there (v. 43). They have been given rest from their enemies (v. 44). Nothing that God promised them has failed (v. 45).

104. **Text signals** in 22:1-34. (i) There is a change from the third-person overarching narrative comment of 21:43-45 to the report of second-person address by Joshua in 22:1-6. (ii) 22:1-6 has Joshua dismiss the Reubenites, the Gadites, and the half-tribe of Manasseh, sending them back east of the Jordan with his blessing, after the commitment of 1:12-18 has been honored. (iii) In v. 1, the term for the half "tribe" of Manasseh is *maṭṭeh*; the significant differences in the distribution of *maṭṭeh* and *šēbeṭ* have already been noted (see the introduction to this book). All told, there are eight occurrences of *maṭṭeh*: Num 34:14; Josh 13:29b; 21:5, 6, 27; 22:1; 1 Chron 6:56; 12:32. In 22:9-34, *šēbeṭ* is used exclusively (22:9, 10, 11, 13, 15, 21; also in 22:7). (iv) In v. 4a, the language of "rest" reflects dtr terminology. (v) In v. 4b, the term for your "possession" is rare, invariably late, and usually priestly; one third of the occurrences are in this chapter (cf. Gen 17:8; 36:43; Lev 14:34; 25:24; Num 35:28; Josh 22:4, 9, 19). (vi) In v. 5, the emphasis on the steadfast observance of the law is obvious, adumbrated earlier in vv. 2-3. (vii) The description of Moses as "the servant of the LORD" (vv. 2, 4, 5) is favored by late dtr editing. (viii) As noted, 22:7 uses the term *šēbeṭ* for tribe. (ix) V. 8 is contrary to the portrayal of the total ban (cf. for Jericho, 6:21), but in line with the policy enunciated for Ai (Josh 8:2; cf. Deut 2:35; 3:7). There is a marked parallel with Exod 12:35-36, with gold, silver, and garments in common. (x) V. 9 opens with the naming of the two and a half tribes, as in 22:1, not using the pronouns as in vv. 2-8 (but *šēbeṭ* is used for Manasseh). (xi) Central to the story of vv. 9-34 is the fear that one day these east-of-Jordan tribes will face the accusation, "You have no portion in the LORD"

Main pre-DH: Conquest Narrative	Other pre-DH:	**Josianic DH:**
and its expansion	single sideline	**from the Dtr**

(vv. 25-27; the phrase is found only here). (xii) The term for treachery (*ma'al*, see vv. 16, 20, 22, 31; cf. Josh 7:1) is priestly or later. (xiii) The term "tabernacle" (*miškan*) is almost exclusive to priestly traditions (cf. 2 Sam 7:6); it occurs here (vv. 19, 29) and nowhere else in the book of Joshua. (xiv) Reference to Peor as an example of sin is found in the DH only at the secondary Deut 4:3 (otherwise, cf. esp. Num 25:3, 5, 18). (xv) The term "congregation of Israel" (vv. 18, 20) is elsewhere priestly or later (cf. 1 Kgs 8:5). (xvi) The concern to specify the offerings (vv. 23, 26, 28, 29) is priestly rather than dtr.

Text-history approach. It seems likely to us that a tradition concerning "the great altar" (vv. 9-34) was already formulated and has been introduced here by 22:1-6, with the added concern of vv. 7-8. The formulation of the tradition was primarily priestly; its introduction drew on a number of characteristics of overall dtr thought and language.

As we have noted, there is a strong likelihood that the traditions dealing with the east-of-Jordan tribes have been incorporated quite late into the DH text.

The core of 22:9-34 could be old tradition; the present formulation is late (cf. J. S. Kloppenborg, "Joshua 22." Whether created or resurrected, some stimulus is needed to trigger the emergence of this tradition in this dress. Clearly, any move to centralize worship in Jerusalem would pose a threat to the belonging of tribes east of the Jordan. If Joshua 14–19 was already in place, late exilic or early post-exilic is a likely date for the text as formulated. East-of-Jordan genealogies are referred to (1 Chron 5:17); successive exiles are noted (1 Chron 5:26; 6:15). The substantial assistance given David (1 Chron 12:1-40, see esp. v. 37) is not corroborated in Samuel; it may be a record of present appeal rather than past activity. An altar was built in Jerusalem by the returning exiles (Ezra 3:1-5) that might have caused fear of exclusion across the river. We are unaware, however, of any textual evidence indicating eastern anxiety. There is no other reference to an altar by the Jordan.

Present-text potential. Joshua's dismissal of Israel in v. 6 is appropriate, because the whole operation has been under Joshua's leadership (cf. 1:1-6) and

7 Now to the one half of the tribe of Manasseh Moses had given a possession in Bashan; but to the other half Joshua had given a possession beside their fellow Israelites in the land west of the Jordan. And when Joshua sent them away to their tents and blessed them, [8]he said to them, "Go back to your tents with much wealth, and with very much livestock, with silver, gold, bronze, and iron, and with a great quantity of clothing; divide the spoil of your enemies with your kindred."

[9]So the Reubenites and the Gadites and the half-tribe of Manasseh returned home, parting from the Israelites at Shiloh, which is in the land of Canaan, to go to the land of Gilead, their own land of which they had taken possession by command of the LORD through Moses.[105]

correlates with the commitment made at the beginning (1:12-18). In Deuteronomy 2–3, Moses allocated the east-of-Jordan land to these tribes. With the completion of the allocation of the land west of the Jordan, it is appropriate to insist on the unity of these tribes who are returning east. It is doubly appropriate to insist on the fidelity to YHWH of these tribes, in the light of Joshua's speech in chap. 23.

105. This extensive block of tradition, 22:9-34, concerns the return of the two and a half tribes to their territories east of the Jordan. Central to the tradition is the fear that one day these tribes will face the accusation, "You have no portion in the LORD" (vv. 25-27). The similarities of language and situation with the cry of Sheba ben Bichri (2 Sam 20:1) and the people of Israel (1 Kgs 12:16) are inescapable. No explanation appears to be to hand. We have no trace, beyond this text, of the occasion when such an accusation might either have been made or been feared. The incorporation of the tradition into the DH appears to be late.

After the Dtr:	Revision:	Other:
indented and sans serif font	*national focus*	double sideline

10 When they came to the region near the Jordan that lies in the land of Canaan, the Reubenites and the Gadites and the half-tribe of Manasseh built there an altar by the Jordan, an altar of great size. [11]The Israelites heard that the Reubenites and the Gadites and the half-tribe of Manasseh had built an altar at the frontier of the land of Canaan, in the region near the Jordan, on the side that belongs to the Israelites. [12]And when the people of Israel heard of it, the whole assembly of the Israelites gathered at Shiloh, to make war against them.

13 Then the Israelites sent the priest Phinehas son of Eleazar to the Reubenites and the Gadites and the half-tribe of Manasseh, in the land of Gilead, [14]and with him ten chiefs, one from each of the tribal families of Israel, every one of them the head of a family among the clans of Israel. [15]They came to the Reubenites, the Gadites, and the half-tribe of Manasseh, in the land of Gilead, and they said to them, [16]"Thus says the whole congregation of the LORD, 'What is this treachery that you have committed against the God of Israel in turning away today from following the LORD, by building yourselves an altar today in rebellion against the LORD? [17]Have we not had enough of the sin at Peor from which even yet we have not cleansed ourselves, and for which a plague came upon the congregation of the LORD, [18]that you must turn away today from following the LORD! If you rebel against the LORD today, he will be angry with the whole congregation of Israel tomorrow. [19]But now, if your land is unclean, cross over into the LORD's land where the LORD's tabernacle now stands, and take for yourselves a possession among us; only do not rebel against the LORD, or rebel against us by building

yourselves an altar other than the altar of the LORD our God. [20]Did not Achan son of Zerah break faith in the matter of the devoted things, and wrath fell upon all the congregation of Israel? And he did not perish alone for his iniquity!' "

21 Then the Reubenites, the Gadites, and the half-tribe of Manasseh said in answer to the heads of the families of Israel, [22]"The LORD, God of gods! The LORD, God of gods! He knows; and let Israel itself know! If it was in rebellion or in breach of faith toward the LORD, do not spare us today [23]for building an altar to turn away from following the LORD; or if we did so to offer burnt offerings or grain offerings or offerings of well-being on it, may the LORD himself take vengeance. [24]No! We did it from fear that in time to come your children might say to our children, 'What have you to do with the LORD, the God of Israel? [25]For the LORD has made the Jordan a boundary between us and you, you Reubenites and Gadites; you have no portion in the LORD.' So your children might make our children cease to worship the LORD. [26]Therefore we said, 'Let us now build an altar, not for burnt offering, nor for sacrifice, [27]but to be a witness between us and you, and between the generations after us, that we do perform the service of the LORD in his presence with our burnt offerings and sacrifices and offerings of well-being; so that your children may never say to our children in time to come, "You have no portion in the LORD."' [28]And we thought, If this should be said to us or to our descendants in time to come, we could say, 'Look at this copy of the altar of the LORD, which our ancestors made, not for burnt offerings, nor for sacrifice, but to be a witness between us and

---

Main pre-DH: Conquest Narrative
and its expansion

Other pre-DH:
single sideline

Josianic DH:
from the Dtr

you.' ²⁹Far be it from us that we should rebel against the Lord, and turn away this day from following the Lord by building an altar for burnt offering, grain offering, or sacrifice, other than the altar of the Lord our God that stands before his tabernacle!"

30 When the priest Phinehas and the chiefs of the congregation, the heads of the families of Israel who were with him, heard the words that the Reubenites and the Gadites and the Manassites spoke, they were satisfied. ³¹The priest Phinehas son of Eleazar said to the Reubenites and the Gadites and the Manassites, "Today we know that the Lord is among us, because you have not committed this treachery against the Lord; now you have saved the Israelites from the hand of the Lord."

32 Then the priest Phinehas son of Eleazar and the chiefs returned from the Reubenites and the Gadites in the land of Gilead to the land of Canaan, to the Israelites, and brought back word to them. ³³The report pleased the Israelites; and the Israelites blessed God and spoke no more of making war against them, to destroy the land where the Reubenites and the Gadites were settled. ³⁴The Reubenites and the Gadites called the altar Witness *(Heb. lacks "Witness")*; "For," said they, "it is a witness between us that the Lord is God."

23 *A long time after the Lord* (Heb.; NRSV, afterward, when the Lord) *had given rest to Israel from all their enemies all around, and Joshua was old and well advanced in years, ²Joshua summoned all Israel, their elders and heads, their judges and officers, and said to them, "I am now old and well advanced in years; ³and you have seen all that the Lord your God has done to all these*

nations for your sake, for it is the Lord your God who has fought for you. ⁴I have allotted to you as an inheritance for your tribes those nations that remain from the Jordan (along with all the nations that I have already cut off) to the Great Sea in the west (Heb.; NRSV rearranges text). *⁵The Lord your God will push them back before you, and drive them out of your sight; and you shall possess their land, as the Lord your God promised you. ⁶Therefore be very steadfast to observe and do all that is written in the book of the law of Moses, turning aside from it neither to the right nor to the left, ⁷so that you may not be mixed with these nations left here among you, or make mention of the names of their gods, or swear by them, or serve them, or bow yourselves down to them, ⁸but hold fast to the Lord your God, as you have done to this day. ⁹For the Lord has driven out before you great and strong nations; and as for you, no one has been able to withstand you to this day. ¹⁰One of you puts to flight a thousand, since it is the Lord your God who fights for you, as he promised you. ¹¹Be very careful, therefore, to love the Lord your God. ¹²For if you turn back, and join the survivors of these nations left here among you, and intermarry with them, so that you marry their women and they yours, ¹³know assuredly that the Lord your God will not continue to drive out these nations before you; but they shall be a snare and a trap for you, a scourge on your sides, and thorns in your eyes, until you perish from this good land that the Lord your God has given you.*[106]

---

106. It is the great merit of Smend's study to have pointed to the association between Josh 1:7-9 and

---

After the Dtr:	Revision:	Other:
indented and sans serif font	*national focus*	double sideline

14 "And now I am about to go the way of all the earth, and you know in your hearts and souls, all of you, that not one thing has failed of all the good things that the LORD your God promised concerning

you; all have come to pass for you, not one of them has failed. 15But just as all the good things that the LORD your God promised concerning you have been fulfilled for you, so the LORD will bring upon you all the bad things, until he has destroyed you from this good land that the LORD your God has given you. 16If you transgress the covenant of the LORD your God, which he enjoined on you, and go and serve other gods and bow down to them, then the anger of the LORD will be kindled against you, and you shall perish quickly from the good land that he has given to you."

24 Then Joshua gathered all the tribes of Israel to Shechem, and summoned the elders, the heads, the judges, and the officers

---

Josh 23:1-16, attributing both to later revision ("Das Gesetz und die Völker"). A similar service was rendered in his time by Noth with regard to Josh 24:1-28, which he attributed to later dtr editing (*DH*, 23-24)—a position reversed by Smend.

Text signals in 23:1-16. (i) V. 1 situates this discourse long after ("many days") YHWH had given rest to Israel, effective in 11:23 and reported in 21:44. (ii) Joshua is reported as old (v. 1) and describes himself as old (v. 2). (iii) In Joshua's speech, the reference is to "nations" (vv. 3, 4, 7, 9, 12, 13); by contrast, in 21:44b, repeated in 23:1, the reference is to "enemies." (iv) In v. 4 nations are said to remain between the Jordan and the Mediterranean, contrasting with those that have been "cut off." (v) The verb "to allot" is the one used in 13:6 and 17:5; it is not the usual verb in chaps. 14–19. (vi) In v. 5 these peoples will be driven out of Israel's sight and their land will be possessed, as God promised. In 21:45 and in 23:14, all God's promises had come to pass. (vii) Intermingling with these nations is prohibited; but they will have been driven out of Israel's sight ("from before you"). (viii) Intermarriage with these nations is prohibited; but, again, they will have been driven out. (ix) These peoples will be a snare, a trap, a scourge, and thorns for Israel. (x) "All the bad things" in v. 15 suggests something that has been said and that is not in the text. "All the good things" are referred to in 21:45.

Text-history approach. There has been discussion over the unity of this chapter; it need not concern us here. As a commentary on 21:43-45, it is a good example of inner biblical exegesis. Vv. 3-8 pick up 21:43, applying it to land still to be won, depending on Israel's fidelity to the law. Note the relation to Deut 6:19; 9:4 for v. 5 and to Josh 1:7 for v. 6. Vv. 9-13 pick up 21:44 and add the modification of "to this day," more suited to a context of peoples yet to be con-

quered, again requiring obedience to the law and, in the event of infidelity, threatening disaster. Vv. 14-16 develop 21:45, with the reference to the good things allowing for introduction of the bad things that follow breach of covenant and apostasy. There is a development across these three moments: from exhortation (vv. 6-7) through warning (vv. 11-13) to a threat that functions as a prophecy of disaster (vv. 15-16).

The relation to 21:43-45, the emphasis on unswerving observance of the law (cf. Josh 1:7-9), and the focus on the people all indicate attribution to the national focus within the dtr process of revision. The shift from "enemies" to "nations" (conquered and yet to be conquered) is a shift away from the language of the Dtr.

The danger of the peoples, described in v. 13, is not paralleled elsewhere in the DH (i.e., "snare," "scourge," and "thorns" are found only here; "trap" occurs also at Deut 7:16; Judg 2:3; 8:27).

Present-text potential. The presence in v. 4 of "those nations that remain" and "the nations that I have already cut off" symbolizes something of the tension within this chapter. Even taking Josh 13:2-6 into

---

Main pre-DH: Conquest Narrative
and its expansion

Other pre-DH:
single sideline

**Josianic DH:
from the Dtr**

of Israel; and they presented themselves before God. ²And Joshua said to all the people, "Thus says the LORD, the God of Israel: Long ago your ancestors—Terah and his sons Abraham and Nahor—lived beyond the Euphrates and served other gods. ³Then I took your father Abraham from beyond the River and led him through all the land of Canaan and made his offspring many. I gave him Isaac; ⁴and to Isaac I gave Jacob and Esau. I gave Esau the hill country of Seir to possess, but Jacob and his children went down to Egypt. ⁵Then I sent Moses and Aaron, and I plagued Egypt with what I did in its midst; and afterwards I brought you out. ⁶When I brought your ancestors out of Egypt, you came to the sea; and the Egyptians pursued your ancestors with chariots and horsemen to the Red Sea. ⁷When they cried out to the LORD, he put darkness between you and the Egyptians, and made the sea come upon them and cover them; and your eyes saw what I did to Egypt. Afterwards you lived in the wilderness a long time. ⁸Then I brought you to the land of the Amorites, who lived on the other side of the Jordan; they fought with you, and I handed them over to you, and you took possession of their land, and I destroyed them before you. ⁹Then King Balak son of Zippor of Moab, set out to fight against Israel. He sent and invited Balaam son of Beor to curse you, ¹⁰but I would not listen to Balaam; therefore he blessed you; so I rescued you out of his hand. ¹¹When you went over the Jordan and came to Jericho, the citizens of Jericho fought against you, and also the Amorites, the Perizzites, the Canaanites, the Hittites, the Girgashites, the Hivites, and the Jebusites; and I handed them over to you. ¹²I sent the hornet ahead of you, which drove out before you the two kings of the Amorites; it was not by your sword or by your bow. ¹³I gave you a land on which you had not labored, and towns that you had not built, and you live in them; you eat the fruit of vineyards and oliveyards that you did not plant.[107]

---

account, there is tension between this chapter and the book as a whole. 13:2-6 has a far wider reach than merely from the Jordan to the Mediterranean (23:4). In the book so far, obedience has been manifest and the local populations have been eliminated. In chap. 23, the local populations are envisaged as a danger and obedience is not to be presumed. Whether read as a prophecy of times to come or as a retrospective reflection on times past, chap. 23 reiterates the emphasis on obedience raised in 1:7-9 and introduces the theme of potential fragility (i.e., intermingling, intermarriage, and apostasy) otherwise absent from the book so far—with the exception of the Achan story (Joshua 7).

The chapter reflects something of the tension inherent in the book of Joshua between the total conquest of chaps. 1–12 and the unfinished conquest within chaps. 13–22—i.e., the peoples or cities that held out: Geshurites and Maacathites; Jerusalem, Gezer, and Beth-shean; Tanaach, Dor, Ibleam, and Megiddo. The conflictual reality of this situation, reflected in the text, is a background to Joshua's exhortation to obedience. The ceremony of commitment in Joshua 24 functions as a response.

---

107. **Text signals** in 24:1-28. (i) 24:1 has Joshua assemble Israel at Shechem; but 23:2 has already had Joshua assemble Israel and there has been no dismissal. The participants listed are the same. (ii) Vv. 2-10 reach back in Israel's history before the book of Deuteronomy. (iii) Vv. 11-12 differ significantly from the text of Joshua 2–11, which has: a) no battle over Jericho; b) no battle with the seven peoples listed; c) no hornet mentioned; and d) no mention of the "two kings of the Amorites" in Canaan. (iv) Vv. 14-15

| After the Dtr: indented and sans serif font | Revision: national focus | Other: double sideline |

14 "Now therefore revere the LORD, and serve him in sincerity and in faithfulness; put away the gods that your ancestors served beyond the River and in Egypt, and serve the LORD. ¹⁵Now if you are unwilling to serve the LORD, choose this day whom you will serve, whether the gods your ancestors served in the region beyond the River or the gods of the Amorites in whose land you are living; but as for me and my household, we will serve the LORD."

16 Then the people answered, "Far be it from us that we should forsake the LORD to serve other gods; ¹⁷for it is the LORD our God who brought us and our ancestors up from the land of Egypt, out of the house of slavery, and who did those great signs in our sight. He protected us along all the way that we went, and among all the peoples through whom we passed; ¹⁸and the LORD drove out before us all the peoples, the Amorites who lived in the land. Therefore we also will serve the LORD, for he is our God."

19 But Joshua said to the people, "You cannot serve the LORD, for he is a holy God. He is a jealous God; he will not forgive your transgressions or your sins. ²⁰If you forsake the LORD and serve foreign gods, then he will turn and do you harm, and consume you, after having done you good." ²¹And the people said to Joshua, "No, we will serve the LORD!" ²²Then Joshua said to the people, "You are witnesses against yourselves that you have chosen the LORD, to serve him." And they said, "We are witnesses." ²³He said, "Then put away the foreign gods that are among you, and incline your hearts to the LORD, the God of Israel." ²⁴The people said to Joshua, "The LORD our God we will serve, and him we will obey." ²⁵So Joshua made a covenant with the people that day, and made statutes and ordinances for them at Shechem. ²⁶Joshua wrote these words in the book of the law of God; and he took a large stone, and set it

---

propose a choice that appears out of place. (v) Vv. 16-18, like the preceding, extend well beyond the book of Deuteronomy. (vi) "You cannot serve the LORD" is not a statement to be expected of the Dtr and is not grounded in the book of Joshua. (vii) Vv. 23-24 presume apostasy and the presence of foreign gods. (viii) Vv. 25-27 portray Joshua performing the role that in the DH belongs to Moses.

Text-history approach. Nelson's comment—"This chapter has been a focus of a great deal of scholarly controversy. There is no consensus about its compositional history, time of origin, or possible relationship to the history or cultic life of Israel" (*Joshua*, 265)—is somewhat of an understatement. This book is not the place to enter these controversies. As the text signals show, there are broad areas of tension with dtr positions. As the history of scholarship shows, traces of dtr editing can be identified (see O'Brien, *Deuteronomistic History Hypothesis* 77-79; and Nelson, *Joshua*, 265-73). It seems to us most likely that Joshua 24, whatever of its history, was not part of the Josianic DH and was introduced later, where it was most appropriate. The addition may not be unconnected with the Shechem texts of Deut 11:29-32; 27:1-26; and Josh 8:30-35.

Present-text potential. The chapter provides a fitting conclusion to the book of Joshua. At one level, it functions as a response to the exhortation of Joshua 23; the threat of failure is met by a solid commitment to YHWH. At another level, it situates the achievement of Joshua's generation within the broad sweep of Israel's history, beginning with Abraham's ancestor. At a further level, it portrays Joshua as covenant-maker and lawgiver (v. 25); the stone at Shechem stands as symbol for Israel's future, its past dominated by the figures of Moses and Joshua.

Main pre-DH: Conquest Narrative
and its expansion

Other pre-DH:
single sideline

**Josianic DH:
from the Dtr**

up there under the oak in the sanctuary of the LORD. [27]Joshua said to all the people, "See, this stone shall be a witness against us; for it has heard all the words of the LORD that he spoke to us; therefore it shall be a witness against you, if you deal falsely with your God." [28]So Joshua sent the people away to their inheritances.[108]

29 After these things Joshua son of Nun, the servant of the LORD, died, being one hundred ten years old. [30]They buried him in his own inheritance at Timnath-serah, which is in the hill country of Ephraim, north of Mount Gaash.[109]

31 Israel served the LORD all the days of Joshua, and all the days of the elders who outlived Joshua and had known all the work that the LORD did for Israel.[110]

32 The bones of Joseph, which the Israelites had brought up from Egypt, were buried at Shechem, in the portion of ground that Jacob had bought from the children of Hamor, the father of Shechem, for one hundred pieces of money; it became an inheritance of the descendants of Joseph.[111]

33 Eleazar son of Aaron died; and they buried him at Gibeah, the town of his son Phinehas, which had been given him in the hill country of Ephraim.[112]

---

108. The reference to "the book of the law of God" in v. 26 is unparalleled. Whether understood as a rival book or as an addition made in the book of Moses, it gives Joshua a rank equivalent to Moses. He is more than military leader (cf. Deut 31:7-8; Josh 1:2-6); he is lawmaker. The dismissal of the people in v. 28 corresponds with the convening of "all the tribes of Israel" (v. 1a).

109. The DH provides notices of death and burial for almost all the kings of Israel and Judah. It is appropriate to do so for Joshua. There is a parallel notice for Moses in Deut 34:5-6, with the statement that the grave site is unknown, "in a valley in the land of Moab" (Deut 34:6). The notice for Joshua is not much more revealing, "in his own inheritance at Timnath-serah" (Josh 24:30). It is repeated in Judg 2:9 (see below).

110. We attribute Josh 24:29-31 here to the Josianic Dtr rather than the almost identical Judg 2:7-9. The reasons will be repeated below; they are: (i) Judg 2:10 follows naturally on Josh 24:31; (ii) note the reference to "that whole generation" (2:10a), inappropriate after 2:8-9 but most appropriate following 24:31; (iii) note also the use of the verb "to know" in

Josh 24:31 and Judg 2:10, by way of contrast with the verb "to see" in Judg 2:7; (iv) Judg 2:10 assures the transition of the generations.

111. The significance of the burial of Joseph's bones at Shechem eludes us. It follows on the oath sworn to the dying patriarch (Gen 50:25) and the report of Israel's compliance with it (Exod 13:19). Abraham rests at Hebron, Joseph at Shechem. The tradition could have been given written form at any time. Its position here, by way of a footnote after 24:31, suggests that its incorporation into this text is late.

112. Eleazar was successor to Aaron, as Joshua was to Moses. He was Joshua's collaborator in the distribution of the land. Like v. 32, this tradition too could have been given written form at almost any time. Its position, after 24:31, suggests that its incorporation here is late.

| After the Dtr: indented and sans serif font | *Revision: national focus* | Other: double sideline |

The Book of Judges

INTRODUCTION

Alas, the book of Judges has been badly served in much biblical theology.[1] Aspects of the book have been placed on a pedestal, when more than its feet are of clay. Its spectacular emphasis on deliverer figures raised up by God has led to visions of a theocratic ideal. The reality of the book is far from any ideal.

In the "Deliverance Collection," as the analytical table shows, Israel is portrayed first, regularly and repetitively, doing evil (e.g., Judg 3:12a; 4:1a; 6:1a). God's response to Israel's evil is given as oppression, raising up foreign powers to oppress Israel for eight, eighteen, twenty, and seven years (beyond that eighteen [10:8] and forty years [13:1b]). So far, in many eyes neither Israel nor God is looking good.

The first "right" thing that oppressed Israel does is to cry out to God. God is then claimed to

have raised up a deliverer and Israel keeps to the straight and narrow during the deliverer's lifetime. At this point, both Israel and God are looking better. Except that it will happen all over again—at least four times.

This "four times" raises the question of the structural components of the book. Estimates would range between three and five such components. At the beginning and the end, the boundaries are clear; boundaries in the middle are not so clear. At the beginning there is conquest; at the end there is anarchy. In between, there are the deliverer-judges, three major figures, and several minor ones. The major figures are Abimelech, murderous beneficiary of the first unauthorized seizure of power in Israel; Jephthah, who leveraged military success into political power; and Samson, a truly mysterious and not very noble figure.[2] The lesser figures are the minor judges, two before Jephthah and three after him.

The conquest traditions are clearly packaged between a reference to and a report of Joshua's death (1:1 and 2:8-9). The portrayal of the conquest is radically different from the scenario of Joshua 1–12. Firstly, it appears to disregard any

---

1. Von Rad cites Martin Buber calling the book of Judges the "Plato's *Republic*" of the Bible (*Old Testament Theology*, 1.332). Well aware of the complex currents in the book, von Rad himself still says: "The Deuteronomist clearly regards the office of the judge as the form of government most appropriate to Israel: it was a tragedy that she asserted her own autonomy over against Jahweh by means of her kings" (ibid.). With all due respect to two great scholars, we must now acknowledge that this is a fearful misreading of the book of Judges and the Deuteronomistic History.

2. Von Rad again: "The oddest figure amongst the judges is Samson: the reader will indeed find it absolutely impossible to understand him as judge over Israel" (ibid., 333).

prior activity under Joshua: "Who shall go up first for us . . . ?" (1:1b, *battĕḫillâ*; literally, in the beginning). Israel inquires of the LORD; Judah is designated. The cities named are Bezek, Jerusalem, Hebron, Debir, Zephath/Hormah, Gaza, Ashkelon, and Ekron; the house of Joseph took Luz/Bethel. There follows the well-known "negative conquest," the list of the major towns Israel did not capture (vv. 27-36). 2:1-5 attributes this failure to Israel's disobedience: "But you have not obeyed my command" (v. 2). The extent of martial activity—"in the hill country, in the Negeb, and in the lowland" (1:9) and well beyond—points to a tradition very different from that of Joshua 1–12. Jericho, Ai, and Gibeon are not mentioned; nor are Gilgal or Makkedah.

The traditions at the end of the book are packaged between two statements of anarchy: "In those days there was no king in Israel; all the people did what was right in their own eyes" (17:6 and 21:25; cf. the shortened version in 18:1 and 19:1). It is an increasingly gruesome picture: a shrine is begun with stolen silver, a Levite is kidnapped, an unsuspecting people is butchered (18:27), a concubine is murdered, a tribe (Benjamin) is almost exterminated (20:46-48), and all this is compounded by organized murder (21:1-12) and organized rape (21:19-21).

Apart from the dtr contributions, the blocks in between include the Deliverance Collection (3:7—8:28), the abortive kingship of Abimelech, the tradition of Jephthah and the minor judges, and finally Samson. Here uncertainty reigns. In our formatting, we have had the Josianic Dtr make use of the Deliverance Collection and the traditions of Jephthah and some of the minor judges. The forty years of Philistine oppression (13:1) is figuratively ended only with the emergence of Samuel, the establishment of Saul as king, and the final victories of David (2 Sam 5:17-25; 8:1). In our judgment, the traditions of Abimelech and Samson are later additions. In both the large picture and the details, uncertainty must prevail. Details will be discussed for each text.

This leaves the Deliverance Collection with a relatively lame ending in 8:28. It must be admitted that the Abimelech episode does not offer much better. A local feud over the control of Shechem has been jumped up into an issue of wider importance. One swallow does not make a spring, and two verses do not make a national king (cf. 9:22, 55). It may be wiser to regard the Deliverance Collection as no more than what it is: a collection of three studies in deliverance.

One thing remains clear: the book of Judges does not present a theocratic ideal—"the form of government most appropriate to Israel." The book of Judges, at the level of the Josianic Dtr, portrays an Israel that did not have the effective leadership to keep it out of the grips of foreign oppression. Its experience has not curbed its addiction to apostasy. The Josianic book ends with Israel serving a forty-year term (13:1). The additions successfully intensify the picture. The outcome presents a miserable conquest, followed by repeated apostasy and evil as well as oppression and deliverance, and a steady deterioration in which the strong constantly overpower the weak. It presents an anarchic social situation that only the establishment of monarchy could overcome. The need is for both internal security and external defense.

As a reflection on the experience of deliverance, the Deliverance Collection is a valued text for the study of Israel's theological processes. In its early part, it tells the stories of three acts of intense personal bravery that won for Israel moments of respite from foreign oppression. It places those stories within a framing narrative that discerns a regularity within the events and that places a theological interpretation on them. The framed text is preceded by a brief episode that has all the elements of the frame for our contemplation, but that is clearly not a story (Judg 3:7-11). Here there is no act of bravery to be told, but instead a theology to be pondered. For those whose thinking processes need help, the text provides a preface to spell out, in slightly altered terms, what this theology is about. We attribute this preface to the Josianic Dtr; its contents are classically identified as 2:11, 14-16, 18-19.[3] There is the move, then, from the experience of event to the distillation of theological conviction. There is the expression of this theology in the framing of the stories and its refinement in the opening stages of the text.

Even here, however, the bravery involved and the emphasis on deliverance in the compositional framing can distract us from the deteriorating picture being painted. In the story of Ehud, Israel went with him from the hill country of Ephraim (3:27) and fought against Moab. There is no sign of disunity. In the next story, that of Deborah and Barak and Jael, trouble is hinted at in one direction and is explicit in another. First is the image of Barak; it is shadowed. He will not carry out YHWH's command unless Deborah goes with him; she assures him that his path will not bring him glory (4:8-9). Second is the image of Israel; it is not one of unity. Why did tribes not respond to the summons (5:15b-17)? Ephraim and others came, but not Reuben, Gilead, Dan, or Asher. The Gideon story descends into complexity and confusion. The essence of the deliverer story lies in the small number of troops involved (7:4-7). There is strife with Ephraim over the level of their participation (7:24—8:3). There is disunity with savage consequences for Succoth and Penuel

3. See Noth, *DH*, 23.

(8:4-17). It is worse than it was in the preceding story. The framing organization gives the land peace for forty years; within the stories, the inner unity of Israel is becoming increasingly stressed and unpeaceful.

This deterioration peaks in the story of Jephthah. He is not raised up by YHWH as a deliverer. He is summoned by the elders of Gilead and he comes only after he has struck a political bargain with them (11:4-11). The Jephthah story ends with two disasters for social structure: one familial and one national. On the family level, he sacrifices his daughter in an apparently stupid and unnecessary vow (11:30-40). On the national level, there is a rupture with Ephraim, leading to war and bloodshed (12:1-6).

The framing elements for the stories of the judges can portray a period with substantial patches where the relationship with God is idyllic. Increasingly, the content of the stories disputes this. There is deterioration.

Two elements have probably had a primary role in deterring the full recognition of this deterioration in the stories of the deliverer-judges. The first element was the conviction that the DH viewed monarchy negatively. The judges provided the counterimage and so were viewed positively. To demand a king was to turn from trust in YHWH and turn away from the protection and deliverance provided through the judges. What this thinking conveniently overlooked was that the oppression from which the judges delivered Israel so effectively was a punishment inflicted on Israel by YHWH because of their evil. The second element was the identification of Samuel as the last of the deliverer-judges. As long as Samuel was given this role, the idyllic image of the deliverer-judges had to extend to include him. Deterioration was out of the question. The deterioration of the final chapters (17–21) was out of place and a late addition.

The possibility of a Josianic DH eliminates the first element. A text advocating reform under King Josiah could have looked favorably on the institution of kingship. At this point, a number of the features of 1 Samuel 8–11 make more lucid sense. A close examination of 1 Samuel 7 eliminates the second element. Whatever the reality of the deliverance Samuel achieved (7:5-12), he is not portrayed as a deliverer-judge. The book of Judges is freed to be evaluated for its own sake.

The process of dtr revision (within its national focus) signals something of this deterioration when it has YHWH unambiguously break from Israel: "Go and cry to the gods whom you have chosen; let them deliver you in the time of your distress" (10:14). From this outburst, the outcome in the text is ambiguous. Translations render the four words of v. 16b as reconciling God and Israel (e.g., the NRSV: and God "could no longer bear to see Israel suffer"). The Hebrew is equally susceptible of a translation that dismisses reconciliation and points to irreconcilable breakdown: "but God could no longer bear the burden of Israel." The text of 1 Samuel 4–6, with the departure of the ark from the sanctuary of Shiloh, risks raising this question: will God leave us and go elsewhere?

One of the questions raised by these reflections concerns what Israel's thinkers here understood by the "spirit of the LORD." 1 Samuel 19:9 speaks of "an evil spirit of the LORD" (literal rendering; cf. 1 Sam 16:14, "from the LORD"; also, the "lying spirit" in 1 Kgs 22:19-23). The spirit of YHWH came upon Othniel and he judged Israel (3:10); it came upon Gideon and the Abiezrites were called out to follow him (6:34). It came upon Jephthah (11:29) and, instead of leading on to victory, the present text has him make a misguided and most unfortunate vow that, in the context, must be considered totally unneces-

sary (11:30-31). In the rest of the book of Judges, the spirit of YHWH is attributed to Samson four times (13:25; 14:6, 19; 15:14). Samson is not portrayed as a noble figure; he dies in a paroxysm of selfish revenge (16:28). It is possible that in the trajectory of these texts, the spirit of YHWH is being viewed in an increasingly unfavorable light. In 1 Sam 10:6 and 16:13, the spirit of YHWH is associated with the activity of Samuel; in 16:14 and 19:9, it is not dissociated from that activity. "The spirit" is an uncertain quantity.

In the closing chapters of the book, there are tales that are indeed terrible. They too have been presented in a frame that states a conviction: "there was no king in those days" (cf. 17:6; 18:1; 19:1; 21:25). In these days of democracy, the conclusion is not one we might have wanted to draw. The extension, "all the people did what was right in their own eyes" (17:6; 21:25), was a plea for central government against the forces of anarchy. Israel's appeal was not to theory; it was to experience.

The DH's view of human fidelity and integrity becomes visible in the book of Joshua. In Deuteronomy, the narrative has only one sinful action of Israel's—the episode of the spies (Deut 1:22-40). It cost their leader his entry into the promised land. The dtr book of Joshua presents Israel in a state close almost to pristine innocence. The sole sin was Achan's; otherwise, "Israel served the LORD all the days of Joshua" (Josh 24:31). With the warning against "these nations left here among you" (see Josh 23:1-16), the national focus within the dtr process of revision introduced an understanding of Israel that is closer to the pentateuchal wilderness stories and far from innocence. For the Josianic DH, there was a watershed between the fidelity of Joshua's generation and the infidelity of the next. It is explained as the difference between those who had "known all the work that the LORD did for

Israel" (Josh 24:31) and those who had not (Judg 2:10). The national focus of revision of the DH introduces a different anthropology; warnings were needed against failure from the outset, and even for Joshua's generation. Failure is in the far background of Joshua; it comes to the fore in Judges—except for the years of undisturbed "innocence" in the remaining lifetime of each deliverer-judge. For Josiah, so many lifetimes later, failure is in the far background; with his death, it comes to the fore.

THE BOOK OF JUDGES

1 After the death of Joshua, the Israelites inquired of the LORD, "Who shall go up first for us against the Canaanites, to fight against them?" [2]The LORD said, "Judah shall go up. I hereby give the land into his hand." [3]Judah said to his brother Simeon, "Come up with me into the territory allotted to me, that we may fight against the Canaanites; then I too will go with you into the territory allotted to you." So Simeon went with him. [4]Then Judah went up and the LORD gave the Canaanites and the Perizzites into their hand; and they defeated ten thousand of them at Bezek. [5]They came upon Adoni-bezek at Bezek, and fought against him, and defeated the Canaanites and the Perizzites. [6]Adoni-bezek fled; but they pursued him, and caught him, and cut off his thumbs and big toes. [7]Adoni-bezek said, "Seventy kings with their thumbs and big toes cut off used to pick up scraps under my table; as I have done, so God has paid me back." They brought him to Jerusalem, and he died there.[1]

---

1. **Text signals** in Judg 1:1–2:10. (i) The passage opens with its location in time: "after the death of Joshua" (v. 1a). (ii) The opening question posed by the Israelites appears to present a process that is just starting, ignoring the book of Joshua (v. 1b). (iii) The passage contains a collection of traditions: Judah's defeat of the Canaanites and Adoni-bezek (vv. 1-7); Judah's capture of Jerusalem, Hebron, and the south (vv. 8-10); Caleb's gift of land to Achsah, his daughter and Othniel's wife (vv. 11-15; = Josh 15:15-19); various Judahite conquests but not Jerusalem (vv. 16-21); the Josephite capture of Bethel (vv. 22-26); a list of tribes (Manasseh, Ephraim, Zebulun, Asher, Naphtali, and Dan) and the towns that they did not capture (vv. 27-

[8] Then the people of Judah fought against Jerusalem and took it. They put it to the sword and set the city on fire. [9]Afterward the people of Judah went down to fight against the Canaanites who lived in

---

36); the tradition of the angel of the LORD's appearance at Bochim, with the accusation of Israel's breach of covenant and the consequence that nations would remain and their gods would be a snare to Israel (2:1-5); the traditions from Josh 24:28-31. (iv) The passage ends with this material from Josh 24:28-31, rearranged and slightly modified, with the addition of 2:10. The rearrangement involves distributing the traditions of Joshua's generation (24:31) over two verses (2:7 and 10a).

Text-history approach. The striking factor for this material is that the traditions of Judg 1:1–2:7 are located between two reports of Joshua's death and burial (Josh 24:29-30 and Judg 2:8-9); they are introduced as "after the death of Joshua" (Judg 1:1a) and concluded with his death and burial (Judg 2:8-9). In terms of narrative sequence, 1:1–2:7 are outside of time. The only parallel is in 2 Kgs 13–14, where King Joash is buried in 13:13 and visits the dying Elisha in vv. 14-19, followed by further storytelling material; the regnal formula for Joash is given at 13:12 and repeated at 14:15. Alternatively, the resumptive repetition of Josh 24:28-31 in Judg 2:6-9 may be understood as the standard practice of redactors when resuming the thread of a narrative. The inclusion of Joshua's death in this repeated material, however, makes this alternative less appealing.

What Judg 1:1—2:5 presents is a radically different view of Israel's conquest of the land from that offered in the book of Joshua, which may explain why it is presented apparently outside of time. The Josianic DH took over the substantial picture of Joshua 1–12. These differing traditions have been subsequently inserted; there is no certainty about their dating. Our formatting simply indicates the belief that insertion followed the completion of the Josianic DH. The limited correlation with Joshua has been noted (cf. Josh 15:63; 16:10; 17:11-13); Josh 13:13 is east of Jordan

---

Main pre-DH: Deliverance *Collection*
    its sources *and its framing*

Other pre-DH:
    single sideline

Josianic DH:
from the Dtr

the hill country, in the Negeb, and in the lowland. [10]Judah went against the Canaanites who lived in Hebron (the name of Hebron was formerly Kiriath-arba); and they defeated Sheshai and Ahiman and Talmai.

---

and not mentioned in Judges 1, which in its turn notes traditions not mentioned in Joshua.

The traditions of Judg 1:1—2:5 need not have been inserted as a package or a single entity. However, Judg 2:6-9 creates the space into which these differing traditions can be inserted. In our judgment, the modifications and rearrangement visible in 2:6-9 suggest that it is later than Josh 24:29-31.

Within the Josianic DH, Josh 21:43-45 followed 12:7-24; in its turn, it was followed by 24:29-31, bringing Joshua's era to a close. Judg 2:10 follows naturally on Josh 24:31. Note the reference to "that whole generation" (2:10a), inappropriate after 2:8-9 but most appropriate following 24:31. Note also v. 31's "had known" and v. 10's "did not know" (by way of contrast with v. 7's "had seen"). V. 10 assures the transition of the generations.

Judg 2:1-5 contradicts both Josh 24:31 and its parallel in Judg 2:7. For these latter two, Israel was faithful to YHWH; for 2:1-5, Israel did not obey YHWH's command. An independent insertion is likely. The differences from Judg 2:20—3:6 should be noted; they are subtle. The verbs used with covenant are different. The covenant itself is understood differently. In 2:1, the covenant is made with Joshua's generation, who are not to make a covenant with the inhabitants of the land; in 2:20, the covenant was made with their ancestors. The "you" and "you" of 2:1 should not be manipulated into harmony with 2:20. Whatever of the complexity of the traditions about who died in the desert—whether the spies alone or a whole generation—some of the exodus generation were to enter the land (cf. Deut 1:39). The formulation of the accusation against Israel is extended; "you have not obeyed" (v. 2) and "this people has transgressed my covenant . . . and have not obeyed" (v. 20). Subtle differences exist over the status of the nations remaining. "Adversaries" in 2:3 does not correlate with intermar-

11 From there they went against the inhabitants of Debir (the name of Debir was formerly Kiriath-sepher). [12]Then Caleb said, "Whoever attacks Kiriath-sepher and takes it, I will give him my daughter Achsah as wife." [13]And Othniel son of Kenaz, Caleb's younger brother, took it; and he gave him his daughter Achsah as wife. [14]When she

---

riage in 3:6. Their gods as "snares" in 2:3 is one step prior to their gods as worshiped in 3:6; temptation is not quite apostasy. In Josh 23:13, it is the nations themselves that are the snare. 2:1-5 as an independent insertion may serve to account for the situation portrayed in the traditions of 1:1-36.

Present-text potential for Judg 1:1—2:10. Two understandings can be brought to bear on the present text. In one, this material provides details filling in some of the gaps left by the book of Joshua. In the other, this material provides a panorama of different traditions concerning Israel's occupation of the land.

In the first, the aspect of battle (cf. 1:1) is reflected in Josh 11:18 ("Joshua made war a long time with all those kings"). Caleb's achievement at Hebron (1:20) correlates with his faith in Josh 14:12. His gift to Othniel and Achsah is not an advance on Josh 15:16-19. The details of Judg 1:11, 16-19, 22-26 can be understood as completing the more sweeping narrative of Joshua, however unhistorical. The uncaptured cities of Judges 1 extend those already noted in Joshua. The episode at Bochim can be seen as bearing out Joshua's warning (Joshua 23) and his blunt assertion (24:19). Those who prefer in 1:1—3:6 to examine "the various shifts in perspective on the psychological, spatial-temporal, and phraseological planes of the text" will find them treated in Polzin, *Moses and the Deuteronomist*, 146–56.

In the second, the present text serves as a particularly good example of the broad palette of traditions from which Israel's theologians painted their pictures of its identity. The portrayal in Joshua 1–12 follows one such tradition. The collection in Judges 1 is a reminder that totally different views existed.

After the Dtr:	*Revision:*	Other:
indented and sans serif font	*national focus*	double sideline

came to him, she urged him to ask her father for a field. As she dismounted from her donkey, Caleb said to her, "What do you wish?" [15]She said to him, "Give me a present; since you have set me in the land of the Negeb, give me also Gulloth-mayim." So Caleb gave her Upper Gulloth and Lower Gulloth.

16 The descendants of Hobab the Kenite, Moses' father-in-law, went up with the people of Judah from the city of palms into the wilderness of Judah, which lies in the Negeb near Arad. Then they went and settled with the Amalekites. [17]Judah went with his brother Simeon, and they defeated the Canaanites who inhabited Zephath, and devoted it to destruction. So the city was called Hormah. [18]Judah took Gaza with its territory, Ashkelon with its territory, and Ekron with its territory. [19]The LORD was with Judah, and he took possession of the hill country, but could not drive out the inhabitants of the plain, because they had chariots of iron. [20]Hebron was given to Caleb, as Moses had said; and he drove out from it the three sons of Anak. [21]But the Benjaminites did not drive out the Jebusites who lived in Jerusalem; so the Jebusites have lived in Jerusalem among the Benjaminites to this day.

22 The house of Joseph also went up against Bethel; and the LORD was with them. [23]The house of Joseph sent out spies to Bethel (the name of the city was formerly Luz). [24]When the spies saw a man coming out of the city, they said to him, "Show us the way into the city, and we will deal kindly with you." [25]So he showed them the way into the city; and they put the city to the sword, but they let the man and all his family go. [26]So the man went to the land of the Hittites and built a city, and named it Luz; that is its name to this day.

27 Manasseh did not drive out the inhabitants of Beth-shean and its villages, or Taanach and its villages, or the inhabitants of Dor and its villages, or the inhabitants of Ibleam and its villages, or the inhabitants of Megiddo and its villages; but the Canaanites continued to live in that land. [28]When Israel grew strong, they put the Canaanites to forced labor, but did not in fact drive them out.

29 And Ephraim did not drive out the Canaanites who lived in Gezer; but the Canaanites lived among them in Gezer.

30 Zebulun did not drive out the inhabitants of Kitron, or the inhabitants of Nahalol; but the Canaanites lived among them, and became subject to forced labor.

31 Asher did not drive out the inhabitants of Acco, or the inhabitants of Sidon, or of Ahlab, or of Achzib, or of Helbah, or of Aphik, or of Rehob; [32]but the Asherites lived among the Canaanites, the inhabitants of the land; for they did not drive them out.

33 Naphtali did not drive out the inhabitants of Beth-shemesh, or the inhabitants of Beth-anath, but lived among the Canaanites, the inhabitants of the land; nevertheless the inhabitants of Beth-shemesh and of Beth-anath became subject to forced labor for them.

34 The Amorites pressed the Danites back into the hill country; they did not allow them to come down to the plain. [35]The Amorites continued to live in Har-heres, in Aijalon, and in Shaalbim, but the hand of the house of Joseph rested heavily on them, and they became subject to forced labor. [36]The border of the Amorites ran from the ascent of Akrabbim, from Sela and upward.

Main pre-DH: Deliverance *Collection*
its sources *and its framing*

Other pre-DH:
single sideline

Josianic DH:
from the Dtr

2 Now the angel of the LORD went up from Gilgal to Bochim, and said, "I brought you up from Egypt, and brought you into the land that I had promised to your ancestors. I said, 'I will never break my covenant with you. ²For your part, do not make a covenant with the inhabitants of this land; tear down their altars.' But you have not obeyed my command. See what you have done! ³So now I say, I will not drive them out before you; but they shall become adversaries to you, and their gods shall be a snare to you." ⁴When the angel of the LORD spoke these words to all the Israelites, the people lifted up their voices and wept. ⁵So they named that place Bochim, and there they sacrificed to the LORD.

6 When Joshua dismissed the people, the Israelites all went to their own inheritances to take possession of the land.⁷The people worshiped the LORD all the days of Joshua, and all the days of the elders who outlived Joshua, who had seen all the great work that the LORD had done for Israel. ⁸Joshua son of Nun, the servant of the LORD, died at the age of one hundred ten years. ⁹So they buried him within the bounds of his inheritance in Timnath-heres, in the hill country of Ephraim, north of Mount Gaash.

¹⁰Moreover, that whole generation was gathered to their ancestors, and another generation grew up after them, who did not know the LORD or the work that he had done for Israel.

11 Then the Israelites did what was evil in the sight of the LORD and worshiped the Baals.²

---

² **Text signals** in 2:11-19. (i) The people of Israel are accused of doing evil in the sight of the LORD. (ii)

¹²and they abandoned the LORD, the God of their ancestors, who had brought them out of the land of Egypt; they followed other gods, from among the gods of the peoples who were all around them, and bowed

---

They are accused of worshiping the Baals. (iii) They are accused of abandoning YHWH, identified as god of their ancestors and god of the exodus. (iv) They are accused of going after other gods from the surrounding peoples. (v) They are accused of provoking YHWH to anger. (vi) They are accused again of abandoning YHWH, a repetition from v. 12. (vii) They are accused of worshiping Baal and the Astartes, a modification over against v. 11. (viii) Vv. 14-16 provide a theological interpretation of events—in terms of divine anger, punishment, and deliverance—that will be resumed with regularity in the narrative to come. (ix) V. 17 displays a theology that is quite different from its context: the people were to obey the judges rather than be delivered by them and the people's infidelity was rife in the judge's generation. (x) Vv. 18-19 continue the theology of vv. 14-16, where the judge is a deliverer and the people of that generation are faithful.

Text-history approach. The regular recurrence of a number of these elements—evil, oppression, cry, deliverance, peace—associates vv. 11, 14-16, 18-19 with the narrative that follows. For Noth, this preface, the Othniel episode, and the framing elements around the subsequent stories were all the work of his Dtr. Painstakingly close study by Richter revealed significant shifts in thought or language between the framing elements, the Othniel episode, and the preface; he attributed these to different stages of development, with principally the preface deriving from the Dtr (*Traditionsgeschichtliche Untersuchungen* and *Bearbeitungen des "Retterbuches"*; for a summary in readable German, see I. Schlauri, "Wolfgang Richters Beitrag," or, in English, Campbell in *Study Companion*, 182-90). Put briefly, the stories tell the experience, the framing universalizes it, the Othniel episode names

---

<table>
<tr><td>After the Dtr:
indented and sans serif font</td><td>*Revision:*
national focus</td><td>Other:
double sideline</td></tr>
</table>

*down to them; and they provoked the L*ORD *to anger.* [13]*They abandoned the L*ORD*, and worshiped Baal and the Astartes.*

[14]So the anger of the LORD **was kindled against Israel, and he gave them over to plunderers who plundered them, and he sold them into the power of their enemies all**

around, so that they could no longer withstand their enemies. [15]Whenever they marched out, the hand of the LORD **was against them to bring misfortune, as the**

---

the evil, and the preface proposes a theological viewpoint for the whole.

For Richter, his Dtr is responsible for the chronological framework, the specific figures, and certain other details (see *Bearbeitungen*, 115). In our judgment, this is unlikely. The specific figures for the periods of oppression (3:8, 14; 4:3; 6:1) more probably belonged in the tradition. The chronological framework of tranquillity for forty years uses a phrase that is unique to these passages, that is close to Josh 11:23, and that is quite different from the standard dtr language of "rest" (cf. Deut 12:8; 25:19; Josh 21:44; 23:1; 2 Sam 7:1, 11; 1 Kgs 5:4 [NRSV; Heb., 5:18]; note Deut 12:9; 1 Kgs 8:56; also 1 Chron 22:9). The "forty years" (or eighty) seems to us (contrary to Richter) to be indispensable to the respective sentences. Attribution to the tradition is therefore more likely than to the Dtr. The Dtr's "all the days of the judge" (2:18) would be derived from these forty-year periods.

At this point, it is extremely important to clarify two ways of reading these chapters. From one point of view, they can be read as proceeding from the stories told to the theology elaborated. From another point of view, they can be taken as a whole, with the theology fully elaborated at the beginning and to be understood in the telling of the stories. In the first instance, which is Richter's, the shifts in theology reveal further stages in the exploration of experience, culminating in the preface attributed to the Dtr. In the second instance, approximating to Noth, what is fully expressed at the beginning provides an understanding that is taken for granted in the interpretative material that follows. This second approach can be satisfactory for the issue of apostasy (2:11 and 3:7), for the kindling of God's anger (2:14a and 3:8a), for only an indirect reference to

the people's cry (2:18). It is less satisfactory for the terminology regarding the deliverer figure: a judge (2:16) a deliverer (3:9-10 and 3:15), and an unspecified figure (4:4 and 6:14-15, 34, 36). The concept of judge fits these stories of deliverance into the overall dtr pattern of the deliverer-judges. Its absence in what follows is not easily explained.

Our own preference, manifest in our formatting, is to allow for stages of development in Israel's storytelling, theological thinking, and extended composition. First, we are well aware that, no matter what hypotheses are adopted, the Dtr used sources extensively in the composition of the DH. There is a lawcode in Deuteronomy, a Conquest Narrative in Joshua, prophetic and Davidic stories in Samuel, and various sources in Kings. A source here in Judges would not be surprising. Second, the development from stories told to theology elaborated and the refining of that theology seems to us to reflect the signals in the text more faithfully. The second approach will come into play with discussion of the present text's potential.

Within the dtr preface (2:11-19), three verses are attributed to the national focus within the dtr process of revision (vv. 12-13, 17). In vv. 12-13, abandoning YHWH, following other gods, and provoking YHWH to anger are predominantly linguistic characteristics of later dtr revision. Other gods return in v. 17, along with an emphasis on obedience to the commandments of the LORD. V. 17 has a different concept of the judge and a different concept of the people's fidelity; the prophet as preacher/teacher occurs elsewhere in this national focus of the revision process. Vv. 12-13 expand v. 11. YHWH's identity is spelled out as the God of Israel's ancestors and the God of Israel's exodus from Egypt. The Baals are identified with the gods of the surrounding peoples and their worship provokes YHWH to anger. V. 13 reduces Baal to the singular and introduces the feminine element of the Astartes (Heb. = Ashtaroth).

Main pre-DH: Deliverance *Collection*
    its sources *and its framing*

Other pre-DH:
    single sideline

Josianic DH:
from the Dtr

LORD had warned them and sworn to them; and they were in great distress.

16 Then the LORD raised up judges, who delivered them out of the power of those who plundered them.

17Yet they did not listen even to their judges; for they lusted after other gods and bowed down to them. They soon turned aside from the way in which their ancestors had walked, who had obeyed the commandments of the LORD; they did not follow their example.

18Whenever the LORD raised up judges for them, the LORD was with the judge, and he delivered them from the hand of their enemies all the days of the judge; for the LORD would be moved to pity by their groaning because of those who persecuted and oppressed them. 19But whenever the judge died, they would relapse and behave worse than their ancestors, following other gods, worshiping them and bowing down to them. They would not drop any of their practices or their stubborn ways.

20So the anger of the LORD was kindled against Israel; and he said, "Because this people have transgressed my covenant that I commanded their ancestors, and have not obeyed my voice, 21I will no longer drive out before them any of the nations that Joshua left when he died." 3

Present-text potential. These verses give theological guidance for the reading of the narrative to come. The stories unfold a pattern of oppression and rescue. Theological reflection claims Israel's apostasy and God's anger as the cause of the oppression; Israel's distress and God's action in raising up deliverer figures as the cause of the rescue. Vv. 12-13 explore the various aspects of apostasy. V. 17 can be read as demythologizing any idealization of Israel under the deliverer-judges.

The differences to come will be highlighted in their place. At a present text level, they can mostly be subsumed under the theological categories formulated here.

---

3. **Text signals** in 2:20–3:6. (i) The opening picks up v. 14 but develops a different concern. Divine anger in v. 14 leads to God's raising up oppressors against Israel; divine anger in v. 20 leads to God's ceasing to drive peoples out of the land. (ii) A further shift in concern is visible between vv. 21 and 23. According to v. 21, God's action is situated after the death of Joshua; according to v. 23, God's action is situated before the death of Joshua. Hebraists will note that the NRSV's pluperfects ("had") appropriately reflect this situation. (iii) Transgression of the covenant is found in Josh 23:16; it points to the national focus within the dtr revision process (see note on Josh 7:11). (iv) The clause, "commanded their ancestors," is found also at 3:4, where Moses is mentioned as mediator. (v) "Obey my voice" as obedience to God is predominantly late (exceptions: Deut 5:25; 1 Sam 15:1, 19-20, 22). Again, the national focus within the dtr revision is likely. (vi) The concept of "testing" is found at 2:22; 3:1, 4. In 2:22 and 3:4, it is a trial; it is different in 3:1-2, where the testing in war would have been seen as beneficial. (vii) The threat in Josh 23:16 is actualized in Judg 2:20-21 and 3:5-6. (viii) The beginning of 3:1 requires a list of nations to follow, provided in 3:3. (ix) 3:2 clarifies the understanding of testing for "all those who did not know all the wars of Canaan" (literal). (x) Repetition is prevalent: "commanded their ancestors" (2:20; 3:4); "to test Israel" (2:22; 3:1, 4); list of nations (3:3, 5).

Text-history approach. The dtr revision process, within its national focus, follows up here on what was begun in Joshua 23. There, Joshua warned against intermarriage and the worship of foreign gods (cf. esp. 23:12, 16). Israel's failure is spelled out in general in 2:20-21 and in detail in 3:5-6. As is to be expected of the revision's national focus, the emphasis is on the failure of the people.

| After the Dtr: indented and sans serif font | Revision: national focus | Other: double sideline |

²²in order to test Israel, whether or not they would take care to walk in the way of the Lord as their ancestors did. ²³And the *(Heb.; NRSV, the)* Lord had left those nations, not driving them out at once, and had not handed them over to Joshua.

3 Now these are the nations that the Lord left to test all those in Israel who had no experience of any war in Canaan ²(it was only that successive generations of Israelites might know war, to teach those who had no experience of it before): ³the five lords of the Philistines, and all the Canaanites, and the Sidonians, and the Hivites who lived on Mount Lebanon, from Mount Baal-hermon as far as Lebo-hamath.

In 2:22-23, two nuances are added, one historical and one theological. Historically, peoples who remained after Joshua clearly were there in his day. Theologically, this was God's doing, measuring Israel's obedience. At issue is the long-term quality of divine providence.

3:1-3 functions as an antidote to this picture of gloom. The test becomes a matter of military training, against such traditional enemies as even the Philistines. The different understanding of testing implies a different understanding of God.

Present-text potential. The present-text potential here is limited. Vv. 11-19 have given a cyclic portrayal of Israel's infidelity on a macroscale; v. 17 has underscored that on the microscale of even a judge's generation. 2:20–3:6 go further to provide a reflection on Israel's infidelity and its consequences, viewed in the light of Joshua 23. Testing is a key theme in these reflections. Differences over providential timing and the nature of this testing are irreconcilable. The God of 2:20-21 can have a change of mind; the God of 2:22-23 does not. The testing of 2:22-23 and 3:4 leads to Israel's failure; the testing of 3:1-3 enhances Israel's defense.

---

⁴*They were for the testing of Israel, to know whether Israel would obey the commandments of the Lord, which he commanded their ancestors by Moses.* ⁵*And* (Heb.; NRSV, so) *the Israelites lived among the Canaanites, the Hittites, the Amorites, the Perizzites, the Hivites, and the Jebusites;* ⁶*and they took their daughters as wives for themselves, and their own daughters they gave to their sons; and they worshiped their gods.*

7 The Israelites did what was evil in the sight of the Lord, forgetting the Lord their God, and worshiping the Baals and the Asherahs. ⁸Therefore the anger of the Lord was kindled against Israel, and he sold them into the hand of King Cushan-rishathaim of Aram-naharaim; and the Israelites served Cushan-rishathaim eight years. ⁹But when the Israelites cried out to the Lord, the Lord raised up a deliverer for the Israelites, who delivered them, Othniel son of Kenaz, Caleb's younger brother. ¹⁰The spirit of the Lord came upon him, and he judged Israel; he went out to war, and the Lord gave King Cushan-rishathaim of Aram into his hand; and his hand prevailed over Cushan-rishathaim. ¹¹So the land was undisturbed for *(Heb.; NRSV, had rest)* forty years. Then Othniel son of Kenaz died.[4]

---

4. **Text signals** in 3:7-11. (i) This text consists of elements to be found in the preceding "preface" (2:11-19*) or in the following framing passages. (ii) There is no independent story. (iii) V. 7 names the evil as apostasy; specified as such in 2:11-13 and unspecified in 3:12a, 4:1a, 6:1a. (iv) In v. 10, the verb "to judge" is found between the coming of the spirit and the going out to war. The context is not of the law but of military deliverance. Note: "undisturbed" replaces the NRSV's "rest" in v. 11 (see also 3:30; 5:31; 8:28; also Josh 11:23). This avoids confusion with the dtr concept of rest, expressed quite differently in Hebrew (see note on Josh 21:45).

Main pre-DH: Deliverance *Collection*
   its sources *and its framing*

Other pre-DH:
single sideline

Josianic DH:
from the Dtr

12 The Israelites again did what was evil in the sight of the LORD; and the LORD strengthened King Eglon of Moab against Israel, because they had done what was evil in the sight of the LORD. 13In alliance with the Ammonites and the Amalekites, he went and defeated Israel; and they took possession of the city of palms. 14So the Israelites served King Eglon of Moab eighteen years.

Text-history approach. The elements constituting this text—i.e., Israel's evil/apostasy, God's anger and Israel's servitude, Israel's cry, God's raising up of Othniel as a deliverer, Israel's deliverance; a forty-year period of peace—are to be found framing the three following stories (Ehud, Deborah/Barak, and Gideon). These elements constitute 3:7-11; there is no story.

There are differences from the elements that follow. The evil is here characterized as apostasy (v. 7b); in what follows, the evil is left unspecified. The deliverance here is characterized as judging (v. 10); in what follows, there is no such characterization. The spirit of YHWH comes upon Othniel; in what follows, the spirit is absent from the framing elements and, in the three stories, present only in Gideon's (6:34).

There are differences from the preceding preface. There the evil is again characterized as apostasy (cf. 2:11-13). It is explicitly stated that Israel was distressed (2:15). It is not explicitly said that the people cried out, although it is implied later (2:18). The deliverers, raised by God, are termed "judges." It is explicitly said that the LORD was with the judge enabling the deliverance itself and the peace that followed in the judge's lifetime (2:18); this is only implicit in the recurring claim that Israel was undisturbed for forty years.

As noted, there are two approaches to the reading of these texts; they are not irreconcilable. The emergence of theological insight is important. At the level of the framed stories, certain generalizations have been drawn from some of Israel's individual experiences: the initial evil, the oppression as punishment, the cry that is heard, the subduing of the oppressor, and the peace of the land. The Othniel episode (3:7-11) offers a further way of understanding these experiences. Israel's evil is perceived as apostasy. God's anger is kindled. The deliverer concept is emphasized (3:9a; cf. 3:15). The onrush of the spirit is given a role.

Without the framing elements, each of the deliverances (Othniel, Ehud, Deborah/Barak, Gideon) constitutes a one-off experience. The framing elements create an association and draw out a pattern; however, in the framing elements a cyclic understanding of these traditions is only implicit. Beyond this again, the Josianic dtr preface (2:11, 14-16, 18-19) offers a further understanding of the experiences preserved in these texts. First and foremost, it makes the cyclic aspect explicit, generalizing Israel's repeated experience of God's punishment and deliverance and thereby creating a period of the judges. Furthermore, the evil is confirmed as apostasy and the anger of God is affirmed. God's punishment, the oppression, is noted as giving rise to Israel's distress; a specific cry to God can be taken for granted. The deliverers, raised up by God, are named as judges and the deliverance is made explicit for all their days. The concept of the deliverer as judge allows the integration of these traditions with those of the minor judges. In this way, the overarching conceptualization of the Josianic DH can be served.

This perception of the history of the text offers three distinct levels in which theological insight can be grasped. The framing of the single stories gives insight into Israel's experience of God as a force for liberation. Read under the influence of the Othniel composition, apostasy is seen as the primary evil in Israel, causing God's anger; the people's cry is seen as effective in causing God to raise up a deliverer coupled with the power of God's spirit. Finally, with the dtr preface, a move is made from the individual to the typical, reading the traditions as a sporadic cycle. From this dtr organization in the preface, the judges emerge favorably, raised up by God, enabled by God to deliver their people from punishing oppression and to sustain peace. There is a shadow side: after the death of each judge, the people fall relentlessly into evil and so are again punished by oppression. At this

| After the Dtr: indented and sans serif font | *Revision: national focus* | Other: double sideline |

15 But when the Israelites cried out to the LORD, the LORD raised up for them a deliverer, Ehud son of Gera, the Benjaminite, a left-handed man.[5]

stage, the potential of multiple experiences has been made explicit in an overarching perception. In our judgment, this reading most accurately reflects the history of the text.

An alternative approach to reading proceeds from the outcome, leapfrogging the stages. The dtr preface, incorporating the previous insights, exercises an overall influence on the reading of what follows. So Israel's apostasy and God's anger are mentioned a couple of times and need not be reiterated. The distress of oppressed Israel is evident and need not be emphasized; God's pity for the people is implied in God's response to their cry. God's response is spelled out in the raising up of deliverer figures and the subduing of the oppressing foe. Finally, there is the peace that comes with divinely inspired leadership. In such a reading, the cyclic is unfolded in the individual instances.

Present-text potential of 2:11–3:11. The potential of the present text lies largely in the alternative reading approach. A fully informed reader will be aware of Israel's prayer and confession in 1 Sam 7:3-6, coupled with the deliverance from Philistine oppression (7:7-14). Within the text of the book of Judges, the conquest has been a patchy affair. Blame has been laid on Israel's breach of covenant (2:1-5). A stabilizing pattern is offered in 2:11-19 that gives intelligibility to a variety of Israel's traditions. The pattern deteriorates as the book of Judges proceeds. Under the Elide priesthood, even worship has been sullied by greed. God will depart from Israel. The ark will not return to a central place in Israel until the great prophetic figure of Samuel has singled out for the throne of Israel a man after God's own heart (1 Sam 13:14; 15:28). The interpretation offered by Judg 2:11-19 reaches deep into the trajectory of Israel's story.

5. The elements here are the evil (again), the oppression, the cry to the LORD, and the raising up of a deliverer, named as Ehud. Without this last element which is integrated into the framing elements, there is

The Israelites sent tribute by him to King Eglon of Moab. [16]Ehud made for himself a sword with two edges, a cubit in length; and he fastened it on his right thigh under his clothes. [17]Then he presented the tribute to King Eglon of Moab. Now Eglon was a very fat man. [18]When Ehud had finished presenting the tribute, he sent the people who carried the tribute on their way. [19]But he himself turned back at the sculptured stones near Gilgal, and said, "I have a secret message for you, O king." So the king said, "Silence!" and all his attendants went out from his presence. [20]Ehud came to him, while he was sitting alone in his cool roof chamber, and said, "I have a message from God for you." So he rose from his seat. [21]Then Ehud reached with his left hand, took the sword from his right thigh, and thrust it into Eglon's belly; [22]the hilt also went in after the blade, and the fat closed over the blade, for he did not draw the sword out of his belly; and the dirt came out. [23]Then Ehud went out into the vestibule, and closed the doors of the roof chamber on him, and locked them.

24 After he had gone, the servants came. When they saw that the doors of the roof chamber were locked, they thought, "He must be relieving himself in the cool chamber." [25]So they waited until they were embarrassed. When he still did not open the doors of the roof chamber, they took the key and opened them. There was their lord lying dead on the floor.

no independent story (cf. "by him," v. 15b). For this reason, we speak of framing elements rather than frame. The story itself is remarkably secular, apart from vv. 20 and 28. It should be noted that in 3:12 and 4:1 it is said that the Israelites "again" did what was evil. The phrase is verbal ("they added to" = did again); it is not to be taken lightly. It expresses an association of the stories, but cannot bear too much weight. It is not present in 6:1.

| Main pre-DH: Deliverance *Collection* its sources *and its framing* | Other pre-DH: single sideline | **Josianic DH: from the Dtr** |

26 Ehud escaped while they delayed, and passed beyond the sculptured stones, and escaped to Seirah. ²⁷When he arrived, he sounded the trumpet in the hill country of Ephraim; and the Israelites went down with him from the hill country, having him at their head. ²⁸He said to them, "Follow after me; for the LORD has given your enemies the Moabites into your hand." So they went down after him, and seized the fords of the Jordan against the Moabites, and allowed no one to cross over. ²⁹At that time they killed about ten thousand of the Moabites, all strong, able-bodied men; no one escaped.

³⁰*So Moab was subdued that day under the hand of Israel. And the land was undisturbed for* (Heb.; NRSV, had rest) *eighty years.*[6]

31 After him came Shamgar son of Anath, who killed six hundred of the Philistines with an oxgoad. *He too delivered Israel.*[7]

4 *The Israelites again did what was evil in the sight of the LORD, after Ehud died.* ²*So the LORD sold them into the hand of King Jabin of Canaan, who reigned in Hazor; the commander of his army was Sisera,* *who lived in Harosheth-ha-goiim.* ³*Then the Israelites cried out to the LORD for help;*[8] for he had nine hundred chariots of iron, and had oppressed the Israelites cruelly twenty years.

4 At that time Deborah, a prophetess, wife of Lappidoth, was judging Israel. ⁵She used to sit under the palm of Deborah between Ramah and Bethel in the hill country of Ephraim; and the Israelites came up to her for judgment. ⁶She sent and summoned Barak son of Abinoam from Kedesh in Naphtali, and said to him, "The LORD, the God of Israel, commands you, 'Go, take position at Mount Tabor, bringing ten thousand from the tribe of Naphtali and the tribe of Zebulun. ⁷I will draw out Sisera, the general of Jabin's army, to meet you by the Wadi Kishon with his chariots and his troops; and I will give him into your hand.' " ⁸Barak said to her, "If you will go with me, I will go; but if you will not go with me, I will not go." ⁹And she said, "I will surely go with you; nevertheless, the road on which you are going will not lead to your glory, for the LORD will sell Sisera into the hand of a woman." Then Deborah got up and went with Barak to Kedesh. ¹⁰Barak summoned Zebulun and Naphtali to Kedesh; and ten thousand warriors went up behind him; and Deborah went up with him.

---

6. With v. 30, the framing elements are completed. The foe is subdued and the land is at peace. The eighty years is understood to create space for a Shamgar story (cf. v. 31).

7. The single verse on Shamgar is a source of embarrassment rather than enlightenment. Presumably a story was available, to be associated with the name (cf. Judg 5:6); clearly it has not been recorded. The name is unlikely to be Israelite; even if the patronymic Anath is considered more likely to reflect a place name than the name of the goddess. If reference to the death of Ehud in 4:1 is original, the verse concerning Shamgar will be later. The interconnectedness of these issues is such that any change in the text must be hypothetical.

8. The elements here are the evil (with the "again"), the oppression, and the cry to YHWH. It is not said that YHWH raised up a deliverer; instead, the deliverer is to be found within the original story. Deborah gives a command from God to Barak (4:6-7); the two of them win victory for Israel over Sisera's army (4:14-16). The death of Sisera, the enemy general, is achieved by Jael, a non-Israelite woman (4:17-22). Within this story, the sacral element is evident at vv. 6-7, 9, 14-15. It is interesting that the action of God permeates the main battle account (4:6-16), while the story of Jael's deed is entirely secular.

| After the Dtr: indented and sans serif font | Revision: national focus | Other: double sideline |

11 Now Heber the Kenite had separated from the other Kenites, that is, the descendants of Hobab the father-in-law of Moses, and had encamped as far away as Elon-bezaanannim, which is near Kedesh.

12 When Sisera was told that Barak son of Abinoam had gone up to Mount Tabor, [13]Sisera called out all his chariots, nine hundred chariots of iron, and all the troops who were with him, from Harosheth-ha-goiim to the Wadi Kishon. [14]Then Deborah said to Barak, "Up! For this is the day on which the LORD has given Sisera into your hand. The LORD is indeed going out before you." So Barak went down from Mount Tabor with ten thousand warriors following him. [15]And the LORD threw Sisera and all his chariots and all his army into a panic before Barak; Sisera got down from his chariot and fled away on foot, [16]while Barak pursued the chariots and the army to Harosheth-ha-goiim. All the army of Sisera fell by the sword; no one was left.

17 Now Sisera had fled away on foot to the tent of Jael wife of Heber the Kenite; for there was peace between King Jabin of Hazor and the clan of Heber the Kenite. [18]Jael came out to meet Sisera, and said to him, "Turn aside, my lord, turn aside to me; have no fear." So he turned aside to her into the tent, and she covered him with a rug. [19]Then he said to her, "Please give me a little water to drink; for I am thirsty." So she opened a skin of milk and gave him a drink and covered him. [20]He said to her, "Stand at the entrance of the tent, and if anybody comes and asks you, 'Is anyone here?' say, 'No.'" [21]But Jael wife of Heber took a tent peg, and took a hammer in her hand, and went softly to him and drove the peg into his temple, until it went down into the ground—he was lying fast asleep from weariness—and he died. [22]Then, as Barak came in pursuit of Sisera, Jael went out to meet him, and said to him, "Come, and I will show you the man whom you are seeking." So he went into her tent; and there was Sisera lying dead, with the tent peg in his temple.

23 So on that day God subdued King Jabin of Canaan before the Israelites. [24]Then the hand of the Israelites bore harder and harder on King Jabin of Canaan, until they destroyed King Jabin of Canaan.[9]

5 Then Deborah and Barak son of Abinoam sang on that day, saying:

  2 "When locks are long in Israel,
      when the people offer themselves
        willingly—
      bless the LORD!
  3 "Hear, O kings; give ear, O princes;
      to the LORD I will sing,
    I will make melody to the LORD, the
        God of Israel.
  4 "LORD, when you went out from Seir,
      when you marched from the region
        of Edom,

---

9. The framing element of the subduing of King Jabin's forces is given in v. 23; the report of the land being at peace is not given until the end of chap. 5 (i.e., 5:31b). 4:24 is difficult. It refers to King Jabin, not to Sisera. Therefore, it is not easily situated within the story; the difficulty of correlation with Josh 11:1-15 is well known (cf. Noth, *DH*, 73-74). The phrasing ("bore harder and harder") looks to an extensive period, beyond the simple act of subduing; it may mean no more than a balance to 5:31b. The reference, "on that day" of v. 23, refers to Israel's victory in battle, with the destruction of Jabin's army and the death of its general (Sisera). The separation of Jabin's destruction (4:24) from Israel's tranquillity (5:31) suggests that 4:24 may function to allow space for Judges 5, even though the song ends with the fate of Sisera. The song rehearses the victory of Deborah and Barak and Jael's killing of Sisera; it is not clear that it describes a time of Israel's oppression.

Main pre-DH: *Deliverance* Collection
  its sources *and its framing*

Other pre-DH:
single sideline

**Josianic DH:
from the Dtr**

the earth trembled,
 and the heavens poured,
 the clouds indeed poured water.
5 The mountains quaked before the LORD,
 the One of Sinai,
 before the LORD, the God of Israel.
6 "In the days of Shamgar son of Anath,
 in the days of Jael, caravans ceased
 and travelers kept to the byways.
7 The peasantry prospered in Israel,
 they grew fat on plunder,
because you arose, Deborah,
 arose as a mother in Israel.
8 When new gods were chosen,
 then war was in the gates.
Was shield or spear to be seen
 among forty thousand in Israel?
9 My heart goes out to the commanders of
 Israel
 who offered themselves willingly
  among the people.
 Bless the LORD.
10 "Tell of it, you who ride on white
  donkeys,
 you who sit on rich carpets
 and you who walk by the way.
11 To the sound of musicians at the
  watering places,
 there they repeat the triumphs of
  the LORD,
 the triumphs of his peasantry in Israel.
"Then down to the gates marched the
  people of the LORD.
12 "Awake, awake, Deborah!
 Awake, awake, utter a song!
Arise, Barak, lead away your captives,
 O son of Abinoam.
13 Then down marched the remnant of
  the noble;
 the people of the LORD marched down
  for him against the mighty.

14 From Ephraim they set out into the
  valley,
 following you, Benjamin, with
  your kin;
from Machir marched down the
  commanders,
 and from Zebulun those who bear
  the marshal's staff;
15 the chiefs of Issachar came with
  Deborah,
 and Issachar faithful to Barak;
 into the valley they rushed out at
  his heels.
Among the clans of Reuben
 there were great searchings of heart.
16 Why did you tarry among the
  sheepfolds,
 to hear the piping for the flocks?[10]
Among the clans of Reuben
 there were great searchings of heart.
17 Gilead stayed beyond the Jordan;
 and Dan, why did he abide with
  the ships?
Asher sat still at the coast of the sea,
 settling down by his landings.
18 Zebulun is a people that scorned death;
 Naphtali too, on the heights of
  the field.
19 "The kings came, they fought;
 then fought the kings of Canaan,
at Taanach, by the waters of Megiddo;
 they got no spoils of silver.

---

10. Insignificant enough in itself, the disunity in Israel alluded to here—with the explicit absence of at least Reuben and Gilead, Dan and Asher—becomes more significant as it is heightened in the deliverer stories to come (cf. Gideon and Jephthah). The framing emphasizes deliverance; the stories sow seeds of disunity as well.

After the Dtr: *Revision:*   Other:
indented and sans serif font   *national focus*   double sideline

²⁰ The stars fought from heaven,
   from their courses they fought
      against Sisera.
²¹ The torrent Kishon swept them away,
   the onrushing torrent, the torrent
      Kishon.
   March on, my soul, with might!
²² "Then loud beat the horses' hoofs
   with the galloping, galloping of
      his steeds.
²³ "Curse Meroz, says the angel of
      the Lord,
   curse bitterly its inhabitants,
because they did not come to the help
      of the Lord,
   to the help of the Lord against
      the mighty.
²⁴ "Most blessed of women be Jael,
   the wife of Heber the Kenite,
   of tent-dwelling women most blessed.
²⁵ He asked water and she gave him milk,
   she brought him curds in a lordly bowl.
²⁶ She put her hand to the tent peg
   and her right hand to the workmen's
      mallet;
she struck Sisera a blow,
   she crushed his head,
   she shattered and pierced his temple.
²⁷ He sank, he fell,
   he lay still at her feet;
at her feet he sank, he fell;
   where he sank, there he fell dead.
²⁸ "Out of the window she peered,
   the mother of Sisera gazed through
      the lattice:
'Why is his chariot so long in coming?
   Why tarry the hoofbeats of his
      chariots?'
²⁹ Her wisest ladies make answer,
   indeed, she answers the question
      herself:

³⁰ 'Are they not finding and dividing the
spoil?—
   A girl or two for every man;
spoil of dyed stuffs for Sisera,
   spoil of dyed stuffs embroidered,
   two pieces of dyed work embroidered
      for my neck as spoil?'
³¹ "So perish all your enemies, O Lord!
   But may your friends be like the sun
      as it rises in its might."
And the land was undisturbed for (Heb.; NRSV, had
rest) *forty years.*

6 *The Israelites did what was evil in the sight of the*
Lord, and the Lord gave them into the hand of
Midian seven years.[11]
²The hand of Midian prevailed over Israel; and
because of Midian the Israelites provided for
themselves hiding places in the mountains,
caves and strongholds. ³For whenever the

---

11. The framing elements here are the evil (but
without the "again") and the oppression. The cry to
YHWH and the commissioning of a deliverer are both
to be found within the tradition (6:6, 14). These
observations make it tempting to suggest that the
Gideon tradition originates this association of deliverance stories. Any reconstruction, however, is too complex and too uncertain to carry conviction. Complexity and uncertainty are heightened by the multiple
stories that form the Gideon tradition itself.

Within these Gideon stories, the secular has little
place. From the initial theophany, God's presence permeates the stories. It is all the more noteworthy that
the strategies involved in the actual attack are secular,
suitable, and carry considerable risk. The basic strategy is a night attack, panicking the enemy with noise
and flares. With a view to coordination, a small number of fighters would have been essential. Around this
secular core, however, a mass of much less secular tradition has been assembled. Detailed analysis of the
three chapters does not belong here.

Israelites put in seed, the Midianites and the Amalekites and the people of the east would come up against them. ⁴They would encamp against them and destroy the produce of the land, as far as the neighborhood of Gaza, and leave no sustenance in Israel, and no sheep or ox or donkey. ⁵For they and their livestock would come up, and they would even bring their tents, as thick as locusts; neither they nor their camels could be counted; so they wasted the land as they came in. ⁶Thus Israel was greatly impoverished because of Midian; and the Israelites cried out to the Lord for help.

> *7 When the Israelites cried to the Lord on account of the Midianites, ⁸the Lord sent a prophet to the Israelites; and he said to them, "Thus says the Lord, the God of Israel: I led you up from Egypt, and brought you out of the house of slavery; ⁹and I delivered you from the hand of the Egyptians, and from the hand of all who oppressed you, and drove them out before you, and gave you their land; ¹⁰and I said to you, 'I am the Lord your God; you shall not pay reverence to the gods of the Amorites, in whose land you live.' But you have not given heed to my voice."¹²*

11 Now the angel of the Lord came and sat under the oak at Ophrah, which belonged to Joash the Abiezrite, as his son Gideon was beating out wheat in the wine press, to hide it from the Midianites. ¹²The angel of the Lord appeared to him and said to him, "The Lord is with you, you mighty warrior." ¹³Gideon answered him, "But sir, if the Lord is with us, why then has all this happened to us? And where are all his wonderful deeds that our ancestors recounted to us, saying, 'Did not the Lord bring us up from Egypt?' But now the Lord has cast us off, and given us into the hand of Midian." ¹⁴Then the Lord turned to him and said, "Go in this might of yours and deliver Israel from the hand of Midian; I hereby commission you." ¹⁵He responded, "But sir, how can I deliver Israel? My clan is the weakest in Manasseh, and I am the least in my family." ¹⁶The Lord said to him, "But I will be with you, and you shall strike down the Midianites, every one of them." ¹⁷Then he said to him, "If now I have found favor with you, then show me a sign that it is you who speak with me. ¹⁸Do not depart from here until I come to you, and bring out my present, and set it before you." And he said, "I will stay until you return."

19 So Gideon went into his house and prepared a kid, and unleavened cakes from an ephah of flour; the meat he put in a basket, and the broth he put in a pot, and brought them to him under the oak and presented them. ²⁰The angel of God said to him, "Take the meat and the

---

12. The dtr concerns of 6:7-10 are evident. Attribution to the national focus, within the dtr revision, is suggested by the role of the prophet as a preacher of the law (cf. Judg 2:17), by the warning given the people (cf. Joshua 23), and by the accusation that Israel failed to give heed to yhwh's voice (cf. Judg 2:20). What these few verses do is situate Israel's oppression and their appeal to God within the trajectory of their saving history that began with the slavery of Egypt and the deliverance of the exodus.

Within the trajectory of the story of the judges, it is worth noting that in 2:1-5 an accusation is brought against Israel by the angel of the Lord. Here, it is a prophet who accuses Israel. In 10:10-16, it will be yhwh who levels the ultimate accusation against Israel. There is a movement across these accusations: from apostasy as threat (2:3), to apostasy as reality (6:10), and finally to the threat of abandonment by yhwh because of apostasy (10:13-14). This movement mirrors something of the sense of an image of Israel declining as the narrative progresses.

After the Dtr:	*Revision:*	Other:
indented and sans serif font	*national focus*	double sideline

unleavened cakes, and put them on this rock, and pour out the broth." And he did so. [21]Then the angel of the Lᴏʀᴅ reached out the tip of the staff that was in his hand, and touched the meat and the unleavened cakes; and fire sprang up from the rock and consumed the meat and the unleavened cakes; and the angel of the Lᴏʀᴅ vanished from his sight. [22]Then Gideon perceived that it was the angel of the Lᴏʀᴅ; and Gideon said, "Help me, Lord Gᴏᴅ! For I have seen the angel of the Lᴏʀᴅ face to face." [23]But the Lᴏʀᴅ said to him, "Peace be to you; do not fear, you shall not die." [24]Then Gideon built an altar there to the Lᴏʀᴅ, and called it, The Lᴏʀᴅ is peace. To this day it still stands at Ophrah, which belongs to the Abiezrites.

25 That night the Lᴏʀᴅ said to him, "Take your father's bull, the second bull seven years old, and pull down the altar of Baal that belongs to your father, and cut down the sacred pole that is beside it; [26]and build an altar to the Lᴏʀᴅ your God on the top of the stronghold here, in proper order; then take the second bull, and offer it as a burnt offering with the wood of the sacred pole that you shall cut down." [27]So Gideon took ten of his servants, and did as the Lᴏʀᴅ had told him; but because he was too afraid of his family and the townspeople to do it by day, he did it by night.

28 When the townspeople rose early in the morning, the altar of Baal was broken down, and the sacred pole beside it was cut down, and the second bull was offered on the altar that had been built. [29]So they said to one another, "Who has done this?" After searching and inquiring, they were told, "Gideon son of Joash did it." [30]Then the townspeople said to Joash, "Bring out your son, so that he may die, for he has pulled down the altar of Baal and cut down the sacred pole beside it." [31]But Joash said to all who were arrayed against him, "Will you contend for Baal? Or will you defend his cause? Whoever contends for him shall be put to death by morning. If he is a god, let him contend for himself, because his altar has been pulled down." [32]Therefore on that day Gideon was called Jerubbaal, that is to say, "Let Baal contend against him," because he pulled down his altar.

33 Then all the Midianites and the Amalekites and the people of the east came together, and crossing the Jordan they encamped in the Valley of Jezreel. [34]But the spirit of the Lᴏʀᴅ took possession of Gideon; and he sounded the trumpet, and the Abiezrites were called out to follow him. [35]He sent messengers throughout all Manasseh, and they too were called out to follow him. He also sent messengers to Asher, Zebulun, and Naphtali, and they went up to meet them.

36 Then Gideon said to God, "In order to see whether you will deliver Israel by my hand, as you have said, [37]I am going to lay a fleece of wool on the threshing floor; if there is dew on the fleece alone, and it is dry on all the ground, then I shall know that you will deliver Israel by my hand, as you have said." [38]And it was so. When he rose early next morning and squeezed the fleece, he wrung enough dew from the fleece to fill a bowl with water. [39]Then Gideon said to God, "Do not let your anger burn against me, let me speak one more time; let me, please, make trial with the fleece just once more; let it be dry only on the fleece, and on all the ground let there be dew." [40]And God did so that night. It was dry on the fleece only, and on all the ground there was dew.

7 Then Jerubbaal (that is, Gideon) and all the troops that were with him rose early and encamped beside the spring of Harod; and the camp of Midian was north of them, below the hill of Moreh, in the valley.

Main pre-DH: Deliverance *Collection* its sources *and its framing*	Other pre-DH: single sideline	**Josianic DH:** **from the Dtr**

2 The LORD said to Gideon, "The troops with you are too many for me to give the Midianites into their hand. Israel would only take the credit away from me, saying, 'My own hand has delivered me.' [3]Now therefore proclaim this in the hearing of the troops, 'Whoever is fearful and trembling, let him return home.' " Thus Gideon sifted them out; twenty-two thousand returned, and ten thousand remained.

4 Then the LORD said to Gideon, "The troops are still too many; take them down to the water and I will sift them out for you there. When I say, 'This one shall go with you,' he shall go with you; and when I say, 'This one shall not go with you,' he shall not go." [5]So he brought the troops down to the water; and the LORD said to Gideon, "All those who lap the water with their tongues, as a dog laps, you shall put to one side; all those who kneel down to drink, putting their hands to their mouths, you shall put to the other side." [6]The number of those that lapped was three hundred; but all the rest of the troops knelt down to drink water. [7]Then the LORD said to Gideon, "With the three hundred that lapped I will deliver you, and give the Midianites into your hand. Let all the others go to their homes." [8]So he took the jars of the troops from their hands, and their trumpets; and he sent all the rest of Israel back to their own tents, but retained the three hundred. The camp of Midian was below him in the valley.

9 That same night the LORD said to him, "Get up, attack the camp; for I have given it into your hand. [10]But if you fear to attack, go down to the camp with your servant Purah; [11]and you shall hear what they say, and afterward your hands shall be strengthened to attack the camp." Then he went down with his servant Purah to the outposts of the armed men that were in the camp. [12]The Midianites and the Amalekites and all the people of the east lay along the valley as

thick as locusts; and their camels were without number, countless as the sand on the seashore. [13]When Gideon arrived, there was a man telling a dream to his comrade; and he said, "I had a dream, and in it a cake of barley bread tumbled into the camp of Midian, and came to the tent, and struck it so that it fell; it turned upside down, and the tent collapsed." [14]And his comrade answered, "This is no other than the sword of Gideon son of Joash, a man of Israel; into his hand God has given Midian and all the army."

15 When Gideon heard the telling of the dream and its interpretation, he worshiped; and he returned to the camp of Israel, and said, "Get up; for the LORD has given the army of Midian into your hand." [16]After he divided the three hundred men into three companies, and put trumpets into the hands of all of them, and empty jars, with torches inside the jars, [17]he said to them, "Look at me, and do the same; when I come to the outskirts of the camp, do as I do. [18]When I blow the trumpet, I and all who are with me, then you also blow the trumpets around the whole camp, and shout, 'For the LORD and for Gideon!' "

19 So Gideon and the hundred who were with him came to the outskirts of the camp at the beginning of the middle watch, when they had just set the watch; and they blew the trumpets and smashed the jars that were in their hands. [20]So the three companies blew the trumpets and broke the jars, holding in their left hands the torches, and in their right hands the trumpets to blow; and they cried, "A sword for the LORD and for Gideon!" [21]Every man stood in his place all around the camp, and all the men in camp ran; they cried out and fled. [22]When they blew the three hundred trumpets, the LORD set every man's sword against his fellow and against all the army; and the army fled as far as Beth-shittah toward Zererah, as far as the border of Abel-

---

After the Dtr:
indented and sans serif font

Revision:
national focus

Other:
double sideline

meholah, by Tabbath. [23]And the men of Israel were called out from Naphtali and from Asher and from all Manasseh, and they pursued after the Midianites.

24 Then Gideon sent messengers throughout all the hill country of Ephraim, saying, "Come down against the Midianites and seize the waters against them, as far as Beth-barah, and also the Jordan." So all the men of Ephraim were called out, and they seized the waters as far as Beth-barah, and also the Jordan. [25]They captured the two captains of Midian, Oreb and Zeeb; they killed Oreb at the rock of Oreb, and Zeeb they killed at the wine press of Zeeb, as they pursued the Midianites. They brought the heads of Oreb and Zeeb to Gideon beyond the Jordan.

8 Then the Ephraimites said to him, "What have you done to us, not to call us when you went to fight against the Midianites?" And they upbraided him violently. [2]So he said to them, "What have I done now in comparison with you? Is not the gleaning of the grapes of Ephraim better than the vintage of Abiezer? [3]God has given into your hands the captains of Midian, Oreb and Zeeb; what have I been able to do in comparison with you?" When he said this, their anger against him subsided.[13]

4 Then Gideon came to the Jordan and crossed over, he and the three hundred who were with him, exhausted and famished. [5]So he said to the people of Succoth, "Please give some loaves of bread to my followers, for they are exhausted, and I am pursuing Zebah and Zalmunna, the kings of Midian." [6]But the officials of Succoth said, "Do you already have in your possession the hands of Zebah and Zalmunna, that we should give bread to your army?" [7]Gideon replied, "Well then, when the LORD has given Zebah and Zalmunna into my hand, I will trample your flesh on the thorns of the wilderness and on briers." [8]From there he went up to Penuel, and made the same request of them; and the people of Penuel answered him as the people of Succoth had answered. [9]So he said to the people of Penuel, "When I come back victorious, I will break down this tower."

10 Now Zebah and Zalmunna were in Karkor with their army, about fifteen thousand men, all who were left of all the army of the people of the east; for one hundred twenty thousand men bearing arms had fallen. [11]So Gideon went up by the caravan route east of Nobah and Jogbehah, and attacked the army; for the army was off its guard. [12]Zebah and Zalmunna fled; and he pursued them and took the two kings of Midian, Zebah and Zalmunna, and threw all the army into a panic.

13 When Gideon son of Joash returned from the battle by the ascent of Heres, [14]he caught a young man, one of the people of Succoth, and questioned him; and he listed for him the officials and elders of Succoth, seventy-seven people. [15]Then he came to the people of Succoth, and said, "Here are Zebah and Zalmunna, about whom you taunted me, saying, 'Do you already have in your possession the hands of Zebah and Zalmunna, that we should give bread to your troops who are exhausted?'" [16]So he took the elders of the city and he took thorns of the wilderness and briers and with them he trampled the people of Succoth. [17]He also broke down the tower of Penuel, and killed the men of the city.

18 Then he said to Zebah and Zalmunna, "What about the men whom you killed at

---

13. The seeds of disunity sown in the stories (cf. note on Judg 5:16) reappear here. There is strife with Ephraim and slaughter for Succoth and Penuel. In the Song of Deborah, disunity received an allusion; here, a couple of episodes are given to it (cf. 8:1-17).

Tabor?" They answered, "As you are, so were they, every one of them; they resembled the sons of a king." [19]And he replied, "They were my brothers, the sons of my mother; as the LORD lives, if you had saved them alive, I would not kill you." [20]So he said to Jether his firstborn, "Go kill them!" But the boy did not draw his sword, for he was afraid, because he was still a boy. [21]Then Zebah and Zalmunna said, "You come and kill us; for as the man is, so is his strength." So Gideon proceeded to kill Zebah and Zalmunna; and he took the crescents that were on the necks of their camels.

> 22 Then the Israelites said to Gideon, "Rule over us, you and your son and your grandson also; for you have delivered us out of the hand of Midian." [23]Gideon said to them, "I will not rule over you, and my son will not rule over you; the LORD will rule over you." [24]Then Gideon said to them, "Let me make a request of you; each of you give me an earring he has taken as booty." (For the enemy had golden earrings, because they were Ishmaelites.) [25]"We will willingly give them," they answered. So they spread a garment, and each threw into it an earring he had taken as booty. [26]The weight of the golden earrings that he requested was one thousand seven hundred shekels of gold (apart from the crescents and the pendants and the purple garments worn by the kings of Midian, and the collars that were on the necks of their camels). [27]Gideon made an ephod of it and put it in his town, in Ophrah; and all Israel prostituted themselves to it there, and it became a snare to Gideon and to his family.[14]

---

14. These verses sit oddly in their context. Despite various attempts to establish links, they are not associated with what follows in chap. 9 or with what pre-

[28]*So Midian was subdued before the Israelites, and they lifted up their heads no more. So the land was undisturbed for* (Heb.; NRSV, had rest) *forty years in the days of Gideon.*[15]

---

cedes. With classic orthodoxy, Gideon rejects the offer of dynastic rule (vv. 22-23; for the language of "rule over," cf. Abimelech in 9:2; Philistines in 14:4; 15:11). In a tradition that cannot be separated from this (cf. "Gideon said to them," v. 24a), Gideon makes and sets up an ephod to which "all Israel prostituted themselves" and which was a snare to Gideon and his family. The language of Israel's prostituting itself (as apostasy) is rare (e.g., 8:33; cf. Hos 4:15; 5:3). The language of gods as snare here is found also in Deut 7:16; Josh 23:13; and Judg 2:3. The ephod evokes the traditions of Judges 17–18.

The function of the passage is not easy to discern. Gideon is exculpated from the implications of 9:2, but he makes an ephod and provides the occasion for Israel to prostitute themselves. This aspect does not sit well with 8:35b ("all the good he had done to Israel"). The passage begins with hope and ends with sin; so did the monarchy. There are thematic associations with Judges 17–21. Noth is not helpful (*DH*, 74-75). No adequate account can be given for the introduction of the verses here; they would appear to be later than 8:33-35.

The tradition's survival is a remarkable tribute to the breadth of Israel's theological holdings. No human being is without its shadow. Alongside Gideon the deliverer hero, Israel's theology retained a memory of Gideon the apostate.

15. As before, we have in v. 28 the two framing elements of the oppressor's being subdued and the land being at peace for the generation of the deliverer—with the added "in the days of Gideon." In v. 32, the death of the deliverer is noted, as with Ehud (4:1). This notice, following v. 28, may confirm that Gideon's death occurred at the end of the forty-year period (cf. Noth, *DH*, 74). Alternatively, the emphasis on burial may derive from the minor judges (cf. 10:2, 5; 12:7, 10, 12, 15). Note the differing nomenclature in v. 29 and v. 32a.

After the Dtr:	*Revision:*	Other:
indented and sans serif font	*national focus*	double sideline

29 Jerubbaal son of Joash went to live in his own house. [30]Now Gideon had seventy sons, his own offspring, for he had many wives. [31]His concubine who was in Shechem also bore him a son, and he named him Abimelech.[16]

32 Then Gideon son of Joash died at a good old age, and was buried in the tomb of his father Joash at Ophrah of the Abiezrites.

33 As soon as Gideon died, the Israelites relapsed and prostituted themselves with the Baals, making Baal-berith their god. [34]The Israelites did not remember the LORD their God, who had rescued them from the hand of all their enemies on every side. [35]And they did not exhibit loyalty to the house of Jerubbaal (that is, Gideon) in return for all the good that he had done to Israel.[17]

9 Now Abimelech son of Jerubbaal went to Shechem to his mother's kinsfolk and said to them and to the whole clan of his mother's family, [2]"Say in the hearing of all the lords of Shechem, 'Which is better for you, that all seventy of the sons of Jerubbaal rule over you, or that one rule over you?' Remember also that I am your bone and your flesh." [3]So his mother's kinsfolk spoke all these words on his behalf in the hearing of all the lords of Shechem; and their hearts inclined to follow Abimelech, for they said, "He is our brother." [4]They gave him seventy pieces of silver out of the temple of Baal-berith with which Abimelech hired worthless and reckless fellows, who followed him. [5]He went to his father's house at Ophrah, and killed his brothers the sons of Jerubbaal, seventy men, on one stone; but Jotham, the youngest son of Jerubbaal, survived, for he hid himself. [6]Then all the lords of Shechem and all Beth-millo came together, and they went and

---

16. Verses 29-31 function in two ways. They bring Abimelech on to the scene, before bringing the Gideon story to a close. The name Jerubbaal (used here in v. 29) is given to Gideon in 6:32 and reiterated in 7:1; these prepare for the story in chap. 9, where Jerubbaal is used exclusively. In the possible hypothesis that chap. 9 was added by the royal focus of the dtr revision process (blaming the evil of the kings), these preparatory verses could belong with that addition (but uncertain, hence the double sideline).

17. In vv. 33-35, the dtr pattern established for the deliverer-judges is not followed. In the pattern, apostasy is followed by foreign oppression and deliverance, which is not the case here. Some linguistic aspects are significant. "Prostituted themselves with" occurs elsewhere in the DH only twice (Deut 31:16; Judg 2:17); Judg 2:17 belongs within the national focus of the revision process. "Did not remember the LORD" (v. 34) occurs only here. "Rescued them" (√NṢL) is nowhere attributed to the Josianic Dtr and occurs several times within the revision's national focus (Judg 6:9; 10:15; 1 Sam 7:3; 10:18; 12:10, 11, 21). "Rescued

them from the hand of their enemies on every side" occurs only here and in 1 Sam 12:11. The cyclic theology—with the death of the judge, Israel relapses into apostasy—echoes that of the dtr preface, but the Abimelech story is not of foreign oppression at the hands of the LORD and it is not followed by the people's cry. The singular focus on Baal-berith in v. 33b reflects the presence of Judges 9 (cf. 9:4), as does the use of Jerubbaal and the reference to disloyalty (v. 35; cf. 9:5). In the hypothesis—which is possible but far from certain—that the Abimelech story of chap. 9 was added as part of the royal focus of the dtr revision process (blaming the kings), the factors just noted suggest the possibility of situating vv. 33-35 within the dtr revision's national focus, directing attention to the people's apostasy as the setting for the Abimelech story (as above: uncertain, hence the double sideline).

Main pre-DH: Deliverance *Collection*
  its sources *and its framing*

Other pre-DH:
single sideline

Josianic DH:
from the Dtr

made Abimelech king, by the oak of the pillar at Shechem.[18]

7 When it was told to Jotham, he went and stood on the top of Mount Gerizim,

---

18. **Text signals** in 9:1-57. (i) There is no sign of any editorial activity by the Josianic Dtr. The Abimelech story is not integrated into the dtr pattern; nor is any judgment expressed by the Dtr. (ii) The Abimelech story deals with internal strife rather than external oppression. (iii) The name Jerubbaal is used for Gideon throughout 9:1-57; otherwise, only 6:32; 7:1; 8:29, 35; and 1 Sam 12:11. (iv) Vv. 1-6 rehearse how Abimelech won power by agreement with the citizens of Shechem and by the fratricidal elimination of his seventy brothers. Over against this stands the parable of Jotham (vv. 7-21). It is linked into the Abimelech story by v. 5b (assuming that the seventy is a round figure; cf. the Jehu story, 2 Kgs 10:1-11). After v. 21, Jotham does not reappear as a character in the story (cf. by contrast, Joash in 2 Kings 11). (v) Abimelech is portrayed as king of Shechem; but his rule over Israel is put on record at v. 22 and Israelites are mentioned at v. 55. (vi) Hostility between Abimelech and the citizens of Shechem is attributed to an evil spirit sent by God (v. 23). The development of this in v. 24 fingers first Abimelech and then the citizens of Shechem. This is mirrored in v. 56, dealing with Abimelech and v. 57a dealing with the people of Shechem. V. 57b returns to the curse of Jotham.

Text-history approach. The Abimelech story (9:1-57) is not without its difficulties. It may be the counterposition to the deliverer-judges expressed in the Deliverance Collection (with Richter). The stories of the judges reveal how tranquillity is restored in Israel; the story of Abimelech shows how it is not—particularly in the person of a king, and a self-appointed king at that. It is a strange story. It may have belonged in the Josianic DH, associated with the Deliverance Collection, in which case the absence of any comment from the Josianic Dtr is surprising.

An alternative conclusion from the Josianic Dtr's silence and the oddness of the story at this point in the DH is, as we have noted, the possibility that its inser-

tion occurred as part of the royal focus of the dtr process of revision (blaming the evil of kings). This possibility is envisaged in conjunction with the conviction that it was as part of the dtr revision's "royal" focus (blaming kings) that the bulk of 1 Samuel 7–8 and some of 10 was introduced into the DH. See below in 1 Samuel.

Two observations are important. First, this is a discussion of possibilities; there is nothing to claim it as necessary. As a conjecture about the history of the text, these possibilities may make attractive sense. As hypotheses, they make no more claim than that they make attractive sense. Second, these suggestions are consonant with three moves that seem to have occurred within dtr circles and that can be seen mirrored in dtr text. The Josianic Dtr looked to right kingship to operate effectively in Israel; those hopes were dashed by events. With this failure, a movement within dtr circles placed the blame squarely on the monarchy; these reflections produced the texts we attribute to a royal focus (blaming the evil of kings) within the dtr process of revision. This disappointment led to further theologizing in these dtr circles and the conviction that the blame for failure was shared by the people; this thinking produced the texts we situate within the national focus of the dtr revision.

Against this background, we can visualize the following possibilities. The Josianic Dtr took over the Deliverance Collection and created the understanding of deliverer-judges. With or without the Abimelech story and with or without the Samson stories, God's interaction with Israel on the pattern of the deliverer-judges ran into the sands. It petered out with Jephthah and the remnant of minor judges (or worse: with Samson). In Israel, and within the DH, the emergence of a prophet heralded something that was new. The divinely controlled departure of the ark from Shiloh signaled something that was ended in Israel. For the Josianic Dtr, building toward hope under Josiah, it would make good sense for the prophet as God's intermediary to establish a totally new institution in Israel, monarchy.

For the dtr revision's royal focus, confronted by the reality of the monarchy's failure, a different under-

---

After the Dtr:
indented and sans serif font

Revision:
national focus

Other:
double sideline

and cried aloud and said to them, "Listen to me, you lords of Shechem, so that God may listen to you.
⁸ The trees once went out
 to anoint a king over themselves.
So they said to the olive tree,
 'Reign over us.'
⁹ The olive tree answered them,
 'Shall I stop producing my rich oil
  by which gods and mortals
   are honored
  and go to sway over the
   trees?'
¹⁰ Then the trees said to the fig tree,
 'You come and reign over us.'
¹¹ But the fig tree answered them,
 'Shall I stop producing my
  sweetness
  and my delicious fruit,
  and go to sway over the
   trees?'

¹² Then the trees said to the vine,
 'You come and reign over us.'
¹³ But the vine said to them,
 'Shall I stop producing my wine
  that cheers gods and mortals,
  and go to sway over the trees?'
¹⁴ So all the trees said to the bramble,
 'You come and reign over us.'
¹⁵ And the bramble said to the trees,
 'If in good faith you are anointing
  me king over you,
  then come and take refuge in
   my shade;
  but if not, let fire come out of the
   bramble
  and devour the cedars of
   Lebanon.'
16 "Now therefore, if you acted in good faith and honor when you made Abimelech king, and if you have dealt well with Jerubbaal and his house, and have done to him as his actions deserved—¹⁷for

---

standing of Israel was called for. For this revision, the self-initiated kingship of Abimelech would have been a strong example of all that was wrong with monarchy and an excellent imagistic balance to the portrayal of the deliverer-judges as God's instruments to bring tranquillity to Israel. For this royal focus of the dtr revising, blaming evil kings, the story of Abimelech has a purpose that it did not have for the Josianic Dtr. It is a cautionary tale, an exemplary horror story of how kings go wrong. It would be appropriate for the royal focus to have inserted this story, with 8:29-31 as lead-in. Hostility to the monarchy, characteristic of this focus, would underlie the claim of rule over Israel, a claim that goes beyond the story (cf. 9:22; the verb is unique in the DH) and the somewhat forced involvement of Israelites, otherwise absent from the story (cf. 9:55). Resuming part of v. 24, it concludes with an insistence that God's justice repaid Abimelech for his fratricide (9:56). Uncertainty remains; hence the double sideline.

The dtr revision's national focus—aware of the destructive illusion "that it is 'they,' the naughty statesmen, who are always responsible for war while 'we,' the innocent people, are merely led" (Tuchman, *Proud Tower*, xiv)—might well have been responsible for the emphasis on the failure of the people, for Israel in 8:33-35, and for Shechem in 9:57 (note: *'anšê* [men of Shechem; NRSV, people] not *ba'ălê* [citizens of Shechem; NRSV, lords]).

Present-text potential. The deliverer stories end with Gideon under something of a cloud; he made an ephod and "it became a snare to Gideon," to his family, and to Israel (8:27). God's involvement had been first for punishment and then for deliverance; at this point, the deliverance is becoming less evident. On the other hand, the civil strife of the closing chapters has its beginning here in the discord and violence of this story. Jotham's repudiation of kingship will be balanced by Samuel's synthesis in 1 Samuel 12.

| Main pre-DH: Deliverance *Collection* | Other pre-DH: | **Josianic DH:** |
| its sources *and its framing* | single sideline | **from the Dtr** |

my father fought for you, and risked his life, and rescued you from the hand of Midian; ¹⁸but you have risen up against my father's house this day, and have killed his sons, seventy men on one stone, and have made Abimelech, the son of his slave woman, king over the lords of Shechem, because he is your kinsman—¹⁹if, I say, you have acted in good faith and honor with Jerubbaal and with his house this day, then rejoice in Abimelech, and let him also rejoice in you; ²⁰but if not, let fire come out from Abimelech, and devour the lords of Shechem, and Beth-millo; and let fire come out from the lords of Shechem, and from Beth-millo, and devour Abimelech." ²¹Then Jotham ran away and fled, going to Beer, where he remained for fear of his brother Abimelech.

22 Abimelech ruled over Israel three years.

23 But God sent an evil spirit between Abimelech and the lords of Shechem; and the lords of Shechem dealt treacherously with Abimelech. ²⁴This happened so that the violence done to the seventy sons of Jerubbaal might be avenged and their blood be laid on their brother Abimelech, who killed them, and on the lords of Shechem, who strengthened his hands to kill his brothers. ²⁵So, out of hostility to him, the lords of Shechem set ambushes on the mountain tops. They robbed all who passed by them along that way; and it was reported to Abimelech.

26 When Gaal son of Ebed moved into Shechem with his kinsfolk, the lords of Shechem put confidence in him. ²⁷They went out into the field and gathered the grapes from their vineyards, trod them, and celebrated. Then they went into the temple of their god, ate and drank, and ridiculed Abimelech. ²⁸Gaal son of Ebed said, "Who is Abimelech, and who are we of Shechem, that we should serve him? Did not the son of Jerubbaal and Zebul his officer serve the men of Hamor father of Shechem? Why then should we serve him? ²⁹If only this people were under my command! Then I would remove Abimelech; I would say to him, 'Increase your army, and come out.' "

30 When Zebul the ruler of the city heard the words of Gaal son of Ebed, his anger was kindled. ³¹He sent messengers to Abimelech at Arumah, saying, "Look, Gaal son of Ebed and his kinsfolk have come to Shechem, and they are stirring up the city against you. ³²Now therefore, go by night, you and the troops that are with you, and lie in wait in the fields. ³³Then early in the morning, as soon as the sun rises, get up and rush on the city; and when he and the troops that are with him come out against you, you may deal with them as best you can."

34 So Abimelech and all the troops with him got up by night and lay in wait against Shechem in four companies. ³⁵When Gaal son of Ebed went out and stood in the entrance of the gate of the city, Abimelech and the troops with him rose from the ambush. ³⁶And when Gaal saw them, he said to Zebul, "Look, people are coming down from the mountain tops!" And Zebul said to him, "The shadows on the mountains look like people to you." ³⁷Gaal spoke again and said, "Look, people are coming down from Tabbur-erez, and one company is coming from the direction of Elon-meonenim." ³⁸Then Zebul said to him, "Where is your boast now, you who said, 'Who is Abimelech, that we should serve him?' Are not these the troops you made light of? Go out now and fight with them." ³⁹So Gaal went

After the Dtr:	Revision:	Other:
indented and sans serif font	national focus	double sideline

out at the head of the lords of Shechem, and fought with Abimelech. [40]Abimelech chased him, and he fled before him. Many fell wounded, up to the entrance of the gate. [41]So Abimelech resided at Arumah; and Zebul drove out Gaal and his kinsfolk, so that they could not live on at Shechem.

42 On the following day the people went out into the fields. When Abimelech was told, [43]he took his troops and divided them into three companies, and lay in wait in the fields. When he looked and saw the people coming out of the city, he rose against them and killed them. [44]Abimelech and the company that was with him rushed forward and stood at the entrance of the gate of the city, while the two companies rushed on all who were in the fields and killed them. [45]Abimelech fought against the city all that day; he took the city, and killed the people that were in it; and he razed the city and sowed it with salt.

46 When all the lords of the Tower of Shechem heard of it, they entered the stronghold of the temple of El-berith. [47]Abimelech was told that all the lords of the Tower of Shechem were gathered together. [48]So Abimelech went up to Mount Zalmon, he and all the troops that were with him. Abimelech took an ax in his hand, cut down a bundle of brushwood, and took it up and laid it on his shoulder. Then he said to the troops with him, "What you have seen me do, do quickly, as I have done." [49]So every one of the troops cut down a bundle and following Abimelech put it against the stronghold, and they set the stronghold on fire over them, so that all the people of the Tower of Shechem also died, about a thousand men and women.

50 Then Abimelech went to Thebez, and encamped against Thebez, and took it. [51]But there was a strong tower within the city, and all the men and women and all the lords of the city fled to it and shut themselves in; and they went to the roof of the tower. [52]Abimelech came to the tower, and fought against it, and came near to the entrance of the tower to burn it with fire. [53]But a certain woman threw an upper millstone on Abimelech's head, and crushed his skull. [54]Immediately he called to the young man who carried his armor and said to him, "Draw your sword and kill me, so people will not say about me, 'A woman killed him.'" So the young man thrust him through, and he died. [55]When the Israelites saw that Abimelech was dead, they all went home. [56]Thus God repaid Abimelech for the crime he committed against his father in killing his seventy brothers. [57]And God also made all the wickedness of the people of Shechem fall back on their heads, and on them came the curse of Jotham son of Jerubbaal.

10 After Abimelech, Tola son of Puah son of Dodo, a man of Issachar, who lived at Shamir in the hill country of Ephraim, rose to deliver Israel. [2]He judged Israel twenty-three years. Then he died, and was buried at Shamir.

3 After him rose (*Heb.; NRSV, came*) Jair the Gileadite, who judged Israel twenty-two years. [4]He had thirty sons who rode on thirty donkeys; and they had thirty towns, which are in the land of Gilead, and are called Havvoth-jair to this day. [5]Jair died, and was buried in Kamon.[19]

---

19. In 10:1-5, we have the notices of the first two so-called "minor judges" (Tola and Jair). Four

more are noted at 12:7-15 (Jephthah, Ibzan, Elon, and Abdon). There are differences between these two groupings that need to be accounted for. However, certain patterned information is common to both groupings: personal name (with patronymic or tribal affiliation or both); fact of judging Israel and length of time; notice of death and place of burial. Other details given include for Jair, his sons, their donkeys and towns; for Ibzan, his sons and daughters and marriage practices; and for Abdon, his sons and grandsons and their donkeys.

We know almost nothing of these figures. The disparate details suggest tradition rather than invention. The claim that each "judged Israel" suggests an office or activity of a national nature. We have no hard information on what it was. The presence of Jephthah in this list as well as in a story of deliverance led Noth to the hypothesis that the Dtr combined these figures with the deliverers to create the idea of the judges of Israel (cf. *DH*, 69-72). Closer examination of these texts has forced us to distance ourselves from aspects of Noth's view.

Text signals in 10:1-5 and 12:7-15. Despite the assumption that the "minor judges" derive from a single list (cf., for example, Noth, *DH*, 69-70), key differences emerge. (i) The sentence structure of 10:1-5 is different from that of 12:7-15. The sentence structures are best represented as follows:

| 10:1-5 | And rose | after (him) | PN | and he | Israel |
| | | | | judged | |

| 12:7 | And judged | PN | Israel |

| 12:8-14 | And judged | after him | Israel | PN |

While 12:7 could be aligned with either pattern, the basics are clear: two verbs over against one; the PN (proper name) early over against late. The language of "rose" and "judged" is important, but it will be treated under the second signal. (ii) 10:1-5 has "and he rose" (*wayyāqom*) for both Tola and Jair, with "to deliver Israel" for Tola. 12:7-15 has "and he judged" for all four figures. Within the close context of the deliverer-judges, the verb "to rise" inevitably evokes an echo of "the LORD raised up" from 2:16; 3:9, 15. The presence in 10:1 of "to deliver Israel" heightens this evocation, again echoing 2:16; 3:9, 15.

The absence of YHWH from the raising up creates a silence that is deafeningly loud. The absence of a situation of oppression from which Tola delivers Israel is also troubling.

Text-history approach. Whatever of the possible origin of these "minor judges" from a single ancient tradition, the present text clearly lists them in two different structures. To put it simply, the use of "and he rose" for both Tola and Jair and of "to deliver Israel" for Tola cry out for explanation. Our formatting offers what we believe to be the most economic solution: first, the Josianic Dtr included the story of Jephthah with the following three "minor judges"; second, Tola and Jair were introduced later—by whom is uncertain, but possibly within the "royal" focus of the dtr revision, in conjunction with the story of Abimelech.

The value within this "royal" focus is first that the Abimelech story casts the monarchy in an extremely bad light and, second, that the inclusion of Tola and Jair brings some respite from violence in Israel, with some echoes of the earlier cycle, before blending into the Josianic Dtr's accusation against Israel at 10:6. As we see it, no other solution accounts for all the signals noted.

Present-text potential. From a narrower point of view, the two "minor judges" preceding the Jephthah story are closer in their language to the earlier cycle of the deliverer-judges; those after are not. Nevertheless, Tola's "rose to deliver Israel" is hardly enough to situate him within the cyclic pattern of deliverer-judges (despite Amit, *Judges*, 44-45). The absences are too many: no formula of Israel's doing evil, no formula of YHWH's anger or action to oppress, no cry from the people, no story of deliverance, no formula for a foe subdued, and no formula for a period of quiet. God is notably absent.

Reviewing a wide sweep of the text, it seems that deliverance is trickling into the sand. Or, differently expressed, God is increasingly less visible in the biblical text. Tola "rose to deliver Israel" (10:1); it is not said that he was raised up by God (cf. 2:16; 3:9, 15). After Tola, it is said (in the Hebrew) that Jair "rose" (10:3); it is not said that he was raised up by God nor that he rose to deliver Israel. In neither case is

| After the Dtr: | Revision: | Other: |
| indented and sans serif font | national focus | double sideline |

6 The Israelites again did what was evil in the sight of the LORD, worshiping the Baals and the Astartes.[20]

the gods of Aram, the gods of Sidon, the gods of Moab, the gods of the Ammonites, and the gods of the Philistines. Thus they abandoned the LORD, and did not worship him

[7]**So the anger of the LORD was kindled against Israel, and he sold them into the hand of the Philistines and into the hand of the Ammonites,** [8]**and they crushed and oppressed the Israelites that year.**[21]

---

deliverance to oppression by YHWH or deliverance by YHWH from that oppression noted. Jephthah is not raised up by God; he negotiates with the elders of Gilead (11:4-11). His story is not wrapped up with the generation of peace given to the other deliverer-judges; instead it is completed with the formulas for the minor judges. The last three do not rise and do not deliver and God is not mentioned. These thoughts may have been implicit in the (Josianic) dtr text of 10:6-9. They are bluntly explicit in the (revised) dtr text of 10:13-14 and 16—especially if the full ambiguity of 10:16 is allowed (see below).

20. It is important to recognize the break between 10:6-9 and 10:10-16. At first sight, there is the standard Josianic dtr pattern of apostasy, anger, oppression, Israel's cry to YHWH, and YHWH's response. On closer inspection, in v. 10b, Israel itself confesses to apostasy; this is unprecedented. In the preceding stories, the narrator reported Israel's evil, rather than Israel confessing it. The response of YHWH is equally unprecedented; it is a refusal (v. 14). The ambiguity of the outcome in v. 16 cannot be avoided. Verse 15 is little more than a repetition of v. 10. In v. 16a, Israel's confession is followed by thoroughgoing reform.

The ambiguity lies in whether God's response in v. 16b goes beyond v. 14. The phrase, "he could not bear" (literally: and his being was shortened), occurs in three other places (Num 21:4; Judg 16:16; Zech 11:8); in all three, impatience is central, not sympathy. The phrase "suffering of Israel" (literally: trouble of Israel) is unique (cf. Num 23:21). The word "trouble" (*'āmāl*) can mean one's own trouble or the trouble one causes others. In v. 16b, it can clearly be rendered as in traditional translations: "he could no longer bear to

see Israel suffer." Alternatively, it can be rendered: "he was impatient with the trouble of Israel" (i.e., the trouble Israel caused God). Such theological thought is not unheard of. The ark of the covenant went into exile under God's direction; it did not return to Israel's life for "a long time" (1 Sam 7:2). There are occurrences such as Exod 33:3 and Hos 1:9. Something of a combination of the two creates a frame within Deuteronomy (cf. Deut 4:25-31; 30:1-5). Could it be that, at a remote and therefore safe distance, the text has a faint pointer to the possibility raised by Josiah's future failure (i.e., his death)?

21. **Text signals** in 10:6-9. Much energy has been invested in these few verses; for Israel's theologians, the moment had meaning. After the report of Israel's apostasy and God's anger, there are two oppressors, two verbs of oppression, two mentions of the object of oppression, two statements of time—and more. There is much to ponder.

(i) The detail of Israel's apostasy includes, after the Baals and Astartes, the gods of Aram, Sidon, and Moab, and the gods of the Ammonites and Philistines. (ii) Israel is accused of abandoning YHWH. (iii) Two oppressors are named: Philistines and Ammonites. (iv) Two verbs of oppression are used: crushed and oppressed. (v) Israel, the object of oppression, is mentioned twice: in v. 8a and v. 8b. (vi) The time involved is stated twice: in v. 8a (that year) and v. 8b (18 years). (vii) V. 8b locates the Ammonite oppression of Israelites in Gilead, across the Jordan. (viii) V. 9 has the Ammonites cross the Jordan and oppress Judah, Benjamin, and Ephraim.

Text-history approach. If the theological patterns of the deliverer-judge stories are applied here, considerable editorial activity must be postulated. If these patterns are believed to be portrayed as disin-

---

eighteen years *(the* NRSV *here begins a new sentence, supplies "For," and repeats "they oppressed" which in the Hebrew occurs only once at v. 8a)* all the Israelites that were beyond the Jordan in the land of the Amor-

ites, which is in Gilead. ⁹The Ammonites also crossed the Jordan to fight against Judah and against Benjamin and against the house of Ephraim so that Israel was greatly distressed.

tegrating, less editorial activity is required. For example, the presence of two oppressors, Philistines and Ammonites, breaks the earlier pattern; the Philistines would be secondary. On the other hand, if these patterns are disintegrating, mention of Philistines and Ammonites may indicate the trouble that is sandwiching Israel from either side. The Ammonite problem will be swiftly resolved with Jephthah; that of the Philistines will have to wait for David (2 Sam 5:17-25; 8:1). The two verbs, "crushed and oppressed," go beyond the earlier pattern. In a disintegrating situation, they may be seen as expressing intensified oppression. The two statements of time are difficult to interpret under any hypothesis.

What we have opted for is to preserve a clean text for the Josianic DH and to allow for disintegration in the framing patterns. Acknowledging the difficulties of the verses (esp. "that year" and "eighteen years"), we assume that the time statement, "that year," probably reflects the Jephthah story and its portrayal of a single campaign, east of the Jordan (cf. 10:17; 11:4). Within this context of a single east-of-Jordan campaign, the later specification of the Israelites (who were crushed and oppressed that year) as those east of the Jordan (v. 8b) is intelligible. Probably more theological reflection and closer attention to the earlier framing patterns then suggested the need for a period of oppression (i.e., the eighteen years) and for this oppression to fall on all Israel (i.e., v. 9). Israel's distress here can be read in the light of "distress" (Heb.) in either Judg 2:15 (dtr) or 1 Sam 30:6 (non-dtr); attribution to the Josianic Dtr is possible, but not necessary.

If we have read the text signals correctly, editing has busied itself with two aspects of this moment in Israel's DH text: Israel's apostasy and Ammon's oppression. The Israelite apostasy has been notably expanded. We cannot pin the list down to any specific source or interest; the five groups, however, surround

Israel—Aram and Sidon to the north (cf. Judg 18:28); Moab and Ammonites to the east; and Philistines on the southwest. Aram is mentioned in Judg 3:8, 10 (in the Othniel passage); also in 2 Chron 28:23 (in the time of Ahaz). Moab, of course, figures in the Ehud story. Ammonites and Philistines feature in what is to come. The Sidonians only recur, linked with Moab and the Ammonites, in the accusation against Solomon (1 Kgs 11:33, national focus of the dtr revision; but the reference is to "Astarte, goddess of the Sidonians," identifying Astarte as a deity of Sidon). Attribution to the national focus (reinforced by the preferred usage of "abandon YHWH") sees the expansion pointing not just to the evil of Israel at this moment in time, but to the history of the people's crumbling under the influences surrounding them.

The Ammonite oppression has its own problems, addressed in the added material of vv. 8b-9. The action of the Jephthah story takes place in Gilead, across the Jordan (so v. 8b). V. 9, on the contrary, brings the Ammonite oppression into the heartland of Israel—Judah, Benjamin, and Ephraim. In v. 8b, the Jephthah story is unsatisfactory for national deliverance. V. 9 offers a remedy by portraying national oppression.

Present-text potential. After the turmoil of Abimelech and the sway of Tola and Jair, the text has Israel return to apostasy. It is no minor apostasy; it involves capitulation to the surrounding cultures. The essentials of Israel's identity are at stake. The implications of this apostasy are grave, spelled out both near and far. Near: the Ammonite oppression is embodied in the Jephthah story; the Philistine oppression (13:1) lasts for forty years and lies behind the Samson cycle. Far: the Ammonites will return with Nahash (1 Samuel 11) and the Philistines will not succumb until David (2 Samuel 5).

| After the Dtr:
indented and sans serif font | *Revision:*
national focus | Other:
double sideline |

10 So the Israelites cried to the Lord, *saying, "We have sinned against you, because we have abandoned our God and have worshiped the Baals." ¹¹And the* Lord *said to the Israelites, "Did I not deliver you from the Egyptians and from the Amorites, from the Ammonites and from the Philistines? ¹²The Sidonians also, and the Amalekites, and the Maonites, oppressed you; and you cried to me, and I delivered you out of their hand. ¹³Yet you have abandoned me and worshiped other gods; therefore I will deliver you no more. ¹⁴Go and cry to the gods whom you have chosen; let them deliver you in the time of your distress." ¹⁵And the Israelites said to the* Lord, *"We have sinned; do to us whatever seems good to you; but deliver us this day!" ¹⁶So they put away the foreign gods from among them and worshiped the* Lord; *and he could no longer bear to see Israel suffer.*[22]

17 Then the Ammonites were called to arms, and they encamped in Gilead; and the Israelites came together, and they encamped at Mizpah. ¹⁸The commanders of the people of Gilead said to one another, "Who will begin the fight against the Ammonites? He shall be head over all the inhabitants of Gilead."[23]

11 Now Jephthah the Gileadite, the son of a prostitute, was a mighty warrior. Gilead was the father of Jephthah. ²Gilead's wife also bore him sons; and when his wife's sons grew up, they drove Jephthah away, saying to him, "You shall not inherit anything in our father's house; for you are the son of another woman." ³Then Jephthah fled from his brothers and lived in the land

---

22. **Text signals** in 10:10-16. (i) Israel cries to the Lord. (ii) Israel itself confesses apostasy, unprecedented in the book of Judges. (iii) The usage "abandon the Lord" occurs in vv. 10 and 13. (iv) The list of seven oppressors of Israel ranges from Egypt to Maon. (v) God refuses to deliver Israel (vv. 13-14), also unprecedented in the book of Judges. (vi) The "foreign gods" are described as *ʾĕlōhê hannēkār* (v. 16a). (vii) V. 16b is unprecedented and ambiguous (see note on 10:6).

Text-history approach. These signals suggest attribution to the dtr revision's national focus. The usage "abandon the Lord" is characteristically late and is a preferred term of the national focus. The oppressors range beyond the book of Judges. The "foreign gods," described as *ʾĕlōhê hannēkār,* may reflect Gen 35:2, 4; other occurrences are late (Deut 31:16; Josh 24:20, 23; 1 Sam 7:3; Jer 5:19; 2 Chron 33:15). If weight is given to the *ʾĕlōhê hannēkār* of

---

Genesis 35, a divestiture from early in Israel's history (Jacob) is being recommended again at a very late stage of that history.

Present-text potential. The text is a watershed in the DH, in relation to both Israel and God. For Israel, it is the first time in the DH that they have confessed sin and undertaken thoroughgoing reform. For God, no matter how v. 16b is understood, the possibility has been raised in vv. 13-14 of God's walking away from Israel. V. 16b is ambiguous; the context, with the "deliverance" attributed to Jephthah, is hardly helpful. The way lies open to reconciliation or divorce.

23. **Text signals** in 10:17—12:6. (i) 10:17 reports the encampments of both sides, a preliminary to battle (cf. 1 Sam 4:1b; 17:1-2; 29:1). (ii) 10:18—11:11 presents the negotiations that led to Jephthah's command. (iii) 11:12-28 are regarded as an addition to the Josianic DH text. (iv) 11:29 reports that the spirit of yhwh came upon Jephthah. (v) 11:30-31 reports Jephthah's ill-fated vow (cf. vv. 34-40). (vi) 11:32 attributes Jephthah's victory to the Lord; v. 33 reports that the Ammonites were subdued (cf. 3:30; 4:23; 8:28). (vii) There is no statement of the land being undisturbed. (viii) 12:1-6 reports Israel's first civil war with its deadly consequences.

Main pre-DH: Deliverance *Collection*
    its sources *and its framing*

Other pre-DH:
    single sideline

Josianic DH:
from the Dtr

of Tob. Outlaws collected around Jephthah and went raiding with him.

4 After a time the Ammonites made war against Israel. [5]And when the Ammonites made war against Israel, the elders of Gilead went to bring Jephthah from the land of Tob. [6]They said to Jephthah, "Come and be our commander, so that we may fight with the Ammonites." [7]But Jephthah said to the elders of Gilead, "Are you not the very ones who rejected me and drove me out of my father's house? So why do you come to me now when you are in trouble?" [8]The elders of Gilead said to Jephthah, "Nevertheless, we have now turned back to you, so that you may go with us and fight with the Ammonites, and become head over us, over all the inhabitants of Gilead." [9]Jephthah said to the elders of Gilead, "If you bring me home again to fight with the Ammonites, and the LORD gives them over to me, I will be your head." [10]And the elders of Gilead said to Jephthah, "The LORD will be witness between us; we will surely do as you say." [11]So Jephthah went with the elders of Gilead, and the people made him head and commander over them; and Jephthah spoke all his words before the LORD at Mizpah.

Text-history approach. The Jephthah tradition is understood to have been used for the DH by the Josianic Dtr. It has not been given the framing found in the earlier stories. So Jephthah is not raised up as a deliverer and there is no tranquillity at the end. The fratricidal dissension of civil war is not canceled out in the text by 12:7-15. Signs of disintegration abound.

In the understanding presented here, the Jephthah story in the Josianic DH followed immediately on the Gideon story. The framing elements are starting to break up. The principal figures are less squeaky clean; Gideon negotiates with God and Jephthah negotiates with the elders of Gilead. The outcome is less satisfactory; suppression of Succoth and Penuel for Gideon and civil strife with the Ephraimites for Jephthah.

12 Then Jephthah sent messengers to the king of the Ammonites and said, "What is there between you and me, that you have come to me to fight against my land?" [13]The king of the Ammonites answered the messengers of Jephthah, "Because Israel, on coming from Egypt, took away my land from the Arnon to the Jabbok and to the Jordan; now therefore restore it peaceably." [14]Once again Jephthah sent messengers to the king of the Ammonites [15]and said to him: "Thus says Jephthah: Israel did not take away the land of Moab or the land of the Ammonites, [16]but when they came up from Egypt, Israel went through the wilderness to the Red Sea and came to Kadesh. [17]Israel then sent messengers to the king of Edom, saying, 'Let us pass through your land'; but the king of Edom would not listen. They also sent to the king of Moab, but he would not consent. So Israel remained at Kadesh. [18]Then they journeyed through the wilderness, went around the land of Edom and the land of Moab, arrived on the east side of the land of Moab, and camped on the other side of the Arnon. They did not enter the territory of Moab, for the Arnon was the boundary of Moab. [19]Israel then sent messengers to King Sihon of the Amorites, king of Heshbon; and Israel said to him, 'Let us pass through your land to our country.' [20]But Sihon did not trust Israel to pass

---

Present-text potential. Coming after the Abimelech story, this story of Jephthah ends with Israel in an even worse position. Abimelech's death ended with the Israelites all returning home (9:55); Jephthah's victory ends with civil war (12:1-6). Although victory is attributed to YHWH (11:9, 32), Jephthah's leadership is not; his vow is appallingly misplaced and tranquillity is not achieved.

| After the Dtr: indented and sans serif font | *Revision: national focus* | Other: double sideline |

through his territory; so Sihon gathered all his people together, and encamped at Jahaz, and fought with Israel. ²¹Then the Lord, the God of Israel, gave Sihon and all his people into the hand of Israel, and they defeated them; so Israel occupied all the land of the Amorites, who inhabited that country. ²²They occupied all the territory of the Amorites from the Arnon to the Jabbok and from the wilderness to the Jordan. ²³So now the Lord, the God of Israel, has conquered the Amorites for the benefit of his people Israel. Do you intend to take their place? ²⁴Should you not possess what your god Chemosh gives you to possess? And should we not be the ones to possess everything that the Lord our God has conquered for our benefit? ²⁵Now are you any better than King Balak son of Zippor of Moab? Did he ever enter into conflict with Israel, or did he ever go to war with them? ²⁶While Israel lived in Heshbon and its villages, and in Aroer and its villages, and in all the towns that are along the Arnon, three hundred years, why did you not recover them within that time? ²⁷It is not I who have sinned against you, but you are the one who does me wrong by making war on me. Let the Lord, who is judge, decide today for the Israelites or for the Ammonites." ²⁸But the king of the Ammonites did not heed the message that Jephthah sent him.[24]

29 Then the spirit of the Lord came upon Jephthah, and he passed through Gilead and Manasseh. He passed on to Mizpah of Gilead, and from Mizpah of Gilead he passed on to the Ammonites. ³⁰And Jephthah made a vow to the Lord, and said, "If you will give the Ammonites

into my hand, ³¹then whoever comes out of the doors of my house to meet me, when I return victorious from the Ammonites, shall be the Lord's, to be offered up by me as a burnt offering." ³²So Jephthah crossed over to the Ammonites to fight against them; and the Lord gave them into his hand. ³³He inflicted a massive defeat on them from Aroer to the neighborhood of Minnith, twenty towns, and as far as Abel-keramim. So the Ammonites were subdued before the people of Israel.[25]

34 Then Jephthah came to his home at Mizpah; and there was his daughter coming out to meet him with timbrels and with dancing. She was his only child; he had no son or daughter except her. ³⁵When he saw her, he tore his clothes, and said, "Alas, my daughter! You have brought me very low; you have become the cause of great trouble to me. For I have opened my mouth to the Lord, and I cannot take back my vow." ³⁶She said to him, "My father, if you have opened your mouth to the Lord, do to me according to what has gone out of your mouth, now that the Lord has given you vengeance against your enemies, the Ammonites." ³⁷And

---

24. On vv. 12-28, see Noth, *DH*, 76, n. 2.

---

25. Two aspects of this text appear to be in tension. The spirit of YHWH came upon Jephthah (v. 29) and he made a foolish vow (v. 30). In usual circumstances, the spirit of YHWH is a sign of effective power; a vow is unnecessary and an ill-fated vow unlikely. Within the book of Judges, the spirit of YHWH is appealed to for Othniel (3:10) and Gideon (6:34), here, and four times for Samson (13:25; 14:6, 19; 15:14). Within the book, the spirit of YHWH appears as a rather uncertain quantity.

Even though the fulfillment of Jephthah's vow is urged on him by his daughter (v. 36), its fearful outcome, without further consultation or change (cf. Lev 27:1-7), leaves an unholy pall over the text.

Main pre-DH: Deliverance *Collection*
  its sources *and its framing*

Other pre-DH:
single sideline

Josianic DH:
from the Dtr

she said to her father, "Let this thing be done for me: Grant me two months, so that I may go and wander on the mountains, and bewail my virginity, my companions and I." ³⁸"Go," he said and sent her away for two months. So she departed, she and her companions, and bewailed her virginity on the mountains. ³⁹At the end of two months, she returned to her father, who did with her according to the vow he had made. She had never slept with a man. So there arose an Israelite custom that ⁴⁰for four days every year the daughters of Israel would go out to lament the daughter of Jephthah the Gileadite.

12 The men of Ephraim were called to arms, and they crossed to Zaphon and said to Jephthah, "Why did you cross over to fight against the Ammonites, and did not call us to go with you? We will burn your house down over you!" ²Jephthah said to them, "My people and I were engaged in conflict with the Ammonites who oppressed us severely. But when I called you, you did not deliver me from their hand. ³When I saw that you would not deliver me, I took my life in my hand, and crossed over against the Ammonites, and the LORD gave them into my hand. Why then have you come up to me this day, to fight against me?" ⁴Then Jephthah gathered all the men of Gilead and fought with Ephraim; and the men of Gilead defeated Ephraim, because they said, "You are fugitives from Ephraim, you Gileadites—in the heart of Ephraim and Manasseh." ⁵Then the Gileadites took the fords of the Jordan against the Ephraimites. Whenever one of the fugitives of Ephraim said, "Let me go over," the men of Gilead would say to him, "Are you an Ephraimite?" When he said, "No," ⁶they said to him, "Then say Shibboleth," and he said, "Sibboleth," for he could not pronounce it right. Then they seized him and killed him at the fords

of the Jordan. Forty-two thousand of the Ephraimites fell at that time.²⁶

7 Jephthah judged Israel six years. Then Jephthah the Gileadite died, and was buried in his town in Gilead.²⁷

8 After him Ibzan of Bethlehem judged Israel. ⁹He had thirty sons. He gave his thirty daughters in marriage outside his clan and brought in thirty young women from outside for his sons. He judged Israel seven years. ¹⁰Then Ibzan died, and was buried at Bethlehem.

11 After him Elon the Zebulunite judged Israel; and he judged Israel ten years. ¹²Then Elon the Zebulunite died, and was buried at Aijalon in the land of Zebulun.

13 After him Abdon son of Hillel the Pirathonite judged Israel. ¹⁴He had forty sons and thirty grandsons, who rode on seventy donkeys; he judged Israel eight years. ¹⁵Then Abdon son of Hillel the Pirathonite died, and was buried at Pirathon in the land of Ephraim, in the hill country of the Amalekites.

13 **The Israelites again did what was evil in the sight of the LORD, and the LORD gave them into the hand of the Philistines forty years.**²⁸

---

26. Jephthah's triumph is not only told in the context of disastrous effects for his daughter. The disunity in Israel is brought to a peak. What merited an allusion under Deborah and a couple of episodes under Gideon has now become a deadly conflict across the Jordan, with corresponding cost of lives (cf. 12:6; note Amit: "relations of intertribal alienation and estrangement are alluded to throughout the book [5:15c, 16, 17, 23; 8:1-21; 12:1-6]," *Judges*, 335).

27. For 12:7-15, see the note above on 10:1-5.

28. **Text signals** in 13:1. (i) The framing element of "doing evil" recurs for the last time (cf. 2:11; 3:7,

---

200 UNFOLDING THE DEUTERONOMISTIC HISTORY

2 There was a certain man of Zorah, of the tribe of the Danites, whose name was Manoah. His wife was barren, having borne no children. ³And the angel of the LORD appeared to the woman and said to her, "Although you are barren, having borne no children, you shall conceive and bear a son. ⁴Now be careful not to drink wine or strong drink, or to eat anything unclean, ⁵for you shall conceive and bear a son. No razor is to come on his head, for the boy shall be a nazirite to God from birth. It is he who shall begin to deliver Israel from the hand of the Philistines." ⁶Then the woman came and told her husband, "A man of God came to me, and his appearance was like that of an angel of God, most awe-inspiring; I did not ask him where he came from, and he did not tell me his name; ⁷but he said to me, 'You shall conceive and bear a son. So then drink no wine or strong drink, and eat nothing unclean, for the boy shall be a nazirite to God from birth to the day of his death.' "²⁹

12a; 4:1a; 6:1a; 10:6). (ii) The framing element of handing over to "oppression" recurs, with a much longer period of time, a period in fact equivalent to the time of quiet (a generation) following each deliverer-judge (oppression: 8 yrs, 18 yrs, 20 yrs, 7 yrs, 18 yrs, and here 40 years; undisturbed for 40 years: 3:11a, 30b; 5:31b; 8:28b). (iii) There are no other framing elements. The kindling of YHWH's anger (2:14a; 3:8a; 10:7a) is absent, but it is absent also from the three main stories (cf. Ehud, Deborah, Gideon). It is not said that Samson was "raised up" (cf. Judg 2:16). He is described as one "who shall begin to deliver Israel from the hand of the Philistines" (cf. 13:5); ultimately, he did not do so. The statements that Samson judged Israel (15:20; 16:31b) mirror the language of the minor judges, not that of the deliverer-judges.

Text-history approach. This is a statement from the Josianic Dtr. It lies behind the call of Saul to be king (1 Sam 9:16); it declares a threat that is not eliminated historically until David (2 Sam 5:17-25; 8:1). The forty-year period of oppression is left unterminated. Without the other framing elements, the text does not bring the period to closure. In our judgment, the next section of the Josianic DH presented the Samuel story, beginning with 1 Samuel 1–3, then 4–6, followed by 9:1. This Philistine oppression, the longest in the period, highlights the failure of deliverer-judge leadership and prepares the way for the leadership of prophetically designated kings.

Present-text potential. This notice of Philistine oppression flows smoothly into the stories of Samson, with his struggles against the Philistines. However it should be noted that this may not be the most appropriate way to read the text. This note of Philistine oppression may take the text into the time of Samuel and beyond. Probably it is best to understand these "forty years" as symbolic of the failure of the generations after Joshua, doomed by recurrent infidelity and sporadic leadership. Alternatively, if emphasis is laid on accommodating the figures, the twenty years of Samson can be combined with the twenty years of 1 Sam 7:2, and Eli's forty-year judgeship relegated to being considered in parallel with these.

29. **Text signals** in 13:2—16:31. (i) On a broader scale than the Gideon traditions, these traditions of Samson form a cycle rather than a story. (ii) In miniform, the cycle travels the trajectory of the book of Judges: it begins relatively well and ends relatively badly. (iii) As noted above, the framing pattern has ceased and Samson does not in fact deliver Israel. (iv) There are similarities between the birth story of Samson and that of Samuel; for example: the barren wife, divine intervention in the child's conception, dedication of the child to God, and the nazirite vow.

Text-history approach. The absence of an identifiable dtr contribution after 13:1 weakens any argument for attributing the Samson cycle to the Josianic DH. This largely intuitive judgment—reflected in our formatting—is supported by the other signals from the text. Nevertheless, the possibility remains that the

---

| Main pre-DH: Deliverance *Collection* | Other pre-DH: | **Josianic DH:** |
| its sources *and its framing* | single sideline | **from the Dtr** |

8 Then Manoah entreated the Lord, and said, "O, Lord, I pray, let the man of God whom you sent come to us again and teach us what we are to do concerning the boy who will be born." ⁹God listened to Manoah, and the angel of God came again to the woman as she sat in the field; but her husband Manoah was not with her. ¹⁰So the woman ran quickly and told her husband, "The man who came to me the other day has appeared to me." ¹¹Manoah got up and followed his wife, and came to the man and said to him, "Are you the man who spoke to this woman?" And he said, "I am." ¹²Then Manoah said, "Now when your words come true, what is to be the boy's rule of life; what is he to do?" ¹³The angel of the Lord said to Manoah, "Let the woman give heed to all that I said to her. ¹⁴She may not eat of anything that comes from the vine. She is not to drink wine or strong drink, or eat any unclean thing. She is to observe everything that I commanded her."

15 Manoah said to the angel of the Lord, "Allow us to detain you, and prepare a kid for you." ¹⁶The angel of the Lord said to Manoah, "If you detain me, I will not eat your food; but if you want to prepare a burnt offering, then offer it to the Lord." (For Manoah did not know that he was the angel of the Lord.) ¹⁷Then Manoah said to the angel of the Lord, "What is your name, so that we may honor you when your words come true?" ¹⁸But the angel of the Lord said to him, "Why do you ask my name? It is too wonderful."

19 So Manoah took the kid with the grain offering, and offered it on the rock to the Lord, to him who works wonders. ²⁰When the flame went up toward heaven from the altar, the angel of the Lord ascended in the flame of the altar while Manoah and his wife looked on; and they fell on their faces to the ground. ²¹The angel of the Lord did not appear again to Manoah and his wife. Then Manoah realized that it was the angel of the Lord. ²²And Manoah said to his wife, "We shall surely die, for we have seen God." ²³But his wife said to him, "If the Lord had meant to kill us, he would not have accepted a burnt offering and a grain offering at our hands, or shown us all these things, or now announced to us such things as these."

24 The woman bore a son, and named him Samson. The boy grew, and the Lord blessed him. ²⁵The spirit of the Lord began to stir him in Mahaneh-dan, between Zorah and Eshtaol.

14 Once Samson went down to Timnah, and at Timnah he saw a Philistine woman. ²Then he came up, and told his father and mother, "I saw a Philistine woman at Timnah; now get her for me as my wife." ³But his father and mother said to him, "Is there not a woman among your kin, or among all

---

cycle was part of the Josianic DH, heightening the disintegration already noticed.

Present-text potential. The Samson cycle is illustrative of the difficult relationships implied by 13:1 (cf. "the Philistines are rulers over us," 15:11), although the cycle's stories more strongly reflect Samson's aggression toward the Philistines. His failure to achieve any lasting success for his people is indicative of the disintegration observed in the text. It leads into the anarchy of chaps. 17–21. The Samson cycle is dominated by personal vendettas; no Israelite army is called out, no leadership exercised over Israel. The way is open to the vacuum of chaps. 17–21, where "there was no king in Israel; all the people did what was right in their own eyes" (17:6; 21:25).

After the Dtr:	*Revision:*	Other:
indented and sans serif font	*national focus*	double sideline

our people, that you must go to take a wife from the uncircumcised Philistines?" But Samson said to his father, "Get her for me, because she pleases me." [4]His father and mother did not know that this was from the LORD; for he was seeking a pretext to act against the Philistines. At that time the Philistines had dominion over Israel.

5 Then Samson went down with his father and mother to Timnah. When he came to the vineyards of Timnah, suddenly a young lion roared at him. [6]The spirit of the LORD rushed on him, and he tore the lion apart barehanded as one might tear apart a kid. But he did not tell his father or his mother what he had done. [7]Then he went down and talked with the woman, and she pleased Samson. [8]After a while he returned to marry her, and he turned aside to see the carcass of the lion, and there was a swarm of bees in the body of the lion, and honey. [9]He scraped it out into his hands, and went on, eating as he went. When he came to his father and mother, he gave some to them, and they ate it. But he did not tell them that he had taken the honey from the carcass of the lion.

10 His father went down to the woman, and Samson made a feast there as the young men were accustomed to do. [11]When the people saw him, they brought thirty companions to be with him. [12]Samson said to them, "Let me now put a riddle to you. If you can explain it to me within the seven days of the feast, and find it out, then I will give you thirty linen garments and thirty festal garments. [13]But if you cannot explain it to me, then you shall give me thirty linen garments and thirty festal garments." So they said to him, "Ask your riddle; let us hear it." [14]He said to them,

"Out of the eater came something
    to eat.
Out of the strong came something
    sweet."
But for three days they could not explain the riddle.

15 On the fourth day they said to Samson's wife, "Coax your husband to explain the riddle to us, or we will burn you and your father's house with fire. Have you invited us here to impoverish us?" [16]So Samson's wife wept before him, saying, "You hate me; you do not really love me. You have asked a riddle of my people, but you have not explained it to me." He said to her, "Look, I have not told my father or my mother. Why should I tell you?" [17]She wept before him the seven days that their feast lasted; and because she nagged him, on the seventh day he told her. Then she explained the riddle to her people. [18]The men of the town said to him on the seventh day before the sun went down,

"What is sweeter than honey?
What is stronger than a lion?"
And he said to them,
"If you had not plowed with my heifer,
    you would not have found out my
    riddle."
[19]Then the spirit of the LORD rushed on him, and he went down to Ashkelon. He killed thirty men of the town, took their spoil, and gave the festal garments to those who had explained the riddle. In hot anger he went back to his father's house. [20]And Samson's wife was given to his companion, who had been his best man.

15 After a while, at the time of the wheat harvest, Samson went to visit his wife, bringing along a kid. He said, "I want to go

---

Main pre-DH: Deliverance *Collection*
    its sources *and its framing*

Other pre-DH:
single sideline

Josianic DH:
from the Dtr

into my wife's room." But her father would not allow him to go in. ²Her father said, "I was sure that you had rejected her; so I gave her to your companion. Is not her younger sister prettier than she? Why not take her instead?" ³Samson said to them, "This time, when I do mischief to the Philistines, I will be without blame." ⁴So Samson went and caught three hundred foxes, and took some torches; and he turned the foxes tail to tail, and put a torch between each pair of tails. ⁵When he had set fire to the torches, he let the foxes go into the standing grain of the Philistines, and burned up the shocks and the standing grain, as well as the vineyards and olive groves. ⁶Then the Philistines asked, "Who has done this?" And they said, "Samson, the son-in-law of the Timnite, because he has taken Samson's wife and given her to his companion." So the Philistines came up, and burned her and her father. ⁷Samson said to them, "If this is what you do, I swear I will not stop until I have taken revenge on you." ⁸He struck them down hip and thigh with great slaughter; and he went down and stayed in the cleft of the rock of Etam.

9 Then the Philistines came up and encamped in Judah, and made a raid on Lehi. ¹⁰The men of Judah said, "Why have you come up against us?" They said, "We have come up to bind Samson, to do to him as he did to us." ¹¹Then three thousand men of Judah went down to the cleft of the rock of Etam, and they said to Samson, "Do you not know that the Philistines are rulers over us? What then have you done to us?" He replied, "As they did to me, so I have done to them." ¹²They said to him, "We have come down to bind you, so that we may give you into the hands of the

Philistines." Samson answered them, "Swear to me that you yourselves will not attack me." ¹³They said to him, "No, we will only bind you and give you into their hands; we will not kill you." So they bound him with two new ropes, and brought him up from the rock.

14 When he came to Lehi, the Philistines came shouting to meet him; and the spirit of the Lᴏʀᴅ rushed on him, and the ropes that were on his arms became like flax that has caught fire, and his bonds melted off his hands. ¹⁵Then he found a fresh jawbone of a donkey, reached down and took it, and with it he killed a thousand men. ¹⁶And Samson said,

"With the jawbone of a donkey,
  heaps upon heaps,
with the jawbone of a donkey
  I have slain a thousand men."

¹⁷When he had finished speaking, he threw away the jawbone; and that place was called Ramath-lehi.

18 By then he was very thirsty, and he called on the Lᴏʀᴅ, saying, "You have granted this great victory by the hand of your servant. Am I now to die of thirst, and fall into the hands of the uncircumcised?" ¹⁹So God split open the hollow place that is at Lehi, and water came from it. When he drank, his spirit returned, and he revived. Therefore it was named En-hakkore, which is at Lehi to this day. ²⁰And he judged Israel in the days of the Philistines twenty years.

16 Once Samson went to Gaza, where he saw a prostitute and went in to her. ²The Gazites were told, "Samson has come here." So they circled around and lay in wait for him all night at the city gate. They kept quiet all night, thinking, "Let us wait until

After the Dtr:
indented and sans serif font   *Revision:* *national focus*   Other:
double sideline

the light of the morning; then we will kill him." [3]But Samson lay only until midnight. Then at midnight he rose up, took hold of the doors of the city gate and the two posts, pulled them up, bar and all, put them on his shoulders, and carried them to the top of the hill that is in front of Hebron.

4 After this he fell in love with a woman in the valley of Sorek, whose name was Delilah. [5]The lords of the Philistines came to her and said to her, "Coax him, and find out what makes his strength so great, and how we may overpower him, so that we may bind him in order to subdue him; and we will each give you eleven hundred pieces of silver." [6]So Delilah said to Samson, "Please tell me what makes your strength so great, and how you could be bound, so that one could subdue you." [7]Samson said to her, "If they bind me with seven fresh bowstrings that are not dried out, then I shall become weak, and be like anyone else." [8]Then the lords of the Philistines brought her seven fresh bowstrings that had not dried out, and she bound him with them. [9]While men were lying in wait in an inner chamber, she said to him, "The Philistines are upon you, Samson!" But he snapped the bowstrings, as a strand of fiber snaps when it touches the fire. So the secret of his strength was not known.[30]

10 Then Delilah said to Samson, "You have mocked me and told me lies; please tell me how you could be bound." [11]He said to her, "If they bind me with new ropes that have not been used, then I shall become weak, and be like anyone else." [12]So Delilah took new ropes and bound him with them, and said to him, "The Philistines are upon you, Samson!" (The men lying in wait were in an inner chamber.) But he snapped the ropes off his arms like a thread.

13 Then Delilah said to Samson, "Until now you have mocked me and told me lies; tell me how you could be bound." He said to her, "If you weave the seven locks of my head with the web and make it tight with the pin, then I shall become weak, and be like anyone else." [14]So while he slept, Delilah took the seven locks of his head and wove them into the web, and made them tight with the pin. Then she said to him, "The Philistines are upon you, Samson!" But he awoke from his sleep, and pulled away the pin, the loom, and the web.

15 Then she said to him, "How can you say, 'I love you,' when your heart is not with me? You have mocked me three times now and have not told me what makes your strength so great." [16]Finally, after she had nagged him with her words day after day, and pestered him, he was tired to death. [17]So he told her his whole secret, and said to her, "A razor has never come upon my

---

30. Questions have to be asked about the source of such a story. Three times, Samson lies to Delilah and the story reveals that he was right to lie to her; she was in alliance with the Philistines and had deceived him. So the fourth time, he tells her the truth and pays the predictable consequences. Stupid or besotted or both? Where does such a story come from? The Delilah story and the death of Samson are by far the most negative in the cycle, leaving open the question whether a more positive cycle ended with 15:20. For reflection and literature on the implications of 15:20 and 16:31b, see Amit, *Judges*, 266-67. According to Amit, the presentation of Samson, "as a judge who disappointed . . . highlights the need for changing the system" (ibid., 267).

Main pre-DH: Deliverance *Collection*
its sources *and its framing*

Other pre-DH:
single sideline

Josianic DH:
from the Dtr

head; for I have been a nazirite to God from my mother's womb. If my head were shaved, then my strength would leave me; I would become weak, and be like anyone else."

18 When Delilah realized that he had told her his whole secret, she sent and called the lords of the Philistines, saying, "This time come up, for he has told his whole secret to me." Then the lords of the Philistines came up to her, and brought the money in their hands. [19]She let him fall asleep on her lap; and she called a man, and had him shave off the seven locks of his head. He began to weaken, and his strength left him. [20]Then she said, "The Philistines are upon you, Samson!" When he awoke from his sleep, he thought, "I will go out as at other times, and shake myself free." But he did not know that the LORD had left him. [21]So the Philistines seized him and gouged out his eyes. They brought him down to Gaza and bound him with bronze shackles; and he ground at the mill in the prison. [22]But the hair of his head began to grow again after it had been shaved.

23 Now the lords of the Philistines gathered to offer a great sacrifice to their god Dagon, and to rejoice; for they said, "Our god has given Samson our enemy into our hand." [24]When the people saw him, they praised their god; for they said, "Our god has given our enemy into our hand, the ravager of our country, who has killed many of us." [25]And when their hearts were merry, they said, "Call Samson, and let him entertain us." So they called Samson out of the prison, and he performed for them. They made him stand between the pillars; [26]and Samson said to the attendant who held him by the hand, "Let me feel the pillars on which the house rests, so that I may lean against them." [27]Now the house was full of men and women; all the lords of the Philistines were there, and on the roof there were about three thousand men and women, who looked on while Samson performed.

28 Then Samson called to the LORD and said, "LORD God, remember me and strengthen me only this once, O God, so that with this one act of revenge I may pay back the Philistines for my two eyes." [29]And Samson grasped the two middle pillars on which the house rested, and he leaned his weight against them, his right hand on the one and his left hand on the other. [30]Then Samson said, "Let me die with the Philistines." He strained with all his might; and the house fell on the lords and all the people who were in it. So those he killed at his death were more than those he had killed during his life. [31]Then his brothers and all his family came down and took him and brought him up and buried him between Zorah and Eshtaol in the tomb of his father Manoah. He had judged Israel twenty years.[31]

17 There was a man in the hill country of Ephraim whose name was Micah. [2]He said

---

31. The self-seeking revenge in Samson's prayer is remarkable and has to cast its shadow on this chapter at least, if not on the significance of the Samson cycle as a whole. In his prayer, there is no mention of Israel, no mention of the knowledge or honor of God; the concern is solely "for my two eyes" (v. 28). Nowhere in biblical text is a representative of Israel so unmindful of God and God's people.

For Noth's view of the two chronological notices (15:20 and 16:31b), see *DH*, 39-40.

to his mother, "The eleven hundred pieces of silver that were taken from you, about which you uttered a curse, and even spoke it in my hearing,—that silver is in my possession; I took it; but now I will return it to you." And his mother said, "May my son be blessed by the Lord!" [3]Then he returned the eleven hundred pieces of silver to his mother; and his mother said, "I consecrate the silver to the Lord from my hand for my son, to make an idol of cast metal." [4]So when he returned the money to his mother, his mother took two hundred pieces of silver, and gave it to the silversmith, who made it into an idol of cast metal; and it was in the house of Micah. [5]This man Micah had a shrine, and he made an ephod and teraphim, and installed one of his sons, who became his priest.[32]

[6]In those days there was no king in Israel; all the people did what was right in their own eyes.[36]

7 Now there was a young man of Bethlehem in Judah, of the clan of Judah. He

---

32. **Discussion** of 17:1–18:31. In these two chapters, as in the three that follow, the text does not present stories of leadership and deliverance; instead, leadership is absent and, in classic terms, the weak are subject to the strong. The stories are not such as to elicit the patterns associated with the deliverer stories (no formulas about Israel's evil, no oppression, no cry of the people, no deliverer, no deliverance, no quiet, and no chronology); linguistic evidence of dtr editing is not forthcoming. In these two chapters, there are attitudes toward idols that are thoroughly undeuteronomistic. While both groupings (17–18; 19–21) fit suitably into the portrayal of deterioration in the book of Judges, in our judgment, it is unlikely that they share a common text history with the earlier material (2–8). Among the additional materials, Samson is a Danite (13:2) and scarcely a positive figure; chap. 18 features Danites and not in a positive role. Their seizure of land is almost a reversal of the Joshua story.

These stories as "texts of terror" (Phyllis Trible) have been well rehearsed. Here, we will briefly highlight a few aspects only. The silver, from part of which

the idol is made, originally involved both theft and curse. In what follows, Micah exercises control and money provides the means. He installed one of his sons as priest, then a Levite, and then concluded "Now I know that the Lord will prosper me" (17:13). Such confident knowledge is a continued theme; the Levite has it (18:6) and the Danites have it, "God has indeed given it into your hands" (18:10). The next scene reflects power, with the weak subjected to the strong; six hundred armed Danites (18:16) cast their shadow over the story. The Danites take the objects, take over the priest, terrorize Micah, and butcher a quiet and unsuspecting people (18:27). Contrary to his expectations (17:13), Micah's prosperity has been plundered, his Levite lost. The Danite five are given God's blessing "in peace" (18:5-6, 10) and the Danites slaughter a "quiet and unsuspecting" people, without any reference to God (18:27-28). It is an ungodly story, a strange and contradictory story, and a story that is far from edifying.

Present-text potential. The story continues the unraveling of God's leadership, so evident at the start of the Judges period. Edifying statements are surrounded by most unedifying events. God is identified with the gods Micah has made (cf. 17:13; 18:24). All of this is placed under the rubric: "there was no king in Israel." As noted, while such material suits the DH context, its appropriateness does not justify dtr attribution (despite Veijola, *Königtum*, 15-29).

36. This refrain is repeated verbatim in 21:25. The first part recurs in 18:1 and 19:1. Our formatting separates the refrain from its surrounding text on the assumption that it was not an integral part of the stories. To the best of our knowledge, there is no evidence that determines whether the refrain was added to these traditions before or after their being appended to the DH.

Main pre-DH: Deliverance *Collection*	Other pre-DH:	**Josianic DH:**
its sources *and its framing*	single sideline	**from the Dtr**

was a Levite residing there. [8]This man left the town of Bethlehem in Judah, to live wherever he could find a place. He came to the house of Micah in the hill country of Ephraim to carry on his work. [9]Micah said to him, "From where do you come?" He replied, "I am a Levite of Bethlehem in Judah, and I am going to live wherever I can find a place." [10]Then Micah said to him, "Stay with me, and be to me a father and a priest, and I will give you ten pieces of silver a year, a set of clothes, and your living." [11]The Levite agreed to stay with the man; and the young man became to him like one of his sons. [12]So Micah installed the Levite, and the young man became his priest, and was in the house of Micah. [13]Then Micah said, "Now I know that the LORD will prosper me, because the Levite has become my priest."

18 In those days there was no king in Israel.

And in those days the tribe of the Danites was seeking for itself a territory to live in; for until then no territory among the tribes of Israel had been allotted to them. [2]So the

Danites sent five valiant men from the whole number of their clan, from Zorah and from Eshtaol, to spy out the land and to explore it; and they said to them, "Go, explore the land." When they came to the hill country of Ephraim, to the house of Micah, they stayed there. [3]While they were at Micah's house, they recognized the voice of the young Levite; so they went over and asked him, "Who brought you here? What are you doing in this place? What is your business here?" [4]He said to them, "Micah did such and such for me, and he hired me, and I have become his priest." [5]Then they said to him, "Inquire of God that we may know whether the mission we are undertaking will succeed." [6]The priest replied, "Go in peace. The mission you are on is under the eye of the LORD."

7 The five men went on, and when they came to Laish, they observed the people who were there living securely, after the manner of the Sidonians, quiet and unsuspecting, lacking nothing on earth, and possessing wealth. Furthermore, they were far from the Sidonians and had no dealings with Aram. [8]When they came to their kinsfolk at Zorah and Eshtaol, they said to them, "What do you report?" [9]They said, "Come, let us go up against them; for we have seen the land, and it is very good. Will you do nothing? Do not be slow to go, but enter in and possess the land. [10]When you go, you will come to an unsuspecting people. The land is broad—God has indeed given it into your hands—a place where there is no lack of anything on earth."

11 Six hundred men of the Danite clan, armed with weapons of war, set out from Zorah and Eshtaol, [12]and went up and encamped at Kiriath-jearim in Judah. On

---

Clearly, the presence of the refrain shapes the stories of these five chapters into a single collection illustrating the appalling implications of anarchy. The chapters, refrain included, could have been appended as a collection, indicating the disastrous state of disintegration. Alternatively, the chapters could have been appended, again illustrating the social disintegration, and the refrain added subsequently to enhance the unity of this vision.

As always, the double sideline says nothing about the date of composition; it indicates our judgment that the material so marked did not form part of the Josianic DH, but was appended later.

After the Dtr:	Revision:	Other:
indented and sans serif font	national focus	double sideline

this account that place is called Mahaneh-dan to this day; it is west of Kiriath-jearim. [13]From there they passed on to the hill country of Ephraim, and came to the house of Micah.

14 Then the five men who had gone to spy out the land (that is, Laish) said to their comrades, "Do you know that in these buildings there are an ephod, teraphim, and an idol of cast metal? Now therefore consider what you will do." [15]So they turned in that direction and came to the house of the young Levite, at the home of Micah, and greeted him. [16]While the six hundred men of the Danites, armed with their weapons of war, stood by the entrance of the gate, [17]the five men who had gone to spy out the land proceeded to enter and take the idol of cast metal, the ephod, and the teraphim. The priest was standing by the entrance of the gate with the six hundred men armed with weapons of war. [18]When the men went into Micah's house and took the idol of cast metal, the ephod, and the teraphim, the priest said to them, "What are you doing?" [19]They said to him, "Keep quiet! Put your hand over your mouth, and come with us, and be to us a father and a priest. Is it better for you to be priest to the house of one person, or to be priest to a tribe and clan in Israel?" [20]Then the priest accepted the offer. He took the ephod, the teraphim, and the idol, and went along with the people.

21 So they resumed their journey, putting the little ones, the livestock, and the goods in front of them. [22]When they were some distance from the home of Micah, the men who were in the houses near Micah's house were called out, and they overtook the Danites. [23]They shouted to the Danites, who turned around and said to Micah, "What is the matter that you come with such a company?" [24]He replied, "You take my gods that I made, and the priest, and go away, and what have I left? How then can you ask me, 'What is the matter?'" [25]And the Danites said to him, "You had better not let your voice be heard among us or else hot-tempered fellows will attack you, and you will lose your life and the lives of your household." [26]Then the Danites went their way. When Micah saw that they were too strong for him, he turned and went back to his home.

27 The Danites, having taken what Micah had made, and the priest who belonged to him, came to Laish, to a people quiet and unsuspecting, put them to the sword, and burned down the city. [28]There was no deliverer, because it was far from Sidon and they had no dealings with Aram. It was in the valley that belongs to Beth-rehob. They rebuilt the city, and lived in it. [29]They named the city Dan, after their ancestor Dan, who was born to Israel; but the name of the city was formerly Laish. [30]Then the Danites set up the idol for themselves. Jonathan son of Gershom, son of Moses, and his sons were priests to the tribe of the Danites until the time the land went into captivity. [31]So they maintained as their own Micah's idol that he had made, as long as the house of God was at Shiloh.

19 In those days, when there was no king in Israel.

A certain Levite, residing in the remote parts of the hill country of Ephraim, took to himself a concubine from Bethlehem in Judah. [2]But his concubine became angry with him, and she went away from him to her father's

---

house at Bethlehem in Judah, and was there some four months. ³Then her husband set out after her, to speak tenderly to her and bring her back. He had with him his servant and a couple of donkeys. When he reached her father's house, the girl's father saw him and came with joy to meet him. ⁴His father-in-law, the girl's father, made him stay, and he remained with him three days; so they ate and drank, and he stayed there. ⁵On the fourth day they got up early in the morning, and he prepared to go; but the girl's father said to his son-in-law, "Fortify yourself with a bit of food, and after that you may go." ⁶So the two men sat and ate and drank together; and the girl's father said to the man, "Why not spend the night and enjoy yourself?" ⁷When the man got up to go, his father-in-law kept urging him until he spent the night there again. ⁸On the fifth day he got up early in the morning to leave; and the girl's father said, "Fortify yourself." So they lingered until the day declined, and the two of them ate and drank. ⁹When the man with his concubine and his servant got up to leave, his father-in-law, the girl's father, said to him, "Look, the day has worn on until it is almost evening. Spend the night. See, the day has drawn to a close. Spend the night here and enjoy yourself. Tomorrow you can get up early in the morning for your journey, and go home."³⁴

10 But the man would not spend the night; he got up and departed, and arrived opposite Jebus (that is, Jerusalem). He had with him a couple of saddled donkeys, and his concubine was with him. ¹¹When they were near Jebus, the day was far spent, and the servant said to his master, "Come now, let us turn aside to this city of the Jebusites, and spend the night in it." ¹²But his master said to him, "We will not turn aside into a

---

man "in the hill country of Ephraim," who hires a Levite from the town of Bethlehem. Chap. 19 begins with a Levite, "residing in the remote parts of the hill country of Ephraim," who has a concubine from Bethlehem. The link is unexploited, but it is there.

The story of the Levite and his concubine is appalling. The story of the crime's avenging in the near-annihilation of Benjamin is equally appalling. The story of the winning of wives for the survivors of Benjamin, "that a tribe may not be blotted out from Israel" (21:17), is no less appalling. The horror is evident; so is the complexity of the composition. The murder of the concubine is avenged by the near-destruction of a tribe. In the campaign that achieves this, three battles are fought at God's command; the first two are lost. In order to achieve the survival of Benjamin, two oaths are invoked (21:1, 5), a town in Israel is wiped out (cf. 2 Sam 20:19) and daughters of Israel are betrayed (21:18-22). Such casuistry; such unholy deeds to keep Israel and vows intact. Wrongs are righted by the commission of equally terrible wrongs. And again, all of this is placed under the rubric: "there was no king in Israel."

Present-text potential. The deterioration is evident. In the book of Judges' portrayal, Israel is at a low point. It is difficult to envisage the situation being allowed to deteriorate further. The situation is ripe for remedy. The refrain points to what may be to come. "In those days, there was no king in Israel." A change in leadership is inevitable. God will raise up a prophet. God's prophet will anoint Israel's king.

---

34. **Discussion** of 19:1—21:24. As above, there are no patterns, no formulas, no dtr concerns to suggest any attribution to the circles responsible for the early chapters of Judges. While the material of chaps. 19–21 is different from that of chaps. 17–18, a point of contact should not be overlooked. Chap. 17 begins with a

---

After the Dtr:	Revision:	Other:
indented and sans serif font	*national focus*	double sideline

city of foreigners, who do not belong to the people of Israel; but we will continue on to Gibeah." [13]Then he said to his servant, "Come, let us try to reach one of these places, and spend the night at Gibeah or at Ramah." [14]So they passed on and went their way; and the sun went down on them near Gibeah, which belongs to Benjamin. [15]They turned aside there, to go in and spend the night at Gibeah. He went in and sat down in the open square of the city, but no one took them in to spend the night.

16 Then at evening there was an old man coming from his work in the field. The man was from the hill country of Ephraim, and he was residing in Gibeah. (The people of the place were Benjaminites) [17]When the old man looked up and saw the wayfarer in the open square of the city, he said, "Where are you going and where do you come from?" [18]He answered him, "We are passing from Bethlehem in Judah to the remote parts of the hill country of Ephraim, from which I come. I went to Bethlehem in Judah; and I am going to my home. Nobody has offered to take me in. [19]We your servants have straw and fodder for our donkeys, with bread and wine for me and the woman and the young man along with us. We need nothing more." [20]The old man said, "Peace be to you. I will care for all your wants; only do not spend the night in the square." [21]So he brought him into his house, and fed the donkeys; they washed their feet, and ate and drank.

22 While they were enjoying themselves, the men of the city, a perverse lot, surrounded the house, and started pounding on the door. They said to the old man, the master of the house, "Bring out the man who came into your house, so that we

may have intercourse with him." [23]And the man, the master of the house, went out to them and said to them, "No, my brothers, do not act so wickedly. Since this man is my guest, do not do this vile thing. [24]Here are my virgin daughter and his concubine; let me bring them out now. Ravish them and do whatever you want to them; but against this man do not do such a vile thing." [25]But the men would not listen to him. So the man seized his concubine, and put her out to them. They wantonly raped her, and abused her all through the night until the morning. And as the dawn began to break, they let her go. [26]As morning appeared, the woman came and fell down at the door of the man's house where her master was, until it was light.

27 In the morning her master got up, opened the doors of the house, and when he went out to go on his way, there was his concubine lying at the door of the house, with her hands on the threshold. [28]"Get up," he said to her, "we are going." But there was no answer. Then he put her on the donkey; and the man set out for his home. [29]When he had entered his house, he took a knife, and grasping his concubine he cut her into twelve pieces, limb by limb, and sent her throughout all the territory of Israel. [30]Then he commanded the men whom he sent, saying, "Thus shall you say to all the Israelites, 'Has such a thing ever happened since the day that the Israelites came up from the land of Egypt until this day? Consider it, take counsel, and speak out.' "

20 Then all the Israelites came out, from Dan to Beer-sheba, including the land of Gilead, and the congregation assembled in one body before the LORD at Mizpah. [2]The

---

Main pre-DH: Deliverance *Collection*
    its sources *and its framing*

Other pre-DH:
single sideline

Josianic DH:
from the Dtr

chiefs of all the people, of all the tribes of Israel, presented themselves in the assembly of the people of God, four hundred thousand foot-soldiers bearing arms. ³(Now the Benjaminites heard that the people of Israel had gone up to Mizpah.) And the Israelites said, "Tell us, how did this criminal act come about?" ⁴The Levite, the husband of the woman who was murdered, answered, "I came to Gibeah that belongs to Benjamin, I and my concubine, to spend the night. ⁵The lords of Gibeah rose up against me, and surrounded the house at night. They intended to kill me, and they raped my concubine until she died. ⁶Then I took my concubine and cut her into pieces, and sent her throughout the whole extent of Israel's territory; for they have committed a vile outrage in Israel. ⁷So now, you Israelites, all of you, give your advice and counsel here."

8 All the people got up as one, saying, "We will not any of us go to our tents, nor will any of us return to our houses. ⁹But now this is what we will do to Gibeah: we will go up against it by lot. ¹⁰We will take ten men of a hundred throughout all the tribes of Israel, and a hundred of a thousand, and a thousand of ten thousand, to bring provisions for the troops, who are going to repay Gibeah of Benjamin for all the disgrace that they have done in Israel." ¹¹So all the men of Israel gathered against the city, united as one.

12 The tribes of Israel sent men through all the tribe of Benjamin, saying, "What crime is this that has been committed among you? ¹³Now then, hand over those scoundrels in Gibeah, so that we may put them to death, and purge the evil from Israel." But the Benjaminites would not lis-

ten to their kinsfolk, the Israelites. ¹⁴The Benjaminites came together out of the towns to Gibeah, to go out to battle against the Israelites. ¹⁵On that day the Benjaminites mustered twenty-six thousand armed men from their towns, besides the inhabitants of Gibeah. ¹⁶Of all this force, there were seven hundred picked men who were left-handed; every one could sling a stone at a hair, and not miss. ¹⁷And the Israelites, apart from Benjamin, mustered four hundred thousand armed men, all of them warriors.

18 The Israelites proceeded to go up to Bethel, where they inquired of God, "Which of us shall go up first to battle against the Benjaminites?" And the LORD answered, "Judah shall go up first."

19 Then the Israelites got up in the morning, and encamped against Gibeah. ²⁰The Israelites went out to battle against Benjamin; and the Israelites drew up the battle line against them at Gibeah. ²¹The Benjaminites came out of Gibeah, and struck down on that day twenty-two thousand of the Israelites. ²³The Israelites went up and wept before the LORD until the evening; and they inquired of the LORD, "Shall we again draw near to battle against our kinsfolk the Benjaminites?" And the LORD said, "Go up against them." ²²The Israelites took courage, and again formed the battle line in the same place where they had formed it on the first day.

24 So the Israelites advanced against the Benjaminites the second day. ²⁵Benjamin moved out against them from Gibeah the second day, and struck down eighteen thousand of the Israelites, all of them armed men. ²⁶Then all the Israelites, the whole army, went back to Bethel and wept, sitting

there before the LORD; they fasted that day until evening. Then they offered burnt offerings and sacrifices of well-being before the LORD. [27]And the Israelites inquired of the LORD (for the ark of the covenant of God was there in those days, [28]and Phinehas son of Eleazar, son of Aaron, ministered before it in those days), saying, "Shall we go out once more to battle against our kinsfolk the Benjaminites, or shall we desist?" The LORD answered, "Go up, for tomorrow I will give them into your hand."

29 So Israel stationed men in ambush around Gibeah. [30]Then the Israelites went up against the Benjaminites on the third day, and set themselves in array against Gibeah, as before. [31]When the Benjaminites went out against the army, they were drawn away from the city. As before they began to inflict casualties on the troops, along the main roads, one of which goes up to Bethel and the other to Gibeah, as well as in the open country, killing about thirty men of Israel. [32]The Benjaminites thought, "They are being routed before us, as previously." But the Israelites said, "Let us retreat and draw them away from the city toward the roads." [33]The main body of the Israelites drew back its battle line to Baal-tamar, while those Israelites who were in ambush rushed out of their place west of Geba. [34]There came against Gibeah ten thousand picked men out of all Israel, and the battle was fierce. But the Benjaminites did not realize that disaster was close upon them.

35 The LORD defeated Benjamin before Israel; and the Israelites destroyed twenty-five thousand one hundred men of Benjamin that day, all of them armed.

36 Then the Benjaminites saw that they were defeated.

The Israelites gave ground to Benjamin, because they trusted to the troops in ambush that they had stationed against Gibeah. [37]The troops in ambush rushed quickly upon Gibeah. Then they put the whole city to the sword. [38]Now the agreement between the main body of Israel and the men in ambush was that when they sent up a cloud of smoke out of the city [39]the main body of Israel should turn in battle. But Benjamin had begun to inflict casualties on the Israelites, killing about thirty of them; so they thought, "Surely they are defeated before us, as in the first battle." [40]But when the cloud, a column of smoke, began to rise out of the city, the Benjaminites looked behind them—and there was the whole city going up in smoke toward the sky! [41]Then the main body of Israel turned, and the Benjaminites were dismayed, for they saw that disaster was close upon them. [42]Therefore they turned away from the Israelites in the direction of the wilderness; but the battle overtook them, and those who came out of the city were slaughtering them in between. [43]Cutting down the Benjaminites, they pursued them from Nohah and trod them down as far as a place east of Gibeah. [44]Eighteen thousand Benjaminites fell, all of them courageous fighters. [45]When they turned and fled toward the wilderness to the rock of Rimmon, five thousand of them were cut down on the main roads, and they were pursued as far as Gidom, and two thousand of them were slain. [46]So all who fell that day of Benjamin were twenty-five thousand arms-bearing men, all of them courageous fighters. [47]But six hundred turned and fled toward the wilderness to the rock of Rimmon, and remained at the rock of Rimmon

---

Main pre-DH: Deliverance *Collection*
its sources *and its framing*

Other pre-DH:
single sideline

Josianic DH:
from the Dtr

for four months. [48]Meanwhile, the Israelites turned back against the Benjaminites, and put them to the sword—the city, the people, the animals, and all that remained. Also the remaining towns they set on fire.

21 Now the Israelites had sworn at Mizpah, "No one of us shall give his daughter in marriage to Benjamin." [2]And the people came to Bethel, and sat there until evening before God, and they lifted up their voices and wept bitterly. [3]They said, "O Lord, the God of Israel, why has it come to pass that today there should be one tribe lacking in Israel?" [4]On the next day, the people got up early, and built an altar there, and offered burnt offerings and sacrifices of well-being. [5]Then the Israelites said, "Which of all the tribes of Israel did not come up in the assembly to the Lord?" For a solemn oath had been taken concerning whoever did not come up to the Lord to Mizpah, saying, "That one shall be put to death." [6]But the Israelites had compassion for Benjamin their kin, and said, "One tribe is cut off from Israel this day. [7]What shall we do for wives for those who are left, since we have sworn by the Lord that we will not give them any of our daughters as wives?"

8 Then they said, "Is there anyone from the tribes of Israel who did not come up to the Lord to Mizpah?" It turned out that no one from Jabesh-gilead had come to the camp, to the assembly. [9]For when the roll was called among the people, not one of the inhabitants of Jabesh-gilead was there. [10]So the congregation sent twelve thousand soldiers there and commanded them, "Go, put the inhabitants of Jabesh-gilead to the sword, including the women and the little ones. [11]This is what you shall do; every male

and every woman that has lain with a male you shall devote to destruction." [12]And they found among the inhabitants of Jabesh-gilead four hundred young virgins who had never slept with a man and brought them to the camp at Shiloh, which is in the land of Canaan.

13 Then the whole congregation sent word to the Benjaminites who were at the rock of Rimmon, and proclaimed peace to them. [14]Benjamin returned at that time; and they gave them the women whom they had saved alive of the women of Jabesh-gilead; but they did not suffice for them.

15 The people had compassion on Benjamin because the Lord had made a breach in the tribes of Israel. [16]So the elders of the congregation said, "What shall we do for wives for those who are left, since there are no women left in Benjamin?" [17]And they said, "There must be heirs for the survivors of Benjamin, in order that a tribe may not be blotted out from Israel. [18]Yet we cannot give any of our daughters to them as wives." For the Israelites had sworn, "Cursed be anyone who gives a wife to Benjamin." [19]So they said, "Look, the yearly festival of the Lord is taking place at Shiloh, which is north of Bethel, on the east of the highway that goes up from Bethel to Shechem, and south of Lebonah." [20]And they instructed the Benjaminites, saying, "Go and lie in wait in the vineyards, [21]and watch; when the young women of Shiloh come out to dance in the dances, then come out of the vineyards and each of you carry off a wife for himself from the young women of Shiloh, and go to the land of Benjamin. [22]Then if their fathers or their brothers come to complain to us, we will say to them, 'Be generous and allow us to

---

| After the Dtr: | Revision: | Other: |
| indented and sans serif font | *national focus* | double sideline |

have them; because we did not capture in battle a wife for each man. But neither did you incur guilt by giving your daughters to them.' " [23]The Benjaminites did so; they took wives for each of them from the dancers whom they abducted. Then they went and returned to their territory, and rebuilt the towns, and lived in them. [24]So the Israelites departed from there at that time by tribes and families, and they went out from there to their own territories.

25 In those days there was no king in Israel; all the people did what was right in their own eyes.[35]

---

35. With this concluding refrain, the book of Judges closes off a despairing picture of Israel without monarchical leadership. The next section will begin with the emergence of the prophet Samuel who, as God's prophet, will designate David as king-to-be in Israel. Out of despair comes hope. The hope is embodied in a leadership that combines the benefits of prophet and king.

Main pre-DH: Deliverance *Collection*	Other pre-DH:	**Josianic DH:**
its sources *and its framing*	single sideline	**from the Dtr**

The Books of Samuel

INTRODUCTION

When we step back from the intricacies of inter-pretation to look at the rhythms that begin with the books of Samuel, we may be in for a surprise.

The downward rhythm of deteriorating situ-ations that we have seen in Judges is halted. A rising rhythm starts slowly developing that will culminate in David's establishment in Jerusalem as king of all Israel, with his military and politi-cal successes. The upbeat rhythm of David's rise toward power starts to sag from the moment that he sins with Bathsheba and murders her hus-band. After the revolts of Absalom and Sheba, David's hold on power is fragile. Israel's hold on stability is just as fragile. The succession of Solomon and the construction of the temple in Jerusalem hold out hope of a return to the upbeat rising rhythm. Solomon's apostasy dashes that hope and the downward rhythm of deterio-ration returns—except for short surges of hope with Hezekiah and Josiah—until the end of the monarchy and the end of independence.

The emergence of Samuel, a prophet, a new figure untainted by the old order, dispels the cloud of instability and evil in the text of the book of Judges: "In those days there was no king in Israel; all the people did what was right in their own eyes" (Judg 21:25). The movement of God's ark from a major sanctuary of Israel into the power of the Philistines and finally to a

peripheral and insignificant town in Israel inserts a glaring question mark into Israel's history: where to next? The emergence of the new (a prophet) and the departure of a symbol of the old (the ark at Shiloh) offers a choice to Israel such as Moses offered. "See, I have set before you today life and prosperity, death and adver-sity" (Deut 30:15). Renaissance may bring life; recalcitrance will surely bring death. As prophet, Samuel is God's medium of communication to Israel (1 Sam 3:20), with an immediacy given no other since Moses. Samuel's establishment of the monarchy opens the way to an initial stability. The rest of Israel's pre-exilic history is the story of this stability, its strengths and weaknesses.

The treatment in this chapter of *Unfolding the Deuteronomistic History* differs from traditional approaches to the books of Samuel in two signif-icant areas. First, there is the introduction of the hypothesis of a Prophetic Record (PR), extend-ing from the emergence of Samuel to the seizure of power by Jehu (1 Samuel 1—2 Kings 10). Second, there is a substantial reassessment of the role of the Dtr and the dtr movement in pre-senting the emergence of the monarchy in Israel (1 Samuel 7–12).

If the hypothesis of a PR withstands critical scrutiny, it offers a backbone to the DH in Samuel—Kings. The text presents prophets who set up and demote kings. Samuel presides over the process by which Saul became king, anointing him king-designate (*nāgîd*) and, in turn, dismissing him from the kingship for failure of obedience. Samuel's life climaxes with the anointing of David as king-to-be. Ahijah of Shiloh legitimates Jeroboam and later withdraws that legitimation. Elijah condemns the dynasty of Ahab. Elisha's disciple gives effect to this in the anointing of Jehu. In its own way, the PR is an extended reflection on the traditions of David's rise to royal power and the traditions associated with Elijah. Again, in its own way, the Josianic DH is an extended reflection on the PR. There is continuity in the story of Israel.

As an expanded version of the Story of David's Rise (or the equivalent narrative), the PR first establishes the figure of the prophet. Samuel is prophet to all Israel and the PR traces the sequence that leads to Samuel's anointing David as Israel's king-to-be (1 Sam 16:1-13). From there, the Story of David's Rise comes to the fore, culminating in David's assumption of royal power over all Israel. The kingdom was at its high point. The PR then takes up the narrative again, with a terse summary of Solomon's reign: he busied himself in three areas—with Pharaoh's daughter, building projects in Jerusalem, and the use of forced labor (1 Kgs 3:1; 9:15-24*). The beginning of the kingdom's decline is signaled by Solomon's apostasy; he built high places for Chemosh and Molech (1 Kgs 11:7). The prophet Ahijah announces God's division of the kingdom into north and south and the designation of Jeroboam as king over the north. But Jeroboam fails. The PR traces the prophetic struggle against northern Israel's apostasy down to the assertion that Elisha initiated Jehu's rebellion and so could claim the elimination of Baal worship from Israel (cf. 2 Kgs 10:28).

The DH has substantially expanded the PR, taking Israel's story back to Moses and continuing it down to Josiah. On the establishment of the monarchy, within 1 Samuel 7–12, both the tradi-

tion and the dtr movement played a major role. Noth himself was well aware of his Dtr's dependence on earlier traditions for the story of Saul and David: "the existence of this traditional material [Saul and David traditions] absolved Dtr. from the need to organize and construct the narrative himself."[1] As prologue to these traditions, Noth's Dtr drew a picture of Samuel as Israel's last deliverer-judge, of "the wicked self-will of the people" demanding a king and of God empowering Samuel to set up the monarchy, so leading into 1 Sam 9:1–10:16; further, he found a place for "a traditional story of Saul's accession" (10:17-27a), inserted the Nahash tradition (10:27b-11:15), and finally composed 1 Samuel 12 to assure Israel that "despite the institution of the monarchy things can remain as they were before"—that Israel has a choice between obedience and disobedience, preservation and annihilation.[2] Noth's conclusion signals his awareness of the significant difficulties involved in the interpretation he was advocating: "it was not without obvious effort and contrivance that Dtr. supplemented the old account which dealt favorably with the institution of the monarchy by adding long passages reflecting his disapproval of the institution."[3] Beyond this, Noth's Dtr sharpened aspects of the promise to David (2 Samuel 7), otherwise leaving 1–2 Samuel much as he found it.

Since 1943 and the launching of Noth's hypothesis of a DH—written in the time of Israel's exile, deploring the total failure of the monarchy in Israel—it has been traditional wisdom to attribute to the Dtr a negative portrayal in 1 Samuel 7–12 of the emergence of kingship in Israel. This view will not be sustained here. For Noth, "Dtr. simply traces the institution of the monarchy, of which he disapproves, back to

---

1. *DH*, 86.
2. *Ibid.*, 78-84.
3. *Ibid.*, 83-84; for the classic resolution, see H. J. Boecker, *Die Beurteilung der Anfänge des Königtums*.

the wicked self-will of the people."[4] When this viewpoint changes, a great deal changes—as will become apparent.

For Noth, certain factors made the assumption of an extensive and negative dtr contribution in 1 Samuel 7–12 almost automatic. Key factors were: (i) the exilic date postulated for the DH with the correlative view that it understood the monarchy as a failure; (ii) the perception of a negative attitude toward kingship on the part of the Dtr throughout the DH; (iii) the presence of limited but clear dtr language.

Developments since Noth change this picture substantially. The case for a Josianic edition of the DH recognizes the existence of support for a potentially positive attitude toward the monarchy on the part of the Josianic Dtr. The identification of movement within the dtr process of revision reveals that the dtr language, which occurs in only a very few verses, reflects a late stage in dtr convictions. The absence of clear dtr thought and language in the rest of the so-called dtr sections of 1 Samuel 7–12 then becomes glaring. Nevertheless, this changing perception should not be read as diminishing dtr responsibility for portraying the origins of the monarchy in Israel. The concept of "the" single Deuteronomistic Historian has been expanded to include at least two stages for consideration, the Josianic Dtr and the later revisers of the DH; within the texts attributed to the revision of the DH, it is possible to identify a royal focus (blaming the evil of kings) and a national focus (blaming a disobedient people). Less text may be attributed to dtr sources as authors; that does not mean that the editorial, compositional, and conceptual-theological role of the dtr sources is dwindling toward some sort of vanishing point. Far from it.

The major dtr intervention in 1 Samuel is seen to be here, in chaps. 7–12; discussion at this

4. *DH*, 80.

introductory level will lighten the already extensive notes later. We believe it essential from the outset to insist that no single reconstruction of its history can be imposed on this text. There are several ways that the text history of 1 Samuel 7–12 can be approached.

As just noted, identifiably dtr language "occurs in only a very few verses" in these chapters, so linguistic controls are few. Attitudes to monarchy are important and helpful, but not determinative. In 1 Samuel 8, the core statements of these attitudes are easily identified: positive to monarchy is God's command (vv. 7a, 22); unspecified negativity is voiced in Samuel's "displeasure" (v. 6, from an individual); negativity is specified in the warning (vv. 11-17, to the people); outright hostility identifies monarchy with rejection of YHWH (vv. 7b-8); the possibility of reconciling these attitudes is given in 1 Samuel 12—which is unquestionably a later text, of enigmatic origin.

The way these attitudes are combined determines how the history of the text is reconstructed. The evidence invites rather than overwhelms the interpreter. Different interpreters will without question be invited in different directions. There are at least three axes along which interpretations will divide; multiple combinations are possible. These three axes are: (i) whether the base text of 1 Samuel 8 is analyzed as positive or negative toward monarchy; (ii) whether the basic integration of traditions into the composition was done simultaneously by the Josianic Dtr or was sequential across the composition and revision of the DH; and (iii), if a simultaneous integration is postulated, whether the basic traditions integrated were in opposition to each other or in substantial harmony.

The view we prefer and have adopted in our formatting opts for a negative (unspecified) base text in 1 Samuel 8 and a sequential integration of the traditions. In this understanding, multiple traditions existed in Israel that came to be organized into two narrative strands: 9:1—10:16 with 11:1-11, 15 (the "prophetic" strand, where the monarchy is God's initiative and gift) and 7:5-17; 8:1-6, 22; 10:17, 20-24 (the "assembly" strand, where the monarchy is asked for by the people and given by God). In our view, the first of these (the "prophetic" strand) was taken up by the Josianic Dtr, whose model was David and whose hope was Josiah. The second (the "assembly" strand) was adopted by the dtr revision's royal focus (blaming evil kings), was specified in its negativity, and introduced into the DH, countering the Josianic optimism and giving a voice to the view that blamed monarchy for the failure of hope and reform in Israel. Subsequently, the national focus of the dtr revision process injected a note of outright hostility to monarchy into these traditions, identifying the move to monarchy with a rejection of YHWH as God of Israel. Arguments and evidence can wait for the discussion of the text. We may simply note here that the "assembly" strand, with its focus on the demand from the people, was an apt vehicle for expressing a negative view of the monarchy and later an intensified insistence on the negative role of the people.

As will be seen, an alternative analysis of 1 Samuel 8 is possible, with 8:1-5 and 21-22 (or equivalent) forming the base text. In this analysis, the base text is unreservedly positive to monarchy. Similarly, the compositional integration of the major traditions can be attributed to the Josianic Dtr or spread over the DH's composition and revision. Finally, where simultaneous composition is attributed to the Josianic Dtr, this can involve two favorable traditions ("prophetic" and "assembly") or one favorable ("prophetic") and one unfavorable (revised "assembly"). It would unduly complicate a book of this kind to explore these options in detail. It would be dishonest even to imply that they did not exist and were not legitimately possible.

Before proceeding, it may be helpful to point out that we can no longer appeal to 1 Samuel 12 as the Josianic Dtr's resolution of the conflicting traditions that the Dtr had combined with "obvious effort and contrivance" (Noth). As the treatment in the text below will make clear, there are formidable arguments that point to a later origin for 1 Samuel 12. The chapter is not the culmination of the original dtr composition; it may be read now as a resolution to these chapters.

It may help to review and contextualize the two major narrative strands in play. Their difference is barely veiled by Samuel's "and there renew the kingship" in 11:14. It is worth insisting that these strands may have been assembled from multiple components over the course of Israel's history. What matters most is the picture they now present. In both strands, Saul emerges as king with God's backing. In one, Saul is sent by God, anointed by Samuel, victorious over Nahash, and crowned by the people (11:15); in the other, a king is requested by the elders and ordered by God, and Saul is selected by divination (lot and oracle) and presented by Samuel to the people for acclamation (10:24). In the first of these, kingship emerges from God's initiative, with Samuel's authority, and directed to the long-term defense of Israel against the Philistines (9:16; necessary, but not achieved until David, also anointed by Samuel). This first strand was itself formed by the prophetic rewriting of the account of an earlier defense initiative directed toward the short-term threat posed by the Ammonites under Nahash, involving the commissioning of Saul by an anonymous prophet. The second major narrative strand, as we have it now, opens with an account of the efficacy of Samuel's intercession in having divine thunder rout the Philistines (7:5-14) and then provides a text with kingship emerging from a call for social justice by Israel's elders, supported by God and carried through by Samuel. It is this second strand that was or became the bearer of the traditions negative or hostile to monarchy, above all in 8:7-21 (or 8:6-20) and 10:18-19.

To return for a moment to the main components of 1–2 Samuel, the chapters often referred to as the Ark Narrative (cf. 1 Samuel 4–6; 2 Samuel 6) should not be overlooked. One issue concerns what sort of literary entity might have actually existed in ancient Israel. At least two major options are current: (i) an actual Ark Narrative, comprising text from both 1 and 2 Samuel, and focusing exclusively on the ark as the symbol of God's activity in Israel; (ii) a virtual ark narrative, comprising text from 1 Samuel and also later taking into account text from 2 Samuel, both blocks focusing exclusively on the ark as the symbol of God's activity in Israel (for discussion and some select bibliography, see Campbell, "Yahweh and the Ark").

In 1 Samuel, the narrative about the ark may communicate a major theological conviction: that God has abandoned the Israel of Shiloh, has not abandoned Israel, but has not signaled acceptance of a particular shape to a changed Israel; the ark has left Shiloh and returned to Kiriath-jearim. Correlatively, in 2 Samuel, the narrative about the ark may communicate the conviction that God has endorsed Israel's shape under David; the ark has come to Jerusalem. As consolidated text, an actual Ark Narrative could have communicated this conviction. In their present situation, as a virtual ark narrative, the traditions can effectively communicate this conviction in the broader context of Israel's story.

The Prophetic Record has already been mentioned. In part, it is an expansion of the traditions of David's rise to power. Whether there ever existed a text that might be called the Story of David's Rise is debated, as are issues of its beginning and end. The likely narrative organization around areas such as 1 Samuel 17–18, 23–26, and 28–31 points to the probability of such a text having existed. It may have begun with the earliest traditions of Saul's rise to kingship, a prerequisite for David's; it would have ended with David's accession to the throne of Judah and Israel (perhaps including early texts of the ark's coming to Jerusalem and YHWH's commitment to David's dynastic security, concluding with 8:15; for details and discussion, see Campbell, *1 Samuel*). Some of Israel's finest storytelling has been consecrated to dramas of David's reign. The usual designation, "Succession Narrative," is an unfortunate misnomer; it is more appropriately termed the Story of David's Later Years. Its characteristically high quality narrative is most evident in 2 Samuel 11–20 (see below).

In the books of Samuel, the outcome of these diverse traditions was ultimately the figure of David, king of Judah and Israel. Given the detailed portrayal of David's sin (above all, concerning Bathsheba and Uriah), it may come as a surprise and an enigma for modern readers to find that David is treated as the standard for future kings (cf. 1 Kgs 11:32-34, 38; 14:8; 15:11; 2 Kgs 14:3; 16:2; 18:3; 22:2). Like Peter in the NT, David had cause to weep bitterly. Unlike Peter, David's sin never included denial. Dtr theology focuses intensely on fidelity to YHWH, God of Israel, and on the centralization of worship in Jerusalem. David captured Jerusalem; there is no evidence of his worshipping elsewhere afterwards. David sinned, above all in regard to Bathsheba and Uriah; he did not add apostasy to his sins. He is shown with an admirable, perhaps uncanny, and almost fatalistic trust in YHWH (see, for example, 1 Sam 24:15; 26:8-11; 2 Sam 16:12). He is quick to confess when charged with sin (2 Sam 12:13a). The traditions show David as a deeply flawed human being; yet the DH used David as a model figure, a measure for the kings of Israel and Judah of what was "right in the sight of the LORD." The breadth of Israel's theological thinking is sometimes stunning.

THE FIRST BOOK OF SAMUEL

1 There was a certain man of Ramathaim, a Zuphite from the hill country of Ephraim, whose name was Elkanah son of Jeroham son of Elihu son of Tohu son of Zuph, an Ephraimite. [2]He had two wives; the name of the one was Hannah, and the name of the other Peninnah. Peninnah had children, but Hannah had no children.[1]

3 Now this man used to go up year by year from his town to worship and to sacrifice to the LORD of hosts at Shiloh, where the two sons of Eli, Hophni and Phinehas, were priests of the LORD. [4]On the day when Elkanah sacrificed, he would give portions to his wife Peninnah and to all her sons and daughters; [5]but to Hannah he gave a double portion, because he loved her, though the LORD had closed her womb. [6]Her rival used to provoke her severely, to irritate her, because the LORD had closed her womb. [7]So it went on year by year; as often as she went up to the house of the LORD, she used to provoke her. Therefore Hannah wept and would not eat.

---

1. **Text signals.** The formulaic introduction to the reign of Saul, in 1 Sam 13:1, begins the portrayal of Israel's monarchy. 1 Samuel 1–12 can be identified as the preparation for this monarchy. Within it, chaps. 1–3 focus almost exclusively on the emerging figure of the prophet Samuel, without any echo of the Philistine oppression (see Judg 13:1); chaps. 4–6 focus almost exclusively on the ark as symbol of YHWH's power and purpose; chaps. 9–12 focus on the emergence of the monarchy in Israel, with chaps. 7–8 functioning to some degree as a transition.

Text-history approach. These signals can be understood as pointing to the Prophetic Record (PR) that begins in chaps. 1–3, to the Ark Narrative in chaps. 4–6, and to the dtr interweaving of dtr contributions with earlier sources (especially the PR) in chaps. 7–12. At the level of the Josianic DH, the text here is a continuation from Judg 13:1. 1 Samuel 1–3 is the beginning of a new source, the PR. Samuel emerges as prophet (1 Sam 3:19-21); he is also portrayed as the midwife for Israel's monarchy (1 Sam 9:1—10:16; 11:1-15). The structure of the composition brings the PR into the wider horizon of the Josianic DH. The PR is represented by the roman and italic text—roman for its sources and italic for the contributions of the prophetic editors (see the footer on even-numbered pages). The revision of the DH that focused on the failure of the kings had to have its start in these chapters. We term it the "royal" focus. The concern for Israel's sin and the failure of the people comes to expression in these chapters too. We call it

the "national" focus (see the footer on odd-numbered pages).

Present-text potential. The present text has to be read in the light of Joshua's generation and its fidelity, a fidelity that has been diminishing as the text proceeds through the book of Judges. Deliverance was last achieved by Jephthah, with its problems. Samson won personal victories; he failed for Israel. Israel's relationship with God has been running down. "All the people did what was right in their own eyes" contrasting sharply with the dtr requirement to do what was right in the eyes of the LORD. The Danites get land for their tribe, but they have procured a priest, beggared his employer, and butchered a village (Judges 17–18). The Israelites avenge a fearful wrong and nearly eliminate a tribe; they commit another fearful wrong and so preserve the tribe (Judges 19–21). For all of the stories' ambiguity and the neutrality of the telling, their content is appalling; the relationship with God is at a low ebb. "There was no king in Israel."

Against this backdrop, 1 Samuel 1–3 offers the hope of a new figure; chaps. 4–6 end an era and lie open to a future; and in chaps. 8–12, Samuel ushers in the king. If Samuel's guidance is followed, Israel's relationship with God will be renewed.

Main pre-DH: *Prophetic* Record
its sources *and prophetic contribution*

Other pre-DH:
single sideline

**Josianic DH:
from the Dtr**

[8]Her husband Elkanah said to her, "Hannah, why do you weep? Why do you not eat? Why is your heart sad? Am I not more to you than ten sons?"[2]

9 After they had eaten and drunk at Shiloh, Hannah rose and presented herself before the Lord. Now Eli the priest was sitting on the seat beside the doorpost of the temple of the Lord. [10]She was deeply distressed and prayed to the Lord, and wept bitterly. [11]She made this vow: "O Lord of hosts, if only you will look on the misery of your servant, and remember me, and not forget your servant, but will give to your servant a male child, then I will set him before you as a nazirite until the day of his death. He shall drink neither wine nor intoxicants, and no razor shall touch his head."

12 As she continued praying before the Lord, Eli observed her mouth. [13]Hannah was praying silently; only her lips moved, but her voice was not heard; therefore Eli thought she was drunk. [14]So Eli said to her, "How long will you make a drunken spectacle of yourself? Put away your wine." [15]But Hannah answered, "No, my lord, I am a woman deeply troubled; I have drunk neither wine nor strong drink, but I have been pouring out my soul before the Lord. [16]Do not regard your servant as a worthless woman, for I have been speaking out of my great anxiety and vexation all this time." [17]Then Eli answered, "Go in peace; the God of Israel grant the petition you have made to him." [18]And she said, "Let your servant find favor in your sight." Then the woman went to her quarters, ate and drank with her husband, and her countenance was sad no longer.

19 They rose early in the morning and worshiped before the Lord; then they went back to their house at Ramah. Elkanah knew his wife Hannah, and the Lord remembered her. [20]In due time Hannah conceived and bore a son. She named him Samuel, for she said, "I have asked him of the Lord."

21 The man Elkanah and all his household went up to offer to the Lord the yearly sacrifice, and to pay his vow. [22]But Hannah did not go up, for she said to her husband, "As soon as the child is weaned, I will bring him, that he may appear in the presence of the Lord, and remain there forever; I will offer him as a nazirite for all time." [23]Her husband Elkanah said to her, "Do what seems best to you, wait until you have weaned him; only—may the Lord establish his word." So the woman remained and nursed her son, until she weaned him. [24]When she had weaned him, she took him up with her, along with a three-year-old bull, an ephah of flour, and a skin of wine. She brought him to the house of the Lord at Shiloh; and the child was young. [25]Then they slaughtered the bull, and they brought the child to Eli. [26]And she said, "Oh, my lord! As you live, my lord, I am the woman who was standing here in your presence, praying to the Lord. [27]For this child I prayed; and the Lord has granted me the petition that I made to him. [28]Therefore I have lent him to the Lord; as long as he lives, he is given to the Lord." She left him there for the Lord.

2 Hannah prayed and said,[3]
> "My heart exults in the Lord;
> > my strength is exalted in my God.
> My mouth derides my enemies,
> > because I rejoice in my victory.

---

2. Whatever its historical value, this story in its context assumes that Shiloh as sanctuary was symbolic of its era in Israel (cf. Judg 18:31; Ps 78:60; Jer 7:12-14).

3. As it stands, the Song of Hannah with its culminating reference to the king cannot be contempo-

---

| After the Dtr: indented and sans serif font | **Revision: royal focus** | *Revision: national focus* | Other: double sideline |

2 "There is no Holy One like the LORD,
    no one besides you;
    there is no Rock like our God.
3 Talk no more so very proudly,
    let not arrogance come from
        your mouth;
    for the LORD is a God of knowledge,
    and by him actions are weighed.
4 The bows of the mighty are broken,
    but the feeble gird on strength.
5 Those who were full have hired
        themselves out for bread,
    but those who were hungry are fat
        with spoil.
    The barren has borne seven,
    but she who has many children is
        forlorn.
6 The LORD kills and brings to life;
    he brings down to Sheol and raises up.
7 The LORD makes poor and makes rich;
    he brings low, he also exalts.
8 He raises up the poor from the dust;
    he lifts the needy from the ash heap,
    to make them sit with princes
    and inherit a seat of honor.

For the pillars of the earth are the LORD's,
    and on them he has set the world.
9 "He will guard the feet of his faithful ones,
    but the wicked shall be cut off in
        darkness;
    for not by might does one prevail.
10 The LORD! His adversaries shall be
        shattered;
    the Most High will thunder in heaven.
    The LORD will judge the ends of the
        earth;
    he will give strength to his king,
    and exalt the power of his anointed."

11 Then Elkanah went home to Ramah, while the boy remained to minister to the LORD, in the presence of the priest Eli.

12 Now the sons of Eli were scoundrels; they had no regard for the LORD [13]or for the duties of the priests to the people. When anyone offered sacrifice, the priest's servant would come, while the meat was boiling, with a three-pronged fork in his hand, [14]and he would thrust it into the pan, or kettle, or caldron, or pot; all that the fork brought up the priest would take for himself. This is what they did at Shiloh to all the Israelites who came there. [15]Moreover, before the fat was burned, the priest's servant would come and say to the one who was sacrificing, "Give meat for the priest to roast; for he will not accept boiled meat from you, but only raw." [16]And if the man said to him, "Let them burn the fat first, and then take whatever you wish," he would say, "No, you must give it now; if not, I will take it by force." [17]Thus the sin of the young men was very great in the sight of the LORD; for they treated the offerings of the LORD with contempt.[4]

---

raneous with Hannah and Samuel. Situated here at the narrative's start, it sounds three themes that will echo through the texts to come: first, momentous change is about to occur; second, Israel will triumph over its foes; third, God will empower the king. Samuel the prophet will replace Eli the priest; Israel will triumph over the Philistines; Samuel will anoint kings. The Song may be secondary, but it is suited to its place—not particularly apt as a song for a mother who has just given up a child to God; far more apt as the song for a woman who is a symbol of Israel on the brink of new life. It is difficult to date; it is even more difficult to say when it came into the text. Opinions include an early date for composition and a late date for inclusion; post-dtr seems less likely.

---

4. **Text signals.** (i) Three blocks of anti-Elide tradition (2:12-17, 22-25, 27-36) as well as the word to

---

Main pre-DH: *Prophetic* Record
its sources *and prophetic contribution*

Other pre-DH:
single sideline

**Josianic DH:
from the Dtr**

*18 Samuel was ministering before the L*ORD*, a boy wearing a linen ephod. *[19]*His mother used to make for him a little robe and take it to him each year, when she went up with her husband to offer the yearly sacrifice. *[20]*Then Eli would bless Elkanah and his wife, and say, "May the L*ORD* repay you with children by this woman for the gift that she made to the L*ORD*"; and then they would return to their home.*

*21 And the L*ORD* took note of Hannah; she conceived and bore three sons and two daughters. And the boy Samuel grew up in the presence of the L*ORD*.*

22 Now Eli was very old. He heard all that his sons were doing to all Israel.

|| and how they lay with the women who served at the entrance to the tent of meeting.[5]

Samuel (3:2-18) are separated by material about Samuel (2:18-21, 26; 3:1; 3:19—4:1a). (ii) The anti-Elide traditions cover a wide palette: vv. 12-17 name liturgical abuse, vv. 22-25 focus on obdurate deafness to their father's reproach, adding sexual abuse and commenting on the divine will to kill. Vv. 27-36 reiterate the charge of liturgical abuse and turn the reproach against the father, an accusation intensified in 3:10-14. (iii) The Samuel material is repetitious, with minimal information about Samuel interposed in alternating contrast with the Elides.

Text-history approach. The hypothesis of a PR allows the anti-Elide material to be drawn from traditional sources and interwoven with prophetic contributions focused on Samuel. The birth story (1:1—2:11) and the temple story (3:2-18) sound traditional, contrasting with the intervening Samuel material. The prophetic goal is the grown Samuel who is prophet to all Israel (3:19—4:1a)—here somewhat superimposed on the narrative of childhood and youth.

Present-text potential. The overall picture is of a declining Elide priesthood and an emerging prophetic figure in Samuel. There has been no such figure in Israel since Moses and Joshua.

5. On textual and other grounds, this accusation of sexual abuse may be judged quite late. The tent of

[23]He said to them, "Why do you do such things? For I hear of your evil dealings from all these people. [24]No, my sons; it is not a good report that I hear the people of the LORD spreading abroad. [25]If one person sins against another, someone can intercede for the sinner with the LORD; but if someone sins against the LORD, who can make intercession?" But they would not listen to the voice of their father; for it was the will of the LORD to kill them.[6]

*26 Now the boy Samuel continued to grow both in stature and in favor with the L*ORD* and with the people.*

27 A man of God came to Eli and said to him, "Thus the LORD has said, 'I revealed myself to the family of your ancestor in Egypt when they were slaves to the house of Pharaoh. [28]I chose him out of all the tribes of Israel to be my priest, to go up to my altar, to offer incense, to wear an ephod before me; and I gave to the family of your ancestor all my offerings by fire from the people of Israel. [29]Why then look with greedy eye at my sacrifices and my offerings that I commanded, and honor your sons more than me by fattening yourselves on the choicest parts of every offering of my people Israel?' [30]Therefore the LORD the God of Israel declares: 'I promised that your family and the family of your ancestor should go in and out before me forever'; but now the LORD declares: 'Far be it from me; for those who honor me I will honor, and those who despise me shall be treated with contempt. [31]See, a time is coming when I will cut off your

---

meeting is a priestly term. The present text is drawing in both the issues of worship and ethics.

6. Noth gives 2:25b to his Dtr as a "characteristic reflection" (*DH*, 84). There is nothing in thought or language to compel this attribution. Stoebe regards v. 25b as expressing prophetic thought (*Erste Buch Samuelis*, 114).

| After the Dtr: indented and sans serif font | **Revision: royal focus** | Revision: national focus | Other: double sideline |

strength and the strength of your ancestor's family, so that no one in your family will live to old age. [32]Then in distress you will look with greedy eye on all the prosperity that shall be bestowed upon Israel; and no one in your family shall ever live to old age. [33]The only one of you whom I shall not cut off from my altar shall be spared to weep out his eyes and grieve his heart; all the members of your household shall die by the sword. **[34]The fate of your two sons, Hophni and Phinehas, shall be the sign to you—both of them shall die on the same day. [35]I will raise up for myself a faithful priest, who shall do according to what is in my heart and in my mind. I will build him a sure house, and he shall go in and out before my anointed one forever. [36]Everyone who is left in your family shall come to implore him for a piece of silver or a loaf of bread, and shall say, Please put me in one of the priest's places, that I may eat a morsel of bread.' "[7]**

3 *Now the boy Samuel was ministering to the* LORD *under Eli. The word of the* LORD *was rare in those days; visions were not widespread.*

2 At that time Eli, whose eyesight had begun to grow dim so that he could not see, was lying down in his room; [3]the lamp of God had not yet gone out, and Samuel was lying down in the temple of the LORD, where the ark of God was. [4]Then the LORD called, "Samuel! Samuel!" and he said, "Here I am!" [5]and ran to Eli, and said,

---

7. This man-of-God speech (2:27-36) has been a highly controverted passage, from Wellhausen to the present day. Its difficulties are compounded by textual uncertainties.

Text signals in 2:27-36. (i) "Man of God" marks the first irruption of God's word into the narrative. (ii) This prophetic speech is situated uncomfortably close to the comment that God's word was rare in those days. (iii) That none will live to old age sits uncomfortably with Abiathar in Solomon's day (1 Kgs 2:26-27). (iv) The death of two sons as sign, pointing to a broader catastrophe, widens the narrower horizon of 2:25b. (v) Vv. 35-36 reflect the situation under Solomon (1 Kgs 2:26-27, 35).

Text-history approach. Since Wellhausen, this passage has been described as deuteronomistic (recently, for example, Hertzberg, Veijola, McCarter, Klein). For Noth, however, it is pre-dtr, part of what was originally "a self-contained prophetic tradition";

according to Noth, the Dtr added only 2:25b, 34-35 (*DH*, 84).

The substance of the prophecy makes good sense within the PR. The Elides are to be superseded; the future belongs to Samuel and the prophets—the unfolding narrative gives them religious hegemony. The solemn and eternal divine promise can be canceled (v. 30); in the PR, what the prophets solemnly promised to David they will transfer to Jeroboam (1 Kgs 11:38b). Vv. 31-32 foreshadow the wholesale slaughter of those Elide descendants who had sought sanctuary at Nob; v. 33 sharpens this with a reference to Abiathar, the sole survivor (1 Samuel 22; cf. 14:3).

This attribution accounts satisfactorily for the first signals in the text. (i) "Man of God" is generally used for anonymous prophets or Elijah and Elisha (64 out of 76 occurrences); 7 are in Elijah and 29 in Elisha stories. Since the Elisha circle is the assumed setting for the PR, this speech sits well within that horizon. (ii) The prophetic compilers, who brought together traditions without imposing total uniformity, needed a prophecy against the Elides in preparation for the temple story of chap. 3; a speech by one of their own meets this need admirably—if somewhat uncomfortably. (iii) Vv. 31-33 (with vv. 31b and 32a textually suspect) outline the punishment and its sole exception. The "cutting off" may be understood in terms of chronological age, requiring a formulation before Abiathar reached old age (see M. Tsevat, "I Sam. 2:27-36," 191-216, esp. pp. 192-95); or it may be understood later as loss of honored status (see H. J. Stoebe, *Erste Buch Samuelis*, 119).

Main pre-DH: *Prophetic* Record
its sources *and prophetic contribution*

Other pre-DH:
single sideline

Josianic DH:
from the Dtr

"Here I am, for you called me." But he said, "I did not call; lie down again." So he went and lay down. [6]The LORD called again, "Samuel!" Samuel got up and went to Eli, and said, "Here I am, for you called me." But he said, "I did not call, my son; lie down again." [7]Now Samuel did not yet know the LORD, and the word of the LORD had not yet been revealed to him. [8]The

LORD called Samuel again, a third time. And he got up and went to Eli, and said, "Here I am, for you called me." Then Eli perceived that the LORD was calling the boy. [9]Therefore Eli said to Samuel, "Go, lie down; and if he calls you, you shall say, 'Speak, LORD, for your servant is listening.' " So Samuel went and lay down in his place.

10 Now the LORD came and stood there, calling as before, "Samuel! Samuel!" And Samuel said, "Speak, for your servant is listening." [11]Then the LORD said to Samuel, "See, I am about to do something in Israel that will make both ears of anyone who hears of it tingle. [12]On that day I will fulfill against Eli all that I have spoken concerning his house, from beginning to end. [13]For I have told him that I am about to punish his house forever, for the iniquity that he knew, because his sons were blaspheming God, and he did not restrain them. [14]Therefore I swear to the house of Eli that the iniquity of Eli's house shall not be expiated by sacrifice or offering forever."[8]

15 Samuel lay there until morning; then he opened the doors of the house of the LORD. Samuel was afraid to tell the vision to Eli. [16]But Eli called Samuel and said, "Samuel, my son." He said, "Here I am." [17]Eli said, "What was it that he told you? Do not hide it from me. May God do so to you and more also, if you hide anything from me of all that he told you." [18]So Samuel told him everything and hid nothing from him. Then he said, "It is the LORD; let him do what seems good to him."

On the other hand, signals in later verses suggest a different attribution. (iv) V. 34 points clearly to chap. 4; chaps. 4–6 were not part of the PR and were most probably inserted here by the Josianic Dtr in the composition of the DH. (v) V. 35 points to the Zadokite replacement of the Elide line (cf. 1 Kgs 2:26-27 and 2:35). V. 36, with its reference to "him," the faithful priest, depends on v. 35. It is usually associated with Josiah's reform (cf. 2 Kgs 23:9), but there are differences. In 2 Kgs 23:9, priestly service at the altar is denied and food is provided; in 1 Sam 2:36, priestly service is being sought as the means to earn food. This may be merely circumstantial; it may be more.

The verses (vv. 34-36) may be from the Dtr (hence the boldface type), but it is by no means certain. V. 35 could be earlier—the PR was interested in a "sure house," *bayit ne'ĕmān* (cf. 2 Sam 7:16 [source] and 1 Kgs 11:38b [prophetic contribution]); v. 36 could be later. We are left with a breadth of options. Priestly quarrels are a quagmire, and this is a priestly quarrel.

Present-text potential. The present text looks to the total impact of this divine message. It will fall upon the whole house of Eli. It will hit home with the death of the two sons. Note that a sign points to the future; it is not itself the event that it signifies. The two sons of Eli are caught up in the disaster of chap. 4; they alone are not its cause. The loss of the ark cannot be disregarded, but Elide sin is still only part of the mystery of God's option to depart from Shiloh. The punishment of that sin is yet to come. It will have its full impact with the slaughter of Eli's descendants at Nob. It will become permanent when the Zadokites assume the central priesthood (cf. 1 Kgs 2:26-27, 35). Its reverberations may reach to the reform of Josiah.

---

8. Veijola attributed 3:11-14 to his DtrP, replacing an older oracle about the Nob slaughter (*Ewige Dynastie*, 38-43). "Two ears" is found in 2 Kgs 21:12 (Heb.); "tingling" is found in 2 Kgs 21:12 and Jer 19:3. Given the respective contexts, no assured associations can be made.

| After the Dtr: indented and sans serif font | *Revision: royal focus* | *Revision: national focus* | Other: double sideline |

19 As Samuel grew up, the LORD was with him and let none of his words fall to the ground. 20And all Israel from Dan to Beer-sheba knew that Samuel was a trustworthy prophet of the LORD. 21The LORD continued to appear at Shiloh, for the LORD revealed himself to Samuel at Shiloh by the word of the LORD.

4 *And the word of Samuel came to all Israel.*[9]

In those days the Philistines mustered for war against Israel, and Israel went out to battle against them; they encamped at Ebenezer, and the Philistines encamped at Aphek.[10] 2The Philistines drew up in line against Israel, and when the battle was joined, Israel was defeated by the Philistines, who killed about four thousand men on the field of battle. 3When the troops came to the camp, the elders of Israel said, "Why has the LORD put us to rout today before the Philistines? Let us bring the ark of the covenant of the LORD here from Shiloh, so that he may come among us and save us from the power of our enemies."[11] 4So the people sent to

---

9. This ends the PR's presentation of the emergence of Samuel to be a prophet to all Israel, replacing the Elide priestly order. It portrays a rapid transition from youthful temple servant to national prophet. It prepares the way for the prophetic narrative to come (9:1—10:16 etc.). It is possible that the PR also contained a brief notice of the events of chap. 4, but it is not necessary. The recognition that 7:3-4 belongs as part of the dtr process of revision, in its national focus, clarifying vv. 5-6 (see below), allows 7:5-14 to be seen as source material most probably used by the royal focus of the dtr revision (for an earlier view, see Campbell, *Of Prophets and Kings*, 67-68). The continuation of the PR is to be found at 9:1.

10. **Text signals** in chaps. 4–6. (i) As has been classically recognized, Samuel is central to chaps. 1–3 and totally absent from chaps. 4–6, while the ark is totally peripheral to chaps. 1–3 and central to chaps. 4–6 (Wellhausen). (ii) The storytelling is quite different between the two blocks. In chaps. 1–3, relatively independent traditions are juxtaposed; in chaps. 4–6, the narrative is tightly structured and sustained. (iii) An inexorable logic drives chaps. 4–6 from question to question: Why did YHWH defeat Israel? Will YHWH return to Israel? Will YHWH bless Israel? (iv) The question in 4:3 remains unanswered until 2 Samuel 6. "Why has the LORD put us to rout today before the

Philistines?" is explained by the Lord's determination to depart from the Israel of Eli and Shiloh and return to the Israel of David and Jerusalem.

Text-history approach. The hypothesis of an independent ark narrative (1 Samuel 4–6 and 2 Samuel 6, focused on the ark as revealing God's power and purpose) accounts for the signals in the text. Differences in the extent of the narrative cannot be discussed here (see Campbell, "Yahweh and the Ark").

In our judgment, this ark narrative would have been incorporated as part of the Josianic DH. It demarcates the division of Israel's history into major periods, here basically from the end of the judges to the establishment of the monarchy under David in Jerusalem.

Present-text potential. The ark narrative combines with the Samuel traditions in pointing to the decline of Israel and the end of an era. 1 Samuel 1–3 signals the coming of the new; 1 Samuel 4–6 signals the passing of the old. In this, the drift of Judges 13–21 is echoed and reinforced.

Note. The NRSV emends 4:1b with the Greek. The Greek has considerably more than the Hebrew: a further negative comment on Eli and his sons within 3:21; within 4:1b, a statement of Philistine initiative in the war. The initiative for the battles is thus transferred to the Philistines, reducing Israel's responsibility for its defeat and disaster. Scribal oversight is certainly possible (haplography); alternatively, it may be that two traditions existed about the onus for this critical engagement.

11. It should be noted that the ark narrative suggests an interpretation of these two defeats that

---

| Main pre-DH: *Prophetic* Record | Other pre-DH: | **Josianic DH:** |
| its sources *and prophetic contribution* | single sideline | **from the Dtr** |

Shiloh, and brought from there the ark of the covenant of the Lord of hosts, who is enthroned on the cherubim. The two sons of Eli, Hophni and Phinehas, were there with the ark of the covenant of God.

5 When the ark of the covenant of the Lord came into the camp, all Israel gave a mighty shout, so that the earth resounded. [6]When the Philistines heard the noise of the shouting, they said, "What does this great shouting in the camp of the Hebrews mean?" When they learned that the ark of the Lord had come to the camp, [7]the Philistines were afraid; for they said, "Gods have come into the camp." They also said, "Woe to us! For nothing like this has happened before. [8]Woe to us! Who can deliver us from the power of these mighty gods? These are the gods who struck the Egyptians with every sort of plague in the wilderness. [9]Take courage, and be men, O Philistines, in order not to become slaves to the Hebrews as they have been to you; be men and fight."

10 So the Philistines fought; Israel was defeated, and they fled, everyone to his home. There was a very great slaughter, for there fell of Israel thirty thousand foot soldiers. [11]The ark of God was captured; and the two sons of Eli, Hophni and Phinehas, died.

12 A man of Benjamin ran from the battle line, and came to Shiloh the same day, with his clothes torn and with earth upon his head. [13]When he arrived, Eli was sitting upon his seat by the road watching, for his heart trembled for the ark of God. When the man came into the city and told the news, all the city cried out. [14]When Eli heard the sound of the outcry, he said, "What is this uproar?" Then the man came quickly and told Eli. [15]Now Eli was ninety-eight years old and his eyes were set, so that he could not see. [16]The man said to Eli, "I have just come from the battle; I fled from the battle today." He said, "How did it go, my son?" [17]The messenger replied, "Israel has fled before the Philistines, and there has also been a great slaughter among the troops; your two sons also, Hophni and Phinehas, are dead, and the ark of God has been captured." [18]When he mentioned the ark of God, Eli fell over backward from his seat by the side of the gate; and his neck was broken and he died, for he was an old man, and heavy.

|| He had judged Israel forty years.[12]

19 Now his daughter-in-law, the wife of Phinehas, was pregnant, about to give birth. When she heard the news that the ark of God was captured, and that her father-in-law and her husband were dead, she bowed and gave birth; for her labor pains overwhelmed her. [20]As she was about to die, the women attending her said to her, "Do not be afraid, for you have borne a son." But she did not answer or give heed. [21]She named the child Ichabod, meaning, "The glory has departed from Israel," because the ark of God had been captured and because of her father-in-law and her husband. [22]She said, "The glory has departed from Israel, for the ark of God has been captured."[13]

---

attributes to God responsibility for the departure of the ark. The events are no mere loss in battle; they are presented as caused by the God of the ark, who chooses to depart into exile, away from God's people, to return to mainstream Israel and Jerusalem only in the time of David. As Samuel has no part whatsoever in this narrative, it is not likely to have formed part of the PR.

---

12. 4:18b is seen by Noth as a later, post-dtr addition, seeking inappropriately to bring Eli into the series of judges (see *DH*, 39-40).

13. Veijola attributed 4:4b, 11b, 17bα, 19aγ, 21b, 22a to his DtrH.

| After the Dtr: indented and sans serif font | **Revision: royal focus** | *Revision: national focus* | Other: double sideline |

5 When the Philistines captured the ark of God, they brought it from Ebenezer to Ashdod; [2]then the Philistines took the ark of God and brought it into the house of Dagon and placed it beside Dagon. [3]When the people of Ashdod rose early the next day, there was Dagon, fallen on his face to the ground before the ark of the Lord. So they took Dagon and put him back in his place. [4]But when they rose early on the next morning, Dagon had fallen on his face to the ground before the ark of the Lord, and the head of Dagon and both his hands were lying cut off upon the threshold; only the trunk of Dagon was left to him. [5]This is why the priests of Dagon and all who enter the house of Dagon do not step on the threshold of Dagon in Ashdod to this day.[14]

6 The hand of the Lord was heavy upon the people of Ashdod, and he terrified and struck them with tumors, both in Ashdod and in its territory. [7]And when the inhabitants of Ashdod saw how things were, they said, "The ark of the God of Israel must not remain with us; for his hand is heavy on us and on our god Dagon." [8]So they sent and gathered together all the lords of the Philistines, and said, "What shall we do with the ark of the God of Israel?" The inhabitants of Gath replied, "Let the ark of God be moved on to us." So they moved the ark of the God of Israel to Gath. [9]But after they had brought it to Gath, the hand of the Lord was against the city, causing a very great panic; he struck the inhabitants of the city, both young and old, so that tumors broke out on them. [10]So they sent the ark of the God of Israel to Ekron. But when the ark of God came to Ekron, the people of Ekron cried out, "Why have they brought around to us the ark of the God of Israel to kill us and our people?" [11]They sent therefore and gathered together all the lords of the Philistines, and said, "Send away the ark of the God of Israel, and let it return to its own place, that it may not kill us and our people." For there was a deathly panic throughout the whole city. The hand of God was very heavy there; [12]those who did not die were stricken with tumors, and the cry of the city went up to heaven.

6 The ark of the Lord was in the country of the Philistines seven months. [2]Then the Philistines called for the priests and the diviners and said, "What shall we do with the ark of the Lord? Tell us what we should send with it to its place." [3]They said, "If you send away the ark of the God of Israel, do not send it empty, but by all means return him a guilt offering. Then you will be healed and will be ransomed; will not his hand then turn from you?" [4]And they said, "What is the guilt offering that we shall return to him?" They answered, "Five gold tumors and five gold mice, according to the number of the lords of the Philistines; for the same plague was upon all of you and upon your lords. [5]So you must make images of your tumors and images of your mice that ravage the land, and give glory to the God of Israel; perhaps he will lighten his hand on you and your gods and your land. [6]Why should you harden your hearts as the Egyptians and Pharaoh hardened their hearts? After he had made fools of them, did they not let the people go, and they departed? [7]Now then, get ready a new cart and two milch cows that have never borne a yoke,

---

14. The narrative reality here is tragic, not triumphant. If the God of Israel is in control within the precincts of Dagon's temple in Ashdod, then the narrative logic is clear: the God of Israel was in control on the battlefield in Israel. The elders of Israel had asked: "Why has the Lord put us to rout today?" (4:3a). The story of this episode does not answer that question. It makes clear, however, that it was indeed the Lord who put Israel to rout that day. The question's answer emerges with the ark's move to Jerusalem.

| Main pre-DH: *Prophetic* Record | Other pre-DH: | **Josianic DH:** |
| its sources *and prophetic contribution* | single sideline | **from the Dtr** |

and yoke the cows to the cart, but take their calves home, away from them. [8]Take the ark of the LORD and place it on the cart, and put in a box at its side the figures of gold, which you are returning to him as a guilt offering. Then send it off, and let it go its way. [9]And watch; if it goes up on the way to its own land, to Beth-shemesh, then it is he who has done us this great harm; but if not, then we shall know that it is not his hand that struck us; it happened to us by chance."[15]

10 The men did so; they took two milch cows and yoked them to the cart, and shut up their calves at home. [11]They put the ark of the LORD on the cart, and the box with the gold mice and the images of their tumors. [12]The cows went straight in the direction of Beth-shemesh along one highway, lowing as they went; they turned neither to the right nor to the left, and the lords of the Philistines went after them as far as the border of Beth-shemesh.

13 Now the people of Beth-shemesh were reaping their wheat harvest in the valley. When they looked up and saw the ark, they went with rejoicing to meet it. [14]The cart came into the field of Joshua of Beth-shemesh, and stopped there. A large stone was there; so they split up the wood of the cart and offered the cows as a burnt offering to the LORD. [15]The Levites took down the ark of the LORD and the box that was beside it, in which were the gold objects, and set them upon the large stone. Then the people of Beth-shemesh offered burnt offerings and presented sacrifices on that day to the LORD. [16]When the five lords of the Philistines saw it, they returned that day to Ekron.

---

15. Those who believe that a skeptical approach to religion is a modern prerogative might well ponder this verse. The ritual of divination is put in place to determine whether "this great harm" was done by God or happened by chance.

17 These are the gold tumors, which the Philistines returned as a guilt offering to the LORD: one for Ashdod, one for Gaza, one for Ashkelon, one for Gath, one for Ekron; [18]also the gold mice, according to the number of all the cities of the Philistines belonging to the five lords, both fortified cities and unwalled villages. The great stone, beside which they set down the ark of the LORD, is a witness to this day in the field of Joshua of Beth-shemesh.

19 The descendants of Jeconiah did not rejoice with the people of Beth-shemesh when they greeted the ark of the LORD; and he killed seventy men of them. The people mourned because the LORD had made a great slaughter among the people. [20]Then the people of Beth-shemesh said, "Who is able to stand before the LORD, this holy God? To whom shall he go so that we may be rid of him?" [21]So they sent messengers to the inhabitants of Kiriath-jearim, saying, "The Philistines have returned the ark of the LORD. Come down and take it up to you."

7 And the people of Kiriath-jearim came and took up the ark of the LORD, and brought it to the house of Abinadab on the hill. They consecrated his son, Eleazar, to have charge of the ark of the LORD.[16]

---

16. In 7:1, the ark has apparently found a resting place in Kiriath-jearim, in the house of Abinadab. Someone has been consecrated to take care of it, Abinadab's son Eleazar. With 7:1, the ark narrative is at an end—at least temporarily. Nothing as cultically significant as the ark could remain long at so cultically insignificant a location as Kiriath-jearim.

1 Samuel 7–12 is a classic example of complex and controverted text. It is also a classic specimen of Israel's theological processes, expressing critical reflection in story, juxtaposing differing traditions, drawing on new material to update views, and often blending the whole into a final text of remarkable artistry and elegance.

| After the Dtr: indented and sans serif font | **Revision: royal focus** | *Revision: national focus* | Other: double sideline |

In these chapters, the issue is the origin of the monarchy in Israel—in modern language, the emergence of central government. In our judgment, the redactors of the PR had at their disposal an old story involving a seer and a short-term defense concern associated with the Ammonites. They reshaped it to involve the prophet Samuel and associated it with the long-term defense threat constituted by the Philistines (so, the "prophetic" strand). Integrated into the present text are traditions of Samuel and traditions invoking assemblies of Israel in which Samuel established monarchy as a response to popular demand primarily for social justice (so, the "assembly" strand). It is extremely important for those used to the traditional interpretation of these texts to realize what is being claimed here. This sequence of "assembly" texts may well be old. It is our assertion that it has been introduced into the DH at this point by the later post-Josianic revision (hence the double sideline formatting), specifically by what we term the "royal" (blaming the evil of kings) focus of that revision. The further overwriting of this "assembly" strand with views negative or hostile to the origin of kingship, in our judgment, derives from both the "royal" and "national" focuses of the dtr revision process.

The combination of these "prophetic" and "assembly" texts offers the following sequence. **Assembly:** Samuel's adequacy as an intercessor and deliverer at Mizpah and as circuit judge at Bethel, Gilgal, and Mizpah (7:5-14, 15-17); the inadequacy of Samuel's sons as keepers of justice that triggers the demand for a king by the elders of Israel, coming to Ramah, ending with God's command to Samuel to establish a king (8:1-6, 22). **Prophetic:** the story of Samuel's secret anointing of Saul as king-designate (9:1–10:16). **Assembly:** an assembly at Mizpah for the public selection of Saul by processes of divination and his acclamation as king (10:17, 20-24). **Prophetic:** the continuation of the prophetic story with Saul winning popular acclaim by military victory and his coronation in a national assembly at Gilgal (11:1-11, 15).

The negative or hostile views of kingship were added within the framework of the national assemblies (8:7-21; 10:18-19, 25); and, above all, the major speech composed for Samuel in 1 Sam 12:1-25. Two little fragments, 10:26-27 and 11:12-13, require the integration of the major strands of tradition but otherwise escape attribution. They acknowledge the passing of epochs.

> 2 From the day that the ark was lodged at Kiriath-jearim, a long time passed (some twenty years),[17] and all the house of Israel lamented after the Lord.[18]

Present-text potential. The voices of the final text allow us to hear the varying views of Israel on the role of so important an institution as Israel's central government. The themes are multiple: national deliverance as direct dependence on divine power; Israel's need for social justice, frustrated by Samuel's sons; Israel's need for defense, whether short-term or long-term (short-term: against the Ammonites, nearly lost to sight in the prophetic overwriting of 9:1—10:16 but reemerging in the Nahash episode; long-term: against the Philistines in 9:1—10:16, nearly lost to sight in the Nahash episode but finally achieved with David); God as initiator, bringing Saul to Samuel; God as responder, meeting Israel's demand with the selection of Saul; royal power as a social danger, occasioning exploitation of the people; royal presence as a theological danger, occasioning rejection of YHWH. Beyond these is the possibility of holding all in harmony by the obedient loyalty of faith (12:14).

As a strategy or metaphor for reading the final text, these voices are to be heard as polyphony and not flattened into a single melodic line, either in theme or in time. Rather, 1 Samuel 7–12 is a richly orchestrated polyphonic composition, employing significant voices and strains, some old, some new.

17. The first part of v. 2a, up to and including "a long time passed," may have functioned as a coda to 7:1. It no longer retains that function; if it did, it would now be part of 2 Samuel 6. The specification of time, "some twenty years," may relate to the 40 years of Philistine oppression (Judg 13:1) combined with the 20 years attributed to Samson (Judg 15:20; 16:31b). Alternatively, the 20 years for Samson may depend on Judg 13:1 and this passage (cf. Noth, *DH*, 39–40). Richter argues for the "some twenty years" as either a post-dtr addition or alternatively a matter of sequence not chronology (*Bearbeitung*, 138). Certainty is out of the question.

18. It is possible that 7:2a, with or without the specification of 20 years, functioned as an introduc-

---

Main pre-DH: *Prophetic* Record	Other pre-DH:	**Josianic DH:**
its sources *and prophetic contribution*	single sideline	**from the Dtr**

3 Then Samuel said to all the house of Israel, "If you are returning to the LORD with all your heart, then put away the foreign gods and the Astartes from among you. Direct your heart to the LORD, and serve him only, and he will deliver you out of the hand of the Philistines." ⁴So Israel put away the Baals and the Astartes, and they served the LORD only.[19]

5 Then Samuel said, "Gather all Israel at Mizpah, and I will pray to the LORD for you." ⁶So they gathered at Mizpah, and drew water and poured it out before the LORD. They fasted that day, and said, "We have sinned against the LORD." And Samuel judged the people of Israel at Mizpah.[20]

tion to 7:5-14. It is clear that now 7:2 is the introduction to 7:3-4, 5-14. There is nothing in 7:2b to suggest dtr usage; any translation of what is rendered here as "lamented" must be recognized as uncertain (see Barthélemy, *Critique textuelle*, 157–58). The term "all the house of Israel" (v. 2b) is unlikely to be early. Of nineteen occurrences, it is found ten times in Ezekiel, twice here, twice in 2 Samuel 6 (see below), twice in Jeremiah, and otherwise in Exod 40:38; Lev 10:16; and Num 20:29. In the present state of v. 2, the double sideline is appropriate, associating it with the text to follow. Part may be older than the national focus of dtr revision; the whole is unlikely to be.

Verses 5-14 portray a ceremony of penitence at Mizpah, perhaps related to 7:2's "lament"; the gathering attracts Philistine attention and aggression. This may be picked up in the overt reference to Philistine oppression in v. 3. In vv. 7-14, Samuel's intercession brings God's intervention, and the Philistine threat is eliminated for the lifetime of Samuel (see below). All this suggests that the "lamentation" resulted from Philistine aggression, associated with the loss of the ark. The "long time" and "twenty years" move to an observation point in the future, looking back from the period's end; the report of lamentation returns to the present. The presentation is of hiatus rather than sequence.

19. **Text signals** in 7:3-4. (i) Repentance and return are here a condition for deliverance; this is not the case with the Josianic DH in Judges—in the framing elements, the people cry out, while in the dtr contribution God is moved to pity by the people's groaning (Judg 2:18). (ii) The phrase "foreign gods" occurs in Josh 24:20, 23; Judg 10:16 (elsewhere, Gen 35:2, 4; Deut 31:16; 2 Chron 33:15; Jer 5:19). (iii) The formu-

lation of v. 4 has strong echoes of Judg 10:16, although its abstract "foreign gods" has been replaced here by the concrete "the Baals and the Astartes." (iv) There is a degree of repetition between vv. 3-4 and 5-6.

Text-history approach. These signals can be accounted for by situating vv. 3-4 with the national focus of the dtr revision process, which is concerned with the responsibility of the people. Here too the concern is with the responsibility of the people, i.e., "all the house of Israel." Genesis 35 could well be the source of the "foreign gods" language; its occurrence here and in Judg 10:16 is consistent with the dtr revision's national focus; Deut 31:16 and Josh 24:20, 23 are located in otherwise later texts. The significance for the national focus of the revising is to clarify both the preceding "lamentation" and the nature of the penitential ritual in vv. 5-6. The "lamentation" relates to Philistine oppression; the ritual is a ceremony of repentance for the sin of apostasy.

Present-text potential. The overall text portrays a situation of apostasy from which, with some similarity to the dtr pattern of deliverance in the book of Judges, Israel is delivered through the intercession of the prophet Samuel (named as judge, v. 6b; see below). In the dtr preface, Israel was merely in great distress (Judg 2:15); in the collected deliverer stories, oppressed Israel cried to the LORD (Judg 3:9, 15; 4:3; 6:6); in Judg 10:10-16 and here, confession of apostasy is specifically mentioned (see also 1 Sam 12:10). So here, the movement of the text is: exhortation with appropriate response (vv. 3-4), sealed by a solemn liturgy of repentance (vv. 5-6), all of which prepares the ground for vv. 7-14.

20. **Text signals** in 7:5-14. (i) The concept of judging in v. 6b is unusual. It is located at Mizpah and associated with repentance. Samuel is not said to be

| After the Dtr: indented and sans serif font | *Revision:* **royal focus** | *Revision: national focus* | Other: double sideline |

7 When the Philistines heard that the people of Israel had gathered at Mizpah, the lords of the Philistines went up against Israel. And when the people of Israel heard of it they were afraid of the Philistines. [8]The people of Israel said to Samuel, "Do not cease to cry out to the LORD our God for us, and pray that he may save us from the hand of the Philistines." [9]So Samuel took a sucking lamb and offered it as a whole burnt offering to the LORD; Samuel cried out to the LORD for Israel, and the LORD answered him. [10]As Samuel was offering up the burnt offering, the Philistines drew near to attack Israel; but the LORD thundered with a mighty voice that day against the Philistines and threw them into confusion; and they were routed before Israel. [11]And the men of Israel went out of Mizpah and pursued the Philistines, and struck them down as far as beyond Beth-car.

12 Then Samuel took a stone and set it up between Mizpah and Jeshanah, and named it Ebenezer; for he said, "Thus far the LORD has helped us." [13]So the Philistines

---

"raised up" by the LORD as judge, nor does his behavior correspond with the warlike activities of the deliverer-judges. (ii) Unusual too is the feature of crying to the LORD. Here it is not phrased as an act of the people, followed by the emergence of a deliverer; instead, the people ask Samuel not to cease crying out to YHWH on their behalf. (iii) "Subdued" is used to describe the Philistine defeat in v. 13a, as for most of the deliverer texts in Judges. (iv) Unusual again is v. 13b in its claim that "the hand of the LORD" was against the Philistines all the days of Samuel; the earlier phrasing was that "the land was undisturbed."

Text-history approach. Given the unusual features noted under "text signals," we do not believe that attribution to dtr circles can be justified (to the contrary, cf. Noth, *DH*, 77-79). An independent Samuel tradition is likely. It may have inspired the framing of the deliverer stories; it may have been modeled to some extent on them.

If the "judging" comment of v. 6b and the subsequent deliverance creates an echo of Judges 3–9, it is not that Samuel is the last of the deliverer-judges but that the mantle of the deliverer-judge has passed to the prophet. Deliverer-judges were "raised up" by YHWH for the occasion; as prophet, Samuel has been on the scene since 1 Samuel 1–3 (cf. esp. 3:19-21).

As before, it is most important to recognize, in this context, the meaning of a double sideline. The double sideline denotes our judgment that a passage is best understood as incorporated into the text after the completion of the Josianic DH. A double sideline says nothing about the date of composition of a passage. In our judgment, the passages in this context that are marked with a double sideline are most probably pre-dtr in their composition.

Our assumption here bears repeating: these "assembly" texts can most probably be old, but their introduction here is situated within the "royal" focus of the later dtr revision.

Present-text potential. This story of the restoration of Israel's relationship with God and of Israel's deliverance by God goes against the deteriorating trend visible in Judges 13–21 and even earlier. The story places Samuel firmly at center stage, in a position to play the key role in the emergence of Israel's monarchy. It goes beyond the merely prophetic figure of chaps. 1–3; it opens the way for the prophet to be God's instrument in establishing the monarchy (cf. 10:20-25). At the same time, however, the tradition allows for an alternative view: the monarchy was unnecessary for the deliverance of Israel.

The story is unique. It contrasts with the conditions of David's rise to power in constant conflict with the Philistines—even during the latter days of Samuel (cf. 1 Sam 17:1—25:1). It portrays Samuel as almost akin to Moses (the Amalekite war, Exod 17:8-16) and not entirely unlike Elijah (on Mt. Carmel, 1 Kgs 18:36-40).

Main pre-DH: *Prophetic* Record	Other pre-DH:	**Josianic DH:**
its sources *and prophetic contribution*	single sideline	**from the Dtr**

were subdued and did not again enter the territory of Israel; the hand of the LORD was against the Philistines all the days of Samuel. [14]The towns that the Philistines had taken from Israel were restored to Israel, from Ekron to Gath; and Israel recovered their territory from the hand of the Philistines. There was peace also between Israel and the Amorites.

15 Samuel judged Israel all the days of his life. [16]He went on a circuit year by year to Bethel, Gilgal, and Mizpah; and he judged Israel in all these places. [17]Then he would come back to Ramah, for his home was there; he administered justice there to Israel, and built there an altar to the LORD.[21]

8 When Samuel became old, he made his sons judges over Israel. [2]The name of his firstborn son was Joel, and the name of his second, Abijah; they were judges in Beer-sheba. [3]Yet his sons did not follow in his ways, but turned aside after gain; they took bribes and perverted justice.[22]

---

21. **7:15-17**. The modifier, "all the days of his life," must not be allowed to mislead. Samuel is here portrayed as a judge, not a deliverer; from Ramah, he goes on circuit to Bethel, Gilgal, and Mizpah. Precisely what he did is unknown to us (as for Deborah, Judg 4:4-5). Some form of leadership is often assumed for the minor judges; Samuel's circuit suggests administrative duties and adjudication of disputes, but we do not know.

22. **8:1-22**. The focus on Samuel as judge for the rest of his life (whether on circuit or back at Ramah, cf. 7:15-17) sets the scene for a radically new development in the text. Biblical scholarship has no sources of information to throw light on what Samuel did on circuit year by year; nor on his power to appoint his sons as judges for Israel; nor on the nature of their appointments in Beer-sheba (so far to the south). All we are

told is that, in his old age, Samuel "made his sons judges over Israel" and that his sons did not follow in Samuel's ways, but turned to profiteering, taking bribes, and perverting justice. Invention is improbable; but we have no context to shed light on this as tradition. What is portrayed, however, is the transition of institutions. It is not a question of replacing corrupt judges with incorrupt ones; it is a question of replacing judges with kings.

The failure of justice is presented as triggering the demand for a king. To this degree, the attitude to kingship is positive; the king is to be a remedy against injustice (Hammurabi: "to cause justice to prevail in the land"). The appeal to Samuel in 8:4-5 is attached to the tradition of 7:15—8:3; it attributes to Samuel the authority to appoint a king—an authority otherwise unknown to us before 9:15-17 (but not impossible in the light of 8:1). In our judgment, the most probable pre-dtr text is 8:1-6, 22; vv. 7-21 will be accounted for below. V. 6's "Samuel prayed to the LORD" makes the same communication as v. 21. In v. 22a, God endorses the demand for a king. The dismissal in v. 22b and the reconvening at Mizpah (10:17) can be natural enough. The repentance ceremony for "all Israel" was at Mizpah (7:5-6, 7, 11). Those who come to Samuel at Ramah, where his house was, were the elders (although the dismissal in 8:22b refers to the "men of Israel"). It would be appropriate that all Israel assemble at the sanctuary of Mizpah to crown their king.

The dialogical nature of 8:1-22 needs to be noted; it allows easily for expansion. The elders speak to Samuel (vv. 4-5). Samuel speaks to God (v. 6). God speaks to Samuel (vv. 7-9). Samuel speaks to the people (vv. 10-18). The people speak to Samuel (vv. 19-20). Samuel speaks to God (v. 21). God speaks to Samuel (v. 22a). Finally, Samuel speaks to the people (v. 22b).

The material assembled in vv. 7-21 runs counter to 8:1-6, 22. Contrary to Noth and others, 1 Sam 7:2—8:22 cannot be read as a literary unity, even allowing for diversity of origin. Close attention to the details of the present text points to a largely positive base layer that has been expanded to express strongly negative concerns. As will be argued below, even these

---

| After the Dtr: indented and sans serif font | **Revision: royal focus** | Revision: national focus | Other: double sideline |

4 Then all the elders of Israel gathered together and came to Samuel at Ramah, [5]and said to him, "You are old and your sons do not follow in your ways; appoint for us, then, a king to govern us, like all the nations *(Heb.; NRSV, other nations)."* [6]But the thing displeased Samuel when they said, "Give us a king to govern us." And Samuel prayed to the LORD.

---

negative concerns are not the work of one hand. In the analysis of 8:1-22, minor variations have been proposed: a dtr base layer in 8:1-5, 20b-22 with subsequent dtr revision in vv. 6-20a (Lohfink, *Rückblick im Zorn*, 61); a dtr base layer in 8:1-5, 22b with nomistic dtr revision in vv. 6-22a (Veijola, *Königtum*, 55-60); a dtr base layer in 8:1-6a, 11-22 with a subsequent dtr revision in vv. 6b-10 (Mayes, *Story of Israel*, 98). Stoebe leaves options open (*Erste Buch Samuelis*, 184). McCarter maintains a safe distance from the structure of the wider text. His king is not welcomed but indulged, sanctioned in a "backhanded way" by a God who "consents" (*I Samuel*, 162). For Klein, rather than kingship itself (elsewhere sometimes "God-pleasing"), Israel's request for a king was sinful to Dtr, but granted generously by God; later, the final text presents "a paradoxical message" (*1 Samuel*, 79, 97). The chapter is a minefield; probability and plausibility are more attainable goals than certainty. The range from positive to hostile, however, should be clear.

The retention of v. 6 in the original base layer is allowed by the text rather than compelled by it. Retaining Samuel's negativity at the core of this "assembly" strand gives the royal focus within the dtr revision an attachment point for the insertion of its more strongly negative editing, in turn providing an opening for the hostile view of the national focus of the dtr revision. Samuel's negativity is appropriate in the overall context. In the text, Israel has just been delivered by direct divine intervention (7:5-12). Samuel has put plans in place for the administration of justice for Israel (8:1-2). The special status of Israel as chosen people is demeaned by the request to be treated like "all the nations" (*kĕkol haggôyim*), although this is not repeated in v. 6. V. 6b leads helpfully into v. 22 and brings v. 6a with it. Israel has retained contrasting views in almost all its major areas of tradition

(e.g., creation, flood, deliverance at the sea, wilderness, conquest, providence); it would be surprising if the monarchy alone was uncontested.

The uncertainties of reconstruction have been clearly stated. While it is our preference to attribute the insertion of this "assembly" strand to the dtr revision's royal focus and, in our formatting, to attribute the formulation of part of vv. 7-21 to the same royal focus, the possibility must be left open that this formulation was earlier. Dtr language is found in "only a very few verses" and these, in our judgment, represent the national focus of the revision. Our formatting represents only one possibility among others. It is noteworthy that the dtr concern for fidelity to YHWH is found here only in this national focus.

1 Samuel 8 uses various terms: elders (v. 4), the people (vv. 7 and 10, 19 and 21), and men (v. 22b). When 8:1-6, 22 is taken as the base and vv. 7-21 are seen as the expansion, the references to "the people" all fall within the expansion and, indeed, within those parts of the expansion attributed to the royal focus of the dtr revision process (see also Veijola, *Königtum* 55-60). This may reflect this focus's heritage in 10:17, 23-24; and 11:14; coming between "the elders of Israel" of v. 4 and "the men of Israel" of v. 22, it may be a hermeneutic move to mark out the addition as new. The term "the people" (*'ām*) is not used in chap. 7. The elders occur in both assembly and prophetic strands, once each: the elders of Israel in 8:4 and the elders of Jabesh in 11:3.

Samuel's "displeasure" at the request for a king in 8:6 is unspecified. The elders' request is stripped to its bare essentials, "a king to govern us." "Like all the nations" (8:5) is not repeated; there is no mention of the rejection of Samuel's sons. Yet the displeasure should not be understood too mildly. Literally translated, it reads: and the thing was evil in the eyes of Samuel. The same language is used to express YHWH's

---

Main pre-DH: *Prophetic* Record
its sources *and prophetic contribution*

Other pre-DH:
single sideline

Josianic DH:
from the Dtr

⁷And the Lord** said to Samuel, "Listen to the voice of the people in all that they say to you.**

For they have not rejected you, but they have rejected me from being king over them. ⁸According to all (Heb.; NRSV, Just as) *they have done to me, from the day I brought them up out of Egypt to this day, they are* (Heb.) *forsaking me and are* (Heb.) *serving other gods.*

|| *so also they are doing to you*
⁹Now then, listen to their voice.

Only—you shall solemnly warn them, and show them the ways of the king who shall reign over them."

"displeasure" at David's sins of rape and murder (2 Sam 11:27b); the same word is used for the condemnation of kings who "did what was evil in the sight of the Lord." It is Samuel's displeasure, it is unspecified, it may not be mild, it is balanced by yhwh's command to comply with the request. The more righteous weight given to Samuel's "displeasure" at the demand, the more difficult it becomes to excuse God's order to comply with it.

The connectedness of this passage with 10:17-27 is affirmed by both Noth (*DH*, 81: "essentially homogeneous action") and Stoebe (*Erste Buch Samuelis*, 214-25). If weight is given to the distinction between a delegation of elders at Ramah and an assembly of Israel at Mizpah, some interval is appropriate.

With the action begun in chaps. 7–12, the DH moves away from the charismatic figures of the deliverer-judges into the opening stages of what will be the end game in the leadership of Israel, the monarchy. First office, with Moses, directly accountable to God, and Joshua, assistant to Moses. Then charisma, with the deliverer-judges, raised up by God. Now office, with the kings, their accountability to God mediated by the prophet.

10 So Samuel reported all the words of the Lord** to the people who were asking him for a king.**²³

---

¹¹He said, "These will be the ways of the king who will reign over you: he will take your sons and appoint them to his chariots and to be his horsemen, and to run before his chariots; ¹²and he will appoint for himself commanders of thousands and commanders of fifties, and some to plow his ground and to reap his harvest, and to make his implements of war and the equipment of his chariots. ¹³He will take your daughters to be perfumers and cooks and bakers. ¹⁴He will take the best of your fields and vineyards and olive orchards and give them to his courtiers. ¹⁵He will levy (*Heb.; NRSV, take*) one-tenth of your grain and of your vineyards and give it to his officers and his courtiers. ¹⁶He will take your male and female slaves, and the best of your cattle and donkeys, and put them to his work. ¹⁷He will levy (*Heb.; NRSV, take*) one-tenth of your flocks, and you shall be his slaves.

---

23. **Text signals** in 8:7-21. (i) In v. 7a, Samuel is to comply with the people in what is, according to v. 7b, a rejection of their God. (ii) V. 7b introduces the rejection of God and v. 8 extends it to characterize Israel since the exodus, going beyond rejection to apostasy and the service of other gods. (iii) According to v. 7, the people have not rejected Samuel; according to the last clause of v. 8, they have. (iv) V. 9a repeats the command to listen to the people (cf. v. 7a); v. 9b requires a warning for the people about the ways of the king. This "ways of the king" will be picked up in v. 11 (cf. 10:25a). (v) V. 10 has Samuel take God's words to the people. (vi) Vv. 11-17 describe the behavior of the

---

| After the Dtr: indented and sans serif font | **Revision: royal focus** | *Revision: national focus* | Other: double sideline |

18And in that day you will cry out because of your king, whom you have chosen for yourselves; but the LORD will not answer you in that day."

19 But the people refused to listen to the voice of Samuel; they said, "No! but we are determined to have a king over us, 20so that we also may be like all the nations (Heb.; NRSV, other nations),

king, strongly structured around the fourfold repetition of "he will take" *preceded* by its objects: your sons, your daughters, your best lands (with tithing of produce), and your slaves and flocks (and tithing again). It ends: "and you shall be his slaves" (v. 17). Noteworthy is that this is not the dtr criticism leveled against kings; apostasy and cultic abuse are not mentioned. (vii) V. 18 moves from the behavior of the king to that of the people. It raises a number of tensions. The reference to the future is indeterminate, "in that day." The description of the king as "whom you have chosen for yourselves" is in some tension with both the people's demand (not choice) and God's command (v. 22). In the light of God's command to make a king, the claim that "the LORD will not answer you in that day" is strange (cf. Judg 10:14). (viii) The people's demand is reiterated (v. 19). Again, two aspects stand out: the demand is characterized as a refusal to listen to Samuel; to the issue of justice is now added the issue of defense. (ix) What Samuel hears from the people (*hāʿām*; cf. vv. 7, 10, 19) he repeats to YHWH (v. 21).

Text-history approach. These signals become intelligible when it is assumed that the basic text has been modified in three distinct stages. First, an extensive interpolation has been made between vv. 1-6 (elders and Samuel) and v. 22 (Samuel and God). It opens with the positive note of God's command (v. 7a, echoing in advance v. 22a), acknowledging that what is to come, in all its negativity, will not alter what God has determined in v. 22a. The negative aspect is specified in God's calling for a solemn warning (v. 9b), conveyed to the people in Samuel's words (vv. 11-17). The interpolation concludes with vv. 19-21, where Samuel's warning is set aside, the demand for a king is reiterated and extended to include defense, and finally the people's response is brought to God by Samuel. The basic text resumes with v. 22: the LORD's command to establish a king and the dismissal by Samuel.

At a second level, the negativity within the interpolation is heightened; the demand for a king is viewed with hostility. The demand is judged as a rejection of the LORD from being Israel's king, and situated within a perception of Israel's history as marked by apostasy. V. 9a's "Listen to their voice" resumes v. 7a and enables the text to blend back into the interpolation. In this way, the revising retains what has already been decided (cf. vv. 22a and 7a); otherwise, God would be aiding and abetting apostasy—a most serious matter. This negative view of rejection by the people is coherent with the national focus of the revision; cf. also 10:19. The tone is echoed in 8:18, equally reflecting this focus's negative view of the people. V. 18 is Samuel's warning added to God's words. "In that day" leads in and out of the comment. Its theology—that their cry will not be answered—reflects Judg 10:13-14 (national focus). "Whom you have chosen" is both echoed and nuanced in 12:13; it does not occur earlier. To the contrary, the lot indicates God's choice (10:24a); the initiative for Gilgal is from Samuel (11:14).

At the end of v. 8, a clause notes "so also they are doing to you." This flatly contradicts v. 7's affirmation, "for they have not rejected you." For some, the contradiction can be overlooked; otherwise it expresses a contrasting view, affirming that the rejection of God did indeed involve a rejection of Samuel, God's prophet.

We obviously believe that modifications are visible here and that any attempt to harmonize their differences is achieved at the cost of the clarity of the text. We freely admit there is less clarity about the distribution across specific editorial levels.

Present-text potential. From what has just been said, it is clear that vv. 7-21 do not form a unified literary text; they express competing views. The warning against kingship is incompatible with the rejection of

Main pre-DH: *Prophetic* Record	Other pre-DH:	**Josianic DH:**
its sources *and prophetic contribution*	single sideline	**from the Dtr**

and that our king may govern us and go out before us and fight our battles." 21When Samuel had heard all the words of the people, he repeated them in the ears of the LORD.

22The LORD said to Samuel, "Listen to their voice and set a king over them." Samuel then said to the men (*Heb.; NRSV people*) of Israel, "Each of you return home."

9 There was a man of Benjamin whose name was Kish son of Abiel son of Zeror son of Becorath son of Aphiah, a Benjaminite, a man of wealth. 2He had a son whose name was Saul, a handsome young man. There was not a man among the people of Israel more handsome than he; he stood head and shoulders above everyone else.24

God—unless we wish to view the text advocating faith in God as weak (permit it) or God as cruel (punish them). Displeasure at the prospect of a king is quite different from constant apostasy that goes back to the exodus.

The warning alone, i.e., the first modification, can be read in continuity with the surrounding context. The displeased Samuel prays to the LORD and is instructed to warn the people; the polemic expresses this warning commanded by God about the ways of a king (vv. 11-17); when this warning is rejected and the demand repeated (vv. 19-21), the original authorization follows (v. 22). When due weight is given to the emphasis on Israel's rejection of God (in vv. 7b-8) and to the prediction of God's refusal to listen to Israel's cry (v. 18), contrasting theologies must be heard.

Where vv. 11-17 are concerned, in this reconstruction their insertion is situated within the royal focus of the dtr revision. It matters little whether they originated from Israelite or Canaanite experience, whether they were early or late. They are clearly a polemic against kingship. It matters a lot that the audience of a modern war-weary democracy will hear them quite differently than will the audiences of a thriving and patriotic monarchy, ancient or not. The polemic appeals to the disaffected; the patriotic, on the other hand, are honored to be invited into the service of their king (cf. 1 Sam 16:22; 2 Sam 23:13-17). To be effective, Samuel's polemic must play to a measure of disaffection. In the present text's demand, the popular resistance to taxes is presumably outweighed by the people's need for social justice (8:3-4). Kings take soldiers and servants, lands and crops; do they ensure stability and justice in return? 1 Sam 12:13-15 resolves the issue on the quite different grounds of fidelity to YHWH (cf. Deut 17:14-20). Hence the double-sideline and box on 8:11-17: composition, uncertain; insertion, royal focus of the dtr revision.

---

24. Resumption of the PR from 4:1a. As discussed in the Introduction, 1 Sam 9:1—10:16 is the first of three occurrences where a prophet anoints a future king: Samuel anoints Saul king-designate (*nāgîd*); Samuel anoints David king-to-be; Elisha's disciple anoints Jehu king (*melek*). We refer to David as king-to-be because in 1 Sam 16:1-13, while king (*melek*) is used in v. 1 and Samuel anoints David in v. 13, king-designate (*nāgîd*) is not used.

In the hypothesis of a PR, this is the task for which Samuel was established as a prophet to all Israel (1 Sam 3:19—4:1a). In the present text, Samuel has also routed the Philistines and presided over a different process that led to Saul's establishment as king.

A number of observations, to be noted under "Text signals," point to a reworking of an older story. The older story told of a chance encounter with an anonymous prophet who prophesied an empowering change that would come over Saul in the future. It was a chance encounter; Saul was looking for his father's asses, not for royal power. The reworking has sharpened the older story considerably, yet its substance has been left visible, above all at the beginning and end. The anonymous prophet has been changed to the established figure of Samuel, known to all Israel (3:20). The chance encounter has been changed to an event guided by the design of God ("I will send to you," 9:16aα). The future foreseen for Saul is explicit—anointed to deliver Israel from the

---

| After the Dtr: indented and sans serif font | **Revision: royal focus** | Revision: national focus | Other: double sideline |

3 Now the donkeys of Kish, Saul's father, had strayed. So Kish said to his son Saul, "Take one of the boys with you; go and look for the donkeys." [4]He passed through the hill country of Ephraim and passed through the land of Shal-

ishah, but they did not find them. And they passed through the land of Shaalim, but they were not there. Then he passed through the land of Benjamin, but they did not find them.

Philistines (9:16aβ); it reflects the conditions of 1 Samuel 13—2 Samuel 5.

Text signals in 9:1—10:16. (i) In 9:6-8, we meet a nameless seer, who might find things for a fee, but who is not the national figure of Samuel. (ii) Suddenly, at the end of 9:13, there is reference to "those eat who are invited"; so far there has been no mention of invitation, but the unfolding story will make Saul an honored guest whose coming has been foreseen (9:23). (iii) In 9:14, the seer becomes Samuel and stays Samuel for the story. (iv) With 9:15-17, the story ceases to be about lost asses and becomes a story of divine design; Samuel is God's instrument in anointing Saul *nāgîd* over Israel (for a thorough study of *nāgîd*, see Campbell, *Of Prophets and Kings*, 47-61). Here and later, *nāgîd*, king-designate, is a useful term; it allows the text to claim for the prophet the exercise of God's responsibility for an event that is still in the future, the coronation of Saul at Gilgal (11:15). (v) According to 9:19b, Samuel will address Saul's concerns in the morning; he may need the night to receive God's revelation (cf. Num 22:8-13; 1 Sam 3:2-15). In the reworked story, God has already made clear to Samuel what is happening (9:15-17). In the reworked story, furthermore, Samuel promptly removes the issue of the asses from Saul's mind and hints at what his destiny holds (9:20-21). (vi) Similarly, 9:20 preempts the role of 10:2. (vii) The reworked material in 9:22-24 implies the foreknowledge given Samuel by God in 9:15-17; the place of honor is not for a farmer's son but for the future king of Israel. (viii) The word *ĕlōhîm* is used for God in 9:27, as in 9:9 and 10:2-4, 7, and 9; in contrast, *yhwh* is used for God in 9:15-17 and 10:1.

Beyond these issues that concern the reworking of an older story, there are other signals that may draw attention to a different activity. (ix) 10:6 speaks of the

coming of the spirit and becoming a different person in ways that do not correspond in circumstances or timing with 10:9a or 11:6. (x) In 10:7, Saul is left free; in 10:8, he is given strict instructions that take away the freedom. (xi) 10:9b reads like the conclusion of a story, referring to "all these signs" being fulfilled; 10:10-13a goes on to relate the fulfillment of only one sign, the one mentioned in 10:5-6.

Text-history approach. Compositional analysis has seen three processes involved in this text, indicated by its signals. The first process is the reworking of the older story; it accounts for the signals from (i) to (viii). The older story, which was continued in chap. 11, had an anonymous seer commission Saul for some mysterious future event that turns out to be the deliverance of Jabesh-gilead. A prophetic reworking has upped the ante considerably; God has directed Samuel to anoint Saul as future king for the deliverance of Israel from the Philistines.

The second process is the attachment here of a story explaining the saying, "Is Saul also among the prophets?" It is set up by 10:5-6 and accomplished in 10:10-13a. It is paralleled in 1 Sam 19:18-24.

The third process prepares for the alternative version of Saul's rejection, told in 1 Sam 13:7b-15a. The command that Saul is there blamed for transgressing is the command given here in 10:8.

One of the best analyses of 1 Sam 9:1—10:16 is unfortunately untranslated: Ludwig Schmidt, *Menschlicher Erfolg und Jahwes Initiative*, 58-102. Its results are incorporated here.

Present-text potential. 1 Sam 9:1–10:16 is a good example of where a dogmatic insistence on a unified literary reading may not best reflect the signals set by the text. The older story, for example, is not replaced by the reworked Samuel story. The older story is undisturbed in 9:1-12. The reworking begins with

---

Main pre-DH: *Prophetic* Record
its sources *and prophetic contribution*

Other pre-DH:
single sideline

Josianic DH:
from the Dtr

5 When they came to the land of Zuph, Saul said to the boy who was with him, "Let us turn back, or my father will stop worrying about the donkeys and worry about us." ⁶But he said to him, "There is a man of God in this town; he is a man held in honor. Whatever he says always comes true. Let us go there now; perhaps he will tell us about the journey on which we have set out." ⁷Then Saul replied to the boy, "But if we go, what can we bring the man? For the bread in our sacks is gone, and there is no present to bring to the man of God. What have we?" ⁸The boy answered Saul again, "Here, I have with me a quarter shekel of silver; I will give it to the man

of God, to tell us our way." ⁹(Formerly in Israel, anyone who went to inquire of God would say, "Come, let us go to the seer"; for the one who is now called a prophet was formerly called a seer.)²⁵ ¹⁰Saul said to the boy, "Good; come, let us go." So they went to the town where the man of God was.

11 As they went up the hill to the town, they met some girls coming out to draw water, and said to them, "Is the seer here?" ¹²They answered, "Yes, there he is just ahead of you. Hurry; he has come just now to the town, because the people have a sacrifice today at the shrine. ¹³As soon as you enter the town, you will find him, before he goes up to the shrine to eat. For the people will not eat until he comes, since he must bless the sacrifice; *afterward those eat who are invited.* Now go up, for you will meet him immediately." ¹⁴So they went up to the town. *As they were entering the town, they saw Samuel coming out toward them on his way up to the shrine.*

15 Now the day before Saul came, the LORD *had revealed to Samuel:* ¹⁶*"Tomorrow about this time I will send to you a man from the land of Benjamin, and you shall anoint him to be ruler over my people Israel. He shall save my people from the hand of the Philistines; for I have seen the suffering of my people, because their outcry has come to me."*²⁶ ¹⁷*When Samuel saw Saul, the* LORD *told him, "Here is the man of whom I spoke to you. He it is who shall rule*

---

the theme of invitation in v. 13. But the seer remains in vv. 18-19; the overnight delay also remains (v. 19). The old story continues in 10:2-4, with its veiled commission in v. 7, and its conclusion in v. 9.

The story could have been entirely rewritten; instead, it has been reworked. Those who reworked it, however, left the substance of the older story clearly visible. An interpretation is scarcely responsible that overlooks this older story. A storyteller may choose to tell either version; the reworked text keeps the storyteller aware of its origins.

The text equally tells the storyteller that the occasion of Saul's encounter with a seer or Samuel during his search for his father's asses is an appropriate one for explaining the saying, "Is Saul also among the prophets?" The text may not be claiming that the explanation of the saying has to be integrated into the anointing story in just the way it is. Similarly, the anointing story may provide a fitting situation in which to prepare for the story of Saul's dismissal in 13:7b-15a. How it is best done may be left to the storyteller's discretion.

Instead of a unified literary text, 1 Sam 9:1—10:16 may be a good example of the text serving as a base for storytelling, rather than being the record of a storyteller's performance or an example of literary skill in composition.

---

25. An explanatory comment like this can be added at any time, once the need is felt.

26. As we have seen above in Judges, Israel's cry to God is a feature of the framing elements of the deliverer stories, hence pre-dtr; it is not found in the dtr preface (Judg 2:11-19*). There is no reason to deny it to the PR (against Veijola, *Königtum*, 73-75; Klein, *1 Samuel*, 89). Conflict with the Philistines is the constant background to the stories of David's struggle with Saul.

| After the Dtr: indented and sans serif font | **Revision: royal focus** | Revision: national focus | Other: double sideline |

over my people." [18]Then Saul approached *Samuel* inside the gate, and said, "Tell me, please, where is the house of the seer?"[27] [19]*Samuel* answered Saul, "I am the seer; go up before me to the shrine, for today you shall eat with me, and in the morning I will let you go and will tell you all that is on your mind. [20]*As for your donkeys that were lost three days ago, give no further thought to them, for they have been found. And on whom is all Israel's desire fixed, if not on you and on all your ancestral house?"* [21]Saul answered, *"I am only a Benjaminite, from the least of the tribes of Israel, and my family is the humblest of all the families of the tribe of Benjamin. Why then have you spoken to me in this way?"*

22 Then *Samuel* took Saul and his servant-boy and brought them into the hall, *and gave them a place at the head of those who had been invited, of whom there were about thirty.* [23]*And Samuel said to the cook, "Bring the portion I gave you, the one I asked you to put aside."* [24]*The cook took up the thigh and what went with it and set them before Saul. Samuel said, "See, what was kept is set before you. Eat; for it is set before you at the appointed time, so that you might eat with the guests."*

So Saul ate with *Samuel* that day. [25]When they came down from the shrine into the town, a bed was spread for Saul on the roof, and he lay down to sleep. [26]Then at the break of dawn *Samuel* called to Saul upon the roof, "Get up, so that I may send you on your way." Saul got up, and both he and *Samuel* went out into the street.

27 As they were going down to the outskirts of the town, *Samuel* said to Saul, "Tell the boy to go on before us, and when he has passed on, stop

here yourself for a while, that I may make known to you the word of God."[28]

10 *Samuel took a vial of oil and poured it on his head, and kissed him; he said, "The LORD has anointed you ruler over his people Israel. You shall reign over the people of the LORD and you will save them from the hand of their enemies all around. Now this shall be the sign to you that the LORD has anointed you ruler over his heritage:* [2]When you depart from me today you will meet two men by Rachel's tomb in the territory of Benjamin at Zelzah; they will say to you, 'The donkeys that you went to seek are found, and now your father has stopped worrying about them and is worrying about you, saying: What shall I do about my son?' [3]Then you shall go on from there further and come to the oak of Tabor; three men going up to God at Bethel will meet you there, one carrying three kids, another carrying three loaves of bread, and another carrying a skin of wine. [4]They will greet you and give you two loaves of bread, which you shall accept from them.

[5]After that you shall come to Gibeath-elohim, at the place where the Philistine garrison is; there, as you come to the town, you will meet a band of prophets coming down from the shrine with harp, tambourine, flute, and lyre playing in front of them; they will be in a prophetic frenzy. [6]Then the spirit of the LORD will possess you, and you will be in a prophetic frenzy along with them and be turned into a different person.[29]

---

27. In the older story, the prophetic figure is called "the seer," but the prophetic editing identifies "the seer" as Samuel and uses his name from v. 14. To follow the original story (roman type), from here on for *Samuel*, read "the seer."

28. If one is following the older story, there is a gap here before the continuation in 10:2. The introduction to Samuel's speech in 10:1 takes the place of an introduction to the speech in v. 2.

29. The single sideline here identifies verses that are an explanation of a saying about Saul, "Is Saul also among the prophets?" (10:5-6, 10-13a); another explanation of the same saying is given in 1 Sam

---

Main pre-DH: *Prophetic* Record
its sources *and prophetic contribution*

Other pre-DH:
single sideline

Josianic DH:
from the Dtr

7Now when these signs meet you, do whatever you see fit to do, for God is with you.30

8And you shall go down to Gilgal ahead of me; then I will come down to you to present burnt offerings and offer sacrifices of well-being. Seven days you shall wait, until I come to you and show you what you shall do."31

9 As he turned away to leave *Samuel*, God gave him another heart; and all these signs were fulfilled that day.32

19:18-24 (see the introductory note at 9:2). 10:9 concludes with "all these signs were fulfilled that day." After this, however, vv. 10-13a report the fulfillment of what is predicted in vv. 5-6, but not the signs in vv. 2-4. This suggests that 10:5-6, 10-13a may be an addition, attaching to this episode the explanation of the saying in v. 12b.

30. After a careful study of the occurrences, Schmidt concludes that the central phrase here does not refer to the possibilities of some future situation, but concerns the potential of the person acting. The phrase means: when these signs meet you, *do whatever you are able to,* for God is with you (*Menschlicher Erfolg,* 77). The old story is understood to prepare the way for Saul's military prowess in 1 Samuel 11. This prowess could be explained by the coming of the spirit in 11:6, without any prior prophetic encounter. The older prophetic story, however, serves to single out Saul and designate him for the task ahead for which he will be empowered by the spirit (11:6). A prior disposition prepares the way for the receipt of the spirit in this case.

31. 10:8 is to be differentiated from 10:5-6, 10-13a (see above, introductory note at 9:2). It contrasts with the freedom given in v. 7 and prepares for the story of 13:7b-15a, itself an alternative account of Saul's rejection as the LORD's anointed (for the other, cf. 1 Samuel 15). We have here an example of the practice of preserving variant traditions, offering alternative versions for storytelling.

32. There is a certain unevenness between 10:7 and 9 and 11:6, with 10:7 placing the signs before a

10When they were going from there to Gibeah, a band of prophets met him; and the spirit of God possessed him, and he fell into a prophetic frenzy along with them. 11When all who knew him before saw how he prophesied with the prophets, the people said to one another, "What has come over the son of Kish? Is Saul also among the prophets?" 12A man of the place answered, "And who is their father?" Therefore it became a proverb, "Is Saul also among the prophets?" 13And his prophetic frenzy ended. (*Heb.;* NRSV, *When his prophetic frenzy had ended,*)

And he (Heb.; NRSV, he) *went home.*

14 *Saul's uncle said to him and to the boy, "Where did you go?" And he replied, "To seek the donkeys; and when we saw they were not to be found, we went to Samuel."* 15*Saul's uncle said, "Tell me what Samuel said to you."* 16*Saul said to his uncle, "He told us that the donkeys had been found." But about the matter of the kingship, of which Samuel had spoken, he did not tell him anything.*33

---

change, 10:9 apparently placing a change before the signs, and 11:6 showing no evidence of change before the coming of the spirit. For the text, the changes envisaged in 10:7 and 9 may not be the same; the terminology is different. The change of heart (v. 9) precedes the fulfillment of the signs (vv. 7 and 9), and is followed by the impact of the prophetic commission (v. 7). On the other hand, the impression left by v. 7 is of an action to be undertaken ("do") when the signs are fulfilled, but despite this, nothing happens until 11:6 and Saul's seizure there by God's spirit.

This tension may result from the combination of two originally independent stories (see Stoebe, independent and parallel, *Erste Buch Samuelis,* 224). According to the combined text, the seer predisposes Saul for the experience of 11:6. The power given by the seer is activated in chap. 11 by the spirit.

33. The reference to "the matter of the kingship" and the insistence on secrecy about the anointing point to these verses belonging to the prophetic edit-

---

After the Dtr: indented and sans serif font	**Revision: royal focus**	Revision: national focus	Other: double sideline

|| 17 Samuel summoned the people to the LORD at Mizpah.[34]

18and said to them, "Thus says the LORD, the God of Israel, 'I brought up Israel out of Egypt, and I rescued you from the hand of the Egyptians and from the hand of all the kingdoms that were oppressing you.' 19But today you have rejected your God, who saves you from all your calamities and your distresses; and you have said, 'No! but set a king over us.' Now therefore present your-selves before the LORD by your tribes and by your clans."[35]

20 Then Samuel brought all the tribes of Israel near, and the tribe of Benjamin was taken by lot. 21He brought the tribe of Ben-jamin near by its families, and the family of the Matrites was taken by lot. Finally he brought the family of the Matrites near man by man, and Saul the son of Kish was taken by lot.

But when they sought him, he could not be found. 22So they inquired again of the LORD, "Is someone still to come here (*Heb.; NRSV, Did the man come here*)?" and the LORD said, "See, he has hidden himself among the baggage." 23Then they ran and brought him from there. When he took his stand

---

ing. The reference to secrecy here highlights its importance in the three prophetic episodes of anoint-ing preceding political realization. For Saul, it is already present in the older story—the servant is sent on ahead (9:27); for David, it is a relatively private family affair (16:5; cf. v. 2); for Jehu, he is summoned inside, away from the military council (2 Kgs 9:2, 6). The continuation of the PR is to be found at 11:1.

34. Attempts to present 10:17, 20-25 as the origi-nal sequence from 9:1–10:16 need to be resisted. There is a twofold danger. First, if Saul's hiding among the baggage is seen as cowardice, it would be a denial of the power conferred in 10:7 and 9. Second, if the divine lot and the divine oracle were used to dis-cover publicly and clumsily what God had already made known to the prophet, an element of charade would be unavoidable (Stoebe: sacrilege, *Erste Buch Samuelis*, 214). Narrative strands are being combined here; a unified text is not created.

35. **Text signals** in 10:18-19. Vv. 18-19 present Israel's request for a king as a rejection of their God, whereas vv. 20-24 present the identification of the king as directed and guided by God.

Text-history approach. The movement here from rejection of God to gift from God is the same as that noted in chap. 8. In both cases, the accusation of rejecting God is voiced in the form of a speech (8:7b-8; 10:18-19), prior to the action of the assembly. The overall theme suggests attribution to the national

focus of the dtr revision. This is confirmed by an investigation of the language used. (i) "I brought up Israel out of Egypt": cf. Deut 20:1; Josh 24:17; Judg 2:1; 6:8, 13; 1 Sam 8:8; 10:18; 12:6; 2 Sam 7:6; 1 Kgs 12:28; 2 Kgs 17:7, 36. (ii) "I rescued you from the hand of the Egyptians": cf. Josh 24:10; Judg 6:9; 10:15; 1 Sam 7:3; 10:18; 12:11, 21; 2 Kgs 17:39. (iii) "Oppressing": cf. Judg 4:3; 10:12; 2 Kgs 13:4, 22; and for "oppressors," cf. Judg 2:18; 6:9. (iv) For "calami-ties and distresses," cf. Deut 31:17, 21; Judg 10:14. This list is not exhaustive for such phrases, but is com-prehensive for the DH; it points substantially toward a late date and attribution to the revision's national focus for 10:18-19. In our judgment, vv. 18-19 are best taken together, as a unity.

Present-text potential. As at 8:7-21, there is no unified literary text here. The strong emphasis on the rejection of God is on a par with and in similar lan-guage to the national focus of the dtr revision within 8:7b-8, also 8:18. 8:22a provides the divine command motivating 10:17, 20-24. 10:18-19 resumes the expression of a contrary view (see 8:7b-8, 18) that characterizes the move to monarchy as a rejection of God by the people. After the positive attitude of 9:1—10:16 and before the divine choice by lot and oracle, it is appropriate to restate this hostile view.

Main pre-DH: *Prophetic* Record
its sources *and prophetic contribution*

Other pre-DH:
single sideline

Josianic DH:
from the Dtr

among the people, he was head and shoulders taller than any of them. ²⁴Samuel said to all the people, "Do you see the one whom the LORD has chosen? There is no one like him among all the people." And all the people shouted, "Long live the king!"³⁶

*25 Samuel told the people the rights and duties of the kingship; and he wrote them in a book and laid it up before the LORD. Then Samuel sent all the people back to their homes.*³⁷

36. **Text signals** in 10:20-24. Verses 20-21bα are about people who are present; vv. 21bβ-24 are about someone who is absent and needs to be found. The use of "again" in v. 22 implies a prior inquiry (inquiry implies oracle not choice by lot); further, the use of "man/someone" in v. 22 and the absence of any proper name in v. 24 caution against understanding the query as being about the whereabouts of "Saul the son of Kish" identified in v. 21.

Text-history approach. The assumption of two traditions accounts for the text signals. In this assumption, procedure by lot is used in the first tradition and procedure by oracle in the second. In the light of v. 24, the oracle would have been equivalent to: "He shall be king who is head and shoulders taller than any other." When lined up for comparison, no man stood out as head and shoulders taller. Hence the second question to the oracle: "Is someone still to come here?" (v. 22) and Samuel's declaration when the man hidden among the baggage was found to be head and shoulders taller than any of them (cf. vv. 23-24).

For Noth, his Dtr composed the procedure by lot, replacing part of the first oracle with it, in order to involve God's will more clearly in the choice—against the "too primitive" oracle of the tallest man (*DH*, 81-82). The text at 10:20 can assume an oracle from YHWH; in 8:22a there was direct communication from YHWH to Samuel, but there has been no identification of the future king. The procedure by lot may have been introduced before the Josianic Dtr or within the royal focus of the dtr revision. There is no linguistic evidence for composition by dtr people (Veijola recognizes the sparseness of the linguistic evidence, *Königtum*, 48-51). The language used here for the lot procedure is found only with Achan (Josh 7:16-18) and Jonathan (1 Sam 14:41-42). The insertion of this

narrative strand into the DH may be attributed to the royal focus of the dtr process of revision.

Present-text potential. Two options present themselves to readers. First, to recognize the presence of two different traditions in the procedures of lot and oracle and to accept that variant traditions agree in affirming God's choice of the man to be king. Second, to read the traditions as complementary, difficulties notwithstanding. Respectable commentators take this second option; it cannot be denied to readers. The message is the same: God chose the man to be king.

37. **Text signals** in 10:25. (i) The phrase "rights and duties of the kingship" (*mišpaṭ hammĕlukâ*) occurs nowhere else in the Bible. The nearest equivalent is "the ways of the king" (*mišpaṭ hammelek*) in 1 Sam 8:9, 11. 1 Sam 11:14 uses the same term for kingship (*hammĕlukâ*). (ii) Dismissal of the people is not mentioned at either 11:15 or 12:25, suggesting it is not needed after the acclamation of the king (v. 24).

Text-history approach. The content envisaged for such a document is unknown to us. Given the similarity of the phrases, while it is unlikely that the tone of the polemic in 8:11-17 could be thought appropriate, the document probably was heard as limiting the various rights of the king, including lands, services, and taxes. More may have been envisaged, but what we do not know. There is nothing to associate it with the Josianic Dtr, but association with the royal focus of the dtr revising is appropriate and plausible. God's warning was introduced by this revision (8:9b, 11-17) and may have been reemphasized here as an indication that Israel's kings should have known to behave better than they did. In dtr eyes, such a statement of royal "rights and duties" would have included responsibilities regarding fidelity and worship. The idea that the royal role might be prescribed in a document is akin to the prescriptions for the king in Deut 17:14-20. Both may be derived from the impact of the dis-

| After the Dtr:
indented and sans serif font | *Revision:*
royal focus | *Revision:*
national focus | Other:
double sideline |

²⁶Saul also went to his home at Gibeah, and with him went warriors whose hearts God had touched. ²⁷But some worthless fellows said, "How can this man save us?" They despised him and brought him no present. But he held his peace.³⁸

Now Nahash, king of the Ammonites, had been grievously oppressing the Gadites and the Reubenites. He would gouge out the right eye of each of them and would not grant Israel a deliv-

erer. No one was left of the Israelites across the Jordan whose right eye Nahash, king of the Ammonites, had not gouged out. But there were seven thousand men who had escaped from the Ammonites and had entered Jabesh-gilead.³⁹

11 About a month later, Nahash the Ammonite went up and besieged Jabesh-gilead; and all the men of Jabesh said to Nahash, "Make a treaty with us, and we will serve you." ²But Nahash the Ammonite said to them, "On this condition I will make a treaty with you, namely that I gouge out everyone's right eye, and thus put disgrace upon all Israel." ³The elders of Jabesh said to him, "Give us seven days' respite that we may send messengers through all the territory of Israel. Then, if there is no one to save us, we will give ourselves up to you." ⁴When the messengers came to Gibeah of Saul, they reported the matter in the hearing of the people; and all the people wept aloud.⁴⁰

5 Now Saul was coming from the field behind the oxen; and Saul said, "What is the matter with the people, that they are weeping?" So they told him the message from the inhabitants of Jabesh. ⁶And the spirit of God came upon Saul in power when he heard these words,

---

covered scroll on the behavior of King Josiah. Joshua's activity, as presented in Josh 24:25-27, shows a similar concern; naturally, given its context, it concerns the people.

Present-text potential. Saul is publicly established as Israel's king. In 11:14, the text speaks of renewing the kingship (*ûnĕḥaddēš šām hammĕlûkâ*). The obstacle to a unified reading of 10:20-25 with 11:14-15 is that there is no hint in 11:1-11 of Saul's exercising kingship or being known as king.

38. **Text signals** in 10:26-27. There is a stark contrast between the laudable "warriors whose hearts God had touched" who went with Saul and the "worthless fellows" who proclaimed yesterday's orthodoxy ("How can this man save us?"); it points to a change of epochs. There is a close thematic link to 11:12-13, where amnesty is offered to heresy; what is now heresy—the rejection of a king (11:12)—was previously orthodoxy in Samuel's eyes (8:6a). As these epoch-creating verses stand, 10:26-27 is associated with the "assembly" strand and 11:12-13 is associated with the "prophetic" strand.

Text-history approach. There is no trace of dtr language. When such fragments might have originated cannot be pinpointed. Here, they come within the combination of the traditions; their insertion would not be earlier than the dtr revision's royal focus.

Present-text potential. These verses highlight what has just taken place. A king has been installed, sanctioned by God. Those who despise this king are described as "worthless fellows." Yesterday's orthodoxy is today's heresy.

39. The NRSV text here derives from Qumran (4QSamᵃ). In 11:1, the temporal clause "about a month later" is also from Qumran (4QSamᵃ). See the NRSV footnotes. The mutilation of almost two whole tribes seems to anticipate the "disgrace" of 11:2; similarly, a deliverer is refused here but equivalently allowed in 11:3. Possibly, different textual traditions coexist here.

40. **Text signals** in 11:1-11. (i) There is no indication here that Saul has already been acclaimed king (cf. 10:24). (ii) The spirit of God comes upon Saul in v. 6, so that there is no need for dependence on any prior story of Saul's establishment as king. (iii) The first mention of Samuel in the message of v. 7 comes late enough in the story to arouse suspicion.

Main pre-DH: *Prophetic* Record	Other pre-DH:	**Josianic DH:**
its sources *and prophetic contribution*	single sideline	**from the Dtr**

and his anger was greatly kindled. ⁷He took a yoke of oxen, and cut them in pieces and sent them throughout all the territory of Israel by messengers, saying, "Whoever does not come out after Saul **and Samuel,** so shall it be done to his oxen!" Then the dread of the LORD fell upon the people, and they came out as one. ⁸When he mustered them at Bezek, those from Israel were three hundred thousand, and those from Judah seventy thousand. ⁹They said to the messengers who had come, "Thus shall you say to the inhabitants of Jabesh-gilead: 'Tomorrow, by the time the sun is hot, you shall have deliverance.' " When the messengers came and told the inhabitants of Jabesh, they rejoiced. ¹⁰So the inhabitants of Jabesh said, "Tomorrow we will give ourselves up to you, and you may do to us whatever seems good to you." ¹¹The next day Saul put the people in three companies. At the morning watch they came into the camp and cut down the Ammonites until the heat of the day; and those who survived were scattered, so that no two of them were left together.

> 12 The people said to Samuel, "Who is it that said, 'Shall Saul reign over us?' Give them to us so that we may put them to death." ¹³But Saul said, "No one shall be put to death this day, for today the LORD has brought deliverance to Israel."⁴¹

¹⁴Samuel said to the people, "Come, let us go to Gilgal and there renew the kingship."⁴²

¹⁵And *(Heb.; NRSV, So)* all the people went to Gilgal, and there they made Saul king before the LORD in Gilgal. There they sacrificed offerings of well-being before the LORD, and there Saul and all the Israelites rejoiced greatly.⁴³

> **12** Samuel said to all Israel, "I have listened to you in all that you have said to me, and have set a king over you. ²See, it is the king who leads you now; I am old and gray, but my sons are with you. I have led you from my youth until this day. ³Here I am; testify against me before the LORD and before his

---

Text-history approach. Resumption of the PR from 10:16. The Jabesh-gilead story may have been originally independent, was most probably associated with the old story of the anonymous seer, and so became part of the PR with 9:1—10:16, fitting the model of a prophetic anointing as king-designate (*nāgîd*) preceding acclamation as king—retrojected from Jehu to David and Saul. In this combination, the coming of the spirit (v. 6) is understood to actualize the power conferred in the anointing. The involvement of Samuel (vv. 7, 14) is best situated at the level of the combination of traditions as part of the royal focus within the dtr revision process.

Present-text potential. The pointer to a reading of the present text is given by v. 14's "renew the kingship." Saul's kingly power is actualized by the impact of the spirit (v. 6); the liberation of Jabesh-gilead is celebrated in a full-scale coronation festival at Gilgal—unmentioned in the account in 10:24-25.

---

41. The association of 11:12-13 with 10:26-27, and their place in the combined narrative, was noted above. The pardon decreed by Saul is appropriate to his new role as king and marks the transition of leadership from Samuel (v. 12) to Saul (v. 13).

42. The old story has no need and no place for the seer; his task was completed in 10:9. In the PR, the prophet is needed for the anointing as *nāgîd* (king-designate) not for the anointing as king (cf. 1 Sam 16:13 [king-to-be] and 2 Sam 2:4; 5:3; Jehu is the exception, where there is no delay). The concern to introduce Samuel here and in v. 7 is associated with the combination of the traditions (in our formatting, attributed to the royal focus).

43. The continuation of the PR is to be found at 14:52.

<table>
<tr><td>After the Dtr:
indented and sans serif font</td><td>*Revision:*
royal focus</td><td>Revision:
national focus</td><td>Other:
double sideline</td></tr>
</table>

anointed. Whose ox have I taken? Or whose donkey have I taken? Or whom have I defrauded? Whom have I oppressed? Or from whose hand have I taken a bribe to blind my eyes with it? Testify against me and I will restore it to you." [4]They said, "You have not defrauded us or oppressed us or taken anything from the hand of anyone." [5]He said to them, "The LORD is witness against you, and his anointed is witness this day, that you have not found anything in my hand." And they said, "Witness." (*Heb.; NRSV, "He is witness."*)[44]

‖   6 Samuel said to the people:

‖ The LORD (*Heb.; NRSV, is witness*), who made (*Heb.; NRSV, appointed*) Moses and Aaron and who brought (*Heb.; NRSV, and brought*)

---

44. Text signals. In 12:1-25 the signals need to be noted at two different levels, one surprisingly clear and the second subtle and discreet.

(i) Clearly, 1 Samuel 12 does not bring together the preceding traditions. It is remarkably different. Despite all text-critical efforts at reconciliation, it remains different.

a) Samuel's sons are portrayed differently. In 8:1-5, the dissatisfaction with Samuel's sons is defined by contrast with Samuel: "his sons did not follow in his ways." In 12:1-5, the sons are presented neutrally and it is Samuel's ways that need to be judicially declared right.

b) The enemies are different. In the preceding text, the enemies were Aram, Moab, Philistines, Canaan, Midian, Ammon, and Philistines; here, they are Canaanites, Philistines, and Moabites (v. 9).

c) The deliverers are different. In the preceding text, the deliverer-judges were Othniel, Ehud, Shamgar, Deborah/Barak, Gideon (Jerubbaal), Jephthah (and grave doubts about Samson, and Samuel as intercessor rather than deliverer-judge); here, they are Jerubbaal (Gideon), Bedan (various conjectures), Jephthah, and Samuel (LXX[L], Samson). For details, see McCarter, *I Samuel*, 211.

d) The Nahash episode is portrayed differently. In the preceding text (1 Samuel 11), no king is apparent before the victory over Nahash, and Samuel proposes kingship afterwards; here, it is fear of Nahash that causes demand for a king. In the preceding text,

demand for a king is expressed in 1 Sam 8:4-5 on grounds of social justice. The king in 1 Samuel 10:20-25 depends on divine choice, by lot and oracle, not on victory over Nahash.

(ii) At a more subtle and discreet level, the following need to be noted.

a) The theology is different from the Dtr. First, the explicit confession of sin is not found in the Josianic Dtr's contributions; it is found in Judg 10:10-16 and 1 Sam 7:3-4, attributed to the national focus within the dtr process of revision. Second, the plea for deliverance is not found in the Josianic Dtr's contributions; it is found in Judg 10:10-16. Third, repentance as a condition before deliverance is not found in Dtr's contributions; it is found in 1 Sam 7:3-4. Fourth, to have asked for monarchy is sin (12:19).

b) There is similarity of thought with passages situated within the national focus of the dtr revising. First, in 12:14-15, the focus is on the obedience of the people; the king is mentioned only in the apodoses. In the Josianic Dtr's contributions, the focus is on the king. The shift of attention to the people is one of the characteristics of the national focus of the dtr revising. Second, in 12:14-15 and 23, Samuel is a preacher of the law, as in Judg 2:17 and 2 Kgs 17:13, both from the national focus of revision.

(c) Beyond the differences of historical presentation and theological reflection, the identification of dtr thinking or language in a passage of this kind needs careful investigation and evaluation. Critical reading of the Hebrew does not evoke echoes of dtr composition; to the contrary, it is an unfamiliar style. Some examples: the "thunder" of vv. 17-18 is not dtr; the "we have added to our sins" of v. 19 is not dtr; the "turn aside after" of vv. 20-21 is not dtr; neither the "useless things" nor the expression of their unprofitability are dtr (v. 21); to "serve YHWH" does not occur within the dtr contributions to the Josianic DH; "with all your hearts" (12:20, 24) evokes the national focus of the dtr

---

Main pre-DH: *Prophetic* Record   Other pre-DH: **Josianic DH:**
its sources *and prophetic contribution*   single sideline   **from the Dtr**

revision (cf. Josh 23:14; 1 Sam 7:3), but there are also Jer 29:13 and Joel 2:12; God's casting off or forsaking his people is not a dtr idiom (v. 22); "the good and right way" of 12:23 is unique in the Hebrew Bible (one commentator describes it as "surely" dtr—it may be, but it is unique). Minor editorial touches are always possible. Imitation and influence by the center on the periphery has to be allowed for. Evaluation is important; what is not exclusive is not likely to have much demonstrative clout. However, it is worth noting that the formulation of 12:10 follows closely that of Judg 10:10.

Text-history approach. The enigma of this chapter is how close it is to the complex of dtr thinking and how far away it is so often from dtr tradition and expression. There is a basic contextual relationship with the issues in the present text of the DH. The details and the linguistic expression are puzzlingly distant from the DH.

The particular characteristics of 12:1-25 need to be evaluated for their own worth, but it is different from the Dtr. At least three options are possible and not necessarily exclusive. (i) The text presents a distorted picture because of uncertain recall of the same tradition, written presumably without access to the dtr scroll. (ii) The text follows a different tradition. (iii) The text draws on elements from the past and selects three; symbols suffice. First, oppressors; second, deliverance; third, threat. Three oppressors, four deliverers, and Nahash supply these needs. Starting from these elements, the text goes on to create an acceptable theology of kingship (cf. O'Brien, *Deuteronomistic History Hypothesis*, 120–28).

Our formatting opts for an understanding in which this tradition (chap. 12) has been added early enough to be available for revision by the national focus, above all in 12:10. The royal focus was probably responsible for introducing this, in conjunction with its preceding additions. Alternatively, the material was composed later with v. 10 reflecting the national focus.

Present-text potential. Two options are open to the reader of the present text. One is to read the chapter as a reflection on the preceding traditions, without focusing on the discrepancies. These traditions are brought to constitutional settlement in vv. 14-15; a right relationship between God and people is estab-

|| your ancestors up out of the land of Egypt. [45]

|| [7]"Now therefore take your stand, so that I may enter into judgment with you before the LORD, and I will declare to you all the saving deeds of the LORD that he performed

lished, and the people are assured of Samuel's intercession. Yet the chapter ends on a note of warning.

The other option is to focus more intensely on the discrepancies between chap. 12 and the preceding traditions and to see the chapter as giving expression to a less optimistic viewpoint. This less optimistic view has already been given sharp expression in 8:7b, 18, and 10:18-19. Chap. 12 holds together this pessimistic outlook and the other traditions that recognized the role in the emergence of kingship of both the people's request and God's gift. The constitutional relationship is established between God and people (vv. 14-15). God's power is also established. The more jaundiced view of kingship comes to the fore in the declaration that the people's request was evil. The reconciliation is manifest in Samuel's promise of intercession. The pessimism remains in the final warning.

45. **Text signals** in 12:6. The Hebrew text says literally: The LORD who made Moses and Aaron and who brought your ancestors up out of the land of Egypt. The problems this raises are: (i) its function in the context; (ii) its relationship with vv. 5 and 8; (iii) its text-critical aspects. LXX adds "witness" as in the NRSV; McCarter assumes conflation and eliminates v. 6a, reading two statements from Samuel.

Text-history approach. Compositional approaches here are not very helpful; but neither are any others. The reconstruction with two consecutive statements from Samuel reads oddly, eliminating the reply of the people. The presence of Moses and Aaron together is legitimated by v. 8. Their presence in v. 8, however, performs a different function from v. 6. In v. 6, they are a testimony to YHWH's activity; in v 8, they are agents sent by YHWH. V. 5 has both YHWH and his anointed, while v. 6 has only YHWH. Deleting "and his anointed" does not resolve the syntactical and text-critical difficulties.

| After the Dtr: indented and sans serif font | **Revision: royal focus** | Revision: national focus | Other: double sideline |

for you and for your ancestors. [8]When Jacob went into Egypt and the Egyptians oppressed them, then your ancestors cried to the LORD and the LORD sent Moses and Aaron, who brought forth your ancestors out of Egypt, and settled them in this place. [9]But they forgot the LORD their God; and he sold them into the hand of Sisera, commander of the army of King Jabin of Hazor, and into the hand of the Philistines, and into the hand of the king of Moab; and they fought against them.

[10]*Then they cried to the LORD, and said, 'We have sinned, because we have forsaken the LORD, and have served the Baals and the Astartes; but now rescue us out of the hand of our enemies, and we will serve you.'*

[11]And the LORD sent Jerubbaal and Barak, and Jephthah, and Samson, and rescued you out of the hand of your enemies on every side; and you lived in safety. [12]But when you saw that King Nahash of the Ammonites came against you, you said to me, 'No, but a king shall reign over us,' though the LORD your God was your king. [13]See, here is the king whom you have chosen, for whom you have asked; see, the LORD has set a king over you. [14]If you will fear the LORD and serve him and heed his voice and not rebel against the command-

ment of the LORD, then *(Heb.; NRSV, and if)* both you and the king who reigns over you will follow the LORD your God *(Heb.; NRSV, it will be well);*[46] [15]but if you will not heed the voice of the LORD, but rebel against the commandment of the LORD, then the hand of the LORD will be against you and your king. [16]Now therefore take your stand and see this great thing that the LORD will do before your eyes. [17]Is it not the wheat harvest today? I will call upon the LORD, that he may send thunder and rain; and you shall know and see that the wickedness that you have done in the sight of the LORD is great in demanding a king for yourselves." [18]So Samuel called upon the LORD, and the LORD sent thunder and rain that day; and all the people greatly feared the LORD and Samuel.

19 All the people said to Samuel, "Pray to the LORD your God for your servants, so that we may not die; for we have added to all our sins the evil of demanding a king for ourselves." [20]And Samuel said to the people, "Do not be afraid; you have done all this evil, yet do not turn aside from following the LORD, but serve the LORD with all

---

The least unsatisfactory solution is most probably to regard v. 6b as a marginal gloss that has come into the text. V. 6b is declarative praise, without the hymnic participle, of YHWH who is witness (v. 5), or of YHWH before whom the people take their stand (v. 7).

Present-text potential. In its present position in the text, v. 6b facilitates the transition from YHWH as witness to Samuel's integrity (v. 5) to YHWH before whom all Israel must stand in judgment under Samuel (v. 7).

---

46. The structure of the Hebrew in v. 14 is the same as in v. 15. If the conditions are observed, there is loyalty (v. 14); if the conditions are breached, there is conflict (v. 15). Translational difficulty arose because the second half of v. 14 was thought to be tautological. The adjusted translation (above) is based on the recognition that the Hebrew idiom, here translated "follow the LORD" (literal: be after the LORD), is specifically an expression of loyalty (cf. 2 Sam 2:10; 15:13; 17:9; 1 Kgs 12:20; 16:21). If the conditions are observed, people and king will be in loyal relationship with the LORD. The assumption of ellipsis, requiring the phrase, "it will be well" which is not in the Hebrew, is unnecessary. See D. J. McCarthy, *Treaty and Covenant*, 215.

| Main pre-DH: *Prophetic* Record | Other pre-DH: | **Josianic DH:** |
| its sources *and prophetic contribution* | single sideline | **from the Dtr** |

your heart; ²¹and do not turn aside after useless things that cannot profit or save, for they are useless. ²²For the LORD will not cast away his people, for his great name's sake, because it has pleased the LORD to make you a people for himself. ²³Moreover as for me, far be it from me that I should sin against the LORD by ceasing to pray for you; and I will instruct you in the good and the right way. ²⁴Only fear the LORD, and serve him faithfully with all your heart; for consider what great things he has done for you. ²⁵But if you still do wickedly, you shall be swept away, both you and your king."

13 Saul was . . . years old when he began to reign; and he reigned . . . and two years over Israel.⁴⁷

2 Saul chose three thousand out of Israel; two thousand were with Saul in Michmash and the hill country of Bethel, and a thousand were with Jonathan in Gibeah of Benjamin; the rest of the people he sent home to their tents. ³Jonathan defeated the garrison of the Philistines that was at Geba; and the Philistines heard of it. And Saul blew the trumpet throughout all the land, saying, "Let the Hebrews hear!" ⁴When all Israel heard that Saul had defeated the garrison of the Philistines, and also that Israel had become odious to the Philistines, the people were called out to join Saul at Gilgal.⁴⁸

---

47. 13:1 is a text-critically troubling verse. The dtr formulas for each king's accession include his age and the length of his reign, so the verse is attributed to the Dtr. Stoebe considers both 13:1 and 14:47-52 to be late editorial framing passages (*Erste Buch Samuelis*, 246, 277).

48. **Text signals.** 1 Samuel 13–14 contains a variety of traditions, assembled around the story of Jonathan's victory over a Philistine garrison at Mich-

5 The Philistines mustered to fight with Israel, thirty thousand chariots, and six thousand horsemen, and troops like the sand on the seashore in multitude; they came up and encamped at Michmash, to the east of Beth-aven. ⁶When the Israelites saw that they were in distress (for the troops were hard pressed), the people hid themselves in caves and in holes and in rocks and in tombs and in cisterns. ⁷Some Hebrews crossed the Jordan to the land of Gad and Gilead.

---

mash. Among these traditions is a story of Saul's being rebuked by Samuel, to be replaced by a man after YHWH's own heart. The collection ends with the summaries of activities and officials that often conclude the account of a king's reign.

Text-history approach. 1 Samuel 13–14 can be understood as a self-contained collection of traditions about Saul and Jonathan, similar to the collection of Davidic traditions in 2 Samuel 21–24. It is presented here as a pre-dtr tradition. As pre-dtr, it will have been attached to the PR for the purposes of storage and retrieval; it is stored in the appropriate place where one would look in order to retrieve it. Stoebe expresses doubt whether so Benjaminite an episode belongs within the period of Saul's kingship (*Erste Buch Samuelis*, 246). It is inappropriate to go into further detail, except for 13:7b-15a (see below). Information can be found in the commentaries.

Present-text potential. 1 Samuel 13–14 can be read as the sequel to Saul's coronation as king. His victory over the Ammonites at Jabesh-gilead brought him the kingship; now he is expected to produce results against Israel's principal foe, the Philistines. The main story has its share of oddity. The victory is Jonathan's; Saul's contribution is to go close to turning victory into disaster. His rejection by Samuel (13:7b-15a) might be seen as the cause for his almost signal failure. It would tie in with 1 Samuel 12; if you do not heed God's voice but rebel against God's commandment, God's hand will be against you (cf. 12:15)—alas, Saul failed in obedience.

After the Dtr: indented and sans serif font	**Revision: royal focus**	Revision: national focus	Other: double sideline

Saul was still at Gilgal, and all the people followed him trembling.[49]

8 He waited seven days, the time appointed by Samuel; but Samuel did not come to Gilgal, and the people began to slip away from Saul. [9]So Saul said, "Bring the burnt offering here to me, and the offerings of well-being." And he offered the burnt offering. [10]As soon as he had finished offering the burnt offering, Samuel arrived; and Saul went out to meet him and salute him. [11]Samuel said, "What have you done?" Saul replied, "When I saw that the people were slip-ping away from me, and that you did not come within the days appointed, and that the Philistines were mustering at Michmash, [12]I said, 'Now the Philistines will come down upon me at Gilgal, and I have not entreated the favor of the LORD'; so I forced myself, and offered the burnt offering." [13]Samuel said to Saul, "You have done foolishly; **you have not kept the commandment of the LORD your God, which he commanded you.** The LORD would have established your kingdom over Israel forever, [14]but now your kingdom will not continue; the LORD has sought out a man after his own heart; and the LORD has appointed him to be ruler over his people, **because you have not kept what the LORD commanded you.**" [15]And Samuel left and went on his way from Gilgal. The rest of the people followed Saul to join the army; they went up from Gilgal toward Gibeah of Benjamin.[50]

---

49. **Text signals** in 13:7b-15a. (i) Saul's wait for Samuel is dependent on 1 Sam 10:8, a verse that is secondary in its context. (ii) Samuel's declaration rejecting Saul's kingship and future dynasty is out of context preceding a story of Jonathan's remarkable success against the Philistines. (iii) 13:7b-15a is a duplicate of 15:1-35; this latter flows smoothly into 16:1-13. 15:1-35 and 16:1 reflect the departure of YHWH's spirit from Saul (16:14a).

Text-history approach. The text signals can be explained as reflecting the process of making room for a tradition downgrading Saul's kingdom from the start. Two questions are present. Where does the tradition come from? What does it mean? The tradition in vv. 7b-15a is likely to have been formulated in the prophetic circles responsible for the PR. Obedience to the prophet is demanded, even in apparently irrational circumstances. These circles that gave Saul the legitimation of anointing clearly believed that they had the right and authority to withdraw that legitimation (cf. 15:1-35).

The second question—what does the tradition mean?—is not strictly a present text question. It is a composition question: how did this insertion come to be made here? If the Michmash story was once the kernel of an independent collection, celebrating Jonathan perhaps more than Saul, vv. 7b-15a might have served to explain both Saul's near failure and the brevity of the account of his reign. The absence of 10:8 creates a difficulty for an independent collection, but is not crippling; with the text as "base for performance," 13:8 could provide the storyteller with adequate information. 10:8 becomes attractive when the texts are combined. Alternatively, the passage met a need to express Saul's downfall as early as possible in his reign, accounting for the absence of any significant achievement by Saul. Thirdly, as a last resort, the episode may have been in the tradition and to be preserved needed to be placed in the text before chap. 15.

Present-text potential. It is likely that history is here subordinate to theology. Issues of charismatic and dynastic kingship are not the question. Kingship is of its essence dynastic (cf. for example, 1 Sam 20:31; Ishida, *The Royal Dynasties in Ancient Israel*, 151-82; Campbell, *Of Prophets and Kings*, 113). The issue is whether or not kingship is successful. This passage deprives Saul of the long-term legitimacy of a dynasty, before he nearly bungles Jonathan's victorious exploit and before the Amalekite episode is used to declare his immediate rejection as king.

50. **Text signals.** Verses 13-14 determine the sentence passed by Samuel. (i) "You have done foolishly"

Main pre-DH: *Prophetic* Record
its sources *and prophetic contribution*

Other pre-DH:
single sideline

Josianic DH:
from the Dtr

Saul counted the people who were present with him, about six hundred men. [16]Saul, his son Jonathan, and the people who were present with them stayed in Geba of Benjamin; but the Philistines encamped at Michmash. [17]And raiders came out of the camp of the Philistines in three companies; one company turned toward Ophrah, to the land of Shual, [18]another company turned toward Beth-horon, and another company turned toward the mountain that looks down upon the valley of Zeboim toward the wilderness.

19 Now there was no smith to be found throughout all the land of Israel; for the Philistines said, "The Hebrews must not make swords or spears for themselves"; [20]so all the Israelites went down to the Philistines to sharpen their plowshare, mattocks, axes, or sickles; [21]the charge was two-thirds of a shekel for the plowshares and for the mattocks, and one-third of a shekel for sharpening the axes and for setting the goads. [22]So on the day of the battle neither sword nor spear was to be found in the possession of any of the people with Saul and Jonathan; but Saul and his son Jonathan had them.

23 Now a garrison of the Philistines had gone out to the pass of Michmash.

14 One day Jonathan son of Saul said to the young man who carried his armor, "Come, let us go over to the Philistine garrison on the other side." But he did not tell his father. [2]Saul was staying in the outskirts of Gibeah under the pomegranate tree that is at Migron; the troops that were with him were about six hundred men, [3]along with Ahijah son of Ahitub, Ichabod's brother, son of Phinehas son of Eli, the priest of the Lord in Shiloh, carrying an ephod. Now the people did not know that Jonathan had gone. [4]In the pass, by which Jonathan tried to go over to the Philistine garrison, there was a rocky crag on one side and a rocky crag on the other; the name of the one was Bozez, and the name of the other Seneh. [5]One crag rose on the north in front of Michmash, and the other on the south in front of Geba.

6 Jonathan said to the young man who carried his armor, "Come, let us go over to the garrison of these uncircumcised; it may be that the Lord will act for us; for nothing can hinder the Lord from saving by many or by few." [7]His armor-bearer said to him, "Do all that your mind inclines to. I am with you; as your mind is, so is mine." [8]Then Jonathan said, "Now we will cross over to those men and will show ourselves to them. [9]If they say to us, 'Wait until we come to you,' then we will stand still in our place, and we

---

is spelled out in v. 13bα. (ii) V. 14bβ repeats what has been said in v. 13bα. (iii) In 10:8, the order is from Samuel not YHWH.

Text-history approach. These observations would be unhelpful nit-picking if it were not important to determine the origin of vv. 13-14. For Veijola, both verses 13 and 14 are from his DtrN (*Ewige Dynastie*, 55-57); as a result, Saul is not even rebuked by Samuel until late in the development of the text. Modern resistance to prophetic absolutism should not lead us to eviscerate an ancient story. The transfer of the kingdom to David is already central to the PR and would be expected in traditions from these prophetic circles.

To "keep the commandment of the Lord" (v. 13bα and equivalent in 14bβ) is recognized as a dtr formula (Weinfeld, *Deuteronomic School*, 336, #16). The "establishing of the kingdom" is not peculiarly dtr. The precise phrase, "a man after his own heart," occurs only here; talk of God's heart is not a dtr preserve (e.g., Gen 6:6; 8:21; Hos 11:8). The Dtr may have added the motivation, making clear that an order from the prophet in this case was the equivalent of a commandment from YHWH. Our formatting allows for such an addition and highlights the possibility—no more.

Present-text potential. The present text of vv. 13-14 stipulates that Saul's sin was disobedience to the command of God, implicit in the order of the prophet.

| After the Dtr: indented and sans serif font | *Revision:* *royal focus* | *Revision:* *national focus* | Other: double sideline |

will not go up to them. [10]But if they say, 'Come up to us,' then we will go up; for the Lord has given them into our hand. That will be the sign for us." [11]So both of them showed themselves to the garrison of the Philistines; and the Philistines said, "Look, Hebrews are coming out of the holes where they have hidden themselves." [12]The men of the garrison hailed Jonathan and his armor-bearer, saying, "Come up to us, and we will show you something." Jonathan said to his armor-bearer, "Come up after me; for the Lord has given them into the hand of Israel." [13]Then Jonathan climbed up on his hands and feet, with his armor-bearer following after him. The Philistines fell before Jonathan, and his armor-bearer, coming after him, killed them. [14]In that first slaughter Jonathan and his armor-bearer killed about twenty men within an area about half a furrow long in an acre of land. [15]There was a panic in the camp, in the field, and among all the people; the garrison and even the raiders trembled; the earth quaked; and it became a very great panic.

16 Saul's lookouts in Gibeah of Benjamin were watching as the multitude was surging back and forth. [17]Then Saul said to the troops that were with him, "Call the roll and see who has gone from us." When they had called the roll, Jonathan and his armor-bearer were not there. [18]Saul said to Ahijah, "Bring the ark of God here." For at that time the ark of God went with the Israelites. [19]While Saul was talking to the priest, the tumult in the camp of the Philistines increased more and more; and Saul said to the priest, "Withdraw your hand." [20]Then Saul and all the people who were with him rallied and went into the battle; and every sword was against the other, so that there was very great confusion. [21]Now the Hebrews who previously had been with the Philistines and had gone up with them into the camp turned and joined the Israelites

who were with Saul and Jonathan. [22]Likewise, when all the Israelites who had gone into hiding in the hill country of Ephraim heard that the Philistines were fleeing, they too followed closely after them in the battle. [23]So the Lord gave Israel the victory that day.

The battle passed beyond Beth-aven, and the troops with Saul numbered altogether about ten thousand men. The battle spread out over the hill country of Ephraim.

24 Now Saul committed a very rash act on that day. He had laid an oath on the troops, saying, "Cursed be anyone who eats food before it is evening and I have been avenged on my enemies." So none of the troops tasted food. [25]All the troops came upon a honeycomb; and there was honey on the ground. [26]When the troops came upon the honeycomb, the honey was dripping out; but they did not put their hands to their mouths, for they feared the oath. [27]But Jonathan had not heard his father charge the troops with the oath; so he extended the staff that was in his hand, and dipped the tip of it in the honeycomb, and put his hand to his mouth; and his eyes brightened. [28]Then one of the soldiers said, "Your father strictly charged the troops with an oath, saying, 'Cursed be anyone who eats food this day.' And so the troops are faint." [29]Then Jonathan said, "My father has troubled the land; see how my eyes have brightened because I tasted a little of this honey. [30]How much better if today the troops had eaten freely of the spoil taken from their enemies; for now the slaughter among the Philistines has not been great."

31 After they had struck down the Philistines that day from Michmash to Aijalon, the troops were very faint; [32]so the troops flew upon the spoil, and took sheep and oxen and calves, and slaughtered them on the ground; and the troops ate them with the blood. [33]Then it was reported

---

Main pre-DH: *Prophetic* Record
its sources *and prophetic contribution*

Other pre-DH:
single sideline

Josianic DH:
from the Dtr

to Saul, "Look, the troops are sinning against the LORD by eating with the blood." And he said, "You have dealt treacherously; roll a large stone before me here." [34]Saul said, "Disperse yourselves among the troops, and say to them, 'Let all bring their oxen or their sheep, and slaughter them here, and eat; and do not sin against the LORD by eating with the blood.' " So all of the troops brought their oxen with them that night, and slaughtered them there. [35]And Saul built an altar to the LORD; it was the first altar that he built to the LORD.

36 Then Saul said, "Let us go down after the Philistines by night and despoil them until the morning light; let us not leave one of them." They said, "Do whatever seems good to you." But the priest said, "Let us draw near to God here." [37]So Saul inquired of God, "Shall I go down after the Philistines? Will you give them into the hand of Israel?" But he did not answer him that day. [38]Saul said, "Come here, all you leaders of the people; and let us find out how this sin has arisen today. [39]For as the LORD lives who saves Israel, even if it is in my son Jonathan, he shall surely die!" But there was no one among all the people who answered him. [40]He said to all Israel, "You shall be on one side, and I and my son Jonathan will be on the other side." The people said to Saul, "Do what seems good to you." [41]Then Saul said, "O LORD God of Israel, why have you not answered your servant today? If this guilt is in me or in my son Jonathan, O LORD God of Israel, give Urim; but if this guilt is in your people Israel, give Thummim." And Jonathan and Saul were indicated by the lot, but the people were cleared. [42]Then Saul said, "Cast the lot between me and my son Jonathan." And Jonathan was taken.

43 Then Saul said to Jonathan, "Tell me what you have done." Jonathan told him, "I tasted a little honey with the tip of the staff that was in my hand; here I am, I will die." [44]Saul said, "God do so to me and more also; you shall surely die, Jonathan!" [45]Then the people said to Saul, "Shall Jonathan die, who has accomplished this great victory in Israel? Far from it! As the LORD lives, not one hair of his head shall fall to the ground; for he has worked with God today." So the people ransomed Jonathan, and he did not die. [46]Then Saul withdrew from pursuing the Philistines; and the Philistines went to their own place.

47 When Saul had taken the kingship over Israel, he fought against all his enemies on every side—against Moab, against the Ammonites, against Edom, against the kings of Zobah, and against the Philistines; wherever he turned he routed them. [48]He did valiantly, and struck down the Amalekites, and rescued Israel out of the hands of those who plundered them.

49 Now the sons of Saul were Jonathan, Ishvi, and Malchishua; and the names of his two daughters were these: the name of the firstborn was Merab, and the name of the younger, Michal. [50]The name of Saul's wife was Ahinoam daughter of Ahimaaz. And the name of the commander of his army was Abner son of Ner, Saul's uncle; [51]Kish was the father of Saul, and Ner the father of Abner was the son of Abiel.[51]

---

51. **Text signals** in 14:47-51. (i) The reference to Saul's *seizure* of power (*lākad*, but cf. 1 Sam 10:20, 21; 14:41, 42) sits oddly at this point, both in expression and location. (ii) The list of enemies routed does not correspond with the traditions about Saul available to us. (iii) The reference to the Amalekites precedes the story about them in the next chapter and differs from it markedly in tone. (iv) The glowing picture of Saul's success contrasts with the traditions of 1 Sam 16:14—31:13. (v) Abinadab is missing from the list of sons (cf. 1 Sam 31:2), and Ishvi needs to be identified with Ishbaal (cf. 2 Sam 2:10). (vi) Rizpah is unmentioned. (vii) The relationship of Abner to Saul is uncertain.

| After the Dtr: indented and sans serif font | **Revision: royal focus** | *Revision: national focus* | Other: double sideline |

52 There was hard fighting against the Philistines all the days of Saul; and when Saul saw any strong or valiant warrior, he took him into his service.[52]

15 Samuel said to Saul, *"The* LORD *sent me to anoint you king over his people Israel;* now therefore listen to the words of the LORD. [2]Thus says the LORD of hosts, 'I will punish the Amalekites for what they did in opposing the Israelites when they came up out of Egypt. [3]Now go and attack Amalek, and utterly destroy all that they have; do not spare them, but kill both man and woman, child and infant, ox and sheep, camel and donkey.' "[53]

Text-history approach. Clearly vv. 47-51 are a summary about Saul. A similar summary of military successes is given for David in 2 Samuel 8 and of David's wives and children in 2 Sam 3:2-5; 5:13-16. David's army commanders and officials are listed at 2 Sam 8:15-18 and 20:23-26; for Saul, only Abner is listed. There is debate over the provenance of the traditions; the discrepancies cannot be easily accounted for. If the story of the battle at Michmash goes back before Saul was king, there is a lot that we do not know about the time of Saul—which is hardly surprising when we consider that most of the Saul traditions come down to us through Davidic sources. We may have to be content with the acknowledgment of ignorance. Given the discrepancies, a pre-dtr origin seems more likely than dtr or post-dtr. A break separates it from its preceding context.

Present-text potential. Where it stands, the summary performs a remarkable function; it, in fact, draws attention to the end of Saul's reign. This summary marks a watershed before Saul's rejection takes effect and the figure of David comes on the scene as YHWH's anointed. 2 Samuel 8 performs a similar function for David, before his relative decline in 2 Samuel 11–20.

52. Resumption of the PR from 11:15. V. 52 is often seen as belonging better after v. 46; it is oddly placed following the summary in vv. 47-51. As a part of the PR, it picks up the prophetic anointing of Saul to deliver Israel from the Philistine threat and it prepares for the role of David in what is to come. Belonging to the PR, it might well have been kept in close proximity to the continuing text in 15:1-35, where the continuation of the PR is to be found.

Veijola attributed 14:3, 18*, 47-52 to his DtrH.

---

53. **Text signals.** 1 Samuel 15 is like 9:1—10:16, in that there is a more recent layer superimposed over an older story. The particular interest here is to note the associations of language and concern with the prophetic editing in 9:1—10:16. Most of these are italicized, signifying their attribution to the prophetic contribution. Note that refusal in v. 26 becomes acquiescence in v. 31.

(i) In v. 1, Saul's anointing is recalled and attributed to God's command. 15:1 says, "to anoint you king"; in 10:1, Saul is anointed *nāgîd* (king-designate). *Nāgîd* appears to be used by prophetic editors to place their claim within pre-existing texts, earlier than the actual fact of kingship. The prophets designate beforehand. In 16:1-13, however, *nāgîd* is not used (see below).

(ii) In vv. 10-12, the establishment of Saul as king is directly attributed to God, "I regret that I made Saul king," as in 9:1-10:16.

(iii) Verse 16 reflects both God's prior communication to Samuel (v.v. 10-11a) and Samuel's night of angry prayer (v. 11b). It implies what is not stated earlier: that God's communication came during that night (cf. 9:19).

(iv) Verse 17b, once again, attributes Saul's anointing directly to God.

(v) Verses 26-30 present the symbolism of the torn garment and the judgment it expresses; it prepares for the prophetic contribution in 16:1-13. The symbol of the torn garment is used formally by the prophet Ahijah (1 Kgs 11:29-31). The rejection is attributed directly to God, "the LORD has rejected you." V. 30, an intensified repetition of v. 25, forms the link back into the older story. V. 29 is grounded in the prophetic tradition (cf. Balaam, Num 23:19); it conflicts with God's repentance in 15:11 and 35. Whether from a prophetic editor or a later hand, the conflict is presumably resolved by the understanding that this

---

| Main pre-DH: *Prophetic* Record | Other pre-DH: | **Josianic DH:** |
| its sources *and prophetic contribution* | single sideline | **from the Dtr** |

4 So Saul summoned the people, and numbered them in Telaim, two hundred thousand foot soldiers, and ten thousand soldiers of Judah. [5]Saul came to the city of the Amalekites and lay in wait in the valley. [6]Saul said to the Kenites, "Go! Leave! Withdraw from among the Amalekites, or I will destroy you with them; for

---

saying applies to Saul in this particular situation without question—there will be no change of heart on this one (cf. Stoebe, *Erste Buch Samuelis*, 295).

(vi) Verse 35 is fully within the horizon of the prophetic editing. 1 Sam 19:18-24 is not part of the PR. V. 34 provides the conclusion of the older story. Verse 23 will be treated in its own right (see below).

Text-history approach. These text signals point to the same procedure as in 9:1–10:16. An older story has been reworked by the prophetic redactors. The reworked text expresses the prophetic conviction that the prophets of old were God's instruments in the establishment and dismissal of kings. The older story is preserved in its entirety; Saul is not rejected but rebuked. Saul is sternly rebuked in v. 22, confesses and repents in vv. 24-25, and is accepted by Samuel in v. 31. The sequence is similar to that of the putative original text for David and Nathan (2 Sam 12:7a, 13a, 13b). The prophetic editing transforms Samuel's rebuke into God's rejection, basing it on God's action in 9:1–10:16 and ignoring other aspects of the tradition. V. 26 refuses Saul's repentance, because his repentance will not prevent his rejection as king. Once the rejection has been proclaimed, however, Samuel can return with him (v. 31). The prophetic editors knew that Saul stays on the scene until 1 Samuel 31. Note that, in the old story, there is no explicit reference to Saul as king.

Present-text potential. Unless the difficulties are brought into the foreground, 1 Sam 15:1-35 reads well as an account of Saul's rejection, preparing the way for David's presentation as God's anointed. It builds on and goes beyond the prophetic condemnation in 13:7b-15a.

you showed kindness to all the people of Israel when they came up out of Egypt." So the Kenites withdrew from the Amalekites. [7]Saul defeated the Amalekites, from Havilah as far as Shur, which is east of Egypt. [8]He took King Agag of the Amalekites alive, but utterly destroyed all the people with the edge of the sword. [9]Saul and the people spared Agag, and the best of the sheep and of the cattle and of the fatlings, and the lambs, and all that was valuable, and would not utterly destroy them; all that was despised and worthless they utterly destroyed.

10 The word of the LORD came to Samuel: [11]"I regret that I made Saul king, for he has turned back from following me, and has not carried out my commands." Samuel was angry; and he cried out to the LORD all night. [12]Samuel rose early in the morning to meet Saul, and Samuel was told, "Saul went to Carmel, where he set up a monument for himself, and on returning he passed on down to Gilgal." [13]And Samuel (Heb.; NRSV, *When Samuel*) came to Saul, and Saul (Heb.; NRSV, *Saul*) said to him, "May you be blessed by the LORD; I have carried out the command of the LORD." [14]But Samuel said, "What then is this bleating of sheep in my ears, and the lowing of cattle that I hear?" [15]Saul said, "They have brought them from the Amalekites; for the people spared the best of the sheep and the cattle, to sacrifice to the LORD your God; but the rest we have utterly destroyed." *[16]Then Samuel said to Saul, "Stop! I will tell you what the LORD said to me last night." He replied, "Speak."*

17 Samuel said, "Though you are little in your own eyes, are you not the head of the tribes of Israel? *The LORD anointed you king over Israel.* [18]And the LORD sent you on a mission, and said, 'Go, utterly destroy the sinners, the Amalekites, and fight against them until they are consumed.' [19]Why then did you not obey the voice of the LORD? Why did you swoop down on the spoil,

---

| After the Dtr: indented and sans serif font | **Revision: royal focus** | Revision: national focus | Other: double sideline |

and do what was evil in the sight of the Lord?" [20]Saul said to Samuel, "I have obeyed the voice of the Lord, I have gone on the mission on which the Lord sent me, I have brought Agag the king of Amalek, and I have utterly destroyed the Amalekites. [21]But from the spoil the people took sheep and cattle, the best of the things devoted to destruction, to sacrifice to the Lord your God in Gilgal." [22]And Samuel said,

"Has the Lord as great delight in burnt
offerings and sacrifices,
as in obeying the voice of the Lord?
Surely, to obey is better than sacrifice,
and to heed than the fat of rams.
[23]*For rebellion is no less a sin than divination,*
and stubbornness is like iniquity and idolatry.
Because you have rejected the word of the Lord,
he has also rejected you from being king."[54]

---

54. **Text signals.** (i) V. 23a is only indirectly linked to v. 22, where there is no question of divination. (ii) Its concerns and language are closer to 1 Samuel 28 (cf. 28:8) than to 1 Samuel 15. (iii) There are echoes of Num 23:18-24, as also in v. 29 (v. 19, the portrayal of God, for 15:29; v. 23, divination, for 15:23). (iv) V. 23b as part of the old story is in some tension with v. 31, but the rejection need not preclude worship. (v) As part of the prophetic reworking, v. 23b anticipates v. 26.

Text-history approach. These signals are significant enough to raise the possibility that v. 23 is later than v. 22 (for v. 23a, see A. Tosato, "La colpa di Saul."). It would be possible within the PR as preparation for 1 Sam 28:17-19a. If this is the case, the similarity to a Balaam text needs explanation. It is again possible that the saying, "Obedience is better than sacrifice," evoked the reflection that Balak, king of Moab, stood beside the burnt offerings while Balaam, the prophet, was obedient to the word of God (Num 22:18-20; 23:5, 16).

Present-text potential. The aphoristic power of v. 22 in summing up the sin of Saul ("obedience is better than sacrifice," *šĕmōʿa mizzebaḥ ṭôb*) and the similar density of expression in v. 23b passing judgment on

24 Saul said to Samuel, "I have sinned; for I have transgressed the order *(Heb., literally "mouth"; NRSV, commandment)* of the Lord and your words, because I feared the people and obeyed their voice. [25]Now therefore, I pray, pardon my sin, and return with me, so that I may worship the Lord." [26]*Samuel said to Saul, "I will not return with you; for you have rejected the word of the Lord, and the Lord has rejected you from being king over Israel." [27]As Samuel turned to go away, Saul caught hold of the hem of his robe, and it tore. [28]And Samuel said to him, "The Lord has torn the kingdom of Israel from you this very day, and has given it to a neighbor of yours, who is better than you. [29]Moreover the Glory of Israel will not recant or change his mind; for he is not a mortal, that he should change his mind." [30]Then Saul said, "I have sinned; yet honor me now before the elders of my people and before Israel, and return with me, so that I may worship the Lord your God." [31]*So Samuel turned back after Saul; and Saul worshiped the Lord.

32 Then Samuel said, "Bring Agag king of the Amalekites here to me." And Agag came to him haltingly. Agag said, "Surely this is the bitterness of death." [33]But Samuel said,

"As your sword has made women childless,
so your mother shall be childless among
women."
And Samuel hewed Agag in pieces before the Lord in Gilgal.

34 Then Samuel went to Ramah; and Saul went up to his house in Gibeah of Saul. [35]*Samuel did not see Saul again until the day of his death, but Samuel grieved over Saul. And the Lord was sorry that he had made Saul king over Israel.*

16 *The Lord said to Samuel, "How long will you grieve over Saul? I have rejected him from being king*

Saul sum up within the poetic passage the point of the whole story.

---

over Israel. Fill your horn with oil and set out; I will send you to Jesse the Bethlehemite, for I have provided for myself a king among his sons." ²Samuel said, "How can I go? If Saul hears of it, he will kill me." And the LORD said, "Take a heifer with you, and say, 'I have come to sacrifice to the LORD.' ³Invite Jesse to the sacrifice, and I will show you what you shall do; and you shall anoint for me the one whom I name to you." ⁴Samuel did what the LORD commanded, and came to Bethlehem. The elders of the city came to meet him trembling, and said, "Do you come peaceably?" ⁵He said, "Peaceably; I have come to sacrifice to the LORD; sanctify yourselves and come with me to the sacrifice." And he sanctified Jesse and his sons and invited them to the sacrifice.⁵⁵

---

55. **Text signals.** Signals in the text of 1 Sam 16:1-13 point to close similarities with the anointings of Saul and Jehu. (i) David is anointed by a prophet, Samuel. (ii) There is concern for a degree of privacy: it is to be kept from Saul (v. 2); it is portrayed within the family circle (vv. 6-13, esp. 13a "in the presence of his brothers"). The place of the elders is uncertain (vv. 4b-5a). (iii) God's control of the anointing is noted repeatedly (vv. 1, 3, 7-9, 12). (iv) The purpose of the anointing was to replace the rejected Saul with a king from among Jesse's sons (v. 1). Surprisingly, there is no reference to *nāgîd* in what follows. The term will be used later of David (1 Sam 25:30; 2 Sam 5:2; 6:21; 7:8). 1 Sam 25:30 refers to the future, not to 16:1-13, and so probably has the older and secular meaning of chief or leader (see Campbell, *Of Prophets and Kings*, 54-60); 2 Sam 5:2 is not part of a story and is a quote from the tribes; 2 Sam 6:21 and 7:8 are not part of the stories of David's rise—with 6:21 pre-PR (ibid., 56-57). With Saul on the throne and exercising royal power, the prophetic editors appear to have discreetly avoided the use of *nāgîd* (as king-designate) for David in the story of David's rise to power. Amid such discretion, 16:1 is blunt—but not yet associated with David and downplayed as the identification of David approaches. (v) As a result of the anointing, David is empowered by the spirit "from that day forward" (16:13).

6 When they came, he looked on Eliab and thought, "Surely the LORD's anointed is now before the LORD." ⁷But the LORD said to Samuel, "Do not look on his appearance or on the height of his stature, because I have rejected him; for the LORD does not see as mortals see; they look on the outward appearance, but the LORD looks on the heart." ⁸Then Jesse called Abinadab, and made him pass before Samuel. He said, "Neither has the LORD chosen this one." ⁹Then Jesse made Shammah pass by. And he said, "Neither has the LORD chosen this one." ¹⁰Jesse made seven of his sons pass before Samuel, and Samuel said to Jesse, "The LORD has not chosen any of these." ¹¹Samuel said to Jesse, "Are all the youths (Heb.; NRSV, your sons) here?" And he said, "There remains yet the youngest, but he is keeping the sheep." And Samuel said to Jesse, "Send and bring him; for we will not sit down until he comes here." ¹²He sent and brought him in. Now he was ruddy, and had beautiful eyes, and was handsome. The LORD said, "Rise and anoint him; for this is the one." ¹³Then Samuel took the horn of oil, and anointed him in the presence of his brothers; and the spirit of the LORD came mightily upon David from that day forward. Samuel then set out and went to Ramah.⁵⁶

Text-history approach. Given these signals and the silence regarding this episode within the following text, 16:1-13 can be seen as the creation of the prophetic circles claiming their mandate to establish and dismiss kings. In the stories that follow (above all, David's combat with the Philistine), it is constantly noted that YHWH is with him. The prophetic editors do not create fiction; they articulate what they see in the unfolding narrative of events. So Samuel's anointing of David is prefaced to the narrative.

Present-text potential. Following on Saul's rejection, the anointing of David seems a natural consequence. It illuminates the narrative ahead, without actually playing an explicit role within it.

56. At this point the PR has fully delineated the prophetic role in the establishment of David as king.

| After the Dtr:
indented and sans serif font | *Revision:*
royal focus | *Revision:*
national focus | Other:
double sideline |

14 Now the spirit of the LORD departed from Saul, and an evil spirit from the LORD tormented him.[57] [15]And Saul's servants said to him, "See now, an evil spirit from God is tormenting you. [16]Let our lord now command the servants who attend you to look for someone who is skillful in playing the lyre; and when the evil spirit from God is upon you, he will play it, and you will feel better." [17]So Saul said to his servants, "Provide for me someone who can play well, and bring him to me." [18]One of the young men answered, "I have seen a son of Jesse the Bethlehemite who is skillful in playing, a man of valor, a warrior, prudent in speech, and a man of good presence; and the LORD is with him." [19]So Saul sent messengers to Jesse, and said, "Send me your son David who is with the sheep." [20]Jesse took a donkey loaded with bread, a skin of wine, and a kid, and sent them by his son David to Saul. [21]And David came to Saul, and entered his service. Saul loved him greatly, and he became his armor-bearer. [22]Saul sent to Jesse, saying, "Let David remain in my service, for he has found favor in my sight." [23]And whenever the evil spirit from God came upon Saul, David took the lyre and played it with his hand, and Saul

---

It can leave the unfolding of the subsequent events substantially to the older Davidic narrative, the Story of David's Rise to power (belonging to both Judah and Israel). The minimal contributions of the prophetic editors are in 1 Sam 25:1; 28:17-19a; and 2 Sam 5:2bβ. The more extensive prophetic editing resumes in 2 Samuel 7.

57. 1 Sam 16:14 is a hugely significant verse, perhaps an interpretative development of what is in v. 15. It is important to note that 9:1—10:16 and 11:1-11, 15 as well as 15:1-35 and 16:1-13 are all, in their own way, preparing expansively for what is said succinctly in 16:14. 16:14 is both experiential observation and theological interpretation. The prophetic contribution gives concrete shape to the theological interpretation; it may well derive from the experiential observation, preserved in the tradition. The subsequent stories of David's rise to power exemplify what 16:14 puts in a nutshell.

16:14 is often seen as the start of a narrative compilation, the Story of David's Rise, ending in 2 Sam 5:10 or 12. Both beginning and end are debated, as is even the existence of such a compilation. Our treatment of David's single combat with the Philistine will show an interpretation of tradition that increases the likelihood of a Story of David's Rise. It is important to be aware that the Story of David's Rise to power is not a piece of unified discursive writing. It is a composition, bringing together all manner of stories, story outlines, and traditions regarding David and the circumstances of his becoming king in Israel (cf. Rendtorff, "Beobachtungen zur altisraelitischen Geschichtsschreibung").

Our study of the prophetic contributions between 9:1 and 16:13 suggests that the Story of David's Rise might well have begun with the oldest level from 9:1 onwards (i.e., the plain roman text only). The contents of such a beginning would be: the original story of Saul's commission by an anonymous seer; the relief of Jabesh-gilead and Saul's coronation; the rebuke from Samuel (there is no trace of an older story without Samuel as there is in 9:1–10:16); and now, with 16:14, the seeds of Saul's destruction. The stories following 16:14 exemplify what it means to have lost the spirit of YHWH and to be tormented by an evil spirit from YHWH. Note that Samuel is present in the tradition, but in a restricted role.

Reconstructions are of course tentative. When the prophetic contributions are traced, this is what appears to precede them in the tradition. It is appropriate. An anonymous seer commissions Saul. He is made king and will be on the scene for some twenty chapters. The prophet Samuel rebukes him. The spirit of YHWH is declared to be no longer with him (16:14). The following stories depict the details of Saul's steady decline, while YHWH is portrayed as constantly with David.

| Main pre-DH: *Prophetic* Record | Other pre-DH: | **Josianic DH:** |
| its sources *and prophetic contribution* | single sideline | **from the Dtr** |

would be relieved and feel better, and the evil spirit would depart from him.[58]

17 Now the Philistines gathered their armies for battle; they were gathered at Socoh, which belongs to Judah, and encamped between Socoh and Azekah, in Ephes-dammim. ²Saul and the Israelites gathered and encamped in the valley of Elah, and formed ranks against the Philistines. ³The Philistines stood on the mountain on the

---

58. **Text signals.** The text of the story of David and Goliath—better, David and the Philistine; Goliath is named only twice (17:4, 23)—is complex, controverted, and bedeviled by misunderstanding. The signals in the text, both Hebrew and Greek, need careful attention. Comparison of the Hebrew and Greek texts reveals the presence of more than one tradition, the differences are preserved in the different textual witnesses (see E. Tov, *Textual Criticism*, 334-36 and, for a full discussion, A. Campbell, "Structure Analysis and the Art of Exegesis" also below, under **text-history approach**).

(i) **In 16:1-13,** David is the youngest son, is keeping the sheep, and is a good-looking redhead. His age is not given; his brothers are referred to as youths, *nĕʿārîm*, a key word in 17:33, here rendered "sons" in the NRSV.

(ii) **In 16:14-23,** Saul seeks a good lyre-player (vv. 16-17); a courtier, one of the young men, (*nĕʿārîm*, that word again) recommends "a son of Jesse"—nameless—who is described as "skillful in playing, a man of valor, a warrior, prudent in speech, and a man of good presence; and the LORD is with him" (v. 18); Saul sends for "your son David who is with the sheep" (v. 19) and makes him his armor-bearer (v. 21). This adds details to the picture of David, but also creates problems. David is described in v. 18, but not named; in v. 19, Saul knows his name and what he does. The description in v. 18 consists of six pairs of Hebrew words, itemizing six qualities of the kind expected of an applicant for the more sophisticated courts of David or Solomon rather than Saul's. It has been suggested that such later official requirements have been read back for David in v. 18, suppressing an earlier, less exalted description, reflected still in v. 19 (von Rad, *OT Theology*, 1.430). Whatever of the description, David is lyre-player and armor-bearer to the king.

(iii) **In 17:1-11,** a set-piece battle is prepared, a challenge is thrown down by a Philistine champion, and Saul and all Israel respond with dismay and fear.

(iv) **In 17:12-31,** this challenge scenario is repeated for forty days, morning and evening, with David shuttling between Bethlehem and his three elder brothers at the front. Vv. 19-21 suggest an army going forth to battle, not troops lining up to hear the Philistine champion for the seventy-ninth or eightieth time. All Israel flee and are afraid at the sight of the Philistine (v. 24), again difficult to reconcile with a twice-daily performance extending over forty days. The troops react as if to a challenge heard for the first time (v. 25a) and speculate on the likely reward from the king to the man who kills him (v. 25b). David works the troops to hear this reward repeated; word reaches Saul who sends for him. Here David is not the armor-bearer, standing at the king's side.

(v) **In 17:32-40,** David is the armor-bearer, standing at the king's side. With Saul and all Israel in the grip of unkingly fear, David displays kingly courage. Saul's reply has bedeviled the understanding of this story. Saul's refusal is based on his assessment, according to the NRSV, that "you are just a boy and he has been a warrior from his youth." The word translated "boy" is *naʿar*. It has a wide range of meanings from infant to youth to royal overseer; it is used of soldiers who kill each other (2 Sam 2:12-17), of soldiers who have sexual intercourse (1 Sam 21:2-5), of Absalom as leader of a rebellion (2 Sam 18:5, 12), and of Jeroboam as Solomon's royal overseer (1 Kgs 11:28). Its root meaning is of dependence, either within the family or in service (see H. P. Stähli, *Knabe-Jüngling-Knecht*—who gets 17:33 wrong!). David's brothers were still within the family (16:11); David is in the service of Saul. Its precise meaning depends on the context. The context here describes David as capable of killing a

---

| After the Dtr: indented and sans serif font | *Revision: royal focus* | *Revision: national focus* | Other: double sideline |

one side, and Israel stood on the mountain on the other side, with a valley between them. [4]And there came out from the camp of the Philistines a champion named Goliath, of Gath, whose height was six cubits and a span. [5]He had a helmet of bronze on his head, and he was armed

---

lion or a bear (17:34-35); he is quick, tough, with excellent reflexes. He is big enough that the offer of Saul's armor is not bereft of all verisimilitude. He is equipped with a sling, a standard weapon of the Israelite military (cf. Judg 20:16; 2 Chron 26:14); it is not to be confused with the US slingshot (in the UK, a schoolboy's catapult). In the text, David has the capacity to kill the Philistine; faith enables him to use it.

(vi) **In 17:40-54,** there are reflections of two accounts of the combat, one extended and the other succinct (indicated in the text: see vv. 40b/48b; vv. 41/48a; vv. 50/51). In particular, the killing is explicitly reported twice.

(vii) **In 17:55–18:5,** David is portrayed as unknown to Saul, as entering Saul's service for the first time (cf. 16:22 and 18:2), and serving successfully in the army. This is not David the lyre-player and armor-bearer.

(viii) **Finally, in 18:6-30,** the two textual witnesses offer different portrayals of the jealousy of Saul for David and his attempt to kill David.

Text-history approach. These signals point to a base text that has been added to. The base text is found in both the Hebrew and Greek (LXX[B], the Codex Vaticanus); the additions are found, in the first instance, only in the Hebrew. Under any circumstances, the chapters would have demanded source-critical study; in the event, the source materials have been preserved separately in the differing textual witnesses. The interpretative question is how these materials are to be understood. The absence of the additions from the LXX does not determine dating, but it makes a post-dtr date more likely (cf. McCarter, *1 Samuel,* 306-9). In our format here, the base text is treated as original and the "additions" are marked by indent and double sideline.

---

with a coat of mail; the weight of the coat was five thousand shekels of bronze. [6]He had greaves of bronze on his legs and a javelin of bronze slung between his shoulders. [7]The shaft of his spear was like a weaver's beam, and his spear's head weighed six hundred shekels of iron; and his shield-bearer went before him. [8]He stood and shouted to the ranks of Israel, "Why have you come out to draw up for battle? Am I not a Philistine, and are you not servants of Saul? Choose a man for yourselves, and let him come down to me. [9]If he is able to fight with me and kill me, then we will be your servants; but if I prevail against him and kill him, then you shall be our servants and serve us." [10]And the Philistine said, "Today I defy the ranks of Israel! Give me a man, that we may fight together." [11]When Saul and all Israel heard these words of the Philistine, they were dismayed and greatly afraid.

> 12 Now David was the son of an Ephrathite of Bethlehem in Judah, named Jesse, who had eight sons. In the days of Saul the man was already old and advanced in years. [13]The three eldest sons of Jesse

---

Present-text potential. The text of chaps. 16–18 cannot be read as a unity. Attempts to do so invariably deal only with part of the text, not its total horizon. The text offers two versions of David's emergence at Saul's court. As a summary outline of the two stories, the text offers opportunities and choices to both the ancient storyteller and the modern reader. Both stories are scarcely to be actualized in the same telling or reading. In both stories, however, David comes to prominence by killing the Philistine challenger. In the base text, David is empowered by faith in God and acts out of the best of theological motives. In the additions, David is motivated by ambition and the hope of reward (17:25b etc.). In both, the outcome is Saul's jealousy regarding David and David's popularity and success.

Main pre-DH: *Prophetic* Record its sources *and prophetic contribution*	Other pre-DH: single sideline	**Josianic DH:** **from the Dtr**

had followed Saul to the battle; the names of his three sons who went to the battle were Eliab the firstborn, and next to him Abinadab, and the third Shammah. [14]David was the youngest; the three eldest followed Saul.[59]

[15]But David went back and forth from Saul to feed his father's sheep at Bethlehem. [16]For forty days the Philistine came forward and took his stand, morning and evening.[60]

17 Jesse said to his son David, "Take for your brothers an ephah of this parched grain and these ten loaves, and carry them quickly to the camp to your brothers; [18]also take these ten cheeses to the commander of their thousand. See how your brothers fare, and bring some token from them."

19 Now Saul, and they, and all the men of Israel, were in the valley of Elah, fighting with the Philistines. [20]David rose early in the morning, left the sheep with a keeper, took the provisions, and went as Jesse had commanded him. He came to the encampment as the army was going forth to the battle line, shouting the war cry. [21]Israel and the Philistines drew up for battle, army against army. [22]David left the things in charge of the keeper of the baggage, ran to the ranks, and went and greeted his brothers. [23]As he talked with them, the champion, the Philistine of Gath, Goliath by name, came up out of the ranks of the Philistines, and spoke the same words as before. And David heard him.[61]

24 All the Israelites, when they saw the man, fled from him and were very much afraid. [25]The Israelites said, "Have you seen this man who has come up? Surely he has come up to defy Israel. The king will greatly enrich the man who kills him, and will give him his daughter and make his family free in Israel." [26]David said to the men who stood by him, "What shall be done for the man who kills this Philistine, and takes away the reproach from Israel? For who is this uncircumcised Philistine that he should defy the armies of the living God?" [27]The people

---

59. The use of the definite article for "the battle" in v. 13 might suggest reference to the scene already told in vv. 1-11. That need not be the case; despite the article, the Hebrew usage may be simply "to battle/to war" (cf. 1 Sam 4:1; 7:10; 17:1; 23:8 and most occurrences).

60. **Text signals.** Verse 15 is in tension with 16:14-23. It would be difficult to perform the function of Saul's armor-bearer and to be available to soothe Saul with lyre music whenever the evil spirit came upon him, while at the same time acting as shepherd back at Bethlehem. V. 16 is in tension with 17:19-25, which gives the strong impression of narrating the confrontation for the first time—especially the details in v. 19 and the introduction by name of the Philistine in v. 23.

Text-history approach. Both vv. 15 and 16 are bridge passages, offering a possibility for blending the two stories into a single superficial context. To the experienced storyteller or reader, they signal where the text is changing from one version to another.

Present-text potential. Even with these verses, the text cannot be read as a unity except at a most superficial level. These bridge verses, along with v. 31, are evidence that the text holds both versions of David's exploit within a single context, as versions of a single triumph. Multiple or complex motivation for a single act is not a modern discovery.

61. As in vv. 15-16, a bridging function is operating here with the phrase "the same words as before." It avoids the repetition of vv. 8-10. The Hebrew is literally "as these words," a possible introduction but without any following speech.

| After the Dtr:
indented and sans serif font | *Revision:*
royal focus | *Revision:*
national focus | Other:
double sideline |

answered him in the same way, "So shall it be done for the man who kills him."

28 His eldest brother Eliab heard him talking to the men; and Eliab's anger was kindled against David. He said, "Why have you come down? With whom have you left those few sheep in the wilderness? I know your presumption and the evil of your heart; for you have come down just to see the battle." [29]David said, "What have I done now? It was only a question." [30]He turned away from him toward another and spoke in the same way; and the people answered him again as before.

31 When the words that David spoke were heard, they repeated them before Saul; and he sent for him.[62]

[32]David said to Saul, "Let no one's heart fail because of him; your servant will go and fight with this Philistine." [33]Saul said to David, "You are not able to go against this Philistine to fight with him; for you are just a youth (*Heb.*; NRSV, *boy)*, and he has been a warrior from his youth." [34]But David said to Saul, "Your servant used to keep sheep for his father; and whenever a lion or a bear came, and took a lamb from the flock, [35]I

went after it and struck it down, rescuing the lamb from its mouth; and if it turned against me, I would catch it by the jaw, strike it down, and kill it. [36]Your servant has killed both lions and bears; and this uncircumcised Philistine shall be like one of them, since he has defied the armies of the living God." [37]David said, "The LORD, who saved me from the paw of the lion and from the paw of the bear, will save me from the hand of this Philistine." So Saul said to David, "Go, and may the LORD be with you!"[63]

38 Saul clothed David with his armor; he put a bronze helmet on his head and clothed him with a coat of mail. [39]David strapped Saul's sword over the armor, and he tried in vain to walk, for he was not used to them. Then David said to Saul, "I cannot walk with these; for I am not used to them." So David removed them. [40]Then he took his staff in his hand, and chose five smooth stones from the wadi, and put them in his shepherd's bag, in the pouch; his sling was in his hand, and he drew near to the Philistine.

41 The Philistine came on and drew near to David, with his shield-bearer in front of him.

---

62. **Text signals.** Verse 31 is in tension with several parts of the surrounding text. (i) As Saul's armor-bearer, he should be at Saul's side and not need to be sent for. (ii) V. 32 has David speak first to Saul, without waiting to be spoken to; David's words to Saul do not address the issues raised in vv. 25-27. (iii) Saul's summoning of David sits uncomfortably with his questions about David's identity in vv. 55-58.

Text-history approach. Like vv. 15-16, v. 31 makes sense as a bridge passage, leading back from the variant version into the base story.

Present-text potential. As with vv. 15-16, v. 31 is evidence that the text holds both versions of David's exploit within a single context, as versions of a single triumph.

63. This is the passage where misunderstanding has been most harmful. David's description as a youth (*na'ar*) does not disqualify him from serving with Saul's army any more than the same designation disqualified his three elder brothers (cf. 16:11). The comparison with the Philistine should make it clear: David now is what the Philistine once was—a raw recruit (not boy vs. man but beginner vs. veteran, Stoebe, *Erste Buch Samuelis*, 335). No matter how good Goliath's armor, as long as his shield is being carried for him by his shield-bearer, the Philistine is vulnerable to a projectile in the face. Slingers do not miss (Judg 20:16). David has the physical qualities and the military weapon. All he needs is nerve. According to the text, faith supplies this nerve.

Main pre-DH: *Prophetic* Record
its sources *and prophetic contribution*

Other pre-DH:
single sideline

Josianic DH:
from the Dtr

⁴²When the Philistine looked and saw David, he disdained him, for he was only a youth, ruddy and handsome in appearance. ⁴³The Philistine said to David, "Am I a dog, that you come to me with sticks?" And the Philistine cursed David by his gods. ⁴⁴The Philistine said to David, "Come to me, and I will give your flesh to the birds of the air and to the wild animals of the field." ⁴⁵But David said to the Philistine, "You come to me with sword and spear and javelin; but I come to you in the name of the LORD of hosts, the God of the armies of Israel, whom you have defied. ⁴⁶This very day the LORD will deliver you into my hand, and I will strike you down and cut off your head; and I will give the dead bodies of the Philistine army this very day to the birds of the air and to the wild animals of the earth, so that all the earth may know that there is a God in Israel, ⁴⁷and that all this assembly may know that the LORD does not save by sword and spear; for the battle is the LORD's and he will give you into our hand."

48 When the Philistine drew nearer to meet David,

> David ran quickly toward the battle line to meet the Philistine.

⁴⁹David put his hand in his bag, took out a stone, slung it, and struck the Philistine on his forehead; the stone sank into his forehead, and he fell face down on the ground.

> 50 So David prevailed over the Philistine with a sling and a stone, striking down the Philistine and killing him; there was no sword in David's hand.

⁵¹Then David ran and stood over the Philistine; he grasped his sword, drew it out of its sheath, and killed him; then he cut off his head with it.

When the Philistines saw that their champion was dead, they fled. ⁵²The troops of Israel and Judah rose up with a shout and pursued the Philistines as far as Gath and the gates of Ekron, so that the wounded Philistines fell on the way from Shaaraim as far as Gath and Ekron. ⁵³The Israelites came back from chasing the Philistines, and they plundered their camp. ⁵⁴David took the head of the Philistine and brought it to Jerusalem; but he put his armor in his tent.

> 55 When Saul saw David go out against the Philistine, he said to Abner, the commander of the army, "Abner, whose son is this young man?" Abner said, "As your soul lives, O king, I do not know." ⁵⁶The king said, "Inquire whose son the stripling is." ⁵⁷On David's return from killing the Philistine, Abner took him and brought him before Saul, with the head of the Philistine in his hand. ⁵⁸Saul said to him, "Whose son are you, young man?" And David answered, "I am the son of your servant Jesse the Bethlehemite."[64]

> **18** When David had finished speaking to Saul, the soul of Jonathan was bound to the soul of David, and Jonathan loved him as his own soul. ²Saul took him that day and would not let him return to his father's house. ³Then Jonathan made a covenant with David, because he loved him as his own soul. ⁴Jonathan stripped himself of the robe that he was wearing, and gave it to David, and his armor, and even his sword and his bow and his belt. ⁵David went out

---

64. The term "stripling" (*'elem*) does not determine David's age here, any more than "youth" (*na'ar*) elsewhere. It occurs twice, here and in 1 Sam 20:22 (parallel with *na'ar*), where it may well refer to a young soldier accompanying Jonathan (not necessarily in the same version of the story as the "small boy" of 20:35—see below). The feminine form (*'almâ*) refers to a sexually mature young woman, unmarried or newly married.

| After the Dtr:
indented and sans serif font | **Revision:**
royal focus | Revision:
national focus | Other:
double sideline |

and was successful wherever Saul sent him; as a result, Saul set him over the army. And all the people, even the servants of Saul, approved.

6 As they were coming home, when David returned from killing the Philistine,

The women came out of all the towns of Israel, singing and dancing, to meet King Saul *(Heb.; LXX^B, to meet David)*, with tambourines, with songs of joy, and with musical instruments. [7]And the women sang to one another as they made merry,

"Saul has killed his thousands,
and David his ten thousands."

[8]Saul was very angry, for this saying displeased him *(Heb.; LXX, And the matter displeased Saul concerning this saying)*. He said, "They have ascribed to David ten thousands, and to me they have ascribed thousands."

what more can he have but the kingdom?

[9]So Saul eyed David from that day on.

10 The next day an evil spirit from God rushed upon Saul, and he raved within his house, while David was playing the lyre, as he did day by day. Saul had his spear in his hand; [11]and Saul threw the spear, for he thought, "I will pin David to the wall." But David eluded him twice.[65]

12 Saul was afraid of David.

because the LORD was with him but had departed from Saul.

[13]So Saul removed him from his presence, and made him a commander of a thousand; and David marched out and came in, leading the army. [14]David had success in all his undertakings; for the LORD was with him. [15]When Saul saw that he had great success, he stood in awe of him. [16]But all Israel and Judah loved David; for it was he who marched out and came in leading them.[66]

17 Then Saul said to David, "Here is my elder daughter Merab; I will give her to you as a wife; only be valiant for me and fight the LORD's battles." For Saul thought, "I will not raise a hand against him; let the Philistines deal with him." [18]David said to Saul, "Who am I and who are my kinsfolk, my father's family in Israel, that I should be son-in-law to the king?" [19]But at the time when Saul's daughter Merab should have been given to David, she was given to Adriel the Meholathite as a wife.

20 Now Saul's daughter Michal loved David. Saul was told, and the thing pleased him. [21]Saul thought, "Let me give her to him that she may be a snare for him and that the hand of the Philistines may be against him."

Therefore Saul said to David a second time, "You shall now be my son-in-law."

[22]Saul commanded his servants, "Speak to David in private and say, 'See, the king is delighted with you, and all his servants love you; now then, become the king's son-in-law.' " [23]So Saul's servants reported these words to David in private. And David said, "Does it seem to you a little thing to become the king's son-in-law, seeing that I am a poor man and of no repute?" [24]The servants of Saul told him, "This is what David said." [25]Then Saul said, "Thus shall you say to David, 'The king desires no marriage present except a hundred foreskins of the Philistines, that he may be avenged on the king's enemies.' " Now Saul planned to make David fall by the hand of the Philistines. [26]When his servants told David

---

65. This particular portrayal of the jealousy of Saul clearly belongs with the lyre-player/armor-bearer version of the story, rather than that of the ambitious young man on the make. The verses are marked with a double sideline because they are absent from LXX^B.

---

66. With these verses (18:14-16), the end of the story of David's rise to power is anticipated as achieved.

Main pre-DH: *Prophetic* Record
its sources and prophetic contribution

Other pre-DH:
single sideline

**Josianic DH:
from the Dtr**

these words, David was well pleased to be the king's son-in-law. Before the time had expired, *(Heb.; LXX^B lacks "Before the time had expired,")* [27]David rose and went, along with his men, and killed one hundred of the Philistines; and David brought their foreskins, which were given in full number to the king *(Heb.; LXX^B lacks "in full number"),* that he might become the king's son-in-law. Saul gave him his daughter Michal as a wife. [28]But when Saul realized that the LORD was with David, and that Saul's daughter Michal loved him, [29]Saul was still more afraid of David.

> So Saul was David's enemy from that time forward.
>
> 30 Then the commanders of the Philistines came out to battle; and as often as they came out, David had more success than all the servants of Saul, so that his fame became very great.[67]

19 Saul spoke with his son Jonathan and with all his servants about killing David. But Saul's son Jonathan took great delight in David. [2]Jonathan told David, "My father Saul is trying to kill you; therefore be on guard tomorrow morning; stay in a secret place and hide yourself. [3]I will go out and stand beside my father in the field where you are,[68] and I will speak to my father about you; if I learn anything I will tell you." [4]Jonathan spoke well of David to his father Saul, saying to him, "The king should not sin against his servant David, because he has not sinned against you, and because his deeds have been of good service to you; [5]for he took his life in his hand when he attacked the Philistine, and the LORD brought about a great victory for all Israel. You saw it, and rejoiced; why then will you sin against an innocent person by killing David without cause?" [6]Saul heeded the voice of Jonathan; Saul swore, "As the LORD lives, he shall not be put to death." [7]So Jonathan called David and related all these things to him. Jonathan then brought David to Saul, and he was in his presence as before.

8 Again there was war, and David went out to fight the Philistines. He launched a heavy attack on them, so that they fled before him. [9]Then an evil spirit from the LORD came upon Saul, as he sat in his house with his spear in his hand, while David was playing music. [10]Saul sought to pin David to the wall with the spear; but he eluded Saul, so that he struck the spear into the wall. David fled and escaped that night.

11 Saul sent messengers to David's house to keep watch over him, planning to kill him in the morning. David's wife Michal told him, "If you do not save your life tonight, tomorrow you will be killed." [12]So Michal let David down through the window; he fled away and escaped. [13]Michal took an idol and laid it on the bed; she put a net of goats' hair on its head, and covered it with the clothes. [14]When Saul sent messengers to take David, she said, "He is sick." [15]Then Saul sent the messengers to see David for themselves. He said, "Bring him up to me in the bed, that I may kill him." [16]When the messengers came in, the idol was in the bed, with the covering of goats' hair on its head. [17]Saul said to Michal, "Why have you deceived me like this, and let my enemy go, so that he has escaped?" Michal answered

---

67. The extensive discrepancy between the MT and LXX^B ends at this point.

68. The early part of v. 3 assumes a specific hiding place that is known to David and Jonathan, so that Jonathan can speak to Saul near the place and David can overhear their conversation. Within a reported story or base for storytelling, it offers a different way of telling the story from the version implied by v. 7, where Jonathan needs to tell David what was said. If the text is read this way, such variants belong in the original, offering choices to storyteller and reader.

| After the Dtr: indented and sans serif font | **Revision: royal focus** | *Revision: national focus* | Other: double sideline |

Saul, "He said to me, 'Let me go; why should I kill you?' "

18 Now David fled and escaped; he came to Samuel at Ramah, and told him all that Saul had done to him. He and Samuel went and settled at Naioth. [19]Saul was told, "David is at Naioth in Ramah." [20]Then Saul sent messengers to take David. When they saw the company of the prophets in a frenzy, with Samuel standing in charge of them, the spirit of God came upon the messengers of Saul, and they also fell into a prophetic frenzy. [21]When Saul was told, he sent other messengers, and they also fell into a frenzy. Saul sent messengers again the third time, and they also fell into a frenzy. [22]Then he himself went to Ramah. He came to the great well that is in Secu; he asked, "Where are Samuel and David?" And someone said, "They are at Naioth in Ramah." [23]He went there, toward Naioth in Ramah; and the spirit of God came upon him. As he was going, he fell into a prophetic frenzy, until he came to Naioth in Ramah. [24]He too stripped off his clothes, and he too fell into a frenzy before Samuel. He lay naked all that day and all that night. Therefore it is said, "Is Saul also among the prophets?"[69]

20 David fled.
from Naioth in Ramah.[70]
He came before Jonathan and said, "What have I done? What is my guilt? And what is my sin against your father that he is trying to take my life?" [2]He said to him, "Far from it! You shall not die. My father does nothing either great or small without disclosing it to me; and why should my father hide this from me? Never!" [3]But David also swore, "Your father knows well that you like me; and he thinks, 'Do not let Jonathan know this, or he will be grieved.' But truly, as the LORD lives and as you yourself live, there is but a step between me and death." [4]Then Jonathan said to David, "Whatever you say, I will do for you." [5]David said to Jonathan, "Tomorrow is the new moon, and I should not fail to sit with the king at the meal; but let me go, so that I may hide in the field until the third evening. [6]If your father misses me at all, then say, 'David earnestly asked leave of me to run to Bethlehem his city; for there is a yearly sacrifice there for all the family.' [7]If he says, 'Good!' it will be well with your servant; but if he is angry, then know that evil has been determined by him. [8]Therefore deal kindly with your servant, for you have brought your servant into a sacred covenant with you. But if there is guilt in me, kill me yourself; why should you bring me to your father?" [9]Jonathan said, "Far be it from you! If I knew that it was decided by my father that evil

---

69. This anecdote is presented as an explanation of the saying "Is Saul also among the prophets?" (v. 24b). The same saying is differently explained at 1 Sam 10:10-11. The single sideline serves to note the potential independence of the anecdote in relation to the surrounding text and the probability that it was not part of the PR. The explanation of this saying was not part of the PR at 1 Sam 10:5-6, 10-13a; there is nothing to suggest that it is original here. In the present text, it is one of three covert attempts to save David from Saul: Michal, 19:11-17; Samuel, 19:18-24; Jonathan, 20:1-42.

---

70. The presence of "from Naioth in Ramah" here can be understood as an insertion that would have accompanied the insertion of the anecdote in 19:18-24. "David fled" picks up the "Now David fled and escaped" of 19:18. Where David met Jonathan is unspecified and uncertain. It would depend on the location of the independent story and its integration into the context.

Main pre-DH: *Prophetic* Record
its sources *and prophetic contribution*

Other pre-DH:
single sideline

Josianic DH:
from the Dtr

should come upon you, would I not tell you?" [10]Then David said to Jonathan, "Who will tell me if your father answers you harshly?" [11]Jonathan replied to David, "Come, let us go out into the field." So they both went out into the field.

12 Jonathan said to David, "By the LORD, the God of Israel! When I have sounded out my father, about this time tomorrow, or on the third day, if he is well disposed toward David, shall I not then send and disclose it to you? [13]But if my father intends to do you harm, the LORD do so to Jonathan, and more also, if I do not disclose it to you, and send you away, so that you may go in safety. May the LORD be with you, as he has been with my father.

[14]If I am still alive, show me the faithful love of the LORD; but if I die, [15]never cut off your faithful love from my house, even if the LORD were to cut off every one of the enemies of David from the face of the earth." [16]Thus Jonathan made a covenant with the house of David, saying, "May the LORD seek out the enemies of David." [17]Jonathan made David swear again by his love for him; for he loved him as he loved his own life.

18 Jonathan said to him, "Tomorrow is the new moon; you will be missed, because your place will be empty. [19]On the day after tomorrow, you shall go a long way down; go to the place where you hid yourself earlier, and remain beside the stone there. [20]I will shoot three arrows to the side of it, as though I shot at a mark. [21]Then I will send the boy, saying, 'Go, find the arrows.' If I say to the boy, 'Look, the arrows are on this side of you, collect them,' then you are to come, for, as the LORD lives, it is safe for you and there is no danger. [22]But if I say to the young man, 'Look, the arrows are beyond you,' then go; for the LORD has sent you away. [23]As for the matter about which you and I have

spoken, the LORD is witness between you and me forever."[71]

24 So David hid himself in the field. When the new moon came, the king sat at the feast to eat. [25]The king sat upon his seat, as at other times, upon the seat by the wall. Jonathan stood, while Abner sat by Saul's side; but David's place was empty.

26 Saul did not say anything that day; for he thought, "Something has befallen him; he is not clean, surely he is not clean." [27]But on the second day, the day after the new moon, David's place was empty. And Saul said to his son Jonathan, "Why has the son of Jesse not come to the feast, either yesterday or today?" [28]Jonathan answered Saul, "David earnestly asked leave of me to go to Bethlehem; [29]he said, 'Let me go; for our family is holding a sacrifice in the city, and my brother has commanded me to be there. So now, if I have found favor in your sight, let me

---

71. Verses 14-23 are best understood as belonging to the text as part of a reported story, offering choices or opportunities to ancient storyteller and modern reader. Vv. 14-17 and v. 23 develop the theme of the future fidelity of the house of David to the house of Jonathan. It is not integrated as it could be with the flow of the present narrative. The theme would be of obvious concern to the descendants of Jonathan's son Mephibosheth (cf. 2 Sam 9:1-13; 21:7). Vv. 18-22 offer a variant version of the base story. In the base story, Jonathan conceals his intention of meeting with David by taking a boy with him for archery practice (cf. Josephus, *Antiquities* 6.239). When the boy has been sent away (v. 40), Jonathan is at liberty to meet with David. In the variant version, instead of a well-camouflaged meeting between David and Jonathan, David is to go to a hiding place he and Jonathan know (cf. 19:3a) and in due course Jonathan will shout a coded message within his hearing (cf. 20:37-39). The variant is situated within vv. 14-23.

---

get away, and see my brothers.' For this reason he has not come to the king's table."

30 Then Saul's anger was kindled against Jonathan. He said to him, "You son of a perverse, rebellious woman! Do I not know that you have chosen the son of Jesse to your own shame, and to the shame of your mother's nakedness? [31]For as long as the son of Jesse lives upon the earth, neither you nor your kingdom shall be established. Now send and bring him to me, for he shall surely die." [32]Then Jonathan answered his father Saul, "Why should he be put to death? What has he done?" [33]But Saul threw his spear at him to strike him; so Jonathan knew that it was the decision of his father to put David to death. [34]Jonathan rose from the table in fierce anger and ate no food on the second day of the month, for he was grieved for David, and because his father had disgraced him.

35 In the morning Jonathan went out into the field to the appointment with David, and with him was a little boy. [36]He said to the boy, "Run and find the arrows that I shoot." As the boy ran, he shot an arrow beyond him. [37]When the boy came to the place where Jonathan's arrow had fallen, Jonathan called after the boy and said, "Is the arrow not beyond you?" [38]Jonathan called after the boy, "Hurry, be quick, do not linger." So Jonathan's boy gathered up the arrows and came to his master. [39]But the boy knew nothing; only Jonathan and David knew the arrangement.[72]

[40]Jonathan gave his weapons to the boy and said to him, "Go and carry them to the city." [41]As soon as the boy had gone, David rose from beside the stone heap and prostrated himself with his face to the ground. He bowed three times, and they kissed each other, and wept with each other; David wept the more. [42]Then Jonathan said to David, "Go in peace, since both of us have sworn in the name of the LORD, saying, 'The LORD shall be between me and you, and between my descendants and your descendants, forever.'" He got up and left; and Jonathan went into the city.[73]

21 David came to Nob to the priest Ahimelech. Ahimelech came trembling to meet David, and said to him, "Why are you alone, and no one with you?" [2]David said to the priest Ahimelech, "The king has charged me with a matter, and said to me, 'No one must know anything of the matter about which I send you, and with which I have charged you.' I have made an appointment with the young men for such and such a place. [3]Now then, what have you at hand? Give me five loaves of bread, or whatever is here." [4]The priest answered David, "I have no ordinary bread at hand, only holy bread—provided that the young men have kept themselves from women." [5]David answered the priest, "Indeed women have been kept from us as always when I go on an expedi-

---

72. Verses 37-39 offer a continuation of the variant version. One arrow is shot rather than three, and the instruction to hurry is probably meant for David rather than the boy. What might happen in the event is not to be confused with what is narrated in the text. In the present text, it would always be possible for a storyteller to have Jonathan overcome by emotion and move beyond the arranged signal to a personal

meeting and final farewell. The text allows for the possibility, but it may be set up as a base for story-telling, offering further choices—the agreed signals or the personal meeting or both, with a change in plan. In such a text, Jonathan's message to David has been clear enough not to need repeating in v. 41.

73. Verse 42a resumes the concern of the descendants, from vv. 14-17, 23. Note that the Heb. verse numbering designates the NRSV's 20:42b as 21:1.

Veijola attributed 20:12-17, 42b to his DtrH.

Main pre-DH: *Prophetic* Record	Other pre-DH:	**Josianic DH:**
its sources *and prophetic contribution*	single sideline	**from the Dtr**

tion; the vessels of the young men are holy even when it is a common journey; how much more today will their vessels be holy?" [6]So the priest gave him the holy bread; for there was no bread there except the bread of the Presence, which is removed from before the Lord, to be replaced by hot bread on the day it is taken away.

7 Now a certain man of the servants of Saul was there that day, detained before the Lord; his name was Doeg the Edomite, the chief of Saul's shepherds.

8 David said to Ahimelech, "Is there no spear or sword here with you? I did not bring my sword or my weapons with me, because the king's business required haste." [9]The priest said, "The sword of Goliath the Philistine, whom you killed in the valley of Elah, is here wrapped in a cloth behind the ephod; if you will take that, take it, for there is none here except that one." David said, "There is none like it; give it to me."

10 David rose and fled that day from Saul; he went to King Achish of Gath. [11]The servants of Achish said to him, "Is this not David the king of the land? Did they not sing to one another of him in dances,

'Saul has killed his thousands,
and David his ten thousands'?"

[12]David took these words to heart and was very much afraid of King Achish of Gath. [13]So he changed his behavior before them; he pretended to be mad when in their presence. He scratched marks on the doors of the gate, and let his spittle run down his beard. [14]Achish said to his servants, "Look, you see the man is mad; why then have you brought him to me? [15]Do I lack madmen, that you have brought this fellow to play the madman in my presence? Shall this fellow come into my house?"[74]

---

74. **Text signals** in 21:10-15. The signal that raises the alarm about this text is the brief report to King

22 David left there and escaped to the cave of Adullam; when his brothers and all his father's house heard of it, they went down there to him. [2]Everyone who was in distress, and everyone who was in debt, and everyone who was discontented gathered to him; and he became captain over them. Those who were with him numbered about four hundred.

3 David went from there to Mizpeh of Moab. He said to the king of Moab, "Please let my father and mother come to you, until I know what God will do for me." [4]He left them with the king of Moab, and they stayed with him all the time that David was in the stronghold. [5]Then the prophet Gad said to David, "Do not remain in the stronghold; leave, and go into the land of Judah." So David left, and went into the forest of Hereth.

6 Saul heard that David and those who were with him had been located. Saul was sitting at Gibeah, under the tamarisk tree on the height,

---

Achish of David's identity and recent history. Can either Achish or the audience be so short of memory as to have forgotten this by 1 Sam 27:1-12?

Text-history approach. A growth-of-text hypothesis assumes that the anecdote was known and valued as a record of David's ingenuity and so needed to be preserved. It could not be situated earlier than David's definitive break with Saul. It needed to be situated as far away from 1 Sam 27:1-12 as possible.

Present-text potential. The anecdote provides a rationale for what is basically David's civil war with Saul. David's choices were limited. Taking refuge with Achish had proved impossible. So the life of a resistance fighter in Judah was all that was left to him (chaps. 22–26). Later, the Achish option proves possible; the text leaves storyteller and reader the task of rendering this plausible. In the later episode, a storyteller might cope with both (e.g., by having a courtier say, "Be careful of this man, my lord; remember, he can be treacherous."); the text, however, does not.

| After the Dtr: indented and sans serif font | **Revision: royal focus** | Revision: national focus | Other: double sideline |

with his spear in his hand, and all his servants were standing around him. ⁷Saul said to his servants who stood around him, "Hear now, you Benjaminites; will the son of Jesse give every one of you fields and vineyards, will he make you all commanders of thousands and commanders of hundreds? ⁸Is that why all of you have conspired against me? No one discloses to me when my son makes a league with the son of Jesse, none of you is sorry for me or discloses to me that my son has stirred up my servant against me, to lie in wait, as he is doing today." ⁹Doeg the Edomite, who was in charge of Saul's servants, answered, "I saw the son of Jesse coming to Nob, to Ahimelech son of Ahitub; ¹⁰he inquired of the Lord for him, gave him provisions, and gave him the sword of Goliath the Philistine."

11 The king sent for the priest Ahimelech son of Ahitub and for all his father's house, the priests who were at Nob; and all of them came to the king. ¹²Saul said, "Listen now, son of Ahitub." He answered, "Here I am, my lord." ¹³Saul said to him, "Why have you conspired against me, you and the son of Jesse, by giving him bread and a sword, and by inquiring of God for him, so that he has risen against me, to lie in wait, as he is doing today?"

14 Then Ahimelech answered the king, "Who among all your servants is so faithful as David? He is the king's son-in-law, and is quick to do your bidding, and is honored in your house. ¹⁵Is today the first time that I have inquired of God for him? By no means! Do not let the king impute anything to his servant or to any member of my father's house; for your servant has known nothing of all this, much or little." ¹⁶The king said, "You shall surely die, Ahimelech, you and all your father's house." ¹⁷The king said to the guard who stood around him, "Turn and kill the priests of the Lord, because their hand also is with David; they knew

that he fled, and did not disclose it to me." But the servants of the king would not raise their hand to attack the priests of the Lord. ¹⁸Then the king said to Doeg, "You, Doeg, turn and attack the priests." Doeg the Edomite turned and attacked the priests; on that day he killed eighty-five who wore the linen ephod. ¹⁹Nob, the city of the priests, he put to the sword; men and women, children and infants, oxen, donkeys, and sheep, he put to the sword.⁷⁵

20 But one of the sons of Ahimelech son of Ahitub, named Abiathar, escaped and fled after David. ²¹Abiathar told David that Saul had killed the priests of the Lord. ²²David said to Abiathar, "I knew on that day, when Doeg the Edomite was there, that he would surely tell Saul. I am responsible for the lives of all your father's house. ²³Stay with me, and do not be afraid; for the one who seeks my life seeks your life; you will be safe with me."

23 Now they told David, "The Philistines are fighting against Keilah, and are robbing the threshing floors." ²David inquired of the Lord, "Shall I go and attack these Philistines?" The Lord said to David, "Go and attack the Philistines and save Keilah." ³But David's men said to him, "Look, we are afraid here in Judah; how much more then if we go to Keilah against the armies of the Philistines?" ⁴Then David inquired of the Lord again. The Lord answered him, "Yes, go down to Keilah; for I will give the Philistines into your hand." ⁵So David and his men went to Keilah, fought with the Philistines, brought away their livestock, and dealt them a heavy defeat. Thus David rescued the inhabitants of Keilah.

---

75. Veijola attributed 22:18βγ to his DtrH and 22:19 to his DtrP.

Main pre-DH: *Prophetic* Record
its sources *and prophetic contribution*

Other pre-DH:
single sideline

Josianic DH:
from the Dtr

6 When Abiathar son of Ahimelech fled to David at Keilah, he came down with an ephod in his hand.[76]

[7]Now it was told Saul that David had come to Keilah. And Saul said, "God has given him into my hand; for he has shut himself in by entering a town that has gates and bars." [8]Saul summoned all the people to war, to go down to Keilah, to besiege David and his men. [9]When David learned that Saul was plotting evil against him, he said to the priest Abiathar, "Bring the ephod here." [10]David said, "O LORD, the God of Israel, your servant has heard that Saul seeks to come to Keilah, to destroy the city on my account. [11]And now, will Saul come down as your servant has heard? O LORD, the God of Israel, I beseech you, tell your servant." The LORD said, "He will come down." [12]Then David said, "Will the men of Keilah surrender me and my men into the hand of Saul?" The LORD said, "They will surrender you." [13]Then David and his men, who were about six hundred, set out and left Keilah; they wandered wherever they could go. When Saul was told that David had escaped from Keilah, he gave up the expedition. [14]David remained in the strongholds in the wilderness, in the hill country of the Wilderness of Ziph. Saul sought him every day, but the LORD did not give him into his hand.[77]

15 David was in the Wilderness of Ziph at Horesh when he learned that Saul had come out to seek his life. [16]Saul's son Jonathan set out and came to David at Horesh; there he strengthened

---

76. As a note explaining how David had the ephod available to him—a privileged means of access to God's will—this could have become part of the text at any time, from its origin on.

77. **Text signals.** Tensions begin here that extend into chap. 26; it will help to see them as a whole. (i) In 23:13, Saul gives up the expedition; in 23:14, Saul is seeking David every day. Having lost a battle, Saul continues the war. Despite the relative proximity of Keilah to Ziph, the narrative flow is abrupt. (ii) Ziphites report David's whereabouts to Saul in

23:19-24; they are not mentioned again until 26:1. (iii) These Ziphites give Saul remarkably precise information on David's whereabouts (23:19), the same information that Saul acts on in 26:1. Yet Saul sends them back to acquire further information (23:22-23). (iv) The same verse that has the Ziphites return "ahead of Saul" begins an anecdote about David and his men in the wilderness of Maon (23:24). This episode leads into the story of Saul's search for David near En-gedi (chap. 24). (v) Signals to be discussed below, under chap. 24, suggest that it is an outline for a story based on chap. 26.

Text-history approach. First, it seems likely that the Ziphite information was associated with the story in chap. 26 and that the pursuit in the wilderness of Maon was preserved in association with chap. 24. Second, assuming that chap. 24 is the derivative text, it seems likely that the material in 23:24b—24:22 has been added to the Ziphite narrative, offering another story of a similar episode with similar emphases. The expansion can have been made at any time, from the origin on (hence our single sideline).

This sequence (associating the Ziphite information with the story in chap. 26) and 23:19 would make much more sense, in view of 23:22-23, if the precise details given at the end of v. 19 were a later migration from 26:1. What is not clear is how they may have found their way to v. 19.

Present-text potential. Taken as a single narrative, the present text interweaves episodes concerning David's friends and foes. It emphasizes Saul's unrelenting pursuit: at Keilah, so ironically; in the wilderness of Maon; in the wilderness of En-gedi; in the wilderness of Ziph. It singles out the support given David: by Jonathan (23:16-18) and Abigail (chap. 25), with emphasis from both on David's future kingship. The Nabal and Abigail story is appropriately associated with David's time in Maon (cf. 25:2). 1 Samuel 26 leads into David's sojourn outside Judah (cf. 26:18-20).

| After the Dtr: indented and sans serif font | **Revision: royal focus** | Revision: national focus | Other: double sideline |

his hand through the LORD. [17]He said to him, "Do not be afraid; for the hand of my father Saul shall not find you; you shall be king over Israel, and I shall be second to you; my father Saul also knows that this is so." [18]Then the two of them made a covenant before the LORD; David remained at Horesh, and Jonathan went home.[78]

19 Then some Ziphites went up to Saul at Gibeah and said, "David is hiding among us in the strongholds of Horesh, on the hill of Hachilah, which is south of Jeshimon. [20]Now, O king, whenever you wish to come down, do so; and our part will be to surrender him into the king's hand." [21]Saul said, "May you be blessed by the LORD for showing me compassion! [22]Go and make sure once more; find out exactly where he is, and who has seen him there; for I am told that he is very cunning. [23]Look around and learn all the hiding places where he lurks, and come back to me with sure information. Then I will go with you; and if he is in the land, I will search him out among all the thousands of Judah." [24]So they set out and went to Ziph ahead of Saul.

David and his men were in the wilderness of Maon, in the Arabah to the south of Jeshimon. [25]Saul and his men went to search for him. When David was told, he went down to the rock and stayed in the wilderness of Maon. When Saul heard that, he pursued David into the wilderness of Maon. [26]Saul went on one side of the mountain, and David and his men on the other side of the mountain. David was hurrying to get away from Saul, while Saul and his men were closing in on David and his men to capture them. [27]Then a messenger came to Saul, saying, "Hurry and come; for the Philistines have made a raid on the land." [28]So Saul stopped pursuing David, and went against the Philistines; there-

fore that place was called the Rock of Escape. [29]David then went up from there, and lived in the strongholds of En-gedi.

24 When Saul returned from following the Philistines, he was told, "David is in the wilderness of En-gedi." [2]Then Saul took three thousand chosen men out of all Israel, and went to look for David and his men in the direction of the Rocks of the Wild Goats. [3]He came to the sheepfolds beside the road, where there was a cave; and Saul went in to relieve himself. Now David and his men were sitting in the innermost parts of the cave. [4]The men of David said to him, "Here is the day of which the LORD said to you, 'I will give your enemy into your hand, and you shall do to him as it seems good to you.' " Then David went and stealthily cut off a corner of Saul's cloak. [5]Afterward David was stricken to the heart because he had cut off a corner of Saul's cloak. [6]He said to his men, "The LORD forbid that I should do this thing to my lord, the LORD's anointed, to raise my hand against him; for he is the LORD's anointed." [7]So David scolded his men severely and did not permit them to attack Saul. Then Saul got up and left the cave, and went on his way.[79]

---

78. Veijola attributed 23:16-18 to his DtrH.

79. **Text signals.** Adumbrated earlier at 23:14, the text signals in chap. 24 must be discussed in more detail. (i) The sequence in vv. 4-7a (Heb., vv. 5-8a) is troubling. It is chiastic: kill—cloak—cloak—kill. When David's men claim that YHWH has given David's enemy into his hand (v. 4a; Heb., v. 5a), they mean no less than the killing of Saul (cf. David's explicit statement in 24:10-11 [Heb., 24:11-12] and also Abishai's proposal in 26:8). This is confirmed by David's (delayed) reaction in vv. 6-7a (Heb., vv. 7-8a). Here, killing is in view and not clipping a cloak. David did not permit the killing; the cloak was already

Main pre-DH: *Prophetic* Record
its sources *and prophetic contribution*

Other pre-DH:
single sideline

**Josianic DH:
from the Dtr**

8 Afterwards David also rose up and went out of the cave and called after Saul, "My lord the king!" When Saul looked behind him, David bowed with his face to the ground, and did obeisance. [9]David said to Saul, "Why do you listen to the words of those who say, 'David seeks to do you harm'? [10]This very day your eyes have seen how the LORD gave you into my hand in the cave; and some urged me to kill you, but I spared you. I said, 'I will not raise my hand against my lord; for he is the LORD's anointed.' [11]See, my father, see the corner of your cloak in my hand; for by the fact that I cut off the corner of your cloak, and did not kill you, you may know for certain that there is no wrong or treason in my hands. I have not sinned against you, though you

are hunting me to take my life. [12]May the LORD judge between me and you! May the LORD avenge me on you; but my hand shall not be against you. [13]As the ancient proverb says, 'Out of the wicked comes forth wickedness'; but my hand shall not be against you. [14]Against whom has the king of Israel come out? Whom do you pursue? A dead dog? A single flea? [15]May the LORD therefore be judge, and give sentence between me and you. May he see to it, and plead my cause, and vindicate me against you."

16 When David had finished speaking these words to Saul, Saul said, "Is this your voice, my son David?" Saul lifted up his voice and wept. [17]He said to David, "You are more righteous than I; for you have repaid me good, whereas I have repaid you evil. [18]Today you have explained how you have dealt well with me, in that you did not kill me when the LORD put me into your hands. [19]For who has ever found an enemy, and sent the enemy safely away? So may the LORD reward you with good for what you have done to me this day. [20]Now I know that you shall surely be king, and that the kingdom of Israel shall be established in your hand. [21]Swear to me therefore by the LORD that you will not cut off my descendants after me, and that you will not wipe out my name from my father's house." [22]So David swore this to Saul. Then Saul went home; but David and his men went up to the stronghold.[80]

---

clipped. (ii) David follows Saul out of the cave, calls out to him, and bows to the ground when Saul looks back (v. 8; Heb., v. 9). David makes a seven-verse speech and shows Saul the corner cut from his cloak. Saul replies: "Is this your voice, my son David?" (v. 16; Heb., v. 17). Two aspects are troubling. Why does the text have Saul refer to David's voice when David is there to be seen in broad daylight? What are Saul's three thousand chosen men doing all this time? It is not a night scenario, as in chap. 26. Broad daylight is assumed in chap. 24, otherwise why the cave and why show Saul the corner of his cloak (contrast with 26:16)?

Text-history approach. Read as a reported story, the text offers storyteller and reader the opportunity to build up a story akin to that of chap. 26, based on Saul's putting his life in David's hands by entering a cave where David was. Imagination will smooth out what the text has left in tension.

Present-text potential. While the text is best recognized as a reported story or base for storytelling, it can be read without attention to the kind of signals noted above, taking up the opportunity it offers without placing a demand on the imagination of the ancient storyteller or the modern reader.

25 *Now Samuel died; and all Israel assembled and mourned for him. They buried him at his home in Ramah.*[81]

---

80. Veijola attributed 24:17-18, (19a), 19b-22a to his DtrH (Heb., 24:18-19, [20a], 20b-23a).

81. It is highly probable that this notice of Samuel's death and burial comes from the PR. The Davidic

---

Then David got up and went down to the wilderness of Paran.

2 There was a man in Maon, whose property was in Carmel. The man was very rich; he had three thousand sheep and a thousand goats. He was shearing his sheep in Carmel. ³Now the name of the man was Nabal, and the name of his wife Abigail. The woman was clever and beautiful, but the man was surly and mean; he was a Calebite. ⁴David heard in the wilderness that Nabal was shearing his sheep. ⁵So David sent ten young men; and David said to the young men, "Go up to Carmel, and go to Nabal, and greet him in my name. ⁶Thus you shall salute him: 'Peace be to you, and peace be to your house, and peace be to all that you have. ⁷I hear that you have shearers; now your shepherds have been with us, and we did them no harm, and they missed nothing, all the time they were in Carmel. ⁸Ask your young men, and they will tell you. Therefore let my young men find favor in your sight; for we have come on a feast day.

Please give whatever you have at hand to your servants and to your son David.' "

9 When David's young men came, they said all this to Nabal in the name of David; and then they waited. ¹⁰But Nabal answered David's servants, "Who is David? Who is the son of Jesse? There are many servants today who are breaking away from their masters. ¹¹Shall I take my bread and my water and the meat that I have butchered for my shearers, and give it to men who come from I do not know where?" ¹²So David's young men turned away, and came back and told him all this. ¹³David said to his men, "Every man strap on his sword!" And every one of them strapped on his sword; David also strapped on his sword; and about four hundred men went up after David, while two hundred remained with the baggage.

14 But one of the young men told Abigail, Nabal's wife, "David sent messengers out of the wilderness to salute our master; and he shouted insults at them. ¹⁵Yet the men were very good to us, and we suffered no harm, and we never missed anything when we were in the fields, as long as we were with them; ¹⁶they were a wall to us both by night and by day, all the while we were with them keeping the sheep. ¹⁷Now therefore know this and consider what you should do; for evil has been decided against our master and against all his house; he is so ill-natured that no one can speak to him."

18 Then Abigail hurried and took two hundred loaves, two skins of wine, five sheep ready dressed, five measures of parched grain, one hundred clusters of raisins, and two hundred cakes of figs. She loaded them on donkeys ¹⁹and said to her young men, "Go on ahead of me; I am coming after you." But she did not tell her husband Nabal. ²⁰As she rode on the donkey and came down under cover of the mountain, David and his men came down toward her; and she met

---

narrative needed Samuel dead before the vision of chap. 28; it is noted at 28:3. Samuel plays a small role in the narrative prior to the PR. In the early version of 1 Samuel 9–10, Saul is commissioned by an anonymous prophet. Samuel rebuked Saul in an early version of 1 Samuel 15. An anecdote may have claimed Samuel's protection of David against Saul (1 Sam 19:18-24). In 1 Samuel 28 (without vv. 17-19a), the dead Samuel foretells Israel's imminent defeat. It is not much.

The prophetic editors responsible for incorporating the traditions of Samuel's birth, his involvement in the emergence of the monarchy, his dismissal of Saul and anointing of David, are much more likely to have insisted on a notice of his death and burial here. The figure of Samuel as a prophet to all Israel, whom "all Israel" mourned, is a figure from the PR.

Main pre-DH: *Prophetic* Record its sources *and prophetic contribution*	Other pre-DH: single sideline	**Josianic DH:** **from the Dtr**

them. [21]Now David had said, "Surely it was in vain that I protected all that this fellow has in the wilderness, so that nothing was missed of all that belonged to him; but he has returned me evil for good. [22]God do so to David and more also, if by morning I leave so much as one male of all who belong to him."

23 When Abigail saw David, she hurried and alighted from the donkey, fell before David on her face, bowing to the ground. [24]She fell at his feet and said, "Upon me alone, my lord, be the guilt; please let your servant speak in your ears, and hear the words of your servant. [25]My lord, do not take seriously this ill-natured fellow, Nabal; for as his name is, so is he; Nabal is his name, and folly is with him; but I, your servant, did not see the young men of my lord, whom you sent.

26 Now then, my lord, as the LORD lives, and as you yourself live, since the LORD has restrained you from bloodguilt and from taking vengeance with your own hand, now let your enemies and those who seek to do evil to my lord be like Nabal. [27]And now let this present that your servant has brought to my lord be given to the young men who follow my lord. [28]Please forgive the trespass of your servant; for the LORD will certainly make my lord a sure house, because my lord is fighting the battles of the LORD; and evil shall not be found in you so long as you live. [29]If anyone should rise up to pursue you and to seek your life, the life of my lord shall be bound in the bundle of the living under the care of the LORD your God; but the lives of your enemies he shall sling out as from the hollow of a sling. [30]When the LORD has done to my lord according to all the good that he has spoken concerning you, and has appointed you prince over Israel, [31]my lord shall have no cause of grief, or pangs of conscience, for having shed blood without cause or for having saved himself. And when the

LORD has dealt well with my lord, then remember your servant."[82]

32 David said to Abigail, "Blessed be the LORD, the God of Israel, who sent you to meet me today! [33]Blessed be your good sense, and blessed be you, who have kept me today from bloodguilt and from avenging myself by my own hand! [34]For as surely as the LORD the God of Israel lives, who has restrained me from hurting you, unless you had hurried and come to meet me, truly by morning there would not have been left to Nabal so much as one male." [35]Then David received from her hand what she had brought him; he said to her, "Go up to your house in peace; see, I have heeded your voice, and I have granted your petition."

36 Abigail came to Nabal; he was holding a feast in his house, like the feast of a king. Nabal's heart was merry within him, for he was very drunk; so she told him nothing at all until the morning light. [37]In the morning, when the wine had gone out of Nabal, his wife told him these things, and his heart died within him; he became like a stone. [38]About ten days later the LORD struck Nabal, and he died.

39 When David heard that Nabal was dead, he said, "Blessed be the LORD who has judged the case of Nabal's insult to me, and has kept back his servant from evil; the LORD has returned the evildoing of Nabal upon his own head." Then David sent and wooed Abigail, to make her his wife. [40]When David's servants

---

82. King-designate would be an unlikely meaning for "prince" (*nāgîd*) in v. 30. "Why should courtly praise stop at the stage of 'almost-but-not-quite king'? But if *nāgîd* were to have become an acceptable way of referring to David's status, as uncrowned leader [while Saul was still king], . . . its use here would be most appropriate" (Campbell, *Of Prophets and Kings*, 59). See 2 Sam 6:21 and 1 Kgs 1:35.

| After the Dtr: indented and sans serif font | **Revision: royal focus** | Revision: national focus | Other: double sideline |

came to Abigail at Carmel, they said to her, "David has sent us to you to take you to him as his wife." [41]She rose and bowed down, with her face to the ground, and said, "Your servant is a slave to wash the feet of the servants of my lord." [42]Abigail got up hurriedly and rode away on a donkey; her five maids attended her. She went after the messengers of David and became his wife.[83]

43 David also married Ahinoam of Jezreel; both of them became his wives. [44]Saul had given his daughter Michal, David's wife, to Palti son of Laish, who was from Gallim.

26 Then the Ziphites came to Saul at Gibeah, saying, "David is in hiding on the hill of Hachilah, which is opposite Jeshimon." [2]So Saul rose and went down to the Wilderness of Ziph, with three thousand chosen men of Israel, to seek David in the Wilderness of Ziph. [3]Saul encamped on the hill of Hachilah, which is opposite Jeshimon beside the road. But David remained in the wilderness. When he learned that Saul came after him into the wilderness, [4]David sent out spies, and learned that Saul had indeed arrived. [5]Then David set out and came to the place where Saul had encamped; and David saw the place where Saul lay, with Abner son of Ner, the commander of his army. Saul was lying within the encampment, while the army was encamped around him.

6 Then David said to Ahimelech the Hittite, and to Joab's brother Abishai son of Zeruiah, "Who will go down with me into the camp to Saul?" Abishai said, "I will go down with you." [7]So David and Abishai went to the army by night; there Saul lay sleeping within the encamp-

ment, with his spear stuck in the ground at his head; and Abner and the army lay around him. [8]Abishai said to David, "God has given your enemy into your hand today; now therefore let me pin him to the ground with one stroke of the spear; I will not strike him twice." [9]But David said to Abishai, "Do not destroy him; for who can raise his hand against the LORD's anointed, and be guiltless?" [10]David said, "As the LORD lives, the LORD will strike him down; or his day will come to die; or he will go down into battle and perish. [11]The LORD forbid that I should raise my hand against the LORD's anointed; but now take the spear that is at his head, and the water jar, and let us go." [12]So David took the spear that was at Saul's head and the water jar, and they went away. No one saw it, or knew it, nor did anyone awake; for they were all asleep, because a deep sleep from the LORD had fallen upon them.

13 Then David went over to the other side, and stood on top of a hill far away, with a great distance between them. [14]David called to the army and to Abner son of Ner, saying, "Abner! Will you not answer?" Then Abner replied, "Who are you that calls to the king?" [15]David said to Abner, "Are you not a man? Who is like you in Israel? Why then have you not kept watch over your lord the king? For one of the people came in to destroy your lord the king. [16]This thing that you have done is not good. As the LORD lives, you deserve to die, because you have not kept watch over your lord, the LORD's anointed. See now, where is the king's spear, or the water jar that was at his head?"

17 Saul recognized David's voice, and said, "Is this your voice, my son David?" David said, "It is my voice, my lord, O king." [18]And he added, "Why does my lord pursue his servant? For what have I done? What guilt is on my hands? [19]Now therefore let my lord the king hear the words of his servant. If it is the LORD

---

83. Veijola attributed 25:21-22, 23b, 24b-26, 28-34, 39a* to his DtrH.

Main pre-DH: *Prophetic* Record its sources *and prophetic contribution*	Other pre-DH: single sideline	**Josianic DH:** **from the Dtr**

who has stirred you up against me, may he accept an offering; but if it is mortals, may they be cursed before the LORD, for they have driven me out today from my share in the heritage of the LORD, saying, 'Go, serve other gods.' 20Now therefore, do not let my blood fall to the ground, away from the presence of the LORD; for the king of Israel has come out to seek a single flea, like one who hunts a partridge in the mountains."

21 Then Saul said, "I have done wrong; come back, my son David, for I will never harm you again, because my life was precious in your sight today; I have been a fool, and have made a great mistake." 22David replied, "Here is the spear, O king! Let one of the young men come over and get it. 23The LORD rewards everyone for his righteousness and his faithfulness; for the LORD gave you into my hand today, but I would not raise my hand against the LORD's anointed. 24As your life was precious today in my sight, so may my life be precious in the sight of the LORD, and may he rescue me from all tribulation." 25Then Saul said to David, "Blessed be you, my son David! You will do many things and will succeed in them." So David went his way, and Saul returned to his place.

27 David said in his heart, "I shall now perish one day by the hand of Saul; there is nothing better for me than to escape to the land of the Philistines; then Saul will despair of seeking me any longer within the borders of Israel, and I shall escape out of his hand." 2So David set out and went over, he and the six hundred men who were with him, to King Achish son of Maoch of Gath. 3David stayed with Achish at Gath, he and his troops, every man with his household, and David with his two wives, Ahinoam of Jezreel, and Abigail of Carmel, Nabal's widow. 4When Saul was told that David had fled to Gath, he no longer sought for him.

5 Then David said to Achish, "If I have found favor in your sight, let a place be given me in one of the country towns, so that I may live there; for why should your servant live in the royal city with you?" 6So that day Achish gave him Ziklag; therefore Ziklag has belonged to the kings of Judah to this day. 7The length of time that David lived in the country of the Philistines was one year and four months.

8 Now David and his men went up and made raids on the Geshurites, the Girzites, and the Amalekites; for these were the landed settlements from Telam on the way to Shur and on to the land of Egypt. 9David struck the land, leaving neither man nor woman alive, but took away the sheep, the oxen, the donkeys, the camels, and the clothing, and came back to Achish. 10When Achish asked, "Against whom have you made a raid today?" David would say, "Against the Negeb of Judah," or "Against the Negeb of the Jerahmeelites," or, "Against the Negeb of the Kenites." 11David left neither man nor woman alive to be brought back to Gath, thinking, "They might tell about us, and say, 'David has done so and so.' " Such was his practice all the time he lived in the country of the Philistines. 12Achish trusted David, thinking, "He has made himself utterly abhorrent to his people Israel; therefore he shall always be my servant."

28 In those days the Philistines gathered their forces for war, to fight against Israel. Achish said to David, "You know, of course, that you and your men are to go out with me in the army." 2David said to Achish, "Very well, then you shall know what your servant can do." Achish said to David, "Very well, I will make you my bodyguard for life."84

84. The sequence of the following text may seem strange until the task is recognized that confronted

³Now Samuel had died, and all Israel had mourned for him and buried him in Ramah, his own city. Saul had expelled the mediums and the wizards from the land. ⁴The Philistines assembled, and came and encamped at Shunem. Saul gathered all Israel, and they encamped at Gilboa. ⁵When Saul saw the army of the Philistines, he was afraid, and his heart trembled greatly. ⁶When Saul inquired of the LORD, the LORD did not answer him, not by dreams, or by Urim, or by prophets. ⁷Then Saul said to his servants, "Seek out for me a woman who is a medium, so that I may go to her and inquire of her." His servants said to him, "There is a medium at Endor."

8 So Saul disguised himself and put on other clothes and went there, he and two men with him. They came to the woman by night. And he said, "Consult a spirit for me, and bring up for me the one whom I name to you." ⁹The woman said to him, "Surely you know what Saul has done, how he has cut off the mediums and the wizards from the land. Why then are you laying a snare for my life to bring about my death?" ¹⁰But Saul swore to her by the LORD, "As the LORD lives, no punishment shall come upon you for this thing." ¹¹Then the woman said, "Whom shall I bring up for you?" He answered, "Bring up Samuel for me." ¹²When the woman saw Samuel, she cried out with a loud voice; and the woman said to Saul, "Why have you deceived me? You are Saul!" ¹³The king said to her, "Have no fear; what do you see?" The woman said to Saul, "I see a divine being coming up out of the ground." ¹⁴He said to her, "What is his appearance?" She said, "An old man is coming up; he is wrapped in a robe." So Saul knew that it was Samuel, and he bowed with his face to the ground, and did obeisance.

15 Then Samuel said to Saul, "Why have you disturbed me by bringing me up?" Saul answered, "I am in great distress, for the Philistines are warring against me, and God has turned away from me and answers me no more, either by prophets or by dreams; so I have summoned you to tell me what I should do." ¹⁶Samuel said, "Why then do you ask me, since the LORD has turned from you and become your enemy?

¹⁷*The LORD has done to you just as he spoke by me; for the LORD has torn the kingdom out of your hand, and given it to your neighbor, David. ¹⁸Because you did not obey the voice of the LORD, and did not carry out his fierce wrath against Amalek, therefore the LORD has done this thing to you today. ¹⁹Moreover the LORD will give Israel along with you into the hands of the Philistines; and tomorrow you and your sons shall be with me.*[85]

---

the Davidic narrators. David, now with a fighting force of 600, might have been able to tip the scales in favor of Israel and Saul at the battle of Gilboa. Such was the view of the Philistine commanders (29:4). For those asserting that David had no part in Saul's downfall, David's failure to help in the all-important confrontation with the Philistines at Gilboa had to be explained. Hence the sequence here: first, the Philistine mustering for war (28:1a); second, David's position with Achish, with all the strategic ambiguity of v. 2 (28:1b-3); third, the episode with Samuel in which Saul's fate is declared as already decreed by God (28:4-25)—help from David is of no avail; fourth, as the Philistines move toward war, the Philistine commanders have David sent back (29:1-11)—help from David is now impossible; fifth, David's successful action against the Amalekites, God being with him (30:1-31, esp. vv. 7-8, 23); sixth, Saul's failure in defeat and death (31:1-13).

---

85. **Text signals** in vv. 17-19. (i) The text quotes Samuel from the prophetic version of 1 Samuel 15, taking the kingdom from Saul in favor of David (15:28; cf. 16:1-13). (ii) The Amalekite episode as

---

Main pre-DH: *Prophetic* Record
its sources *and prophetic contribution*

Other pre-DH:
single sideline

Josianic DH:
from the Dtr

The LORD will indeed (NRSV, *also*) give the army of Israel into the hands of the Philistines."

20 Immediately Saul fell full length on the ground, filled with fear because of the words of Samuel; and there was no strength in him, for he had eaten nothing all day and all night. ²¹The woman came to Saul, and when she saw that he was terrified, she said to him, "Your servant has listened to you; I have taken my life in my hand, and have listened to what you have said to me. ²²Now therefore, you also listen to your servant; let me set a morsel of bread before you. Eat, that you may have strength when you go on your way." ²³He refused, and said, "I will not eat." But his servants, together with the woman, urged him; and he listened to their words. So he got up from the ground and sat on the bed. ²⁴Now the woman had a fatted calf in the house. She quickly slaughtered it, and she took flour, kneaded it, and baked unleavened cakes. ²⁵She

---

cause for Saul's fate goes back to the prophetic version of 1 Samuel 15; the older version dealt with rebuke rather than the rejection implied here. (iii) The theme of God's giving Israel into the hands of the Philistines occurs twice in v. 19. The NRSV's "moreover" in v. 19a renders the same Hebrew (*wĕgam*) as its "also" in v. 19b.

Text-history approach. The prophetic editors, who reshaped the older story of 1 Samuel 15 from a rebuke to Saul into the rejection of Saul, here have inserted a reference to these matters into the older account of Samuel's words of doom and death. The repetition in v. 19 is part of the normal procedure for stitching new material into old cloth.

Present-text potential. The present text can be read here for what it is: a reference to the present text of 1 Samuel 15, indicating beyond doubt that what is going to happen is God's doing, God's will declared already by the prophet. As God's predicted action, it is beyond David's responsibility.

Veijola attributed 28:17-19aα to his DtrP.

put them before Saul and his servants, and they ate. Then they rose and went away that night.

29 Now the Philistines gathered all their forces at Aphek, while the Israelites were encamped by the fountain that is in Jezreel. ²As the lords of the Philistines were passing on by hundreds and by thousands, and David and his men were passing on in the rear with Achish, ³the commanders of the Philistines said, "What are these Hebrews doing here?" Achish said to the commanders of the Philistines, "Is this not David, the servant of King Saul of Israel, who has been with me now for days and years? Since he deserted to me I have found no fault in him to this day." ⁴But the commanders of the Philistines were angry with him; and the commanders of the Philistines said to him, "Send the man back, so that he may return to the place that you have assigned to him; he shall not go down with us to battle, or else he may become an adversary to us in the battle. For how could this fellow reconcile himself to his lord? Would it not be with the heads of the men here? ⁵Is this not David, of whom they sing to one another in dances,

'Saul has killed his thousands,
    and David his ten thousands'?"

6 Then Achish called David and said to him, "As the LORD lives, you have been honest, and to me it seems right that you should march out and in with me in the campaign; for I have found nothing wrong in you from the day of your coming to me until today. Nevertheless the lords do not approve of you. ⁷So go back now; and go peaceably; do nothing to displease the lords of the Philistines." ⁸David said to Achish, "But what have I done? What have you found in your servant from the day I entered your service until now, that I should not go and fight against the enemies of my lord the king?" ⁹Achish replied to David, "I know that you are as blameless in my

---

| After the Dtr: indented and sans serif font | **Revision:** **royal focus** | *Revision:* *national focus* | Other: double sideline |

sight as an angel of God; nevertheless, the commanders of the Philistines have said, 'He shall not go up with us to the battle.' [10]Now then rise early in the morning, you and the servants of your lord who came with you, and go to the place that I appointed for you. As for the evil report, do not take it to heart, for you have done well before me. Start early in the morning, and leave as soon as you have light." [11]So David set out with his men early in the morning, to return to the land of the Philistines. But the Philistines went up to Jezreel.

30 Now when David and his men came to Ziklag on the third day, the Amalekites had made a raid on the Negeb and on Ziklag. They had attacked Ziklag, burned it down, [2]and taken captive the women and all who were in it, both small and great; they killed none of them, but carried them off, and went their way. [3]When David and his men came to the city, they found it burned down, and their wives and sons and daughters taken captive. [4]Then David and the people who were with him raised their voices and wept, until they had no more strength to weep. [5]David's two wives also had been taken captive, Ahinoam of Jezreel, and Abigail the widow of Nabal of Carmel. [6]David was in great danger; for the people spoke of stoning him, because all the people were bitter in spirit for their sons and daughters. But David strengthened himself in the LORD his God.

7 David said to the priest Abiathar son of Ahimelech, "Bring me the ephod." So Abiathar brought the ephod to David. [8]David inquired of the LORD, "Shall I pursue this band? Shall I overtake them?" He answered him, "Pursue; for you shall surely overtake and shall surely rescue." [9]So David set out, he and the six hundred men who were with him. They came to the Wadi Besor, where those stayed who were left behind.

[10]But David went on with the pursuit, he and four hundred men; two hundred stayed behind, too exhausted to cross the Wadi Besor.

11 In the open country they found an Egyptian, and brought him to David. They gave him bread and he ate, they gave him water to drink; [12]they also gave him a piece of fig cake and two clusters of raisins. When he had eaten, his spirit revived; for he had not eaten bread or drunk water for three days and three nights. [13]Then David said to him, "To whom do you belong? Where are you from?" He said, "I am a young man of Egypt, servant to an Amalekite. My master left me behind because I fell sick three days ago. [14]We had made a raid on the Negeb of the Cherethites and on that which belongs to Judah and on the Negeb of Caleb; and we burned Ziklag down." [15]David said to him, "Will you take me down to this raiding party?" He said, "Swear to me by God that you will not kill me, or hand me over to my master, and I will take you down to them."

16 When he had taken him down, they were spread out all over the ground, eating and drinking and dancing, because of the great amount of spoil they had taken from the land of the Philistines and from the land of Judah. [17]David attacked them from twilight until the evening of the next day. Not one of them escaped, except four hundred young men, who mounted camels and fled. [18]David recovered all that the Amalekites had taken; and David rescued his two wives. [19]Nothing was missing, whether small or great, sons or daughters, spoil or anything that had been taken; David brought back everything. [20]David also captured all the flocks and herds, which were driven ahead of the other cattle; people said, "This is David's spoil."

21 Then David came to the two hundred men who had been too exhausted to follow David, and who had been left at the Wadi Besor.

Main pre-DH: *Prophetic* Record
its sources *and prophetic contribution*

Other pre-DH:
single sideline

Josianic DH:
from the Dtr

They went out to meet David and to meet the people who were with him. When David drew near to the people he saluted them. ²²Then all the corrupt and worthless fellows among the men who had gone with David said, "Because they did not go with us, we will not give them any of the spoil that we have recovered, except that each man may take his wife and children, and leave." ²³But David said, "You shall not do so, my brothers, with what the LORD has given us; he has preserved us and handed over to us the raiding party that attacked us. ²⁴Who would listen to you in this matter? For the share of the one who goes down into the battle shall be the same as the share of the one who stays by the baggage; they shall share alike." ²⁵From that day forward he made it a statute and an ordinance for Israel; it continues to the present day.

26 When David came to Ziklag, he sent part of the spoil to his friends, the elders of Judah, saying, "Here is a present for you from the spoil of the enemies of the LORD"; ²⁷it was for those in Bethel, in Ramoth of the Negeb, in Jattir, ²⁸in Aroer, in Siphmoth, in Eshtemoa, ²⁹in Racal, in the towns of the Jerahmeelites, in the towns of the Kenites, ³⁰in Hormah, in Bor-ashan, in Athach, ³¹in Hebron, all the places where David and his men had roamed.

31 Now the Philistines fought against Israel; and the men of Israel fled before the Philistines, and many fell on Mount Gilboa. ²The Philistines overtook Saul and his sons; and the Philistines killed Jonathan and Abinadab and Malchishua, the sons of Saul. ³The battle pressed hard upon Saul; the archers found him, and he was badly wounded by them. ⁴Then Saul said to his armor-bearer, "Draw your sword and thrust me through with it, so that these uncircumcised may not come and thrust me through, and make sport of me." But his armor-bearer was unwilling; for he was terrified. So Saul took his own sword and fell upon it. ⁵When his armor-bearer saw that Saul was dead, he also fell upon his sword and died with him. ⁶So Saul and his three sons and his armor-bearer and all his men died together on the same day. ⁷When the men of Israel who were on the other side of the valley and those beyond the Jordan saw that the men of Israel had fled and that Saul and his sons were dead, they forsook their towns and fled; and the Philistines came and occupied them.

8 The next day, when the Philistines came to strip the dead, they found Saul and his three sons fallen on Mount Gilboa. ⁹They cut off his head, stripped off his armor, and sent messengers throughout the land of the Philistines to carry the good news to the houses of their idols and to the people. ¹⁰They put his armor in the temple of Astarte; and they fastened his body to the wall of Beth-shan. ¹¹But when the inhabitants of Jabesh-gilead heard what the Philistines had done to Saul, ¹²all the valiant men set out, traveled all night long, and took the body of Saul and the bodies of his sons from the wall of Beth-shan. They came to Jabesh and burned them there. ¹³Then they took their bones and buried them under the tamarisk tree in Jabesh, and fasted seven days.

| After the Dtr: indented and sans serif font | *Revision: royal focus* | *Revision: national focus* | Other: double sideline |

THE SECOND BOOK OF SAMUEL

1 After the death of Saul, when David had returned from defeating the Amalekites, David remained two days in Ziklag. ²On the third day, a man came from Saul's camp, with his clothes torn and dirt on his head. When he came to David, he fell to the ground and did obeisance. ³David said to him, "Where have you come from?" He said to him, "I have escaped from the camp of Israel." ⁴David said to him, "How did things go? Tell me!" He answered, "The army fled from the battle, but also many of the army fell and died; and Saul and his son Jonathan also died." ⁵Then David asked the young man who was reporting to him, "How do you know that Saul and his son Jonathan died?" ⁶The young man reporting to him said, "I happened to be on Mount Gilboa; and there was Saul leaning on his spear, while the chariots and the horsemen drew close to him. ⁷When he looked behind him, he saw me, and called to me. I answered, 'Here sir.' ⁸And he said to me, 'Who are you?' I answered him, 'I am an Amalekite.' ⁹He said to me, 'Come, stand over me and kill me; for convulsions have seized me, and yet my life still lingers.' ¹⁰So I stood over him, and killed him, for I knew that he could not live after he had fallen. I took the crown that was on his head and the armlet that was on his arm, and I have brought them here to my lord."

11 Then David took hold of his clothes and tore them; and all the men who were with him did the same. ¹²They mourned and wept, and fasted until evening for Saul and for his son Jonathan, and for the army of the LORD and for the house of Israel, because they had fallen by the sword. ¹³David said to the young man who had reported to him, "Where do you come from?" He answered, "I am the son of a resident alien, an Amalekite." ¹⁴David said to him, "Were you not afraid to lift your hand to destroy the LORD's anointed?" ¹⁵Then David called one of the young men and said, "Come here and strike him down." So he struck him down and he died. ¹⁶David said to him, "Your blood be on your head; for your own mouth has testified against you, saying, 'I have killed the LORD's anointed.' "

17 David intoned this lamentation over Saul and his son Jonathan. ¹⁸(He ordered that The Song of the Bow be taught to the people of Judah; it is written in the Book of Jashar.) He said:

> ¹⁹Your glory, O Israel, lies slain upon your
> high places!
> How the mighty have fallen!
> ²⁰Tell it not in Gath,
> proclaim it not in the streets of Ashkelon;
> or the daughters of the Philistines will
> rejoice,
> the daughters of the uncircumcised
> will exult.
> ²¹You mountains of Gilboa,
> let there be no dew or rain upon you,
> nor bounteous fields!
> For there the shield of the mighty
> was defiled,
> the shield of Saul, anointed with oil
> no more.
> ²²From the blood of the slain,
> from the fat of the mighty,
> the bow of Jonathan did not turn back,
> nor the sword of Saul return empty.
> ²³Saul and Jonathan, beloved and lovely!
> In life and in death they were not divided;
> they were swifter than eagles,
> they were stronger than lions.
> ²⁴O daughters of Israel, weep over Saul,
> who clothed you with crimson, in luxury,
> who put ornaments of gold on your
> apparel.
> ²⁵How the mighty have fallen

Main pre-DH: *Prophetic* Record
its sources *and prophetic contribution*

Other pre-DH:
single sideline

**Josianic DH:
from the Dtr**

in the midst of the battle!
Jonathan lies slain upon your high places.
   [26]I am distressed for you, my brother
     Jonathan;
greatly beloved were you to me;
   your love to me was wonderful,
   passing the love of women.
   [27]How the mighty have fallen,
   and the weapons of war perished!

2 After this David inquired of the Lord, "Shall I go up into any of the cities of Judah?" The Lord said to him, "Go up." David said, "To which shall I go up?" He said, "To Hebron." [2]So David went up there, along with his two wives, Ahinoam of Jezreel, and Abigail the widow of Nabal of Carmel. [3]David brought up the men who were with him, every one with his household; and they settled in the towns of Hebron. [4]Then the people of Judah came, and there they anointed David king over the house of Judah.

When they told David, "It was the people of Jabesh-gilead who buried Saul," [5]David sent messengers to the people of Jabesh-gilead, and said to them, "May you be blessed by the Lord, because you showed this loyalty to Saul your lord, and buried him! [6]Now may the Lord show steadfast love and faithfulness to you! And I too will reward you because you have done this thing. [7]Therefore let your hands be strong, and be valiant; for Saul your lord is dead, and the house of Judah has anointed me king over them."

8 But Abner son of Ner, commander of Saul's army, had taken Ishbaal son of Saul, and brought him over to Mahanaim. [9]He made him king over Gilead, the Ashurites, Jezreel, Ephraim, Benjamin, and over all Israel. [10]**Ishbaal, Saul's son, was forty years old when he began to reign over Israel, and he reigned two years.** But the house of Judah followed David. [11]**The time that**

David was king in Hebron over the house of Judah was seven years and six months.[1]

12 Abner son of Ner, and the servants of Ishbaal son of Saul, went out from Mahanaim to Gibeon. [13]Joab son of Zeruiah, and the servants of David, went out and met them at the pool of Gibeon. One group sat on one side of the pool, while the other sat on the other side of the pool. [14]Abner said to Joab, "Let the young men come forward and have a contest before us." Joab said, "Let them come forward." [15]So they came forward and were counted as they passed by, twelve for Benjamin and Ishbaal son of Saul, and twelve of the servants of David. [16]Each grasped his opponent by the head, and thrust his sword in his opponent's side; so they fell down together. Therefore that place was called Helkath-hazzurim, which is at Gibeon. [17]The battle was very fierce that day; and Abner and the men of Israel were beaten by the servants of David.

18 The three sons of Zeruiah were there, Joab, Abishai, and Asahel. Now Asahel was as swift of foot as a wild gazelle. [19]Asahel pursued Abner, turning neither to the right nor to the left as he followed him. [20]Then Abner looked back and said, "Is it you, Asahel?" He answered, "Yes, it is." [21]Abner said to him, "Turn to your right or to your left, and seize one of the young men, and

---

1. The DH structures the period of Israel under the monarchy around a chronological list, synchronizing the reigns of the kings of Israel and Judah, as part of a regnal framework with a potential for seven key elements comprising both factual and judgmental statements about a king. Among these elements are the age of the king at the time of his accession and the duration of his reign, as here. These regnal frameworks are attributed to the Dtr by Noth, as being "too well known to warrant detailed examination" (cf. Noth, *DH*, 101, n. 4; also p. 34); closer examination is needed and will be provided below, in 1–2 Kings.

After the Dtr:	Revision:	Other:
indented and sans serif font	*national focus*	double sideline

take his spoil." But Asahel would not turn away from following him. [22]Abner said again to Asahel, "Turn away from following me; why should I strike you to the ground? How then could I show my face to your brother Joab?" [23]But he refused to turn away. So Abner struck him in the stomach with the butt of his spear, so that the spear came out at his back. He fell there, and died where he lay. And all those who came to the place where Asahel had fallen and died, stood still.

24 But Joab and Abishai pursued Abner. As the sun was going down they came to the hill of Ammah, which lies before Giah on the way to the wilderness of Gibeon. [25]The Benjaminites rallied around Abner and formed a single band; they took their stand on the top of a hill. [26]Then Abner called to Joab, "Is the sword to keep devouring forever? Do you not know that the end will be bitter? How long will it be before you order your people to turn from the pursuit of their kinsmen?" [27]Joab said, "As God lives, if you had not spoken, the people would have continued to pursue their kinsmen, not stopping until morning." [28]Joab sounded the trumpet and all the people stopped; they no longer pursued Israel or engaged in battle any further.

29 Abner and his men traveled all that night through the Arabah; they crossed the Jordan, and, marching the whole forenoon, they came to Mahanaim. [30]Joab returned from the pursuit of Abner; and when he had gathered all the people together, there were missing of David's servants nineteen men besides Asahel. [31]But the servants of David had killed of Benjamin three hundred sixty of Abner's men. [32]They took up Asahel and buried him in the tomb of his father, which was at Bethlehem. Joab and his men marched all night, and the day broke upon them at Hebron.

3 There was a long war between the house of Saul and the house of David; David grew stronger and stronger, while the house of Saul became weaker and weaker.

2 Sons were born to David at Hebron: his firstborn was Amnon, of Ahinoam of Jezreel; [3]his second, Chileab, of Abigail the widow of Nabal of Carmel; the third, Absalom son of Maacah, daughter of King Talmai of Geshur; [4]the fourth, Adonijah son of Haggith; the fifth, Shephatiah son of Abital; [5]and the sixth, Ithream, of David's wife Eglah. These were born to David in Hebron.[2]

6 While there was war between the house of Saul and the house of David, Abner was making himself strong in the house of Saul. [7]Now Saul had a concubine whose name was Rizpah daughter of Aiah. And Ishbaal said to Abner, "Why have you gone in to my father's concubine?" [8]The words of Ishbaal made Abner very angry; he said, "Am I a dog's head for Judah? Today I keep showing loyalty to the house of your father Saul, to his brothers, and to his friends, and have not given you into the hand of David; and yet you charge me now with a crime concerning this woman. [9]So may God do to Abner and so may he add to it! For just what the LORD has sworn to David, that will I accomplish for him, [10]to transfer the kingdom from the house of Saul, and set up the throne of David over Israel and over Judah, from Dan to Beer-sheba." [11]And Ishbaal could not answer Abner another word, because he feared him.

---

2. This list of the sons born to David at Hebron (i.e., 3:2-5, with v. 6a as resumptive link) is regarded by Noth as prior to the DH, as is the parallel list for Jerusalem in 2 Sam 5:13-16. Precise attribution remains uncertain. As Noth writes: "probably" not part of the original tradition, "but surely prior to Dtr." (*DH*, 88, n. 1).

Main pre-DH: *Prophetic* Record
its sources *and prophetic contribution*

Other pre-DH:
single sideline

**Josianic DH:
from the Dtr**

12 Abner sent messengers to David at Hebron, saying, "To whom does the land belong? Make your covenant with me, and I will give you my support to bring all Israel over to you." [13]He said, "Good; I will make a covenant with you. But one thing I require of you: you shall never appear in my presence unless you bring Saul's daughter Michal when you come to see me." [14]Then David sent messengers to Saul's son Ishbaal, saying, "Give me my wife Michal, to whom I became engaged at the price of one hundred foreskins of the Philistines." [15]Ishbaal sent and took her from her husband Paltiel the son of Laish. [16]But her husband went with her, weeping as he walked behind her all the way to Bahurim. Then Abner said to him, "Go back home!" So he went back.

17 Abner sent word to the elders of Israel, saying, "For some time past you have been seeking David as king over you. [18]Now then bring it about; for the LORD has promised David: Through my servant David I will save my people Israel from the hand of the Philistines, and from all their enemies." [19]Abner also spoke directly to the Benjaminites; then Abner went to tell David at Hebron all that Israel and the whole house of Benjamin were ready to do.[3]

---

3. Beyond Veijola's position (below), attribution of at least v. 18b to the Dtr has been advocated recently by McCarter, alleging reference to 2 Samuel 7 and to David's future victories and the phrase "my servant David" (*II Samuel*, 116). However, not all oracles cited are attested in our texts (cf. 2 Sam 5:2), and the stories of David are likely to have been composed after his victories had been achieved. The usage "my servant David" is normally late (but see for example Ps 78:70; cf. Campbell, "Psalm 78"). Some expansion is certainly possible, but does not appear absolutely necessary. Its presence or absence does not affect the DH; specific formatting does not seem appropriate.

20 When Abner came with twenty men to David at Hebron, David made a feast for Abner and the men who were with him. [21]Abner said to David, "Let me go and rally all Israel to my lord the king, in order that they may make a covenant with you, and that you may reign over all that your heart desires." So David dismissed Abner, and he went away in peace.

22 Just then the servants of David arrived with Joab from a raid, bringing much spoil with them. But Abner was not with David at Hebron, for David had dismissed him, and he had gone away in peace. [23]When Joab and all the army that was with him came, it was told Joab, "Abner son of Ner came to the king, and he has dismissed him, and he has gone away in peace." [24]Then Joab went to the king and said, "What have you done? Abner came to you; why did you dismiss him, so that he got away? [25]You know that Abner son of Ner came to deceive you, and to learn your comings and goings and to learn all that you are doing."

26 When Joab came out from David's presence, he sent messengers after Abner, and they brought him back from the cistern of Sirah; but David did not know about it. [27]When Abner returned to Hebron, Joab took him aside in the gateway to speak with him privately, and there he stabbed him in the stomach. So he died for shedding the blood of Asahel, Joab's brother. [28]Afterward, when David heard of it, he said, "I and my kingdom are forever guiltless before the LORD for the blood of Abner son of Ner. [29]May the guilt fall on the head of Joab, and on all his father's house; and may the house of Joab never be without one who has a discharge, or who is leprous, or who holds a spindle, or who falls by the sword, or who lacks food!" [30]So Joab and his brother Abishai murdered Abner because he had killed their brother Asahel in the battle at Gibeon.

After the Dtr:	Revision:	Other:
indented and sans serif font	*national focus*	double sideline

31 Then David said to Joab and to all the people who were with him, "Tear your clothes, and put on sackcloth, and mourn over Abner." And King David followed the bier. [32]They buried Abner at Hebron. The king lifted up his voice and wept at the grave of Abner, and all the people wept. [33]The king lamented for Abner, saying,

> "Should Abner die as a fool dies?
> [34]Your hands were not bound,
>   your feet were not fettered;
> as one falls before the wicked
>   you have fallen."

And all the people wept over him again. [35]Then all the people came to persuade David to eat something while it was still day; but David swore, saying, "So may God do to me, and more, if I taste bread or anything else before the sun goes down!" [36]All the people took notice of it, and it pleased them; just as everything the king did pleased all the people. [37]So all the people and all Israel understood that day that the king had no part in the killing of Abner son of Ner. [38]And the king said to his servants, "Do you not know that a prince and a great man has fallen this day in Israel? [39]Today I am powerless, even though anointed king; these men, the sons of Zeruiah, are too violent for me. The LORD pay back the one who does wickedly in accordance with his wickedness!"[4]

4 When Saul's son Ishbaal heard that Abner had died at Hebron, his courage failed, and all Israel was dismayed. [2]Saul's son had two captains of raiding bands; the name of the one was Baanah, and the name of the other Rechab.

They were sons of Rimmon a Benjaminite from Beeroth.
—for Beeroth is considered to belong to Benjamin. [3](Now the people of Beeroth had fled to Gittaim and are there as resident aliens to this day).

4 Saul's son Jonathan had a son who was crippled in his feet. He was five years old when the news about Saul and Jonathan came from Jezreel. His nurse picked him up and fled; and, in her haste to flee, it happened that he fell and became lame. His name was Mephibosheth.[5]

5 Now the sons of Rimmon the Beerothite, Rechab and Baanah, set out, and about the heat of the day they came to the house of Ishbaal, while he was taking his noonday rest. [6]They came inside the house as though to take wheat,

---

4. Veijola attributed 2 Sam 3:9-10, 17-19, 28-29, 38-39 to his DtrH.

5. **Text signals** in 4:2b-4. (i) V. 2b picks up the reference to Rimmon as a Benjaminite and adds the explanation that Beeroth was considered part of Benjamin (cf. Josh 9:17, one of the four Gibeonite towns that were incorporated into Israel; also Josh 18:25). (ii) A further explanation adds that "to this day" the people of Beeroth lived in Gittaim, also a town in Benjamin (Neh 11:33). (iii) The reference to Jonathan's son, Mephibosheth, is not taken up in the context and interrupts the flow of the narrative. (iv) The names from v. 2a are repeated at the start of v. 5.

Text-history approach. Given the flow of the narrative from v. 2a to v. 5, the intervening vv. 2b-4 have the look of later additions. Vv. 2b-3 explain matters associated with Beeroth and Benjamin. V. 4 gives details of Mephibosheth, for reasons that are uncertain—there may be some association with the mention of Ishbaal as Saul's son; there may be some association with 2 Sam 21:1-14

Present-text potential. In the present text, these verses are best regarded as a couple of helpful footnotes.

Veijola attributed 4:2b-4 to his DtrH.

Main pre-DH: *Prophetic* Record	Other pre-DH:	**Josianic DH:**
its sources *and prophetic contribution*	single sideline	**from the Dtr**

and they struck him in the stomach; then Rechab and his brother Baanah escaped. [7]Now they had come into the house while he was lying on his couch in his bedchamber; they attacked him, killed him, and beheaded him. Then they took his head and traveled by way of the Arabah all night long. [8]They brought the head of Ishbaal to David at Hebron and said to the king, "Here is the head of Ishbaal, son of Saul, your enemy, who sought your life; the LORD has avenged my lord the king this day on Saul and on his offspring."

[9] David answered Rechab and his brother Baanah, the sons of Rimmon the Beerothite, "As the LORD lives, who has redeemed my life out of every adversity, [10]when the one who told me, 'See, Saul is dead,' thought he was bringing good news, I seized him and killed him at Ziklag—this was the reward I gave him for his news. [11]How much more then, when wicked men have killed a righteous man on his bed in his own house! And now shall I not require his blood at your hand, and destroy you from the earth?" [12]So David commanded the young men, and they killed them; they cut off their hands and feet, and hung their bodies beside the pool at Hebron. But the head of Ishbaal they took and buried in the tomb of Abner at Hebron.

5 Then all the tribes of Israel came to David at Hebron, and said, "Look, we are your bone and flesh. [2]For some time, while Saul was king over us, it was you who led out Israel and brought it in. The LORD said to you: It is you who shall be shepherd of my people Israel, *you who shall be ruler over Israel.*"[6] [3]So all the elders of Israel came to the king at Hebron; and King David made a covenant with them at Hebron before the LORD, and they anointed David king over Israel. **[4]David was thirty years old when he began to reign, and he reigned forty years. [5]At Hebron he reigned over Judah seven years and six months; and at Jerusalem he reigned over all Israel and Judah thirty-three years.**[7]

[6] The king and his men marched to Jerusalem against the Jebusites, the inhabitants of the land, who said to David, "You will not come in here, even the blind and the lame will turn you back"—thinking, "David cannot come in here." [7]Nevertheless David took the stronghold of Zion, which is now the city of David. [8]David had said on that day, "Whoever would strike down the Jebusites, let him get up the water shaft to attack the lame and the blind, those whom David hates." Therefore it is said, "The blind and the lame shall not come into the house." [9]David occupied the stronghold, and named it the city of David. David built the city all around from the Millo inward. [10]And David

---

6. In the Hebrew of v. 2, the phrase "you shall be ruler over Israel" not only repeats what has been said but also has the appearance of being added. "Ruler" renders the technical term *nāgîd* (king-designate) favored of the Prophetic Record (PR). It may be from the prophetic editors. On the other hand, it may be an imitation of prophetic theology. In the general usage of the PR, the status of *nāgîd* is given with the prophetic anointing; it is not normally used for a state to be achieved in the future. A person is *nāgîd* and will become *melek* (king).

7. As noted at 2:10a and 11, the DH structures the period of Israel under the monarchy around a chronological list, as part of a regnal framework with a potential for seven key elements comprising both factual and judgmental statements about a king. Among these elements are the age of the king at the time of his accession and the duration of his reign, as here. These regnal frameworks are attributed to the Dtr (cf. Noth, *DH*, 101, n. 4; also p. 34).

| After the Dtr: indented and sans serif font | Revision: national focus | Other: double sideline |

became greater and greater, for the Lord, the God of hosts, was with him.[8]

11 King Hiram of Tyre sent messengers to David, along with cedar trees, and carpenters and masons who built David a house. [12]David then perceived that the Lord had established him king over Israel, and that he had exalted his kingdom for the sake of his people Israel.

13 In Jerusalem, after he came from Hebron, David took more concubines and wives; and more sons and daughters were born to David. [14]These are the names of those who were born to him in Jerusalem: Shammua, Shobab, Nathan, Solomon, [15]Ibhar, Elishua, Nepheg, Japhia, [16]Elishama, Eliada, and Eliphelet.[9]

17 When the Philistines heard that David had been anointed king over Israel, all the Philistines went up in search of David; but David heard about it and went down to the stronghold. [18]Now the Philistines had come and spread out in the valley of Rephaim. [19]David inquired of the Lord, "Shall I go up against the Philistines? Will you give them into my hand?" The Lord said to David, "Go up; for I will certainly give the Philistines into your hand." [20]So David came to Baal-perazim, and David defeated them there. He said, "The Lord has burst forth against my enemies before me, like a bursting flood." Therefore that place is called Baal-perazim. [21]The Philistines abandoned their idols there, and David and his men carried them away.[10]

22 Once again the Philistines came up, and were spread out in the valley of Rephaim. [23]When David inquired of the Lord, he said, "You shall not go up; go around to their rear, and come upon them opposite the balsam trees. [24]When you hear the sound of marching in the tops of the balsam trees, then be on the alert; for then the Lord has gone out before you to strike down the army of the Philistines." [25]David did just as the Lord had commanded him; and he struck down the Philistines from Geba all the way to Gezer.[11]

6 David again gathered all the chosen men of Israel, thirty thousand. [2]David and all the people with him set out and went from Baale-judah, to bring up from there the ark of God, which is called by the name of the Lord of hosts who is enthroned on the cherubim. [3]They carried the ark of God on a new cart, and brought it out of the house of Abinadab, which was on the hill. Uzzah and Ahio, the sons of Abinadab, were driving the new cart [4]with the ark of God; and Ahio went in front of the ark. ([5]David and all the house of Israel were dancing before the Lord with all their might, with

---

8. The association made between 5:17 and 5:3 is evident. If the account of David's rise to power began with the defeat of the Philistine Goliath, it has to end in some association with the defeat of the Philistines. However 5:17-25 does resemble old tradition that need not have originated in its present context (cf. McCarter, *II Samuel*, 157-60). At the same time, a king needs a capital and David needed Jerusalem; once a king has a capital, he needs a palace. The text history of 5:6-10, 11-12, 17-25 comes under the rubric of the possible rather than the necessary. It need not attract source comment here.

9. This list of the sons born to David in Jerusalem is regarded by Noth as prior to the DH, as is the parallel list for Hebron in 2 Sam 3:2-5. Precise attribution remains uncertain. As Noth writes: "probably" not part of the original tradition, "but surely prior to Dtr" (*DH*, 88, n. 1).

10. Veijola attributed 5:1-2, 4-5, 11, 12a, 17a to his DtrH and 5:12b to his DtrN.

11. The continuation of the PR is to be found at 7:1.

Main pre-DH: *Prophetic* Record	Other pre-DH:	**Josianic DH:**
its sources *and prophetic contribution*	single sideline	**from the Dtr**

songs and lyres and harps and tambourines and castanets and cymbals.)[12]

6 When they came to the threshing floor of Nacon, Uzzah reached out his hand to the ark of God and took hold of it, for the oxen shook it. [7]The anger of the LORD was kindled against Uzzah; and God struck him there because he reached out his hand to the ark; and he died there beside the ark of God. [8]David was angry because the LORD had burst forth with an outburst upon Uzzah; so that place is called Perez-uzzah, to this day. [9]David was afraid of the LORD that day; he said, "How can the ark of the LORD come into my care?" [10]So David was unwilling to take the ark of the LORD into his care in the city of David; instead David took it to the house of Obed-edom the Gittite. [11]The ark of the LORD remained in the house of Obed-edom the Gittite

---

12. Along with 1 Samuel 4–6, 2 Sam 6:1-19 constitutes the only biblical tradition focused exclusively on the ark and, in particular, focusing on the ark as the manifestation of God's power and purpose. As such, 2 Sam 6:1-19 either forms the final section of the Ark Narrative or is a slightly later reflection that practically forms a single text with 1 Samuel 4–6. As noted in connection with 1 Samuel 4–6, in this tradition God's will is made known by the ark; the prophet plays no role. There would have been no place for the Ark Narrative within the PR. It is an old tradition that the Dtr took over and used to express the change of epochs within the story of Israel. For the PR, this new epoch was initiated by the prophet Samuel. For the Josianic DH, the move of the ark from Shiloh, via Kiriath-jearim, to Jerusalem is confirmation that an epoch-making change has taken place in Israel. The exchange between David and Michal, as the king returned to bless his household, most probably highlights the passing of epochs, signaled by the ark's coming to David's city. The phrase "all the house of Israel" is unlikely to be early (cf. note on 1 Sam 7:2b). The status of 6:5, 15 as later additions is probable but not demonstrable (cf. Psalm 150).

three months; and the LORD blessed Obed-edom and all his household.

12 It was told King David, "The LORD has blessed the household of Obed-edom and all that belongs to him, because of the ark of God." So David went and brought up the ark of God from the house of Obed-edom to the city of David with rejoicing; [13]and when those who bore the ark of the LORD had gone six paces, he sacrificed an ox and a fatling. [14]David danced before the LORD with all his might; David was girded with a linen ephod. ([15]So David and all the house of Israel brought up the ark of the LORD with shouting, and with the sound of the trumpet.)

16 As the ark of the LORD came into the city of David, Michal daughter of Saul looked out of the window, and saw King David leaping and dancing before the LORD; and she despised him in her heart.

17 They brought in the ark of the LORD, and set it in its place, inside the tent that David had pitched for it; and David offered burnt offerings and offerings of well-being before the LORD. [18]When David had finished offering the burnt offerings and the offerings of well-being, he blessed the people in the name of the LORD of hosts, [19]and distributed food among all the people, the whole multitude of Israel, both men and women, to each a cake of bread, a portion of meat, and a cake of raisins. Then all the people went back to their homes.

20 David returned to bless his household. But Michal the daughter of Saul came out to meet David, and said, "How the king of Israel honored himself today, uncovering himself today before the eyes of his servants' maids, as any vulgar fellow might shamelessly uncover himself!" [21]David said to Michal, "It was before the LORD, who chose me in place of your father and all his household, to appoint me as prince over Israel, the people of the LORD, that I have danced

---

| After the Dtr: | Revision: | Other: |
| indented and sans serif font | national focus | double sideline |

before the LORD. [22]I will make myself yet more contemptible than this, and I will be abased in my own eyes; but by the maids of whom you have spoken, by them I shall be held in honor." [23]And Michal the daughter of Saul had no child to the day of her death.[13]

7 Now when the king was settled in his house, **and the LORD had given him rest from all his enemies around him,** [2]the king said to the prophet Nathan, "See now, I am living in a house of cedar, but the ark of God stays in a tent." [3]*Nathan said to the king, "Go, do all that you have in mind; for the LORD is with you."*[14]

---

13. Veijola attributed 6:21* to his DtrH. Rather, the reference to David as "prince [*nāgîd*] over Israel" is earlier than the PR, one of three such uses of *nāgîd* as leader or chief (Campbell, *Of Prophets and Kings*, 54-60, esp. 57; see above 1 Sam 25:30 and below 1 Kgs 1:35).

14. Resumption of the PR from 5:25. The complexity of 2 Samuel 7 is legendary; the literature on it is endless. Our necessarily brief suggestions here are offered as helpful rather than definitive.

Text signals in 7:1-17. (i) To give rest from one's enemies around about is considered a dtr phrase (Weinfeld, *Deuteronomic School*, 343, #8). (ii) The text has Nathan take an affirmative stance toward David's proposal to build a temple (v. 3), followed promptly by a negative reaction from God (vv. 4-7). (iii) The introductory phrase, "and it was," (*wayhî*) occurs twice in v. 4. (iv) Two questions with the interrogative particle (*ha-*; vv. 5b and 7a) are separated by the statement which begins in v. 6 and prematurely implies an answer to both questions. (v) Areas of prophetic concern in 1st person divine address, redolent of the language and thought of the PR, are found in vv. 8-10, 12, 14-15. (vi) In v. 11, as well as "giving rest from enemies" (see above), the concept of appointing judges over Israel is a dtr creation. (vii) The essential communication to David that God will build him a dynasty is contained in vv. 11b and 16. (viii) Describing the temple as "a house for my name" uses dtr

name theology (cf. Weinfeld, ibid., 324-25, esp. #6). (ix) Mention of the temple interrupts discourse about the dynasty and kingdom. (x) The reference back to Saul's rejection picks up an issue significant to the PR.

Text-history approach. A growth-of-text hypothesis would see a core here applicable to David's time: an introduction (v. 1a), a discreet proposal (v. 2), a discreet divine negative (vv. 5-7*), a divine promise of a dynasty (house, v. 11b), and the promise that this dynasty will be secure (house and kingdom, v. 16).

A considerable expansion of this Davidic core bears the marks of prophetic interest: by inserting Nathan's acquiescence (v. 3), an emphasis is placed on God's will in the enterprise, mediated by a prophet; the summary of history in vv. 8-10 picks up the prophetic *nāgîd* language and uses the 1st person speech of the prophetic editing; in vv. 12, 14-15, the turn to the future prepares discreetly for the prophetic intervention of Ahijah against Solomon, tearing from him a substantial component of his kingdom (i.e., northern Israel); nevertheless, the dynastic promise is maintained, Judah alone remaining (v. 15; cf. 1 Kgs 12:20b). Part of this preparation is the restriction of the original promise of a dynasty to a narrower focus on Solomon (vv. 12, 14-15). The PR does not follow the Davidic dynasty beyond Solomon.

The Dtr's contribution, as identified here, lays stress on the perception of "rest" (cf. 1 Chron 28:2) and on Solomon's building of the temple. V. 13 continues v. 12's focus on Solomon alone. The promise of a Davidic dynasty is endorsed (v. 13b), within the context of the prophetic editing and restriction noted above (i.e., over Judah alone).

The insertion comprising vv. 6-7a* points to a strongly negative view of the Jerusalem temple, preempting the two questions that are otherwise left unanswered (see Campbell, *Of Prophets and Kings*, 72-81, especially for the language involved).

Present-text potential. This famous David passage has pivotal position in the narrative. Well after Abimelech, Israel's monarchy began with the failure of Saul. The prophets anointed David as king and now his kingship is securely established. Prophetic action will strip ten tribes from David's kingdom, but the

---

Main pre-DH: *Prophetic* Record	Other pre-DH:	**Josianic DH:**
its sources *and prophetic contribution*	single sideline	**from the Dtr**

4 But that same night the word of the Lord came to Nathan: [5]Go and tell my servant David: Thus says the Lord: Are you the one to build me a house to live in?[15]

[6]I have not lived in a house since the day I brought up the people of Israel from Egypt to this day, but I have been moving about in a tent and a tabernacle. [7]Wherever I have moved about among all the people of Israel,

Did I ever speak a word with any of the tribal leaders of Israel, whom I commanded to shepherd my people Israel, saying, "Why have you not built me a house of cedar?" *[8]Now therefore thus you shall say to my servant David: Thus says the Lord of hosts: I took you from the pasture, from following the sheep to be prince over my people Israel; [9]and I have been with you wherever you went, and have cut off all your enemies from before you; and I will make for you a great name, like the name of the great ones of the earth. [10]And I will appoint a place for my people Israel and will plant them, so that they may live in their own place, and be disturbed no more; and evildoers shall afflict them no more, as formerly,* **[11]from the time that I appointed judges over my people Israel; and I will give you rest from all your enemies.** Moreover the Lord declares to you that the Lord will make you a house. *[12]When your days are fulfilled and you lie down with your ancestors, I will raise up your off-spring after you, who shall come forth from your body, and I will establish his kingdom.* **[13]He shall build a house for my name, and I will establish the throne of his kingdom forever.** *[14]I will be a father to him, and he shall be a son to me. When he commits iniquity, I will punish him with a rod such as mortals use, with blows inflicted by human beings. [15]But I will not take my steadfast love from him, as I took it from Saul, whom I put away from before you.* [16]Your house and your kingdom shall be made sure forever before me; your throne shall be established forever. *[17]In accordance with all these words and with all this vision, Nathan spoke to David.*[16]

18 Then King David went in and sat before the Lord, and said, "Who am I, O Lord God, and what is my house, that you have brought me thus far? [19]And yet this was a small thing in your eyes, O Lord God; you have spoken also of your servant's house for a great while to come. May this be instruction for the people, O Lord God! [20]And what more can David say to you? For you know your servant, O Lord God! [21]Because of your promise, and according to your own heart, you have wrought all this greatness, so that your servant may know it.[17]

---

kingdom will not be taken from David's descendants as it was from Saul. The temple in Jerusalem that is of such central importance will be built by Solomon. A pinnacle has been reached in Israel's history and the text insists that it was God's doing.

15. The Hebrew repeats the preposition in v. 5, "to my servant to David"; rather than a title, the proper name is in apposition (cf. 1 Sam 19:4, contrasted with Pss 78:70; 89:4; 144:10). It may well be original and have been echoed by the prophetic text in v. 8, with a similar repetition.

16. The continuation of the PR is to be found at 8:15.

17. The bulk of the Davidic prayer here (i.e., vv. 18-21, 25-29) does not admit of easy attribution. Noth, fundamentally following Rost, allowed it to the original text (see Noth, *DH*, 89). It is clear that this prayer would not have come from the prophetic editors; it is focused on the dynasty of David (cf. vv. 11b, 16), with no reference to the prophetic concerns evident in the rewriting of 7:1-17. The prayer's fulsomeness is reminiscent of aspects of 1 Sam 26:18-20. The repeated use of "Lord God" (*ʾădōnāy yhwh*; cf. the NRSV's preface) does not exclude an early origin; at the same time it does not favor one. Apart from the difficult Gen 15:2 and 8, it is found as lament in Josh 7:7

After the Dtr:	Revision:	Other:
indented and sans serif font	national focus	double sideline

22Therefore you are great, O Lord God; for there is no one like you, and there is no God besides you, according to all that we have heard with our ears. 23Who is like your people, like Israel? Is there another nation on earth whose God went to redeem it as a people, and to make a name for himself, doing great and awesome things for them, by driving out before his people nations and their gods? 24And you established your people Israel for yourself to be your people forever; and you, O Lord, became their God.18

25And now, O Lord God, as for the word that you have spoken concerning your servant and concerning his house, confirm it forever; do as you have promised. 26Thus your name will be magnified forever in the saying, 'The Lord of hosts is God over Israel'; and the house of your servant David will be established before you. 27For you, O Lord of hosts, the God of Israel, have made this revelation to your servant, saying, 'I will build you a house'; therefore your servant has found courage to pray this prayer to you. 28And now, O Lord God, you are God, and your words are true, and you have promised this good thing to your servant; 29now therefore may it please you to bless the house of your servant, so that it may continue forever before you; for you, O Lord God, have spoken, and with your blessing shall the house of your servant be blessed forever."19

8 **Some time afterward,** David attacked the Philistines and subdued them; David took Metheg-ammah out of the hand of the Philistines.

2 He also defeated the Moabites and, making them lie down on the ground, measured them off with a cord; he measured two lengths of cord for those who were to be put to death, and one length for those who were to be spared. And the Moabites became servants to David and brought tribute.

3 David also struck down King Hadadezer son of Rehob of Zobah, as he went to restore his monument at the river Euphrates. 4David took from him one thousand seven hundred horsemen, and twenty thousand foot soldiers. David hamstrung all the chariot horses, but left enough for a hundred chariots. 5When the Arameans of Damascus came to help King Hadadezer of Zobah, David killed twenty-two thousand men of the Arameans. 6Then David put garrisons among the Arameans of Damascus; and the Arameans became servants to David and brought tribute. The Lord gave victory to David wherever he went. 7David took the gold shields that were carried by the servants of Hadadezer, and brought them to Jerusalem. 8From Betah and from Berothai, towns of Hadadezer, King David took a great amount of bronze.

---

and Judg 6:22, as well as in Jeremiah. It is also found in Judg 16:28; 1 Kgs 2:26 (non-dtr), and in Amos. Other occurrences in the DH include Deut 3:24; 9:26; 1 Kgs 8:53. Its use in Ezekiel is massive. The half-dozen or more occurrences in 2 Sam 7:18-29 are exceptional for the DH. A Jerusalem addition, with a focus on the dynasty seems likely. The dating for such an addition remains difficult; if vv. 22-24 are rightly assigned to the national focus within the dtr process of revision, the addition of vv. 18-21, 25-29 would have had to be earlier.

18. The similarity between 2 Sam 7:22-24 and Deut 4:7-8, 34-39 suggests attribution to the national focus; note the shift of attention from king to people, characteristic of this focus. "Lord God" (*'ādonāy yhwh*) occurs only in the initial v. 22, blending into the context.

---

19. Veijola attributed 7:8b, 11b, 13, 16, 18-21, 25-29 to his DtrH and 7:1b, 6, 11a, 22-24 to his DtrN.

| Main pre-DH: *Prophetic* Record | Other pre-DH: | **Josianic DH:** |
| its sources *and prophetic contribution* | single sideline | **from the Dtr** |

9 When King Toi of Hamath heard that David had defeated the whole army of Hadadezer, [10]Toi sent his son Joram to King David, to greet him and to congratulate him because he had fought against Hadadezer and defeated him. Now Hadadezer had often been at war with Toi. Joram brought with him articles of silver, gold, and bronze; [11]these also King David dedicated to the LORD, together with the silver and gold that he dedicated from all the nations he subdued, [12]from Edom, Moab, the Ammonites, the Philistines, Amalek, and from the spoil of King Hadadezer son of Rehob of Zobah.

13 David won a name for himself. When he returned, he killed eighteen thousand Edomites in the Valley of Salt. [14]He put garrisons in Edom; throughout all Edom he put garrisons, and all the Edomites became David's servants.

And the LORD gave victory to David wherever he went.[20]

15 So David reigned over all Israel; and David administered justice and equity to all his people.[21]

[16]Joab son of Zeruiah was over the army; Jehoshaphat son of Ahilud was recorder;

[17]Zadok son of Ahitub and Ahimelech son of Abiathar were priests; Seraiah was secretary; [18]Benaiah son of Jehoiada was over the Cherethites and the Pelethites; and David's sons were priests.

9 David asked, "Is there still anyone left of the house of Saul to whom I may show kindness for Jonathan's sake?" [2]Now there was a servant of the house of Saul whose name was Ziba, and he was summoned to David. The king said to him, "Are you Ziba?" And he said, "At your service!" [3]The king said, "Is there anyone remaining of the house of Saul to whom I may show the kindness of God?" Ziba said to the king, "There remains a son of Jonathan; he is crippled in his feet." [4]The king said to him, "Where is he?" Ziba said to the king, "He is in the house of Machir son of Ammiel, at Lo-debar." [5]Then King David sent and brought him from the house of Machir son of Ammiel, at Lo-debar. [6]Mephibosheth son of Jonathan son of Saul came to David, and fell on his face and did obeisance. David said, "Mephibosheth!" He answered, "I am your servant." [7]David said to him, "Do not be afraid, for I will show you kindness for the sake of your father Jonathan; I will restore to you all the land of your grandfather Saul, and you yourself shall eat at my table always." [8]He did obeisance and said, "What is your servant, that you should look upon a dead dog such as I?"[22]

---

20. Noth suggests that the Dtr added 8:1aα and 14b (*DH*, 89-90). If this is correct, it is likely that the Dtr was working with a southern list of David's achievements and inserted it before v. 15, which may well be the PR's summary of David's reign. The list of officials is then restricted to vv. 16-18, which (like 2 Sam 20:23-26 and 1 Kgs 4:2-6) was taken by the Dtr from official records.

21. Resumption of the PR from 7:17. The PR regularly provides a summary of the reign. The list of David's achievements (8:1b-14a), postulated by Noth, could provide this. 8:15 alone, however, is adequate and satisfactory. For the notice in the PR of David's death, see below in the initial note for 1 Kings 1–2, under **text-history approach**. The continuation of the PR is to be found at 1 Kgs 3:1 (but cf. 2:10, 12).

Veijola attributed 8:1a, 14b-15 to his DtrH.

22. 2 Sam 9:1-13 belongs to relatively early tradition. For McCarter, 2 Sam 21:1-14 and 9:1-13 "once stood in continuous narrative sequence" (*II Samuel*, 263). It is clear that the question in 9:1 presupposes the killing of Saul's descendants (cf. 21:1-14); the order of the events is therefore the reverse of the present order of the texts. But it should be equally clear that the question in 9:1 does not presuppose the

---

After the Dtr:
indented and sans serif font

Revision:
national focus

Other:
double sideline

9 Then the king summoned Saul's servant Ziba, and said to him, "All that belonged to Saul and to all his house I have given to your master's grandson. [10]You and your sons and your servants shall till the land for him, and shall bring in the produce, so that your master's grandson may have food to eat; but your master's grandson Mephibosheth shall always eat at my table." Now Ziba had fifteen sons and twenty servants. [11]Then Ziba said to the king, "According to all that my lord the king commands his servant, so your servant will do." Mephibosheth ate at David's table, like one of the king's sons. [12]Mephibosheth had a young son whose name was Mica. And all who lived in Ziba's house became Mephibosheth's servants. [13]Mephibosheth lived in Jerusalem, for he always ate at the king's table. Now he was lame in both his feet.[23]

10 Some time afterward, the king of the Ammonites died, and his son Hanun succeeded him. [2]David said, "I will deal loyally with Hanun son of Nahash, just as his father dealt loyally with me." So David sent envoys to console him concerning his father. When David's envoys came into the land of the Ammonites, [3]the princes of the Ammonites said to their lord Hanun, "Do you really think that David is honoring your father just because he has sent messengers with condolences to you? Has not David sent his envoys to you to search the city, to spy it out, and to overthrow it?" [4]So Hanun seized David's envoys, shaved off half the beard of each, cut off their garments in the middle at their hips, and sent them away. [5]When David was told, he sent to meet them, for the men were greatly ashamed. The king said, "Remain at Jericho until your beards have grown, and then return."[24]

6 When the Ammonites saw that they had become odious to David, the Ammonites sent and hired the Arameans of Beth-rehob and the Arameans of Zobah, twenty thousand foot soldiers, as well as the king of Maacah, one thousand men, and the men of Tob, twelve thousand men. [7]When David heard of it, he sent Joab and all the army with the warriors. [8]The Ammonites came out and drew up in battle array at the

---

sparing of Mephibosheth (21:7); here David does not know of his existence. Within 2 Samuel 11–20, Mephibosheth's statement to David, "all my father's house were doomed to death before my lord the king; but you set your servant among those who eat at your table" (2 Sam 19:28), presupposes the scenario of chap. 21 where descendants of Saul are still alive, but adds the fact of eating at David's table, given in chap. 9 but not in chap. 21. In all probability, we have three independent reflections of one event.

Practically, 2 Sam 9:1-13 is an appendix that has some bearing on the subsequent text. It introduces two characters, Mephibosheth and Ziba, who reappear in 2 Sam 16:1-4; 19:24-30 (Heb., 19:25-31). Their role in the narrative there is not dependent on 9:1-13 as text. The difference between 9:1 and 19:28 suggests that 9:1-13 was in all probability not part of the longer narrative.

23. Veijola attributed 9:1, 7*, 10*, 11b, 13aβ to his DtrH.

24. 2 Sam 10:1-19 is an appendix with some bearing on the following text. It provides a context to the Davidic campaign against Ammon and the siege of Rabbah that forms the frame in 2 Samuel 11–12. The narrative of 2 Samuel 11–12, however, does not depend on 10:1-19 and does not refer to it. There is no evidence to justify the claim that 10:1-19 necessarily belonged within the same narrative as 2 Samuel 11–12. There is equally no evidence against its having been prefaced to chaps. 11–12 as an introduction. It is possible but not necessary.

| Main pre-DH: *Prophetic* Record | Other pre-DH: | **Josianic DH:** |
| its sources *and prophetic contribution* | single sideline | **from the Dtr** |

entrance of the gate; but the Arameans of Zobah and of Rehob, and the men of Tob and Maacah, were by themselves in the open country.

9 When Joab saw that the battle was set against him both in front and in the rear, he chose some of the picked men of Israel, and arrayed them against the Arameans; [10]the rest of his men he put in the charge of his brother Abishai, and he arrayed them against the Ammonites. [11]He said, "If the Arameans are too strong for me, then you shall help me; but if the Ammonites are too strong for you, then I will come and help you. [12]Be strong, and let us be courageous for the sake of our people, and for the cities of our God; and may the LORD do what seems good to him." [13]So Joab and the people who were with him moved forward into battle against the Arameans; and they fled before him. [14]When the Ammonites saw that the Arameans fled, they likewise fled before Abishai, and entered the city. Then Joab returned from fighting against the Ammonites, and came to Jerusalem.

15 But when the Arameans saw that they had been defeated by Israel, they gathered themselves together. [16]Hadadezer sent and brought out the Arameans who were beyond the Euphrates; and they came to Helam, with Shobach the commander of the army of Hadadezer at their head. [17]When it was told David, he gathered all Israel together, and crossed the Jordan, and came to Helam. The Arameans arrayed themselves against David and fought with him. [18]The Arameans fled before Israel; and David killed of the Arameans seven hundred chariot teams, and forty thousand horsemen, and wounded Shobach the commander of their army, so that he died there. [19]When all the kings who were servants of Hadadezer saw that they had been defeated by Israel, they made peace with Israel, and became

subject to them. So the Arameans were afraid to help the Ammonites any more.

11 In the spring of the year, the time when kings go out to battle, David sent Joab with his officers and all Israel with him; they ravaged the Ammonites, and besieged Rabbah. But David remained at Jerusalem.[25]

---

25. 2 Samuel 11–12 introduces the major narrative sequence of chaps. 11–20. While there are links between 2 Sam 12:7b-12 and the PR (see below), the balance of evidence suggests that 2 Samuel 11–20 was not part of the PR. It is treated here as a source for the Josianic DH, but not as part of the PR. Despite Rost's immense contribution (*The Succession to the Throne of David*) the focus on succession has been a distraction. For a fuller treatment of 2 Samuel 11–20, see Campbell and O'Brien, "1–2 Samuel," in *The International Bible Commentary*, 572-607.

The evidence against the inclusion of 2 Samuel 11–20 in the PR is: (i) Beyond 2 Sam 12:7b-12, there is no trace of prophetic influence in 2 Samuel 11–20. Of course, there is precious little in the later stages of the Story of David's Rise. (ii) 2 Sam 7:1-17, at the level of the PR, does not speak of any sin of David's, as it does of Solomon. This would be inappropriate if 2 Samuel 11–20 was in view. (iii) 2 Sam 7:1-17, at the level of the PR, is focused on Solomon—despite exegetical efforts to the contrary. This stands in contrast with 2 Sam 12:7b-12's regard for a more distant future (literally, "the sword shall not depart from your house forever," v. 10a). Beyond the deaths of Amnon, Absalom, and Adonijah, Jehu slaughtered Ahaziah and his kin (2 Kings 9–10) and Queen Athaliah murdered the descendants of David, save one (2 Kgs 11:1-3). (iv) The PR is concerned with the election and rejection of kings; to the contrary, 2 Samuel 11–20 is concerned with the internal events of a royal reign. The long story of David's rise to power works out the realization in history and the political process of the prophetic

---

After the Dtr:	*Revision:*	Other:
indented and sans serif font	*national focus*	double sideline

2 It happened, late one afternoon, when David rose from his couch and was walking about on the roof of the king's house, that he saw from the roof a woman bathing; the woman was very beautiful. [3]David sent someone to inquire about the woman. It was reported, "This is Bathsheba daughter of Eliam, the wife of Uriah the Hittite." [4]So David sent messengers to get

---

anointing in 1 Sam 16:1-13, as for Saul between 10:1 and 11:15. (v) The long-recognized sacral overtones of the Story of David's Rise are congenial to the attitudes of the prophetic circles. The equally long-recognized secular overtones of 2 Samuel 11–20 are not. The place of prophet or priest is practically usurped by the counselors, behind whose influence God's will may be discerned (2 Sam 17:14). (vi) The highly negative aspects of the portrayal of David in 2 Samuel 11–20 sit uncomfortably with his role in the PR. David is not rejected as Saul was; he is the neighbor of Saul's "who is better than you" (1 Sam 15:28).

Finding a satisfactory setting for these stories of David's later years has long baffled scholarship—unless the hypothesis of a Succession Narrative is taken more seriously than it warrants. The signals from the text—the central role of wise counsel at some points, the evident absence of wise counsel at others, and the wonderful ability of the narrative to open avenues everywhere and close none—all point to its origin in the circles of royal counselors. It is likely that these were stories that kings' counselors either told themselves or had told for them with a view to evoking the kind of real-life situation where wise counsel was needed and, as so often in real life, was not at all easy to find.

In our judgment, 2 Samuel 11–20 probably originated relatively close to the time with which it is concerned. If a setting among counselors is right, an origin at the newly founded court of Jeroboam, many of whose courtiers would have come from David's court in Jerusalem, is open to consideration.

Quite another question is the incorporation of this material into our present text. It must be noted that, surprising as it may seem, the material has little or no substantial bearing on the interpretation of the DH, Josianic or later. There is no comment or other revision that can be attributed to the Dtr. The question must be asked what in the text of 2 Samuel 11–20

might have been of sufficient interest to a Josianic Dtr to motivate its inclusion in the DH.

We moderns may well focus on David's sin and folly in the early chapters; monarchists might choose to focus on David's undoubted success once he had left Jerusalem. The rich ambiguity of the text throughout allows both admirers and belittlers of David to find plenty to their liking. The Josianic Dtr held David in high esteem. The text of 2 Samuel 11–20 holds much to fuel that admiration. For example:

- David sins most grievously, but he confesses, asks forgiveness, and is forgiven; and furthermore he is blessed with a favored son (chaps. 11–12);
- David, faced with rebellion and leaving Jerusalem, receives Ittai's loyalty (15:19-22);
- David is deeply pious with regard to the ark, as well as astute (15:24-29);
- David prays to God, commissions Hushai, and ultimately his prayer is heard (15:30-37; 17:1-14, esp. v. 14b);
- David's piety is to the fore in the episode with Shimei (16:5-13);
- David finds more than adequate political and military support east-of-Jordan (17:27—18:5);
- David's forces are victorious in the military confrontation (18:6—19:8);
- David's return to Jerusalem is marked by political skill and success (19:9-43);
- David achieves the unification of the people centered on Jerusalem (20:3-22).

An incorporation earlier than the Josianic DH is unlikely. A later incorporation is frankly less than likely. The potential for esteem of David can motivate the inclusion of 2 Samuel 11–20 in the Josianic DH. Above all, despite the sinfulness of the king and his sons, David's commitment to YHWH as God of Israel never wavers and David is founder of YHWH's worship in Jerusalem.

Main pre-DH: *Prophetic* Record
its sources *and prophetic contribution*

Other pre-DH:
single sideline

Josianic DH:
from the Dtr

her, and she came to him, and he lay with her. (Now she was purifying herself after her period.) Then she returned to her house. [5]The woman conceived; and she sent and told David, "I am pregnant."

6 So David sent word to Joab, "Send me Uriah the Hittite." And Joab sent Uriah to David. [7]When Uriah came to him, David asked how Joab and the people fared, and how the war was going. [8]Then David said to Uriah, "Go down to your house, and wash your feet." Uriah went out of the king's house, and there followed him a present from the king. [9]But Uriah slept at the entrance of the king's house with all the servants of his lord, and did not go down to his house. [10]When they told David, "Uriah did not go down to his house," David said to Uriah, "You have just come from a journey. Why did you not go down to your house?" [11]Uriah said to David, "The ark and Israel and Judah remain in booths; and my lord Joab and the servants of my lord are camping in the open field; shall I then go to my house, to eat and to drink, and to lie with my wife? As you live, and as your soul lives, I will not do such a thing." [12]Then David said to Uriah, "Remain here today also, and tomorrow I will send you back." So Uriah remained in Jerusalem that day. On the next day, [13]David invited him to eat and drink in his presence and made him drunk; and in the evening he went out to lie on his couch with the servants of his lord, but he did not go down to his house.

14 In the morning David wrote a letter to Joab, and sent it by the hand of Uriah. [15]In the letter he wrote, "Set Uriah in the forefront of the hardest fighting, and then draw back from him, so that he may be struck down and die." [16]As Joab was besieging the city, he assigned Uriah to the place where he knew there were valiant warriors. [17]The men of the city came out and fought with Joab; and some of the servants of David among the people fell. Uriah the Hittite was killed as well. [18]Then Joab sent and told David all the news about the fighting; [19]and he instructed the messenger, "When you have finished telling the king all the news about the fighting, [20]then, if the king's anger rises, and if he says to you, 'Why did you go so near the city to fight? Did you not know that they would shoot from the wall? [21]Who killed Abimelech son of Jerubbaal? Did not a woman throw an upper millstone on him from the wall, so that he died at Thebez? Why did you go so near the wall?' then you shall say, 'Your servant Uriah the Hittite is dead too.' "[26]

22 So the messenger went, and came and told David all that Joab had sent him to tell. [23]The messenger said to David, "The men gained an advantage over us, and came out against us in the field; but we drove them back to the entrance of the gate. [24]Then the archers shot at your servants from the wall; some of the king's servants are dead; and your servant Uriah the Hittite is dead also." [25]David said to the messenger, "Thus you shall say to Joab, 'Do not let this matter trouble you, for the sword devours now one and now another; press your attack on the city, and overthrow it.' And encourage him."

26 When the wife of Uriah heard that her husband was dead, she made lamentation for him. [27]When the mourning was over, David sent and brought her to his house, and she became his wife, and bore him a son. But the thing that David had done displeased the LORD,

---

26. The episode of Abimelech's death, too close to the wall, is part of the story now in Judges 9; in Joab's time, it was clearly part of the military tradition.

After the Dtr:
indented and sans serif font

Revision:
national focus

Other:
double sideline

12 and the LORD sent Nathan to David. He came to him, and said to him, "There were two men in a certain city, the one rich and the other poor. [2]The rich man had very many flocks and herds; [3]but the poor man had nothing but one little ewe lamb, which he had bought. He brought it up, and it grew up with him and with his children; it used to eat of his meager fare, and drink from his cup, and lie in his bosom, and it was like a daughter to him. [4]Now there came a traveler to the rich man, and he was loath to take one of his own flock or herd to prepare for the wayfarer who had come to him, but he took the poor man's lamb, and prepared that for the guest who had come to him." [5]Then David's anger was greatly kindled against the man. He said to Nathan, "As the LORD lives, the man who has done this deserves to die; [6]he shall restore the lamb fourfold, because he did this thing, and because he had no pity."

7 Nathan said to David, "You are the man! Thus says the LORD, the God of Israel: I anointed you king over Israel, and I rescued you from the hand of Saul; [8]I gave you your master's house, and your master's wives into your bosom, and gave you the house of Israel and of Judah; and if that had been too little, I would have added as much more. [9]Why have you despised the word of the LORD, to do what is evil in his sight? You have struck down Uriah the Hittite with the sword, and have taken his wife to be your wife, and have killed him with the sword of the Ammonites. [10]Now therefore the sword shall never depart from your house, for you have despised me, and have taken the wife of Uriah the Hittite to be your wife. [11]Thus says the LORD: I will raise up trouble against you from within your own house; and I will take your wives before your eyes, and give them to your neighbor, and he shall lie with your wives in the sight of this very sun. [12]For you did it secretly; but I will do this thing before all Israel, and before the sun."[27]

[13]David said to Nathan, "I have sinned against the LORD." Nathan said to David, "Now the LORD has put away your sin; you shall not die.

---

27. **Text signals.** Within 12:7b-12, following Nathan's "You are the man!" there are text signals to be noted. (i) "I anointed you king over Israel" recalls texts from the PR (e.g., 1 Sam 9:16; 10:1; 15:1, 17; 16:3, 12-13). (ii) 12:9a expresses the same concern as 1 Sam 15:19. (iii) The summary of David's rise in Nathan's prophetic speech (vv. 7b-8) expresses God's involvement in the 1st person, a characteristic of such speeches in the PR (cf. McCarter, *II Samuel*, 300).

Text-history approach. Without including 2 Samuel 11–20 in the PR and without assuming prophetic authorship for chaps. 11–12 (against McCarter, ibid.), it is plausible to assume that the similarities just noted could derive from editing by the prophetic circles assumed to have been responsible for the PR or by other prophetic circles with similar thought and theology. 2 Samuel 11–20 is too significant a literary treasure and too multivalent a document to be restricted to the kingdom of Judah.

2 Sam 12:7b-12 reflects on the episodes of sexual and homicidal violence in the subsequent narrative and traces these back to David's own sexual and homicidal violence. In a complex text, two prophetic words of judgment are present. If the *'ēqeb kî* in v. 10b is read with vv. 11-12 (not to be confused with *'ēqeb 'ăšer* in v. 6; cf. Amos 4:12), both prophecies of judgment are complete with accusation and announcement. One looks primarily at the homicidal violence (retrospect in vv. 7b-8, accusation in v. 9, and announcement in v. 10a). The other, beginning with v. 10b, looks primarily at the sexual violence (with the accusation in v. 10b, and an announcement moving from the general to the specific in vv. 11-12; note the renewed introduction at v. 11, preceding the announcement). Both interpretations of 2 Samuel 11–20 appear to be prophetic in origin, without requiring chaps. 11–12 as part of the PR.

Main pre-DH: *Prophetic* Record
its sources *and prophetic contribution*

Other pre-DH:
single sideline

Josianic DH:
from the Dtr

¹⁴Nevertheless, because by this deed you have utterly scorned the Lord, the child that is born to you shall die." ¹⁵Then Nathan went to his house.

The Lord struck the child that Uriah's wife bore to David, and it became very ill. ¹⁶David therefore pleaded with God for the child; David fasted, and went in and lay all night on the ground. ¹⁷The elders of his house stood beside him, urging him to rise from the ground; but he would not, nor did he eat food with them. ¹⁸On the seventh day the child died. And the servants of David were afraid to tell him that the child was dead; for they said, "While the child was still alive, we spoke to him, and he did not listen to us; how then can we tell him the child is dead? He may do himself some harm." ¹⁹But when David saw that his servants were whispering together, he perceived that the child was dead; and David said to his servants, "Is the child dead?" They said, "He is dead."

20 Then David rose from the ground, washed, anointed himself, and changed his clothes. He went into the house of the Lord, and worshiped; he then went to his own house; and when he asked, they set food before him and he ate. ²¹Then his servants said to him, "What is this thing that you have done? You fasted and wept for the child while it was alive; but when the child died, you rose and ate food." ²²He said,

"While the child was still alive, I fasted and wept; for I said, 'Who knows? The Lord may be gracious to me, and the child may live.' ²³But now he is dead; why should I fast? Can I bring him back again? I shall go to him, but he will not return to me."

24 Then David consoled his wife Bathsheba, and went to her, and lay with her; and she bore a son, and he named him Solomon. The Lord loved him, ²⁵and sent a message by the prophet Nathan; so he named him Jedidiah, because of the Lord.

26 Now Joab fought against Rabbah of the Ammonites, and took the royal city. ²⁷Joab sent messengers to David, and said, "I have fought against Rabbah; moreover, I have taken the water city. ²⁸Now, then, gather the rest of the people together, and encamp against the city, and take it; or I myself will take the city, and it will be called by my name." ²⁹So David gathered all the people together and went to Rabbah, and fought against it and took it. ³⁰He took the crown of Milcom from his head; the weight of it was a talent of gold, and in it was a precious stone; and it was placed on David's head. He also brought forth the spoil of the city, a very great amount. ³¹He brought out the people who were in it, and set them to work with saws and iron picks and iron axes, or sent them to the brickworks. Thus he did to all the cities of the Ammonites. Then David and all the people returned to Jerusalem.²⁸

Present-text potential. While Nathan's expanded speech interrupts the dramatic conjunction of his "You are the man!" and David's "I have sinned against the Lord" (12:7a, 13a), it links brilliantly the sins of David, just narrated, with the future turmoil that will contribute to the fragility of David's kingdom.

Veijola attributed 12:7b-10*, 13-14 to his DtrP. Dietrich attributed to his DtrP the insertion of 12:1-14, with 11:27b and 12:15a as literary seams and the addition of 12:7b, 8aβγ, 9aα (from "to do") βγ, 10abα.

28. **Text-history approach.** The question needs to be raised whether these associated stories (2 Samuel 11–12; 13; 14; 15–19; 20) were originally independent sources or whether they are presented within a single narrative text. While they may have once been independent, they are now combined and have the shape of a single narrative. The appropriate beginnings or endings are no longer there.

| After the Dtr: indented and sans serif font | Revision: national focus | Other: double sideline |

13 Some time passed. David's son Absalom had a beautiful sister whose name was Tamar; and David's son Amnon fell in love with her. [2]Amnon was so tormented that he made himself ill because of his sister Tamar, for she was a virgin and it seemed impossible to Amnon to do anything to her. [3]But Amnon had a friend whose name was Jonadab, the son of David's brother Shimeah; and Jonadab was a very crafty man. [4]He said to him, "O son of the king, why are you so haggard morning after morning? Will you not tell me?" Amnon said to him, "I love Tamar, my brother Absalom's sister." [5]Jonadab said to him, "Lie down on your bed, and pretend to be ill; and when your father comes to see you, say to him, 'Let my sister Tamar come and give me something to eat, and prepare the food in my sight, so that I may see it and eat it from her hand.' " [6]So Amnon lay down, and pretended to be ill; and when the king came to see him,

Amnon said to the king, "Please let my sister Tamar come and make a couple of cakes in my sight, so that I may eat from her hand."

[7] Then David sent home to Tamar, saying, "Go to your brother Amnon's house, and prepare food for him." [8]So Tamar went to her brother Amnon's house, where he was lying down. She took dough, kneaded it, made cakes in his sight, and baked the cakes. [9]Then she took the pan and set them out before him, but he refused to eat. Amnon said, "Send out everyone from me." So everyone went out from him. [10]Then Amnon said to Tamar, "Bring the food into the chamber, so that I may eat from your hand." So Tamar took the cakes she had made, and brought them into the chamber to Amnon her brother. [11]But when she brought them near him to eat, he took hold of her, and said to her, "Come, lie with me, my sister." [12]She answered him, "No, my brother, do not force me; for such

---

Here, for example, while 12:31 provides a satisfactory conclusion to an independent story, 13:1 is not an independent beginning. "Some time passed" forges a link. The statement, "David's son Absalom had a beautiful sister," is not the way ancient Israel's stories normally begin.

Present-text potential. The story of David and Bathsheba is one of the great literary achievements of the OT. Its gaps and silences as well as the themes with which it grapples invite a wealth of interpretation and cannot be glossed over lightly.

It is the lead story in the great succession of stories located in David's later years. Inevitably, given its position, it casts an interpretative shadow over the narrative to come. Its interpretative influence is intensified by the prophetic judgments attributed to Nathan: because of David's homicidal violence, the sword will never depart from his house (12:10a); because of David's sexual violence, what he did secretly will be done before all Israel and before the sun (12:12).

Given what is to come in the narrative—David's concubines will be publicly violated by Absalom (16:21-22); David's prominent sons will die violently: Amnon murdered by Absalom (13:28-29), Absalom killed by Joab (18:14-15), Adonijah executed by Solomon (1 Kgs 2:13-25)—it is difficult not to see this story setting the interpretation of David's later years.

Today, faith faces a dilemma. Does this interpretation point to the impact of divine providence or the influence of genes and paternal nurture and modeling? The stories are subtle enough for both (for example, 2 Sam 13:21 [cf. Qumran and LXX] and 1 Kgs 1:6). The prophetic oracle is suitably ambiguous: "the sword shall never depart from your house" (12:10) is neutral as to the agent; "I will take your wives . . . I will do this before all Israel" (12:11-12) attributes the action to God, while the text gives responsibility to Ahithophel—whose counsel was as the oracle of God! Crime and punishment or act and consequence or both? The text is beguiling in what it brings to light and what it shrouds in shadow.

Main pre-DH: *Prophetic* Record
its sources *and prophetic contribution*

Other pre-DH:
single sideline

Josianic DH:
from the Dtr

a thing is not done in Israel; do not do anything so vile! [13]As for me, where could I carry my shame? And as for you, you would be as one of the scoundrels in Israel. Now therefore, I beg you, speak to the king; for he will not withhold me from you." [14]But he would not listen to her; and being stronger than she, he forced her and lay with her.

15 Then Amnon was seized with a very great loathing for her; indeed, his loathing was even greater than the lust he had felt for her. Amnon said to her, "Get out!" [16]But she said to him, "No, my brother; for this wrong in sending me away is greater than the other that you did to me." But he would not listen to her. [17]He called the young man who served him and said, "Put this woman out of my presence, and bolt the door after her." [18](Now she was wearing a long robe with sleeves; for this is how the virgin daughters of the king were clothed in earlier times.) So his servant put her out, and bolted the door after her. [19]But Tamar put ashes on her head, and tore the long robe that she was wearing; she put her hand on her head, and went away, crying aloud as she went.

20 Her brother Absalom said to her, "Has Amnon your brother been with you? Be quiet for now, my sister; he is your brother; do not take this to heart." So Tamar remained, a desolate woman, in her brother Absalom's house. [21]When King David heard of all these things, he became very angry, but he would not punish his son Amnon, because he loved him, for he was his firstborn. [22]But Absalom spoke to Amnon neither good nor bad; for Absalom hated Amnon, because he had raped his sister Tamar.

23 After two full years Absalom had sheepshearers at Baal-hazor, which is near Ephraim, and Absalom invited all the king's sons. [24]Absalom came to the king, and said, "Your servant has sheepshearers; will the king and his servants please go with your servant?" [25]But the king said to Absalom, "No, my son, let us not all go, or else we will be burdensome to you." He pressed him, but he would not go but gave him his blessing. [26]Then Absalom said, "If not, please let my brother Amnon go with us." The king said to him, "Why should he go with you?" [27]But Absalom pressed him until he let Amnon and all the king's sons go with him. Absalom made a feast like a king's feast. [28]Then Absalom commanded his servants, "Watch when Amnon's heart is merry with wine, and when I say to you, 'Strike Amnon,' then kill him. Do not be afraid; have I not myself commanded you? Be courageous and valiant." [29]So the servants of Absalom did to Amnon as Absalom had commanded. Then all the king's sons rose, and each mounted his mule and fled.

30 While they were on the way, the report came to David that Absalom had killed all the king's sons, and not one of them was left. [31]The king rose, tore his garments, and lay on the ground; and all his servants who were standing by tore their garments. [32]But Jonadab, the son of David's brother Shimeah, said, "Let not my lord suppose that they have killed all the young men the king's sons; Amnon alone is dead. This has been determined by Absalom from the day Amnon raped his sister Tamar. [33]Now therefore, do not let my lord the king take it to heart, as if all the king's sons were dead; for Amnon alone is dead."

34 But Absalom fled. When the young man who kept watch looked up, he saw many people coming from the Horonaim road by the side of the mountain. [35]Jonadab said to the king, "See, the king's sons have come; as your servant said, so it has come about." [36]As soon as he had finished speaking, the king's sons arrived, and raised their voices and wept; and the king and all his servants also wept very bitterly.

After the Dtr:	Revision:	Other:
indented and sans serif font	national focus	double sideline

37 But Absalom fled, and went to Talmai son of Ammihud, king of Geshur. David mourned for his son day after day. [38]Absalom, having fled to Geshur, stayed there three years. [39]And the heart of the king went out, yearning for Absalom; for he was now consoled over the death of Amnon.[29]

14 Now Joab son of Zeruiah perceived that the king's mind was on Absalom. [2]Joab sent to Tekoa and brought from there a wise woman. He said to her, "Pretend to be a mourner; put on mourning garments, do not anoint yourself with oil, but behave like a woman who has been mourning many days for the dead. [3]Go to the king and speak to him as follows." And Joab put the words into her mouth. [4]When the woman of Tekoa came to the king, she fell on her face to the ground and did obeisance, and said, "Help, O king!" [5]The king asked her, "What is your trouble?" She answered, "Alas, I am a widow; my husband is dead. [6]Your servant had two sons, and they fought with one another in the field; there was no one to part them, and one struck the other and killed him. [7]Now the whole family has risen against your servant. They say, 'Give up the man who struck his brother, so that we may kill him for the life of his brother whom he murdered, even if we destroy the heir as well.' Thus they would quench my one remaining ember, and leave to my husband neither name nor remnant on the face of the earth." [8]Then the king said to the woman, "Go to your house, and I will give orders concerning you." [9]The woman of Tekoa said to the king, "On me be the guilt, my lord the king, and on my father's house; let the king and his throne be guiltless." [10]The king said, "If anyone says anything to you, bring him to me, and he shall never touch you again." [11]Then she said, "Please, may the king keep the LORD your God in mind, so that the avenger of blood may kill no more, and my son not be destroyed." He said, "As the LORD lives, not one hair of your son shall fall to the ground."[30]

12 Then the woman said, "Please let your servant speak a word to my lord the king." He said, "Speak." [13]The woman said, "Why then have you planned such a thing against the people of God? For in giving this decision the king convicts himself, inasmuch as the king does not bring his banished one home again. [14]We must all die; we are like water spilled on the ground, which cannot be gathered up. But God will not take away a life; he will devise plans so as not to keep an outcast banished forever from his presence. [15]Now I have come to say this to my lord the king because the people have made me afraid;

---

29. **Text-history approach.** It is possible, perhaps, to settle on a satisfactory ending for the story of chap. 13 in v. 36 or v. 37. In such a hypothesis, vv. 38-39 would be bridging verses, linking chaps. 13 and 14. But 14:1 depends on chap. 13 and a satisfactory beginning cannot be found for the story of chap. 14. As the stories stand in the text, they form a single narrative.

Present-text potential. While there is much that cries out for interpretation in this material and while this book is not the place for interpretation, a comment may be permitted. The shadowy figure of Jonadab is present at the beginning and the end of chap. 13. At the beginning, he knew what Amnon wanted and how to get it (13:4-5). Note: he is described in 13:3 as a very wise man (*'îš ḥākām mĕ'ōd*); translational variants can be accurate but misleading—the snake in Gen 3:1 is described as crafty (*'ārûm*) but Jonadab is described as wise. At the end, he knew exactly what had happened and why (13:32-33). Who is this figure of the wise who knows all, is involved in all, and disappears apparently scot-free? Or are we invited to wonder whether David had knowingly let Amnon go to his death?

---

30. Veijola attributed 14:9 to his DtrH, tentatively.

---

your servant thought, 'I will speak to the king; it may be that the king will perform the request of his servant. [16]For the king will hear, and deliver his servant from the hand of the man who would cut both me and my son off from the heritage of God.' [17]Your servant thought, 'The word of my lord the king will set me at rest'; for my lord the king is like the angel of God, discerning good and evil. The LORD your God be with you!"

18 Then the king answered the woman, "Do not withhold from me anything I ask you." The woman said, "Let my lord the king speak." [19]The king said, "Is the hand of Joab with you in all this?" The woman answered and said, "As surely as you live, my lord the king, one cannot turn right or left from anything that my lord the king has said. For it was your servant Joab who commanded me; it was he who put all these words into the mouth of your servant. [20]In order to change the course of affairs your servant Joab did this. But my lord has wisdom like the wisdom of the angel of God to know all things that are on the earth."

21 Then the king said to Joab, "Very well, I grant this; go, bring back the young man Absalom." [22]Joab prostrated himself with his face to the ground and did obeisance, and blessed the king; and Joab said, "Today your servant knows that I have found favor in your sight, my lord the king, in that the king has granted the request of his servant." [23]So Joab set off, went to Geshur, and brought Absalom to Jerusalem. [24]The king said, "Let him go to his own house; he is not to come into my presence." So Absalom went to his own house, and did not come into the king's presence.

25 Now in all Israel there was no one to be praised so much for his beauty as Absalom; from the sole of his foot to the crown of his head there was no blemish in him. [26]When he cut the hair of his head (for at the end of every year he used to cut it; when it was heavy on him, he cut it), he weighed the hair of his head, two hundred shekels by the king's weight. [27]There were born to Absalom three sons, and one daughter whose name was Tamar; she was a beautiful woman.

28 So Absalom lived two full years in Jerusalem, without coming into the king's presence. [29]Then Absalom sent for Joab to send him to the king; but Joab would not come to him. He sent a second time, but Joab would not come. [30]Then he said to his servants, "Look, Joab's field is next to mine, and he has barley there; go and set it on fire." So Absalom's servants set the field on fire. [31]Then Joab rose and went to Absalom at his house, and said to him, "Why have your servants set my field on fire?" [32]Absalom answered Joab, "Look, I sent word to you: Come here, that I may send you to the king with the question, 'Why have I come from Geshur? It would be better for me to be there still.' Now let me go into the king's presence; if there is guilt in me, let him kill me!" [33]Then Joab went to the king and told him; and he summoned Absalom. So he came to the king and prostrated himself with his face to the ground before the king; and the king kissed Absalom.[31]

---

31. **Text-history approach.** Ill-fated as the overdue reconciliation may be, it would be possible to see a story coming to a close with v. 33. 15:1 begins with a linking clause, and is a little too abrupt for a satisfactory start to a story (contrast 1 Kgs 1:5). If there were to be a break in the narrative, this is probably the most likely place to postulate it. From here, the story continues unbroken until the end of chap. 19.

Present-text potential. Two comments are in place here. While Joab is clearly the power behind David's throne, it is worth noting the agent he employs to influence the king. A skilled storyteller is needed, capable of putting on a good performance in public. Joab chose a woman, although the script could

---

After the Dtr:	Revision:	Other:
indented and sans serif font	*national focus*	double sideline

15 After this Absalom got himself a chariot and horses, and fifty men to run ahead of him. [2]Absalom used to rise early and stand beside the road into the gate; and when anyone brought a suit before the king for judgment, Absalom would call out and say, "From what city are you?" When the person said, "Your servant is of such and such a tribe in Israel," [3]Absalom would say, "See, your claims are good and right; but there is no one deputed by the king to hear you." [4]Absalom said moreover, "If only I were judge in the land! Then all who had a suit or cause might come to me, and I would give them justice." [5]Whenever people came near to do obeisance to him, he would put out his hand and take hold of them, and kiss them. [6]Thus Absalom did to every Israelite who came to the king for judgment; so Absalom stole the hearts of the people of Israel.

7 At the end of four years Absalom said to the king, "Please let me go to Hebron and pay the vow that I have made to the LORD. [8]For your servant made a vow while I lived at Geshur in Aram: If the LORD will indeed bring me back to Jerusalem, then I will worship the LORD in Hebron." [9]The king said to him, "Go in peace." So he got up, and went to Hebron. [10]But Absalom sent secret messengers throughout all the tribes of Israel, saying, "As soon as you hear the sound of the trumpet, then shout: Absalom has become king at Hebron!" [11]Two hundred men from Jerusalem went with Absalom; they were invited guests, and they went in their innocence, knowing nothing of the matter. [12]While Absalom was offering the sacrifices, he sent for Ahithophel the Gilonite, David's counselor, from his city Giloh. The conspiracy grew in strength, and the people with Absalom kept increasing.

13 A messenger came to David, saying, "The hearts of the Israelites have gone after Absalom." [14]Then David said to all his officials who were with him at Jerusalem, "Get up! Let us flee, or there will be no escape for us from Absalom. Hurry, or he will soon overtake us, and bring disaster down upon us, and attack the city with the edge of the sword." [15]The king's officials said to the king, "Your servants are ready to do whatever our lord the king decides." [16]So the king left, followed by all his household, except ten concubines whom he left behind to look after the house. [17]The king left, followed by all the people; and they stopped at the last house. [18]All his officials passed by him; and all the Cherethites, and all the Pelethites, and all the six hundred Gittites who had followed him from Gath, passed on before the king.

---

easily have been modified for a man. She is from the country, Tekoa in the south, so she should not be recognized by King David. She is smart enough to get herself out of trouble when the situation turns dangerous (14:18-20). Her performance is brilliant and gets exactly the result Joab wanted (cf. 14:21). We know next to nothing of Israel's storytellers, but this unnamed woman from Tekoa would surely qualify as one. If, as is likely, they are to be reckoned among Israel's singers at court (*šārîm wĕšārôt*), then both men and women had the role (cf. 2 Sam 19:35 [Heb., v. 36]; Eccl 2:8; 2 Chron 36:25).

Is this story a classic example of "too little too late"? Joab pulls strings to have Absalom brought back from exile; but he is not brought into royal favor (14:24). Joab appears to wash his hands of his project; it takes a fire in Joab's field to get Absalom an interview (14:29-32). An audience with the king is arranged, apparently too late. It would seem that Absalom's heart is set on revolution.

Did Joab realize his mistake and did this experience influence his decision to kill Absalom, trapped in the oak (18:9-15)? The text says nothing. But then the text has nothing to say about Joab while all the action is happening (except that Absalom had given his job to Amasa, 17:25). Joab is a shifty shadow throughout the narrative.

| Main pre-DH: *Prophetic* Record | Other pre-DH: | **Josianic DH:** |
| its sources *and prophetic contribution* | single sideline | **from the Dtr** |

19 Then the king said to Ittai the Gittite, "Why are you also coming with us? Go back, and stay with the king; for you are a foreigner, and also an exile from your home. [20]You came only yesterday, and shall I today make you wander about with us, while I go wherever I can? Go back, and take your kinsfolk with you; and may the LORD show steadfast love and faithfulness to you." [21]But Ittai answered the king, "As the LORD lives, and as my lord the king lives, wherever my lord the king may be, whether for death or for life, there also your servant will be." [22]David said to Ittai, "Go then, march on." So Ittai the Gittite marched on, with all his men and all the little ones who were with him. [23]The whole country wept aloud as all the people passed by; the king crossed the Wadi Kidron, and all the people moved on toward the wilderness.

24 Abiathar came up, and Zadok also, with all the Levites, carrying the ark of the covenant of God. They set down the ark of God, until the people had all passed out of the city. [25]Then the king said to Zadok, "Carry the ark of God back into the city. If I find favor in the eyes of the LORD, he will bring me back and let me see both it and the place where it stays. [26]But if he says, 'I take no pleasure in you,' here I am, let him do to me what seems good to him." [27]The king also said to the priest Zadok, "Look, go back to the city in peace, you and Abiathar, with your two sons, Ahimaaz your son, and Jonathan son of Abiathar. [28]See, I will wait at the fords of the wilderness until word comes from you to inform me." [29]So Zadok and Abiathar carried the ark of God back to Jerusalem, and they remained there.[32]

30 But David went up the ascent of the Mount of Olives, weeping as he went, with his head covered and walking barefoot; and all the people who were with him covered their heads and went up, weeping as they went. [31]David was told that Ahithophel was among the conspirators with Absalom. And David said, "O LORD, I pray you, turn the counsel of Ahithophel into foolishness."

32 When David came to the summit, where God was worshiped, Hushai the Archite came to meet him with his coat torn and earth on his head. [33]David said to him, "If you go on with me, you will be a burden to me. [34]But if you return to the city and say to Absalom, 'I will be your servant, O king; as I have been your father's servant in time past, so now I will be your servant,' then you will defeat for me the counsel of Ahithophel. [35]The priests Zadok and Abiathar will be with you there. So whatever you hear from the king's house, tell it to the priests Zadok and Abiathar. [36]Their two sons are with them there, Zadok's son Ahimaaz and Abiathar's son Jonathan; and by them you shall report to me everything you hear." [37]So Hushai, David's friend, came into the city, just as Absalom was entering Jerusalem.[33]

---

32. Veijola attributed 15:25-26 to his DtrH.

---

33. **Present-text potential.** This chapter raises issues of David's behavior. He is portrayed abandoning Jerusalem without a thought. "Get up! Let us flee, or there will be no escape for us from Absalom" (15:14). Whatever happened to the city ten chapters ago that even the blind and the lame could defend (2 Sam 5:6)? Surely David would not be caught by the water-shaft trick. Did David know for certain that he could win a war across the Jordan? The text does not say. Did David fear that Absalom might die leading his troops in an assault on his father's city? The text does not say. Did David feel sure he could forge a peace settlement with his favored son? The text does not say. Is this why Ahithophel counseled Absalom's public rape of David's concubines? The text does not say so explicitly, but probably (16:21). Is this why Joab

---

After the Dtr:
indented and sans serif font

Revision:
national focus

Other:
double sideline

16 When David had passed a little beyond the summit, Ziba the servant of Mephibosheth met him, with a couple of donkeys saddled, carrying two hundred loaves of bread, one hundred bunches of raisins, one hundred of summer fruits, and one skin of wine. ²The king said to Ziba, "Why have you brought these?" Ziba answered, "The donkeys are for the king's household to ride, the bread and summer fruit for the young men to eat, and the wine is for those to drink who faint in the wilderness." ³The king said, "And where is your master's son?" Ziba said to the king, "He remains in Jerusalem; for he said, 'Today the house of Israel will give me back my grandfather's kingdom.'" ⁴Then the king said to Ziba, "All that belonged to Mephibosheth is now yours." Ziba said, "I do obeisance; let me find favor in your sight, my lord the king."

5 When King David came to Bahurim, a man of the family of the house of Saul came out whose name was Shimei son of Gera; he came out cursing. ⁶He threw stones at David and at all the servants of King David; now all the people and all the warriors were on his right and on his left. ⁷Shimei shouted while he cursed, "Out! Out! Murderer! Scoundrel! ⁸The LORD has avenged on all of you the blood of the house of Saul, in whose place you have reigned; and the LORD has given the kingdom into the hand of your son Absalom. See, disaster has overtaken you; for you are a man of blood."

9 Then Abishai son of Zeruiah said to the king, "Why should this dead dog curse my lord the king? Let me go over and take off his head." ¹⁰But the king said, "What have I to do with you, you sons of Zeruiah? If he is cursing because the LORD has said to him, 'Curse David,' who then shall say, 'Why have you done so?'" ¹¹David said to Abishai and to all his servants, "My own son seeks my life; how much more now may this Benjaminite! Let him alone, and let him curse; for the LORD has bidden him. ¹²It may be that the LORD will look on my distress, and the LORD will repay me with good for this cursing of me today."[34] ¹³So David and his men went on the road, while Shimei went along on the hillside opposite him and cursed as he went, throwing stones and flinging dust at him. ¹⁴The king and all the people who were with him arrived weary at the Jordan; and there he refreshed himself.

15 Now Absalom and all the Israelites came to Jerusalem; Ahithophel was with him. ¹⁶When Hushai the Archite, David's friend, came to Absalom, Hushai said to Absalom, "Long live the king! Long live the king!" ¹⁷Absalom said to Hushai, "Is this your loyalty to your friend? Why did you not go with your friend?" ¹⁸Hushai said to Absalom, "No; but the one whom the

---

kills Absalom when he gets his chance? The text does not say so, but probably (18:14).

The chapter also raises issues about David's faith. As he leaves Jerusalem, David is portrayed as trusting totally in God. If David has God's favor, God will bring him back; if not, let God do what seems good (15:25-26). It is an amazing faith that every now and then is attributed to David (cf. 1 Sam 22:3; 2 Sam 12:22-23; 15:25-26; 16:10-12). It is particularly interesting here in its present context. David has just evacuated the apparently secure Jerusalem in a hurry. With his next breath, David will set up his lines of communication from within the city he has abandoned. Climbing the Mount of Olives, David prays that the LORD "turn the counsel of Ahithophel into foolishness" (15:31). At the summit, a verse later, David meets Hushai and arranges to have his own man in Absalom's cabinet and his communication network in place. David's faith is total and his strategic planning is perfect.

---

34. Veijola attributed 16:11-12 to his DtrH.

Main pre-DH: *Prophetic* Record   Other pre-DH: **Josianic DH:**
its sources *and prophetic contribution*   single sideline   **from the Dtr**

LORD and this people and all the Israelites have chosen, his I will be, and with him I will remain. [19]Moreover, whom should I serve? Should it not be his son? Just as I have served your father, so I will serve you."

20 Then Absalom said to Ahithophel, "Give us your counsel; what shall we do?" [21]Ahithophel said to Absalom, "Go in to your father's concubines, the ones he has left to look after the house; and all Israel will hear that you have made yourself odious to your father, and the hands of all who are with you will be strengthened." [22]So they pitched a tent for Absalom upon the roof; and Absalom went in to his father's concubines in the sight of all Israel. [23]Now in those days the counsel that Ahithophel gave was as if one consulted the oracle of God; so all the counsel of Ahithophel was esteemed, both by David and by Absalom.[35]

---

35. **Present-text potential.** Much attention is given to those whom David meets on his flight and on his return—the loser in flight, the winner on return. Ziba has little hope for patronage with Absalom; so he betrays Mephibosheth and backs David. Shimei ben Gera sounds sincere in his detestation for David; only his later switch of allegiance betrays the perennial turncoat (19:16-23). Why does Shimei make it into the text? Are we invited to wonder how many in Israel felt as he did and switched to the winner as conveniently as he did? Hushai meets Absalom, is questioned over his loyalty, and lies convincingly. Hushai is loyal to the loser; does he know he is backing a winner? David allowed himself to be misled by Amnon (13:6-7) and by Absalom himself (13:26-27). Now it appears Absalom is allowing himself to be deceived by Hushai. As Ahithophel's advice to Absalom makes clear (16:20-23), politics was as dirty then as now.

Did David know of Absalom's deed or of Absalom's pleasure at the prospect of his father's death (17:1-4)? The text does not say. Even the reason for the fate of David's concubines is not given (cf. 20:3). Would

17 Moreover Ahithophel said to Absalom, "Let me choose twelve thousand men, and I will set out and pursue David tonight. [2]I will come upon him while he is weary and discouraged, and throw him into a panic; and all the people who are with him will flee. I will strike down only the king, [3]and I will bring all the people back to you as a bride comes home to her husband. You seek the life of only one man, and all the people will be at peace." [4]The advice pleased Absalom and all the elders of Israel.

5 Then Absalom said, "Call Hushai the Archite also, and let us hear too what he has to say." [6]When Hushai came to Absalom, Absalom said to him, "This is what Ahithophel has said; shall we do as he advises? If not, you tell us." [7]Then Hushai said to Absalom, "This time the counsel that Ahithophel has given is not good." [8]Hushai continued, "You know that your father and his men are warriors, and that they are enraged, like a bear robbed of her cubs in the field. Besides, your father is expert in war; he will not spend the night with the troops. [9]Even now he has hidden himself in one of the pits, or in some other place. And when some of our troops fall at the first attack, whoever hears it will say, 'There has been a slaughter among the troops who follow Absalom.' [10]Then even the valiant warrior, whose heart is like the heart of a lion, will utterly melt with fear; for all Israel knows that your father is a warrior, and that those who are with him are valiant warriors. [11]But my counsel is that all Israel be gathered to you, from Dan to Beer-sheba, like the sand by the sea for multitude, and that you go to battle in person. [12]So we shall come upon him in whatever place he may be found, and we shall light on him as

---

David's ignorance explain his softness toward his son (cf. 18:5)? Was David indeed as soft toward Absalom as the text suggests?

the dew falls on the ground; and he will not survive, nor will any of those with him. ¹³If he withdraws into a city, then all Israel will bring ropes to that city, and we shall drag it into the valley, until not even a pebble is to be found there." ¹⁴Absalom and all the men of Israel said, "The counsel of Hushai the Archite is better than the counsel of Ahithophel." For the Lord had ordained to defeat the good counsel of Ahithophel, so that the Lord might bring ruin on Absalom.

15 Then Hushai said to the priests Zadok and Abiathar, "Thus and so did Ahithophel counsel Absalom and the elders of Israel; and thus and so I have counseled. ¹⁶Therefore send quickly and tell David, 'Do not lodge tonight at the fords of the wilderness, but by all means cross over; otherwise the king and all the people who are with him will be swallowed up.' " ¹⁷Jonathan and Ahimaaz were waiting at En-rogel; a servant-girl used to go and tell them, and they would go and tell King David; for they could not risk being seen entering the city. ¹⁸But a boy saw them, and told Absalom; so both of them went away quickly, and came to the house of a man at Bahurim, who had a well in his courtyard; and they went down into it. ¹⁹The man's wife took a covering, stretched it over the well's mouth, and spread out grain on it; and nothing was known of it. ²⁰When Absalom's servants came to the woman at the house, they said, "Where are Ahimaaz and Jonathan?" The woman said to them, "They have crossed over the brook of water." And when they had searched and could not find them, they returned to Jerusalem.

21 After they had gone, the men came up out of the well, and went and told King David. They said to David, "Go and cross the water quickly; for thus and so has Ahithophel counseled against you." ²²So David and all the people who were

with him set out and crossed the Jordan; by daybreak not one was left who had not crossed the Jordan.

23 When Ahithophel saw that his counsel was not followed, he saddled his donkey and went off home to his own city. He set his house in order, and hanged himself; he died and was buried in the tomb of his father.

24 Then David came to Mahanaim, while Absalom crossed the Jordan with all the men of Israel. ²⁵Now Absalom had set Amasa over the army in the place of Joab. Amasa was the son of a man named Ithra the Ishmaelite, who had married Abigal daughter of Nahash, sister of Zeruiah, Joab's mother. ²⁶The Israelites and Absalom encamped in the land of Gilead.

27 When David came to Mahanaim, Shobi son of Nahash from Rabbah of the Ammonites, and Machir son of Ammiel from Lo-debar, and Barzillai the Gileadite from Rogelim, ²⁸brought beds, basins, and earthen vessels, wheat, barley, meal, parched grain, beans and lentils, ²⁹honey and curds, sheep, and cheese from the herd, for David and the people with him to eat; for they said, "The troops are hungry and weary and thirsty in the wilderness."³⁶

---

36. **Present-text potential.** Observations about this chapter reflect on the relationship between our texts and the practice of storytelling in ancient Israel. Hushai sends a message to David reporting on the counsel given Absalom and advising David to cross the Jordan or be swallowed up (17:15-16)—just what Ahithophel counseled doing to David. But Hushai's counsel had prevailed over Ahithophel's, and Absalom was going to wait while he rallied all the available troops.

So why does the text have Hushai advise David to cross the Jordan at once, as though Ahithophel's counsel was going to be followed? Did he fear a double cross? The text does not say. Did a different version of

---

Main pre-DH: *Prophetic* Record
its sources *and prophetic contribution*

Other pre-DH:
single sideline

Josianic DH:
from the Dtr

18 Then David mustered the men who were with him, and set over them commanders of thousands and commanders of hundreds. ²And David divided the army into three groups: one third under the command of Joab, one third under the command of Abishai son of Zeruiah, Joab's brother, and one third under the command of Ittai the Gittite. The king said to the men, "I myself will also go out with you." ³But the men said, "You shall not go out. For if we flee, they will not care about us. If half of us die, they will not care about us. But you are worth ten thousand of us; therefore it is better that you send us help from the city." ⁴The king said to them, "Whatever seems best to you I will do." So the king stood at the side of the gate, while all the army marched out by hundreds and by thousands. ⁵The king ordered Joab and Abishai and Ittai, saying, "Deal gently for my sake with the young man Absalom." And all the people heard when the king gave orders to all the commanders concerning Absalom.³⁷

6 So the army went out into the field against Israel; and the battle was fought in the forest of Ephraim. ⁷The men of Israel were defeated there by the servants of David, and the slaughter there was great on that day, twenty thousand men. ⁸The battle spread over the face of all the country; and the forest claimed more victims that day than the sword.

9 Absalom happened to meet the servants of David. Absalom was riding on his mule, and the mule went under the thick branches of a great oak. His head caught fast in the oak, and he was left hanging between heaven and earth, while the mule that was under him went on. ¹⁰A man saw it, and told Joab, "I saw Absalom hanging in an oak." ¹¹Joab said to the man who told him, "What, you saw him! Why then did you not strike him there to the ground? I would have been glad to give you ten pieces of silver and a belt." ¹²But the man said to Joab, "Even if I felt in my hand the weight of a thousand pieces of silver, I would not raise my hand against the king's son; for in our hearing the king commanded you and Abishai and Ittai, saying: For my sake protect the young man Absalom! ¹³On the other hand, if I had dealt treacherously against his life (and there is nothing hidden from the king), then you yourself would have stood aloof." ¹⁴Joab said, "I will not waste time like this with you." He took three spears in his hand, and thrust them into the heart of Absalom, while he

---

the story have him leave the king's counsel session before the decision was taken? Quite possibly. But if so, it is different from the full version of the story that we have. The text, then, was a pointer to the performance of the story; the text is not to be confused with the performance.

Jonathan and Ahimaaz, the sons of the priests backing David, Zadok and Abiathar, stood by near Jerusalem, where a servant girl gave them their messages at En-rogel—irony of ironies, near where Adonijah was going to have his ill-fated coronation party (1 Kgs 1:9). A boy spotted them and told Absalom. So they hid in a well at Bahurim.

The information lacking here is essential information. What did the boy see and tell Absalom? What did he know? The text does not say. What did the two messengers see that made them hide? The text does not say. How did Absalom's agents know which house to search at Bahurim (Shimei's village)? The text does not say. Since this is the first message delivered to David (17:21, which suggests a version in which Hushai's counsel was not known to have prevailed), there was no time for patterns to have developed and been observed. A lot here is left to the storyteller.

---

37. Are we to understand this as one more cover for David's complicity? Had David given the nod to Joab, it would help explain something of 19:1-8.

| After the Dtr: indented and sans serif font | *Revision:* *national focus* | Other: double sideline |

was still alive in the oak. [15]And ten young men, Joab's armor-bearers, surrounded Absalom and struck him, and killed him.

16 Then Joab sounded the trumpet, and the troops came back from pursuing Israel, for Joab restrained the troops. [17]They took Absalom, threw him into a great pit in the forest, and raised over him a very great heap of stones. Meanwhile all the Israelites fled to their homes. [18]Now Absalom in his lifetime had taken and set up for himself a pillar that is in the King's Valley, for he said, "I have no son to keep my name in remembrance"; he called the pillar by his own name. It is called Absalom's Monument to this day.

19 Then Ahimaaz son of Zadok said, "Let me run, and carry tidings to the king that the LORD has delivered him from the power of his enemies." [20]Joab said to him, "You are not to carry tidings today; you may carry tidings another day, but today you shall not do so, because the king's son is dead." [21]Then Joab said to a Cushite, "Go, tell the king what you have seen." The Cushite bowed before Joab, and ran. [22]Then Ahimaaz son of Zadok said again to Joab, "Come what may, let me also run after the Cushite." And Joab said, "Why will you run, my son, seeing that you have no reward for the tidings?" [23]"Come what may," he said, "I will run." So he said to him, "Run." Then Ahimaaz ran by the way of the Plain, and outran the Cushite.

24 Now David was sitting between the two gates. The sentinel went up to the roof of the gate by the wall, and when he looked up, he saw a man running alone. [25]The sentinel shouted and told the king. The king said, "If he is alone, there are tidings in his mouth." He kept coming, and drew near. [26]Then the sentinel saw another man running; and the sentinel called to the gatekeeper and said, "See, another man running alone!" The king said, "He also is bringing tidings." [27]The sentinel said, "I think the running

of the first one is like the running of Ahimaaz son of Zadok." The king said, "He is a good man, and comes with good tidings."

28 Then Ahimaaz cried out to the king, "All is well!" He prostrated himself before the king with his face to the ground, and said, "Blessed be the LORD your God, who has delivered up the men who raised their hand against my lord the king." [29]The king said, "Is it well with the young man Absalom?" Ahimaaz answered, "When Joab sent your servant, I saw a great tumult, but I do not know what it was." [30]The king said, "Turn aside, and stand here." So he turned aside, and stood still.

31 Then the Cushite came; and the Cushite said, "Good tidings for my lord the king! For the LORD has vindicated you this day, delivering you from the power of all who rose up against you." [32]The king said to the Cushite, "Is it well with the young man Absalom?" The Cushite answered, "May the enemies of my lord the king, and all who rise up to do you harm, be like that young man."

33 The king was deeply moved, and went up to the chamber over the gate, and wept; and as he went, he said, "O my son Absalom, my son, my son Absalom! Would I had died instead of you, O Absalom, my son, my son!"[38]

---

38. **Present-text potential.** At first sight, the dynamics of the chapter are clear: David wants Absalom alive; Joab wants him dead and kills him. While the dynamics remain, the motivation is mystifying. Did David want Absalom alive because he loved his son. If so, David was either unwise or ill-advised to keep Absalom in exile for three years and at bay in Jerusalem for two years more (13:38; 14:28). Did David's people want to keep the king at a distance from any hint of wanting his own son eliminated? After all, what was David's role in Amnon's death: rat cunning or royal folly (cf. 13:26-27)? Did David believe he could reach a peace settlement and a succession agreement with his son? Who would then lose?

Main pre-DH: *Prophetic* Record
its sources *and prophetic contribution*

Other pre-DH:
single sideline

Josianic DH:
from the Dtr

19 It was told Joab, "The king is weeping and mourning for Absalom." ²So the victory that day was turned into mourning for all the troops; for the troops heard that day, "The king is grieving for his son." ³The troops stole into the city that day as soldiers steal in who are ashamed when they flee in battle. ⁴The king covered his face, and the king cried with a loud voice, "O my son Absalom, O Absalom, my son, my son!" ⁵Then Joab came into the house to the king, and said, "Today you have covered with shame the faces of all your officers who have saved your life today, and the lives of your sons and your daughters, and the lives of your wives and your concubines, ⁶for love of those who hate you and for hatred of those who love you. You have made it clear today that commanders and officers are nothing to you; for I perceive that if Absalom were alive and all of us were dead today, then you would be pleased. ⁷So go out at once and speak kindly to your servants; for I swear by the LORD, if you do not go, not a man will stay with you this night; and this will be worse for you than any disaster that has come upon you from your youth until now." ⁸Then the king got up and took his seat in the gate. The troops were all told, "See, the king is sitting in the gate"; and all the troops came before the king.

Meanwhile, all the Israelites had fled to their homes. ⁹All the people were disputing throughout all the tribes of Israel, saying, "The king delivered us from the hand of our enemies, and saved us from the hand of the Philistines; and now he has fled out of the land because of Absalom. ¹⁰But Absalom, whom we anointed over us, is dead in battle. Now therefore why do you say nothing about bringing the king back?"

11 King David sent this message to the priests Zadok and Abiathar, "Say to the elders of Judah, 'Why should you be the last to bring the king back to his house? The talk of all Israel has come to the king. ¹²You are my kin, you are my bone and my flesh; why then should you be the last to bring back the king?' ¹³And say to Amasa, 'Are you not my bone and my flesh? So may God do to me, and more, if you are not the commander of my army from now on, in place of Joab.'" ¹⁴Amasa swayed the hearts of all the people of Judah as one, and they sent word to the king, "Return, both you and all your servants." ¹⁵So the king came back to the Jordan; and Judah came to Gilgal to meet the king and to bring him over the Jordan.

16 Shimei son of Gera, the Benjaminite, from Bahurim, hurried to come down with the people of Judah to meet King David; ¹⁷with him were a thousand people from Benjamin. And Ziba, the servant of the house of Saul, with his fifteen sons and his twenty servants, rushed down to the Jordan ahead of the king, ¹⁸while the crossing was taking place, to bring over the king's household, and to do his pleasure.

Shimei son of Gera fell down before the king, as he was about to cross the Jordan, ¹⁹and said to the king, "May my lord not hold me guilty or remember how your servant did wrong on the day my lord the king left Jerusalem; may the king not bear it in mind. ²⁰For your servant knows that I have sinned; therefore, see, I have

---

After the Dtr:	*Revision:*	Other:
indented and sans serif font	*national focus*	double sideline

come this day, the first of all the house of Joseph to come down to meet my lord the king." [21]Abishai son of Zeruiah answered, "Shall not Shimei be put to death for this, because he cursed the LORD's anointed?" [22]But David said, "What have I to do with you, you sons of Zeruiah, that you should today become an adversary to me? Shall anyone be put to death in Israel this day? For do I not know that I am this day king over Israel?" [23]The king said to Shimei, "You shall not die." And the king gave him his oath.

24 Mephibosheth grandson of Saul came down to meet the king; he had not taken care of his feet, or trimmed his beard, or washed his clothes, from the day the king left until the day he came back in safety. [25]When he came from Jerusalem to meet the king, the king said to him, "Why did you not go with me, Mephibosheth?" [26]He answered, "My lord, O king, my servant deceived me; for your servant said to him, 'Saddle a donkey for me, so that I may ride on it and go with the king.' For your servant is lame. [27]He has slandered your servant to my lord the king. But my lord the king is like the angel of God; do therefore what seems good to you. [28]For all my father's house were doomed to death before my lord the king; but you set your servant among those who eat at your table. What further right have I, then, to appeal to the king?" [29]The king said to him, "Why speak any more of your affairs? I have decided: you and Ziba shall divide the land." [30]Mephibosheth said to the king, "Let him take it all, since my lord the king has arrived home safely."[39]

31 Now Barzillai the Gileadite had come down from Rogelim; he went on with the king to the Jordan, to escort him over the Jordan.

[32]Barzillai was a very aged man, eighty years old. He had provided the king with food while he stayed at Mahanaim, for he was a very wealthy man. [33]The king said to Barzillai, "Come over with me, and I will provide for you in Jerusalem at my side." [34]But Barzillai said to the king, "How many years have I still to live, that I should go up with the king to Jerusalem? [35]Today I am eighty years old; can I discern what is pleasant and what is not? Can your servant taste what he eats or what he drinks? Can I still listen to the voice of singing men and singing women? Why then should your servant be an added burden to my lord the king? [36]Your servant will go a little way over the Jordan with the king. Why should the king recompense me with such a reward? [37]Please let your servant return, so that I may die in my own town, near the graves of my father and my mother. But here is your servant Chimham; let him go over with my lord the king; and do for him whatever seems good to you." [38]The king answered, "Chimham shall go over with me, and I will do for him whatever seems good to you; and all that you desire of me I will do for you." [39]Then all the people crossed over the Jordan, and the king crossed over; the king kissed Barzillai and blessed him, and he returned to his own home. [40]The king went on to Gilgal, and Chimham went on with him; all the people of Judah, and also half the people of Israel, brought the king on his way.

41 Then all the people of Israel came to the king, and said to him, "Why have our kindred the people of Judah stolen you away, and brought the king and his household over the Jordan, and all David's men with him?" [42]All the people of Judah answered the people of Israel, "Because the king is near of kin to us. Why then are you angry over this matter? Have we eaten at all at the king's expense? Or has he given us any gift?" [43]But the people of Israel answered the

---

39. Veijola attributed 19:21-22, 28 to his DtrH (Heb., 19:22-23, 29).

Main pre-DH: *Prophetic* Record
its sources *and prophetic contribution*

Other pre-DH:
single sideline

**Josianic DH:
from the Dtr**

people of Judah, "We have ten shares in the king, and in David also we have more than you. Why then did you despise us? Were we not the first to speak of bringing back our king?" But the words of the people of Judah were fiercer than the words of the people of Israel.[40]

20 Now a scoundrel named Sheba son of Bichri, a Benjaminite, happened to be there. He sounded the trumpet and cried out,

"We have no portion in David,
no share in the son of Jesse!
Everyone to your tents, O Israel!"
[2]So all the people of Israel withdrew from David and followed Sheba son of Bichri; but the people of Judah followed their king steadfastly from the Jordan to Jerusalem.

3 David came to his house at Jerusalem; and the king took the ten concubines whom he had left to look after the house, and put them in a house under guard, and provided for them, but did not go in to them. So they were shut up until the day of their death, living as if in widowhood.

4 Then the king said to Amasa, "Call the men of Judah together to me within three days, and be here yourself." [5]So Amasa went to summon Judah; but he delayed beyond the set time that had been appointed him. [6]David said to Abishai, "Now Sheba son of Bichri will do us more harm than Absalom; take your lord's servants and pur-

---

40. **Text-history approach.** A story can hardly end with 19:43 (Heb., 19:44); something more is needed by way of David's return. Something is offered in 20:3. It gets David back to Jerusalem, but hardly brings the story to an end. 20:22 ends the story of Sheba's revolt, but still leaves the story of David's return in an unrounded state. 1 Kings 1 is no help in this regard. The start of the story of Sheba's revolt in 20:1 is dependent on what precedes. All told, the text from 2 Samuel 11–12 through to 2 Samuel 20 weaves a single narrative thread with a skill and literary quality unparalleled in Israel's literature.

Present-text potential. The division of chapters has been well done. 19:1-8a (Heb., 19:2-9a) might seem to be the conclusion of the account of the death of Absalom. Instead, it is the beginning of the account of the support of a political winner on his way back to power. As Joab knew, David's power began with his own troops (cf. 19:7; Heb., v. 8). The next block of support to be secured is David's kin, the people of Judah (19:11-15; Heb., vv. 12-16). Shimei ben Gera of the house of Saul is next, symbolic of David's enemies, ready to curse him when he looks a loser and switching allegiance the instant the loser looks a winner (19:16-17a, 18b-23; Heb., 17-18a, 19b-24). Abishai, the soldier, wanted Shimei dead; David, the politician, let him live. Losers are not normally left to live long. Perhaps we wonder how many in Israel Shimei represented beyond his thousand from Benjamin.

Mephibosheth, son of Jonathan, manages to get in ahead of his servant Ziba. Was he an opportunist or

was his servant a liar? The text does not say. Ziba earlier and Mephibosheth here both have their say. One must be lying. The text does not say. David appears not to know and divides the real estate between them. Winners can afford to do that.

After the fair-weather friends, the genuine supporter comes on the scene, Barzillai, very old and very wealthy. He declines the invitation to go further—and gives us an insight into the pleasures of courtly life: food, drink, and singers (19:35; Heb., v. 36). We know nothing of the military support that Barzillai brought to David; we can be certain it was not negligible. There is no mention of the east-of-Jordan tribes.

Finally, a report which began at Gilgal returns there (19:15, 40; Heb., vv. 16, 41). David's tribal support from Judah is there. Israel buys into the support issue. It seems that Israel has the numbers, "ten shares"; but Judah has the best of the debate, the fiercer words (19:43; Heb., v. 44). We do not have a clear picture of the political outcome, except that it seems to pave the way for chap. 20.

After the Dtr:	Revision:	Other:
indented and sans serif font	*national focus*	double sideline

sue him, or he will find fortified cities for him-self, and escape from us." [7]Joab's men went out after him, along with the Cherethites, the Pelethites, and all the warriors; they went out from Jerusalem to pursue Sheba son of Bichri. [8]When they were at the large stone that is in Gibeon, Amasa came to meet them. Now Joab was wearing a soldier's garment and over it was a belt with a sword in its sheath fastened at his waist; as he went forward it fell out. [9]Joab said to Amasa, "Is it well with you, my brother?" And Joab took Amasa by the beard with his right hand to kiss him. [10]But Amasa did not notice the sword in Joab's hand; Joab struck him in the belly so that his entrails poured out on the ground, and he died. He did not strike a second blow.

Then Joab and his brother Abishai pursued Sheba son of Bichri. [11]And one of Joab's men took his stand by Amasa, and said, "Whoever favors Joab, and whoever is for David, let him follow Joab." [12]Amasa lay wallowing in his blood on the highway, and the man saw that all the people were stopping. Since he saw that all who came by him were stopping, he carried Amasa from the highway into a field, and threw a gar-ment over him. [13]Once he was removed from the highway, all the people went on after Joab to pursue Sheba son of Bichri.

14 Sheba passed through all the tribes of Israel to Abel of Beth-maacah; and all the Bichrites assembled, and followed him inside. [15]Joab's forces came and besieged him in Abel of Beth-maacah; they threw up a siege ramp against the city, and it stood against the rampart. Joab's forces were battering the wall to break it down. [16]Then a wise woman called from the city, "Lis-ten! Listen! Tell Joab, 'Come here, I want to speak to you.' " [17]He came near her; and the woman said, "Are you Joab?" He answered, "I am." Then she said to him, "Listen to the words of your servant." He answered, "I am listening."

[18]Then she said, "They used to say in the old days, 'Let them inquire at Abel'; and so they would settle a matter. [19]I am one of those who are peaceable and faithful in Israel; you seek to destroy a city that is a mother in Israel; why will you swallow up the heritage of the Lord?" [20]Joab answered, "Far be it from me, far be it, that I should swallow up or destroy! [21]That is not the case! But a man of the hill country of Ephraim, called Sheba son of Bichri, has lifted up his hand against King David; give him up alone, and I will withdraw from the city." The woman said to Joab, "His head shall be thrown over the wall to you." [22]Then the woman went to all the people with her wise plan. And they cut off the head of Sheba son of Bichri, and threw it out to Joab. So he blew the trumpet, and they dispersed from the city, and all went to their homes, while Joab returned to Jerusalem to the king.[41]

---

41. **Present-text potential.** One element emerges starkly from this story: the fragility of David's restored kingdom. What happens here is a forerunner of what will happen under Solomon's son in 1 Kings 12. Except that in 1 Kings 12, there is no Joab to bring power back to the king.

Sheba ben Bichri gives no reason for his separatist call: simply, "We have no portion in David" (20:1). It is enough for all Israel to withdraw from any national coalition. The secession is along tribal lines (20:2). Where, then, did Absalom's support come from?

Amasa takes too long returning. Treachery or time constraints? The text does not say. David turns to Abishai, not to Joab. Why? The text does not say. Joab kills Amasa. For Amasa's treachery or Joab's ambition? The text does not say. Later the text will favor Amasa (1 Kgs 2:5, 32-33), but the later context is not favor-able to Joab. Here, in 2 Samuel 20, Joab has taken command, Joab negotiates for the head of Sheba ben Bichri, and Joab returns to Jerusalem to the king (20:22). In all this, where does the power lie?

| Main pre-DH: *Prophetic* Record | Other pre-DH: | **Josianic DH:** |
| its sources *and prophetic contribution* | single sideline | **from the Dtr** |

23 Now Joab was in command of all the army of Israel; Benaiah son of Jehoiada was in command of the Cherethites and the Pelethites; [24]Adoram was in charge of the forced labor; Jehoshaphat son of Ahilud was the recorder; [25]Sheva was secretary; Zadok and Abiathar were priests; [26]and Ira the Jairite was also David's priest.[42]

> **21** Now there was a famine in the days of David for three years, year after year; and David inquired of the LORD. The LORD said, "There is bloodguilt on Saul and on his house, because he put the Gibeonites to death." [2]So the king called the Gibeonites and spoke to them. (Now the Gibeonites were not of the people of Israel, but of the remnant of the Amorites; although the people of Israel had sworn to spare them, Saul had tried to wipe them out in his zeal for the people of Israel and Judah.) [3]David said to the Gibeonites, "What shall I do for you? How shall I make expiation, that you may bless the heritage of the LORD?" [4]The Gibeonites said to him, "It is not a matter of silver or gold between us and Saul or his house; neither is it for us to put anyone to death in Israel." He said, "What do you say that I should do for you?" [5]They said to the king, "The man who consumed us and planned to destroy us, so that we should have no place in all the territory of Israel—

> [6]let seven of his sons be handed over to us, and we will impale them before the LORD at Gibeon on the mountain of the LORD." The king said, "I will hand them over."[43]

> 7 But the king spared Mephibosheth, the son of Saul's son Jonathan, because of the oath of the LORD that was between them, between David and Jonathan son of Saul. [8]The king took the two sons of Rizpah daughter of Aiah, whom she bore to Saul, Armoni and Mephibosheth; and the five sons of Merab daughter of Saul, whom she

---

43. For Noth, 2 Samuel 21–24 was added to the DH after it had been divided into books. Noth comments that 2 Sam 21:1-14 and 24:1-25 were added first, then the anecdotes and lists, 21:15-22; 23:8-39, and finally the poetry, 22:1-51; 23:1-7 (*DH*, 86, n. 3). In our view, the division into books is probably unimportant; this collection of traditions could hardly have been inserted anywhere else. It belongs late in the story of David, but before his death. The time of its integration into the text must remain uncertain. The lists of the Three and the Thirty are a reminder to us of how much we do not know about the reign of David, despite the extensive texts preserved.

The concentric structure of this collection is well known. At the core are two poems: a thanksgiving song that is equivalent to Psalm 18 (22:1-51) and the last words of David (23:1-7). Outside these are two collections of traditions from the early days of David's career (21:15-22 and 23:8-39), with information about events and institutions that are totally unknown to us from other parts of Samuel. The collection is framed by two stories of sacral intervention: the expiation of blood guilt (21:1-14) and the staying of divine threat (24:1-25). Despite Noth, there is no convincing evidence indicating how this collection came into being. More than anything else, the coherence of its structural organization suggests that it was preserved as a unity. As noted above, the time of its integration into the text must remain uncertain, with the odds favoring later rather than earlier.

---

42. **Present-text potential.** In the royal service, Joab commands the national army and Benaiah the mercenaries. Joab will back Adonijah and Benaiah will back Solomon. Zadok and Abiathar were priests. Abiathar will side with Adonijah and Zadok will anoint Solomon. The undercurrents of the politics escape us. We can assume they were there!

| After the Dtr: indented and sans serif font | Revision: national focus | Other: double sideline |

bore to Adriel son of Barzillai the Meho-lathite; [9]he gave them into the hands of the Gibeonites, and they impaled them on the mountain before the LORD. The seven of them perished together. They were put to death in the first days of harvest, at the beginning of barley harvest.[44]

10 Then Rizpah the daughter of Aiah took sackcloth, and spread it on a rock for herself, from the beginning of harvest until rain fell on them from the heavens; she did not allow the birds of the air to come on the bodies by day, or the wild animals by night. [11]When David was told what Rizpah daughter of Aiah, the concubine of Saul, had done, [12]David went and took the bones of Saul and the bones of his son Jonathan from the people of Jabesh-gilead, who had stolen them from the public square of Beth-shan, where the Philistines had hung them up, on the day the Philistines killed Saul on Gilboa. [13]He brought up from there the bones of Saul and the bones of his son Jonathan; and they gathered the bones of those who had been impaled. [14]They buried the bones of Saul and of his son Jonathan in the land of Benjamin in Zela, in the tomb of his father Kish; they did all that the king commanded. After that, God heeded supplications for the land.

15 The Philistines went to war again with Israel, and David went down together with his servants. They fought against the Philistines, and David grew weary. [16]Ishbi-benob, one of the descendants of the giants, whose spear weighed three hundred shekels of bronze, and who was fitted out with new weapons, said he would kill

David. [17]But Abishai son of Zeruiah came to his aid, and attacked the Philistine and killed him. Then David's men swore to him, "You shall not go out with us to battle any longer, so that you do not quench the lamp of Israel."

18 After this a battle took place with the Philistines, at Gob; then Sibbecai the Hushathite killed Saph, who was one of the descendants of the giants. [19]Then there was another battle with the Philistines at Gob; and Elhanan son of Jaare-oregim, the Beth-lehemite, killed Goliath the Gittite, the shaft of whose spear was like a weaver's beam. [20]There was again war at Gath, where there was a man of great size, who had six fingers on each hand, and six toes on each foot, twenty-four in number; he too was descended from the giants. [21]When he taunted Israel, Jonathan son of David's brother Shimei, killed him. [22]These four were descended from the giants in Gath; they fell by the hands of David and his servants.

22 David spoke to the LORD the words of this song on the day when the LORD delivered him from the hand of all his enemies, and from the hand of Saul. [2]He said:
The LORD is my rock, my fortress, and my
    deliverer,
    [3]my God, my rock, in whom I take
        refuge,
my shield and the horn of my salvation,
    my stronghold and my refuge,
    my savior; you save me from violence.
[4]I call upon the LORD, who is worthy to be
        praised,
    and I am saved from my enemies.
[5]For the waves of death encompassed me,
    the torrents of perdition assailed me;

---

44. Veijola attributed 21:2b, 7 to his DtrH.

---

⁶the cords of Sheol entangled me,
the snares of death confronted me.
⁷In my distress I called upon the LORD;
to my God I called.
From his temple he heard my voice,
and my cry came to his ears.
⁸Then the earth reeled and rocked;
the foundations of the heavens
trembled
and quaked, because he was angry.
⁹Smoke went up from his nostrils,
and devouring fire from his mouth;
glowing coals flamed forth from him.
¹⁰He bowed the heavens, and came down;
thick darkness was under his feet.
¹¹He rode on a cherub, and flew;
he was seen upon the wings of the wind.
¹²He made darkness around him a canopy,
thick clouds, a gathering of water.
¹³Out of the brightness before him
coals of fire flamed forth.
¹⁴The LORD thundered from heaven;
the Most High uttered his voice.
¹⁵He sent out arrows, and scattered them
—lightning, and routed them.
¹⁶Then the channels of the sea were seen,
the foundations of the world were
laid bare
at the rebuke of the LORD,
at the blast of the breath of his nostrils.
¹⁷He reached from on high, he took me,
he drew me out of mighty waters.
¹⁸He delivered me from my strong enemy,
from those who hated me;
for they were too mighty for me.
¹⁹They came upon me in the day of my
calamity,
but the LORD was my stay.
²⁰He brought me out into a broad place;
he delivered me, because he delighted
in me.

²¹The LORD rewarded me according to my
righteousness;
according to the cleanness of my hands
he recompensed me.
²²For I have kept the ways of the LORD,
and have not wickedly departed from
my God.
²³For all his ordinances were before me,
and from his statutes I did not turn
aside.
²⁴I was blameless before him,
and I kept myself from guilt.
²⁵Therefore the LORD has recompensed
me according to my
righteousness,
according to my cleanness in his sight.
²⁶With the loyal you show yourself loyal;
with the blameless you show yourself
blameless;
²⁷with the pure you show yourself pure,
and with the crooked you show yourself
perverse.
²⁸You deliver a humble people,
but your eyes are upon the haughty to
bring them down.
²⁹Indeed, you are my lamp, O LORD,
the LORD lightens my darkness.
³⁰By you I can crush a troop,
and by my God I can leap over a wall.
³¹This God—his way is perfect;
the promise of the LORD proves true;
he is a shield for all who take refuge
in him.
³²For who is God, but the LORD?
And who is a rock, except our God?
³³The God who has girded me with
strength
has opened wide my path.
³⁴He made my feet like the feet of deer,
and set me secure on the heights.
³⁵He trains my hands for war,

| After the Dtr: indented and sans serif font | Revision: national focus | Other: double sideline |

so that my arms can bend a bow
of bronze.
[36]You have given me the shield of your
salvation,
and your help has made me great.
[37]You have made me stride freely,
and my feet do not slip;
[38]I pursued my enemies and destroyed
them,
and did not turn back until they were
consumed.
[39]I consumed them; I struck them down,
so that they did not rise;
they fell under my feet.
[40]For you girded me with strength for the
battle;
you made my assailants sink under me.
[41]You made my enemies turn their backs
to me,
those who hated me, and I destroyed
them.
[42]They looked, but there was no one to
save them;
they cried to the LORD, but he did not
answer them.
[43]I beat them fine like the dust of the
earth,
I crushed them and stamped them
down like the mire of the streets.
[44]You delivered me from strife with the
peoples;
you kept me as the head of the nations;
people whom I had not known
served me.
[45]Foreigners came cringing to me;
as soon as they heard of me, they
obeyed me.
[46]Foreigners lost heart,
and came trembling out of their
strongholds.
[47]The LORD lives! Blessed be my rock,

and exalted be my God, the rock of my
salvation,
[48]the God who gave me vengeance
and brought down peoples under me,
[49]who brought me out from my enemies;
you exalted me above my adversaries,
you delivered me from the violent.
[50]For this I will extol you, O LORD, among
the nations,
and sing praises to your name.
[51]He is a tower of salvation for his king,
and shows steadfast love to his
anointed,
to David and his descendants forever.[45]

23 Now these are the last words of David:
The oracle of David, son of Jesse,
the oracle of the man whom God
exalted,
the anointed of the God of Jacob,
the favorite of the Strong One of Israel:
[2]The spirit of the LORD speaks through me,
his word is upon my tongue.
[3]The God of Israel has spoken,
the Rock of Israel has said to me:
One who rules over people justly,
ruling in the fear of God,
[4]is like the light of morning,
like the sun rising on a cloudless
morning,
gleaming from the rain on the
grassy land.
[5]Is not my house like this with God?
For he has made with me an everlasting
covenant,
ordered in all things and secure.
Will he not cause to prosper
all my help and my desire?

---

45. Veijola attributed 22:1, 22-25, 51 to his DtrN.

---

⁶But the godless are all like thorns that are
thrown away;
for they cannot be picked up with
the hand;
⁷to touch them one uses an iron bar
or the shaft of a spear.
And they are entirely consumed in fire
on the spot.

8 These are the names of the warriors whom David had: Josheb-basshebeth a Tahchemonite; he was chief of the Three; he wielded his spear against eight hundred whom he killed at one time.

9 Next to him among the three warriors was Eleazar son of Dodo son of Ahohi. He was with David when they defied the Philistines who were gathered there for battle. The Israelites withdrew, ¹⁰but he stood his ground. He struck down the Philistines until his arm grew weary, though his hand clung to the sword. The LORD brought about a great victory that day. Then the people came back to him—but only to strip the dead.

11 Next to him was Shammah son of Agee, the Hararite. The Philistines gathered together at Lehi, where there was a plot of ground full of lentils; and the army fled from the Philistines. ¹²But he took his stand in the middle of the plot, defended it, and killed the Philistines; and the LORD brought about a great victory.

13 Towards the beginning of harvest three of the thirty chiefs went down to join David at the cave of Adullam, while a band of Philistines was encamped in the valley of Rephaim. ¹⁴David was then in the stronghold; and the garrison of the Philistines was then at Bethlehem. ¹⁵David said longingly, "O that someone would give me water to drink from the well of Bethlehem that is by the gate!" ¹⁶Then the three warriors broke through the camp of the Philistines, drew water from the well of Bethlehem that was by the gate, and brought it to David. But he would not drink of it; he poured it out to the LORD, ¹⁷for he said, "The LORD forbid that I should do this. Can I drink the blood of the men who went at the risk of their lives?" Therefore he would not drink it. The three warriors did these things.

18 Now Abishai son of Zeruiah, the brother of Joab, was chief of the Thirty. With his spear he fought against three hundred men and killed them, and won a name beside the Three. ¹⁹He was the most renowned of the Thirty, and became their commander; but he did not attain to the Three.

20 Benaiah son of Jehoiada was a valiant warrior from Kabzeel, a doer of great deeds; he struck down two sons of Ariel of Moab. He also went down and killed a lion in a pit on a day when snow had fallen. ²¹And he killed an Egyptian, a handsome man. The Egyptian had a spear in his hand; but Benaiah went against him with a staff, snatched the spear out of the Egyptian's hand, and killed him with his own spear. ²²Such were the things Benaiah son of Jehoiada did, and won a name beside the three warriors. ²³He was renowned among the Thirty, but he did not attain to the Three. And David put him in charge of his bodyguard.

24 Among the Thirty were Asahel brother of Joab; Elhanan son of Dodo of Bethlehem; ²⁵Shammah of Harod; Elika of Harod; ²⁶Helez the Paltite; Ira son of Ikkesh of Tekoa; ²⁷Abiezer of Anathoth; Mebunnai the Hushathite; ²⁸Zalmon the Ahohite;

After the Dtr:
indented and sans serif font

Revision:
national focus

Other:
double sideline

Maharai of Netophah; [29]Heleb son of Baanah of Netophah; Ittai son of Ribai of Gibeah of the Benjaminites; [30]Benaiah of Pirathon; Hiddai of the torrents of Gaash; [31]Abi-albon the Arbathite; Azmaveth of Bahurim; [32]Eliahba of Shaalbon; the sons of Jashen: Jonathan [33]son of Shammah the Hararite; Ahiam son of Sharar the Hararite; [34]Eliphelet son of Ahasbai of Maacah; Eliam son of Ahithophel the Gilonite; [35]Hezro of Carmel; Paarai the Arbite; [36]Igal son of Nathan of Zobah; Bani the Gadite; [37]Zelek the Ammonite; Naharai of Beeroth, the armor-bearer of Joab son of Zeruiah; [38]Ira the Ithrite; Gareb the Ithrite; [39]Uriah the Hittite—thirty-seven in all.

24 Again the anger of the LORD was kindled against Israel, and he incited David against them, saying, "Go, count the people of Israel and Judah." [2]So the king said to Joab and the commanders of the army, who were with him, "Go through all the tribes of Israel, from Dan to Beer-sheba, and take a census of the people, so that I may know how many there are." [3]But Joab said to the king, "May the LORD your God increase the number of the people a hundredfold, while the eyes of my lord the king can still see it! But why does my lord the king want to do this?" [4]But the king's word prevailed against Joab and the commanders of the army. So Joab and the commanders of the army went out from the presence of the king to take a census of the people of Israel. [5]They crossed the Jordan, and began from Aroer and from the city that is in the middle of the valley, toward Gad and on to Jazer. [6]Then they came to Gilead, and to Kadesh in the land of the Hittites; and they came to Dan, and from Dan they went around to Sidon, [7]and came to the fortress of Tyre and to all the cities of the Hivites and Canaanites; and they went out to the Negeb of Judah at Beer-sheba. [8]So when they had gone through all the land, they came back to Jerusalem at the end of nine months and twenty days. [9]Joab reported to the king the number of those who had been recorded: in Israel there were eight hundred thousand soldiers able to draw the sword, and those of Judah were five hundred thousand.

10 But afterward, David was stricken to the heart because he had numbered the people. David said to the LORD, "I have sinned greatly in what I have done. But now, O LORD, I pray you, take away the guilt of your servant; for I have done very foolishly." [11]When David rose in the morning, the word of the LORD came to the prophet Gad, David's seer, saying, [12]"Go and say to David: Thus says the LORD: Three things I offer you; choose one of them, and I will do it to you." [13]So Gad came to David and told him; he asked him, "Shall three years of famine come to you on your land? Or will you flee three months before your foes while they pursue you? Or shall there be three days' pestilence in your land? Now consider, and decide what answer I shall return to the one who sent me." [14]Then David said to Gad, "I am in great distress; let us fall into the hand of the LORD, for his mercy is great; but let me not fall into human hands."

15 So the LORD sent a pestilence on Israel from that morning until the appointed time; and seventy thousand of the people died, from Dan to Beer-sheba. [16]But when the angel stretched out his hand toward Jerusalem to destroy it, the LORD relented

---

| Main pre-DH: *Prophetic* Record | Other pre-DH: | **Josianic DH:** |
| its sources *and prophetic contribution* | single sideline | **from the Dtr** |

concerning the evil, and said to the angel who was bringing destruction among the people, "It is enough; now stay your hand." The angel of the LORD was then by the threshing floor of Araunah the Jebusite. [17]When David saw the angel who was destroying the people, he said to the LORD, "I alone have sinned, and I alone have done wickedly; but these sheep, what have they done? Let your hand, I pray, be against me and against my father's house."

18 That day Gad came to David and said to him, "Go up and erect an altar to the LORD on the threshing floor of Araunah the Jebusite." [19]Following Gad's instructions, David went up, as the LORD had commanded. [20]When Araunah looked down, he saw the king and his servants coming toward him; and Araunah went out and prostrated himself before the king with his face to the ground. [21]Araunah said, "Why has my lord the king come to his servant?"

David said, "To buy the threshing floor from you in order to build an altar to the LORD, so that the plague may be averted from the people." [22]Then Araunah said to David, "Let my lord the king take and offer up what seems good to him; here are the oxen for the burnt offering, and the threshing sledges and the yokes of the oxen for the wood. [23]All this, O king, Araunah gives to the king." And Araunah said to the king, "May the LORD your God respond favorably to you."

24 But the king said to Araunah, "No, but I will buy them from you for a price; I will not offer burnt offerings to the LORD my God that cost me nothing." So David bought the threshing floor and the oxen for fifty shekels of silver. [25]David built there an altar to the LORD, and offered burnt offerings and offerings of well-being. So the LORD answered his supplication for the land, and the plague was averted from Israel.[46]

---

46. Veijola attributed 24:1, 19b, 23b, 25bα to his DtrH and 24:3-4a, 10-14, 15aβ, 17, 21bβ, 25bβ to his DtrP.

| After the Dtr: indented and sans serif font | *Revision:* *national focus* | Other: double sideline |

The Books of Kings

INTRODUCTION

The books of Kings confront some remarkable theological challenges. First there is celebration, then cause for despondency and diminishment. National celebration is at its height with the successful transfer of the monarchy from David to Solomon, with God's gift to Solomon of great wisdom, and with Solomon's successful building of the temple. The causes for despondency are not far behind.

With Solomon's prayer for the acceptance of his temple answered—God's lovely "my eyes and my heart will be there for all time" (9:3)—comes a warning of what will happen if Solomon turns aside from following God (9:6-9; ostensibly addressed to Solomon, it is in the plural—a pointer to Israel's inclusion). The warning points to consequences that are terminal: Israel will be cut off from both land and temple, banished from God's sight (9:6-9). The warning is in vain. 11:1-13 reports Solomon's apostasy and God's anger. So much for Solomon's kingdom.

The northern kingdom is to do no better. Jeroboam is designated by a prophet, becomes king of the ten northern tribes, and out of political necessity (12:27) creates a cause of sin. The seeds of destruction have been sown for the northern kingdom. Those seeds will be reaped in the exile of 722. The south undergoes reform with Hezekiah (c. 701) and again under Josiah (c.

622). Old habits outweigh reforms and 587 sees the final exile.

It is a book of prophets and kings. Prophets bulk large. Nathan at the start is more a courtier than a prophet. But Ahijah of Shiloh is in full prophetic voice, promising Jeroboam what was given David (11:29-39) and, when he turned apostate, rejecting him (14:1-14). Shemaiah, the man of God, is at hand to prevent Rehoboam joining together by force what God by the prophet has put asunder (12:21-24). The great Elijah is there to reject Ahab. Elisha sends a disciple to anoint Jehu king to replace Ahab's line. Kings are central. David who won a kingdom and Solomon who lost one. Rehoboam who divided a kingdom and Jeroboam who created the snare of sin for a kingdom. Turbulent kings until Ahab rate with Jeroboam as a source of evil.

The evil culminates in the crushing of the northern kingdom by the Assyrian empire. The southern kingdom survives in hope. There is reform under Hezekiah, bolstered by the prophet Isaiah; more radical reform under Josiah, bolstered by the prophetess Huldah. According to the text, the damage done by Manasseh is too deep even for the Josianic reform. The southern kingdom is crushed by the Babylonian empire. The four final kings are puppets.

1 Kings 1–2 echo the drama and intrigue that dominated the story of David's later years in 2 Samuel 11–20. The actions of Adonijah recall

those of Absalom in 2 Samuel 15. The outcome is Solomon's succession.

1 Kings 3–11 are quite different. Here, dramatic storytelling gives way to the measured accounts of the administration of the united kingdom by David's successor, Solomon. The focus is firmly and almost exclusively on Solomon: his conduct and policies at the national and international levels; his provisions for the royal court; his extensive building programs, culminating in the construction and dedication of the temple. There is fulsome approval of Solomon in chapters 3-10 followed by condemnation in chapter 11. The account of his reign ends with the formulaic report in 1 Kgs 11:43 of his death and burial. 1 Kings 12 marks the disintegration of the united monarchy and the emergence of the separate kingdoms of Israel and Judah.

1 Kings 12—2 Kings 25 is a different story again. Drama and achievement are replaced by the sorry succession of human failure. Solomon's son is politically inept and the united kingdom of David and Solomon's Israel is divided. Jeroboam starts on the path of worship apart from Jerusalem. If Jeroboam was a separatist, Ahab was an apostate. Jehu's rebellion, with prophetic backing, eliminated a threat to the worship of YHWH as God of Israel. Jeroboam's sin remained a canker and northern Israel ended in exile. According to the DH, despite the reforming efforts of Hezekiah and Josiah in Judah, the politics and religious practices of Manasseh were too deeply ingrained and southern Israel too ended in exile.

It is a sad chronicle. The notes of hope are there. But they are overrun by the realism of events and the ebb and flow of empires beyond Israel's control. What hope remains in a descendant of David closely watched in Babylon?

It is helpful to be aware of the component elements that we identify in this text of 1–2 Kings, recalling what has been said above in the Introduction. Assuming the Josianic DH, its revision involves three major focuses: the extension that takes the story down to 2 Kgs 25:21; the royal focus that looks particularly to the evil of kings (found in 1 Samuel and 1–2 Kings); and the national focus that looks to the responsibility of the people and their disobedience (found throughout). Among the components available to the Josianic Dtr were the latter part of the Prophetic Record (down to 2 Kgs 10:28), the list of northern kings after Jehu (i.e., the PR's extension, from Jehu to Hoshea), and the Hezekian King List (at its most minimal). Central to the identification of the last two, as well as of the DH's extension, are the patterns discernible in the royal judgment formulas. What matters here is less the variation possible within one author and more the apparent regularity of the formulas' distribution. So we attribute Pattern A to the PR Extension, Pattern B to the HKL, and Pattern C to the Josianic Dtr (for these patterns, see the Tables; for discussion, see the Introduction). Pattern B/C reports on Manasseh, Amon, and Josiah; Pattern D reports on the kings of the DH Extension.

When the text after Solomon is read as a record of faith and its expression, it can be unsettling. The reflective reader may be troubled by two enigmas that the text leaves unresolved. First, what was the role of the northern kingdom in the destiny of Israel? It was brought into existence by God (e.g., 1 Kgs 11:31); its existence was terminated by God (e.g., 2 Kgs 17:18). What role then did northern Israel have in this divine design? Second, what value was left to dtr theology with the death of Josiah? According to dtr theology, explicit in the great exhortation given by Moses, Israel was to choose life, obeying God and holding fast to him, "for that means life to you and length of days" (Deut 30:20). Josiah and Josiah's generation had done just that, choosing life in fidelity to YHWH ("all the people joined in the covenant," 2 Kgs 23:3). But Josiah died in battle at Megiddo and the reform died with him. Should dtr theology have died as well?

The northern kingdom of Israel

The enterprise is clearly presented as of God. It is God who, through a prophet, gives ten tribes to Jeroboam and leaves the Davidic dynasty in Jerusalem. It is God who brings about the ill-advised political decisions of Rehoboam (1 Kgs 12:15). It is God who, through a prophet, prevents political retribution (1 Kgs 12:21-24). The rejection of the enterprise is presented equally as of God. It is through a prophet that the message is delivered: "Go, tell Jeroboam, 'Thus says the LORD, the God of Israel: ... I will bring evil upon the house of Jeroboam' " (1 Kgs 14:7, 10). The final word is no kinder: "The LORD rejected all the descendants of Israel; he punished them and gave them into the hand of plunderers, until he had banished them from his presence" (2 Kgs 17:20). What is the meaning of all this for Israel?

"The sins of Jeroboam son of Nebat, which he caused Israel to commit" is a refrain that runs relentlessly through the story of the northern kingdom. What exactly were Jeroboam's sins? The text is uncharacteristically coy.

In the present biblical text, Saul is given clear instructions (whether 1 Sam 10:8 or 15:3 or both). Solomon is given instructions and warning (1 Kgs 9:4, 6-9). Jeroboam was given a kingdom; amid all that was said, his instructions amount to half a verse (11:38a).[1] Jeroboam is to

be in a new situation, never previously experienced in Israel. There is a newly-built temple in Jerusalem. There will be a Davidic dynasty reigning in Jerusalem always (11:36). What is taken from the Jerusalem dynasty is given to Jeroboam—without his being told what to do with it.[2] The silence is strange.

Saul's sin is clear; he disobeyed. Solomon's sin is clear; an apostate, he turned to other gods. On Jeroboam's sin, the text is almost delphic, shrouding detail in obscurity and double meaning. The account of his rejection will spell out his sin as apostasy (1 Kgs 14:9abα); the account of what he did is less specific. The declaration attached to the golden calves says: "your gods, O Israel, who brought you up out of the land of Egypt" (12:28). Syncretism at least and open to apostasy, if not already there.[3] At no point is

---

1. In the Josianic DH, enormous weight rests on two verses. For Solomon: "if you will walk before me, as David your father walked, with integrity of heart and uprightness, doing according to all that I have commanded you, and keeping my statutes and my ordinances" (9:4); for Jeroboam: "if you will listen to all that I command you, walk in my ways, and do what is right in my sight by keeping my statutes and my commandments, as David my servant did" (11:38a).

2. Reality is reality and royalty is royalty. Two kings with two kingdoms do not have one capital city and worship in one temple. Jeroboam's commission from God can hardly be expected to include political and personal suicide. It is hardly fair to say that "Jeroboam's actions appear reprehensible, given his mandate" (Knoppers, *Two Nations Under God*, 2.37). What is surprising, if not reprehensible, is the lack of any mandate, the lack of any specifics on political and cultic practice.

3. The description of the god as "who brought you up out of the land of Egypt" is thoroughly orthodox. The use of a plural verb is open to double meaning, to syncretism and to apostasy. To one familiar with the DH, the plural speaks of gods not God (e.g., contrast 1 Sam 25:22 or 2 Sam 3:35 or 1 Kgs 1:47 [sing.; from non-Israelites, note 1 Sam 4:7; 2 Kgs 6:31] with 1 Kgs 19:2 [plur.; outside the DH, 1 Kgs 20:10]; cf. the discrimination between sing. and plur. in Psalm 82). So Jones, "a plural verb in the second half of the verse demands the translation **your gods**" (*1 and 2 Kings*, 1.258). Note the comment, "Whatever was intended, the veneration of these animal symbols as deities occurred . . ." (ibid.).

Jerusalem given a characterization equivalent to "the place that the LORD will choose in one of your tribes" (Deut 12:14).

Twice Jeroboam's action is described as sin. First, regarding the placement of the calves in Bethel and Dan (12:29), because the people went there. Going is not quite walking in the way of; the text says only that they went—not to bow down, not to serve, not to prostitute themselves (as with Gideon, Judg 7:27).[4] Second, regarding the indiscriminate consecration of priests, where it is said that the sin impacted on "the house of Jeroboam"—not on Israel (1 Kgs 13:33b-34).[5]

When it comes to Jeroboam's rejection, 1 Kgs 14:9 has specifics enough. "You have done evil above all those who were before you" (v. 9a); that must include Solomon's apostasy. "You have gone and made for yourself other gods, and cast images, provoking me to anger" (v. 9abα); other gods is apostasy. You "have thrust me behind your back" (v. 9abβ); this can range from disobedience through syncretism to apostasy.[6]

To accuse Jeroboam of the worship of Baal is too simple. When Jehu has "wiped out Baal from Israel" (2 Kgs 10:28), he is still accused of not having turned aside "from the sins of Jeroboam son of Nebat, which he caused Israel to commit" (10:29; cf. v. 31b).

What does it mean in the text of the DH that God set up the northern kingdom and that it failed? The Josianic DH has little to say about the north, leaving it to the PR which lays the blame squarely on the people (2 Kgs 17:21-23). The revised DH concludes with two remarkably harsh judgments: "Therefore the LORD was very angry with Israel and removed them out of his sight; none was left but the tribe of Judah alone" (17:18); "The LORD rejected all the descendants of Israel; he punished them and gave them into the hand of the plunderers, until he had banished them from his presence" (17:20). There is a frightening echo here of the dtr preface in Judges (2:14, 16), with an ominous similarity to Judg 10:14, 16. The beginning of it all with Jeroboam's calves recalls the episode with Aaron at Sinai and God's readiness to destroy Israel and start anew (Exod 32:10; cf. Num 14:12). What does the conjunction of these texts say of divine patience? What is the role of the northern kingdom in the destiny of Israel?[7]

---

4. The NRSV helps out by expanding the Hebrew's "went" into "went to worship." As Knoppers notes, "many commentators excise v 30a as a late gloss," and he follows suit (*Two Nations Under God*, 2.25, 27). What such commentators must do is account for the presence of the "gloss" where it is. Its incompleteness argues for its authenticity; a later insertion would surely have had more to say. V. 30b is textually uncertain.

5. Our attribution of 1 Kgs 13:33b-34 to the PR and of 12:31-33 to the royal focus of dtr revision process goes against the views of many commentators. This is not the place for argument in detail. One point may be noted. 12:31a has two actions, using two verbs: 13:33b has one action, using one verb. To speak of inverted quotations and Zeidel's Law is an oversimplification (against Knoppers, *Two Nations Under God*, 2.52-55).

The text—whether PR, Josianic Dtr, or later revision—has no reference to high places in the northern kingdom between 1 Kgs 13:33 (Jeroboam) and 2 Kgs 17:9 and 11 (the later reflective summary).

We need to be aware of Jeroboam's substantial interference in the cultic affairs of his realm listed in 12:31-33. These seem to be corollaries to his sin rather than its core.

6. Not all syncretism is unacceptable. After his capture of Jerusalem, David gave some of his sons names that included the element of the god "El" (cf. 2 Sam 5:13-16). Saul surely saw no harm in giving two of his sons names with the element of "Baal" (cf. Ishbaal and Meribaal), even if later Israel in shame changed the element to "boshet."

7. What cannot be ignored here either is the realization that in 2 Kgs 17:7-20 the accusation touches both northern and southern kingdoms, northern Israel and Judah (see the

The failure of dtr theology

The unsettling element in the DH text becomes clearer. In later eyes, at least, the northern kingdom was established by God as a result of Solomon's apostasy—we might say, therefore, in the hope of stemming apostasy in Israel. The attempt was a failure and its outcome was exile. The southern kingdom recovered from Solomon's apostasy, recovered again from Jehoram, Ahaziah, and Ahaz. Hezekiah righted matters after Ahaz; Josiah righted them after Manasseh and Amon. According to dtr theology, all should have been well. Josiah and his generation ("all the people joined in the covenant," 2 Kgs 23:3) chose life in fidelity to YHWH. According to dtr theology, that should have meant life to them and length of days (Deut 30:19-20). Alas, not so. Josiah went into battle at Megiddo and died. The reform died with him. Not only the reform. At that moment, dtr theology was in deep trouble.

The thought that Huldah's prophecy offered Josiah a mercifully early death so that he would not live to see the reform shatter on the rocks of Manasseh's enduring evil is tempting. But it disavows Deuteronomy. The promise of "life to you and length of days" (Deut 30:20) is not fulfilled by the gift of an early death. Josiah's unexpected death challenged dtr theology at its core.

With the failure of the hoped-for Josianic reform, some revision of the DH was necessary and inevitable. An extension that brought it down to the exile of Judah can be seen within 23:28—25:30. It does no more than catalogue events; there is no theological reflection, beyond the judgment formulas.

Elsewhere within the work of the revision, strong emphasis is laid on the negative impact of Manasseh. 2 Kgs 23:26-27 is a highly explicit statement of this position: "still the LORD did not turn from the fierceness of his great wrath, by which his anger was kindled against Judah, because of all the provocations with which Manasseh had provoked him" (v. 26). While this may make sense politically, it is theologically at odds with dtr doctrine (cf. Deut 30:15-20). The DH places emphasis on the responsibility of kings; they do what is right or what is evil in the sight of YHWH. It is a major shift in theological thinking to move from this apparent individual royal responsibility to a more collective understanding—one where Manasseh's evil can outweigh Josiah's good.

This collective understanding is expanded in what we have termed the "national focus" within the process of revising the DH. Two elements are primary in the texts attributed to this national focus: the responsibility of the people and the failure in obedience to the law of God. At first sight, this theological move eliminates the scandal of Josiah's unexpected death in battle. At stake is not good or evil in the actions of Josiah. The bigger picture includes the actions of the people and their responsibility for obedience to the law of God, revealed by Moses. On closer inspection, even this move does not meet the challenge to dtr theology involved in Josiah's death. If, as we have noted, the dtr text claimed that "all the people joined in the covenant" (2 Kgs 23:3), the blame for failure cannot be placed on the people of that generation. Even if we notice that the national focus of the revision emphasized the nature of the repentance in Samuel's time (cf. 1 Sam 7:3-4), and that nothing of the kind is said for Josiah's time, it would be theological sleight of hand to ignore the affirmation of 23:3, that "all the people joined in the covenant."

discussion of the text below). It is not simply what this says of the north; it is what this says of the destiny of Israel as chosen people of God (cf. 2 Kgs 17:13).

There are times when the realities of faith have to free themselves from the trappings of theological logic. The DH achieves this where it begins rather than where it ends. God's commitment to David and the ambivalent fate of David's last descendant in Babylon (cf. 2 Kgs 25:27-30) might inspire hope in some. Its echo of Mephibosheth at David's table and the end of the road for Saul's dynasty might inspire despair for others. However, at the beginning of the DH, the revision has enveloped Moses' discourse in a combination of realism and hope. In chap. 4, the realism looks to God scattering Israel among the peoples (Deut 4:27-28). The hope has Israel "seek the LORD," "return to the LORD," and be received by the LORD (4:29-31). In chap. 30, after realism has portrayed the agony of exile (Deut 29:18-28), hope comes to the fore, based on the commitment of God: "the LORD your God will restore your fortunes and have compassion on you" (30:3, cf. vv. 1-10).

The Josianic DH started out with a theology closely akin to that of the wisdom literature (cf. Psalm 1). The revised DH, confronted with the limited disorder of its world, opted away from theology to a faith in God's commitment.[8]

---

8. This may come as a surprise after the relentlessly theological logic of the DH. When we recall the dtr passages, before and after Israel's wilderness wanderings, in the episodes of the golden calf and the spies (Exod 32:7-14; Num 14:10b-25), the surprise may be lessened.

THE FIRST BOOK OF KINGS

1 King David was old and advanced in years; and although they covered him with clothes, he could not get warm. ²So his servants said to him, "Let a young virgin be sought for my lord the king, and let her wait on the king, and be his attendant; let her lie in your bosom, so that my lord the king may be warm." ³So they searched for a beautiful girl throughout all the territory of Israel, and found Abishag the Shunammite, and brought her to the king. ⁴The girl was very beautiful. She became the king's attendant and served him, but the king did not know her sexually.¹

5 Now Adonijah son of Haggith exalted himself, saying, "I will be king"; he prepared for himself chariots and horsemen, and fifty men to run before him. ⁶His father had never at any time displeased him by asking, "Why have you

---

1. **Text signals** in 1 Kings 1–2. (i) The passage opens with a notice of David's old age (1:1), notes his death and succession by Solomon (2:10-12), and concludes by noting again the establishment of Solomon as king (2:46; cf. 2:12 and LXX, 2:35).

(ii) Detailed instructions by David in favor of Solomon's succession (1:32-37) contrast with David's notably vague prayer, giving thanks for the succession with no mention of the identity of the individual (1:48; cf. Vulg., *sedentem in solio meo*). The contrast is such—and the gap in v. 48 so surprising, compare LXX and Versions for various fillings of the gap—that even Queen Athaliah (2 Kgs 11:1-3) could have appealed to the verse.

(iii) David's charge to Solomon falls into two clear and distinct parts (2:1-4 and 5-9). Vv. 1-4 focus on obedience to the law; vv. 5-9 focus on the completion of David's business in three political areas. The first of these concerns Joab and his responsibility for the deaths of Abner and Amasa; he supported Adonijah against Solomon (1:7). The second relates to rewarding the loyalty of the sons of Barzillai (2:7; note that here it is the sons of Barzillai who met David in his flight while in 2 Sam 17:27-29 the sons are not mentioned, and in 19:31-40 [Heb., 32-41] only Chimham is involved). The third concerns Shimei, an influential Saul supporter (2 Sam 16:5; 19:16-17 [Heb., 17-18];

David's oath does not bind Solomon. All three instructions look to shoring up support for Solomon.

(iv) In the sequel to this paternal charge, Solomon first eliminates two dangers not mentioned by David: Adonijah, his elder brother and rival; Abiathar who had backed Adonijah. Joab is next; he saw the writing on the wall, sought sanctuary, and died at the altar, replaced by Benaiah. Shimei was the last of the dangers. He gave Solomon a pretext and Solomon took it. "So the kingdom was established in the hand of Solomon" (2:46; the repetition of this phrase in various forms and the state of the textual traditions bear witness to the complexity of the energies expended on these texts). It would have been improbable to have put a reference to either Adonijah (cf. 1:6) or Abiathar (2:26b) on David's lips; the sons of Barzillai were supporters and not dangers, and so need not have been mentioned in this context.

(v) Chap. 1, with the involvement of Bathsheba and Nathan, has echoes of 2 Samuel 11–12. While Solomon's accession may echo 2 Sam 12:24-25, the vagueness of 1 Kgs 1:48 warns against putting too much weight on the succession link. Neither Nathan nor Bathsheba plays a role in 2 Samuel 13–20. The oath noted by Bathsheba (1 Kgs 1:17) is unmentioned in 2 Samuel 13–20.

(vi) Chap. 2 looks exclusively to Solomon's reign. It is a series of accounts rather than a sustained narrative.

Text-history approach. The divergence of well-informed opinion on 1 Kings 1–2 is considerable. For some, this text is the conclusion of the "Succession Narrative"; for others, it is not. It is a text in its own right, with its own beginning, middle, and end. In our reading of the signals, it is unlikely that it belonged with 2 Samuel 11–20 (despite S. Seiler, *Geschichte von der Thronfolge Davids*). Its primary concern is with the legitimation given Solomon as David's heir and

---

| After the Dtr: indented and sans serif font | *Revision: royal focus* | *Revision: national focus* | Other: double sideline |

done thus and so?" He was also a very handsome man, and he was born next after Absalom. [7]He conferred with Joab son of Zeruiah and with the priest Abiathar, and they supported Adonijah.

---

with a justification for the killing of those who were a danger to Solomon's hold on power. As such, a setting in Solomon's reign would be appropriate; a later setting cannot be excluded. Later generations might defend bloodletting by Solomon; others might seek justification from Solomon's behavior for their own (for example, Athaliah in 2 Kings 11 or Amaziah in 2 Kings 14).

It is perfectly possible that the Prophetic Record (PR) moved from the successful establishment of David (cf. 2 Sam 8:15) to the designation of Jeroboam (1 Kgs 11:26ff.). After all, what the prophets who established David promised him was promised to Jeroboam by Ahijah—a dynasty, "an enduring house, as I built for David" (1 Kgs 11:38b). Similar abrupt transitions can be observed at 1 Samuel 9 and 1 Kings 17, for example. However, there are elements in the present text that stand out as unusual and need to be accounted for (i.e., 1 Kgs 3:1; 9:15a, 24; and 11:7); attribution to the PR will be suggested in due course (see below).

These elements belong within the reign of Solomon. They may have served simply to prepare for Jeroboam's elevation. It is also possible that the PR preceded these with a note of Solomon's accession. Despite 1 Kgs 1:48, there is no text actually duplicating such a notice of accession. Given the probable identity of language involved, it is possible that the Dtr took over 2:10 and 12 from the PR. It is not necessary, only possible. To indicate this possibility, however, we have italicized 2:10 and 12.

Present-text potential. After the review of Davidic tradition in 2 Samuel 21–24, 1 Kings 1–2 returns to the court of David in his old age, with David seeing the succession to his throne in his own lifetime, and with Solomon's measures to secure his kingdom. In all of this, the dynastic promise of 2 Samuel 7 may be seen to be fulfilled.

[8]But the priest Zadok, and Benaiah son of Jehoiada, and the prophet Nathan, and Shimei, and Rei, and David's own warriors did not side with Adonijah.

9 Adonijah sacrificed sheep, oxen, and fatted cattle by the stone Zoheleth, which is beside En-rogel, and he invited all his brothers, the king's sons, and all the royal officials of Judah, [10]but he did not invite the prophet Nathan or Benaiah or the warriors or his brother Solomon.

11 Then Nathan said to Bathsheba, Solomon's mother, "Have you not heard that Adonijah son of Haggith has become king and our lord David does not know it? [12]Now therefore come, let me give you advice, so that you may save your own life and the life of your son Solomon. [13]Go in at once to King David, and say to him, 'Did you not, my lord the king, swear to your servant, saying: Your son Solomon shall succeed me as king, and he shall sit on my throne? Why then is Adonijah king?' [14]Then while you are still there speaking with the king, I will come in after you and confirm your words."

15 So Bathsheba went to the king in his room. The king was very old; Abishag the Shunammite was attending the king. [16]Bathsheba bowed and did obeisance to the king, and the king said, "What do you wish?" [17]She said to him, "My lord, you swore to your servant by the LORD your God, saying: Your son Solomon shall succeed me as king, and he shall sit on my throne. [18]But now suddenly Adonijah has become king, though you, my lord the king, do not know it. [19]He has sacrificed oxen, fatted cattle, and sheep in abundance, and has invited all the children of the king, the priest Abiathar, and Joab the commander of the army; but your servant Solomon he has not invited. [20]But you, my lord the king—the eyes of all Israel are on you to tell them who shall sit on the throne of my lord

---

Main pre-DH:	Other pre-DH:	HKL: + single	**Josianic DH:**
Prophetic Record	single sideline	underline	**from the Dtr**

the king after him. ²¹Otherwise it will come to pass, when my lord the king sleeps with his ancestors, that my son Solomon and I will be counted offenders."

22 While she was still speaking with the king, the prophet Nathan came in. ²³The king was told, "Here is the prophet Nathan." When he came in before the king, he did obeisance to the king, with his face to the ground. ²⁴Nathan said, "My lord the king, have you said, 'Adonijah shall succeed me as king, and he shall sit on my throne'? ²⁵For today he has gone down and has sacrificed oxen, fatted cattle, and sheep in abundance, and has invited all the king's children, Joab the commander of the army, and the priest Abiathar, who are now eating and drinking before him, and saying, 'Long live King Adonijah!' ²⁶But he did not invite me, your servant, and the priest Zadok, and Benaiah son of Jehoiada, and your servant Solomon. ²⁷Has this thing been brought about by my lord the king and you have not let your servants know who should sit on the throne of my lord the king after him?"

28 King David answered, "Summon Bathsheba to me." So she came into the king's presence, and stood before the king. ²⁹The king swore, saying, "As the Lord lives, who has saved my life from every adversity, ³⁰as I swore to you by the Lord, the God of Israel, 'Your son Solomon shall succeed me as king, and he shall sit on my throne in my place,' so will I do this day." ³¹Then Bathsheba bowed with her face to the ground, and did obeisance to the king, and said, "May my lord King David live forever!"

32 King David said, "Summon to me the priest Zadok, the prophet Nathan, and Benaiah son of Jehoiada." When they came before the king, ³³the king said to them, "Take with you the servants of your lord, and have my son Solomon ride on my own mule, and bring him down to Gihon. ³⁴There let the priest Zadok and the prophet Nathan anoint him king over Israel; then blow the trumpet, and say, 'Long live King Solomon!' ³⁵You shall go up following him. Let him enter and sit on my throne; he shall be king in my place; for I have appointed him to be ruler over Israel and over Judah." ³⁶Benaiah son of Jehoiada answered the king, "Amen! May the Lord, the God of my lord the king, so ordain. ³⁷As the Lord has been with my lord the king, so may he be with Solomon, and make his throne greater than the throne of my lord King David."

38 So the priest Zadok, the prophet Nathan, and Benaiah son of Jehoiada, and the Cherethites and the Pelethites, went down and had Solomon ride on King David's mule, and led him to Gihon. ³⁹There the priest Zadok took the horn of oil from the tent and anointed Solomon. Then they blew the trumpet, and all the people said, "Long live King Solomon!" ⁴⁰And all the people went up following him, playing on pipes and rejoicing with great joy, so that the earth quaked at their noise.

41 Adonijah and all the guests who were with him heard it as they finished feasting. When Joab heard the sound of the trumpet, he said, "Why is the city in an uproar?" ⁴²While he was still speaking, Jonathan son of the priest Abiathar arrived. Adonijah said, "Come in, for you are a worthy man and surely you bring good news." ⁴³Jonathan answered Adonijah, "No, for our lord King David has made Solomon king; ⁴⁴the king has sent with him the priest Zadok, the prophet Nathan, and Benaiah son of Jehoiada, and the Cherethites and the Pelethites; and they had him ride on the king's mule; ⁴⁵the priest Zadok and the prophet Nathan have anointed him king at Gihon; and they have gone up from there rejoicing, so that the city is in an uproar. This is the noise that you heard. ⁴⁶Solomon now sits on the royal throne.

| After the Dtr:
indented and sans serif font | **Revision:
royal focus** | *Revision:
national focus* | Other:
double sideline |

[47]Moreover the king's servants came to congratulate our lord King David, saying, 'May God make the name of Solomon more famous than yours, and make his throne greater than your throne.' The king bowed in worship on the bed [48]and went on to pray thus, 'Blessed be the LORD, the God of Israel, who today has granted one of my offspring to sit on my throne and permitted me to witness it.' "[2]

49 Then all the guests of Adonijah got up trembling and went their own ways. [50]Adonijah, fearing Solomon, got up and went to grasp the horns of the altar. [51]Solomon was informed, "Adonijah is afraid of King Solomon; see, he has laid hold of the horns of the altar, saying, 'Let King Solomon swear to me first that he will not kill his servant with the sword.' " [52]So Solomon responded, "If he proves to be a worthy man, not one of his hairs shall fall to the ground; but if wickedness is found in him, he shall die." [53]Then King Solomon sent to have him brought down from the altar. He came to do obeisance to King Solomon; and Solomon said to him, "Go home."

2 When David's time to die drew near, he commanded (NRSV, *charged*) his son Solomon, saying:

[2]"I am about to go the way of all the earth. Be strong, be courageous, [3]and keep the charge of the LORD your God, walking in his ways and keeping his statutes, his commandments, his ordinances, and his testimonies, as it is written in the law of Moses, so that you may prosper in all that you do and wherever you turn. [4]Then the LORD will establish his word that he spoke concerning me: 'If your heirs take heed to their way, to walk before me in faithfulness with all their heart and with all their soul, 'there shall not fail you a successor on the throne of Israel.'[3]

5 "And moreover (Heb.; NRSV, moreover, you know also) you know what Joab son of Zeruiah did to me, how he dealt with the two commanders of the armies of Israel, Abner son of Ner, and Amasa son of Jether, whom he murdered, retali-

---

2. Veijola attributed 1:30*, 35-37, 46-48 to his DtrH.

---

3. **Text signals** in 2:2-4. (i) "I am about to go the way of all the earth" seems commonplace enough, but it occurs only here and in Josh 23:14, a text from the national focus within the dtr process of revision. (ii) "Be strong and courageous" is a misleading translation. The literal Hebrew here and only here is "be strong and be a man" (both verbs in the qatal/perfect form). "Be strong and courageous/bold/of good courage" (NRSV) is found in several other places, translating the pair √ḤZQ and √'MṢ (always in the imperative). Probably Deut 31:7 and Josh 1:6 can be attributed to the Dtr. Joshua 1:7, 9 are situated within the dtr revision's national focus. Probably Deut 31:23 and Josh 1:18 should be attributed to a later dtr editor. The remaining occurrences are: Josh 10:25; 1 Chron 22:13; 28:20; 2 Chron 32:7. (iii) "The charge of the Lord" (*mišmeret*) is late and predominantly priestly. (iv) Law-oriented language is present, especially in v. 3. (v) "Establish his word" (*hēkîm dābār*) is probably from the Josianic Dtr in 1 Kgs 8:20; 12:15; probably from the national focus in Deut 9:5; 1 Kgs 6:12. (vi) "There shall not fail you" (v. 4), with reference to a Davidic successor, occurs only here and 1 Kgs 8:25 and 9:5; also Jer 33:17. For the phrase, "throne of Israel," see at 9:5. (vii) The text here explicitly (and conditionally) looks down the track, referring to "children/heirs" (v. 4) as in 8:25, but not in 9:5. (viii) Within vv. 3-4, it needs to be noted that there are three cases of apparent reduplication: a. to walk, to keep—without any conjunction (v. 3a); b. "so that" (*lĕma'an*) twice, in vv. 3b and 4a—again without any conjunction; c. the introduction to speech (v. 4, untranslated, *lē'mōr*), once before "If your heirs" and once before "there shall not fail."

Main pre-DH:	Other pre-DH:	HKL: + single	**Josianic DH:**
Prophetic Record	single sideline	underline	**from the Dtr**

ating in time of peace for blood that had been shed in war, and putting the blood of war on the belt around his waist, and on the sandals on his feet. [6]Act therefore according to your wisdom, but do not let his gray head go down to Sheol in peace. [7]Deal loyally, however, with the sons of Barzillai the Gileadite, and let them be among

those who eat at your table; for with such loyalty they met me when I fled from your brother Absalom. [8]There is also with you Shimei son of Gera, the Benjaminite from Bahurim, who cursed me with a terrible curse on the day when I went to Mahanaim; but when he came down to meet me at the Jordan, I swore to him by the LORD, 'I will not put you to death with the sword.' [9]Therefore do not hold him guiltless, for you are a wise man; you will know what you ought to do to him, and you must bring his gray head down with blood to Sheol."[4]

Text-history approach. An overall assessment of these text signals suggests attribution of vv. 2-4 to the national focus within the dtr revision process. Much of the linguistic evidence identified points in this direction. 2:2-4 constitute a dtr speech, given David at the end of his life. The equivalent speech of Joshua has been attributed to this national focus (Joshua 23). The same is probably the case here.

In the Josianic DH, the basic dynastic promise of God to Solomon is made in 9:4-5, as part of God's response to Solomon (8:28), going beyond the promise of presence (9:3) to the promise of a dynasty over Israel (i.e., the united kingdom). In the promise to David (cf. 2 Samuel 7), there is no condition attached. In 9:4-5, a condition is attached, but it is expressed for Solomon alone, without being injected into the Davidic promise (v. 5b). In 2:4 and in 8:25, the condition is explicitly expressed within the promise to David and explicitly extended to David's descendants (plural). This reformulation of the Davidic promise (in 2:4 and 8:25) accentuates and intensifies the conditional aspect beyond 9:4-5. The reformulation may well reflect the bitter experience of exile. While 2:4 places the conditional element of obedience within the promise to David and applies it to the heirs/children/descendants, it needs to be noted that 2:3 insists on Solomon's obedience to the law (v. 3a) for his personal (singular) success (v. 3b).

The reduplications noted under #viii of the text signals probably indicate activity in the text; in our judgment, the meaning of the text is not illuminated by further speculation about them.

Present-text potential. 1 Kings 2:2-4, with vv. 5-9, is David's farewell speech to Solomon. Its function

is analogous to the final instructions to the people of Israel's earlier leaders: Moses (Deuteronomy), Joshua (Joshua 23), and Samuel (1 Samuel 12). These speeches occur at strategic points in the story of Israel; here it is the crucial transition of royal rule from David to Solomon. Like the earlier dtr speeches, 1 Kgs 2:2-4 emphasizes the dtr requirement of complete fidelity to God in terms of the law of Moses. The requirement is directed initially to Solomon and then to all the members of the Davidic dynasty. In the Josianic DH, the divine promise to Solomon, with its condition, is located after the dedication of the newly built temple (9:1-5), at the peak of Solomon's achievement. In the present text, this conditional promise is anticipated and modified at two preliminary points: at Solomon's accession, the beginning of his achievement (2:2-4); and within the temple dedication, in association with the peak of Solomon's achievement (8:25). The modifications bear in mind the full sweep of the monarchy and the bitter experience of the failure of Josiah's reform.

Cross attributed 2:4 to his Dtr[2]. Dietrich attributed 2:4 to his DtrN. For these early ground-breaking attributions, see for Cross *Canaanite Myth and Hebrew Epic* and for Dietrich *Prophetie und Geschichte*.

4. The introductory "and moreover" (Heb., *wĕgam*) is the bridge from vv. 2-4. David charges Solomon to act wisely with regard to the two who are to die, Joab and Shimei. With regard to the bene-

---

| After the Dtr: indented and sans serif font | **Revision: royal focus** | Revision: national focus | Other: double sideline |

10 Then David slept with his ancestors, and was buried in the city of David.

|| ¹¹The time that David reigned over Israel was forty years; he reigned seven years in Hebron, and thirty-three years in Jerusalem.⁵

*12So Solomon sat on the throne of his father David; and his kingdom was firmly established.*⁶

13 Then Adonijah son of Haggith came to Bathsheba, Solomon's mother. She asked, "Do you come peaceably?" He said, "Peaceably." ¹⁴Then he said, "May I have a word with you?" She said, "Go on." ¹⁵He said, "You know that the kingdom was mine, and that all Israel expected me to reign; however, the kingdom has turned about and become my brother's, for it was his from the LORD. ¹⁶And now I have one request to make of you; do not refuse me." She said to him, "Go on." ¹⁷He said, "Please ask King Solomon—he will not refuse you—to give me Abishag the Shunammite as my wife." ¹⁸Bathsheba said, "Very well; I will speak to the king on your behalf."⁷

19 So Bathsheba went to King Solomon, to speak to him on behalf of Adonijah. The king rose to meet her, and bowed down to her; then he sat on his throne, and had a throne brought for the king's mother, and she sat on his right. ²⁰Then she said, "I have one small request to make of you; do not refuse me." And the king said to her, "Make your request, my mother; for I will not refuse you." ²¹She said, "Let Abishag the Shunammite be given to your brother Adonijah as his wife." ²²King Solomon answered his mother, "And why do you ask Abishag the Shunammite for Adonijah? Ask for him the kingdom as well! For he is my elder brother; ask not only for him but also for the priest Abiathar and for Joab son of Zeruiah!" ²³Then King Solomon swore by the LORD, "So may God do to me, and more also, for Adonijah has devised this scheme at the risk of his life! ²⁴Now therefore as the LORD lives, who has established me and placed me on the throne of my father David, and who has made me a house as he promised, today Adonijah shall be put to death." ²⁵So King

---

factors, the sons of Barzillai, Solomon is to act loyally. The compliance with this charge will be discussed under vv. 13-46, where it will be argued that there is no reason against associating vv. 5-9 with vv. 13-46 in a single composition belonging within chaps. 1–2.

5. The information contained here is normally given at the start of a king's reign (for David, cf. 2 Sam 5:4-5). This slightly abbreviated version may come from the Dtr, given the length of David's reign and the extensive text associated with it. Alternatively, and possibly more likely, v. 11 could be a later addition, condensing 2 Sam 5:4-5, under the influence of 1 Kgs 11:42 (cf. Noth, *DH*, p. 42 [Dtr] and p. 91 [later addition]).

6. See the initial note on 1 Kings 1–2, under **text-history approach**.

7. Verses 13-46 deal fundamentally with the elimination of Solomon's rivals. The differences from

vv. 5-9 should not surprise. Loyalty to Barzillai's heirs (v. 7) is not mentioned; they are not rivals. Adonijah was a serious threat; he was an elder brother who had already made a claim on the throne. Whether the pretext for his death was genuine or fabricated is a matter for reflection. Joab had backed Adonijah. Shimei was dangerous; he had proved shifty. It would be implausible to attribute to David either a command to eliminate Adonijah, his son (cf. 1:6), or to expel Abiathar, his priest (cf. 2:26; also 1 Sam 22:23). Once this is seen, there is no reason to attribute vv. 5-9 to a different hand from vv. 13-46. 1 Kings 1 deals with securing the succession for Solomon and 1 Kings 2 deals with ensuring his hold on power. The two chapters can well form a single document.

Veijola attributed 2:1-2, 4aαb, 5-11, 15bγ, 24, 26b, 27, 31b-33, 35b, 37b, 42-45 to his DtrH and 2:3, 4aβ to his DtrN.

Main pre-DH:	Other pre-DH:	HKL: + single	**Josianic DH:**
Prophetic Record	single sideline	underline	**from the Dtr**

Solomon sent Benaiah son of Jehoiada; he struck him down, and he died.

26 The king said to the priest Abiathar, "Go to Anathoth, to your estate; for you deserve death. But I will not at this time put you to death, because you carried the ark of the Lord GOD before my father David, and because you shared in all the hardships my father endured." [27]So Solomon banished Abiathar from being priest to the LORD,

thus fulfilling the word of the LORD that he had spoken concerning the house of Eli in Shiloh.[8]

28 When the news came to Joab—for Joab had supported Adonijah though he had not supported Absalom—Joab fled to the tent of the LORD and grasped the horns of the altar. [29]When it was told King Solomon, "Joab has fled to the tent of the LORD and now is beside the altar," Solomon sent Benaiah son of Jehoiada, saying, "Go, strike him down." [30]So Benaiah came to the tent of the LORD and said to him, "The king commands, 'Come out.' " But he said, "No, I will die here." Then Benaiah brought the king word again, saying, "Thus said Joab, and thus he answered me." [31]The king replied to him, "Do as he has said, strike him down and bury him; and thus take away from me and from my father's house the guilt for the blood that Joab shed without cause. [32]The LORD will bring back his bloody deeds on his own head, because, without the knowledge of my father David, he attacked and killed with the sword two men more righteous and better than himself, Abner son of Ner, commander of the army of Israel, and Amasa son of Jether, commander of the army of Judah. [33]So shall their blood come back on the head of Joab

---

8. As we have noted, this half-verse "may be from the Dtr . . . but it is by no means certain" (for a full discussion, see above on 1 Sam 2:36).

and on the head of his descendants forever; but to David, and to his descendants, and to his house, and to his throne, there shall be peace from the LORD forevermore." [34]Then Benaiah son of Jehoiada went up and struck him down and killed him; and he was buried at his own house near the wilderness. [35]The king put Benaiah son of Jehoiada over the army in his place, and the king put the priest Zadok in the place of Abiathar.

36 Then the king sent and summoned Shimei, and said to him, "Build yourself a house in Jerusalem, and live there, and do not go out from there to any place whatever. [37]For on the day you go out, and cross the Wadi Kidron, know for certain that you shall die; your blood shall be on your own head." [38]And Shimei said to the king, "The sentence is fair; as my lord the king has said, so will your servant do." So Shimei lived in Jerusalem many days.

39 But it happened at the end of three years that two of Shimei's slaves ran away to King Achish son of Maacah of Gath. When it was told Shimei, "Your slaves are in Gath," [40]Shimei arose and saddled a donkey, and went to Achish in Gath, to search for his slaves; Shimei went and brought his slaves from Gath. [41]When Solomon was told that Shimei had gone from Jerusalem to Gath and returned, [42]the king sent and summoned Shimei, and said to him, "Did I not make you swear by the LORD, and solemnly adjure you, saying, 'Know for certain that on the day you go out and go to any place whatever, you shall die'? And you said to me, 'The sentence is fair; I accept.' [43]Why then have you not kept your oath to the LORD and the commandment with which I charged you?" [44]The king also said to Shimei, "You know in your own heart all the evil that you did to my father David; so the LORD will bring back your evil on your own head. [45]But King Solomon shall be blessed, and the throne of

---

| After the Dtr:
indented and sans serif font | **Revision:**
royal focus | Revision:
national focus | Other:
double sideline |

David shall be established before the LORD forever." [46]Then the king commanded Benaiah son of Jehoiada; and he went out and struck him down, and he died.

So the kingdom was established in the hand of Solomon.

3 *Solomon made a marriage alliance with Pharaoh king of Egypt; he took Pharaoh's daughter and brought her into the city of David, until he had finished building his own house and the house of the LORD and the wall around Jerusalem.*[9]

[2]The people were sacrificing at the high places, however, because no house had yet been built for the name of the LORD.

3 Solomon loved the LORD, walking in the statutes of his father David.

only, he sacrificed and offered incense at the high places.[10]

---

9. Resumption of the PR from 2 Sam 8:15. The primary evidence for prophetic editing exists firstly in the anointing/rejection texts for Saul and David, with their follow-up in the Story of David's Rise, and secondly in the texts of designation or anointing or rejection for Jeroboam, Ahab, and Jehu. The question faced here is whether there was a narrative connecting these two interrelated blocks of material. The specific prophetic concerns and language are not present and would not be expected to be. The question remains whether there is text related to Solomon's reign that would be of interest to the northern prophetic redactors and that can be distinguished and disengaged from the other textual material accumulated around the reign of Solomon (cf. initial note on 1 Kings 1–2).

The brief note of Solomon's marriage to a daughter of Pharaoh and of his building program could well be of interest to the prophetic redactors. Ahab, an arch-enemy in their eyes and an apostate, married Jezebel, a foreign princess. The marriage to a daughter of Pharaoh tars Solomon with the same brush; he too will be seen as an apostate (11:7). Taxes will be the political issue on which the united kingdom will founder (1 Kings 12). Reference to Solomon's building activity is appropriate in the PR, preparing for the objectionable "forced labor" (9:15a). Otherwise it is oddly out of place here, so early in the account of Solomon's reign.

The text postulated for the PR forms a balanced structure. It opens with the marriage to Pharaoh's

---

daughter and her living in the city of David while Solomon's building program proceeds (1 Kgs 3:1); it concludes with a summary of Solomon's building and the princess's move from the city of David to her own house that Solomon had built for her (1 Kgs 9:15a, 24). The continuation of the PR is to be found at 9:15.

The present account of Solomon's administration and building activity (temple and palace) is found between 3:1 and 9:15 etc. It is possible that this account took the place of earlier material from the PR; it would not be surprising if there were no such earlier material. From the northern perspective of the PR, Solomon and the Jerusalem temple would not be of major significance. There is no prophetic designation of Solomon (despite Nathan's scheming in 1 Kings 1); there is no mention of the temple in the prophetic editing of 2 Samuel 7.

Noth proposes that the story of Solomon was constructed by the Dtr from the "Acts of Solomon" and some other material (*DH*, 91-92). In our presentation, the extensive text reflecting southern and deuteronomistic interest in King Solomon has, for the most part, been deftly placed between the two parts of this balanced structure in the PR, forming an inclusion. The account of the Queen of Sheba's visit and the emphasis on Solomon's wealth follow and lead into Solomon's old age and apostasy. For a range of studies concerning Solomon, see L. K. Handy (ed.), *The Age of Solomon*.

10. **Text signals** in 1 Kgs 3:2-3. (i) In v. 2 the focus is on the people, in v. 3 it is on Solomon. (ii) Vv. 2 and 3b speak of sacrifice at the high places. (iii) V. 2 appears to excuse the people for such sacrifice because there was no temple. (iv) V. 3b regards such worship as

---

Main pre-DH:	Other pre-DH:	HKL: + single	**Josianic DH:**
Prophetic Record	single sideline	underline	**from the Dtr**

⁴The king went to Gibeon to sacrifice there, for that was the principal high place; Solomon used to offer a thousand burnt offerings on that altar. ⁵At Gibeon the Lord appeared to Solomon in a dream by night; and God said, "Ask what I should give you." ⁶And Solomon said,¹¹

"You have shown great and steadfast love to your servant my father David,

because he walked before you in faithfulness, in righteousness, and in uprightness of heart toward you

---

a blemish on Solomon's otherwise faultless conduct in v. 3a. (v) Vv. 2 and 3b both begin with the adverb "only" (*raq*).

Text-history approach. The reference to the people (3:2) is out of context in a section devoted entirely to Solomon. V. 1 has already referred to the fact that the temple has not yet been built; moreover, the Dtr did not need to excuse the people here since worship at the temple does not become the norm in the DH until the temple has been erected and dedicated. 3:2 is most likely an addition in the dtr mold by a later hand, concerned to avoid any scandal in relation to the high places. As noted in the Introduction, the indentation and double-sideline indicate additions to the Josianic DH; these may be from dtr circles, but do not have the characteristics that allow attribution to either focus of the dtr revision.

A similar concern to excuse Solomon is expressed in v. 3b. Elsewhere in 1–2 Kings, sacrificing and burning incense at the high places is used disapprovingly to describe the worship of the people of Judah; the one king so described is Ahaz in 2 Kgs 16:1-4, who receives an entirely negative assessment. Sustained concern over the high places probably began in Hezekiah's time and remained a constant issue in dtr circles.

Verse 3a is a judgment formula for Solomon like the judgment formulas for subsequent kings of Israel and Judah. They are a basic structural feature of the DH in the books of Kings. They occur within the report of the king's accession. The usual formula (he did good or evil in the eyes of yhwh) is here replaced by the unique "Solomon loved yhwh."

Present-text potential. The logical sequence running in the text moves from the as-yet-unbuilt temple in Jerusalem through to yhwh's appearance to Solomon at Gibeon. Because the temple has not yet been built, the people are sacrificing at the high places (3:2). Solomon is mentioned with favor (v. 3a); the dream and theophany at Gibeon will follow. Solomon's love of God, uniquely referred to here, forms a striking contrast with 11:1-8 where his love of foreign women turns his heart from yhwh to other gods. Solomon's love of yhwh is presented as a key factor in the realization of the dtr ideal; his failure to maintain that love is presented as an equally important factor in the collapse of the ideal. The term "love" here is to be understood in the dtn sense of complete fidelity to God. The favorable reference to Solomon's observance of the law brings in its train the comment about his worship at the high places (v. 3b), leading to the theophany at Gibeon, the great high place. It is significant that, at the end of the dream, Solomon returns to Jerusalem and the ark before offering worship (v. 15).

11. **Text signals.** Within vv. 6-14, giving Solomon's request and God's response, the language signals are complex and ambivalent. There are phrases that are widely used, but that in this context are appropriately judged to be dtr; there are others where attribution would not be responsible. The specific references given are neither exhaustive nor exclusive.

In v. 6: "great and steadfast love" is only here and 2 Chron 1:8; "your servant David" is widespread in dtr contexts, but not exclusively (cf. 1 Kgs 3:6, 7; 8:24, 25, 26; 11:13, 32, 34, 36, 38; 14:8); "walked before you . . . in uprightness of heart toward you" is a complex combination of elements that here is best situated within the national focus of the dtr revision process (cf. 1 Kgs 2:4; 8:23, 25). V. 6aβ relates not to a promise but to the fulfillment of a condition that is expressed in law-oriented terms.

In v. 7: the title "yhwh my God" is used.

After the Dtr: indented and sans serif font	*Revision:* *royal focus*	Revision: national focus	Other: double sideline

and you have kept for him this great and steadfast love, and have given him a son to sit on his throne today. [7]And now, O LORD my God, you have made your servant king in

place of my father David, although I am only a little child; I do not know how to go out or come in. [8]And your servant is in the midst of the people whom you have chosen, a great

---

In v. 8: "people whom you have chosen" can be dtr but not necessarily (cf. Deut 4:37; 7:6, 7; 10:15; 14:2); "a great people" may be dtr when 3:7-8 and 5:7 (Heb., 5:21) are seen to be expanding 1:48 (cf. also Gen 50:20 [E]; Exod 1:9 [J]); "numerous"—as expressed here it is unique, but the concern may be dtr (cf. Gen 22:17; 26:4; Exod 32:13; Deut 6:3; 13:18).

In v. 9: "an understanding mind" and "to discern between good and evil" are found only here.

In v. 10: the title 'adōnāy is used, as in v. 15.

In v. 11: "to discern what is right" is found only here; the subject of the opening verb is simply "God."

In v. 12: "a wise and discerning mind" is found only here (but cf. Deut 4:6). The particular comparison with others is found here and at 2 Kgs 23:25.

In v. 13: "riches and honor" are wisdom concepts (cf. Prov 3:16; 8:18; 11:16; Qoh 6:2), associated in later texts with worthy royalty (cf. 1 Chron 29:12, 28; 2 Chron 17:5; 18:1; 32:27).

In v. 14: the text signals here include its position outside or after the apparent conclusion in v. 13. As in v. 6aβ, it relates not to a promise but to the fulfillment of conditions dear to the legally focused circle. Length of life as a reward for obedience to the law is a strongly dtr concern (some 15 occurrences; as a late focus of revision, see Deut 4:26, 40; 5:33; 6:2). Cross attributed 3:14 tentatively to his Dtr[2].

Text-history approach. The presence of language that can be responsibly attributed to the dtr circles and of language that, because it is unique, cannot responsibly be restricted to any one circle makes the assessment of these verses unusually complex. This may account for Noth's ambivalence on this text (see *DH*, 93 and *Könige*, 45). The signals point in two directions. First, the final form of the text is most probably to be attributed to dtr circles; second, an earlier pre-dtr form of the text almost certainly existed. With this particular text, for these

reasons, it is not helpful to try to separate an original from later dtr contributions. Because of this, while the tradition requires a request from Solomon and a response from God (as, for example, in vv. 9-10 and part of vv. 12-13a), the whole section will be presented as being formulated by the Josianic Dtr and dtr circles.

In its formulation by the Dtr, this text plays an important role in the structure of the DH. First, it incorporates Solomon into the Davidic promise, identifying him in vv. 6b-7, as the seed referred to in 2 Sam 7:12. Second, the gift of wisdom, requested in v. 9 and granted in v. 12, is in the DH a preparation for the building of the temple (cf. 1 Kgs 5:7; Heb., 5:21).

The linguistic signals and the shift from promise to conditional reward point to vv. 6aβ and 14 as contributions from the dtr revision's national focus.

Present-text potential. This text is unique in the literature of Israel's kings, with the divine gift of wisdom being conferred on the king at his accession. Within the traditions of the ancient Near East, it is entirely appropriate. The language of v. 9a evokes Exodus 18 (cf. vv. 13, 22, 26).

Where the present text goes beyond what is already in place with the Josianic DH is the integration of the entire structure of promise and fulfillment within the overarching dtr theology, whether that theology is understood as consequence or condition (see Introduction). This is highlighted by vv. 6aβ and 14, the work of the national focus within the dtr revision with its emphasis on obedience to the Torah. The failure of Josiah's reform has to be accounted for and that accounting begins with Solomon (in 1 Kings 9 and 11). The text here, that establishes Solomon as David's wise successor, knows that Solomon will be the builder of the temple and also the beginning of Israel's future failure. With Solomon's building of the temple,

---

Main pre-DH:	Other pre-DH:	HKL: + single	**Josianic DH:**
Prophetic Record	single sideline	underline	**from the Dtr**

people, so numerous they cannot be numbered or counted. ⁹**Give your servant therefore an understanding mind to govern your people, able to discern between good and evil; for who can govern this your great people?"**

10 It pleased the Lord that Solomon had asked this. ¹¹God said to him, "Because you have asked this, and have not asked for yourself long life or riches, or for the life of your enemies, but have asked for yourself understanding to discern what is right, ¹²I now do according to your word. Indeed I give you a wise and discerning mind; no one like you has been before you and no one like you shall arise after you. ¹³I give you also what you have not asked, both riches and honor all your life; no other king shall compare with you."

¹⁴If you will walk in my ways, keeping my statutes and my commandments, as your father David walked, then I will lengthen your life."

15 Then Solomon awoke; it had been a dream. **He came to Jerusalem where he stood before the ark of the covenant of the Lord.**¹²

---

the dtr ideal is realized; with Solomon's apostasy, in dtr theology the seeds of Israel's end have been sown (at least for the revised DH).

It is noteworthy that v. 14 picks up an element left over from v. 11 ("long life"), that its condition is restricted to the issue of the length of Solomon's life, and that Solomon is credited with a long life (11:42) despite being accused of apostasy (11:5, 6 and 8, and 9-10). There is much in these texts that defies the definers.

12. This may well be the Dtr giving expression to a concern that is of major importance in the DH: the centralizing of worship in Jerusalem. Solomon's move from Gibeon to Jerusalem, expressed here, can be

He offered up burnt offerings and offerings of well-being, and provided a feast for all his servants.

16 Later, two women who were prostitutes came to the king and stood before him. ¹⁷The one woman said, "Please, my lord, this woman and I live in the same house; and I gave birth while she was in the house. ¹⁸Then on the third day after I gave birth, this woman also gave birth. We were together; there was no one else with us in the house, only the two of us were in the house. ¹⁹Then this woman's son died in the night, because she lay on him. ²⁰She got up in the middle of the night and took my son from beside me while your servant slept. She laid him at her breast, and laid her dead son at my breast. ²¹When I rose in the morning to nurse my son, I saw that he was dead; but when I looked at him closely in the morning, clearly it was not the son I had borne." ²²But the other woman said, "No, the living son is mine, and the dead son is yours." The first said, "No, the dead son is yours, and the living son is mine." So they argued before the king.

23 Then the king said, "The one says, 'This is my son that is alive, and your son is dead'; while the other says, 'Not so! Your son is dead, and my son is the living one.'" ²⁴So the king said, "Bring me a sword," and they brought a sword before the king. ²⁵The king said, "Divide the living boy in two; then give half to the one, and half to the other." ²⁶But the woman whose

---

understood as the first fruits of his God-given wisdom (v. 12). This discreet emphasis on Jerusalem would allow the Dtr to develop the tradition here, focusing the fulfillment of the Davidic promise on Solomon and his building of the temple. It should be noted, however, that the Heb. has *ʾădōnāy* as in v. 10 (not YHWH); elsewhere in Kings, only 1 Kgs 22:6 and 2 Kgs 19:23.

| After the Dtr:
indented and sans serif font | ***Revision:***
royal focus | *Revision:*
national focus | Other:
double sideline |

son was alive said to the king—because compassion for her son burned within her—"Please, my lord, give her the living boy; certainly do not kill him!" The other said, "It shall be neither mine nor yours; divide it." [27]Then the king responded: "Give the first woman the living boy; do not kill him. She is his mother." [28]All Israel heard of the judgment that the king had rendered; and they stood in awe of the king, because they perceived that the wisdom of God was in him, to execute justice.

4 King Solomon was king over all Israel, [2]and these were his high officials: Azariah son of Zadok was the priest; [3]Elihoreph and Ahijah sons of Shisha were secretaries; Jehoshaphat son of Ahilud was recorder; [4]Benaiah son of Jehoiada was in command of the army; Zadok and Abiathar were priests; [5]Azariah son of Nathan was over the officials; Zabud son of Nathan was priest and king's friend; [6]Ahishar was in charge of the palace; and Adoniram son of Abda was in charge of the forced labor.[13]

7 Solomon had twelve officials over all Israel, who provided food for the king and his household; each one had to make provision for one month in the year. [8]These were their names: Ben-hur, in the hill country of Ephraim; [9]Ben-deker, in Makaz, Shaalbim, Beth-shemesh, and Elon-beth-hanan; [10]Ben-hesed, in Arubboth (to him belonged Socoh and all the land of Hepher); [11]Ben-abinadab, in all Naphath-dor (he had Taphath, Solomon's daughter, as his wife); [12]Baana son of Ahilud, in Taanach, Megiddo, and all Beth-shean, which is beside Zarethan below Jezreel, and from Beth-shean to Abel-meholah, as far as the other side of Jokmeam; [13]Ben-geber, in Ramoth-gilead (he had the villages of Jair son of Manasseh, which are in Gilead, and he had the region of Argob, which is in Bashan, sixty great cities with walls and bronze bars); [14]Ahinadab son of Iddo, in Mahanaim; [15]Ahimaaz, in Naphtali (he had taken Basemath, Solomon's daughter, as his wife); [16]Baana son of Hushai, in Asher and Bealoth; [17]Jehoshaphat son of Paruah, in Issachar; [18]Shimei son of Ela, in Benjamin; [19]Geber son of Uri, in the land of Gilead, the country of King Sihon of the Amorites and of King Og of Bashan. And there was one official in the land of Judah.[14]

20 Judah and Israel were as numerous as the sand by the sea; they ate and drank and were happy. [21]Solomon was sovereign over all the kingdoms from the Euphrates to the land of the Philistines, even to the border of Egypt; they brought tribute and served Solomon all the days of his life.[15]

---

13. The information here, in 4:1-28 (Heb., 4:1—5:8), is regarded as based on official records available to the Dtr (with Noth, *DH*, 93).

---

14. In this list (4:7-19), five names have the patronymic only (= son of X) while in six cases there is both personal name and patronymic, with one more personal name and one anonymous official. It has been argued that the list must have been taken from an official document, damaged in the top right-hand corner, so that only the patronymic was available in vv. 8b, 9-11, 13, not the preceding personal name (cf. Noth, *DH*, 93, n. 4 and *Könige*, 59-60); an alternative, based on Canaanite practice, was argued by Alt ("Menschen Ohne Namen," 211-12), and recently favored by E. Würthwein (*Die Bücher der Könige*, 1.44). Both explanations are possible; a decision between them is fraught with difficulty.

15. **Text signals.** Verses 20-28 (Heb., 4:20—5:8) provide a text of remarkable diversity. V. 20 notes the peaceful situation of Judah and Israel; v. 25 (Heb., 5:5) does the same. V. 21 (Heb., 5:1) notes the extent

---

Main pre-DH:	Other pre-DH:	HKL: + single	**Josianic DH:**
Prophetic Record	single sideline	underline	**from the Dtr**

22 Solomon's provision for one day was thirty cors of choice flour, and sixty cors of meal, ²³ten fat oxen, and twenty pasture-fed cattle, one hundred sheep, besides deer, gazelles, roebucks, and fatted fowl. ²⁴For he had dominion over all the region west of the Euphrates from Tiphsah to Gaza, over all the kings west of the Euphrates; and he had peace on all sides. ²⁵During Solomon's lifetime Judah and Israel lived in safety, from Dan even to Beer-sheba, all of them under their vines and fig trees. ²⁶Solomon also had forty thousand stalls of horses for his chariots, and twelve thousand horsemen. ²⁷Those officials supplied provisions for King Solomon and for all who came to King Solomon's table, each one in his month; they let nothing be lacking. ²⁸They also brought to the required place barley and straw for the horses and swift steeds, each according to his charge.

29 God gave Solomon very great wisdom, discernment, and breadth of understanding as vast as the sand on the seashore, ³⁰so that Solomon's wisdom surpassed the wisdom of all the people of the east, and all the wisdom of Egypt. ³¹He was wiser than anyone else, wiser than Ethan the Ezrahite, and Heman, Calcol, and Darda, children of Mahol; his fame spread throughout all the surrounding nations. ³²He composed three thousand proverbs, and his songs numbered a thousand and five. ³³He would speak of trees, from the cedar that is in the Lebanon to the hyssop that grows in the wall; he would speak of animals, and birds, and reptiles, and fish. ³⁴People came from all the nations to hear the wisdom of Solomon; they came from all the kings of the earth who had heard of his wisdom.[16]

---

of Solomon's authority; v. 24 (Heb., 5:4) does the same. Vv. 22-23 (Heb., 5:2-3) note the provisions supplied for people; v. 28 (Heb., 5:8) does the same for the horses. V. 26 (Heb., 5:6) notes the horses and horsemen to be supplied. V. 27 (Heb., 5:7) points to a list of officials, presumably those named in vv. 7-19.

Text-history approach. LXX has a different order and selection of material (see Jones, *Kings*, 1.145-46). Noth was confident that 4:22-23, 27 (NRSV) could be identified as the original account; the first additions were vv. 26 and 28, then vv. 24-25; finally vv. 20-21 were certainly added by the Dtr (*DH*, 93, n. 5). There is no linguistic evidence supporting the attribution of vv. 20-21 to the Dtr; later Noth dropped this attribution and revised the reconstruction (*Könige*, 62, 75-78).

Present-text potential. A chiastic structure is evident in vv. 20-25 (Heb., 4:20–5:5): bliss–authority–provisions–authority–bliss (cf. Nelson, *First and Second Kings*, 40). Vv. 26-28 (Heb., 5:6-8) are also in the form of a rough chiasm: horses and handlers–officials–supplies for horses. Solomon is at the center of each.

16. As so often in this material, the date of the traditions in 4:29-34 (Heb., 5:9-14) is subject to debate. Two issues are separate and often equally insoluble: the time of origin and the time of incorporation into the present text. Noth describes these verses as a passage of old narrative, used by the Dtr to introduce the account of the building of the temple (*DH*, 93-94; also *Könige*, 80-81). Jones too allows for a pre-dtr origin (*Kings*, 1.148). For Würthwein (*Könige*, 1.48) and Scott ("Wisdom in Israel," 262–79), the passage is post-dtr, partly because the names of famous wise men are listed also in 1 Chron 2:6 and partly because v. 32 points to the book of Proverbs and the Song of Songs, both post-exilic works. Gray opts for "a late popular source" while claiming "the antiquity of the tradition itself" (*I & II Kings*, 144-45).

---

5   Now King Hiram of Tyre sent his servants to Solomon, when he heard that they had anointed him king in place of his father; for Hiram had always been a friend to David. [2]Solomon sent word to Hiram, saying,[17]

Whether pre-dtr or post-dtr, it serves as a foil before Solomon's fall. A post-dtr provenance would not significantly alter the shape of the DH.

The format used here reflects this divergence of views. It is an indented paragraph, but with a single dotted sideline. It is used for half a dozen instances in this Solomonic material (i.e., NRSV, 1 Kgs 4:29-34; 5:13-18; 9:16-17a, 23; 9:26–10:29). See the Introduction for further details. Since it designates text as potentially before the dtr or after the dtr, it would be awkward to include it in the footers at the bottom of each page. Its use is rare.

17. **Text signals** in 5:1-7 (Heb., 5:15-21). (i) Solomon's message to Hiram speaks in dtr terms of his intention to build the temple (e.g., name theology, enemies round about, rest, etc.). (ii) In v. 4a, Solomon claims the time is ripe to build the temple because YHWH has given him rest on every side; in v. 5, he claims that the proposed building is in fulfillment of the promise made to David (cf. 2 Sam 7:13). (iii) In vv. 4b and 6, characteristic dtr language is not discernible. (iv) Hiram's enthusiastic reaction to Solomon's message is given in v. 7, with strong echoes of the dtr 3:6-13. His reply to Solomon will follow in vv. 8-9.

Text-history approach. As with 3:4-15, traces of the original account may have been retained but the dialog has been rewritten by the Dtr. Vv. 1-2 and 8-12 are attributed to the original, with dtr material in vv. 3-7. The preponderance of dtr terminology and themes in vv. 3-4a, 5, 7 is evident. These verses are integral to the conceptual plan of the Josianic DH. They claim that the conditions for the completion of the dtn ideal, as outlined in Deut 12:10-11, were realized in the reign of Solomon and that his building of the temple was the fulfillment of the promise to David in 2 Sam 7:13. While some of the material here might be original, it is more economical to regard the whole of vv. 3-7 as the work of the Dtr.

[3]"You know that my father David could not build a house for the name of the LORD his God because of the warfare with which his enemies surrounded him, until the LORD put them under the soles of his feet. [4]But now the LORD my God has given me rest on every side; there is neither adversary nor misfortune. [5]So I intend to build a house for the name of the LORD my God, as the LORD said to my father David, 'Your son, whom I will set on your throne in your place, shall build the house for my name.' [6]Therefore command that cedars from the Lebanon be cut for me. My servants will join your servants, and I will give you whatever wages you set for your servants; for you know that there is no one among us who knows how to cut timber like the Sidonians."

Present-text potential. 3:16—4:28 portrays Solomon as a king who rules his people wisely and brings them peace and prosperity. According to 4:29-34, Solomon is wise beyond any other; people came from all the nations to hear his wisdom. Among them is a delegation from Hiram of Tyre.

The climax of this portrayal is reached here with Solomon's announcement that the time has come to build a temple for the name of the LORD. What is at stake is not just a royal building contract but the achievement of a national goal, involving divine command in the past and the divine gift of wisdom in the present (cf. vv. 7 and 12). The text reaches back to Deut 12:10-11 and situates this climactic moment in Israel's history in terms of security and peace. Israel is poised to realize the ideal of a united people with a wise and just king, living in peace and prosperity, worshiping the one God at the one shrine in Jerusalem. The joy noted for Hiram reflects the significance of this moment. The praise of Sidonian skills (v. 6) emphasizes that for YHWH's temple in Jerusalem only the best will do.

Main pre-DH:	Other pre-DH:	HKL: + single	**Josianic DH:**
Prophetic Record	single sideline	underline	**from the Dtr**

7 When Hiram heard the words of Solomon, he rejoiced greatly, and said, "Blessed be the LORD today, who has given to David a wise son to be over this great people." [8]Hiram sent word to Solomon, "I have heard the message that you have sent to me; I will fulfill all your needs in the matter of cedar and cypress timber. [9]My servants shall bring it down to the sea from the Lebanon; I will make it into rafts to go by sea to the place you indicate. I will have them broken up there for you to take away. And you shall meet my needs by providing food for my household." [10]So Hiram supplied Solomon's every need for timber of cedar and cypress. [11]Solomon in turn gave Hiram twenty thousand cors of wheat as food for his household, and twenty cors of fine oil. Solomon gave this to Hiram year by year. [12]So the LORD gave Solomon wisdom, as he promised him. There was peace between Hiram and Solomon; and the two of them made a treaty.[18]

> 13 King Solomon conscripted forced labor out of all Israel; the levy numbered thirty thousand men. [14]He sent them to the Lebanon, ten thousand a month in shifts;

they would be a month in the Lebanon and two months at home; Adoniram was in charge of the forced labor. [15]Solomon also had seventy thousand laborers and eighty thousand stonecutters in the hill country, [16]besides Solomon's three thousand three hundred supervisors who were over the work, having charge of the people who did the work. [17]At the king's command, they quarried out great, costly stones in order to lay the foundation of the house with dressed stones. [18]So Solomon's builders and Hiram's builders and the Gebalites did the stonecutting and prepared the timber and the stone to build the house.[19]

---

18. Along with vv. 1-2, vv. 8-12 form the pre-dtr text that now frames the dtr material in vv. 3-7 (their dtr emphasis has been addressed above). Hiram's reply refers specifically to the timber supply and its details. The speech given to Solomon requests cedars, seeks Israelite participation in the workforce, and invites a wages settlement (v. 6). Hiram, in reply, specifies cedar and cypress, sets up the division of labor, and lays down the payment he requires. Vv. 10-11 conclude the commercial deal. V. 12 sets the whole within its broader context, including both peace and treaty. V. 12a probably refers to the pre-dtr mention of the gift of wisdom to Solomon at Gibeon, now incorporated into the total dtr presentation of the scene (cf. v. 12 in 3:6-13).

---

19. **Text signals** in 5:13-18 (Heb., 5:27-32). (i) The issue of forced labor is much disputed, whether there is a division between temporary and permanent conscription, and whether the latter applied to Israelites. An overseer of forced labor is noted in 2 Sam 20:24; 1 Kgs 4:6; 12:18. Forced labor specifically for non-Israelites is asserted in 1 Kgs 9:21 and equally specifically denied for Israelites in 9:22. On the other hand, the issue of forced labor is seen as a cause in the division of the kingdom—associating the presence of Adoram in 12:18 with the "yoke" of 12:4 and 14). Forced labor is asserted elsewhere in 1 Kings here and 9:15 (see Soggin, "Compulsory Labor under David and Solomon," 259-67). (ii) V. 14 has been seen to be in tension with v. 9. (iii) Vv. 13-16 are primarily concerned with the numbers of workers involved. (iv) The central focus is on stone quarrying not timber. (v) V. 17 functions as a conclusion to vv. 13-16, while v. 18 concludes the whole enterprise.

Text-history approach. Views have differed between a pre-dtr and post-dtr assessment. The tension between vv. 9 and 14 may not be significant once it is noted that v. 9 applies to timber cutting and vv. 14-15 to stone quarrying (v. 15 provides the numbers and the NRSV's "also" is misleading). How literally

---

After the Dtr: indented and sans serif font	*Revision: royal focus*	*Revision: national focus*	Other: double sideline

6 In the four hundred eightieth year after the Israelites came out of the land of Egypt[20]

In the fourth year of Solomon's reign over Israel, in the month of Ziv, which is the second month, he began to build the house of the LORD.

[2]The house that King Solomon built for the LORD was sixty cubits long, twenty cubits wide, and thirty cubits high. [3]The vestibule in front of the nave of the house was twenty cubits wide, across the width of the house. Its depth was ten cubits in front of the house. [4]For the house he made windows with recessed frames. [5]He also built a structure against the wall of the house, running around the walls of the house, both the nave and the inner sanctuary; and he made side chambers all around. [6]The lowest story was five cubits wide, the middle one was six cubits wide, and the third was seven cubits wide; for around the outside of the house he made offsets on the wall in order that the supporting beams should not be inserted into the walls of the house.[21]

these numbers are to be understood is as difficult here as elsewhere. Stones are required for the building of the temple (cf. 6:7); anticipation of 7:9-12 is not surprising and need not indicate literary dependence. The question of forced labor is unclear, but the use of Canaanite labor on so holy a project as the temple is unlikely (see 7:14; cf. Exod 35:31). The conclusion in vv. 17-18 could just as well be early as late.

For the format used here, see the Introduction and the note on 1 Kgs 4:29-34.

Present-text potential. The arrangements agreed on for the supply of timber are complemented by those for stone. Timber cutting is the responsibility of the Sidonians (vv. 6 and 9); stone quarrying, and the numbers involved, is an Israelite responsibility. The conclusion in v. 18 reviews those involved in the total undertaking. 5:12b brings the negotiations between Hiram and Solomon over the supply of timber to a close. 5:18 brings to a close the report of the acquisition of the necessary building materials, both timber and stone.

20. According to Noth, in 1 Kgs 6:1 "Dtr sums up the whole chronology of the pre-monarchic period in a specific figure and thereby links it firmly to the chronology of the monarchic period" (*DH*, 35; cf. 34-44). However, starting from the chronological information in the text, this figure has been calculated differently by Noth, Richter, *Bearbeitungen*, 132-41, and G. Sauer (two versions), "Chronologischen Angaben." Both Gray (*Kings*, 159-61) and Jones (*Kings*, 1.162-63) opt for different bases of calculation. LXX has 440. Noth's position is further weakened by reliance on the 3-year reign attributed to Abimelech (Judg 9:22)—in our view, a later figure. The round figure could have been introduced at any time, based on one of several possible calculations. For the "fourth year" figure, see 6:37.

21. Beyond the verses noted (6:1*, and possibilities in 6:11-14), there is no linguistic or thematic evidence that indicates dtr authorship for chaps. 6–7, apart from obvious dtr interest in the temple itself. Under these circumstances, the text could be pre-dtr or post-dtr; it could be fictional or traditional. If the bulk of chaps. 6–7 is considered post-dtr, the report of the building (6:1) would be followed closely by the report of its dedication (8:2ff). This text would resemble 6:1 and 1a-1d of the present LXX (= Heb., 6:1; 5:31-32*; 6:37-38*; = NRSV, 6:1; 5:17-18*; 6:37-38*—without any reference to seven years); much of the substance of the Heb. is provided, with some significant variations, in 6:2–7:50 of the LXX. It is worth noting that the Heb. of 1 Kgs 6:1–8:2 has some remarkable similarities and massive differences from 2 Chron 3:1–5:1. If the text is considered pre-dtr, without any prejudice to its origins or the accuracy of its claims, the presence of older chronological terms in 6:37-38 vis-à-vis 6:1 (esp. *yeraḥ* and *ḥōdeš*) is understandable. Our own reasons for formatting this material as pre-dtr are: (i) that some such account is appropriate following the detailed negotiations over the building materials in 5:1-18 (Heb., 5:15-32); (ii) that interest in the details of the temple seems to us more likely in the pre-exilic

Main pre-DH:	Other pre-DH:	HKL: + single	**Josianic DH:**
Prophetic Record	single sideline	underline	**from the Dtr**

7 The house was built with stone finished at the quarry, so that neither hammer nor ax nor any tool of iron was heard in the temple while it was being built.

8 The entrance for the middle story was on the south side of the house: one went up by winding stairs to the middle story, and from the middle story to the third. ⁹So he built the house, and finished it; he roofed the house with beams and planks of cedar. ¹⁰He built the structure against the whole house, each story five cubits high, and it was joined to the house with timbers of cedar.

11 Now the word of the LORD came to Solomon, ¹²"Concerning this house that you are building, if you will walk in my statutes, obey my ordinances, and keep all my commandments by walking in them, then I will establish my promise with you, which I made to your father David. ¹³I will dwell among the children of Israel, and will not forsake my people Israel." 14 So Solomon built the house, and finished it.²²

period than later, when the temple was either in ruins or a lesser structure (cf. Hag 2:3; Ezra 3:12); (iii) the lavish use of gold may be legendary, but is scarcely an issue given the repeated reports of looting or stripping of the temple. A close analysis of J. Van Seters ("Solomon's Temple") does not provide a base for secure conclusions. Allowance must be made in Israel as anywhere else for the possibility of creativity and innovation. Control by ancient Near Eastern models is indispensable; but, unless the possibility of innovation is taken into account, the result may be an endless chain of dependence of each model on some other.

The origins of 7:47-51 have been disputed. As is often the case, the distinction between primary and secondary materials is difficult and the direction of dependence between early and late uncertain. There is nothing identifiably dtr here. There is a distinction between the bronze work done by Hiram (7:15-47) and the gold work for which Solomon was responsible (7:48-50); note the similar distinction between timber and stone in chap. 5. For a variety of views, see Jones (*Kings*, 1.178-79), Noth (*DH*, 95 and differently *Könige*, 147-48; 165-67), and Würthwein (*Könige*, 1.82-84).

We have not attempted to identify the additions in this material. For valuable discussion as well as references to relevant literature, see Jones, *Kings*, 1.160-91.

As is well known, the MT and LXX traditions differ widely in Samuel–Kings, and both differ from the equivalent traditions in Chronicles. Increasing attention is being devoted to these areas (cf. for example, the studies of J. C. Trebolle Barrera and A. G. Auld). The situation has not yet reached a stage suitable for summary here.

22. **Text signals** in vv. 11-14. (i) V. 11 introduces a speech in the middle of reporting the building project. (ii) V. 12 has a strongly law-oriented focus. (iii) V. 13 goes beyond Solomon to bring in the implications for the people. (iv) V. 14 duplicates v. 9a. (v) The verses are missing from LXX.

Text-history approach. The transition from the completed structure of the temple to its interior finishing provides an appropriate moment for the insertion of a speech. The question is: insertion by whom? V. 12 has a clear focus on law, with its emphasis on obedience and its implications for Solomon and the fulfillment of the promise about him made to David (spelled out in 9:4-5, also 2:4 and 8:25; but not spelled out here). The emphasis on the law and its observance suggests the national focus of the dtr revision process or a later imitation; the silence on the content of the promise may point toward the later imitation. The mention of the people, in v. 13, does not involve them in responsibility for failure, as in the national focus of the revision; instead, it is an assurance of divine presence among and commitment to the people of Israel, provided the king is obedient. The notion of God dwelling among the people is found in priestly passages in the Pentateuch (cf. Exod 29:45, 46; Num 5:3;

| After the Dtr: indented and sans serif font | *Revision:* *royal focus* | *Revision:* *national focus* | Other: double sideline |

[15]He lined the walls of the house on the inside with boards of cedar; from the floor of the house to the rafters of the ceiling, he covered them on the inside with wood; and he covered the floor of the house with boards of cypress. [16]He built twenty cubits of the rear of the house with boards of cedar from the floor to the rafters, and he built this within as an inner sanctuary, as the most holy place. [17]The house, that is, the nave in front of the inner sanctuary, was forty cubits long. [18]The cedar within the house had carvings of gourds and open flowers; all was cedar, no stone was seen. [19]The inner sanctuary he prepared in the innermost part of the house, to set there the ark of the covenant of the LORD. [20]The interior of the inner sanctuary was twenty cubits long, twenty cubits wide, and twenty cubits high; he overlaid it with pure gold. He also overlaid the altar with cedar. [21]Solomon overlaid the inside of the house with pure gold, then he drew chains of gold across, in front of the inner sanctuary, and overlaid it with gold. [22]Next he overlaid the whole house with gold, in order that the whole house might be perfect; even the whole altar that belonged to the inner sanctuary he overlaid with gold.

35:34) and in post-exilic prophecy (cf. Zech 2:10, 11 [Heb., 14, 15]; 8:3; Ezek 43:7, 9). The combination of these factors points to the likelihood of a late addition, with some imitation of the national focus.

Cross attributed 6:11-13 to his Dtr[2].

Present-text potential. As is characteristic for the texts about Solomon, YHWH addresses the king directly, without prophetic mediation (cf. 1 Kgs 3:5; 6:11; 9:2-3; 11:11; elsewhere in Kings, only 2 Kgs 10:30, cf. 15:12). The word of the LORD expresses a significant reminder that God's commitment to the Davidic dynasty and the people is secured not by a building but by the king's loyalty to God.

23 In the inner sanctuary he made two cherubim of olivewood, each ten cubits high. [24]Five cubits was the length of one wing of the cherub, and five cubits the length of the other wing of the cherub; it was ten cubits from the tip of one wing to the tip of the other. [25]The other cherub also measured ten cubits; both cherubim had the same measure and the same form. [26]The height of one cherub was ten cubits, and so was that of the other cherub. [27]He put the cherubim in the innermost part of the house; the wings of the cherubim were spread out so that a wing of one was touching the one wall, and a wing of the other cherub was touching the other wall; their other wings toward the center of the house were touching wing to wing. [28]He also overlaid the cherubim with gold.

29 He carved the walls of the house all around about with carved engravings of cherubim, palm trees, and open flowers, in the inner and outer rooms. [30]The floor of the house he overlaid with gold, in the inner and outer rooms.

31 For the entrance to the inner sanctuary he made doors of olivewood; the lintel and the doorposts were five-sided. [32]He covered the two doors of olivewood with carvings of cherubim, palm trees, and open flowers; he overlaid them with gold, and spread gold on the cherubim and on the palm trees.

33 So also he made for the entrance to the nave doorposts of olivewood, four-sided each, [34]and two doors of cypress wood; the two leaves of the one door were folding, and the two leaves of the other door were folding. [35]He carved cherubim, palm trees, and open flowers, overlaying them with gold evenly applied upon the carved work. [36]He built the inner court with three courses of dressed stone to one course of cedar beams.

37 In the fourth year the foundation of the house of the LORD was laid, in the month of Ziv.

Main pre-DH:	Other pre-DH:	HKL: + single	**Josianic DH:**
Prophetic Record	single sideline	underline	**from the Dtr**

[38]In the eleventh year, in the month of Bul, which is the eighth month, the house was finished in all its parts, and according to all its specifications. He was seven years in building it.

7 Solomon was building his own house thirteen years, and he finished his entire house.

2 He built the House of the Forest of the Lebanon one hundred cubits long, fifty cubits wide, and thirty cubits high, built on four rows of cedar pillars, with cedar beams on the pillars. [3]It was roofed with cedar on the forty-five rafters, fifteen in each row, which were on the pillars. [4]There were window frames in the three rows, facing each other in the three rows. [5]All the doorways and doorposts had four-sided frames, opposite, facing each other in the three rows.

6 He made the Hall of Pillars fifty cubits long and thirty cubits wide. There was a porch in front with pillars, and a canopy in front of them.

7 He made the Hall of the Throne where he was to pronounce judgment, the Hall of Justice, covered with cedar from floor to floor.

8 His own house where he would reside, in the other court back of the hall, was of the same construction. Solomon also made a house like this hall for Pharaoh's daughter, whom he had taken in marriage.

9 All these were made of costly stones, cut according to measure, sawed with saws, back and front, from the foundation to the coping, and from outside to the great court. [10]The foundation was of costly stones, huge stones, stones of eight and ten cubits. [11]There were costly stones above, cut to measure, and cedarwood. [12]The great court had three courses of dressed stone to one layer of cedar beams all around; so had the inner court of the house of the LORD, and the vestibule of the house.

13 Now King Solomon invited and received Hiram from Tyre. [14]He was the son of a widow of the tribe of Naphtali, whose father, a man of Tyre, had been an artisan in bronze; he was full of skill, intelligence, and knowledge in working bronze. He came to King Solomon, and did all his work.

15 He cast two pillars of bronze. Eighteen cubits was the height of the one, and a cord of twelve cubits would encircle it; the second pillar was the same. [16]He also made two capitals of molten bronze, to set on the tops of the pillars; the height of the one capital was five cubits, and the height of the other capital was five cubits. [17]There were nets of checker work with wreaths of chain work for the capitals on the tops of the pillars; seven for the one capital, and seven for the other capital. [18]He made the columns with two rows around each latticework to cover the capitals that were above the pomegranates; he did the same with the other capital. [19]Now the capitals that were on the tops of the pillars in the vestibule were of lily-work, four cubits high. [20]The capitals were on the two pillars and also above the rounded projection that was beside the latticework; there were two hundred pomegranates in rows all around; and so with the other capital. [21]He set up the pillars at the vestibule of the temple; he set up the pillar on the south and called it Jachin; and he set up the pillar on the north and called it Boaz. [22]On the tops of the pillars was lily-work. Thus the work of the pillars was finished.

23 Then he made the molten sea; it was round, ten cubits from brim to brim, and five cubits high. A line of thirty cubits would encircle it completely. [24]Under its brim were panels all around it, each of ten cubits, surrounding the sea; there were two rows of panels, cast when it was cast. [25]It stood on twelve oxen, three facing north, three facing west, three facing south, and three facing east; the sea was set on them. The hindquarters of each were toward the inside.

[26]Its thickness was a handbreadth; its brim was made like the brim of a cup, like the flower of a lily; it held two thousand baths.

27 He also made the ten stands of bronze; each stand was four cubits long, four cubits wide, and three cubits high. [28]This was the construction of the stands: they had borders; the borders were within the frames; [29]on the borders that were set in the frames were lions, oxen, and cherubim. On the frames, both above and below the lions and oxen, there were wreaths of beveled work. [30]Each stand had four bronze wheels and axles of bronze; at the four corners were supports for a basin. The supports were cast with wreaths at the side of each. [31]Its opening was within the crown whose height was one cubit; its opening was round, as a pedestal is made; it was a cubit and a half wide. At its opening there were carvings; its borders were four-sided, not round. [32]The four wheels were underneath the borders; the axles of the wheels were in the stands; and the height of a wheel was a cubit and a half. [33]The wheels were made like a chariot wheel; their axles, their rims, their spokes, and their hubs were all cast. [34]There were four supports at the four corners of each stand; the supports were of one piece with the stands. [35]On the top of the stand there was a round band half a cubit high; on the top of the stand, its stays and its borders were of one piece with it. [36]On the surfaces of its stays and on its borders he carved cherubim, lions, and palm trees, where each had space, with wreaths all around. [37]In this way he made the ten stands; all of them were cast alike, with the same size and the same form.

38 He made ten basins of bronze; each basin held forty baths, each basin measured four cubits; there was a basin for each of the ten stands. [39]He set five of the stands on the south side of the house, and five on the north side of the house; he set the sea on the southeast corner of the house.

40 Hiram also made the pots, the shovels, and the basins. So Hiram finished all the work that he did for King Solomon on the house of the LORD: [41]the two pillars, the two bowls of the capitals that were on the tops of the pillars, the two latticeworks to cover the two bowls of the capitals that were on the tops of the pillars; [42]the four hundred pomegranates for the two latticeworks, two rows of pomegranates for each latticework, to cover the two bowls of the capitals that were on the pillars; [43]the ten stands, the ten basins on the stands; [44]the one sea, and the twelve oxen underneath the sea.

45 The pots, the shovels, and the basins, all these vessels that Hiram made for King Solomon for the house of the LORD were of burnished bronze. [46]In the plain of the Jordan the king cast them, in the clay ground between Succoth and Zarethan. [47]Solomon left all the vessels unweighed, because there were so many of them; the weight of the bronze was not determined.

48 So Solomon made all the vessels that were in the house of the LORD: the golden altar, the golden table for the bread of the Presence, [49]the lampstands of pure gold, five on the south side and five on the north, in front of the inner sanctuary; the flowers, the lamps, and the tongs, of gold; [50]the cups, snuffers, basins, dishes for incense, and firepans, of pure gold; the sockets for the doors of the innermost part of the house, the most holy place, and for the doors of the nave of the temple, of gold.

51 Thus all the work that King Solomon did on the house of the LORD was finished. Solomon brought in the things that his father David had dedicated, the silver, the gold, and the vessels, and stored them in the treasuries of the house of the LORD.

| Main pre-DH: | Other pre-DH: | HKL: + single | **Josianic DH:** |
| *Prophetic Record* | single sideline | underline | **from the Dtr** |

8 Then Solomon assembled the elders of Israel[23]

|| and all the heads of the tribes, the leaders of the ancestral houses of the Israelites, before King Solomon in Jerusalem,[24]

---

23. The moment that the text begins here is a major highpoint of the Josianic DH. Fundamental to its understanding is the claim that, with the dedication of the temple, the dtr program outlined in Deut 12:10-12 is fulfilled. The claim of this DH is that Josiah's reform provided Judah with the opportunity to recapture this situation of fulfillment. Solomon was responsible for the fulfillment; the beginning of the demise was equally Solomon's responsibility.

The celebration involves a number of elements: the gift of the land and the gift of rest to Israel; the possession of the place that YHWH has chosen as a dwelling for his name; the building by David's successor of the temple for YHWH's name; the assembly of the people to rejoice and celebrate before YHWH. All of this is seen as the fulfillment of the dtr program in Deut 12:10-12 (cf. 8:56).

The Josianic DH has been building up to this point. In 1 Kgs 11:1-7*, prepared by the condition expressed in 9:1-5 (cf. v. 4), the Josianic DH begins the story of decline, to be reversed in the restoration under Josiah.

Text signals. In 8:1-13, the following signals may point to an original text. (i) The √QHL (assemble, assembly), whether as noun or verb, is very common in later texts. It has a respectable dtr lineage (cf. code: Deut 18:16; 23:1, 2, 3, 8 [Heb., 23:2, 3, 4, 9]; Dtr: 5:22; 9:10; 10:4; national focus within the dtr revision: 4:10; 31:12, 28; and later: 31:30). It is not unknown in potentially earlier passages: 1 Sam 17:47; 2 Sam 20:14; 1 Kgs 12:3, 21(?); Jer 26:9, 17(?). The possibility of dtr origin cannot be disputed; the possibility of an earlier origin cannot be excluded. (ii) "Elders of Israel" can certainly be early and is unlikely to be dtr. (iii) Consideration of the phrase "ark of the covenant of the LORD" in Joshua (3:3, 17; 4:7, 18; 6:8) and 1 Samuel (4:3, 5) leads to the same conclusion: the possibility of dtr origin cannot be disputed; the possibility of an earlier origin cannot be excluded. (iv) In v. 2, the word for "month" (*yeraḥ*) and the name of the month (Ethanim) are regarded as older usages; *yeraḥ* is

by far the less frequent word for month; the more common word is *ḥōdeš* (12 as against c. 277 occurrences). Bul is the month (*yeraḥ*) given in 6:38 for the completion of the building. (v) In v. 6, *debîr* is regarded as the older word for the innermost chamber of the Temple, also called the Holy of Holies; *debîr* is the commoner word in chaps. 6–7. "Even from the outset only priests were allowed into the inner sanctuary of the Temple" (Jones, *Kings*, 1.194). (vi) While not incompatible with dtr views (Deut 4:11; 5:22), vv. 12-13 do not reflect the dtr understanding of God's presence in the temple. (vii) A check in the DH shows that *'āz* (v. 12, "Then Solomon said") is frequently used to express appropriate sequence.

Text-history approach. The text signals just outlined allow for a reasonable probability that the verses indicated by a single sideline are pre-dtr. The possibility of dtr formulation has to be kept open, in which case certain older elements appear to have been preserved. Allowing for the "thick darkness" in association with the mystery of God's nearness, the dtr formulation of God's presence in the temple is normally nuanced in terms of the "name" theology (cf. vv. 16-20, 29). This suggests respect here for an older tradition, rather than a dtr formulation.

If an older narrative has been retained as the frame for the dtr speech (i.e., here and vv. 62-64), then a procedure has been followed similar to that observed in 1 Kgs 3:4-15 and 5:1-12 (Heb., 5:15-27).

There is a potential difference between Solomon's summoning of the elders (v. 1) and the gathering to Solomon of the people (v. 2). A difference of initiative may lie behind the texts but it is far too fragile a foundation for any reconstruction of Israel's religious history. Held together, the text may signify that the elders, summoned by Solomon, were joined by all the people of Israel. Whatever more there may have been is hidden from us.

24. **Text signals.** Further to what has been noted, in 8:1-13 the following signals point to later additions,

---

| After the Dtr: indented and sans serif font | **Revision: royal focus** | *Revision: national focus* | Other: double sideline |

to bring up the ark of the covenant of the LORD out of the city of David, which is Zion. ²All the people of Israel assembled to King Solomon at the festival in the month Ethanim, which is the seventh month.²⁵

³And all the elders of Israel came, and the priests carried the ark. ⁴So they brought up the ark of the LORD, and *(Heb.)* the tent of meeting. and all the holy vessels that were in the tent; the priests and the Levites brought them up. ⁵King Solomon and all the congregation of Israel, who had assembled before him, were with him before the ark, sacrificing so many sheep and oxen that they could not be counted or numbered.

---

often priestly. (i) "Heads of the tribes" is a late usage (cf. Num 30:1; 32:28; Josh 14:1; 21:1). (ii) "Leaders of the ancestral houses" is unique here (and, of course, 2 Chron 5:2; cf. Num 1:16). (iii) The "tent of meeting" is a late and almost exclusively priestly term. (iv) "Holy vessels" and "congregation of Israel" are not found earlier than priestly texts. (v) The "cloud" and the "glory" filling the temple to the exclusion of the priests is very close to the "cloud" covering the tent of meeting and YHWH's "glory" filling the tabernacle to the exclusion of Moses (Exod 40:34-35). (vi) The term "pole" associated with the ark is exclusively priestly.

Text-history approach. As the text signals indicate, this double-sidelined material is primarily of priestly origin. It is not surprising that a passage as significant as the transfer of the ark to the newly built temple should be a locus for intensive priestly literary activity. The concern of vv. 6*-8 is to coordinate the placing of the ark (with the cherubim on its cover, cf. Exod 25:17-20) and Solomon's overarching cherubim (6:23-28).

25. The references to "Zion" (v. 1) and "the seventh month" (v. 2) are unparalleled in the Hebrew scriptures (except for 2 Chron 5:2) and could come from any time. The combination of "city of David" and "Zion" blends two major traditions in Israel.

⁶Then the priests brought the ark of the covenant of the LORD to its place, in the inner sanctuary of the house.

in the most holy place, underneath the wings of the cherubim. ⁷For the cherubim spread out their wings over the place of the ark, so that the cherubim made a covering above the ark and its poles. ⁸The poles were so long that the ends of the poles were seen from the holy place in front of the inner sanctuary; but they could not be seen from outside; they are there to this day.

⁹There was nothing in the ark except the two tablets of stone that Moses had placed there at Horeb, where the Lord made a covenant with the Israelites, when they came out of the land of Egypt.²⁶

¹⁰And when the priests came out of the holy place, a cloud filled the house of the LORD, ¹¹so that the priests could not stand to minister because of the cloud; for the glory of the LORD filled the house of the LORD.

12 Then Solomon said,
"The LORD has said that he would dwell in
         thick darkness.
¹³I have built you an exalted house,
         a place for you to dwell in forever."²⁷

---

26. The use of "Horeb" for Sinai may indicate dtr origin for v. 9. The placing of the tablets within the ark is noted in Deut 10:1-5. A similar priestly concern for the testimony (*hā'ēdut*) is expressed in Exod 25:21. The national focus within the dtr revision might have sought to emphasize the presence of the law. Beyond the reference to Horeb, there are no specific identifying features in the verse. The limited references to the tablets of stone renders identification difficult—apart from 1 Kgs 8:9, only Exod 24:12; 31:18; 34:1, 4; and Deut 4:13; 5:22; 9:9, 10, 11; 10:1, 3.

27. **Present-text potential.** In 1 Kgs 8:1-13, vv. 1-11 portray the transfer of the ark from the city of

---

14 Then the king turned around and blessed all the assembly of Israel, while all the assembly of Israel stood.[28] **15He said,**

David to the newly completed temple as a grand liturgical procession in which the participants are arrayed in due order and in which everything is done with due solemnity and care. The text has a mixture of elements that may be reconciled with more or less ease. The further specification of temple fittings and layout is fully reconcilable with any earlier bare report. The different participating groups—in v. 1, elders, heads, and leaders—may be read as particular emphases rather than exclusive claims. The king and various representatives of the people are introduced first and then all the people. Appropriately, the priests emerge from this vast assembly as the bearers of the ark. On being lodged in the inner sanctuary, the whole temple is suddenly enveloped by the cloud, a dramatic portrayal of the divine presence and a fitting climax to the procession.

The cloud that fills the temple in vv. 10-11 is a sign that from now on the temple is to be the focus of worship, not the ark. Vv. 10-11 function effectively to evoke the significance of the moment: as the completion of the Exodus sanctuary was the beginning of God's enduring presence in the midst of journeying Israel, so here the completion of the temple and the transfer there of the ark is a signal of God's enduring presence in Jerusalem, in the midst of Israel. V. 9 is a reminder that the ark is only a container for the tablets of the Horeb covenant. For this idea in dtr circles, see Deut 10:1-5; in priestly circles, see Exod 25:21. Despite Heb 9:4, the manna is placed "before YHWH" (Exod 16:33) and Aaron's rod is placed "before the covenant" (*lipnê hā'ēdût*, Num 17:10 [Heb., 17:25]). After chap. 8, the ark is not mentioned again in the books of Kings.

With the transfer of the ark of the covenant to the new temple, it is appropriate that the king, as builder of the temple, should give expression to the significance of what has just been celebrated (vv. 12-13).

28. Verses 14-61 present a major prayer offered by Solomon. For a reflective and detailed study of this text, see E. Talstra, *Solomon's Prayer*.

"Blessed be the LORD, the God of Israel, who with his hand has fulfilled what he promised with his mouth to my father David, saying, 16"Since the day that I brought my people Israel out of Egypt, I have not chosen a city from any of the tribes of Israel in which to

---

Verses 14-29 give Solomon's opening blessing and prayer, balancing the concluding vv. 54-61. Vv. 14-21 have Solomon bless God for fulfilling the promises to David (cf. 2 Samuel 7); they also legitimate Solomon as the promised temple-builder. Vv. 22-29 have Solomon petition God in a prayer with two major points of focus. In vv. 22-25, the focus is on the promise to David of an everlasting dynasty, conditional upon obedience (v. 25b). In vv. 26-29, the focus is on the promise to David of the presence of God's name, in the house that Solomon has now built (v. 29).

In the middle, vv. 30-53 present Solomon praying that, in seven typical situations, each described in some detail, God will hear Israel's prayer. The plea in the introductory v. 30, "O hear in heaven your dwelling place," reflects a shift in emphasis that is maintained throughout the series of seven prayers.

Verses 54-61 have Solomon's concluding blessing and prayer which, in the present text, expand Solomon's opening words in vv. 14-29. (i) In vv. 14-21, Solomon blesses God for fulfilling the promises to David; in vv. 54-56, he blesses God for fulfilling the promises spoken through Moses. (ii) In vv. 22-25, Solomon prays that God will be with the Davidic dynasty as with David; in vv. 57-58, he prays that God may be with Israel as with their ancestors. (iii) In vv. 26-53, Solomon prays that God will heed his prayer "today" (v. 28) and in seven critical situations (vv. 31-51), with eyes open "night and day toward this house" (v. 29, cf. v. 52); in v. 59, he prays that his words be near God "day and night" and that God may maintain his cause and the cause of the people, "as each day requires." In conclusion, Solomon prays that all the peoples of the earth may know that "the LORD is God" (v. 60) and calls Israel to fidelity (v. 61).

After the Dtr:	**Revision:**	Revision:	Other:
indented and sans serif font	**royal focus**	national focus	double sideline

build a house, that my name might be there; but I chose David to be over my people Israel.' [17]My father David had it in mind to build a house for the name of the LORD, the God of Israel. [18]But the LORD said to my father David, 'You did well to consider building a house for my name; [19]nevertheless you shall not build the house, but your son who shall be born to you shall build the house for my name.' [20]Now the LORD has upheld the promise that he made; for I have risen in the place of my father David; I sit on the throne of Israel, as the LORD promised, and have built the house for the name of the LORD, the God of Israel. [21]There I have provided a place for the ark, in which is the covenant of the LORD that he made with our ancestors when he brought them out of the land of Egypt."[29]

---

29. **Text signals** in 8:14-21. (i) There is a strong appeal to the promise to David in 2 Samuel 7. (ii) There is a strong emphasis on the temple as a house for God's name.

Text-history approach. Both these signals favor dtr attribution for this passage. Furthermore, references to the temple as a house for the name of YHWH permeate the passage and put the stamp of the Josianic Dtr firmly upon it (cf. 8:16, 17, 18, 19, 20). Within the presentation of the DH advocated here, the focus on the Davidic dynasty and the fulfillment of the prophecy in 2 Samuel 7 point to the work of the Josianic Dtr. The twelve verses of the prophecy have been condensed into five verses here (vv. 16-20). The Samuel text is rearranged and rephrased to advance the Dtr's argument that God's purpose was set unwaveringly on Solomon as builder of the temple. Each stage in the unfolding of the text points in this direction. David was chosen, who took possession of the city where the temple was to be built (8:16; cf. 2 Sam 7:8). According to Solomon, David was commended

22 Then Solomon stood before the altar of the LORD in the presence of all the assembly of Israel, and spread out his hands to heaven. [23]He said, "O LORD, God of Israel,

---

for his desire to build a temple for YHWH (8:17-18; cf. 2 Sam 7:2-3) but the privilege was reserved for a promised son (8:19). According to Nathan, God would make David a house (or dynasty, 7:11b) and give David a son who would build a house for God's name (7:12-13). For the Dtr, the rise of Solomon as David's successor and his construction of the temple confirmed the fulfillment of God's purpose (8:20).

There are notable differences between 2 Samuel 7 and the appeal to it here. 8:15 refers to the promise given in 2 Samuel 7. As quoted in 8:16 however, the promise is a conflation of elements from 2 Sam 7:6-8 and 13a. 8:16 also refers to the choice of a city (Jerusalem), something that is not mentioned in 2 Samuel 7. 8:17 recalls 2 Sam 7:2 but this text does not speak of "a house for the name of the LORD" as does 8:17. The approval by God of David's plan to build a temple (8:18) is not found in 2 Sam 7:3-4, where God promptly overturns the approval given by Nathan. 8:19 draws on 2 Sam 7:12 (the promised offspring) and 7:13a (who shall build a house for God's name). 8:21 brings the ark into focus at the end of the text; in 2 Samuel 7, the ark is the initial focus (7:2). David's purpose was to build a temple for the ark; the Dtr transforms this into a temple for the name of YHWH.

This rearrangement expresses the dtr conceptual association of 2 Samuel 7 with 1 Kings 8, where the promise made to David by God is fulfilled dynastically in the figure of Solomon and cultically in the temple built for the name of YHWH.

The theological culmination is expressed in 8:21, where the ark, the covenant, and the temple are brought into a single focus. The Dtr has associated ark and covenant since Deut 10:1-5. For the Dtr, the ark symbolized the transition from an older epoch to the beginning of something new with David in Jerusalem. The presence of the ancient symbols of ark

| Main pre-DH: *Prophetic Record* | Other pre-DH: single sideline | HKL: + single underline | **Josianic DH: from the Dtr** |

there is no God like you in heaven above or on earth beneath, keeping covenant and steadfast love for your servants who walk before you with all their heart[30]

24who have kept (Heb.; NRSV, the covenant that you kept) **for your servant my father David what** (Heb.; NRSV, as) **you declared to him; you promised with your mouth and have this day fulfilled with your hand. 25And now** (Heb.; NRSV, therefore), **O LORD, God of Israel,**

keep for your servant my father David that which you promised him, saying, 'There

shall never fail you a successor before me to sit on the throne of Israel, if only your children look to their way, to walk before me as you have walked before me.' 26And now (Heb.; NRSV, therefore), *O God of Israel*[31]

let your word be confirmed, which you promised to your servant my father David.

> 27 "But will God indeed dwell on the earth? Even heaven and the highest heaven cannot contain you, much less this house that I have built![32]

and covenant within the newly built temple in Jerusalem intensifies the focus on the temple that Solomon has built in Jerusalem for the name of YHWH and on which, for the Dtr, all Israel's worship will be centered. This will be reflected in the prayers that follow.

Present-text potential. 1 Kgs 8:14-21 fleshes out the meaning of 8:13a—"I have built you an exalted house." According to vv. 14-21, the building of the temple was not Solomon's initiative as v. 13a might of itself imply. It was the fulfillment of God's purpose, a purpose that was first manifested in God's deliverance of Israel from Egypt, manifested subsequently in the choice of David as Israel's king, of Jerusalem as the site of the temple and, above all, of Solomon as David's successor. God is blessed for bringing all this about.

30. **Text signals** in v. 23. (i) The incomparability of God. (ii) God's covenant loyalty to those who are loyal. (iii) The reference to "your servants" is wider than to Solomon alone or David.

Text-history approach. The incomparability of God is emphasized in Deuteronomy 4 (see 4:39). Covenant here stands out from the surrounding context that concerns God's promises to David. Covenant loyalty (*bĕrît* and *ḥesed*) occurs only here and in Deut 7:9 within the DH. The plural "servants" may reflect the move from king to people within the dtr revision's national focus.

Present-text potential. See below on v. 29a.

31. **Text signals** in v. 25. (i) The initial address to God is repeated at the start of v. 25 and at the start of v. 26. (ii) The dynastic promise to David is presented as conditional.

Text-history approach. The repetition at the start of vv. 25 and 26 is best understood as a typical resumption of the main theme after an insertion—i.e., here, the bulk of v. 25. Together with 2:4, 8:25 anticipates 9:5, as noted earlier. In 9:4-5, the Dtr reaffirms the promise to David, while making it conditional on Solomon's obedience. In both 2:4 and 8:25 (using terminology that is almost exclusive to these three passages), the promise to David is rendered conditional in a way that 9:4-5 does not do. The promise to David in 2 Samuel 7 was explicitly unconditional (cf. 7:13b to 16). God's report of it remains unconditional in 9:5 and in 9:4 obedience is demanded of Solomon alone (singular). In 2:4 and 8:25, the condition has been introduced into the Davidic promise itself and it is explicitly laid down for David's descendants (plural). For these reasons, attribution to the national focus of the dtr revision is probable.

The formal aspect is worth noting: direct speech as against reported speech. In 9:4-5, God is speaking to Solomon. In 2:4, David in his charge to Solomon reports God's word. In 8:25, Solomon in his prayer also reports God's word.

Present-text potential. See below on v. 29a.

32. **Text signals** in v. 27. (i) The verse interrupts Solomon's prayer and pleading (vv. 26 & 28). (ii) It forms a contrast to 8:13.

| After the Dtr: indented and sans serif font | **Revision: royal focus** | Revision: national focus | Other: double sideline |

²⁸**Regard your servant's prayer and his plea, O LORD my God, heeding the cry and the prayer that your servant prays to you today; ²⁹that your eyes may be open night and day toward this house, the place of which you said, 'My name shall be there.'**[33]

that you may heed the prayer that your servant prays toward this place. ³⁰Hear the plea of your servant and of your people Israel when they pray toward this place; O hear in heaven your dwelling place; heed and forgive.[34]

Text-history approach. At the level of the Josianic DH, Solomon's prayer of dedication culminates in the plea that God's eyes be open toward the house, where God's name shall be. The theology of the Dtr crystallizes this in God's promise to put his name in the house and the promise that God's eyes and heart "will be there for all time" (9:3). In advance of these, 8:27 expresses a sharp corrective to any overly immanent theology. This sentiment is markedly evident in 2 Chron 2:6 and 6:18. As a theological affirmation, it could have been made in its own right, or it may have been introduced in conjunction with the prayers that follow. It fits with their refrain, "hear in heaven."

Present-text potential. See below on v. 29a.

33. **Text signals** in 8:22-29a. As in 8:14-21, the text signals of dtr presence here are: (i) the appeal to the promise to David in 2 Samuel 7; (ii) the emphasis on the temple as a house for God's name. The signals for the bulk of the material in vv. 23, 25, and 27 have been dealt with in the preceding notes.

Text-history approach. As for vv. 14-21, the substance of these verses is to be attributed to the Dtr. The shift from "my father David" in vv. 15-20 to "your servant my father David" in vv. 24-26 reflects the shift in literary form from report to prayer. The promise of 2 Samuel 7 is taken up here in two stages. In v. 24, the reference has to be to the actual construction of the temple. In v. 26, the word to be confirmed has to refer to the presence of God's name in the temple (cf. v. 29a). A third stage goes beyond the promise of 2 Samuel 7 in Solomon's plea that God's eyes might be open "night and day toward this house" (vv. 28-29a). This culminating prayer of Solomon's, in the text of the Dtr, is met with God's assurance in 9:3, emphasizing all three—house, name, and eyes and heart.

Present-text potential. At the original level of the Dtr, Solomon's plea in 8:28-29a was close in the text to God's response in what is now 9:3. The relationship between plea and response would have been evident. The fine tuning of the plea (see in vv. 23, 25, 27) would not have disturbed the perception of the relationship between plea and response. The additions that have created an extensive gap between plea and response may have accumulated gradually or been introduced as a block. From the time of exile on, the significance of the presence of God's eyes and heart in the temple would have been diminished by its destruction in 587. The prayers ask that God "hear in heaven" (8:30, 32, 34, 36, 39, 43, 45, 49); the sense of God's presence in the temple is diminished.

It is against this background and in this context that the present text of 8:22-29a needs to be interpreted. 8:14-21 was focused on the achievement of the temple building. 8:22-29a, as the prayer of consecration for this building, expresses the (dtr) concern to understand the temple as a place for God's name—not, as in v. 13, "a place for you to dwell in forever." As a present text, the prayer appropriately begins with affirmations of God's incomparability and covenant fidelity. The covenant fidelity is exemplified in the reality of the dynasty and the temple (cf. v. 20). The prayer reflects on the conditions implicit for the future of the dynasty (v. 25) and the proper understanding required of God's presence in the temple (vv. 26-29a).

34. A new perspective is begun with v. 29b, where prayer is made "toward this place"—no longer within the temple. V. 30 involves the people along with the king. 8:29b-30 is the literary seam that introduces the seven prayers in 8:31-53, concerned exclusively with the people. The NRSV in v. 29b must be understood to

Main pre-DH:	Other pre-DH:	HKL: + single	**Josianic DH:**
Prophetic Record	single sideline	underline	**from the Dtr**

31 "If someone sins against a neighbor and is given an oath to swear, and comes and swears before your altar in this house, ³²then hear in heaven, and act, and judge your servants, condemning the guilty by bringing their conduct on their own head, and vindicating the righteous by rewarding them according to their righteousness.

33 "When your people Israel, having sinned against you, are defeated before an enemy but turn again to you, confess your name, pray and plead with you in this house, ³⁴then hear in heaven, forgive the sin of your people Israel, and bring them again to the land that you gave to their ancestors.

35 "When heaven is shut up and there is no rain because they have sinned against you, and then they pray toward this place, confess your name, and turn from their sin, because you punish them, ³⁶then hear in heaven, and forgive the sin of your servants, your people Israel, when you teach them the good way in which they should walk; and grant rain on your land, which you have given to your people as an inheritance.

37 "If there is famine in the land, if there is plague, blight, mildew, locust, or caterpillar; if their enemy besieges them in any of their cities; whatever plague, whatever sickness there is; ³⁸whatever prayer, whatever plea there is from any individual or from all your people Israel, all knowing the afflictions of their own hearts so that they stretch out their hands toward this house; ³⁹then hear in heaven your dwelling place, forgive, act, and render to all whose

hearts you know—according to all their ways, for only you know what is in every human heart— ⁴⁰so that they may fear you all the days that they live in the land that you gave to our ancestors.

41 "Likewise when a foreigner, who is not of your people Israel, comes from a distant land because of your name ⁴²—for they shall hear of your great name, your mighty hand, and your outstretched arm—when a foreigner comes and prays toward this house, ⁴³then hear in heaven your dwelling place, and do according to all that the foreigner calls to you, so that all the peoples of the earth may know your name and fear you, as do your people Israel, and so that they may know that your name has been invoked on this house that I have built.

44 "If your people go out to battle against their enemy, by whatever way you shall send them, and they pray to the LORD toward the city that you have chosen and the house that I have built for your name, ⁴⁵then hear in heaven their prayer and their plea, and maintain their cause.

46 "If they sin against you—for there is no one who does not sin—and you are angry with them and give them to an enemy, so that they are carried away captive to the land of the enemy, far off or near; ⁴⁷yet if they come to their senses in the land to which they have been taken captive, and repent, and plead with you in the land of their captors, saying, 'We have sinned, and have done wrong; we have acted wickedly'; ⁴⁸if they repent with all their heart and soul in the land of their enemies, who took them captive, and pray to you toward their land, which you gave to their ancestors, the city that you have chosen, and the house that I have built for your name; ⁴⁹then hear in

refer to a future prayer of Solomon's, prayed "toward this place." The equivalence of the Hebrew in vv. 29b and 30 indicates a future prayer in both cases.

| After the Dtr:
indented and sans serif font | **Revision:**
royal focus | *Revision:*
national focus | Other:
double sideline |

heaven your dwelling place their prayer and their plea, maintain their cause [50]and forgive your people who have sinned against you, and all their transgressions that they have committed against you; and grant them compassion in the sight of their captors, so that they may have compassion on them [51](for they are your people and heritage, which you brought out of Egypt, from the midst of the iron-smelter). [52]Let your eyes be open to the plea of your servant, and to the plea of your people Israel, listening to them whenever they call to you. [53]For you have separated them from among all the peoples of the earth, to be your heritage, just as you promised through Moses, your servant, when you brought our ancestors out of Egypt, O LORD God."[35]

54 Now when Solomon finished offering all this prayer and this plea to the LORD, he arose from facing the altar of the LORD, where he had knelt with hands outstretched toward heaven; [55]and (Heb.) he stood and blessed all the assembly of Israel with a loud voice:

---

35. 1 Kgs 8:31-51 is a collection of seven prayers: vv. 31-32, 33-34, 35-36, 37-40, 41-43, 44-45, 46-51. The collection is framed by vv. 29b-30 and vv. 52-53 as introduction and conclusion.

Text signals. There are five signals that point to the collection of seven prayers as a later expansion of the Dtr's prayer for the dedication of the temple. (i) The literary seam identified above—vv. 29b-30—that introduces the collection. (ii) The literary seam of vv 52-53 that concludes the collection and links it to the surrounding context. V. 52 provides a link to the immediate context (cf. v. 54) by echoing the language of vv. 29-30 and by reintroducing the king as one in need of prayer; he is not mentioned in any of the seven prayers. V. 53 provides a link to the larger context by recalling the promises to Moses (cf. v. 56). (iii) All the prayers address situations that affect the people, not the king. The prayer for the individual in vv. 31-32 is hardly a reference to the king. (iv) The majority of the prayers are preoccupied with the forgiveness of sin (cf. vv. 34, 36, 39, 46-50). The verb "to forgive," *sālaḥ*, occurs elsewhere in Deuteronomy—2 Kings in passages that are later than the Josianic DH;

Deut 29:20 (Heb., 29:19), and 2 Kgs 5:18; 24:4 (on these, see notes on the respective texts). The occurrence in Deut 29:20 is heading in the reverse direction to the tenor of these prayers; they are unlikely to be from the dtr revision (national focus). (v) The prayers presume divine approval of the temple which, in the text, is not granted until 9:3. Cross attributed 8:25b, 46-53 to his Dtr[2]. Nelson attributed 8:44-51 to his Dtr[2].

Text-history approach. These prayers are close to the concerns for the observance of the law, characteristic of the national focus of the dtr revision process, but their insertion is almost certainly later. Vv. 57-58 and v. 61 belong within this national focus (see below); vv. 59-60, which are a later insertion into this material, belong with the series of prayers. Furthermore, the verb *sālaḥ* is not found in any of the law-focused texts. The national focus within the dtr revision emphasized disobedience and condemnation; it is a move beyond such condemnation that engenders the confidence which longs for forgiveness (see O'Brien, *Deuteronomistic History Hypothesis*, 283).

The late addition of the collection to the DH does not mean that all the prayers are late compositions. Vv. 44-45 may well be a pre-exilic composition since it speaks of a military campaign without any suggestion of defeat. In the present text however, it is to be read in conjunction with vv. 46-51 for which it forms the preface. V. 46 presumes the setting of battle in vv. 44-45 and "they" of v. 46 refers back to "your people" of v. 44. The setting of vv. 46-51, as its language and concerns show, is clearly exilic.

Present-text potential. In vv. 29-53, Solomon's prayer, which up to this point has focused on the future of the Davidic monarchy in Israel and on the

---

Main pre-DH:	Other pre-DH:	HKL: + single	**Josianic DH:**
Prophetic Record	single sideline	underline	**from the Dtr**

56 **"Blessed be the LORD, who has given rest to his people Israel according to all that he promised; not one word has failed of all his good promise, which he spoke through his servant Moses.**[36]

57The LORD our God be with us, as he was with our ancestors; may he not leave us or abandon us, 58but incline our hearts to him, to walk in all his ways, and to keep his commandments, his statutes, and his

ordinances, which he commanded our ancestors.

59Let these words of mine, with which I pleaded before the LORD, be near to the LORD our God day and night, and may he maintain the cause of his servant and the cause of his people Israel, as each day requires; 60so that all the peoples of the earth may know that the LORD is God; there is no other.

61Therefore devote yourselves completely to the LORD our God, walking in his statutes and keeping his commandments, as at this day."[37]

---

temple as the exclusive dwelling place of the divine name, expands to embrace key needs of the people, even foreigners (vv. 41-43). Solomon has built and consecrated the shrine of the united kingdom. Following the prayer of consecration, the focus is turned outward to the people that this shrine serves. The series first situates the supplicant before the altar in the temple (vv. 31-32). Vv. 33-34 contain a contrast between presence in the temple (v. 33) and absence in exile (v. 34); they imply that some who are in the temple pray for others who are not (cf. Jones, *Kings*, 1.202-3). Following these, the supplicants are spoken of as praying "toward this place" (v. 35) or "toward this house" (vv. 38, 42), or "to the LORD toward the city … and the house" (v. 44, not necessarily in exile), and "to you toward their land, … the city … and the house" (v. 48, explicitly in exile). As formulated, the prayers are appropriate to national needs foreseen in Solomon's time as well as to needs experienced later in the diaspora.

36. Verses 54-56 bring to a close the prayer that Solomon began in 8:22. The kneeling is not reported in v. 22; nor is it reported anywhere later. The "prayer and plea" of 8:54 occur also in 8:28 and 9:3, with the "all" of v. 54 as a possible flourish or later expansion. The concept of "rest" confirms the attribution to the Dtr. V. 56 signals the fulfillment of the program outlined in Deut 12:10-12, with stages along the way noted at Josh 21:43-45 and 1 Kgs 5:3-5 (Heb., 5:17-19). What was laid down by Moses there is here uniquely brought under Moses' name (cf. note on 8:1).

---

37. **Text signals** in vv. 57-61. (i) V. 57 refers to Israel's ancestors, as does v. 58. (ii) V. 58 describes the fidelity required of Israel in law-oriented terms, as does v. 61. (iii) V. 58 refers to Israel's heart collectively (our heart), as does v. 61 (your heart/yourselves). (iv) There is a change from the second person plural of vv. 57-58 to the first person singular in v. 59. (v) V. 59 recalls elements of the prayers in vv. 29b-53; "plead", as in vv. 33, 38, 45, 47, 49, 52; "maintain his servant's/Israel's cause," as in vv. 45, 49.

Text-history approach. In vv. 57-58 and 61, three elements point to the dtr revision's national focus: (i) the bringing together of king and people (1st pers. plural, "our" and "us"); (ii) the emphasis on obedience ("incline our hearts," "devote yourselves completely"); (iii) the specific legal focus given to this obedience (commandments, statutes, ordinances). King and people are brought together: in 5:4 (Heb., 5:18), "rest" was noted specifically in relation to Solomon and, in 8:56, it is noted in relation to the people; the development in vv. 57-58 and 61 bring king and people together within a single focus. Obedience: the emphasis on the people's obedience is a characteristic of the national focus of the dtr revision; here, Solomon's prayer is that God will be the source of that obedience (cf. the promise in Deut 30:6-10, also national focus). Throughout the texts of the revision, the focus is on Israel abandoning God (see Deut 29:25 [Heb., v. 24];

After the Dtr: indented and sans serif font	*Revision:* *royal focus*	*Revision:* *national focus*	Other: double sideline

62 Then the king, and all Israel with him, offered sacrifice before the LORD. [63]Solomon offered as sacrifices of well-being to the LORD twenty-two thousand oxen and one hundred twenty thousand sheep. So the king and all the people of Israel dedicated the house of the LORD. [64]The same day the king consecrated the middle

of the court that was in front of the house of the LORD; for there he offered the burnt offerings and the grain offerings and the fat pieces of the sacrifices of well-being, because the bronze altar that was before the LORD was too small to receive the burnt offerings and the grain offerings and the fat pieces of the sacrifices of well-being.[38]

65 So Solomon held the festival at that time, and all Israel with him—a great assembly, people from Lebo-hamath to the Wadi of Egypt—before the LORD our God, seven days. [66]On the eighth day he sent the people away; and they blessed the king,

Judg 2:12, 13, 20; 10:6, 10, 13; 1 Sam 12:10; 1 Kgs 11:33; 2 Kgs 17:18; 22:17); here (1 Kgs 8:57), at a climactic point in the DH, the prayer is that God will not abandon Israel. Vv. 57-58 and 61 are bound together by the repetition of "heart" (Heb.; NRSV, "our hearts," "yourselves") and the legal focus (commandments, statutes).

In vv. 59-60, the change to first person singular and the echoes of vv. 29b-53 point to a different provenance from vv. 57-58 and 61. This is confirmed by the absence of law-oriented language and the absence of emphasis on the people's fidelity. In its place, the emphasis is on Solomon's prayer: that it be accepted and that his cause and Israel's be maintained.

This is an unmistakable echo of the prayers in vv. 29b-53. Solomon does not exhort Israel to obedience; instead, according to v. 60, the plea is that God's support will promote knowledge of the one true God among all the peoples of the earth, echoing v. 43. Vv. 59-60 belong therefore to the same level as vv. 29b-53.

Verses 29b-53, 59-60 look beyond sin and punishment to forgiveness and the renewal of Israel's relationship with God. It is more than likely that this material was added after the national focus of dtr revising that condemned Israel for its disobedience and claimed that the exile was the outcome of its disobedience.

Present-text potential. Verses 57-61 take up v. 56's blessing for past benefits and turn to the future. There is a logical sequence: Solomon prays for Israel, prays for his prayer on behalf of Israel, and exhorts Israel to practice what he has asked of God.

As noted earlier, the function of the various parts within the present text as a whole is best seen by comparing the sequence of blessing and prayer in vv. 14-

53 with a similar sequence in vv. 54-61, but within a consistently broader horizon. In vv. 14-21, Solomon blesses God for fulfilling the promises to David; in vv. 54-56, he blesses God for fulfilling the promises spoken through Moses. In vv. 22-25, Solomon prays that God will be with the Davidic dynasty as with David; in vv. 57-58, he prays that God may be with Israel as with their ancestors. In vv. 26-53, Solomon prays that God will heed his prayer for the temple and the prayers of the people in a number of critical situations; in v. 59, he prays that God may maintain his cause and the cause of the people "as each day requires." V. 60 expands the horizon even further by praying that all peoples of the earth may know that "the LORD is God." V. 61 concludes with the reminder that a critical ingredient in all these prayers is Israel's complete fidelity to the LORD.

Dietrich attributed 8:14-26, 28-30a, 53-61 to his DtrN.

38. With vv. 62-64, the pre-dtr account of the temple's consecration is brought to a close. V. 64 may read as a narrative afterthought. But the consecration of a mid-court area—explicitly without any semblance of an altar—is most surprising, quite unparalleled, and contrary to any known later canons. The repetition within the verse suggests the possibility of some editorial activity.

Main pre-DH:	Other pre-DH:	HKL: + single	**Josianic DH:**
Prophetic Record	single sideline	underline	**from the Dtr**

and went to their tents, joyful and in good spirits because of all the goodness that the LORD had shown to his servant David and to his people Israel.[39]

9 When Solomon had finished building the house of the LORD and the king's house and all that Solomon desired to build, [2]the LORD appeared to Solomon a second time, as he had appeared to him at Gibeon.

[3]The LORD said to him, "I have heard your prayer and your plea, which you made before me; I have consecrated this house that you have built, and put my name there forever; my eyes and my heart will be there for all time. [4]As for you, if you will walk before me, as David your father walked, with integrity of heart and uprightness, doing according to all that I have commanded you, and keeping my statutes and my ordinances, [5]then I will establish your royal throne over Israel forever, as I promised your father David, saying, 'There shall not fail you a successor on the throne of Israel.'[40]

---

39. Noth and others attribute vv. 65-66 to the Dtr. The verses may, however, be later. The phrase "great assembly" is used of Israel only here (and 2 Chron 7:8); it is used in Jer 31:8 of the returning exiles (otherwise, cf. Jer 44:15; Ezek 38:15). The geographical designation "from Lebo-hamath to the Wadi of Egypt," is not a dtr characteristic (only here and 2 Chron 7:8; cf. 1 Chron 13:5; also Amos 6:14). 2 Chron 7:8-9 reflects a twofold seven-day festival, akin to the Heb. text of 1 Kgs 8:65 (contrary to Deut 16:13-15). These may be pointers to a later origin.

40. **Text signals** in 9:1-5. (i) 9:1 refers to the end of the building of the temple, without mention of the immediately preceding ceremonies; with a single infinitive (*libnôt*), it brings into focus the end of a more extensive building program of Solomon's. (ii) The third element, "all that Solomon desired to build,"

opens the focus remarkably wide. For "desire," it uses an unusual noun, found elsewhere only in 9:19; Isa 21:4; and 2 Chron 8:6 (= 1 Kgs 9:19). Literally, the Hebrew reads: all the longing of Solomon which he desired to do. The pleonastic subordinate clause, "which he desired to do," uses a more common verb (desire) and a more general infinitive (to do); 1 Kgs 9:19 and 2 Chron 8:6 repeat the less usual verbal root (longing, √HSQ) and the more appropriate infinitive (to build). (iii) 9:2 explicitly compares the theophany with the previous appearance at Gibeon. (iv) 9:3's use of "prayer and plea" picks up 8:28-29a, 54. (v) Literally, the Hebrew of 9:3 reads: I have consecrated this house—that you have built—to put my name there forever. As it stands, the phrase is unique. It uses "put" rather than "dwell," and the more specific "consecration of the house" in place of the more general "choose." To "put God's name there" is used in Deuteronomy in association with the chosen place (12:5, 21; 14:24) and in Kings in association with the chosen city (1 Kgs 14:21; 2 Kgs 21:4, 7). (vi) 9:4 introduces a condition, applicable to Solomon alone (2nd pers. sing.), formulated outside the promise quoted in v. 5. At the end of v. 4, three terse words in Hebrew spell out upright conduct in legal terms. (vii) 9:5 evokes the unconditional promise to David from 2 Sam 7:12-13, 16. The quoted phrase "there shall not fail you a successor" is not to be found in 2 Samuel 7, but occurs only here, 2:4 and 8:25 (and 2 Chron 6:16; 7:18). The "throne of Israel" here refers to the united kingdom (cf. 1 Kgs 2:4; 8:20, 25; 9:5; 10:9; 2 Chron 6:10, 16; the two exceptions are 2 Kgs 10:30; 15:12).

Text-history approach in 9:1-5. The signals in 9:1-2 suggest the existence of pre-dtr text here, as at the beginning of chaps. 3, 5, and 8. As in these cases, only the frame remains and the present speeches are almost entirely the work of the Dtr. Such replacement of prior tradition is rare in the growth of biblical text. It is not unknown within the DH (cf. Huldah's prophecy, 2 Kgs 22:15-20). It may be indicative of just how substantial the Dtr's authorial activity was in this area, bringing together and significantly shaping traditions to form extensive text.

| After the Dtr: indented and sans serif font | *Revision: royal focus* | *Revision: national focus* | Other: double sideline |

6 "If you turn aside from following me, you (plural) or your children, and do not keep my commandments and my statutes that I have set before you, but go and serve other gods and worship them, [7]then I will cut Israel off from the land that I have given them; and the house that I have consecrated for my name I will cast out of my sight; and Israel will become a proverb and a taunt among all peoples. [8]This house will become a heap of ruins; everyone passing by it will be astonished, and will hiss; and they will say, 'Why has the LORD done such a thing to this land and to this house?' [9]Then they will say, 'Because they have forsaken the LORD their God, who brought their ancestors out of the land of Egypt, and embraced other gods, worshiping them and serving them; therefore the LORD has brought this disaster upon them.' "[41]

Understanding the structural composition of the Josianic DH is of the highest importance here. Conditions envisaged in Deuteronomy 12 have been fulfilled: Israel lives in the land; rest has been given; the temple in Jerusalem has been built for God's name. The text signals God's endorsement of all that has happened; "I have heard your prayer and your plea" (cf. 8:14-29a*, 54-56). The consecration in the present ("I have consecrated this house that you have built") has implications for the future. The Josianic Dtr treats temple and dynasty differently. God's presence in the temple is guaranteed: "my name there forever; my eyes and my heart will be there for all time." God's word for the dynasty is conditioned: the Davidic rule over the united kingdom is dependent on Solomon's fidelity (v. 4; the legal specification, "keeping my statutes and my ordinances," could derive from the national focus. It is possible but not certain; a change in format is not necessary. Cf. 11:34, 38). The infidelity of Solomon will cost his successor the northern kingdom; Judah and Jerusalem will remain, because of the fidelity of David. A base is kept in place for Josiah's reform—to restore what will be lost.

Present-text potential. See note on 9:9.

41. **Text signals** in 9:6-9. (i) While in v. 5 the address is singular, the address in v. 6 is emphatically plural—the five verbs, "you and your children," and "before you"; it reaches out beyond the king to the people. (ii) The possibility of apostasy is raised by God in v. 6 and its consequences affirmed by foreigners in v. 9. (iii) In v. 7, retribution for disobedience is directed against Israel rather than the Davidic dynasty. (iv) The rejection of the temple and its destruction is envisaged in vv. 7-8, in contrast to the promise in v. 3. (v) The destruction envisaged is described in terms found in Jeremiah: for "a proverb and a taunt among all peoples," cf. Jer 24:9; also Deut 28:37; for the combination of verbs "to be astonished" and "to hiss," cf. Jer 19:8; 49:17; 50:13. (vi) The question and answer schema here is found also in Jer 22:8-9; Deut 29:24-28 (Heb., 23-27).

Text-history approach in 9:6-9. The abrupt change to the plural and the shift of focus from Solomon to the people indicates an addition. The transfer of attention from king to people is a characteristic of the national focus of the dtr revision. However, the presence of language and images here shared with the book of Jeremiah suggests caution about the attribution of this text. For the present, it may be unwise to associate the dtr revision (national focus) too closely with the dtr elements in the book of Jeremiah.

Present-text potential in 9:1-9. The focus of this second appearance of God to Solomon is on God's response to Solomon's prayer and plea (9:1-9). At a first stage, the address is directly to Solomon (vv. 3-5). God's presence in the temple is assured. God's commitment to the dynasty is conditioned. At a second stage, the address moves, surprisingly, to the people (vv. 6-9). In relation to God, there is an inseparable bond between king and people. If there is no fidelity to God, there will be no successors on the throne, no people on the land, and no divine presence in the temple.

Main pre-DH:	Other pre-DH:	HKL: + single	**Josianic DH:**
Prophetic Record	single sideline	underline	**from the Dtr**

10 At the end of twenty years, in which Solomon had built the two houses, the house of the LORD and the king's house, ¹¹King Hiram of Tyre having supplied Solomon with cedar and cypress timber and gold, as much as he desired, King Solomon gave to Hiram twenty cities in the land of Galilee. ¹²But when Hiram came from Tyre to see the cities that Solomon had given him, they did not please him. ¹³Therefore he said, "What kind of cities are these that you have given me, my brother?" So they are called the land of Cabul to this day. ¹⁴But Hiram had sent to the king one hundred twenty talents of gold.[42]

There is a reflection here on the whole prayer of Solomon and the dedication of the temple. In vv. 41-43 of Solomon's prayer, both Israel and the foreigner are to know God's name and its invocation on the temple. In the event of Israel's failure in fidelity, the foreigner confronted by the fate of the temple will confess that God "has brought this disaster upon them." "So that all the peoples of the earth may know your name and fear you, as do your people Israel" (v. 43): whether Israel is obedient or disobedient, God's purpose in the temple will be achieved.

Cross attributed 9:4-9 to his Dtr². Nelson attributed 9:6-9 to his Dtr². Dietrich attributed 9:1-9 to his DtrN.

42. Between the response to Solomon's prayer (9:1-9) and the condemnation of Solomon's sin (11:1-13), 9:10–10:29 gathers a variety of traditions, encompassing generally Solomon's activities (9:10-28), wisdom (10:1-13), and wealth (10:14-29). The collection has attracted traditions and comments from a variety of sources that it is neither necessary nor easy to unravel. The absence here of explicit benefit derived by Solomon's subjects, comparable with 1 Kgs 4:20, 25 (Heb., 4:20 and 5:5), invites the suggestion that this section is not as well disposed toward Solomon as the earlier chaps. 3-5.

15 This is the account of the forced labor that King Solomon conscripted to build the house of the LORD and his own house, the Millo and the wall of Jerusalem. Hazor, Megiddo, Gezer,

---

Text signals in 9:10-14. (i) V. 10 needs follow-up that is lacking in the text; it is left hanging in the Hebrew. (ii) V. 11a begins independently and refers to the ongoing provision of building supplies. (iii) With an introductory particle, v. 11b is equally independent. (iv) Vv. 12-13 depend on v. 11b, report a visit to Galilee by Hiram, and pass a disparaging judgment on the twenty cities. The etymology of the name Cabul is far from clear. (v) V. 14 reports a sum of gold given to "the king" by Hiram, either as specification of the quantity of gold in v. 11a or as payment for an unspecified transaction. (vi) 2 Chron 8:2 reverses the situation, with Solomon restoring the cities given him by Hiram.

Text-history approach. Attempts to make sense of the origins and growth of this passage have not been particularly successful. Some begin from vv. 11b and 14, with vv. 12-13 as an added derogatory gloss and vv. 10-11a as a somewhat unsatisfactory introduction and gloss (so Gray, *Kings*, 238-39; Noth, *Könige*, 209-12). The ineptness of such later additions is left unexplained. Jones starts with v. 11b as the reliable archival note, where cities have replaced the produce of 5:11 (Heb., 5:25), due to Solomon's economic difficulties; vv. 10-11a are a dtr introduction, vv. 12-13 a later addition, and v. 14 a gloss specifying the gold in v. 11a (*Kings*, 1.212-14). The awkwardness remains unexplained.

Verse 11b may reflect an accurate tradition; this does not determine the time of its entry into the text. The level of apparently secondary addition militates against a pre-dtr attribution for the passage. In any hypothesis, the unevennesses are difficult to explain.

Present-text potential. 9:10 serves to separate narratively what follows from the preceding account of Solomon's building and the temple dedication. Solomon's story enters a new phase. Whether the collection overall is laudatory or pejorative remains delightfully uncertain. However, 9:10-14 gets it off to a bad start. It sounds the first critical note since 3:3.

After the Dtr:	**Revision:**	Revision:	Other:
indented and sans serif font	**royal focus**	national focus	double sideline

¹⁶(Pharaoh king of Egypt had gone up and captured Gezer and burned it down, had killed the Canaanites who lived in the city, and had given it as dowry to his daughter, Solomon's wife; ¹⁷so Solomon rebuilt Gezer)

Lower Beth-horon, ¹⁸*Baalath, Tamar in the wilderness, within the land,* ¹⁹*as well as all of Solomon's storage cities, the cities for his chariots, the cities for his cavalry, and whatever Solomon desired to build, in Jerusalem, in Lebanon, and in all the land of his dominion.*⁴³

²⁰All the people, who were left of the Amorites, the Hittites, the Perizzites, the Hivites, and the Jebusites, who were not of the people of Israel, ²¹—their descendants who were still left in the land, whom the Israelites were unable to destroy completely—these Solomon conscripted for slave labor, and so they are to this day. ²²But of the Israelites Solomon made no slaves; they were the soldiers, they were his officials, his commanders, his captains, and the commanders of his chariotry and cavalry.⁴⁴

43. **Text signals** in vv. 15-19. (i) The initial phrase is a formulaic opening for a comment (cf. Deut 15:2; 19:4; also 1 Kgs 11:27). It denotes a new beginning. (ii) The "forced labor" is related first to the temple, the palace, and the wall (all specified in 3:1) and the "Millo" (to be found in 9:24), and second to other burdensome projects of Solomon's. (iii) 3:1 and 9:24 are the primary occurrences referring to Pharaoh's daughter, wife of Solomon (derived from these: 1 Kgs 7:8; 11:1; 2 Chron 8:11). (iv) Vv. 16-17a add a historical note about Gezer, interrupting the list of towns. (v) V. 19b moves beyond the particular projects to an overall and general view; it has unusual terminology, found to a more limited degree in 9:1b.

Text-history approach. Resumption of the PR from 3:1. The likelihood is that these verses come from the PR, with their initial focus on Pharaoh's daughter and on Solomon's building in Jerusalem (cf. above, the initial footnote on 1 Kings 1–2, under **text-history approach**). The four items listed in 9:15a are restricted to the concerns of 3:1 and 9:24; together with the other areas listed, they specify the projects on which forced labor was used. The association with Pharaoh (vv. 16-17a, in parentheses in the NRSV) could have been added to this material at any time; for the format used see the Introduction and the note on 1 Kgs 4:29-34. The attribution of v. 19b may be considered dubious (but cf. 9:1b above); it cannot be denied to pre-dtr material (including the PR), nor can it be denied to dtr editing. Certainty is out of the question.

All of this builds up the picture of the burden inherited from Solomon by Rehoboam (12:4). The continuation of the PR is to be found at 9:24.

Present-text potential. In 1 Kings 12 (PR), Rehoboam's escalation of the burdensome yoke inherited from Solomon features as the cause for the division of the kingdom; the origins of that burden are adumbrated here. If parts of 11:1-7 are attributed to the PR, as below, the concern with Solomon's apostasy was present from early on. This is not surprising, given the PR's concern with Jeroboam's disobedience/apostasy (1 Kgs 14:9b), Ahab's Baalism (1 Kgs 16:31b-32, and cf. 2 Kgs 10:28), as well as Saul's disobedience. In the Josianic DH, Solomon's apostasy becomes a principal concern. There is an interplay of politics and religion that is not resolved. As the division of the kingdom approaches, the text here goes beyond the temple in Jerusalem (see 5:13-18). The further projects might be seen as conducive to the glory of Solomon rather than the glory of YHWH.

44. Burden ("yoke"), presumably labor and taxes, is the cause for resistance to Solomon's son in 1 Kings 12, utilized by the PR. For the Dtr, Solomon's failure was due to his apostasy. These verses, vv. 20-22, may be regarded as distinguishing temporary conscripted labor from permanent slave labor (see Gray, *Kings*, 155-56, 250-52 and Jones, *Kings*, 1.157-58, 214). Some consider them original (so Noth, *Könige*, 216-18; see Campbell, *Of Prophets and Kings*, 86-87); others

Main pre-DH:	Other pre-DH:	HKL: + single	**Josianic DH:**
Prophetic Record	single sideline	underline	**from the Dtr**

23 These were the chief officers who were over Solomon's work: five hundred fifty, who had charge of the people who carried on the work.[45]

24 But Pharaoh's daughter went up from the city of David to her own house that Solomon had built for her; then he built the Millo.[46]

25 Three times a year Solomon used to offer up burnt offerings and sacrifices of well-being on the altar that he built for the LORD, offering incense before the LORD. So he completed the house.[47]

26 King Solomon built a fleet of ships at Ezion-geber, which is near Eloth on the shore of the Red Sea, in the land of Edom. [27]Hiram sent his servants with the fleet, sailors who were familiar with the sea, together with the servants of Solomon. [28]They went to Ophir, and imported from there four hundred twenty talents of gold, which they delivered to King Solomon.[48]

---

consider them to be "written by the deuteronomists" (Jones, *Kings*, 1.214; see also Würthwein, *Könige*, 1.112-13). In our judgment, neither the unity of the text nor its provenance can be assured; the more it is seen as excusing Solomon, the later it is likely to be.

45. Verse 23 is generally acknowledged as an old fragment, to be associated with a list of names now missing. However, it is unlikely to have been of interest to the prophetic redactors. It can be variously interpreted—negatively, positively, etc.—and so the time of its addition can scarcely be determined; a possibility is in conjunction with dtr editing or at an even later stage. For the format used, see the Introduction and the note on 1 Kgs 4:29-34.

46. Resumption of the PR from 9:19. This verse is an integral part of the traditions of 3:1 and 9:15. The continuation of the PR is to be found at 11:1.

47. For Noth, this and the following material in chap. 10 was derived by the Dtr from the Book of the Acts of Solomon (*DH*, 97). Of the three components in v. 25, two appear clear: one refers to Solomon's practice at an altar that he built and the other to his completion of the temple. The text and meaning of the incense/burning component is uncertain (cf. Heb.). The verse is unexpected in the context and is self-contained. Its focus on the period before the finished temple suggests an early tradition, in some way associated with the pre-dtr material on Solomon's temple-building. But later composition and incorpo-

ration cannot be discounted. The final element, "So he completed the house," may explain the verse's presence here, at the end of Solomon's building activity.

48. **Text signals** in 9:26–10:29. (i) The text here is overwhelmingly concerned with the affairs of Solomon. (ii) The issue of trade by sea is dealt with in three places. First, 9:26-28, with Solomon's fleet, accompanied by Hiram's sailors, concerned with gold. Second, 10:11-12, with Hiram's fleet, concerned principally with almug wood. Third, 10:22, with the fleets of both Solomon and Hiram, concerned with gold, silver, ivory, apes and peacocks. (iii) The report of the visit of the Queen of Sheba is begun in 10:1-10 and completed in 10:13. (iv) The phrases used by the Queen for the royal roles in 10:9 do not point unequivocally to dtr origin; "the throne of Israel" is from dtr circles, but "to execute justice and righteousness" is a biblical commonplace from Amos to Ezekiel, used rarely outside the prophets (cf. 2 Sam 8:15). (v) The material in 10:14-29 appears to fall into three major blocks: 10:14-21, focused principally on gold; 10:23-25, focusing on Solomon's wealth, wisdom, and world renown; 10:26-29, focusing principally on Solomon's chariots and horses. (vi) 10:27 has a report on Solomon's extensive use of silver and cedar, which appears to duplicate 10:21b without depending on it. (vii) There are echoes from 1 Kings 4–5 (e.g. 4:34 [Heb., 5:14]; 4:26 [Heb., 5:6]). (viii) There is also the absence in 9:26–10:29 of references to the explicit benefit derived by Solomon's subjects, of the sort found in 1 Kgs 4:20 and 25.

Text-history approach. Despite the differences in this material, it is appropriate to treat 9:26–10:29 as a

---

After the Dtr: indented and sans serif font	*Revision:* *royal focus*	*Revision:* *national focus*	Other: double sideline

10 When the queen of Sheba heard of the fame of Solomon, (fame due to the name of the LORD), she came to test him with hard questions. ²She came to Jerusalem with a very great retinue, with camels bearing spices, and very much gold, and precious stones; and when she came to Solomon, she told him all that was on her mind. ³Solomon answered all her questions; there was nothing hidden from the king that he could not explain to her. ⁴When the queen of Sheba had observed all the wisdom of Solomon, the house that he had built, ⁵the food of his table, the seating of his officials, and the attendance of his servants, their clothing, his valets, and his burnt offerings that he offered at the house of the LORD, there was no more spirit in her.

6 So she said to the king, "The report was true that I heard in my own land of your accomplishments and of your wisdom, ⁷but I did not believe the reports until I came and my own eyes had seen it. Not even half had been told me; your wisdom and prosperity far surpass the report that I had heard. ⁸Happy are your wives! Happy are these your servants, who continually attend you and hear your wisdom! ⁹Blessed be the LORD your God, who has delighted in you and set you on the throne of Israel! Because the LORD loved Israel forever, he has made you king to execute justice and righteousness." ¹⁰Then she gave the king one hundred twenty talents of gold, a great quantity of spices, and precious stones; never again did spices come in such quantity as that which the queen of Sheba gave to King Solomon.

11 Moreover, the fleet of Hiram, which carried gold from Ophir, brought from Ophir a great quantity of almug wood and precious stones. ¹²From the almug wood the king made supports for the house of the LORD, and for the king's house, lyres also and harps for the singers; no such almug wood has come or been seen to this day.

13 Meanwhile King Solomon gave to the queen of Sheba every desire that she expressed, as well as what he gave her out of Solomon's royal bounty. Then she returned to her own land, with her servants.

14 The weight of gold that came to Solomon in one year was six hundred sixty-

---

single block. It is clear that here, between the report of Solomon's building achievements, above all the temple, and the report of his fall into apostasy, traditions have been collected that illustrate Solomon's wealth and wisdom. The disparate origins of the material are evident. The sequence does not display any perceptible logic. Since Alt, it has been known that praise of this kind for the monarch has flourished in the ancient Near East. Aspects of the account of the Queen of Sheba's visit have suggested legendary character. The presence of additions and expansions is generally admitted. It is likely that some of the traditions are early and some late. Further precision is not helpful and the resolution of these issues contributes little to the understanding of the DH.

For the format used here, see the Introduction and the note on 1 Kgs 4:29-34.

Present-text potential. As present text, the primary question is whether this collection reads as exalting Solomon or criticizing him. Does it bring to a climax the positive view of his career, before his lapse into apostasy? Or does it signal his excessive (and to some degree prohibited) indulgence, to the neglect of his people, thus introducing his lapse into apostasy? Most probably here too the verdict must be recognized as uncertain or, more accurately, mixed. Without going into details, there are passages that are admiringly laudatory of Solomon and others that are more open to assessment as critical. Modern views differ.

Main pre-DH:	Other pre-DH:	HKL: + single	**Josianic DH:**
Prophetic Record	single sideline	underline	**from the Dtr**

six talents of gold, [15]besides that which came from the traders and from the business of the merchants, and from all the kings of Arabia and the governors of the land. [16]King Solomon made two hundred large shields of beaten gold; six hundred shekels of gold went into each large shield. [17]He made three hundred shields of beaten gold; three minas of gold went into each shield; and the king put them in the House of the Forest of Lebanon. [18]The king also made a great ivory throne, and overlaid it with the finest gold. [19]The throne had six steps. The top of the throne was rounded in the back, and on each side of the seat were arm rests and two lions standing beside the arm rests, [20]while twelve lions were standing, one on each end of a step on the six steps. Nothing like it was ever made in any kingdom. [21]All King Solomon's drinking vessels were of gold, and all the vessels of the House of the Forest of Lebanon were of pure gold; none were of silver—it was not considered as anything in the days of Solomon. [22]For the king had a fleet of ships of Tarshish at sea with the fleet of Hiram. Once every three years the fleet of ships of Tarshish used to come bringing gold, silver, ivory, apes, and peacocks.

23 Thus King Solomon excelled all the kings of the earth in riches and in wisdom. [24]The whole earth sought the presence of Solomon to hear his wisdom, which God had put into his mind. [25]Every one of them brought a present, objects of silver and gold, garments, weaponry, spices, horses, and mules, so much year by year.[49]

26 Solomon gathered together chariots and horses; he had fourteen hundred chariots and twelve thousand horses, which he stationed in the chariot cities and with the king in Jerusalem. [27]The king made silver as common in Jerusalem as stones, and he made cedars as numerous as the sycamores of the Shephelah.[50] [28]Solomon's import of horses was from Egypt and Kue, and the king's traders received them from Kue at a price. [29]A chariot could be imported from Egypt for six hundred shekels of silver, and a horse for one hundred fifty; so through the king's traders they were exported to all the kings of the Hittites and the kings of Aram.

11 *King Solomon loved many foreign women, along with the daughter of Pharaoh.*[51]

Moabite, Ammonite, Edomite, Sidonian, and Hittite women [2]from the nations concerning which the LORD *had said to the Israelites, "You shall not enter into marriage with them, neither shall they with you; for they will surely incline your heart to follow their gods"*

---

49. 10:23-25 is regarded by Noth as a later addition (*DH*, 97).

50. 10:27 is regarded by Noth as a later addition, disrupting the train of thought (ibid.).

51. **Text signals** in 11:1-3. (i) V. 1 has a disrupted sequence, both in Hebrew and the NRSV, but especially noticeable in the Hebrew. The object of the sentence—literally: women foreign many—concludes with two feminine plural adjectives. The second half of the verse lists five ethnic groupings in the feminine plural. In between them, there is the reference in the singular to the daughter of Pharaoh. The NRSV rendering reads more smoothly than the Hebrew. In LXX, the information of v. 3a is found after "Solomon loved women"; it resumes with "and he took foreign wives." (ii) Neither the report of Solomon's loving many foreign women nor the list of five groups has

---

After the Dtr: indented and sans serif font	**Revision: royal focus**	Revision: national focus	Other: double sideline

Solomon clung to these in love. ³Among his wives were seven hundred princesses and three hundred concubines; and his wives turned away his heart.
⁴For when Solomon was old, his wives turned away his heart after other gods; and his heart was not true to the LORD his God, as was the heart of his father David.⁵²

⁵*For Solomon followed Astarte the goddess of the Sidonians.*
‖ and Milcom the abomination of the ‖ Ammonites
⁶So Solomon did what was evil in the sight of the LORD, and did not completely follow the LORD, as his father David had done.
⁷*Then Solomon built a high place for Chemosh the abomination of Moab on the mountain east of Jerusalem.* (Hebrew order)⁵³
and for Molech the abomination of the Ammonites. ⁸He did the same for all his foreign wives, who offered incense and sacrificed to their gods.

any characteristics that can be claimed as dtr. The standard dtr lists (e.g. Deut 7:1) concern local peoples whose land Israel has occupied—not the case here. The listing here is unique; Ezra 9:1 has an 8-nation list, including Moabites, Ammonites, and Hittites, but otherwise different. (iii) The prohibition against intermarriage is in Deut 7:3-4 (content) and refers to the local peoples; they could be understood as embraced in the OT collective term "Hittites." (iv) V. 2b has Solomon cling to these in love. The combination of "to cling" with "in love" is unique in the MT (cf. Gen 2:24; 34:3). "To cling" is used in dtr circles to express Israel's close relationship with YHWH. (v) The phrase "to incline the heart" is used with both the shorter (*lēb*) and longer (*lēbāb*) forms of the word for heart. The shorter form is used here (11:3) and in five other occurrences; none is dtr. The longer form is used three times in this context (11:2, 4, 9), and three times in other texts (Josh 24:23; 1 Kgs 8:58; and 2 Sam 19:15 [NRSV, 19:14]). The wider distribution of these shorter and longer forms for heart is noteworthy; the dtr circles show a preference for the longer form, but they also use the shorter form.

For **text-history approach** and **present-text potential** in 11:1-13, see below.

52. **Text signals** in 11:4-8. (i) V. 3b is repeated within v. 4a, which specifies the time as "when Solomon was old," substitutes the longer *lēbāb* for the shorter *lēb*, and specifies the object as "after other gods." (ii) Fidelity to YHWH, expressed through the metaphor of the heart, is a major dtr concern; the precise language of v. 4b is found elsewhere only at 1 Kgs 15:3. The comparison with David is also in 1 Kgs

3:3. (iii) Most references to Astarte/the Astartes are attributed to the national focus of the revision (cf. Judg 2:13; 10:6; 1 Sam 7:3-4; 12:10; 1 Kgs 11:5, 33; 2 Kgs 23:13; note also 1 Sam 31:10). However 1 Sam 31:10 indicates the possibility of an earlier date. (iv) The reference here to Milcom, along with Astarte, completes the triad named in 1 Kgs 11:33 and 2 Kgs 23:13. (v) V. 6a is the basic formula of judgment on a king. (vi) V. 6b repeats the content of v. 4b, using a verbal construction that is otherwise only used within the DH at Deut 1:36 (secondary). (vii) In the Hebrew, the location "on the mountain east of Jerusalem," is put between the references to the two high places. (viii) The "abomination of the Ammonites" in v. 7b uses the term for "abomination" from v. 7a, not *tô'ēbâ* from 2 Kgs 23:13, and the commoner "children of Ammon" for Ammonites. The addition completes the pair of Moabites and Ammonites (cf. Deut 23:3 [Heb., 23:4]). (ix) The sequence in v. 8b of incense and sacrifice is not that of 1 Kgs 3:3 nor of 1 Kgs 22:43 (Heb., 22:44); 2 Kgs 12:3 (Heb., v. 4); 14:4; 15:4, 35 (HKL).

For **text-history approach** and **present-text potential** in 11:1-13, see below.

53. The continuation of the PR is to be found at 11:26.

Main pre-DH:	Other pre-DH:	HKL: + single	**Josianic DH:**
Prophetic Record	single sideline	underline	**from the Dtr**

*9 Then the L*ORD *was angry with Solomon, because his heart had turned away from the L*ORD*, the God of Israel, who had appeared to him twice,*[54] *¹⁰and had commanded him concerning this matter, that he should not follow other gods; but he did not observe what the L*ORD *commanded. ¹¹Therefore the L*ORD *said to Solomon, "Since this has been your mind and you have not kept my covenant and my statutes that I have commanded you, I will surely tear the kingdom from you and give it to your servant. ¹²Yet for the sake of your father David I will not do it in your lifetime; I will tear it out of the hand of your son. ¹³I will not, however, tear away the entire kingdom; I will give one tribe to your son, for the sake of*

my servant David and for the sake of Jerusalem, which I have chosen."[55]

‖ 14 Then the LORD raised up an adversary against Solomon, Hadad the Edomite;

---

54. **Text signals** in vv. 9-13. (i) "to be angry" (referring to God) whether qal or hithpael, is likely to be late (cf. Deut 1:37; 4:21; 9:8, 20; 1 Kgs 8:46; 2 Kgs 17:18; of these, Deut 1:37 we attribute to the Josianic Dtr and Deut 9:8, 20 are uncertain but scarcely problematic). (ii) In vv. 3-4, the accusation is that Solomon's wives turned away his heart; here the accusation is sharpened, with Solomon responsible, "his heart had turned away." (iii) In vv. 9-13, the focus has shifted from the foreign wives to Solomon's apostasy associated with "their gods" (vv. 2a, 8b). (iv) The issue of "other gods" goes back at least to Hos 3:1 (cf. Exod 20:3; 23:13); going "after other gods" can clearly be Josianic (cf. 1 Kgs 11:4), but can equally be later (cf. Judg 2:12, 17; and prose sections of Jeremiah). (v) In v. 11a, none of the three key phrases is definitively late, but all three tend in that direction. (vi) It may be noted here that phrases like "for the sake of David," "for the sake of Jerusalem," "which I have chosen" are from dtr circles; greater precision is not available.

55. **Text-history approach** of 11:1-13. As the text signals have shown, the resort to hypotheses of composition is both necessary and extremely difficult for this text. The results generated are necessarily uncertain and fragile. The need arises from the irregularity of the Hebrew text; the difficulty comes from phrases that are rare and not easily labeled and from additions that are relatively easy to identify and remarkably difficult to explain.

Attribution to the PR is not a matter of necessity. There is a broad consensus that vv. 3 and 7 are old material. In vv. 1a and 2b there is nothing that indicates dtr origin—which, of course, does not exclude dtr origin. However, if this material is to be pre-dtr, it needs to belong somewhere, either with the PR or with the traditions about Solomon. Of the two, the PR seems more appropriate; the traditions about Solomon offer a more positive view of the king.

Verses 1b and 2a have been attributed to the national focus within the dtr revision process, because of the concern in v. 2a with intermarriage (cf. Deut 7:3; Josh 23:12). In v. 1b, the Moabite, Ammonite, and Sidonian women can be explained from information already in the surrounding text. The Hittites, a collective term in the OT for the local peoples, is appropriate as lead-in to v. 2, where the law refers to local peoples.

Where vv. 4 and 6 are concerned, several signals, including repetition and shifts in language, suggest the attribution of v. 4 to the Dtr. This attribution is also valid for v. 6a. The change of language in v. 6b could suggest a change of author; it could also be attributed to authorial variation of style. The Josianic history is basically favorable to the Davidic dynasty; its condemnation of Solomon is therefore muted. The condemnation has to be there, but it is nuanced—his old age, the initiative of his wives, and his flawed fidelity (in v. 4, the choice between "true" and "wholly

---

| After the Dtr:
indented and sans serif font | **Revision:**
royal focus | *Revision:*
national focus | Other:
double sideline |

he was of the royal house in Edom. [15]For when David was in Edom, and Joab the commander of the army went up to bury the dead, he killed every male in Edom [16](for Joab and all Israel remained there six

months, until he had eliminated every male in Edom); [17]but Hadad fled to Egypt with some Edomites who were servants of his father. He was a young boy at that time. [18]They set out from Midian and came to Paran; they took people with them from Paran and came to Egypt, to Pharaoh king of Egypt, who gave him a house, assigned him an allowance of food, and gave him land. [19]Hadad found great favor in the sight of Pharaoh, so that he gave him his sister-in-law for a wife, the sister of Queen Tahpenes. [20]The sister of Tahpenes gave birth by him to his son Genubath, whom Tahpenes weaned in Pharaoh's house; Genubath was in Pharaoh's house among the children of Pharaoh. [21]When Hadad heard

---

true" is uncertain; v. 6b settles on incompleteness—cf. 1 Kgs 15:3, 14; 2 Chron 25:2). There is no punishment spelled out so far.

Verses 5 and 7 deal with Solomon's foreign deities. The other occurrences for these are 1 Kgs 11:33 and 2 Kgs 23:13. The traditions are tricky. The names are Astarte, Chemosh, Milcom (3x) and Molech (1x); the designations are god/goddess and abomination (šiqqūṣ/tôʿēbâ) and children of Ammon/ Ammonites; the activities are "following" and building high places. Variations are possible. Our formatting, in chronological order, suggests: v. 7a to the PR; v. 7b, after "on the mountain east of Jerusalem," along with v. 8 (appropriately expanding the accusation) as attributable to the royal focus within the dtr revision looking to the king, echoing the abomination-language of v. 7a; v. 5a picks up the national focus's concern with Astarte (goddess); 11:33 with Astarte, Chemosh, and Milcom (goddess/gods) also to the national focus (apostasy; plural = people = national focus); and finally v. 5b (abomination, šiqqūṣ) and 2 Kgs 23:13 (abomination, šiqqūṣ and tôʿēbâ) to a later unidentified revision.

In vv. 9-13, the bulk of the text signals suggests attribution of the whole passage to the royal focus within the dtr revision with its fundamentally negative focus on the kings. Consistently with this, Solomon's guilt is emphasized, YHWH is spoken of as "angry with Solomon," responsibility is sheeted home to Solomon "because his heart had turned away" (his initiative: not "was turned away"), and this from a God who had appeared to him twice before and explicitly commanded that he should not follow other gods. The punishment is spelled out at this point; its location here anticipates the encounter of Ahijah with Jeroboam presented by the Dtr, as 2:4 and 8:25 anticipated the Dtr's 9:4-5.

Present-text potential. 1 Kgs 11:1-13 marks a turning point in the biblical text. A trajectory of Israel's that has been upward to this point turns down. Beginning at 1 Kings 3, the text reports Solomon's love of YHWH, his faithful conduct, and his building of the temple. This is presented as the culmination of God's promise to Moses in Deuteronomy and to David in 2 Samuel 7. Here, in 1 Kgs 11:1-13, all this is turned around. The text reports Solomon's love of foreign women, his unfaithful conduct (apostasy), and his building of the high places (for foreign gods).

On three occasions, YHWH is presented speaking to Solomon. In 1 Kgs 3:4-15, God promises Solomon wisdom and wealth. In 1 Kgs 9:1-9, at the completion of the temple's dedication, God responds to Solomon's prayer and utters a promise that is personal in its focus, coupled with a threat that is national in its dimensions. Here, in 1 Kgs 11:1-13, Solomon has failed the promise and, while the Davidic dynasty remains, the kingdom pays the price. This is developed in speeches to the three main players: Solomon, Jeroboam (11:31-39), and Rehoboam (12:22-24). The speech here looks back to David as a figure of fidelity and forward to the disruption of the kingdom.

Main pre-DH:	Other pre-DH:	HKL: + single	**Josianic DH:**
Prophetic Record	single sideline	underline	**from the Dtr**

in Egypt that David slept with his ancestors and that Joab the commander of the army was dead, Hadad said to Pharaoh, "Let me depart, that I may go to my own country." ²²But Pharaoh said to him, "What do you lack with me that you now seek to go to your own country?" And he said, "No, do let me go."

23 God raised up another adversary against Solomon, Rezon son of Eliada, who had fled from his master, King Hadadezer of Zobah. ²⁴He gathered followers around him and became leader of a marauding band, after the slaughter by David; they went to Damascus, settled there, and made him king in Damascus. ²⁵He was an adversary of Israel all the days of Solomon, making trouble as Hadad did; he despised Israel and reigned over Aram.⁵⁶

26 Jeroboam son of Nebat, an Ephraimite of Zeredah, a servant of Solomon, whose mother's name was Zeruah, a widow, rebelled against the king.⁵⁷ ²⁷The following was the reason he rebelled against the king. Solomon built the Millo, and closed up the gap in the wall of the city of his father David. ²⁸The man Jeroboam was very able, and when Solomon saw that the young man was industrious he gave him charge over all the forced labor of the house of Joseph. ²⁹About that time, when Jeroboam was leaving Jerusalem, the prophet Ahijah the Shilonite found him on the road. Ahijah had clothed himself with a new garment. The two of them were alone in the open country ³⁰when Ahijah laid hold of the new garment he was wearing and tore it into twelve pieces. ³¹He then said to Jeroboam: Take for yourself ten pieces; for thus says the LORD, the God of Israel, "See, I am about to tear the kingdom from the hand of Solomon, and will give you ten tribes.⁵⁸

---

56. 11:14-25, the two passages concerning Hadad and Rezon, are seen to come from early sources (Noth, *Könige*, 251; Gray, *Kings*, 280-85; Jones, *Kings*, 1.237); but differences arise over the time of their incorporation into the DH (Noth, his Dtr; Würthwein and Jones, post-dtr). There is no dtr language. There is no mention of apostasy. There is no focus on the disruption of the kingdom from within. The "adversary" language is restricted here to Hadad and Rezon. A post-dtr incorporation is likely. The absence of adversaries marked Solomon's high point (cf. 1 Kgs 5:4; Heb., 5:18); their introduction here tips the scales downward. The Hadad passage has echoes of the Moses tradition and the Rezon passage has echoes of David's guerrilla days. Jeroboam must be left in third place for continuity with what follows. Note: "all the days of X" is most commonly used to mean "the rest of the days of X"; v. 25, therefore, locates Rezon's activity toward the end of Solomon's life, not throughout it.

57. Resumption of the PR from 11:7. The gift of the northern kingdom is made to Jeroboam by the prophet Ahijah. As God's instruments, what the prophets took from Saul and gave to David they can take from Solomon and give to Jeroboam (see Introduction, under PR). It is probably right to claim older material here (vv. 26-28, 40), where the prophetic story of Ahijah has taken over the principal function. The major feature of the story is Ahijah's speech to Jeroboam.

58. **Text signals** in vv. 29-40. (i) Jeroboam meets Ahijah outside the city, on the road, alone in the open country. (ii) Ahijah is wearing a new garment. (iii) He tears the garment into twelve pieces. (iii) He gives ten pieces to Jeroboam, with echoes of 1 Sam 15:28. (iv) V. 32a, literally: "the tribe the one will be to him," cannot refer to Solomon (cf. v. 31) but must refer to Rehoboam. (v) V. 32b cites two reasons for this, for the sake of David (unmotivated) and for the sake of Jerusalem (motivation: chosen city). (vi) In v. 32b, David is referred to as "my servant David"; in vv. 34b, 36b, and 38a, the order in Hebrew is the reverse,

---

After the Dtr: indented and sans serif font	**Revision: royal focus**	Revision: national focus	Other: double sideline

³²One tribe will remain his, for the sake of my servant David and for the sake of Jerusalem, the city that I have chosen out of all the tribes of Israel.

³³*This is because they have* (Heb.; NRSV, he has) *forsaken me, worshiped Astarte the goddess of the Sidonians, Chemosh the god of Moab, and Milcom the god of the Ammonites, and they have* (Heb.; NRSV, he has) *not walked in my ways, doing what is right in my sight.*

and (Heb.; NRSV, *keeping*) my statutes and my ordinances
as his father David did

"David my servant"; v. 33b has "his father David" and v. 38b has simply "David." (vii) In v. 33, the verbs are in the plural (MT; in LXX, they are singular, "he"); "his father David," however, refers to the singular. (viii) In v. 33a, the three foreign gods mentioned include two from 11:5 (Astarte and Milcom) and one from 11:7 (Chemosh); they are found together in 2 Kgs 23:13. (ix) In v. 33b, the second last pair of words in Hebrew, "and my statutes and my ordinances," has no governing verb (NRSV supplies "keeping") and is absent in LXX. (x) In v. 34a, "from him" refers to Solomon (not Rehoboam, as in v. 32). (xi) In v. 34b, Solomon is referred to as *nāśî*', meaning chief or leader, and unused in the DH for a king. (xii) The concern with ten tribes recurs in v. 35 and, in v. 36, the concern with one tribe. (xiii) V. 38b promises Jeroboam kingship and a dynasty like that promised David, while v. 38a makes this conditional on Jeroboam's fidelity to the law. (xiv) V. 39 surprises with a reversal: the "seed of David" (occurring here for the first time) will be punished "because of this," but not forever; above, punishment is transferred for Solomon (v. 34) and limited for Rehoboam (v. 36a) *because of David* (vv. 34b, 36b). (xv) There is extensive use of dtr language in the passage. Attributable primarily to the Dtr are the motivations associated with David, with Jerusalem, and with the "lamp"—understood as "dominion" (Hanson, "The Song of Heshbon and David's *Nîr*"). Attributable to the national focus of the dtr revision process are the expression of legal concerns and the charge of apostasy directed against the people (v. 33). (xvi) Solomon's seeking to kill Jeroboam is reported without explicit association with the prophecy; no rebellion is described (cf. v. 26).

For **text-history approach** and **present-text potential,** see the note on 11:40.

³⁴**Nevertheless I will not take the whole kingdom away from him** (but will make him ruler) **all the days of his life, for the sake of my servant David whom I chose who kept** (Heb.; NRSV, and who did keep) **my commandments and my statutes;** ³⁵**but I will take the kingdom away from his son and give it to you** (—that is, the ten tribes). ³⁶**Yet to his son I will give one tribe, so that my servant David may always have a lamp before me in Jerusalem, the city where I have chosen to put my name.** ³⁷*I will take you, and you shall reign over all that your soul desires; you shall be king over Israel.*

³⁸**If you will listen to all that I command you, walk in my ways, and do what is right in my sight, by keeping my statutes and my commandments, as David my servant did,** *I will be with you, and will build you an enduring house, as I built for David, and I will give Israel to you.*

³⁹For this reason I will punish the descendants of David, but not forever."

⁴⁰*And Solomon sought* (Heb.; NRSV, therefore) *to kill Jeroboam; but Jeroboam promptly fled to Egypt, to King Shishak of Egypt, and remained in Egypt until the death of Solomon.*⁵⁹

---

59. **Text-history approach** in vv. 29-40. It is hardly surprising that this should be a complex text. It deals with a major failure of political power in Israel and the most significant fracture in Israel's unity.

Main pre-DH:	Other pre-DH:	HKL: + single	**Josianic DH:**
Prophetic Record	single sideline	underline	**from the Dtr**

41 Now the rest of the acts of Solomon, all that he did as well as his wisdom, are they not written in the Book of the Acts of Solomon? **42**The time that Solomon reigned in Jerusalem over all Israel was forty years.

43Solomon slept with his ancestors and was buried in the city of his father David; and his son Rehoboam succeeded him.

12 *Rehoboam went to Shechem, for all Israel had come to Shechem to make him king.*

The text has clearly been subject to intensive study in the ancient world, long before modern scholars came to ponder it. Four "moments" can be identified from the text signals and are reflected in our formatting.

The traces of an older frame. The references to a rebellion against the king by Jeroboam (v. 26), to Solomon's seeking to kill Jeroboam—despite the encounter with Ahijah being "alone in the open country"—and to Jeroboam's flight to Egypt (v. 40), as well as the narrative of the political division after his return, all suggest that an older story has been replaced here. Its traces remain in vv. 26-28 and 40.

The Prophetic Record text. This frame was retained by the PR for a prophetic story in which Ahijah, with the prophetic action of the torn cloak (vv. 29-30), promised to Jeroboam what had been promised to David—both kingdom (v. 37) and dynasty (v. 38b). There is no trace of dtr concern or language in this material. In our view, it is inconceivable that a dtr author would have chosen language such as this to express the handover of northern Israel to Jeroboam. For the PR, on the other hand, this transfer of power is only a stage on the way to Jehu's revolution and Israel's liberation from Baal worship.

The Josianic dtr editing. The viewpoint of the Dtr is very different. To be reckoned with were: (i) the tradition's attribution of the kingdom's division to the sins of Solomon, builder of God's temple; (ii) the delay between Solomon's sin and this division; (iii) the continued existence of the Davidic dynasty. Solomon is treated lightly; the more severe condemnation comes from later generations (cf. 11:9-13; 9:6-9; note that 9:6-9 and 11:33 both use the plural, spreading the blame beyond Solomon). In vv. 34-35, the Dtr leaves the kingdom with Solomon for his lifetime. V. 36 assures the Davidic dynasty's hegemony in Jerusalem.

On this basis, a sure hope could be developed for Josiah. The need for fidelity on the part of the king is emphasized in v. 38a, even for the north.

The subsequent dtr editing. This aspect of human fidelity and obedience to God's law has been given considerable later emphasis in the text. Its breach is the substance of v. 33; it underlies the interventions within vv. 34 and 38a. The same concern is already reflected in 9:4. The exact nature and extent of some of these interventions is most uncertain, as any commentator is well aware. Modern translations attempt to smooth over irregular Hebrew. Appeal to glosses—the last resort of the frustrated—is not uncommon. In v. 33, the Hebrew has plural verbs, pointing to the people; the Greek has singular verbs, pointing to Solomon. To forsake God is a favorite accusation from the national focus of the dtr revision. Near the end of the verse, the phrase "and my statutes and my ordinances" crops up obtrusively. It is not in accord with regular Hebrew syntax; at best, it can be claimed as an apposition, putting the general canons of good behavior in specifically legal terms. If, in some quarters, this was felt to be an imperative concern—and it recurs several times—the unevenness of the resulting text might have been thought a small price to pay for interventions judged to be of great theological importance. The same concern recurs at the end of v. 34 and in v. 38a; attribution to the national focus of the revision is possible, but not necessary. Because of this uncertainty, no change has been made in the formatting.

The unidentifiable. Verse 32 shares with 11:13 the concern for "one tribe" and the issues of loyalty to David and Jerusalem, expanding on v. 36. Situated at the start of a complex passage, it looks like an attempt to open with the clarity of a southern perspective.

| After the Dtr:
indented and sans serif font | **Revision:**
royal focus | Revision:
national focus | Other:
double sideline |

The end of v. 33 is almost impossible. LXX does have "as his father David," which may account for its singular verbs; it does not have the preceding "and my statutes and my ordinances," which, if an addition, must for LXX have come later. Any emendation that adopts the singular verbs must explain the presence of the plural in the Hebrew. The singular reference of "his father" may reflect the commonness of the phrase or, more likely, modulates into the singular of v. 34.

In v. 34a, it has been common to omit the "whole" in reference to the kingdom. In tight logic, if the "whole kingdom" is not taken away, the implication is that some of the kingdom was. In Solomon's case, none of the kingdom was taken during his lifetime. An author emphatically expressing that no part of the kingdom was taken from Solomon might not have seen or accepted the logical consequences of the "whole kingdom." In v. 34b, the designation of Solomon as ruler may be a downgrading or a later reflection of Ezek 34:24; no one claims clarity or certainty. At the end of v. 35, the "ten tribes" are clear enough but unnecessary. Overall, this passage means too much not to have been fine-tuned. The basic moves suggested here reflect the text's signals.

The end of v. 38 ("and I will give Israel to you") along with v. 39 is missing from the original versions of the LXX; it may be an addition. Fundamental to v. 39 is the expression of ultimate hope. Its focus—"seed of David" and "for this"—is odd here. With emphasis on hope, it could be Josianic; with emphasis on punishment, it could be later.

Present-text potential in vv. 29-40. The prophetic intervention of Ahijah with Jeroboam activates what was announced by God in 11:11—"I will surely tear the kingdom from you and give it to your servant." The servant is Jeroboam. The prophet is God's instrument in the direction of Israel's history. Beyond the punishment outlined for Solomon in 11:11-13, the prophecy moves to the surprising promise made Jeroboam: "I will be with you, and will build you an enduring house, as I built for David" (11:38b). The condition is explicit; Jeroboam's conduct must be on a par with David's. The division of the kingdom, politically the outcome of the people's decision over

²When Jeroboam son of Nebat heard of it (for he was still in Egypt, where he had fled from King Solomon), then Jeroboam returned from Egypt. ³And they sent and called him.[60]
And Jeroboam and all the assembly of Israel came and said to Rehoboam, ⁴"Your father made our yoke heavy. Now therefore lighten the hard service of your father and his heavy yoke that he placed on us, and we will serve you." ⁵He said to them, "Go away for three days, then come again to me." So the people went away.

---

taxes, is here identified as the unfolding of God's will (cf. 12:15).

In vv. 29-40, Dietrich attributed 11:29-31, 33a, 34a, 35aβα, 37aβγb to his DtrP and 11:32, 33b, 34b, 35bβ, 36, 37aα, 38abα to his DtrN. The PR continues in 11:43.

60. There is good reason to believe that the break-up of the united kingdom, recounted here, was remembered differently in the north and the south. The PR retains a northern view. A glimpse of a possible southern view is preserved here, involving Jeroboam from the outset in the politics of the assembly; it is missing in the LXX at this point. A more complex view, positively evaluating the LXX miscellanies, is offered by Trebolle Barrera (*Salomón y Jeroboán*, 143, 185; cf. O'Brien, *Deuteronomistic History Hypothesis*, 172-73 and Knoppers, *Two Nations Under God*, 1.206-18). The miscellanies are attracting attention with good reason; in our judgment, more serious study will be needed before a consensus emerges on their contribution within the tradition.

Seen as a possible southern view, the Dtr might have taken this material from tradition in Judah or from the Annals of the Kings of Judah. It serves to cast a southern shadow over the figure of Jeroboam even before his reign has begun. In 11:34-35, the Dtr has been protective of Solomon; negativity toward Jeroboam emerges in the PR at 13:34 and 14:9bβ-13, and as a refrain (the sins of Jeroboam which he made Israel to sin) in the later judgment formulas for northern kings.

Main pre-DH:	Other pre-DH:	HKL: + single	**Josianic DH:**
Prophetic Record	single sideline	underline	**from the Dtr**

6 Then King Rehoboam took counsel with the older men who had attended his father Solomon while he was still alive, saying, "How do you advise me to answer this people?" *7They answered him, "If you will be a servant to this people today and serve them, and speak good words to them when you answer them, then they will be your servants forever."* *8But he disregarded the advice that the older men gave him, and consulted with the young men who had grown up with him and now attended him. 9He said to them, "What do you advise that we answer this people who have said to me, 'Lighten the yoke that your father put on us'?"* *10The young men who had grown up with him said to him, "Thus you should say to this people who spoke to you, 'Your father made our yoke heavy, but you must lighten it for us'; thus you should say to them, 'My little finger is thicker than my father's loins. 11Now, whereas my father laid on you a heavy yoke, I will add to your yoke. My father disciplined you with whips, but I will discipline you with scorpions.' "*

12 So [Jeroboam and][61] *all the people came to Rehoboam the third day, as the king had said, "Come to me again the third day." 13The king answered the people harshly. He disregarded the advice that the older men had given him 14and spoke to them according to the advice of the young men, "My father made your yoke heavy, but I will add to your yoke; my father disciplined you with whips, but I will discipline you with scorpions." 15So the king did not listen to the people,* **because it was a turn of affairs brought about by the Lord that he might fulfill his word, which the Lord had spoken by Ahijah the Shilonite to Jeroboam son of Nebat.**[62]

16 When all Israel saw that the king would not listen to them, the people answered the king,
"What share do we have in David?
  We have no inheritance in the son of Jesse.
To your tents, O Israel!
  Look now to your own house, O David."
So Israel went away to their tents.

[17]But Rehoboam reigned over the Israelites who were living in the towns of Judah.[63]

18When King Rehoboam sent Adoram, who was taskmaster over the forced labor, all Israel stoned him to death. King Rehoboam then hurriedly mounted his chariot to flee to Jerusalem.[64]

19So Israel has been in rebellion against the house of David to this day.[65]

20 When all Israel heard that Jeroboam had returned, they sent and called him to the assembly and made him king over all Israel. There was no one who followed the house of David, except the tribe of Judah alone.[66]

21 When Rehoboam came to Jerusalem, he assembled all the house of Judah

---

bution to the Dtr is appropriate. Dietrich attributed 12:15 to his DtrP.

63. The verse insists that Israelites living in the south remained under Rehoboam's rule; it is missing from the LXX and is generally regarded as a later addition. Nevertheless, it would not be out of place in a Josianic DH, looking to the well-being of northern refugees in the south.

64. Rehoboam's flight to Jerusalem suggests that this episode took place at Shechem. While it is far from explicit, the episode must be situated before the actual dispersal of the assembly.

65. Ahijah's prophecy authorized the division of the kingdom, while 1 Kgs 12:1-16 portrayed it as a tax revolt; 12:15 reconciles the two views. For the Dtr, v. 19 is an acknowledgment of the status quo.

66. The version in vv. 2-3a has Jeroboam present; this verse gives him a later arrival on the scene. The division of the kingdom is complete.

---

61. The mention of Jeroboam is not in the LXX and may have come into the Hebrew at the same time as vv. 2-3a.

62. While the linguistic evidence is not altogether compelling (cf. *Of Prophets and Kings*, 89, n. 55), attri-

---

| After the Dtr: indented and sans serif font | **Revision: royal focus** | Revision: national focus | Other: double sideline |

and the tribe of Benjamin, one hundred eighty thousand chosen troops to fight against the house of Israel, to restore the kingdom to Rehoboam son of Solomon. [22]But the word of God came to Shemaiah the man of God: [23]Say to King Rehoboam of Judah, son of Solomon, and to all the house of Judah and Benjamin, and to the rest of the people, [24]"Thus says the LORD, You shall not go up or fight against your kindred the people of Israel. Let everyone go home, for this thing is from me." So they heeded the word of the LORD and went home again, according to the word of the LORD.[67]

25 Then Jeroboam built Shechem in the hill country of Ephraim, and resided there; he went out from there and built Penuel.[68]
[26]**Then Jeroboam said to himself, "Now the kingdom may well revert to the house of**

---

67. **Text signals** in vv. 21-24. (i) V. 21 refers to the "house of Judah," not the "tribe of Judah" as in v. 20. (ii) V. 21 introduces the tribe of Benjamin, not mentioned before. (iii) V. 24b does not contain the characteristic dtr reference to the fulfillment of prophecy. (iv) The passage, vv. 21-24, is in conflict with 14:30 and 15:6, which refer to continual war between Rehoboam and Jeroboam.

Text-history approach. While the idea expressed is attractive, the passage is generally judged a later addition. Benjamin has not been mentioned in the preceding tribal scenario. The vast majority of occurrences combining Judah and Benjamin are post-exilic (cf. Ezra 1:5; 4:1; 10:9; Neh 11:4, 36; 2 Chron 11:12, 23; 15:2, 8-9; 25:5). Shemaiah as a name occurs here, six times in Jeremiah, and thirty-four times in Ezra-Nehemiah-Chronicles. The overall tone of language and style is not consonant with the context; a later addition is likely. Dtr characteristics are absent.

Present-text potential. The passage moves away from an overly political understanding of the schism, which might be derived from 12:1-16, and emphasizes the role of God's will, expressed in 11:9-13 and Ahijah's prophecy. Solomon has been addressed in 11:9-13, Jeroboam by the prophet Ahijah, and now Rehoboam by the prophet Shemaiah.

68. 12:25-33 and 13:33-34 constitute critical material for reflection on the establishment of religious worship in the kingdom of northern Israel. The moment is of crucial political importance. For a northern king, worship in Jerusalem would have been political suicide—and the calves may have been pedestals for the divinity rather than idols (for a YHWH-interpretation of the calf, see Exod 32:5). Bethel's pedigree in Israel's tradition was vastly superior to that of Jerusalem (see Gen 12:8; 28:16-19; 35:1; 1 Sam 7:16 etc.). From a southern viewpoint, such a move would have sealed the division and given it permanence in the politics of Israel. In dtr eyes, three centuries later, Jeroboam's establishment was damned on two grounds: it was not in Jerusalem and the golden calves were idolatry. Initially, perhaps, the infamous sin of Jeroboam included the indiscriminate consecration of clergy (cf. 13:33b-34).

The text containing this material naturally attracted attention. In the present text, 12:25-33 and 13:33-34 frame a prophetic story. For our purposes, it is appropriate to handle the **text signals of 12:25-33 and 13:33-34** together and then to consider their implications as well as the treatment of the prophetic story in 13:1-32.

Text signals in 12:25-33. (i) 12:25-29 reports the building of Shechem and Penuel and the establishment of the calves at Bethel and Dan. The bare facts are narrated in vv. 25, 28a, and 29; the motivation is given in the speeches of vv. 26-27 and 28b. (ii) These speeches express a strongly southern viewpoint (King Rehoboam of Judah 2x; their master; kill me; your gods). (iii) The southern viewpoint is continued in 12:30-33. (iv) 12:30 reflects the sinfulness onto the people; 13:34 reflects it onto the dynasty. (v) In 12:31, the Hebrew has "a high-place house" (singular; also 2 Kgs 17:29, 32) frequently emended with the Versions

---

Main pre-DH:	Other pre-DH:	HKL: + single	**Josianic DH:**
Prophetic Record	single sideline	underline	**from the Dtr**

David. ²⁷If this people continues to go up to offer sacrifices in the house of the LORD at Jerusalem, the heart of this people will turn again to their master, King Rehoboam of Judah; they will kill me and return to King Rehoboam of Judah."⁶⁹

---

to the "houses on/of (the) high places," found in Kings only in 12:31; 13:32; 2 Kgs 17:29 (sg.), 32 (sg.); 23:19—mostly late dtr texts. (vi) The references to the high places (vv. 31, 32b) draw Jeroboam unfavorably into Solomon's orbit. (vii) 12:31 shows a concern for the appointment of levitical priests; in 13:33, the issue is indiscriminate consecration. (viii) 12:32-33 shows extensive duplication: a festival (2x); day and month (2x); going up to the altar (2x). (ix) 12:32-33 shows considerable negativity toward Jeroboam: he arrogated priestly functions to himself (offering sacrifice and incense); he was guilty of apostasy (sacrificing to the calves); he established his own calendar (v. 33a, cf. Lev 23:34).

Text signals in 13:33-34. (i) 13:33 situates itself "after this event" but returns to duplicate material that preceded the event. (ii) In 13:33a, "turn from his evil way" is a stereotyped phrase typical of the dtr passages in the book of Jeremiah (18:11; 25:5; 26:3; 35:15; 36:3, 7; cf. also Jonah 3:8, 10). (iii) In 13:33b, the accusation specifies the indiscriminate consecration of priests, rather than the consecration of non-levitical priests (12:31). (iv) 13:34 repeats the inherent sinfulness noted in 12:30. In 13:34, the concern is with the dynasty of Jeroboam that is corrupted; in 12:30, the impact is on the people. (v) In 13:34b, the object (NRSV, "it") is not expressed; also, the first infinitive, "to cut off," occurs only here and the second, "to destroy," in the DH is mainly late dtr (but cf. 2 Sam 14:16).

Text-history approach. This will be dealt with under each of the relevant sections, i.e., 12:26-27, 28b, 28a and 29, 30, 31-33; 13:1-32, 33-34.

Present-text potential. This will be dealt with at 13:34.

69. **Text-history approach: 12:26-27.** This comment, cast in the form of a speech, puts a negative,

²⁸So the king took counsel, and made two calves of gold.

He said to the people, "You have gone up to Jerusalem long enough. Here are your gods, O Israel, who brought you up out of the land of Egypt."⁷⁰
²⁹He set one in Bethel, and the other he put in Dan. ³⁰And this thing became a sin, for the people went to worship before the one at Bethel and before the other as far as Dan.⁷¹

---

self-serving, anti-Jerusalem coloring on Jeroboam's action, reported neutrally in the PR (vv. 28a, 29). It is most economically attributed to the overall composition of the Dtr; its strongly southern viewpoint is appropriate enough for dtr ideology. The seeking of counsel without preceding motivation is found, for example, in 1 Chron 13:1 and 2 Chron 25:17; for preceding motivation, see for example 1 Kgs 12:6.

70. **Text-history approach: v. 28b.** A further comment, again in the form of a speech; in the context, it accuses Jeroboam of apostasy—although with the surprising mixture of an unorthodox plural verb (apostasy) and a highly orthodox traditional description. The dtr negativity toward Jeroboam is clear in the accusation leveled in 1 Kgs 14:9*.

71. **Text-history approach: vv. 28a and 29-30.** Vv. 28a and 29 offer a relatively neutral report of Jeroboam's activity; it need not be construed as apostasy, although it opens the way to syncretism at least. In v. 30, it is named as sin and correlated with the people as a whole. Within the PR, greater emphasis is expressed regarding Jeroboam's sin in the indiscriminate consecration of priests (13:33b-34; cf. esp. v. 34 in contrast to 12:30).

As indicated in the introduction to the books of Kings, there is considerable confusion associated with the indictment of Jeroboam's religious policies. The indiscriminate consecration of clergy attracts emphatic condemnation of the house of Jeroboam, "so as to cut it off and destroy it from the face of the earth" (13:34; executed by Baasha, 15:27-29). The setting up of the two calves can be seen as either idolatry

³¹*He* (Heb.; NRSV, He also) **made a high-place house** (Heb.; NRSV, houses on high places)**, and appointed priests from among all the people, who were not Levites.** ³²*Jeroboam appointed a festival on the fifteenth day of the eighth month like the festival that was in Judah, and he offered sacrifices on the altar; so he did in Bethel, sacrificing to the calves that he had made. And he placed in Bethel the priests of the high places that he had made.* ³³*He went up to the altar that he had made in Bethel on the fifteenth day in the eighth month, in the month that he alone had devised; he appointed a festival for the people of Israel, and he went up to the altar to offer incense.* ⁷²

13 While Jeroboam was standing by the altar to offer incense, a man of God came out of Judah by the word of the LORD to Bethel ²and proclaimed against the altar by the word of the LORD, and said:⁷³

(images), or syncretism, or apostasy—which has its impact on the people. What precisely is meant by 14:9's "you have thrust me behind your back" is unclear. The confusion remains in the text; the impact of changing attitudes over time is probable.

A probable direction for resolution points to syncretism or apostasy as the sin that ultimately brought down northern Israel, while the indiscriminate consecration of clergy is to be seen as the sin that brought down the house of Jeroboam (in the next generation).

72. **Text-history approach: vv. 31-33.** The extensive duplication in these verses and their negativity toward Jeroboam have been noted under the text signals. It may be helpful to specify here that a high place (*bāmâ*) is a "built cult place" and a high-place house (*bêt-bāmōt*) is a "sanctuary complex" or its "principal cult building"; the latter occurs only five times (see above, Text signals in 12:25-33, #v.), used for non-Judah installations, and the former appears to have been used indiscriminately (see Barrick, "On the Meaning," esp. pp. 623, 641-42). Barrick's analysis associates the term high-place house with three activities: Jeroboam's building, most probably one

structure at Bethel (1 Kgs 12:31); building at the high places of Samaria (2 Kgs 17:29, 32); destruction attributed to Josiah (1 Kgs 13:32; 2 Kgs 23:19). High places (*bāmâ/bāmōt*) are not mentioned in the deuteronomic lawcode.

The text is such that it is neither appropriate nor helpful to bring a source-critical approach to bear on its issues here. Two concerns overlap and yet contribute to the tension. The verses are providing a framework for the prophetic story of chap. 13; on the other hand, in conjunction with the story, they seek to emphasize the negative impact of Jeroboam on the life of Israel. Material from the end of chap. 13 has been regrouped and reshaped at the end of chap. 12 to locate it all before the Bethel story. Note the reference to high places and non-Levites, absent in 13:33b-34. The negativity toward the king and the lateness of some of the language are indicators in favor of attribution of all three verses to the royal focus of the dtr revision.

73. **Text-history approach: 13:1-32.** The prophetic story has been introduced here as part of the dtr revision's royal focus, updated to associate it with the Josianic reform. Its adaptation and incorporation into the DH within this focus of the revision says nothing about the time of its original composition.

The conflicts between king and prophet and between prophet and prophet never ceased to fascinate ancient Israel. Basic to them are the clashes of interest involved in human living in the sociopolitical sphere (king and prophet) and the religious sphere (prophet and prophet).

The early part of the story is complex and has received various interpretations. The understanding proposed here assumes an original utterance against the altar by the man of God (v. 3b). In order to introduce the association with Josiah, the royal focus of the

---

Main pre-DH: *Prophetic Record*	Other pre-DH: single sideline	HKL: + single underline	**Josianic DH:** **from the Dtr**

*"O altar, altar, thus says the Lᴏʀᴅ: 'A son shall be born to the house of David, Josiah by name; and he shall sacrifice on you the priests of the high places who offer incense on you, and human bones shall be burned on you.' " ³He gave a sign the same day, saying, This is the sign that the Lᴏʀᴅ has spoken:*⁷⁴

"The altar shall be torn down, and the ashes that are on it shall be poured out." ⁴When the king heard what the man of God cried out against the altar at Bethel,

---

dtr revision process has transformed this original utterance into a sign validating the prophecy about Josiah. See below.

At the end of the story, the saying pronounced against Bethel is affirmed as true, and it is extended in v. 32b to apply beyond Bethel to "the cities of Samaria," specifically to "all the houses of the high places" there. Barrick is right to insist on the story's focus on a single event around the altar at Bethel; he is not necessarily right to exclude a concern for the rest of Samaria from the focus of the same editor (cf. 12:32b; 13:32b; 2 Kgs 23:19). Dtr revisers working within the royal focus of the revision process can have held both concerns, restricting the first to Bethel alone and bringing in the second at the end of the story. It is not uncommon to distribute these concerns (here and also 2 Kgs 23:15-20) over several editorial layers; however, they can come together within the compass of a single focus of revision.

Dietrich attributed to his DtrP the insertion of 13:1-32, with 12:33 and 13:2bβ, 32b, 33-34 as literary seams; he later attributed to his DtrP the addition of 2 Kgs 23:15*, 16b, 19b.

74. **Text signals in vv. 2-5.** (i) The specificity of this saying is unusual in Kings, e.g., the reference to Josiah by name. (ii) The singular reference to Josiah ("he shall sacrifice on you") is followed by a plural verb at the end of v. 2 (Heb.: they shall burn on you; nʀsv: "shall be burned on you"). (iii) At the beginning of v. 3, the Hebrew verb can be read as future or past. As future, the sign will be given by Josiah; as past, the sign is given by the man of God. V. 5b clearly interprets the sign as given by the man of God.

Text-history approach. If the specificity is not a problem, the text flows smoothly. Where it is a problem, as it is for us, the resolution can be found in the text's composition. As noted above, what is now the sign was originally the prophetic oracle. The collapse of the altar occurred simultaneously with the withering of the king's outstretched arm. The double demonstration of prophetic power exalted the prophet, debased Jeroboam, and destroyed the altar he had made to rival the authorities of Judah.

The royal focus of the dtr revision associates the prophecy with the reforming action of Josiah and transforms the original utterance (v. 3b) into a sign, validating what is to come. The description of the altar's collapse as "the sign that the man of God had given" (v. 5b) is to be attributed to this revision.

The signals noted above as (ii) and (iii) can be read as in the nʀsv. Read differently, they can be accounted for by a different history of composition (cf. Noth, *Könige*, 295-98). This approach is more complex and, in our judgment, is unnecessary (cf. 2 Kgs 23:15-20). For Noth, a fragment of the original oracle is retained (and they shall burn human bones on you); for Jones and Würthwein, the original utterance has been completely replaced by the insertion; for us, the original word is completely retained, but later transformed.

Present-text potential. In the context, Jeroboam has established a center of worship to rival Jerusalem (12:27-28); from the outset, the text points to the destruction of this center, achieved under Josiah (cf. 2 Kgs 23:15-18). Jeroboam's action may have been one of political pragmatism. In the pitting of king against king, the house of David prevails. In the pitting of Bethel against Jerusalem, Jerusalem prevails. Even in this story of the north, dtr ideology dominates—the promise to David, the place of Jerusalem.

No rebuilding of the altar is reported. Rebuilding might be implied by 13:33; the altar is required for 2 Kgs 23:15.

| After the Dtr:
indented and sans serif font | **Revision:**
royal focus | *Revision:*
national focus | Other:
double sideline |

Jeroboam stretched out his hand from the altar, saying, "Seize him!" But the hand that he stretched out against him withered so that he could not draw it back to himself. [5]The altar also was torn down, and the ashes poured out from the altar.

according to the sign that the man of God had given by the word of the Lord
[6]The king said to the man of God, "Entreat now the favor of the Lord your God, and pray for me, so that my hand may be restored to me." So the man of God entreated the Lord; and the king's hand was restored to him, and became as it was before. [7]Then the king said to the man of God, "Come home with me and dine, and I will give you a gift." [8]But the man of God said to the king, "If you give me half your kingdom, I will not go in with you; nor will I eat food or drink water in this place. [9]For thus I was commanded by the word of the Lord: You shall not eat food, or drink water, or return by the way that you came." [10]So he went another way, and did not return by the way that he had come to Bethel.

11 Now there lived an old prophet in Bethel. One of his sons came and told him all that the man of God had done that day in Bethel; the words also that he had spoken to the king, they told to their father. [12]Their father said to them, "Which way did he go?" And his sons showed him the way that the man of God who came from Judah had gone. [13]Then he said to his sons, "Saddle a donkey for me." So they saddled a donkey for him, and he mounted it. [14]He went after the man of God, and found him sitting under an oak tree. He said to him, "Are you the man of God who came from Judah?" He answered, "I am." [15]Then he said to him, "Come home with me and eat

some food." [16]But he said, "I cannot return with you, or go in with you; nor will I eat food or drink water with you in this place; [17]for it was said to me by the word of the Lord: You shall not eat food or drink water there, or return by the way that you came." [18]Then the other said to him, "I also am a prophet as you are, and an angel spoke to me by the word of the Lord: Bring him back with you into your house so that he may eat food and drink water." But he was deceiving him. [19]Then the man of God went back with him, and ate food and drank water in his house.

20 As they were sitting at the table, the word of the Lord came to the prophet who had brought him back; [21]and he proclaimed to the man of God who came from Judah, "Thus says the Lord: Because you have disobeyed the word of the Lord, and have not kept the commandment that the Lord your God commanded you, [22]but have come back and have eaten food and drunk water in the place of which he said to you, 'Eat no food, and drink no water,' your body shall not come to your ancestral tomb." [23]After the man of God had eaten food and had drunk, they saddled for him a donkey belonging to the prophet who had brought him back. [24]Then as he went away, a lion met him on the road and killed him. His body was thrown in the road, and the donkey stood beside it; the lion also stood beside the body. [25]People passed by and saw the body thrown in the road, with the lion standing by the body. And they came and told it in the town where the old prophet lived.

26 When the prophet who had brought him back from the way heard of it, he said, "It is the man of God who disobeyed the

---

| Main pre-DH:
Prophetic Record | Other pre-DH:
single sideline | HKL: + single
underline | **Josianic DH:**
from the Dtr |

word of the LORD; therefore the LORD has given him to the lion, which has torn him and killed him according to the word that the LORD spoke to him." 27Then he said to his sons, "Saddle a donkey for me." So they saddled one, 28and he went and found the body thrown in the road, with the donkey and the lion standing beside the body. The lion had not eaten the body or attacked the donkey. 29The prophet took up the body of the man of God, laid it on the donkey, and brought it back to the city, to mourn and to bury him. 30He laid the body in his own grave; and they mourned over him, saying, "Alas, my brother!" 31After he had buried him, he said to his sons, "When I die, bury me in the grave in which the man of God is buried; lay my bones beside his bones. 32For the saying shall surely come to pass *(Heb.; NRSV, order rearranged)* that he proclaimed by the word of the LORD against the altar in Bethel."

and against all the houses of the high places that are in the cities of Samaria.

33 Even after this event Jeroboam did not turn from his evil way, but he returned (Heb.)

And he made priests for the high places from among all the people; any who wanted to be priests he consecrated for the high places. 34*This matter became sin to the house of Jeroboam, so as to cut it off and to destroy it from the face of the earth.*[75]

---

75. **Text-history approach:** 13:33-34 (see the text signals in the note on 12:25). The translation has been slightly adjusted in v. 33 to mirror the Hebrew more closely and allow the editorial procedure to be visible. The verb "but he returned" is rendered in the NRSV by "again" after "the high places."

The first part of v. 33 is a link made by the dtr revision (royal focus), in conjunction with its expansion

14 *At that time Abijah son of Jeroboam fell sick.* 2*Jeroboam said to his wife, "Go, disguise yourself, so that it will not be known that you are the wife of Jeroboam, and go to Shiloh; for the prophet Ahijah is there, who said of me that I should be king over this people.* 3*Take with you ten loaves, some cakes, and a*

---

added in v. 32b, blending the inserted story (13:1-32) back into the larger narrative. Its "after this event" and "he returned" attempt to hold together the reality that what follows in vv. 33b-34 has already been dealt with "before" the prophetic story. The phrase "turn from his evil way" is late and appropriate to the dtr redaction's royal focus.

Here the PR resumes from 12:29-30. The two concerns are for the consecration of priests (it is indiscriminate: "any who wanted") and the ongoing impact of this sin (the impact falls on the house of Jeroboam). Any attempt to account for v. 34 as an addition must explain why it has been added here. We note that the reference to the high places in 13:33 is the last such mention for the northern kingdom until 2 Kgs 17:9.

Present-text potential of 12:25–13:34. This text paints the picture of Jeroboam's first acts as king, the inauguration of the northern monarchy. It is a bleak picture, as might be expected from a basically southern text. Jeroboam's establishment as king in the north is recounted in the immediately preceding 11:26–12:24. Jeroboam is promised the northern kingship by a prophet, with specific conditions attached. With his first acts, Jeroboam violates those conditions. He is condemned by a prophet, who is also under specific conditions. The prophet violates his conditions—he ate and drank when he had been told not to. He died for it and is acknowledged as an authentic prophet (13:32). Gathered around this story of two prophets and a king are reflections on Jeroboam and his house. First, the sins of Jeroboam; they are grave. Second, the impact of these sins on Jeroboam's dynasty; it is finished. God's prophet set up the king, under certain conditions. The conditions are ignored and a prophet from God predicts the royal failure.

After the Dtr: indented and sans serif font	**Revision: royal focus**	Revision: national focus	Other: double sideline

jar of honey, and go to him; he will tell you what shall happen to the child."[76]

4 Jeroboam's wife did so; she set out and went to Shiloh, and came to the house of Ahijah. Now Ahijah could not see, for his eyes were dim because of his age. ⁵But the LORD said to Ahijah, "The wife of Jeroboam is coming to inquire of you concerning her son; for he is sick. Thus and thus you shall say to her."

When she came, she pretended to be another woman. ⁶But when Ahijah heard the sound of her feet, as she came in at the door, he said, "Come in, wife of Jeroboam; why do you pretend to be another? For I am charged with heavy tidings for you. ⁷Go, tell Jeroboam, 'Thus says the LORD, the God of Israel: Because I exalted you from among the people, made

---

76. **Text signals** in 14:1-18. (i) Within a prophetic story, there is a prophetic speech dismissing the house of Jeroboam, couched in stereotyped terms (see the Introduction). (ii) A part of vv. 8-9 is made up of characteristic dtr phrases. (iii) V. 14 goes beyond vv. 10-11 to specify God's agent in bringing evil on the house of Jeroboam. (iv) Vv. 15-16 focus on Israel rather than Jeroboam. (v) V. 18b reports the fulfillment of Ahijah's prophecy.

Text-history approach. The "stereotyped terms" noted under text signals point to the PR. "I exalted you": reflects the thought of 1 Sam 15:1; 2 Sam 7:8; 12:7. The specific formulation is found elsewhere only at 1 Kgs 16:2, for Baasha—where there is no accompanying story. "Made you leader (*nāgîd*)" etc.: cf. 1 Sam 9:16; 10:1; (15:1); 2 Sam 5:2; 7:8. and 1 Kgs 16:2—again without any accompanying story. "Tore the kingdom away": cf. 1 Sam 15:27-28; 1 Kgs 11:30-31. For the stereotyped phrases that constitute vv. 10-11, see the Introduction. This pre-dtr text is attributed to the PR.

In vv. 8-9, the references to my servant David, keeping the commandments, all one's heart, right in my eyes, and the comparison with other kings all belong within dtr vocabulary and here, in our judgment, are best attributed to the Josianic Dtr. On the other hand, the distribution of the references to making other gods (predominantly late), cast images (rare and late), and provoking God to anger (predominantly late) point decisively to later dtr editing, here the national focus. The combination of these three elements here is unique.

Verse 14 specifies an agent of God's will (in the occurrence, Baasha), not included in what precedes

nor referred to in what follows. The emphasis on a king suggests the royal focus of the dtr revision.

In vv. 15-16, apart from other issues, the making of sacred poles is not mentioned in the preceding narrative. The focus is on Israel. V. 16, dependent on v. 15, brings the accusation against Israel back to the general context of Jeroboam's sins. "This good land" occurs elsewhere only in Josh 23:13, 15. The image of the reed is unique and v. 15 as a whole is unusual. Our observations suggest that vv. 15-16 are best attributed to the national focus of the dtr revision.

Verse 18b is a fulfillment notice. These do not seem to belong in the PR but do belong in the contributions of the Josianic Dtr. "A survey of the fulfillment notations in Joshua–2 Kings favors an attribution to dtr circles" (Campbell, *Of Prophets and Kings*, 92, n. 61).

Present-text potential. In 1 Kings 11, the northern kingdom was promised to Jeroboam by the prophet Ahijah, subject to certain conditions, relating to "David my servant" (11:38-39). 1 Kings 12:26–13:34 shows these conditions to have been royally breached. The text here (14:1-18) has the consequences of this failure spelled out by the same Ahijah and its realization noted. The editing of the text makes a strong theological observation. The focus is first on Jeroboam, his sin and his punishment, then on the consequences of this for Israel and its exile (v. 15), finally returning to the sin of Jeroboam "which he sinned and which he caused Israel to sin" (v. 16). Such is the power of one ruler to corrupt a whole people and destroy its destiny.

Dietrich attributed to his DtrP the insertion of 14:1-18*, distributed as follows: vv. 1-6, 12-13a, 17-18, old story; vv. 7-8a, 9b-11, 13b, DtrP; vv. 8b-9a, (15-16), DtrN.

---

you leader over my people Israel, ^{8}*and tore the kingdom away from the house of David to give it to you;* **yet you have not been like my servant David, who kept my commandments and followed me with all his heart, doing only that which was right in my sight,** ^{9}**but you have done evil above all those who were before you**

> *and have gone and made for yourself other gods, and cast images, provoking me to anger*

and you (Heb.) *have thrust me behind your back;* ^{10}*therefore, I will bring evil upon the house of Jeroboam. I will cut off from Jeroboam every male, both bond and free in Israel, and will consume the house of Jeroboam, just as one burns up dung until it is all gone.* ^{11}*Anyone belonging to Jeroboam who dies in the city, the dogs shall eat; and anyone who dies in the open country, the birds of the air shall eat; for the* LORD *has spoken.'* ^{12}*Therefore set out, go to your house. When your feet enter the city, the child shall die.* ^{13}*All Israel shall mourn for him and bury him; for he alone of Jeroboam's family shall come to the grave, because in him there is found something pleasing to the* LORD, *the God of Israel, in the house of Jeroboam.*

^{14}*Moreover the* LORD *will raise up for himself a king over Israel, who shall cut off the house of Jeroboam today, even right now!*

> *15 "The* LORD *will strike Israel, as a reed is shaken in the water; he will root up Israel out of this good land that he gave to their ancestors, and scatter them beyond the Euphrates, because they have made their sacred poles, provoking the* LORD *to anger.* ^{16}*He will give Israel up because of the sins of Jeroboam, which he sinned and which he caused Israel to commit."*

17 Then Jeroboam's wife got up and went away, and she came to Tirzah. As she came to the threshold of the house, the child died. ^{18}*All Israel buried him*

and mourned for him, **according to the word of the** LORD, **which he spoke by his servant the prophet Ahijah.**[77]

19 Now the rest of the acts of Jeroboam, how he warred and how he reigned, are written in the Book of the Annals of the Kings of Israel. ^{20}**The time that Jeroboam reigned was twenty-two years;** *then Jeroboam* (proper name restored here; Heb. and NRSV, he) *slept with his ancestors, and his son Nadab succeeded him.*[78]

---

77. As noted briefly, a survey of the fulfillment notations throughout Joshua to Second Kings suggests an attribution of these notations to dtr circles. They do not occur in 1–2 Samuel, although they would have been appropriate for the death of Saul, the crowning of David, and the succession of Solomon. In the Elijah-Elisha stories, fulfillment notations are present, but without the use of "servant" or "prophet." 1 Kings 12:15 and 16:12 show that the usage is not essential to the Dtr. But if 1 Kgs 14:18 (here) and 15:29 (below) are not dtr, they would be the only two occurrences of "servant" in these fulfillment stories that are not (cf. Campbell, *Of Prophets and Kings*, 92, n. 61).

78. The narrative of the northern kingdom, expressed in the PR, was adequately served by a simple linear system for reporting the succession. The advent of the DH, with its focus on both north and south, demanded a more complicated synchronistic system, dating the events of one kingdom in relation to the other. "Where the successor's reign is considered immediately, the unnecessarily formulaic repetition of already reported information can only be due to the pattern elaborated to bring some coherence into the linear reporting of two parallel kingdoms" (Campbell, *Of Prophets and Kings*, 139).

The issue at stake here is whether the linear system existed independently or whether the information it conveyed was merely a part of the synchronistic system. That the linear system could exist independently is evident from Gen 36:31-39. That it did, in fact, exist independently here, in these pre-dtr traditions

---

| After the Dtr: indented and sans serif font | **Revision: royal focus** | *Revision: national focus* | Other: double sideline |

21 <u>Now Rehoboam son of Solomon reigned in Judah.</u>[79]

Rehoboam was forty-one years old when he began to reign, and he reigned seventeen years in Jerusalem, the city that the LORD had chosen out of all the tribes of Israel, to put his name there. His mother's name was Naamah the Ammonite.[80]

[22]<u>Judah did what was evil in the sight of the LORD.</u>[81]

---

of the kings, can be claimed on the basis of the unnecessary repetition where both systems are present. The pre-dtr texts—the PR, its extension, the HKL—were concerned with one kingdom only; a linear system was satisfactory. The DH was concerned with two kingdoms, northern and southern; the synchronistic system was necessary. Examples of the needless repetition are 1 Kgs 16:28-29; 2 Kgs 8:24-25; 13:9-10; 15:22-23; 15:38–16:1. Of these, one reflects the PR and two each belong to its extension and the HKL respectively.

This is the only case where the proper name is absent from the formula "and X slept with his ancestors." Presumably it was dropped following the reference to Jeroboam's reign. The continuation of the PR is to be found at 15:27.

79. The references to Rehoboam and Judah, in vv. 21, 22, and 23, begin the Hezekian King List (HKL). Analysis here is based on the judgment formulas (for a general treatment, see the Introduction). The characteristic and exclusive element that is significant here (pattern B) is the reference to the high places and worship there. Scholarship points to a surge of theological activity, reflection and writing, associated with the reign of Hezekiah. In our judgment, the sole trace of this activity that can be identified in the text with any certainty is the judgment formulas associated with the high places, comprising substantially a list of the southern kings as far as Hezekiah.

We refer to this as the Hezekian King List (HKL). It is identified in our text by dual signals. As pre-dtr, it receives a single sideline; among the pre-dtr materials, it is marked out by a single underline. Options around this king list are noted in the Introduction. A freestanding list is conceivable, with the possibility of oral development for policy or preaching. It is equally conceivable that traditions were collected in association with this list and all it stood for. A document structured around the list is also conceivable. Restricting ourselves to the HKL, we will signal in the notes passages that might have been associated with the HKL, or that might have been part of such a structured document, and that in any case are now found incorporated in the Josianic DH.

In v. 22, the MT has Judah, followed by a plural verb; the LXX has Rehoboam, followed by a singular verb. It would seem that two traditions existed, one fingering the king directly, the other focusing on the people who "still sacrificed and made offerings on the high places." The conflict of traditions remains visible in the text (cf. v. 23; also 1 Kgs 15:3).

80. With Rehoboam, the standard dtr regnal framework is introduced; its elements provide a structural shape for the narrative. Nine elements comprise the framework: synchronism (for the two kingdoms), king's age at his accession (kings of Judah only), length of reign, capital city, name of queen mother (kings of Judah only), judgment formula, source reference, notice of death and burial, succession. These recur regularly, so that normally no comment will be required. Most are attributed to the Josianic Dtr; the synchronisms and chronology reflect the concern for a structured account of the two kingdoms. In contrast with Noth's view, the linear aspect of the framework for northern kings will be attributed to the PR and its extension and for southern kings to the Hezekian King List.

The dtr accession formula for Rehoboam lacks the synchronism. As far as the capital is concerned, here and only here in the accession formulas, Jerusalem is mentioned with the dtr specification that it is "the city that the LORD had chosen out of all the tribes of Israel, to put his name there." The emphasis is on Jerusalem now established as the central place of worship (cf. 1 Kgs 8:16-21).

81. To do "evil in the eyes of YHWH" is a commonplace in the OT, from Gen 38:7 to 2 Chron 36:12,

---

| Main pre-DH:
Prophetic Record | Other pre-DH:
single sideline | HKL: + single
underline | **Josianic DH:
from the Dtr** |

They provoked him to jealousy more than all that their ancestors had done with their sins that they committed (Heb.; NRSV rearranges sentence order, eliminating ambiguity).[82]

23For they also built for themselves high places.
and (*Heb.*) pillars, and sacred poles, on every high hill and under every green tree; 24there were also male temple prostitutes (*NRSV; Heb. singular*) in the land. They committed all the abominations of the nations that the LORD drove out before the people of Israel.[83]

---

with the bulk of occurrences associated with the royal judgment formulas. The attributions given here are based on the patterns of the judgment formulas.

82. The polemical attitude toward the people favors attribution to the dtr revision's national focus. The three elements that comprise the passage are not found in the Josianic Dtr: i) provoke to jealousy (cf. Deut 32:16, 21); ii) the precise formulation of the comparison with the ancestors; iii) the place in the sentence of the reference to "their sins." The precise referents of the plurals are syntactically uncertain. Attribution to the national focus of the dtr revision is likely, without being compelling.

83. An integral part of the judgment formulas in the HKL is the description for most of the kings as doing "what was right in the sight of the LORD" so that presumably the issue of the high places is one of centralization not apostasy (cf. I. W. Provan, *Hezekiah and the Books of Kings*, 65). The triad of high places, pillars, and sacred pole(s) is found here and in 2 Kgs 18:4. In both places, the charge of apostasy appears to be later. "On every high hill and under every green tree" appears to depend on Jeremiah (esp. 2:20; cf. 3:6, 13; 17:2; cf. W. L. Holladay, "On Every High Hill"). The distribution of the phrase "the abominations of the nations" also suggests a later period. Male prostitution is referred to only twice (1 Kgs 14:24; 15:12). We suggest that here it has been added later to antic-

25 In the fifth year of King Rehoboam, King Shishak of Egypt came up against Jerusalem; 26he took away the treasures of the house of the LORD and the treasures of the king's house; he took everything. He also took away all the shields of gold that Solomon had made; 27so King Rehoboam made shields of bronze instead, and committed them to the hands of the officers of the guard, who kept the door of the king's house. 28As often as the king went into the house of the LORD, the guard carried them and brought them back to the guardroom.[84]

29 Now the rest of the acts of Rehoboam, and all that he did, are they not written in the Book of the Annals of the Kings of Judah? 30There was war between Rehoboam and Jeroboam continually.[85]

31Rehoboam slept with his ancestors and was buried with his ancestors in the city of David. His mother's name was Naamah the Ammonite. His son Abijam succeeded him.[86]

15 Now in the eighteenth year of King Jeroboam son of Nebat, Abijam began to reign over Judah. 2He reigned for three years in Jerusalem. His mother's name was Maacah daughter of Abishalom.

---

ipate the removal in 15:12. Overall, no specific attributions can be made for this later material.

84. Verses 25-28 contain a tradition that might well have been associated with the HKL. Its incorporation here is to be attributed to the Dtr.

85. Verses 29-30: note the parallel in 15:7.

86. The notice here, in the regnal framework's conclusion, of the queen mother, Naamah the Ammonite, is unique. The Dtr gives this information in the accession section of the framework (cf. 14:21). No reason suggests that the Dtr might have repeated this. In the absence of other evidence, it is reasonable to attribute it to the source (HKL).

| After the Dtr: indented and sans serif font | ***Revision: royal focus*** | *Revision: national focus* | Other: double sideline |

<u>[3]He committed all the sins that his father did before him.</u>[87]

His heart was not true to the LORD his God, like the heart of his father David. [4]Nevertheless for David's sake the LORD his God gave him a lamp in Jerusalem, setting up his son after him, and establishing Jerusalem.

[5]because David did what was right in the sight of the LORD, and did not turn aside from anything that he commanded him all the days of his life, except in the matter of Uriah the Hittite.[88]

[6]The war begun between Rehoboam and Jeroboam continued all the days of his life.[89]

[7]The rest of the acts of Abijam, and all that he did, are they not written in the Book of the Annals of the Kings of Judah? There was war between Abijam and Jeroboam.

<u>[8]Abijam slept with his ancestors, and they buried him in the city of David. Then his son Asa succeeded him.</u>

9 In the twentieth year of King Jeroboam of Israel, Asa began to reign over Judah; [10]he reigned forty-one years in Jerusalem. His mother's name was Maacah daughter of Abishalom.[90]

<u>[11]Asa did what was right in the sight of the LORD, as his father David had done. [12]He put away the male temple prostitutes out of the land.</u>

and removed all the idols that his ancestors had made[91]

[13]He also removed his mother Maacah from being queen mother, because she had made an abominable image for Asherah; Asa cut down her image and burned it at the Wadi Kidron.[92]

<u>[14]But the high places were not taken away.</u>[93]

---

87. This element for Abijam is unique in the Hezekian judgment formulas. There is no mention of the high places, but such mention is restricted to kings who "did what was right in the sight of the LORD." "His father" is Rehoboam; without prejudice to the textual issues of 14:22, the comment reflects a tradition of Rehoboam's sinfulness.

88. Verse 4 reports the fulfillment of 11:36 (the Dtr). V. 5 repeats the theme of David as the model king. Its focus is on David, not Abijam; its formulation suggests a later spelling out of how David was wholly true to YHWH. The comment revealing embarrassment over the Uriah episode is missing from LXX, as is v. 6. The royal focus within the dtr revision was hostile to the monarchy; here, the emphasis on David's fidelity to all that was commanded suggests attribution to the law-oriented national focus of the dtr revision.

89. Verse 6 draws together the information in 14:30 and 15:7b. It is missing from the LXX.

90. This is the second reference to Maacah, daughter of Abishalom, as queen mother (cf. above, 15:2). The simplest assumption is that she was Asa's grandmother and functioned as "queen mother" (cf. v. 13: *gĕbîrâ*) under both Abijam and Asa (cf. Jones, *Kings*, 1.283).

91. The negativity toward the preceding Davidic kings ("his ancestors") suggests attribution to the royal focus of the dtr revision process. We have no evidence for the establishment of such idols, but the claim may fill out the accusations of sinfulness against Rehoboam and Abijam. The term for idols, used here, is found predominantly in Ezekiel (thirty-nine out of forty-eight) but also in seven dtr contexts that are later (Deut 29:17 [Heb., v. 16]; 1 Kgs 15:12; 21:26; 2 Kgs 17:12; 21:11, 21; 23:24).

92. The HKL is concerned with the high places, not with apostasy. While the precise meaning of the "abominable image for Asherah" is uncertain, it concerns apostasy and is therefore appropriately attributed to the Dtr.

93. It is important to note here the sequence of text with regard to the high places. In 14:23, they are reported as built by the people. Asa is the first reforming king in the southern kingdom, and it is noted here

---

Main pre-DH:	Other pre-DH:	HKL: + single	**Josianic DH:**
Prophetic Record	single sideline	underline	**from the Dtr**

Nevertheless the heart of Asa was true to the LORD all his days. ¹⁵He brought into the house of the LORD the votive gifts of his father and his own votive gifts—silver, gold, and utensils.

16 There was war between Asa and King Baasha of Israel all their days. ¹⁷King Baasha of Israel went up against Judah, and built Ramah, to prevent anyone from going out or coming in to King Asa of Judah. ¹⁸Then Asa took all the silver and the gold that were left in the treasures of the house of the LORD and the treasures of the king's house, and gave them into the hands of his servants. King Asa sent them to King Ben-hadad son of Tabrimmon son of Hezion of Aram, who resided in Damascus, saying, ¹⁹"Let there be an alliance between me and you, like that between my father and your father: I am sending you a present of silver and gold; go, break your alliance with King Baasha of Israel, so that he may withdraw from me." ²⁰Ben-hadad listened to King Asa, and sent the commanders of his armies against the cities of Israel. He conquered Ijon, Dan, Abel-beth-maacah, and all Chinneroth, with all the land of Naphtali. ²¹When Baasha heard of it, he stopped building Ramah and lived in Tirzah. ²²Then King Asa made a proclamation to all Judah, none was exempt: they carried away the stones of Ramah and its timber, with which

Baasha had been building; with them King Asa built Geba of Benjamin and Mizpah.[94]

²³Now the rest of all the acts of Asa, all his power, all that he did, and the cities that he

---

94. This text, 15:16-22, is a clear example of those texts that might have been associated in some way with the activities under Hezekiah. The minimum that we identify here is the HKL. In the Introduction, we have noted the minimal, moderate, and maximal positions that can be taken. In this book, we consider it appropriate to point out that a HKL can be identified, that traditions exist that can be appropriately associated with the HKL, and that these traditions might have come either from a collection associated with the HKL or from a document structured around the HKL. These possibilities seem, at this time, too hypothetical for incorporation into the text of this book.

This text is one of four dealing with kings of Judah who ransacked the temple in Jerusalem to pay for a counter to the threat of invasion (1 Kgs 15:16-22; 2 Kgs 12:17-18; 16:5-9; 18:14-16). Association with the HKL is problematic. 2 Kgs 18:14-16 concerns Hezekiah and portrays a different Hezekiah from the image in HKL. Highlighting the problematic aspect is the fact that three of these kings are characterized as reformers (Asa, Joash, and Hezekiah); only one is characterized as an evil king (Ahaz).

At least three options are possible for these texts. First, all four derive from the royal focus within the dtr process of revision, bringing to the fore traditions that cast the four kings in a less-than-positive light. Second, the first three are associated with the HKL, while the fourth comes from the royal focus of the dtr revision and, against the HKL, expresses a dissenting view of Hezekiah. Third, the one relating to Ahaz comes from the HKL, while the other three derive from the royal focus. What gives the second option a certain credibility is the positive judgment of kings who did not take the high places away. So the HKL apparently assumes that for earlier kings the Jerusalem temple was less significant than later for the Dtr.

---

that, despite his reforms, the high places were not taken away. Under the subsequent southern kings, it will be regularly noted that the high places were not taken away; they remained a locus of worship for the people.

After the Dtr: indented and sans serif font	**Revision:** **royal focus**	Revision: national focus	Other: double sideline

built, are they not written in the Book of the Annals of the Kings of Judah? But in his old age he was diseased in his feet. <u>[24]Then Asa slept with his ancestors, and was buried with his ancestors in the city of his father David; his son Jehoshaphat succeeded him.</u>

25 Nadab son of Jeroboam began to reign over Israel in the second year of King Asa of Judah; he reigned over Israel two years. [26]He did what was evil in the sight of the LORD, walking in the way of his ancestor and in the sin that he caused Israel to commit.[95]

27 And (Heb.) *Baasha son of Ahijah, of the house of Issachar, conspired against him; and Baasha struck him down at Gibbethon, which belonged to the Philistines; for Nadab and all Israel were laying siege to Gibbethon.* *[28]So Baasha killed Nadab* **in the third year of King Asa of Judah.** *And he* (Heb.) *succeeded him. [29]As soon as he was king, he killed all*

the house of Jeroboam; he left to the house of Jeroboam not one that breathed, until he had destroyed it, **according to the word of the LORD that he spoke by his servant Ahijah the Shilonite.**[96]

—[30]because of the sins of Jeroboam that he committed and that he caused Israel to commit, and because of the anger to which he provoked the LORD, the God of Israel.[97]

31 Now the rest of the acts of Nadab, and all that he did, are they not written in the Book of the Annals of the Kings of Israel? [32]There was war between Asa and King Baasha of Israel all their days.

33 In the third year of King Asa of Judah, Baasha son of Ahijah began to reign over all Israel at Tirzah; he reigned twenty-four years. [34]He did what was evil in the sight of the LORD, walking in the way of Jeroboam and in the sin that he caused Israel to commit.[98]

Our own preference, as reflected in the formatting, is for the third option, i.e., to attribute three of these passages to the royal focus of the dtr revision process, but the Ahaz passage to the HKL (2 Kgs 16:5-9). It is highly unlikely that the Josianic text, which gives such prominence to the great reforming kings, Hezekiah and Josiah, should portray negatively these earlier reforming kings—Asa who reversed the policies of Rehoboam and Abijam, on the one hand, and Jehoash who broke with the northern policies of his predecessors, Jehoram and Ahaziah, on the other. The royal focus shows a hostility to the monarchy, in contrast both to the positive view of the Josianic Dtr and to the hostility to the people of the later national focus within the dtr revision. In keeping with this, it is appropriate for the royal focus to emphasize traditions that highlight flaws in the behavior of these otherwise favorably viewed kings. For Ahaz, see below, 2 Kgs 16:5-9.

95. This is the first of the judgment formulas for northern kings before Jehu. For discussion of the pattern (C) and its implications, see the Introduction.

96. 15:27 is the resumption of the PR from 14:20b; the "him," of course, is Nadab. The continuation of the PR is to be found at 16:6.

The synchronism between the two kingdoms is to be attributed to the Dtr. While the killing noted in v. 28 can be read as a doublet of the striking in v. 27 (cf. the same repetition in 16:10), the attribution to the Dtr of the synchronism alone is the least complex approach.

The notice of fulfillment (v. 29b) is from the Dtr; see the note on 14:18 above.

97. Verse 30a echoes v. 26b; v. 30b's language is normally late dtr. It is appropriately located after the note of fulfillment, which it reinforces. It specifies Jeroboam by name, over against the more general formulation of v. 26. Its negativity toward Nadab is in keeping with the tenor of the royal focus of the dtr revision.

Dietrich attributed 15:29 to his DtrP and 15:30 to his DtrN.

98. **Present-text potential.** With the assassination of Nadab and the accession of Baasha to the

---

Main pre-DH:	Other pre-DH:	HKL: + single	**Josianic DH:**
Prophetic Record	single sideline	underline	**from the Dtr**

16 The word of the LORD came to Jehu son of Hanani against Baasha, saying, ²"Since I exalted you out of the dust and made you leader over my people Israel, and you have walked in the way of Jeroboam, and have caused my people Israel to sin, *provoking me to anger with their sins,* ³therefore, I will consume Baasha and his house, and I will make your house like the house of Jeroboam son of Nebat. ⁴Anyone belonging to Baasha who dies in the city the dogs shall eat; and anyone of his who dies in the field the birds of the air shall eat."⁹⁹

throne, Jeroboam's dynasty has come to an end—has been cut off (14:10). The unity of focus for the present text goes back to the prophetic condemnation of Jeroboam's dynasty by Ahijah in 1 Kgs 14:1-18. The overall text moves from the prophecy to its fulfillment. This arch in the understanding of the events is articulated in 15:29b. The text reports the murder of Nadab (v. 28) and the extermination of his house (v. 29). Ultimate responsibility for the regicide and the bloodbath is given to YHWH and his servant the prophet. Understandably, then, v. 30 follows immediately, noting that Jeroboam had sinned, and caused Israel to sin, and provoked YHWH to anger (v. 30). Close attention to the text here shows a phenomenon that occurs across the two chapters: what have been identified as later additions within the DH function to sharpen insight into what is recounted. The signposting provided by the regnal framework offers a means of access to the broader narrative, keeping in view the unfolding stories of the two kingdoms and keeping track of their chronological correlation. That this is not secular history is brought home by the theological accusation recurring regularly in the evaluations of the kings.

99. **Text signals.** (i) 16:1-4 reports a word of the LORD; it does not tell a story with a prophetic speech. (ii) There is no prior story of Baasha's being exalted out of the dust. The reference may be modeled on 14:7; these are the only two occurrences. (iii)

5 Now the rest of the acts of Baasha, what he did, and his power, are they not written in the Book of the Annals of the Kings of

The accusation against Baasha (v. 2b) is composed entirely of three elements found in the judgment formulas on kings, but not found in the accusations attributed to the PR. The third element, "provoking me to anger," is more common in later dtr revision. All three elements together are found only here and in 16:26; the other two elements are found together at 1 Kgs 15:34; 16:19; 22:52 (Heb., 22:53). It is possible that the element of "provoking the LORD to anger" was either a rare usage by the Dtr here or a later dtr embellishment (esp. given its frequency in the context); in the light of this uncertainty, we have used the royal focus font but not disrupted the text. (iv) Despite the possibility offered in 16:11, the threat to cut off every male, bond or free, is absent from 16:1-4 (cf. 1 Kgs 14:10; 21:21; 2 Kgs 9:8). (v) The announcement begins for Jeroboam (14:10) and Ahab (21:21) with a general statement ("I will bring evil/disaster"); here it moves immediately to the particular. Note: the NRSV is not literal in this material. (vi) There is a minor omission in the otherwise highly stereotyped reference to the fate of the dead (v. 4). See Campbell, *Of Prophets and Kings,* 39-41.

Text-history approach. The evidence of these text signals indicates that 16:1-4 is not of a piece with the speeches of designation and rejection attributed to the PR. It is most plausibly attributed to the Dtr. Note that 16:1-4 is a key text for Walter Dietrich (cf. *Prophetie und Geschichte,* 9-10; for critical evaluation, *Of Prophets and Kings,* 6-11).

Present-text potential. It is important to recognize that, with the presence of this text, all the northern dynasties from Jeroboam to Jehu are brought within the orbit of the prophetic word. The dynasties of Jeroboam, Baasha, and Omri/Ahab are all rejected by the LORD. Zimri, murdered after a seven-day reign, has no dynasty; Omri is the founder of the dynasty rejected in Ahab. Jehu's four-generation dynasty is initiated by his prophetic designation (2 Kgs 9:1-13); a word from the LORD set its limits (2 Kgs 10:30).

| After the Dtr: indented and sans serif font | **Revision: royal focus** | Revision: national focus | Other: double sideline |

Israel? *⁶Baasha slept with his ancestors, and was buried at Tirzah; and his son Elah succeeded him.*[100]

⁷Moreover the word of the Lord came by the prophet Jehu son of Hanani against Baasha and his house, both because of all the evil that he did in the sight of the Lord, provoking him to anger with the work of his hands, in being like the house of Jeroboam, and also because he destroyed it.[101]

8 In the twenty-sixth year of King Asa of Judah, Elah son of Baasha began to reign over Israel in Tirzah; he reigned two years. *⁹But his servant Zimri, commander of half his chariots, conspired against him. When he was at Tirzah, drinking himself drunk in the house of Arza, who was in charge of the palace at Tirzah, ¹⁰Zimri came in and struck him down and killed him,* **in the twenty-seventh year of King Asa of Judah,** *and succeeded him.*[102]

11 When he began to reign, as soon as he had seated himself on his throne, he killed all the house of Baasha; he did not leave him a single male of his kindred or his friends. **¹²Thus Zimri destroyed all the house of Baasha, according to the word of the Lord, which he spoke against Baasha by the prophet Jehu.**[103]

— **¹³because of all the sins of Baasha and the sins of his son Elah that they committed, and that they caused Israel to commit, provoking the Lord God of Israel to anger with their idols.**[104]

Jeroboam's designation is the subject of the Ahijah story. There is no narrative of Baasha's designation, but the brief phrase "since I exalted you" claims such a tradition. Naturally, there is no prophetic designation for Omri, who seized power by violence amid the anarchy of a divided nation.

100. The resumption of the PR from 15:29a; the continuation of the PR in this chapter is to be found in vv. 9-11, 15-18, 21-22, 24, 28, and 31b-32. This v. 6 is an example of the linear succession model in contrast to the synchronistic model; see the note on 1 Kgs 14:20.

101. 16:7 is in stark conflict with 16:1-4. V. 7 rehearses much of the content of vv. 1-4; Baasha was as evil as Jeroboam and his house will pay the price. But the first tradition (vv. 1-4) opens with approval of Baasha's regicide; the second tradition (v. 7) ends with its condemnation. V. 7 condemns Baasha for destroying the house of Jeroboam. V. 2, however, can only be read as an endorsement of Baasha's destruction of the house of Jeroboam. "I exalted you" and "I made you" claim God's action in Baasha's rise to power. Politically, Baasha rose to power by conspiring against Nadab son of Jeroboam and striking him down at Gibbethon and killing "all the house of Jeroboam" (cf. 15:27-29). The incompatibility appears to be beyond resolution. In our judgment, the present text is not served by attempted harmonization. Here two differing traditions are being preserved. The negativity shown the king suggests attribution to the royal focus of the dtr revision.

102. For the attribution of the synchronism alone to the Dtr, see above in the note on 15:29.

103. For the attribution of the fulfillment notice to the Dtr, see the note above on 14:18 (and cf. 15:29). It is appropriate to note that the dtr fulfillment notice in v. 12 relates to the prophecy attributed to the Dtr in vv. 1-4. For Noth, the Dtr has taken 16:9-12 from the Chronicles of the Kings of Israel. In fact, much of what we attribute to the PR in reporting this turbulent period in the history of the northern Israelite monarchy is recognized by Noth as older tradition and attributed to these chronicles (cf. vv. 15-18, 21-22, 24, 31; also v. 34).

104. There is no judgment formula for Elah. V. 13 resumes the sins of both Baasha and Elah; somehow it acts as a substitute for Elah's judgment formula. The dtr prophecy, in vv. 1-4, places the responsibility for the failure of the dynasty on Baasha; here the responsibility is laid upon Elah as well as Baasha. The language and the negativity toward the kings suggest

---

Main pre-DH: *Prophetic Record*	Other pre-DH: single sideline	HKL: + single underline	**Josianic DH: from the Dtr**

¹⁴Now the rest of the acts of Elah, and all that he did, are they not written in the Book of the Annals of the Kings of Israel?

15 In the twenty-seventh year of King Asa of Judah, Zimri reigned seven days in Tirzah. *Now the troops were encamped against Gibbethon, which belonged to the Philistines,* ¹⁶*and the troops who were encamped heard it said, "Zimri has conspired, and he has killed the king"; therefore all Israel made Omri, the commander of the army, king over Israel that day in the camp.* ¹⁷*So Omri went up from Gibbethon, and all Israel with him, and they besieged Tirzah.* ¹⁸*When Zimri saw that the city was taken, he went into the citadel of the king's house; he burned down the king's house over himself with fire, and died.*

—¹⁹**because of the sins that he committed, doing evil in the sight of the Lord, walking in the way of Jeroboam, and for the sin that he committed, causing Israel to sin.**¹⁰⁵

²⁰Now the rest of the acts of Zimri, and the conspiracy that he made, are they not written in the Book of the Annals of the Kings of Israel?

21 Then the people of Israel were divided into two parts; half of the people followed Tibni son of Ginath, to make him king, and half followed Omri. ²²*But the people who followed Omri overcame the people who followed Tibni son of Ginath; so Tibni died, and Omri became king.* ²³In the thirty-first year of King Asa of Judah, Omri began to reign over Israel; he reigned for twelve years, six of them in Tirzah.

24 He bought the hill of Samaria from Shemer for two talents of silver; he fortified the hill, and called the city that he built, Samaria, after the name of Shemer, the owner of the hill.

25 Omri did what was evil in the sight of the Lord; he did more evil than all who were before him. ²⁶For he walked in all the way of Jeroboam son of Nebat, and in the sins that he caused Israel to commit, **provoking the Lord, the God of Israel, to anger by their idols.** ²⁷Now the rest of the acts of Omri that he did, and the power that he showed, are they not written in the Book of the Annals of the Kings of Israel? ²⁸*Omri slept with his ancestors, and was buried in Samaria; his son Ahab succeeded him.*¹⁰⁶

29 In the thirty-eighth year of King Asa of Judah, Ahab son of Omri began to reign over Israel; Ahab son of Omri reigned over Israel in Samaria twenty-two years. ³⁰Ahab son of Omri did evil in the sight of the Lord more than all who were before him.

31 And as if it had been a light thing for him to walk in the sins of Jeroboam son of Nebat,¹⁰⁷

---

attribution to the dtr revision's royal focus. The "idols" language in this context is rare; see Deut 32:21; 1 Kgs 16:13, 26; 2 Kgs 17:15 (sing.); Jer 2:5 (phrase identical with 2 Kgs 17:15); 8:19b.

Dietrich attributed 16:1-4, 12 to his DtrP and 16:13 to his DtrN.

105. As for Elah, for Zimri no judgment formula is given. V. 19 offers a substitute for such a judgment formula, rehearsing in general terms the standard accusations against the northern kings. The dtr revision's royal focus is the favored candidate for the attribution.

106. Verse 26b uses the late language of provoking to anger (see note on 14:1-18); for the idols, see v. 13 above. V. 28 is a good example of the linear succession model functioning within the PR.

107. **Text signals** in vv. 31-33. (i) Vv. 31-33 are not set apart by ideology or language. (ii) The proper name of Ahab occurs three times in vv. 29-30 and twice in v. 33; the name does not occur at all in vv. 31-32. (iii) The marriage to Jezebel and the aspects of Baal worship correlate with what is to come in the

---

Elijah narrative. (iv) Although the NRSV's "also" is not in the Hebrew text, it reflects the reality that v. 33a stands outside what can be read as a complete sentence in v. 32, concluding with the location in Samaria. (v) The comparison with "all" in v. 30 becomes a comparison with "all the kings of Israel" in v. 33b.

Text-history approach. Attribution of vv. 31b-32 to the PR prepares for the enmity between Ahab and Elijah (see 18:17-18). If, on the other hand—as is possible since they are not set apart by ideology or language—vv. 31b-32 followed v. 31a as dtr, the Elijah narrative would be understood to have assumed the enmity as part of the tradition. As noted above, the occurrences of the proper name Ahab suggest that at least vv. 31-32 depend (in whole or in part) either on v. 28 or on vv. 29-30; vv. 33-34, with the recurrence of the proper name, are likely to be additions. Our proposal, in the text formatting, represents the earlier possibility: the PR reported Ahab's succession to the throne of his father and his marriage to Jezebel and his worship of Baal. Alternatively, and quite possibly, this material could derive from the Dtr, anticipating the stories to come.

For v. 33a, the earliest attribution would be in association with the negative traditions about Jezebel in the material to come. "A sacred pole" (NRSV) is literally "the Asherah"; Jezebel is portrayed as a devotee of the goddess Asherah (cf. 18:19b). A later date is possible.

For v. 33b, attribution to later editing reflects its repetition of the comparison from v. 30 and the issue of provoking YHWH to anger. The sharpening of the comparison to specify "the kings of Israel" makes its attribution appropriate to the royal focus within the dtr revision with its hostility to the kings.

Present-text potential. The report of accession and the formula of judgment (vv. 29-30) are provided for Ahab before the introduction of the extensive Elijah cycle. The two comparisons (v. 30b and v. 33b) form an inclusion, framing Ahab's evil deeds in vv. 31-33a. It is appropriate that these evil deeds be noted in brief summary before the extensive narrative of Elijah, Ahab's prophetic foe.

With 1 Kings 17, the massive Elijah-Elisha narrative cycle begins. It will lead to the rejection of Ahab and the condemnation of his dynasty (1 Kings 21). The elimination of the dynasty will be completed by Jehu (2 Kings 9–10). At stake in these narratives is the religious identity of Israel: in a minimal scenario, whether Baal can coexist with YHWH as a god in Israel; in a maximal scenario, whether Baal or YHWH is to be the sole god of Israel.

The existence of such a narrative cycle involves both assumptions and knowledge on our part. We know that a wealth of traditions existed, not all of which has come down to us (see the complexity of 1 Kings 21, 2 Kings 9-10, and the interrelationships involved). We assume that such a cycle had a life of its own, acquiring stories and shedding stories. It would be naive and arrogant of us to believe that what we have was all there ever was. The understanding on which much of our analysis of this cycle is based is that the cycle was focused on the figure of Elijah and that the PR was focused on the interaction of prophets with kings. Elijah's confrontation with Ahab centers on the Carmel episode and the story of Naboth's vineyard. As these traditions became text and document, further stories would have been attracted to the figure of Elijah.

Before the introduction of Elijah, the text sets up the three great forces for evil in northern Israel: Jeroboam, Omri, and Ahab. In southern eyes, Jeroboam set up the sinful structures that ultimately destroyed the north; in dtr eyes, he was guilty both of apostasy and the abandonment of Jerusalem, two choices that were never reversed. Jeroboam was worse than all his predecessors (1 Kgs 14:9); dtr rhetoric may have Solomon in mind (cf. 1 Kgs 11:4, 6). Omri, founder of Samaria, the long-term northern capital, is portrayed as worse (16:25); his origins remain uncertain (cf. 16:16). Worst of all is Ahab, singled out in 16:30 and 33, identified with the commitment to Baal worship in Israel; he is portrayed as building on the foundations of Jeroboam and as institutionalizing the worship of Baal in Israel (16:31-32). The evil portrayed is not social injustice; it is the issue of religious infidelity, touching the identity of Israel. The references to

Main pre-DH:	Other pre-DH:	HKL: + single	**Josianic DH:**
Prophetic Record	single sideline	underline	**from the Dtr**

And he (Heb.; NRSV, he) *took as his wife Jezebel daughter of King Ethbaal of the Sidonians, and went and served Baal, and worshiped him. ³²He erected an altar for Baal in the house of Baal, which he built in Samaria.*[108]

³³Ahab also made a sacred pole.

> **Ahab did more to provoke the anger of the LORD, the God of Israel, than had all the kings of Israel who were before him.**

> ³⁴In his days Hiel of Bethel built Jericho; he laid its foundation at the cost of Abiram his firstborn, and set up its gates at the cost of his youngest son Segub, according to the word of the LORD, which he spoke by Joshua son of Nun.[109]

17 *Now Elijah the Tishbite, of Tishbe in Gilead, said to Ahab, "As the LORD the God of Israel lives, before whom I stand, there shall be neither dew nor rain these years, except by my word."*[110]

Jezebel, Baal, and Asherah all prepare the way for what is to come: the confrontation on which the destiny of Israel is to depend.

We cannot overlook the sequence in 2 Kgs 10:28-29, where Jehu "wiped out Baal from Israel" and "did not turn aside from the sins of Jeroboam." The two can, therefore, be viewed differently. In this extensive Elijah cycle, we may have—in the first instance, at least—a power struggle operating on two levels, political and religious. Politically, the house of Omri faces a challenge from the military, in the person of Jehu. Religiously, the prophets of Baal and Asherah, under the patronage of Ahab and Jezebel (cf. 1 Kgs 18:19), face a challenge from Elijah, as the last of the YHWH prophets. From one point of view, perhaps, the foreign imports face a challenge from the local forces. We say "in the first instance" because in such power struggles the destiny of Israel is still at stake. Local issues of orthodoxy may be temporarily in abeyance.

108. The continuation of the PR is to be found at 17:1. The Hebrew of v. 31 can be clearly read as two sentences, with v. 28 followed by v. 31b, as formatted here for the PR. A translation of the present combined text can be equally accommodated to the rules of Hebrew syntax.

109. This annalistic note might have been added at any time once a text concerning Ahab existed; the reference is to Josh 6:26. For Noth, the Dtr took 16:34 from the Chronicles of the Kings of Israel; Dietrich attributed the insertion of 16:34 to his DtrP. Its location at the end of the chapter might favor a late attribution; alternatively, the loose connection with Ahab ("in his days") might suggest that it appropriately be placed last. The dotted sideline emphasizes this uncertainty.

110. Resumption of the PR from 16:32. The continuation of the PR is to be found at 18:2b.

The justification for the presence of the PR reflects three realities. First, while not impossible it is improbable that as extensive a prophetic collection as the Elijah cycle, concerning so significant a figure in the realm of prophecy, should not be touched in some way by the PR with its concern for the activity of the prophets in relation to the kings. Naturally, such a consideration carries no demonstrative weight whatsoever. Second, however, there is Elijah's role in condemning the house of Ahab and the language in which that condemnation is expressed. Third, there is the role played by Elisha's disciple and the language in which that is expressed, along with the appeal in 2 Kings 9-10 to Elijah's prophecy. These factors are significantly weighty.

When proposing a hypothetical text, there is prudence in being guided by the work of others that is quite independent of any such hypothesis. The investigation of the PR in the Elijah cycle was and is guided by and principally indebted to the specialist studies of Georg Hentschel, *Die Elijaerzählungen*, and O. H. Steck, *Überlieferung und Zeitgeschichte in den Elia-Erzählungen*—cf. Campbell, *Of Prophets and Kings*, 93.

| After the Dtr: indented and sans serif font | ***Revision:*** ***royal focus*** | *Revision:* *national focus* | Other: double sideline |

²The word of the Lord came to him, saying, ³"Go from here and turn eastward, and hide yourself by the Wadi Cherith, which is east of the Jordan. ⁴You shall drink from the wadi, and I have commanded the ravens to feed you there." ⁵So he went and did according to the word of the Lord; he went and lived by the Wadi Cherith, which is east of the Jordan. ⁶The ravens brought him bread and meat in the morning, and bread and meat in the evening; and he drank from the wadi. ⁷But after a while the wadi dried up, because there was no rain in the land.¹¹¹

8 Then the word of the Lord came to him, saying, ⁹"Go now to Zarephath, which belongs to Sidon, and live there; for I have commanded a widow there to feed you." ¹⁰So he set out and

---

Specific details may be found in *Of Prophets and Kings*, but it is our desire that the present volume should contain the basic information needed. As part of the life of the cycle, we will encounter additions that emphasize Jezebel's role pejoratively; the PR appears to antedate these.

17:1 sets the scene for the Elijah cycle with the identification of Elijah the Tishbite and the prospect of a drought, under the prophet's control. At the level of the PR, only two Elijah stories are involved here: first, the confrontation on Mount Carmel, with yhwh's triumph over Baal, the end of the drought, and Elijah's move to Jezreel; second, the story of the alienation of Naboth's vineyard in Jezreel. The narrative moves from the prophetic control of the famine, to the encounter with Obadiah and Ahab, and the confrontation on Mount Carmel and yhwh's triumph over Baal, culminating in the slaughter of the Baal prophets, the breaking of the drought, and Elijah's superhuman run to Jezreel (18:46). The stage is then set for the story of Ahab's judicial murder of Naboth and seizure of his vineyard, with the consequent condemnation of Ahab and his dynasty. This condemnation will ultimately become effective in Jehu's revolt.

Around this core, as noted above, a number of Elijah traditions appear to have accumulated. Without going too painstakingly into detail, the evidence for this accumulation will be noted in each case. The meaning of the present text emerging from this process of accumulation will be addressed as appropriate.

---

111. 17:2–18:2a is focused on the figure of the prophet rather than the confrontation with either the king or the prophets. With Hentschel (and against Steck), it seems reasonable to delimit this later material as vv. 2-7 (Elijah's being cared for by the ravens at the Wadi Cherith), vv. 8-16 (Elijah's being cared for by the widow at Sidon), and vv. 17-24 (Elijah's care for the widow's son).

18:1-2a presents the end of the drought as decided before any commitment to yhwh on Israel's part. It anticipates the story to come. The drought story, begun in 17:1, has become inextricably bound up with the confrontation-on-Carmel story in which Israel makes the choice for commitment to yhwh; only after this commitment is the end of the drought narrated. It is worth noting that in the material attributed to the PR, Elijah acts on his own authority; in 17:2—18:2a, on the other hand, it is the word of the Lord that prompts Elijah's actions (17:2, 8; 18:1).

Dietrich attributed to his DtrP the insertion of 17:2-24, with the addition of 17:2-4, 5a, 8-9, 14aα* and 18:1-2a.

Regarding the **present-text potential** (17:1–18:2), the material enhances the figure of the prophet, as cared for by God (vv. 2-7), doing God's will (vv. 8-10), whose word comes true (vv. 11-16), and whose exercise of power brings recognition and acknowledgment (v. 24: "Now I know that you are a man of God, and that the word of the Lord in your mouth is truth."). This presentation prepares appropriately for the coming confrontation with the prophets of Baal (who is to be god in Israel?) and the power of the state (who is to be king in Israel?). For the former, see the **present-text potential** note on 19:21, and for the latter on 22:40.

Main pre-DH:	Other pre-DH:	HKL: + single	**Josianic DH:**
Prophetic Record	single sideline	underline	**from the Dtr**

went to Zarephath. When he came to the gate of the town, a widow was there gathering sticks; he called to her and said, "Bring me a little water in a vessel, so that I may drink." [11]As she was going to bring it, he called to her and said, "Bring me a morsel of bread in your hand." [12]But she said, "As the LORD your God lives, I have nothing baked, only a handful of meal in a jar, and a little oil in a jug; I am now gathering a couple of sticks, so that I may go home and prepare it for myself and my son, that we may eat it, and die." [13]Elijah said to her, "Do not be afraid; go and do as you have said; but first make me a little cake of it and bring it to me, and afterwards make something for yourself and your son. [14]For thus says the LORD the God of Israel: The jar of meal will not be emptied and the jug of oil will not fail until the day that the LORD sends rain on the earth." [15]She went and did as Elijah said, so that she as well as he and her household ate for many days. [16]The jar of meal was not emptied, neither did the jug of oil fail, according to the word of the LORD that he spoke by Elijah.

17 After this the son of the woman, the mistress of the house, became ill; his illness was so severe that there was no breath left in him. [18]She then said to Elijah, "What have you against me, O man of God? You have come to me to bring my sin to remembrance, and to cause the death of my son!" [19]But he said to her, "Give me your son." He took him from her bosom, carried him up into the upper chamber where he was lodging, and laid him on his own bed. [20]He cried out to the LORD, "O LORD my God, have you brought calamity even upon the widow with whom I am staying, by killing her son?" [21]Then he stretched himself upon the child three times, and cried out to the LORD, "O LORD my God, let this child's life come into him again." [22]The LORD listened to the voice of Elijah; the life of the child came into him again, and he revived.

[23]Elijah took the child, brought him down from the upper chamber into the house, and gave him to his mother; then Elijah said, "See, your son is alive." [24]So the woman said to Elijah, "Now I know that you are a man of God, and that the word of the LORD in your mouth is truth."

18 After many days the word of the LORD came to Elijah, in the third year of the drought, saying, "Go, present yourself to Ahab; I will send rain on the earth." [2]So Elijah went to present himself to Ahab.

The famine was severe in Samaria. [3]*Ahab summoned Obadiah, who was in charge of the palace.*[112] (Now Obadiah revered the LORD greatly; [4]when Jezebel was killing off the prophets of the LORD, Obadiah took a hundred prophets, hid them fifty to a cave, and provided them with bread and water.)[113]

[5]*Then Ahab said to Obadiah, "Go through the land to all the springs of water and to all the wadis; perhaps we may find grass to keep the horses and mules alive, and not lose some of the animals." [6]So they divided the land between them to pass through it; Ahab went in one direction by himself, and Obadiah went in another direction by himself.*

---

112. Resumption of the PR from 17:1.

113. 18:3b-4 is associated with 18:12b-14 by the allusion to Jezebel's persecution of the prophets and the emphasis on Obadiah's protection of a hundred. In vv. 3b-4, it is said of Obadiah; in vv. 12b-14 Obadiah says it of himself. Vv. 3b-4 are inserted between Ahab's summons to Obadiah and Ahab's speech to Obadiah. Vv. 12b-14 are worked in with a skillful repetition, v. 14 resuming vv. 11-12a.

This material on Obadiah reflects a tradition in which Jezebel was responsible for the killing of YHWH prophets. This negative focus on Jezebel and her part in Ahab's evil occurs at several points across the Elijah narratives. It opens up possibilities for storytelling; it can also simply damn this foreign princess.

| After the Dtr: indented and sans serif font | **Revision: royal focus** | *Revision: national focus* | Other: double sideline |

7 *As Obadiah was on the way, Elijah met him; Obadiah recognized him, fell on his face, and said, "Is it you, my lord Elijah?"* [8]*He answered him, "It is I. Go, tell your lord that Elijah is here."* [9]*And he said, "How have I sinned, that you would hand your servant over to Ahab, to kill me?* [10]*As the* LORD *your God lives, there is no nation or kingdom to which my lord has not sent to seek you; and when they would say, 'He is not here,' he would require an oath of the kingdom or nation, that they had not found you.* [11]*But now you say, 'Go, tell your lord that Elijah is here.'* [12]*As soon as I have gone from you, the spirit of the* LORD *will carry you I know not where; so, when I come and tell Ahab and he cannot find you, he will kill me.*

although I your servant have revered the LORD from my youth. [13]Has it not been told my lord what I did when Jezebel killed the prophets of the LORD, how I hid a hundred of the LORD's prophets fifty to a cave, and provided them with bread and water? [14]Yet now you say, 'Go, tell your lord that Elijah is here'; he will surely kill me."[114]

[15]*Elijah said, "As the* LORD *of hosts lives, before whom I stand, I will surely show myself to him today."* [16]*So Obadiah went to meet Ahab, and told him; and Ahab went to meet Elijah.*

17 *When Ahab saw Elijah, Ahab said to him, "Is it you, you troubler of Israel?"* [18]*He answered, "I have not troubled Israel, but you have.*

and your father's house, because you have forsaken the commandments of the LORD and followed the Baals.[115]

[19]*Now therefore have all Israel assemble for me at Mount Carmel, with the four hundred fifty prophets of Baal."*

and the four hundred prophets of Asherah, who eat at Jezebel's table."[116]

20 *So Ahab sent to all the Israelites, and assembled the prophets at Mount Carmel.* [21]*Elijah then came near to all the people, and said, "How long will you go limping with two different opinions? If the* LORD *is God, follow him; but if Baal, then follow him." The people did not answer him a word.* [22]*Then Elijah said to the people, "I, even I only, am left a prophet of the* LORD; *but Baal's prophets number four hundred fifty.* [23]*Let two bulls be given to us; let them choose one bull for themselves, cut it in pieces, and lay it on the wood, but put no fire to it; I will prepare the other bull and lay it on the wood, but put no fire to it.* [24]*Then you call on the name of your god and I will call on the name of the* LORD; *the god who answers by fire is indeed God." All the people answered, "Well spoken!"* [25]*Then Elijah said to the prophets of Baal, "Choose for yourselves one bull and prepare it first, for you are many; then call on the name of your god, but put no fire to it."* [26]*So they took the bull that was given them, prepared it, and called on the name of Baal from morning until noon, crying, "O Baal, answer us!" But there was no voice, and no answer. They limped about the altar that they had made.* [27]*At noon Elijah mocked them, saying, "Cry aloud! Surely*

---

114. See above, on 18:3b-4.

115. The latter part of v. 18 is problematic. The reference to "your father's house" is uncertain. Omri, Ahab's father, is not accused of Baal worship; a reference to the house of Ahab—Ahab, Ahaziah, and Joram—could betray the interests of a later (dtr ?) hand. In v. 18b, the first part (forsaking) is in the

plural; the second part (following) is in the singular. "Forsaking YHWH" is a favored accusation from the dtr revision's national focus. "Following Baal" might come from the same (cf. Deut 4:3b). While possible, this attribution is not certain. The plural might include Omri, with the singular referring to Ahab; otherwise, the alternation is unexplained.

116. An addition offering an anti-Jezebel variant. There is no subsequent reference to these prophets of Asherah. The variant opens up the possibility of exploiting this aspect in telling the story.

Main pre-DH:	Other pre-DH:	HKL: + single	**Josianic DH:**
Prophetic Record	single sideline	underline	**from the Dtr**

he is a god; either he is meditating, or he has wandered away, or he is on a journey, or perhaps he is asleep and must be awakened." ²⁸Then they cried aloud and, as was their custom, they cut themselves with swords and lances until the blood gushed out over them. ²⁹As midday passed, they raved on until the time of the offering of the oblation, but there was no voice, no answer, and no response.

30 Then Elijah said to all the people, "Come closer to me"; and all the people came closer to him. First he repaired the altar of the LORD that had been thrown down; ³¹Elijah took twelve stones, according to the number of the tribes of the sons of Jacob, to whom the word of the LORD came, saying, "Israel shall be your name"; ³²with the stones he built an altar in the name of the LORD. Then he made a trench around the altar, large enough to contain two measures of seed. ³³Next he put the wood in order, cut the bull in pieces, and laid it on the wood. He said, "Fill four jars with water and pour it on the burnt offering and on the wood." ³⁴Then he said, "Do it a second time"; and they did it a second time. Again he said, "Do it a third time"; and they did it a third time, ³⁵so that the water ran all around the altar, and filled the trench also with water.

36 At the time of the offering of the oblation, the prophet Elijah came near and said, "O LORD, God of Abraham, Isaac, and Israel,[117] let it be known this day that you are God in Israel, that I am your servant, and that I have done all these things at your bidding. ³⁷Answer me, O LORD, answer me, so that this people may know that you, O LORD, are God, and that you have turned their hearts back." ³⁸Then the fire of the LORD fell and consumed the burnt offering, the wood, the stones, and the dust, and even licked up the water that was in the trench. ³⁹When all the people saw it, they fell on their faces and said,

"The LORD indeed is God; the LORD indeed is God." ⁴⁰Elijah said to them, "Seize the prophets of Baal; do not let one of them escape." Then they seized them; and Elijah brought them down to the Wadi Kishon, and killed them there.

41 Elijah said to Ahab, "Go up, eat and drink; for there is a sound of rushing rain." ⁴²So Ahab went up to eat and to drink.[118]
Elijah went up to the top of Carmel; there he bowed himself down upon the earth and put his face between his knees.
⁴³He said to his servant, "Go up now, look toward the sea." He went up and looked, and said, "There is nothing." Then he said, "Go again seven times." ⁴⁴At the seventh time he said, "Look, a little cloud no bigger than a person's hand is rising out of the sea." Then he said, "Go say to Ahab, 'Harness your chariot and go down before the rain stops you.'"
⁴⁵In a little while the heavens grew black with clouds and wind; there was a heavy rain. Ahab rode off and went to Jezreel. ⁴⁶But the hand of the LORD was on

---

117. Cf. Hos 12:13 (NRSV, 12:12); note also 1 Chron 29:18; 2 Chron 30:6.

118. Together with vv. 43-44, vv. 41-42a reflect various ways in which the end of the drought story might have been told, beyond what is already in vv. 42b, 45-46. In v. 41a and 42a, there is emphasis on Ahab's eating and drinking ("go up": the drought and famine are about to end) and in v. 41b the rain is imminent. In vv. 43-44, there is a servant on the scene (not present earlier) and the rain is far from imminent. V. 44b could belong with v. 45, but the presence of the servant associates it with v. 43. V. 42b makes no mention of any servant; Elijah "went up" because v. 40 had him in the Wadi Kishon. V. 45 has Ahab leave Mount Carmel; without vv. 41-42a, he will have been there since v. 20. V. 46 gives symbolic expression to Elijah's triumph over Ahab.

In the present text, the servant is left behind in 19:3 and replaced by Elisha in 19:21. In the Elisha cycle, Elisha's servant, Gehazi, figures prominently (2 Kings 4; 5; 8:1-6).

After the Dtr:	**Revision:**	Revision:	Other:
indented and sans serif font	**royal focus**	national focus	double sideline

Elijah; he girded up his loins and ran in front of Ahab to the entrance of Jezreel.[119]

19 Ahab told Jezebel all that Elijah had done, and how he had killed all the prophets with the sword. [2]Then Jezebel sent a messenger to Elijah, saying, "So may the gods do to me, and more also, if I do not make your life like the life of one of them by this time tomorrow." [3]Then he was afraid; he got up and fled for his life, and came to Beer-sheba, which belongs to Judah *[note: possibly replacing a northern location in a hypothetical early text]*; he left his servant there.[120]

---

119. The continuation of the PR is to be found at 21:1.

120. 1 Kgs 19:1-21 belongs to another prophetic tradition altogether; it is not to be attributed to the PR. There is no confrontation with Ahab; instead, the hostility is from Jezebel. There is no trace of the theme of drought or famine. Instead of the triumph achieved on Mount Carmel in conflict with Ahab, the narrative portrays a sense of Elijah's loss of nerve in conflict with Jezebel.

Elijah's encounter with God at Horeb, source of Israel's spiritual energy, reinvigorates the prophet and reasserts God's control over Israel's destiny (19:15-18). In the chapter, however, Israel has forsaken YHWH (19:10) rather than committed itself to YHWH (18:39). Israel has "killed your prophets with the sword" (19:10); in the preceding text, only Jezebel has been mentioned as killer of prophets (18:4, 13). As it stands, chap. 19 also clashes with the rest of the Elijah-Elisha cycle. According to vv. 15-16, Elijah is to anoint Hazael, Jehu, and Elisha; in the following narrative, Elijah does none of these things.

The origins of this chapter are unquestionably complex (cf. for example, Jones, *Kings*, 2.326-28). A further overview is appropriate for the question of the unity of the chapter.

Text signals. (i) Elijah's flight from Jezebel is said to take him to "Beer-sheba, which belongs to Judah."

4 But he himself went a day's journey into the wilderness, and came and sat down under a solitary broom tree. He asked that he might die: "It is enough; now, O LORD, take away my life, for I am no better than

---

(ii) The specification of Beer-sheba here as belonging to Judah is unique in the OT. (iii) The contents of the exchange between YHWH and Elijah in vv. 9b-10 are repeated verbatim in vv. 13b-14. (iv) The three commissions given Elijah by YHWH in vv. 15-18—anoint Hazael, Jehu, and Elisha—are not carried out in the subsequent text. (v) The enlisting of Elisha which follows immediately (vv. 19-21) does not involve anointing. (vi) Elisha is said to "serve" Elijah (v. 21) and so replaces the "young man" (*na'ar*) left in v. 3.

Text-history approach. It is possible that the core of the chapter involves the enlisting of Elisha as Elijah's disciple and servant. The tradition that Elijah had a servant is found also in 18:43-44. The servant would be dismissed in 19:3 and Elisha enlisted in 19:19-21. Supporting this is the use of "there" (*šām*) in both v. 3 and v. 19. But there is a grave difficulty. V. 3 has the servant left in Beer-sheba and Elisha ben Shaphat does not come from Judah. The only reference to his origin in Abel-meholah is in the highly unhistorical vv. 15-18, but there is no reason to doubt that Elisha is a northerner. The presence of Beer-sheba in 19:3 is most likely associated with the following Horeb traditions; Elijah is understood to have left his servant there, on his way to Horeb. If a sequence is assumed from 19:1-3 to 19:19-21, almost certainly another place name must be assumed in v. 3 instead of Beer-sheba. Such an assumption, however, has no support in the manuscripts.

The repetition of vv. 9b-10 and vv. 13b-14 can be understood as an editorial signal indicating the insertion of vv. 11-13a, an insertion that is highly intelligible. It heightens and solemnizes YHWH's intervention at Horeb. Prior to this insertion being made, the text from vv. 4-9a and vv. 15-18 took Elijah to Horeb where, in the face of Jezebel's persecution, he is com-

---

Main pre-DH:	Other pre-DH:	HKL: + single	**Josianic DH:**
Prophetic Record	single sideline	underline	**from the Dtr**

my ancestors." ⁵Then he lay down under the broom tree and fell asleep. Suddenly an angel touched him and said to him, "Get up and eat." ⁶He looked, and there at his head was a cake baked on hot stones, and a jar

of water. He ate and drank, and lay down again. ⁷The angel of the LORD came a second time, touched him, and said, "Get up and eat, otherwise the journey will be too much for you." ⁸He got up, and ate and drank; then he went in the strength of that food forty days and forty nights to Horeb the mount of God. ⁹At that place he came to a cave, and spent the night there.

Then the word of the LORD came to him, saying, "What are you doing here, Elijah?" ¹⁰He answered, "I have been very zealous for the LORD, the God of hosts; for the Israelites have forsaken your covenant, thrown down your altars, and killed your prophets with the sword. I alone am left, and they are seeking my life, to take it away."

11 He said, "Go out and stand on the mountain before the LORD, for the LORD is about to pass by." Now there was a great wind, so strong that it was splitting mountains and breaking rocks in pieces before the LORD, but the LORD was not in the wind; and after the wind an earthquake, but the LORD was not in the earthquake; ¹²and after the earthquake a fire, but the LORD was not

---

missioned by YHWH to anoint Hazael, Jehu, and Elisha. In this text, despite the differences from subsequent reports, the whole subsequent disposition of history is placed under YHWH's direct control and mandate. The insertion (vv. 11-13a) emphasizes the mysteriousness of God's communication.

Finally, the reference to "Beer-sheba, which belongs to Judah" can be understood as a substitution needed to introduce the theme of Elijah's journey to Horeb.

While all this is hypothetical, without any support in the manuscripts or versions, it allows some sense to be made of an otherwise very difficult text. It is understandable that the subsequent developments should be brought under YHWH's authority. The language of anointing was probably best suited to the purpose, even though it did not correspond with what was reported in the following traditions. Precision would have been intolerably unwieldy. This commission from God at Horeb had, of course, to precede its implementation, so to precede the enlisting of Elisha. Hence the commission's location in this place in the text.

Present-text potential. In the present text, vv. 4-18 overwhelm what might have been an early core. Two elements stand out now in this chapter. First, the commission from God is received at Horeb, the place of Israel's original and intimate encounter with its God, under Moses. Second, the subsequent unfolding of events, from Elisha through Jehu to Hazael, is under the mandate and authority of YHWH. What is to come in the immediate future is not a deviation from Israel's destiny, revealed to Moses. Rather, the work of Elijah and Elisha is a reinforcement of Israel's destiny, in continuity with and fidelity to the God of Sinai (contrast the unfavorable view of Elijah in J. T. Walsh, *1 Kings*, 264–82).

Two aspects of the present text need noting. The repetition of Elijah's self-description in vv. 9b-10 and 13b-14 creates an ambiguity. At one level, despite the meeting with God of vv. 11-13a, for Elijah nothing changes. At another level, Elijah is reinvigorated for the confrontation with Ahab in 1 Kings 21. The formulation of the divine commission in vv. 15-18 creates another ambiguity. At the level of the manner of the commission ("anoint"), nothing happens; Elijah does not anoint any of the three. At the level of the matter, everything happens; Hazael, Jehu, and Elisha are well and truly involved in the subsequent developments for Israel.

| After the Dtr:
indented and sans serif font | *Revision:*
royal focus | *Revision:*
national focus | Other:
double sideline |

in the fire; and after the fire a sound of sheer silence. [13]When Elijah heard it, he wrapped his face in his mantle and went out and stood at the entrance of the cave. Then there came a voice to him that said, "What are you doing here, Elijah?" [14]He answered, "I have been very zealous for the LORD, the God of hosts; for the Israelites have forsaken your covenant, thrown down your altars, and killed your prophets with the sword. I alone am left, and they are seeking my life, to take it away."

[15]Then the LORD said to him, "Go, return on your way to the wilderness of Damascus; when you arrive, you shall anoint Hazael as king over Aram. [16]Also you shall anoint Jehu son of Nimshi as king over Israel; and you shall anoint Elisha son of Shaphat of Abel-meholah as prophet in your place. [17]Whoever escapes from the sword of Hazael, Jehu shall kill; and whoever escapes from the sword of Jehu, Elisha shall kill. [18]Yet I will leave seven thousand in Israel, all the knees that have not bowed to Baal, and every mouth that has not kissed him."[121]

[19]So he set out from there, and found Elisha son of Shaphat, who was plowing. There were twelve yoke of oxen ahead of him, and he was with the twelfth. Elijah passed by him and threw his mantle over him. [20]He left the oxen, ran after Elijah, and said, "Let me kiss my father and my mother, and then I will follow you." Then Elijah said to him, "Go back again; for what have I done to you?" [21]He returned from following him, took the yoke of oxen, and slaughtered them; using the equipment from the oxen, he boiled their flesh, and gave it to the people, and they ate. Then he set out and followed Elijah, and became his servant.[122]

---

121. Whatever of the origin of the traditions constituting vv. 4-18, the issue must be addressed of their present formulation and their incorporation into the DH. Elijah's self-description (vv. 10 and 14) contains two elements that can scarcely be pre-dtr. The term for covenant (*bĕrît*), naming the relationship between YHWH and Israel, is almost non-existent in the DH before later revisions and secondary material (prescinding from references to the ark). The verb "abandon/forsake" (*'āzab*), naming Israel's apostasy from YHWH, is equally late in the DH. Both terms are present in Elijah's self-description (19:10, 14). It would not be responsible to suggest that this material was given its present formulation before the Dtr.

It is not unlikely that "covenant" replaces an original "you" in 19:10, 14. The differences in the LXX for vv. 10 and 14 point in the direction of alterations to the text or variations in the tradition (i.e., LXX has "you" in v. 10 and in v. 14 some MSS. have "you" and some "your covenant"). It might have been realized that forsaking the covenant was less severe than "forsaking you," with its implication of a breach in the relationship with God. It is worth emphasizing that covenant is only one way in which Israel's relationship with God is expressed. The covenant may be spoken of as broken, the relationship never—with the sole exception of Hos 1:9, immediately restored in 2:1-3 (NRSV, 1:10–2:1). The use of "abandon/forsake" means that changes in the text regarding covenant are unlikely to affect its date of origin.

Both passages, and the material in which they are embedded, make eminent sense for the disaster after Josiah. Whatever their origin, these traditions have the potential to be enormously encouraging for supporters of the Josianic reform after it collapsed under Egyptian pressure and, presumably, Israel's acquiescence if not approval.

122. **Present-text potential** of chaps. 18–19. There is a striking and surprising contrast between these two chapters. In chap. 18, Elijah triumphs over the prophets of Baal and Ahab, the troubler of Israel; on Mount Carmel, he wins the absolute allegiance of

---

Main pre-DH:	Other pre-DH:	HKL: + single	**Josianic DH:**
Prophetic Record	single sideline	underline	**from the Dtr**

20 King Ben-hadad of Aram gathered all his army together; thirty-two kings were with him, along with horses and chariots. He marched against Samaria, laid siege to it, and attacked it. ²Then he sent messengers into the city to King Ahab of Israel, and said

to him: "Thus says Ben-hadad: ³Your silver and gold are mine; your fairest wives and children also are mine." ⁴The king of Israel answered, "As you say, my lord, O king, I am yours, and all that I have." ⁵The messengers came again and said: "Thus says Ben-hadad: I sent to you, saying, 'Deliver to me your silver and gold, your wives and children'; ⁶nevertheless I will send my servants to you tomorrow about this time, and they shall search your house and the houses of your servants, and lay hands on whatever pleases them, and take it away."[123]

7 Then the king of Israel called all the elders of the land, and said, "Look now! See how this man is seeking trouble; for he sent to me for my wives, my children, my silver, and my gold; and I did not refuse him." ⁸Then all the elders and all the people said to him, "Do not listen or consent." ⁹So he

---

Israel to YHWH. In chap. 19, Elijah is cowed by and flees from Jezebel, queen of Israel and worshiper of Baal; Elijah is the exact opposite of triumphant. The encounter at Horeb brings God to the fore and reasserts God's sovereignty over the destiny of Israel. In the following narrative, while this fulfillment is achieved, the means are quite different.

It would be dishonest not to note that 19:15-18 is in conflict with the surrounding context; it implies massive defection by Israel to the worship of Baal. As noted, it is in conflict with the subsequent narrative; Elijah does not anoint Hazael, Jehu, or Elisha. The attempts to harmonize either the traditions or the events is an option of last resort. Something of this divine destructiveness (19:17) runs as a refrain through the prophetic tradition: e.g., Amos (9:1-4), Hosea (9:11-17), Isaiah (6:11-13, cf. v. 10), Jeremiah (15:1-3), Ezekiel (5:1-4), and Zechariah (13:7-9).

The occurrence here of Horeb is not without significance. The close juxtaposition of intimacy and apostasy—Moses and YHWH, Aaron and the golden calf—at Mount Sinai (Exod 32:1-14) finds an echo in Israel's allegiance to YHWH on Mount Carmel and the sense immediately afterwards of Israel's apostasy and Elijah's isolation.

The realization that 19:4-18 is probably post-Josianic sharpens the impact of this Elijah experience for exilic Israel. The high hopes set on the deuteronomic reform find an echo in Israel's traditions of Moses on Mount Sinai and Elijah on Mount Carmel. The failure of the dtn reform—with the death of Josiah and the apostasy of his sons, Jehoahaz and Jehoiakim—finds its echo in the traditions of Israel's apostasy with the golden calf and Israel's apostasy in Elijah's time (19:10, 14, 18). Yet survival and hope followed on both. So why not for exilic Israel?

---

123. The associated traditions of 1 Kgs 20:1-43, 21:19b, and 22:1-38 represent a view of Ahab and his death that is in contrast with both the PR and the Josianic DH. In both these, Ahab "slept with his ancestors" (22:40), classically accepted as indicating a peaceful death. A violent death is foretold for Ahab in 20:42, further specified in 21:19b, and brought to fulfillment in 22:34-38. The introduction of these traditions into the biblical narrative offers a different understanding of Ahab's end. For this reason, we have treated them as incorporated after the contribution of the Josianic Dtr.

The negative focus on the king makes these traditions candidates for the royal focus within the dtr revision. It may well be that this is the case. In our judgment, however, this indicator is rather too slight for the attribution of over eighty verses of text. Our formatting has, therefore, left the issue of attribution open (indented and with a double sideline).

Dietrich attributed the insertion of 1 Kings 20 to his DtrP.

| After the Dtr:
indented and sans serif font | **Revision:**
royal focus | Revision:
national focus | Other:
double sideline |

said to the messengers of Ben-hadad, "Tell my lord the king: All that you first demanded of your servant I will do; but this thing I cannot do." The messengers left and brought him word again. [10]Ben-hadad sent to him and said, "The gods do so to me, and more also, if the dust of Samaria will provide a handful for each of the people who follow me." [11]The king of Israel answered, "Tell him: One who puts on armor should not brag like one who takes it off." [12]When Ben-hadad heard this message—now he had been drinking with the kings in the booths—he said to his men, "Take your positions!" And they took their positions against the city.

13 Then a certain prophet came up to King Ahab of Israel and said, "Thus says the LORD, Have you seen all this great multitude? Look, I will give it into your hand today; and you shall know that I am the LORD." [14]Ahab said, "By whom?" He said, "Thus says the LORD, By the young men who serve the district governors." Then he said, "Who shall begin the battle?" He answered, "You." [15]Then he mustered the young men who serve the district governors, two hundred thirty-two; after them he mustered all the people of Israel, seven thousand.

16 They went out at noon, while Ben-hadad was drinking himself drunk in the booths, he and the thirty-two kings allied with him. [17]The young men who serve the district governors went out first. Ben-hadad had sent out scouts, and they reported to him, "Men have come out from Samaria." [18]He said, "If they have come out for peace, take them alive; if they have come out for war, take them alive."

19 But these had already come out of the city: the young men who serve the dis-trict governors, and the army that followed them. [20]Each killed his man; the Arameans fled and Israel pursued them, but King Ben-hadad of Aram escaped on a horse with the cavalry. [21]The king of Israel went out, attacked the horses and chariots, and defeated the Arameans with a great slaughter.

22 Then the prophet approached the king of Israel and said to him, "Come, strengthen yourself, and consider well what you have to do; for in the spring the king of Aram will come up against you."

23 The servants of the king of Aram said to him, "Their gods are gods of the hills, and so they were stronger than we; but let us fight against them in the plain, and surely we shall be stronger than they. [24]Also do this: remove the kings, each from his post, and put commanders in place of them; [25]and muster an army like the army that you have lost, horse for horse, and chariot for chariot; then we will fight against them in the plain, and surely we shall be stronger than they." He heeded their voice, and did so.

26 In the spring Ben-hadad mustered the Arameans and went up to Aphek to fight against Israel. [27]After the Israelites had been mustered and provisioned, they went out to engage them; the people of Israel encamped opposite them like two little flocks of goats, while the Arameans filled the country. [28]A man of God approached and said to the king of Israel, "Thus says the LORD: Because the Arameans have said, 'The LORD is a god of the hills but he is not a god of the valleys,' therefore I will give all this great multitude into your hand, and you shall know that I am the LORD." [29]They encamped opposite one another seven days. Then on the seventh day the battle

Main pre-DH:	Other pre-DH:	HKL: + single	**Josianic DH:**
Prophetic Record	single sideline	underline	**from the Dtr**

began; the Israelites killed one hundred thousand Aramean foot soldiers in one day. [30]The rest fled into the city of Aphek; and the wall fell on twenty-seven thousand men that were left.

Ben-hadad also fled, and entered the city to hide. [31]His servants said to him, "Look, we have heard that the kings of the house of Israel are merciful kings; let us put sackcloth around our waists and ropes on our heads, and go out to the king of Israel; perhaps he will spare your life." [32]So they tied sackcloth around their waists, put ropes on their heads, went to the king of Israel, and said, "Your servant Ben-hadad says, 'Please let me live.' " And he said, "Is he still alive? He is my brother." [33]Now the men were watching for an omen; they quickly took it up from him and said, "Yes, Ben-hadad is your brother." Then he said, "Go and bring him." So Ben-hadad came out to him; and he had him come up into the chariot. [34]Ben-hadad said to him, "I will restore the towns that my father took from your father; and you may establish bazaars for yourself in Damascus, as my father did in Samaria." The king of Israel responded, "I will let you go on those terms." So he made a treaty with him and let him go.

35 At the command of the LORD a certain member of a company of prophets said to another, "Strike me!" But the man refused to strike him. [36]Then he said to him, "Because you have not obeyed the voice of the LORD, as soon as you have left me, a lion will kill you." And when he had left him, a lion met him and killed him. [37]Then he found another man and said, "Strike me!" So the man hit him, striking and wounding him. [38]Then the prophet departed, and waited for the king along the road, disguis-

ing himself with a bandage over his eyes. [39]As the king passed by, he cried to the king and said, "Your servant went out into the thick of the battle; then a soldier turned and brought a man to me, and said, 'Guard this man; if he is missing, your life shall be given for his life, or else you shall pay a talent of silver.' [40]While your servant was busy here and there, he was gone." The king of Israel said to him, "So shall your judgment be; you yourself have decided it." [41]Then he quickly took the bandage away from his eyes. The king of Israel recognized him as one of the prophets. [42]Then he said to him, "Thus says the LORD, 'Because you have let the man go whom I had devoted to destruction, therefore your life shall be for his life, and your people for his people.' " [43]The king of Israel set out toward home, resentful and sullen, and came to Samaria.

21 *Later the following events took place: Naboth the Jezreelite had a vineyard in Jezreel, beside the palace of King Ahab of Samaria.* [2]*And Ahab said to Naboth, "Give me your vineyard, so that I may have it for a vegetable garden, because it is near my house; I will give you a better vineyard for it; or, if it seems good to you, I will give you its value in money."* [3]*But Naboth said to Ahab, "The LORD forbid that I should give you my ancestral inheritance."* [4]*Ahab went home resentful and sullen because of what Naboth the Jezreelite had said to him; for he had said, "I will not give you my ancestral inheritance." He lay down on his bed, turned away his face, and would not eat.*[124]

---

124. Resumption of the PR from 18:46.

Text signals in 1 Kings 21. (i) There is a story that runs through to v. 16 and a prophecy that follows it. (ii) It can be argued that vv. 7b, 9-10, and 11b-13 repeat some elements that are already in the narrative and constitute a heightened emphasis on the negative

---

| After the Dtr: indented and sans serif font | **Revision: royal focus** | *Revision: national focus* | Other: double sideline |

5 His wife Jezebel came to him and said, "Why are you so depressed that you will not eat?" 6He said to her, "Because I spoke to Naboth the Jezreelite and said to him, 'Give me your vineyard for money; or else, if you prefer, I will give you another vineyard *for it'; but he answered, 'I will not give you my vineyard.' " 7His wife Jezebel said to him, "Do you now govern Israel? Get up, eat some food, and be cheerful; I will give you the vineyard of Naboth the Jezreelite."*

role of Jezebel. (iii) V. 19 contains two parallel formulas of prophetic address to Ahab; the first is followed by an accusation, the second by an announcement. (iv) Following on the accusation and announcement in v. 19, there is a further accusation against Ahab in v. 20 and a further announcement for Ahab within vv. 21-24. (v) V. 23, within the announcement of vv. 21-24, contains a new introduction and an announcement of YHWH against Jezebel. (vi) In the present text, the sequence of vv. 20 and 21 means that the announcement against Ahab (vv. 21-22, 24) is presented as a word of Elijah—which is highly unusual. (vii) V. 25a repeats the identical accusation of v. 20; v. 25b adds Jezebel's urging and v. 26 adds Ahab's apostasy. (viii) Vv. 27-29 are in harmony with 22:40 and in conflict with 22:37. The verses have been the subject of considerable controversy. The verb "humble himself" (nifal of *kāna'*) occurs, apart from Chronicles, in the following: Lev 26:41; Judg 3:30; 8:28; 11:33; 1 Sam 7:13; 2 Kgs 22:19; Ps 106:42; in the hifil, there are: Deut 9:3; Judg 4:23; 2 Sam 8:1; Job 40:12; Pss 81:15; 107:12; Isa 25:5; Neh 9:24. The spread precludes any conclusions, except that the term is not dtr.

Text-history approach. Verses 7b, 9-10, and 11b-13 do strongly emphasize the negative role of Jezebel; they do not necessarily form a separate rendering of the story (despite Hentschel, *Elijaerzählungen*, 151-53; Campbell, *Of Prophets and Kings*, 97, n. 78). That some elements negative to Jezebel have been added elsewhere from tradition (i.e., within 18:3b-4, 12b-14; and 18:19b; within 19:1-2; and 21:23; 2 Kgs 9:7b, 10, 36b-37) does not mean that a coherent anti-Jezebel editing has been performed. For example, we see the earlier of these as pre-dtr and the last four as dtr.

Within the prophecy, the material attributed to the PR has the same view of the prophet's role and power that is found elsewhere in the PR; this attribution avoids the repetition in v. 19 and the problems of v. 20.

The prophetic material is comparable to that within 1 Kgs 14:1-18 (for Jeroboam) and 2 Kgs 9:1-10 (for Jehu). In our judgment, there is a core of pre-dtr material in all these passages (cf. Campbell, *Of Prophets and Kings*, 23-41 and Table II there); the subsequent dtr editing is clearly identifiable.

Where vv. 27-29 are concerned, there is no characteristically dtr language evident and no good reason requiring later attribution. The parallels with the royal pleading of David (2 Sam 12:15b-17) and Hezekiah (2 Kgs 20:1-6) and with the sequence both of Saul and Solomon (Saul: transfer to David after Saul's death; Solomon: transfer named by the Dtr as postponement, 1 Kgs 11:34) make a pre-dtr attribution likely. Within the biblical text, the manner of Ahab's death remains uncertain (cf. 22:37 and 40).

Within vv. 22-23, the text attributed to the Dtr (i.e., vv. 22aβ-23) deals with the house of Baasha, the provocation of God, and the fate of Jezebel. The pronouncement concerning Baasha and his house has been discussed at 1 Kgs 16:1-4; it is most plausibly attributed to the Dtr. The same is to be said of the subsequent references (here and 2 Kgs 9:9). The provocation of YHWH to anger is a motif common to both focuses of the dtr revision. Here it may be original to the Dtr or it may be a precision from later dtr revision. It is unusual in that it uses "cause to sin" in a singular address (so 1 Kgs 16:2) and that it does not express an object regarding provocation (so 2 Kgs 21:6; 23:19, both royal focus). The former might perhaps favor attribution to the Dtr; the latter might favor attribution to the revision's royal focus. Either is possible. The prophecy against Jezebel is used with dtr formulation (servant and prophet) in 2 Kgs 9:7b and again in 9:36 and is therefore attributed to the Dtr. Here it follows the dtr references to Baasha and to provocation, confirming this attribution. Note that punishment of Ahab is proclaimed in v. 21; the pun-

Main pre-DH:	Other pre-DH:	HKL: + single	**Josianic DH:**
Prophetic Record	single sideline	underline	**from the Dtr**

8 So she wrote letters in Ahab's name and sealed them with his seal; she sent the letters to the elders and the nobles who lived with Naboth in his city. 9She wrote in the letters, "Proclaim a fast, and seat Naboth at the head of the assembly; 10seat two scoundrels opposite him, and have them bring a charge against him, saying, 'You have cursed God and the king.' Then take him out, and stone him to death." 11The men of his city, the elders and the nobles who lived in

---

ishment of his wife is not integral to the punishment of the dynasty. For a different view, see M. C. White, *Elijah Legends and Jehu's Coup.*

Verses 20 and 25-26 belong together and are to be situated within the royal focus of the dtr revision. As noted above, v. 20 offers an accusation over and above the two crimes of which Ahab is accused in v. 19a. It would be stylistically possible for v. 20 to follow v. 18, but it is unlikely that God's word to Elijah merely concerned Ahab's whereabouts. In v. 20, three elements are noteworthy: (i) Ahab's comment (cf. 18:17); (ii) the formulation by Elijah of the accusation; (iii) the content of the accusation.

Ahab's comment reveals the king's hostility to the prophet. Elijah's formulation of the accusation would be most unusual on two counts. First, it preempts an accusation from God, if it follows v. 18; and, following v. 19, it shifts the focus of the earlier accusation. Second, the "I" in the following announcement becomes Elijah rather than God. The content of the accusation—"because you have sold yourself to do what is evil in the sight of the LORD"—is picked up and specified in vv. 25-26, as worse than any other (v. 25) and as idolatry (v. 26). The focus on the king as enemy, evildoer, and apostate suggests attribution to the royal focus within the dtr revision. Both stylistically and in its quality of abstraction, this material intrudes on and goes beyond the dynastic concern. With its repetition of the accusation in v. 20b and v. 25a (sold self to do evil in the sight of LORD), this material forms an envelope around the series of announcements that were in the text at the time. From Ahab's specific crimes, it distills the abstraction of "evil in the sight of the LORD." It goes beyond these crimes to reaffirm the earlier accusation of apostasy (cf. 16:30-33).

Verse 19b is an evident parallel to v. 19a and reflects the wealth of the ongoing Elijah traditions. Its content is associated with chap. 20 (death sentence on

the king, 20:42) and 22:37-38 (death of the king). In the latter, of course, Ahab was brought to Samaria. This may reflect the circulation within Israel of multiple versions of a single story. In this context, it is important to be aware of the following: in 21:1, the LXX lacks "in Jezreel" for Naboth's vineyard; equally in 21:1, the Hebrew preposition, *'ēṣel*, ("beside" the palace) can mean "near" or "in the vicinity of" (cf. Deut 11:30; Judg 19:14; 1 Kgs 4:12; 21:2; Jer 41:17; Prov 7:8; Neh 4:6 [NRSV, 12]; 2 Chron 28:15)—the vineyard need not be within the town; in 21:18a, the phrase rendered "who rules in Samaria" (NRSV) among other things can be understood to designate Ahab's whereabouts ("who is in Samaria," [RSV]); 2 Kgs 9:25-26 can be understood in terms of a further version of the story. To focus these observations, we need to be aware that more than one version of the story may have circulated in Israel. In one version, the vineyard may have been in Jezreel, where Naboth died (21:11-13); in another version, the vineyard may have been in Samaria, where Ahab ended (22:37-38); in yet another version, the vineyard may have been "a plot of ground" (2 Kgs 9:21, 25-26, but cf. Jer 12:10; Job 24:18).

The tradition expressed in v. 19b is coherent with chaps. 20 and 22 (MT). Along with them, it is believed to have been introduced into the text here after the composition of the Josianic DH. It has come into the text later than v. 20; without v. 20 intervening, its detail would be odd before the general announcement that begins v. 21 (cf. 14:10; also 2 Kgs 17:17 for selling themselves to do evil in the sight of YHWH).

Present-text potential of 21:1-29. According to the way the text is understood (or translated), the story is told with Naboth's vineyard located in Jezreel or told with pointers to variant versions (see above).

| After the Dtr: indented and sans serif font | **Revision:** **royal focus** | *Revision: national focus* | Other: double sideline |

his city, did as Jezebel had sent word to them. Just as it was written in the letters that she had sent to them, [12]*they proclaimed a fast and seated Naboth at the head of the assembly.* [13]*The two scoundrels came in and sat opposite him; and the scoundrels brought a charge against Naboth, in the presence of the people, saying, "Naboth cursed God and the king." So they took him outside the city, and stoned him to death.* [14]*Then they sent to Jezebel, saying, "Naboth has been stoned; he is dead."*

[15] *As soon as Jezebel heard that Naboth had been stoned and was dead, Jezebel said to Ahab, "Go, take possession of the vineyard of Naboth the Jezreelite, which he refused to give you for money; for Naboth is not alive, but dead."* [16]*As soon as Ahab heard that Naboth was dead, Ahab set out to go down to the vineyard of Naboth the Jezreelite, to take possession of it.*

[17] *Then the word of the LORD came to Elijah the Tishbite, saying:* [18]*Go down to meet King Ahab of Israel, who rules in Samaria; he is now in the vineyard of Naboth, where he has gone to take possession.* [19]*You shall say to him, "Thus says the LORD: Have you killed, and also taken possession?"*

> You shall say to him, "Thus says the LORD: In the place where dogs licked up the blood of Naboth, dogs will also lick up your blood."

Once Elijah is on the scene, the text reveals God's condemnation of Ahab, Ahab's enmity for Elijah, and Elijah's expression of the impact of God's condemnation, for Ahab, his dynasty, and those connected with him. A narrator's comment precedes the report of Ahab's repentance. In this context, it is important to bear in mind that the interpretation of 22:40, "slept with his ancestors," as denoting a peaceful death is a conclusion of modern scholarship; how widely it was shared in ancient Israel, we do not know. Once this is accepted, the death of Ahab and the disaster for his dynasty can be retained within an overall narrative thread.

20 Ahab said to Elijah, "Have you found me, O my enemy?" He answered, "I have found you. Because you have sold yourself to do what is evil in the sight of the LORD.
[21]*I will bring disaster on you; I will consume you, and will cut off from Ahab every male, bond or free, in Israel;* [22]*and I will make your house like the house of Jeroboam son of Nebat,* **and like the house of Baasha son of Ahijah, because you have provoked** (Heb.; NRSV, me) **to anger and have caused Israel to sin.** [23]**Also concerning Jezebel the LORD said, 'The dogs shall eat Jezebel within the bounds of Jezreel.'**
[24]*Anyone belonging to Ahab who dies in the city the dogs shall eat; and anyone of his who dies in the open country the birds of the air shall eat."*[125]

25 (Indeed, there was no one like Ahab, who sold himself to do what was evil in the sight of the LORD, urged on by his wife Jezebel. [26]**He acted most abominably in going after idols, as the Amorites had done, whom the LORD drove out before the Israelites.)**

[27] When Ahab heard those words, he tore his clothes and put sackcloth over his bare flesh; he fasted, lay in the sackcloth, and went about dejectedly. [28]Then the word of the LORD came to Elijah the Tishbite: [29]"Have you seen how Ahab has humbled himself before me? Because he has humbled himself before me, I will not bring the disaster in his days; but in his son's days I will bring the disaster on his house."[126]

---

125. The continuation of the PR is to be found at 22:40.

126. See the discussion above under **text-history approach**. For the diversity of dates proposed, see Campbell, *Of Prophets and Kings*, 98, n. 82. Dietrich attributed 21:19b, 20bβ-24, 27-29 to his DtrP.

Main pre-DH:	Other pre-DH:	HKL: + single	**Josianic DH:**
Prophetic Record	single sideline	underline	**from the Dtr**

22 For three years Aram and Israel continued without war. ²But in the third year King Jehoshaphat of Judah came down to the king of Israel. ³The king of Israel said to his servants, "Do you know that Ramoth-gilead belongs to us, yet we are doing nothing to take it out of the hand of the king of Aram?" ⁴He said to Jehoshaphat, "Will you go with me to battle at Ramoth-gilead?" Jehoshaphat replied to the king of Israel, "I am as you are; my people are your people, my horses are your horses."

5 But Jehoshaphat also said to the king of Israel, "Inquire first for the word of the Lord." ⁶Then the king of Israel gathered the prophets together, about four hundred of them, and said to them, "Shall I go to battle against Ramoth-gilead, or shall I refrain?" They said, "Go up; for the Lord will give it into the hand of the king." ⁷But Jehoshaphat said, "Is there no other prophet of the Lord here of whom we may inquire?" ⁸The king of Israel said to Jehoshaphat, "There is still one other by whom we may inquire of the Lord, Micaiah son of Imlah; but I hate him, for he never prophesies anything favorable about me, but only disaster." Jehoshaphat said, "Let the king not say such a thing." ⁹Then the king of Israel summoned an officer and said, "Bring quickly Micaiah son of Imlah." ¹⁰Now the king of Israel and King Jehoshaphat of Judah were sitting on their thrones, arrayed in their robes, at the threshing floor at the entrance of the gate of Samaria; and all the prophets were prophesying before them. ¹¹Zedekiah son of Chenaanah made for himself horns of iron, and he said, "Thus says the Lord: With these you shall gore the Arameans until they are destroyed." ¹²All the prophets were prophesying the same and saying, "Go up to Ramoth-gilead and triumph; the Lord will give it into the hand of the king."

13 The messenger who had gone to summon Micaiah said to him, "Look, the words of the prophets with one accord are favorable to the king; let your word be like the word of one of them, and speak favorably." ¹⁴But Micaiah said, "As the Lord lives, whatever the Lord says to me, that I will speak."

15 When he had come to the king, the king said to him, "Micaiah, shall we go to Ramoth-gilead to battle, or shall we refrain?" He answered him, "Go up and triumph; the Lord will give it into the hand of the king." ¹⁶But the king said to him, "How many times must I make you swear to tell me nothing but the truth in the name of the Lord?" ¹⁷Then Micaiah said, "I saw all Israel scattered on the mountains, like sheep that have no shepherd; and the Lord said, 'These have no master; let each one go home in peace.' " ¹⁸The king of Israel said to Jehoshaphat, "Did I not tell you that he would not prophesy anything favorable about me, but only disaster?"

19 Then Micaiah said, "Therefore hear the word of the Lord: I saw the Lord sitting on his throne, with all the host of heaven standing beside him to the right and to the left of him. ²⁰And the Lord said, 'Who will entice Ahab, so that he may go up and fall at Ramoth-gilead?' Then one said one thing, and another said another, ²¹until a spirit came forward and stood before the Lord, saying, 'I will entice him.' ²²'How?' the Lord asked him. He replied, 'I will go out and be a lying spirit in the mouth of all his prophets.' Then the Lord said, 'You are to entice him, and you shall succeed; go out

After the Dtr: indented and sans serif font	**Revision: royal focus**	Revision: national focus	Other: double sideline

and do it.' [23]So you see, the LORD has put a lying spirit in the mouth of all these your prophets; the LORD has decreed disaster for you."

24 Then Zedekiah son of Chenaanah came up to Micaiah, slapped him on the cheek, and said, "Which way did the spirit of the LORD pass from me to speak to you?" [25]Micaiah replied, "You will find out on that day when you go in to hide in an inner chamber." [26]The king of Israel then ordered, "Take Micaiah, and return him to Amon the governor of the city and to Joash the king's son, [27]and say, 'Thus says the king: Put this fellow in prison, and feed him on reduced rations of bread and water until I come in peace.' " [28]Micaiah said, "If you return in peace, the LORD has not spoken by me." And he said, "Hear, you peoples, all of you!"

29 So the king of Israel and King Jehoshaphat of Judah went up to Ramoth-gilead. [30]The king of Israel said to Jehoshaphat, "I will disguise myself and go into battle, but you wear your robes." So the king of Israel disguised himself and went into battle. [31]Now the king of Aram had commanded the thirty-two captains of his chariots, "Fight with no one small or great, but only with the king of Israel." [32]When the captains of the chariots saw Jehoshaphat, they said, "It is surely the king of Israel." So they turned to fight against him; and Jehoshaphat cried out. [33]When the captains of the chariots saw that it was not the king of Israel, they turned back from pursuing him. [34]But a certain man drew his bow and unknowingly struck the king of Israel between the scale armor and the breastplate; so he said to the driver of his chariot, "Turn around, and carry me out of the battle, for I am wounded." [35]The battle grew hot that day, and the king was propped up in his chariot facing the Arameans, until at evening he died; the blood from the wound had flowed into the bottom of the chariot. [36]Then about sunset a shout went through the army, "Every man to his city, and every man to his country!"

37 So the king died, and was brought to Samaria; they buried the king in Samaria. [38]They washed the chariot by the pool of Samaria; the dogs licked up his blood, and the prostitutes washed themselves in it, according to the word of the LORD that he had spoken.[127]

[39]Now the rest of the acts of Ahab, and all that he did, and the ivory house that he built, and all the cities that he built, are they not written in the Book of the Annals of the Kings of Israel?

[40]So Ahab slept with his ancestors; and his son Ahaziah succeeded him.[128]

---

127. This story of the conflict between king and prophet and between prophet and prophet (22:1-38) need not originally have concerned Ahab as king of Israel (for indications of the intense scholarly discussion, see Jones, *Kings*, 2.360-62). In all probability, it is the identification of "the king of Israel" with Ahab in 22:20 that is responsible for the insertion of the story here. Thematically, it fits well. In the total text, Elijah and Micaiah are lined up with God against Ahab; God uses Ahab's own prophets to bring him down. Ahab, like any king, acts on political rather than religious grounds—and, in the story, dies for it.

Dietrich attributed to his DtrP the insertion of 22:1-38, with the addition of "Ahab" and 22:38.

128. Resumption of the PR from 21:24. The continuation of the PR is to be found at 2 Kgs 1:2.

Present-text potential of 20:1—22:40. 1 Kings 18–19 faced the issue of who was god in Israel. With 1 Kings 20–22, the text turns to the question of who is

---

Main pre-DH:	Other pre-DH:	HKL: + single	**Josianic DH:**
Prophetic Record	single sideline	underline	**from the Dtr**

41 Jehoshaphat son of Asa began to reign over Judah in the fourth year of King Ahab of Israel. **42**Jehoshaphat was thirty-five years old when he began to reign, and he reigned twenty-five years in Jerusalem. His mother's name was Azubah daughter of Shilhi. 43He walked in all the way of his father Asa; he did not turn aside from it, doing what was right in the sight of the Lord; yet the high places were not taken away, and the people still sacrificed and offered incense on the high places.

44And Jehoshaphat (Heb.; NRSV, Jehoshaphat also) made peace with the king of Israel.129

45 Now the rest of the acts of Jehoshaphat, and his power that he showed, and how he waged war, are they not written in the Book of the Annals of the Kings of Judah?

---

to be king in Israel. Elijah says: neither Ahab nor his dynasty (chap. 21, recognizing the difference between Ahab's death [v. 19b] and the disaster for his dynasty [v. 22]). Framing this story, the man of God says: not Ahab (chap. 20) and Micaiah ben Imlah too says: not Ahab (chap. 22). The LXX has a different order, with the Elijah traditions together and the traditions of the Syrian war together, so that Elijah, then the man of God, and finally Micaiah, all in turn reject Ahab. Both chaps. 20 and 22 focus on "the king of Israel"; Ahab is named three times in chap. 20 (vv. 2, 13, 14) and once only in the story of chap. 22 (v. 20).

In chap. 20, God intervenes through the prophets on behalf of Israel either when Israel's honor (vv. 9, 13) or God's honor (vv. 23, 28) is threatened. An agreement on property and trade led to a treaty between Israel's king and the enemy king God had defeated. The chapter ends with a prophet pronouncing sentence of death on the king of Israel. Broadly speaking, the king of Israel is condemned by one of the prophetic company on grounds of international relations. In chap. 21, the prophet Elijah condemns Ahab, king of Israel, on the grounds of internal social justice. In chap. 22, God deceives Ahab (v. 20) through the prophets, bringing the earlier prophecies to fulfillment.

In the Hebrew order, chap. 20 brings prophetic condemnation of the king as military leader on the international scene; chap. 21 brings Elijah's condemnation of both king and dynasty, as source of social justice on the national scene; and chap. 22 brings

God's action to initiate fulfillment of these prophecies through Ahab's violent death. In the LXX order, the move is from national to international to divine realms. Furthermore, the LXX moves from the condemnation of king and dynasty to the condemnation of the king alone, to God's fulfillment against the king alone—leaving the fate of the dynasty for the traditions to come.

129. For us, 1 Kgs 22:43 (Heb., vv. 43-44) is from the HKL, with its concern for the high places. We found the King List's beginnings within 14:21-23a. The refrain complaining about the high places not being taken away begins with 15:14a. Asa's death and Jehoshaphat's succession were reported in 15:24. Here the text presents an evaluation of Jehoshaphat's reign (v. 43; Heb., vv. 43-44) and the succession of his son, Jehoram (v. 50; Heb., v. 51). For the first time, the continued existence of the high places is joined to a statement of the continued sacrifice and offering of incense there by the people. These two elements continue until Hezekiah's reform. Note that Chronicles has differing judgments on Jehoshaphat: "he removed the high places and the sacred poles from Judah" (2 Chron 17:6); "yet the high places were not removed" (2 Chron 20:33).

Verse 44 (Heb., v. 45) is attributed to the Josianic Dtr. The justification for this is extremely precarious—as for many such fragments of text. The later PR Extension is focused on the northern kingdom, the HKL on the southern kingdom, and the DH embraces both kingdoms. Here, therefore, the notice of peace between north and south is attributed to the Dtr (cf. similarly: 1 Kgs 14:30; 15:7b; also 2 Kgs 15:37, HKL). For Jones, the peace referred to involved Jehoshaphat and Ahab, sealed by Jehoram's marriage

---

| After the Dtr: indented and sans serif font | **Revision: royal focus** | Revision: national focus | Other: double sideline |

⁴⁶The remnant of the male temple prostitutes who were still in the land in the days
of his father Asa, he exterminated.

47 There was no king in Edom; a
deputy was king. ⁴⁸Jehoshaphat made ships
of the Tarshish type to go to Ophir for gold;
but they did not go, for the ships were
wrecked at Ezion-geber. ⁴⁹Then Ahaziah
son of Ahab said to Jehoshaphat, "Let my
servants go with your servants in the ships,"
but Jehoshaphat was not willing.¹³⁰

⁵⁰Jehoshaphat slept with his ancestors and was
buried with his ancestors in the city of his father
David; his son Jehoram succeeded him.

**51 Ahaziah son of Ahab began to reign
over Israel in Samaria in the seventeenth
year of King Jehoshaphat of Judah; he
reigned two years over Israel. ⁵²He did what
was evil in the sight of the LORD, and walked
in the way of his father and mother, and in
the way of Jeroboam son of Nebat, who
caused Israel to sin. ⁵³He served Baal and
worshiped him; he provoked the LORD, the
God of Israel, to anger, just as his father had
done.¹³¹**

---

to Athaliah, Ahab's daughter (cf. 2 Kgs 8:18; *Kings*, 2.373).

130. Because they lie outside the dtr concluding formula in v. 45 (Heb., v. 46), vv. 46-49 (Heb., vv. 47-50) may be regarded as post-dtr. The information relates to Jehoshaphat's reign and needs to be included before the report of his death (v. 50; Heb., v. 51). Had they been part of the Dtr's editing, we would expect them to have followed on v. 44 (Heb., v. 45).

131. As we have seen, "provoking God to anger" is a concern shared almost equally by both focuses of the dtr revision process (about eight occurrences each in the DH); but it is not completely foreign to the Dtr (cf. at least Deut 9:18; 1 Kgs 21:22). The concern with a father's modeling is rather more balanced between earlier and later texts (cf. HKL 4x and the Dtr 2x; later 6x). As a result, v. 53b (Heb., v. 54b) could well be original to the Dtr or be an added intensification from the revision. It would be imprudent to do more than indicate the options.

Main pre-DH:	Other pre-DH:	HKL: + single	**Josianic DH:**
Prophetic Record	single sideline	underline	**from the Dtr**

THE SECOND BOOK OF KINGS

1 After the death of Ahab, Moab rebelled against Israel.[1]

2 Ahaziah had fallen through the lattice in his upper chamber in Samaria, and lay injured; so he sent messengers, telling them, "Go, inquire of Baal-zebub, the god of Ekron, whether I shall recover from this injury." [3]But the angel of the LORD said to Elijah the Tishbite, "Get up, go to meet the messengers of the king of Samaria, and say to them, 'Is it because there is no God in Israel that you are going to inquire of Baal-zebub, the god of Ekron?' [4]Now therefore thus says the LORD, 'You shall not leave the bed to which you have gone, but you shall surely die.' " So Elijah went.[2]

5 The messengers returned to the king, who said to them, "Why have you returned?" [6]They answered him, "There came a man to meet us, who said to us, 'Go back to the king who sent you, and say to him: Thus says the LORD: Is it because there is no God in Israel that you are sending to inquire of Baal-zebub, the god of Ekron? Therefore you shall not leave the bed to which you have gone, but shall surely die.' " [7]He said to them, "What sort of man was he who came to meet you and told you these things?" [8]They answered him, "A hairy man, with a leather belt around his waist." He said, "It is Elijah the Tishbite."

9 Then the king sent to him a captain of fifty with his fifty men. He went up to Elijah, who was sitting on the top of a hill, and said to him, "O man of God, the king says, 'Come down.' " [10]But Elijah answered the captain of fifty, "If I am a man of God, let fire come down from heaven and consume you and your fifty." Then fire came down from heaven, and consumed him and his fifty.[3]

---

1. This venture into foreign affairs is a strange way to begin a biblical book. The Hebrew word order puts rebellion first: "And Moab rebelled against Israel after the death of Ahab." Ahaziah is on his father's throne; his death is the theme of what follows. The discordant note harks back to the death of Ahab and unavoidably forward to the rebellion of Moab (3:4-27).

There are no identifying features of thought or language to point to the source of 1:1 (cf. 3:5). What may be seen in the verse is the growing deterioration of Israel's fortunes. After subduing the Philistines, victory over the Moabites came high on the list of David's successes (2 Sam 8:2). David's kingdom was torn from Solomon's son. As Samuel tore the kingdom from Saul to give it to David (1 Sam 15:28), so Ahijah tore the kingdom from Solomon and gave ten tribes to Jeroboam (1 Kgs 11:31). The Davidic kingdom was divided. Jeroboam failed in fidelity and was condemned. From the turbulence that followed, the Omrides emerged, Baal worship was established, and Ahab "did evil in the sight of the LORD more than all who were before him" (1 Kgs 16:30). With Ahab's death, not only the Davidic kingdom but now the Davidic empire begins to crumble.

The overarching view of Israel's history can well be attributed to the Josianic Dtr for whom this deterioration is to be reversed by the fidelity of Josiah and his reform.

2. Resumption of the Prophetic Record (PR) from 1 Kgs 22:40. This prophetic tradition is appropriate within the horizon of the PR. It is in line with the portrayal of Elijah: he comes and goes; he confronts kings. The fashion sense attributed to Elijah (v. 8) is unique in the OT. Within the PR, the death of Ahaziah is the beginning of what was prophesied: disaster brought on the house of Ahab (1 Kgs 21:21-22). It is the work of Elijah, pronounced first to Ahab, now to Ahaziah.

3. Verses 9-16 are often seen as an addition from the Elisha circle (Jones, *Kings*, 2.376; perhaps in two stages, vv. 9 and 15-16 first, then vv. 10-14, cf. Hentschel, *Eliaerzählungen*, 11-12, 145-48), expanding and enriching the story.

Text signals in vv. 9-16. (i) Elijah is described as a "man of God" (vv. 9, 10, 11, 12, 13). Elsewhere, this

---

| After the Dtr: indented and sans serif font | DH Extension | *Revision: royal focus* | Revision: national focus | Other: double sideline |

11 Again the king sent to him another captain of fifty with his fifty. He went up and said to him, "O man of God, this is the king's order: Come down quickly!" [12]But Elijah answered them, "If I am a man of God, let fire come down from heaven and consume you and your fifty." Then the fire of God came down from heaven and consumed him and his fifty.

13 Again the king sent the captain of a third fifty with his fifty. So the third captain of fifty went up, and came and fell on his knees before Elijah, and entreated him, "O man of God,

please let my life, and the life of these fifty servants of yours, be precious in your sight. [14]Look, fire came down from heaven and consumed the two former captains of fifty men with their fifties; but now let my life be precious in your sight." [15]Then the angel of the LORD said to Elijah, "Go down with him; do not be afraid of him." So he set out and went down with him to the king, [16]and said to him, "Thus says the LORD: Because you have sent messengers to inquire of Baal-zebub, the god of Ekron,—is it because there is no God in Israel to inquire of his word?—therefore you shall not leave the bed to which you have gone, but you shall surely die."

17 So he died according to the word of the LORD that Elijah had spoken. His brother, Jehoram succeeded him as king,

‖ in the second year of King Jehoram son of Jehoshaphat of Judah

because he (Heb.; NRSV, Ahaziah) *had no son.*[4]

---

description is used only twice for Elijah (1 Kgs 17:18, 24), regarded as later material (see above); for Elisha, the term is frequent (twenty-six times). (ii) The soldiers come to Elijah on his hilltop, whereas in vv. 3-4 the angel of the LORD instructs him to go to meet the messengers. (iii) Elijah is portrayed in the role of wonder-worker calling down fire from heaven, whereas in vv. 2-8 he is the messenger of God's word to the king (cf. 1 Kings 21). Contrast 2 Kgs 1:10-12 with 1 Kgs 18:36-38. (iv) In vv. 13-14, it is the captain who fears for his life; on the other hand, in v. 15, it is Elijah who fears for his life.

Text-history approach. There is little question that the vignette in vv. 9-16 is closer to the stories told of Elisha than to those told of Elijah. On the other hand, if we accept that the Elijah stories were told and preserved within the Elisha circle, it is not particularly surprising that these traits should be combined. The stages of growth indicated by the text signals do not point to tensions sufficient to prevent the telling of this as a single prophetic story.

Present-text potential. The condemnation of Ahaziah in the PR's story reflects a concern for how life is to be sought and found in Israel—by consultation of the God of Israel, not other gods. Vv. 9-16, in rather gruesome fashion, underline that this is indeed a matter of life and death. They highlight as well the dominance of the prophetic power over both the military and the monarchy. Note the multiple mission to a prophet in 1 Sam 19:18-24.

4. There is no pointer to dtr formulation in the fulfillment note (v. 17aα). It may well have been in the story taken over by the prophetic editors (cf. 1 Kgs 17:16; 2 Kgs 2:22; 4:17; 7:16, 17; 10:17). The comment that "he" (Ahaziah) had no son follows naturally on the linear statement of succession, appropriate to the PR. This is the only case where it is said that the king had no son. Note: the Hebrew has simply "he"; in naming Ahaziah, the NRSV has clarified the sentence—necessary in the sequence of the present text.

The reference to "Jehoram ben Jehoshaphat, king of Judah" (v. 17) causes massive problems. Both chronology and syntax point to the name of another king. If the text read "King Ahaziah," the "second year" would agree with what is known of the royal chronology. Ahaziah reigned for two years over Israel (1 Kgs 22:51 [Heb., v. 52]). There would then be an antecedent for the pronoun at the end of v. 17: there was not "to him" a son. Ahaziah was childless, not Jehoram of Judah. But, beyond omission, there is no textual support for this possibility—which is, however,

---

18Now the rest of the acts of Ahaziah that he did, are they not written in the Book of the Annals of the Kings of Israel?

2 Now when the LORD was about to take Elijah up to heaven by a whirlwind, Elijah and Elisha were on their way from Gilgal. ²Elijah said to Elisha, "Stay here; for the LORD has sent me as far as Bethel." But Elisha said, "As the LORD lives, and as you yourself live, I will not leave you." So they went down to Bethel. ³The company of prophets who were in Bethel came out to Elisha, and said to him, "Do you know that today the LORD will take your master away from you?" And he said, "Yes, I know; keep silent."5

4 Elijah said to him, "Elisha, stay here; for the LORD has sent me to Jericho." But he said, "As the LORD lives, and as you yourself live, I will not leave you." So they came to Jericho.

---

the only one that makes sense of the chronology and syntax. The reference to a king of Judah may have come from a sense of the need for parallel chronicling of the two kingdoms—the synchronistic system. Why the chronology should conflict so starkly with 2 Kgs 3:1 and 8:16 is unknown. Appeals to a co-regency or to independent chronological sources (cf. Jones, *Kings*, 2.380, 392) merely underline the well-known difficulties associated with the chronologies of the kings of Israel and Judah.

The continuation of the PR is to be found at 9:1. The transition is no more abrupt than in the present text of 1 Sam 9:1 and 1 Kgs 17:1. The PR's concern appears to be for the role of the prophets in the rise and fall of Israel's kings. After Ahaziah, the fall of Jehoram will bring the house of Ahab to the end that Elijah prophesied.

Dietrich attributed to DtrP the insertion of 2 Kings 1, with 1:17aβb as a literary seam.

5. With the transfer of Elijah's spirit to Elisha, the focus of the text shifts from stories of the highly individualistic Elijah's confrontations with kings to stories of the more community-oriented Elisha and his circle. With 2 Kings 9–10, the Elisha circle takes up the completion of Elijah's task of confrontation with the house of Ahab.

We do not see signals in the text that indicate later composition. Except for 3:4-27, we do not see signals pointing with any clarity to incorporation of these stories after the composition of the Josianic DH. On the other hand, composition of the stories while the Elisha circle still existed is possible. Those responsible for the composition of the Josianic DH inherited material—whether in the form of the PR or in some other form—that evidenced strong prophetic influence, including Jehu's anointing and commissioning by a disciple of Elisha. The Elisha stories could, therefore, have been of interest.

Supporting this possibility is the insight that Elisha is portrayed as far more than a mere worker of wonders. The stories present the prophet as provider or preserver of life and a counterpart to kings. As such, this cluster of stories might well have been of interest to the Josianic Dtr. Later incorporation is not to be excluded; in the present situation, we do not see evidence for it.

2 Kings 3:4-27 is a different kettle of fish. The strong positive role of Jehoshaphat, king of Judah, is surprising in the context. Jehoshaphat has a similar role in 1 Kings 22. In both stories, Jehoshaphat's role in the consultation of a prophet is significant. It is possible that neither Jehoshaphat nor Elisha featured in an original story of the campaign against Moab. As the story stands now, it is likely that it was introduced into the DH along with 1 Kings 20 and 22.

While in this book we try to refrain from interpretation, the marked tendency in scholarship to dismiss the Elisha material as focused merely on marvels and wonders will be balanced by brief sketches pointing to other understandings. For fuller treatment, see O'Brien and Campbell, "1–2 Kings," in *The International Bible Commentary*, 608-43.

In the present text, there are five major Elisha stories, along with a number of less extensive traditions. The major stories probe the prophetic role and the

⁵The company of prophets who were at Jericho drew near to Elisha, and said to him, "Do you know that today the LORD will take your master away from you?" And he answered, "Yes, I know; be silent."

6 Then Elijah said to him, "Stay here; for the LORD has sent me to the Jordan." But he said, "As the LORD lives, and as you yourself live, I will not leave you." So the two of them went on. ⁷Fifty men of the company of prophets also went, and stood at some distance from them, as they both were standing by the Jordan. ⁸Then Elijah took his mantle and rolled it up, and struck the water; the water was parted to the one side and to the other, until the two of them crossed on dry ground.

---

accompanying understanding of the prophet. Stories of the prophet in times of war frame stories of the prophet concerned with care for others. In the war with King Mesha of Moab, where Israel is the aggressor, as the present text tells the story the prophet under royal pressure provides all that is requested and nevertheless Israel ends up in withdrawal and rout. Both the woman of Shunem and the Syrian Naaman experience the prophet's care. In the war with the king of Aram, where Israel is the victim, Elisha's intervention achieves Israel's deliverance—providing food without bloodshed.

Some prophets confront kings. Samuel confronted Saul. Ahijah confronted Jeroboam. Elijah confronted Ahab. Some kings consult prophets. David consulted Nathan over the temple (2 Sam 7:2). Hezekiah consulted Isaiah over the Assyrians (2 Kgs 19:2). Josiah consulted Huldah over the book (2 Kgs 22:13-14). After Elisha's disciple initiates the action that brings Elijah's word to fulfillment, no prophet will again claim to exercise such confrontational control over the monarchy, designating and deposing kings. The Elisha circle has made its claim for the past. The stories and traditions surrounding Elisha do not carry such confrontation beyond Jehu into the future.

9 When they had crossed, Elijah said to Elisha, "Tell me what I may do for you, before I am taken from you." Elisha said, "Please let me inherit a double share of your spirit." ¹⁰He responded, "You have asked a hard thing; yet, if you see me as I am being taken from you, it will be granted you; if not, it will not." ¹¹As they continued walking and talking, a chariot of fire and horses of fire separated the two of them, and Elijah ascended in a whirlwind into heaven. ¹²Elisha kept watching and crying out, "Father, father! The chariots of Israel and its horsemen!" But when he could no longer see him, he grasped his own clothes and tore them in two pieces.

13 He picked up the mantle of Elijah that had fallen from him, and went back and stood on the bank of the Jordan. ¹⁴He took the mantle of Elijah that had fallen from him, and struck the water, saying, "Where is the LORD, the God of Elijah?" And he struck the water (*Heb.; NRSV, When he had struck the water*), the water was parted to the one side and to the other, and Elisha went over.

15 When the company of prophets who were at Jericho saw him at a distance, they declared, "The spirit of Elijah rests on Elisha." They came to meet him and bowed to the ground before him. ¹⁶They said to him, "See now, we have fifty strong men among your servants; please let them go and seek your master; it may be that the spirit of the LORD has caught him up and thrown him down on some mountain or into some valley." He responded, "No, do not send them." ¹⁷But when they urged him until he was ashamed, he said, "Send them." So they sent fifty men who searched for three days but did not find him. ¹⁸When they came back to him (he had remained at Jericho), he said to them, "Did I not say to you, Do not go?"[6]

---

6. The story of prophetic transition (2:1-18) points to something of the experience of prophecy. There is

---

| Main pre-DH: | Other pre-DH: | HKL: + single | **Josianic DH:** |
| *Prophetic Record and PR Extension* | single sideline | underline | **from the Dtr** |

19 Now the people of the city said to Elisha, "The location of this city is good, as my lord sees; but the water is bad, and the land is unfruitful." [20]He said, "Bring me a new bowl, and put salt in it." So they brought it to him. [21]Then he went to the spring of water and threw the salt into it, and said, "Thus says the LORD, I have made this water wholesome; from now on neither death nor miscarriage shall come from it." [22]So the water has been wholesome to this day, according to the word that Elisha spoke.

23 He went up from there to Bethel; and while he was going up on the way, some small boys came out of the city and jeered at him, saying, "Go away, baldhead! Go away, baldhead!" [24]When he turned around and saw them, he

cursed them in the name of the LORD. Then two she-bears came out of the woods and mauled forty-two of the boys. [25]From there he went on to Mount Carmel, and then returned to Samaria.[7]

3 In the eighteenth year of King Jehoshaphat of Judah, Jehoram son of Ahab became king over Israel in Samaria; he reigned twelve years. [2]He did what was evil in the sight of the LORD, though not like his father and mother, for he removed the pillar of Baal that his father had made. [3]Nevertheless he clung to the sin of Jeroboam son of Nebat, which he caused Israel to commit; he did not depart from it.

4 Now King Mesha of Moab was a sheep breeder, who used to deliver to the king of Israel one hundred thousand lambs, and the wool of one hundred thousand rams. [5]But when Ahab died, the king of Moab rebelled against the king of Israel. [6]So King Jehoram marched out of Samaria at that time and mustered all Israel. [7]As he went he sent word to King Jehoshaphat of Judah, "The king of Moab has rebelled against me; will you go with me to battle against Moab?" He answered, "I will; I am with you, my people are your people, my horses are your horses." [8]Then he asked, "By which way shall we march?" Jehoram

---

certainly power exercised by the prophets (here: parting of the Jordan); equally, certainty is elusive. Certain passages are instructive: "Stay here." "I will not leave you." "Yes, I know; keep silent." "Let me inherit a double share of your spirit." "You have asked a hard thing; yet, if you see me as I am being taken from you, it will be granted you; if not, it will not." Elisha disobeys, knows, and demands. Is this behavior independence, or loyalty, or discernment? Is the demand self-seeking or not, granted or not? Did he miss seeing Elijah? He picks up the mantle—and is still asking.

Seeing Elijah: was it condition or sign? Parting the waters: Elijah's mantle or Elisha's power (the NRSV's translation closes an open issue)? Searching for the master: did they already know or were they uncertain? Or was the mantle a sign for Elisha, the search a sign for the company, and the city water a sign for the community at large? Elijah's spirit: the handing on of charisma or the handing over of office or both? As Elisha disobeyed his master (vv. 2, 4, 6), so the company acknowledges its new master (v. 15) and is far from docile and obedient (vv. 16-18).

Kings are regularly succeeded by their sons. Succession among prophets is difficult ("a hard thing," v. 10) and rare; this case is unique in the OT.

---

7. The report that has Elisha leave Benjaminite territory for Mount Carmel and finally Samaria fits coherently with the story of the woman of Shunem, in the valley of Esdraelon, who goes to Elisha at Mount Carmel (cf. 4:8-37, esp. v. 25). The whereabouts of Elisha in 3:4-27 is not specified. Later stories have Elisha back at Gilgal, also at Dothan, and again in Samaria.

| After the Dtr: indented and sans serif font | DH Extension | *Revision: royal focus* | Revision: national focus | Other: double sideline |

answered, "By the way of the wilderness of Edom."

9 So the king of Israel, the king of Judah, and the king of Edom set out; and when they had made a roundabout march of seven days, there was no water for the army or for the animals that were with them. [10]Then the king of Israel said, "Alas! The LORD has summoned us, three kings, only to be handed over to Moab." [11]But Jehoshaphat said, "Is there no prophet of the LORD here, through whom we may inquire of the LORD?" Then one of the servants of the king of Israel answered, "Elisha son of Shaphat, who used to pour water on the hands of Elijah, is here." [12]Jehoshaphat said, "The word of the LORD is with him." So the king of Israel and Jehoshaphat and the king of Edom went down to him.

13 Elisha said to the king of Israel, "What have I to do with you? Go to your father's prophets or to your mother's." But the king of Israel said to him, "No; it is the LORD who has summoned us, three kings, only to be handed over to Moab." [14]Elisha said, "As the LORD of hosts lives, whom I serve, were it not that I have regard for King Jehoshaphat of Judah, I would give you neither a look nor a glance. [15]But get me a musician." And then, while the musician was playing, the power of the LORD came on him. [16]And he said, "Thus says the LORD, 'I will make this wadi full of pools.' [17]For thus says the LORD, 'You shall see neither wind nor rain, but the wadi shall be filled with water, so that you shall drink, you, your cattle, and your animals.' [18]This is only a trifle in the sight of the LORD, for he will also hand Moab over to you. [19]You shall conquer every fortified city and every choice city; every good tree you shall fell, all springs of water you shall stop up, and every good piece of land you shall ruin with stones." [20]The next day, about the time of the morning offering, suddenly water began to flow from the direction of Edom, until the country was filled with water.

21 When all the Moabites heard that the kings had come up to fight against them, all who were able to put on armor, from the youngest to the oldest, were called out and were drawn up at the frontier. [22]When they rose early in the morning, and the sun shone upon the water, the Moabites saw the water opposite them as red as blood. [23]They said, "This is blood; the kings must have fought together, and killed one another. Now then, Moab, to the spoil!" [24]But when they came to the camp of Israel, the Israelites rose up and attacked the Moabites, who fled before them; as they entered Moab they continued the attack. [25]The cities they overturned, and on every good piece of land everyone threw a stone, until it was covered; every spring of water they stopped up, and every good tree they felled. Only at Kir-hareseth did the stone walls remain, until the slingers surrounded and attacked it. [26]When the king of Moab saw that the battle was going against him, he took with him seven hundred swordsmen to break through, opposite the king of Edom; but they could not. [27]Then he took his firstborn son who was to succeed him, and offered him as a burnt offering on the wall. And great wrath came upon Israel, so they withdrew from him and returned to their own land.[8]

---

8. As noted above, the place of Jehoshaphat, king of Judah, in this story and his role in it associates it with 1 Kings 22. The traditions of 1 Kgs 20:1-43;

| Main pre-DH: *Prophetic Record and PR Extension* | Other pre-DH: single sideline | HKL: + single underline | **Josianic DH: from the Dtr** |

4 Now the wife of a member of the company of prophets cried to Elisha, "Your servant my husband is dead; and you know that your servant feared the Lord, but a creditor has come to take my two children as slaves." [2]Elisha said to her,

"What shall I do for you? Tell me, what do you have in the house?" She answered, "Your servant has nothing in the house, except a jar of oil." [3]He said, "Go outside, borrow vessels from all your neighbors, empty vessels and not just a few. [4]Then go in, and shut the door behind you and your children, and start pouring into all these vessels; when each is full, set it aside." [5]So she left him and shut the door behind her and her children; they kept bringing vessels to her, and she kept pouring. [6]When the vessels were full, she said to her son, "Bring me another vessel." But he said to her, "There are no more." Then the oil stopped flowing. [7]She came and told the man of God, and he said, "Go sell the oil and pay your debts, and you and your children can live on the rest."[9]

8 One day Elisha was passing through Shunem, where a wealthy woman lived, who urged him to have a meal. So whenever he passed that way, he would stop there for a meal. [9]She said to her husband, "Look, I am sure that this man who regularly passes our way is a holy man of God. [10]Let us make a small roof chamber with walls, and put there for him a bed, a table, a chair, and a lamp, so that he can stay there whenever he comes to us."

21:19b; and 22:1-38 predicate a violent death for Ahab, while the traditions of the Josianic DH assume his peaceful death (22:40). The web of associations suggests that all these texts (1 Kgs 20:1-43; 21:19b; 22:1-38), in their present form, were incorporated into the DH later than the contribution of the Josianic Dtr.

In its own strange way, the present text of 2 Kgs 3:4-27 is a story of the prophet's consummate freedom with regard to kings and consummate contempt for the king of Israel—whose replacement Elisha's people are going to claim to have authorized (2 Kgs 9:1-13). The kings, all three of them, make their decisions without consulting the prophet. They run into trouble—no water. Jehoram, king of Israel, who launched the campaign and outlined the strategy (3:6-8), now blames the God of Israel for the failure. Jehoshaphat, king of Judah, suggests consulting a prophet (cf. 1 Kgs 22:5, 7). So need forces them to consult the prophet and all three kings go down to Elisha "here" (wherever "here" may have been, cf. 3:11-12). Elisha is contemptuously rude to Jehoram, but surprisingly respectful of Jehoshaphat. The kings are in need; the rudeness goes unheeded. The word of YHWH is extraordinary: without wind or rain the wadi will be filled (vv. 16-17). The prophet goes beyond the word of the Lord to announce the seizure and devastation of Moab (vv. 18-19). What the prophet does not say is what will happen when both the word of YHWH and the word of his prophet are fulfilled. There are two consequences in the story, one spelled out and the other left unsaid. Spelled out is the sacrifice that brings "great wrath" upon Israel and their withdrawal. Unsaid is that the devastation of Moab will eliminate any worthwhile tribute for years to come. The kings' project has come to naught. What the king of Israel began God finished—God's way.

The ending (with v. 27) has been a major source of difficulty. The sacrifice of the son as a burnt offering on the city wall must be understood by the Moabites as a prayer to Chemosh, their god. To the Israelites, on the other hand, the "great wrath" (cf. Deut 29:28 [Heb., v. 27]; Jer 21:5; 32:37; Zech 7:12) is YHWH's and they rightly pull back.

9. Four traditions comprise this chapter, beginning and ending with the maintenance of life (4:1-7, 42-44) and with death to life as the focus of the other two (4:8-37, 38-41). One is developed: the restoration to life of the woman's son. In all four, the contrast with chap. 3 is marked.

| After the Dtr:
indented and sans serif font | DH
Extension | **Revision:**
royal focus | Revision:
national focus | Other:
double sideline |

11 One day when he came there, he went up to the chamber and lay down there. ¹²He said to his servant Gehazi, "Call the Shunammite woman." When he had called her, she stood before him. ¹³He said to him, "Say to her, Since you have taken all this trouble for us, what may be done for you? Would you have a word spoken on your behalf to the king or to the commander of the army?" She answered, "I live among my own people." ¹⁴He said, "What then may be done for her?" Gehazi answered, "Well, she has no son, and her husband is old." ¹⁵He said, "Call her." When he had called her, she stood at the door. ¹⁶He said, "At this season, in due time, you shall embrace a son." She replied, "No, my lord, O man of God; do not deceive your servant."

17 The woman conceived and bore a son at that season, in due time, as Elisha had declared to her.

18 When the child was older, he went out one day to his father among the reapers. ¹⁹He complained to his father, "Oh, my head, my head!" The father said to his servant, "Carry him to his mother." ²⁰He carried him and brought him to his mother; the child sat on her lap until noon, and he died. ²¹She went up and laid him on the bed of the man of God, closed the door on him, and left. ²²Then she called to her husband, and said, "Send me one of the servants and one of the donkeys, so that I may quickly go to the man of God and come back again." ²³He said, "Why go to him today? It is neither new moon nor sabbath." She said, "It will be all right." ²⁴Then she saddled the donkey and said to her servant, "Urge the animal on; do not hold back for me unless I tell you." ²⁵So she set out, and came to the man of God at Mount Carmel.

When the man of God saw her coming, he said to Gehazi his servant, "Look, there is the Shunammite woman; ²⁶run at once to meet her, and say to her, Are you all right? Is your husband all right? Is the child all right?" She answered, "It is all right." ²⁷When she came to the man of God at the mountain, she caught hold of his feet. Gehazi approached to push her away. But the man of God said, "Let her alone, for she is in bitter distress; the LORD has hidden it from me and has not told me." ²⁸Then she said, "Did I ask my lord for a son? Did I not say, Do not mislead me?" ²⁹He said to Gehazi, "Gird up your loins, and take my staff in your hand, and go. If you meet anyone, give no greeting, and if anyone greets you, do not answer; and lay my staff on the face of the child." ³⁰Then the mother of the child said, "As the LORD lives, and as you yourself live, I will not leave without you." So he rose up and followed her. ³¹Gehazi went on ahead and laid the staff on the face of the child, but there was no sound or sign of life. He came back to meet him and told him, "The child has not awakened."

32 When Elisha came into the house, he saw the child lying dead on his bed. ³³So he went in and closed the door on the two of them, and prayed to the LORD. ³⁴Then he got up on the bed and lay upon the child, putting his mouth upon his mouth, his eyes upon his eyes, and his hands upon his hands; and while he lay bent over him, the flesh of the child became warm. ³⁵He got down, walked once to and fro in the room, then got up again and bent over him; the child sneezed seven times, and the child opened his eyes. ³⁶Elisha summoned Gehazi and said, "Call the Shunammite woman." So he called her. When she came to him, he said, "Take your son." ³⁷She came and fell at his feet, bowing to the ground; then she took her son and left.¹⁰

---

10. There is more focus on the woman here than in the parallel Elijah story (1 Kgs 17:17-24). She is wealthy and she takes the initiative (4:8-10). As Elisha

---

Main pre-DH: *Prophetic Record and PR Extension* — Other pre-DH: single sideline — HKL: + single underline — **Josianic DH: from the Dtr**

38 When Elisha returned to Gilgal, there was a famine in the land. As the company of prophets was sitting before him, he said to his servant, "Put the large pot on, and make some stew for the company of prophets." ³⁹One of them went out into the field to gather herbs; he found a wild vine and gathered from it a lapful of wild gourds, and came and cut them up into the pot of stew, not knowing what they were. ⁴⁰They served some for the men to eat. But while they were eating the stew, they cried out, "O man of God, there is death in the pot!" They could not eat it. ⁴¹He said, "Then bring some flour." He threw it into the pot, and said, "Serve the people and let them eat." And there was nothing harmful in the pot.¹¹

42 A man came from Baal-shalishah, bringing food from the first fruits to the man of God: twenty loaves of barley and fresh ears of grain in his sack. Elisha said, "Give it to the people and let them eat." ⁴³But his servant said, "How can I set this before a hundred people?" So he repeated, "Give it to the people and let them eat, for thus says the LORD, 'They shall eat and have some left.' " ⁴⁴He set it before them, they ate,

and had some left, according to the word of the LORD.

5 Naaman, commander of the army of the king of Aram, was a great man and in high favor with his master, because by him the LORD had given victory to Aram. The man, though a mighty warrior, suffered from leprosy. ²Now the Arameans on one of their raids had taken a young girl captive from the land of Israel, and she served Naaman's wife. ³She said to her mistress, "If only my lord were with the prophet who is in Samaria! He would cure him of his leprosy." ⁴So Naaman went in and told his lord just what the girl from the land of Israel had said. ⁵And the king of Aram said, "Go then, and I will send along a letter to the king of Israel."

He went, taking with him ten talents of silver, six thousand shekels of gold, and ten sets of garments. ⁶He brought the letter to the king of Israel, which read, "When this letter reaches you, know that I have sent to you my servant Naaman, that you may cure him of his leprosy." ⁷When the king of Israel read the letter, he tore his clothes and said, "Am I God, to give death or life, that this man sends word to me to cure a man of his leprosy? Just look and see how he is trying to pick a quarrel with me."

8 But when Elisha the man of God heard that the king of Israel had torn his clothes, he sent a message to the king, "Why have you torn your clothes? Let him come to me, that he may learn that there is a prophet in Israel." ⁹So Naaman came with his horses and chariots, and halted at the entrance of Elisha's house. ¹⁰Elisha sent a messenger to him, saying, "Go, wash in the Jordan seven times, and your flesh shall be restored and you shall be clean." ¹¹But Naaman became angry and went away, saying, "I thought that for me he would surely come out, and stand and call on the name of the LORD his God, and would

---

was servant to Elijah (1 Kgs 19:21), so she provides for Elisha. As Elisha refused to leave Elijah, she refuses to leave Elisha (2 Kgs 2:2, 4, 6 and 4:30—identical wording). Her insight is greater than Elisha's; she knows that Gehazi will not revive the child. The paralleling of her role with Elisha's serves only to cast Elisha in the Elijah mold.

11. The prophet is pictured as giving life (4:16) and restoring life (4:32-37). Within the broader picture of a weakened Israel, these stories present the prophet as one who can give new life where there is need and who can restore life when there is trouble and despair. Children spared, a pot rendered harmless, and a multitude fed all contribute to the picture of the prophet, preserver of life.

---

wave his hand over the spot, and cure the leprosy! [12]Are not Abana and Pharpar, the rivers of Damascus, better than all the waters of Israel? Could I not wash in them, and be clean?" He turned and went away in a rage. [13]But his servants approached and said to him, "Father, if the prophet had commanded you to do something difficult, would you not have done it? How much more, when all he said to you was, 'Wash, and be clean'?" [14]So he went down and immersed himself seven times in the Jordan, according to the word of the man of God; his flesh was restored like the flesh of a young boy, and he was clean.

15 Then he returned to the man of God, he and all his company; he came and stood before him and said, "Now I know that there is no God in all the earth except in Israel; please accept a present from your servant." [16]But he said, "As the Lord lives, whom I serve, I will accept nothing!" He urged him to accept, but he refused. [17]Then Naaman said, "If not, please let two mule-loads of earth be given to your servant; for your servant will no longer offer burnt offering or sacrifice to any god except the Lord. [18]But may the Lord pardon your servant on one count: when my master goes into the house of Rimmon to worship there, leaning on my arm, and I bow down in the house of Rimmon, when I do bow down in the house of Rimmon, may the Lord pardon your servant on this one count." [19]He said to him, "Go in peace."

But when Naaman had gone from him a short distance, [20]Gehazi, the servant of Elisha the man of God, thought, "My master has let that Aramean Naaman off too lightly by not accepting from him what he offered. As the Lord lives, I will run after him and get something out of him." [21]So Gehazi went after Naaman. When Naaman saw someone running after him, he jumped down from the chariot to meet him and said, "Is everything all right?" [22]He replied, "Yes, but my master has sent me to say, 'Two members of a company of prophets have just come to me from the hill country of Ephraim; please give them a talent of silver and two changes of clothing.' " [23]Naaman said, "Please accept two talents." He urged him, and tied up two talents of silver in two bags, with two changes of clothing, and gave them to two of his servants, who carried them in front of Gehazi. [24]When he came to the citadel, he took the bags from them, and stored them inside; he dismissed the men, and they left.

25 He went in and stood before his master; and Elisha said to him, "Where have you been, Gehazi?" He answered, "Your servant has not gone anywhere at all." [26]But he said to him, "Did I not go with you in spirit when someone left his chariot to meet you? Is this a time to accept money and to accept clothing, olive orchards and vineyards, sheep and oxen, and male and female slaves? [27]Therefore the leprosy of Naaman shall cling to you, and to your descendants forever." So he left his presence leprous, as white as snow.[12]

6 Now the company of prophets said to Elisha, "As you see, the place where we live under your charge is too small for us. [2]Let us go to the Jordan, and let us collect logs there, one for each of us, and build a place there for us to live." He answered, "Do so." [3]Then one of them said,

---

12. The domestic scene changes to the international. The prophet will heal where the king cannot. Obedience to the prophetic word brings healing, even to the foreign military. And indeed it brings peace.

The parallel with Moses is strong. As Moses interceded for Miriam's leprosy, so Elisha intervenes for the great Syrian general, Naaman. Miriam incurred leprosy for challenging the authority of Moses; Gehazi incurs leprosy for usurping the authority of Elisha.

| Main pre-DH: | Other pre-DH: | HKL: + single | **Josianic DH:** |
| *Prophetic Record and PR Extension* | single sideline | underline | **from the Dtr** |

"Please come with your servants." And he answered, "I will." [4]So he went with them. When they came to the Jordan, they cut down trees. [5]But as one was felling a log, his ax head fell into the water; he cried out, "Alas, master! It was borrowed." [6]Then the man of God said, "Where did it fall?" When he showed him the place, he cut off a stick, and threw it in there, and made the iron float. [7]He said, "Pick it up." So he reached out his hand and took it.

8 Once when the king of Aram was at war with Israel, he took counsel with his officers. He said, "At such and such a place shall be my camp." [9]But the man of God sent word to the king of Israel, "Take care not to pass this place, because the Arameans are going down there." [10]The king of Israel sent word to the place of which the man of God spoke. More than once or twice he warned such a place so that it was on the alert.

11 The mind of the king of Aram was greatly perturbed because of this; he called his officers and said to them, "Now tell me who among us sides with the king of Israel?" [12]Then one of his officers said, "No one, my lord king. It is Elisha, the prophet in Israel, who tells the king of Israel the words that you speak in your bedchamber." [13]He said, "Go and find where he is; I will send and seize him." He was told, "He is in Dothan." [14]So he sent horses and chariots there and a great army; they came by night, and surrounded the city.

15 When an attendant of the man of God rose early in the morning and went out, an army with horses and chariots was all around the city. His servant said, "Alas, master! What shall we do?" [16]He replied, "Do not be afraid, for there are more with us than there are with them." [17]Then Elisha prayed: "O Lord, please open his eyes that he may see." So the Lord opened the eyes of the servant, and he saw; the mountain was full of horses and chariots of fire all around

Elisha. [18]When the Arameans came down against him, Elisha prayed to the Lord, and said, "Strike this people, please, with blindness." So he struck them with blindness as Elisha had asked. [19]Elisha said to them, "This is not the way, and this is not the city; follow me, and I will bring you to the man whom you seek." And he led them to Samaria.

20 As soon as they entered Samaria, Elisha said, "O Lord, open the eyes of these men so that they may see." The Lord opened their eyes, and they saw that they were inside Samaria. [21]When the king of Israel saw them he said to Elisha, "Father, shall I kill them? Shall I kill them?" [22]He answered, "No! Did you capture with your sword and your bow those whom you want to kill? Set food and water before them so that they may eat and drink; and let them go to their master." [23]So he prepared for them a great feast; after they ate and drank, he sent them on their way, and they went to their master. And the Arameans no longer came raiding into the land of Israel.

24 Some time later King Ben-hadad of Aram mustered his entire army; he marched against Samaria and laid siege to it. [25]As the siege continued, famine in Samaria became so great that a donkey's head was sold for eighty shekels of silver, and one-fourth of a kab of dove's dung for five shekels of silver. [26]Now as the king of Israel was walking on the city wall, a woman cried out to him, "Help, my lord king!" [27]He said, "No! Let the Lord help you. How can I help you? From the threshing floor or from the wine press?" [28]But then the king asked her, "What is your complaint?" She answered, "This woman said to me, 'Give up your son; we will eat him today, and we will eat my son tomorrow.' [29]So we cooked my son and ate him. The next day I said to her, 'Give up your son and we will eat him.' But she has hidden her son." [30]When the king

After the Dtr: indented and sans serif font	DH Extension	**Revision: royal focus**	Revision: national focus	Other: double sideline

heard the words of the woman he tore his clothes—now since he was walking on the city wall, the people could see that he had sackcloth on his body underneath— [31]and he said, "So may God do to me, and more, if the head of Elisha son of Shaphat stays on his shoulders today." [32]So he dispatched a man from his presence.

Now Elisha was sitting in his house, and the elders were sitting with him. Before the messenger arrived, Elisha said to the elders, "Are you aware that this murderer has sent someone to take off my head? When the messenger comes, see that you shut the door and hold it closed against him. Is not the sound of his master's feet behind him?" [33]While he was still speaking with them, the king came down to him and said, "This trouble is from the LORD! Why should I hope in the LORD any longer?"

7 But Elisha said, "Hear the word of the LORD: thus says the LORD, Tomorrow about this time a measure of choice meal shall be sold for a shekel, and two measures of barley for a shekel, at the gate of Samaria." [2]Then the captain on whose hand the king leaned said to the man of God, "Even if the LORD were to make windows in the sky, could such a thing happen?" But he said, "You shall see it with your own eyes, but you shall not eat from it."

3 Now there were four leprous men outside the city gate, who said to one another, "Why should we sit here until we die? [4]If we say, 'Let us enter the city,' the famine is in the city, and we shall die there; but if we sit here, we shall also die. Therefore, let us desert to the Aramean camp; if they spare our lives, we shall live; and if they kill us, we shall but die." [5]So they arose at twilight to go to the Aramean camp; but when they came to the edge of the Aramean camp, there was no one there at all. [6]For the Lord had caused the Aramean army to hear the sound of chariots, and of horses, the sound of a great army, so that they said to one another, "The king of Israel has hired the kings of the Hittites and the kings of Egypt to fight against us." [7]So they fled away in the twilight and abandoned their tents, their horses, and their donkeys leaving the camp just as it was, and fled for their lives. [8]When these leprous men had come to the edge of the camp, they went into a tent, ate and drank, carried off silver, gold, and clothing, and went and hid them. Then they came back, entered another tent, carried off things from it, and went and hid them.

9 Then they said to one another, "What we are doing is wrong. This is a day of good news; if we are silent and wait until the morning light, we will be found guilty; therefore let us go and tell the king's household." [10]So they came and called to the gatekeepers of the city, and told them, "We went to the Aramean camp, but there was no one to be seen or heard there, nothing but the horses tied, the donkeys tied, and the tents as they were." [11]Then the gatekeepers called out and proclaimed it to the king's household. [12]The king got up in the night, and said to his servants, "I will tell you what the Arameans have prepared against us. They know that we are starving; so they have left the camp to hide themselves in the open country, thinking, 'When they come out of the city, we shall take them alive and get into the city.'" [13]One of his servants said, "Let some men take five of the remaining horses, since those left here will suffer the fate of the whole multitude of Israel that have perished already; let us send and find out." [14]So they took two mounted men, and the king sent them after the Aramean army, saying, "Go and find out." [15]So they went after them as far as the Jordan; the whole way was littered with garments and equipment that the Arameans had thrown away in their haste. So the messengers returned, and told the king.

Main pre-DH:	Other pre-DH:	HKL: + single	**Josianic DH:**
Prophetic Record and PR Extension	single sideline	underline	**from the Dtr**

16 Then the people went out, and plundered the camp of the Arameans. So a measure of choice meal was sold for a shekel, and two measures of barley for a shekel, according to the word of the Lord. [17]Now the king had appointed the captain on whose hand he leaned to have charge of the gate; the people trampled him to death in the gate, just as the man of God had said when the king came down to him. [18]For when the man of God had said to the king, "Two measures of barley shall be sold for a shekel, and a measure of choice meal for a shekel, about this time tomorrow in the gate of Samaria," [19]the captain had answered the man of God, "Even if the Lord were to make windows in the sky, could such a thing happen?" And he had answered, "You shall see it with your own eyes, but you shall not eat from it." [20]It did indeed happen to him; the people trampled him to death in the gate.[13]

---

13. Iron ax heads do not float; but one does for Elisha. As a general rule the prophets do not know the thoughts and secrets of kings. But Elisha does. And Balaam claimed to see what God saw (Num 24:4, 16). Elisha sees and hears what the king of Syria says and does—including the king's plans to seize Elisha. The vast superiority of Elisha's forces over against the king of Syria is revealed (6:16-17) and—irony of ironies—the one who sees into the king's cabinet blinds those whom the king has sent to seize him. Prophetic power so fully overwhelms royal power that the prophet can wine and dine his would-be captors and then release them.

The second time around, the king of Syria no longer seeks to capture Elisha but to capture the city of Samaria. The king of Samaria blames Elisha for the appalling suffering of the siege. His words are paradigmatic for kings: "Why should I hope in the Lord any longer?" (6:33). The prophet has demonstrated total awareness of royal moves; now he demonstrates total power where the king has failed wretchedly: the siege is broken and food is supplied.

8 Now Elisha had said to the woman whose son he had restored to life, "Get up and go with your household, and settle wherever you can; for the Lord has called for a famine, and it will come on the land for seven years." [2]So the woman got up and did according to the word of the man of God; she went with her household and settled in the land of the Philistines seven years. [3]At the end of the seven years, when the woman returned from the land of the Philistines, she set out to appeal to the king for her house and her land. [4]Now the king was talking with Gehazi the servant of the man of God, saying, "Tell me all the great things that Elisha has done." [5]While he was telling the king how Elisha had restored a dead person to life, the woman whose son he had restored to life appealed to the king for her house and her land. Gehazi said, "My lord king, here is the woman, and here is her son whom Elisha restored to life." [6]When the king questioned the woman, she told him. So the king appointed an official for her, saying, "Restore all that was hers, together with all the revenue of the fields from the day that she left the land until now."[14]

7 Elisha went to Damascus while King Ben-hadad of Aram was ill. When it was told him, "The man of God has come here," [8]the king said to Hazael, "Take a present with you and go to meet the man of God. Inquire of the Lord through him, whether I shall recover from this illness." [9]So Hazael went to meet him, taking a present with him, all kinds of goods of Damascus, forty camel loads. When he entered and stood before him, he said, "Your son King Ben-hadad of Aram has sent me to you, saying, 'Shall

---

14. According to the prophetic tradition, lives can be transformed in Israel through the word of the prophet. Here, a life is transformed even by a word about the prophet.

| After the Dtr: indented and sans serif font | DH Extension | **Revision: royal focus** | *Revision: national focus* | Other: double sideline |

I recover from this illness?' " [10]Elisha said to him, "Go, say to him, 'You shall certainly recover'; but the LORD has shown me that he shall certainly die." [11]He fixed his gaze and stared at him, until he was ashamed. Then the man of God wept. [12]Hazael asked, "Why does my lord weep?" He answered, "Because I know the evil that you will do to the people of Israel; you will set their fortresses on fire, you will kill their young men with the sword, dash in pieces their little ones, and rip up their pregnant women." [13]Hazael said, "What is your servant, who is a mere dog, that he should do this great thing?" Elisha answered, "The LORD has shown me that you are to be king over Aram." [14]Then he left Elisha, and went to his master Ben-hadad, who said to him, "What did Elisha say to you?" And he answered, "He told me that you would certainly recover." [15]But the next day he took the bed-cover and dipped it in water and spread it over the king's face, until he died. And Hazael succeeded him.[15]

16 In the fifth year of King Joram son of Ahab of Israel, Jehoram son of King Jehoshaphat of Judah began to reign. [17]He was thirty-two years old when he became king, and he reigned eight years in Jerusalem.

[18]He walked in the way of the kings of Israel, as the house of Ahab had done, for the daughter of Ahab was his wife. He did what was evil in the sight of the LORD.[16]

[19]**Yet the LORD would not destroy Judah, for the sake of his servant David, since he had promised to give a lamp to him and to his descendants forever.**[17]

20 In his days Edom revolted against the rule of Judah, and set up a king of their own. [21]Then Joram crossed over to Zair with all his chariots. He set out by night and attacked the Edomites and their chariot commanders who had surrounded him; but his army fled home. [22]So Edom has been in revolt against the rule of Judah to this day. Libnah also revolted at the same time.[18]

[23]**Now the rest of the acts of Joram, and all that he did, are they not written in the Book of the Annals of the Kings of Judah?**

[24]So Joram slept with his ancestors, and was buried with them in the city of David; his son Ahaziah succeeded him.

25 In the twelfth year of King Joram son of Ahab of Israel, Ahaziah son of King Jeho-

---

15. An odd little story reflecting the power of the prophet, the vision of the prophet, and the strangely remorseless word of the prophet. The prophet's power: Ben-hadad, king of Syria, sends Hazael to inquire of YHWH through Elisha, whose power is worth forty camel loads of Damascus's best. The prophet's vision: Elisha sees the accession of Hazael to power, the brutality of Hazael in power, and Elisha weeps for the pain of his people. The prophet's word: Elisha's word for Ben-hadad is "life"; to Hazael it is the awful truth of "death." Hazael murdered Ben-hadad and succeeded him. Shades of Jehu to come!

16. Jehoram is a king of Judah. Between Rehoboam and Hezekiah, the three kings of Judah accused of evil (Jehoram, Ahaziah, and Ahaz) are charged with walking in the way of the kings of Israel (Ahaziah: house of Ahab). As a result, their judgment formulas differ notably from those of the other kings of Judah, who as a rule in the HKL were deemed to have done "what was right in the sight of the LORD" except that "the high places were not taken away."

17. This is the third and last reference to the "lamp" for David (cf. 1 Kgs 11:36; 15:4). Dietrich attributed 8:19 to his DtrN.

18. This further evidence of the fragmentation of David's empire might have been preserved in association with the HKL, in some official or semi-official records, or otherwise independently.

Main pre-DH:	Other pre-DH:	HKL: + single	**Josianic DH:**
Prophetic Record and PR Extension	single sideline	underline	**from the Dtr**

ram of Judah began to reign. ²⁶Ahaziah was twenty-two years old when he began to reign; he reigned one year in Jerusalem. His mother's name was Athaliah, a granddaughter of King Omri of Israel.

²⁷He also walked in the way of the house of Ahab, doing what was evil in the sight of the Lord, as the house of Ahab had done, for he was son-in-law to the house of Ahab.¹⁹

28 He went with Joram son of Ahab to wage war against King Hazael of Aram at Ramoth-gilead, where the Arameans wounded Joram. ²⁹King Joram returned to be healed in Jezreel of the wounds that the Arameans had inflicted on him at Ramah, when he fought against King Hazael of Aram. King Ahaziah son of Jehoram of Judah went down to see Joram son of Ahab in Jezreel, because he was wounded.²⁰

9 *Then the prophet Elisha called a member of the company of prophets and said to him, "Gird up your loins; take this flask of oil in your hand, and go to Ramoth-gilead. ²When you arrive, look there for Jehu son of Jehoshaphat, son of Nimshi; go in and get him to leave his companions, and take him into an inner chamber. ³Then take the flask of oil, pour it on his head, and say, 'Thus says the LORD: I anoint you king over Israel.' Then open the door and flee; do not linger."²¹*

---

19. Ahaziah is another king of Judah charged with evil (see note on v. 18 above). The third is Ahaz.

20. There is a notable overlap here with 9:14-15a. The material could be derived from 9:14-15a or from some other source; in either case, it is likely to have been formulated by the Dtr for the composition of the Josianic DH, combining the reigns of north and south.

21. Resumption of the PR from 1:17a*.

Text signals in 9:1–10:28. (i) The instruction to anoint Jehu is given by Elisha to a member of the

4 So the young man, the young prophet, went to Ramoth-gilead. ⁵He arrived while the commanders of the army were in council, and he announced, "I have a message for you, commander." "For which one of us?" asked Jehu. "For you, commander." ⁶So Jehu

---

company of prophets. (ii) The action of anointing Jehu in private is reminiscent of the anointing of Saul and David. (iii) The accompanying speech has the same core identifiable for Ahab (1 Kgs 21:17-24) and Jeroboam (1 Kgs 14:7-11), and it has much the same dtr expansions as these. (iv) Jehu is given a full presentation in 9:14, for the second time, following v. 2. Note that the other occurrences do not mention Jehoshaphat as his father (1 Kgs 19:16; 2 Kgs 9:20; 2 Chron 22:7). (v) Jehu's words in 9:15b refer at least to the hurried proclamation of Jehu as king (vv. 11-13). (vi) The oracle in 9:25-26 is not attributed to a prophet and differs from the story in 1 Kings 21— where the designation "plot of ground" does not occur and there is no reference to Naboth's children. (vii) In 9:36-37, specific mention is made of the fulfillment of the word of the Lord, spoken by his servant Elijah the Tishbite. (viii) In 10:10, specific mention is made of the fulfillment of the word of the Lord, spoken by his servant Elijah.

Text-history approach. Three items of evidence signal the possible existence of an older story that was taken over by the PR. First, 9:14 could be the start of an older story. Second, 9:25-26, as noted, differ from 1 Kings 21. It is conceivable that a story could have been built up around them; it is difficult to envisage their being introduced into the existing story. Third, concern for the details of Ahaziah's burial in Jerusalem (v. 28) is not likely to be reflected in the PR.

It is possible that substantially the present story began at 9:14, to which was subsequently prefaced the prophetic claim in vv. 1-13. This hypothesis requires v. 15b to be regarded as a bridging verse, linking at least to vv. 11-13. Alternatively, and more economically, what is substantially the present text can be seen as a prophetic composition, from 9:1 to 10:28, possibly incorporating an older story. It would be the

---

After the Dtr: indented and sans serif font	DH Extension	**Revision: royal focus**	*Revision: national focus*	Other: double sideline

*got up and went inside; the young man poured the oil on his head, saying to him, "Thus says the LORD the God of Israel: I anoint you king over the people of the LORD, over Israel. *⁷You shall strike down the house of your master Ahab,* **so that I may avenge on**

---

culmination of the PR, claiming that the prophetic authorization of Jehu's coup was grounded in the traditions associating Samuel with Saul and David, Ahijah with Jeroboam, and Elijah with Ahab and his house. The elimination of Baal worship from Israel fits perfectly within this horizon. It is more difficult to envisage it within an independent story.

The action of anointing and commissioning Jehu is attributed to a member of the company of prophets, instructed by Elisha. Why this should be is puzzling. Historical reality has to be among the options. What is claimed for Elijah (the anointing of Hazael, Jehu, and Elisha, 1 Kgs 19:15-18) and for Elisha (the Damascus visit, 2 Kgs 8:7-15) imposes caution on any appeal to historical reality. Another possibility is that the endorsement of Jehu's coup—and even the composition of the PR—was the work of circles associated with the Elisha movement but not central enough to claim Elisha's personal action. We are left without certainty but, remarkably, the claim made is not extravagant. Another area of general ambivalence may be adverted to here. Hebrew syntax allows for a verbal form to be chosen that can be either command/commission or future foretelling (e.g., "you shall strike down" in v. 7). Often the context is clear, but not always. The now largely superseded distinction in English between "shall" and "will" is a similar case.

The dtr additions are identifiable by their language (esp. the reference to prophets as "servants") and will be discussed in turn.

Present-text potential. The unashamedly appalling story of Jehu's revolt, reveling in the killing and the bloodshed, is an appropriate culmination to a tradition claimed to go back to Samuel in distant antiquity and in recent generations to Elijah's confrontation on Mount Carmel. We do not know precisely when or why Israel turned against this particu-

---

Jezebel the blood of my servants the prophets, and the blood of all the servants of the LORD.

⁸For the whole house of Ahab shall perish; I will cut off from Ahab every male, bond or free, in Israel. ⁹I will make the house of Ahab like the house of Jeroboam son of Nebat, **and like the house of Baasha son of Ahijah. ¹⁰The dogs shall eat Jezebel in the territory of Jezreel, and no one shall bury her."**²²

Then he opened the door and fled.

11 When Jehu came back to his master's officers, they said to him, "Is everything all right? Why did

---

lar Baalism, with the ferocity, for example, embodied in Elijah. In the text attributed to the PR, Ahab bears the responsibility for its establishment in Israel. Elijah forces the confrontation and articulates the condemnation. Jehu sees to its political implementation. According to 2 Kgs 10:28, "Jehu wiped out Baal from Israel." According to Hosea, that was wishful thinking, to say the least—unless it is an issue of the foreign import versus the homegrown variety.

22. 9:7b, 9b-10a, and 36-37 are attributed to the Dtr; they need to be looked at together. The reference to the house of Baasha goes back to the dtr concerns in 1 Kgs 16:1-4, bringing all the northern dynasties under the prophetic word. The references to Jezebel are inextricably involved with the dtr formulation, "my servants the prophets" (9:7b) and the reference to Elijah the Tishbite as "his servant" (9:36). The traditions related to Ahab and Jezebel have been brought together in some cases prior to and in other cases in the composition of the Josianic DH (cf. 1 Kg 18:1-16); vv. 7b and 9b-10a bring the pronouncement of the PR up-to-date (cf. 1 Kgs 21:21-24). For 9:36-37, we may note the dtr concern for the fulfillment of the prophetic word (cf. note on 1 Kgs 14:18). The words (1 Kgs 21:23; 2 Kgs 9:10a, 36) may go back to an old saying regarding the fate of Jezebel. Note the development: v. 10a adds "and no one shall bury her"; and v. 37 explains "so that no one can say, This is Jezebel."

Dietrich attributed 9:7-10a to his DtrP.

| Main pre-DH: *Prophetic Record and PR Extension* | Other pre-DH: single sideline | HKL: + single underline | **Josianic DH: from the Dtr** |

that madman come to you?" He answered them, "You know the sort and how they babble." ¹²They said, "Liar! Come on, tell us!" So he said, "This is just what he said to me: 'Thus says the LORD, I anoint you king over Israel.' " ¹³Then hurriedly they all took their cloaks and spread them for him on the bare steps; and they blew the trumpet, and proclaimed, "Jehu is king."

14 Thus Jehu son of Jehoshaphat son of Nimshi conspired against Joram. Joram with all Israel had been on guard at Ramoth-gilead against King Hazael of Aram; ¹⁵but King Joram had returned to be healed in Jezreel of the wounds that the Arameans had inflicted on him, when he fought against King Hazael of Aram. So Jehu said, "If this is your wish, then let no one slip out of the city to go and tell the news in Jezreel." ¹⁶Then Jehu mounted his chariot and went to Jezreel, where Joram was lying ill. King Ahaziah of Judah had come down to visit Joram.

17 In Jezreel, the sentinel standing on the tower spied the company of Jehu arriving, and said, "I see a company." Joram said, "Take a horseman; send him to meet them, and let him say, 'Is it peace?' " ¹⁸So the horseman went to meet him; he said, "Thus says the king, 'Is it peace?' " Jehu responded, "What have you to do with peace? Fall in behind me." The sentinel reported, saying, "The messenger reached them, but he is not coming back." ¹⁹Then he sent out a second horseman, who came to them and said, "Thus says the king, 'Is it peace?' " Jehu answered, "What have you to do with peace? Fall in behind me." ²⁰Again the sentinel reported, "He reached them, but he is not coming back. It looks like the driving of Jehu son of Nimshi; for he drives like a maniac."

21 Joram said, "Get ready." And they got his chariot ready. Then King Joram of Israel and King Ahaziah of Judah set out, each in his chariot, and went to meet Jehu; they met him at the property of Naboth the Jezreelite. ²²When Joram saw Jehu, he said, "Is it peace, Jehu?" He answered, "What peace can there be, so long as the many whoredoms and sor-

ceries of your mother Jezebel continue?" ²³Then Joram reined about and fled, saying to Ahaziah, "Treason, Ahaziah!" ²⁴Jehu drew his bow with all his strength, and shot Joram between the shoulders, so that the arrow pierced his heart; and he sank in his chariot. ²⁵Jehu said to his aide Bidkar, "Lift him out, and throw him on the plot of ground belonging to Naboth the Jezreelite; for remember, when you and I rode side by side behind his father Ahab how the LORD uttered this oracle against him: ²⁶'For the blood of Naboth and for the blood of his children that I saw yesterday, says the LORD, I swear I will repay you on this very plot of ground.' Now therefore lift him out and throw him on the plot of ground, in accordance with the word of the LORD."

27 When King Ahaziah of Judah saw this, he fled in the direction of Beth-haggan. Jehu pursued him, saying, "Shoot him also!" And they shot him in the chariot at the ascent to Gur, which is by Ibleam. Then he fled to Megiddo, and died there. ²⁸His officers carried him in a chariot to Jerusalem, and buried him in his tomb with his ancestors in the city of David.

29 In the eleventh year of Joram son of Ahab, Ahaziah began to reign over Judah.

30 When Jehu came to Jezreel, Jezebel heard of it; she painted her eyes, and adorned her head, and looked out of the window. ³¹As Jehu entered the gate, she said, "Is it peace, Zimri, murderer of your master?" ³²He looked up to the window and said, "Who is on my side? Who?" Two or three eunuchs looked out at him. ³³He said, "Throw her down." So they threw her down; some of her blood spattered on the wall and on the horses, which trampled on her. ³⁴Then he went in and ate and drank; he said, "See to that cursed woman and bury her; for she is a king's daughter." ³⁵But when they went to bury her, they found no more of her than the skull and the feet and the palms of her hands. **³⁶When they came back and told him, he said, "This is the word of the LORD, which he spoke by his servant Elijah the Tishbite,**

| After the Dtr: indented and sans serif font | DH Extension | **Revision: royal focus** | *Revision: national focus* | Other: double sideline |

'In the territory of Jezreel the dogs shall eat the flesh of Jezebel; [37]the corpse of Jezebel shall be like dung on the field in the territory of Jezreel, so that no one can say, This is Jezebel.' "[23]

10 *Now Ahab had seventy sons in Samaria. So Jehu wrote letters and sent them to Samaria, to the rulers of Jezreel, to the elders, and to the guardians of the sons of Ahab, saying, [2]"Since your master's sons are with you and you have at your disposal chariots and horses, a fortified city, and weapons, [3]select the son of your master who is the best qualified, set him on his father's throne, and fight for your master's house." [4]But they were utterly terrified and said, "Look, two kings could not withstand him; how then can we stand?" [5]So the steward of the palace, and the governor of the city, along with the elders and the guardians, sent word to Jehu: "We are your servants; we will do anything you say. We will not make anyone king; do whatever you think right." [6]Then he wrote them a second letter, saying, "If you are on my side, and if you are ready to obey me, take the heads of your master's sons and come to me at Jezreel tomorrow at this time." Now the king's sons, seventy persons, were with the leaders of the city, who were charged with their upbringing. [7]When the letter reached them, they took the king's sons and killed them, seventy persons; they put their heads in baskets and sent them to him at Jezreel. [8]When the messenger came and told him, "They have brought the heads of the king's sons," he said, "Lay them in two heaps at the entrance of the gate until the morning." [9]Then in the morning when he went out, he stood and said to all the people, "You are innocent. It was I who conspired against my master and killed him; but who struck down all these?*

[10]**Know then that there shall fall to the earth nothing of the word of the LORD, which the LORD spoke concerning the house of Ahab; for the LORD has done what he said through his servant Elijah."[24]**

[11]*So Jehu killed all who were left of the house of Ahab in Jezreel, all his leaders, close friends, and priests, until he left him no survivor.*

12 Then he set out and went to Samaria. On the way, when he was at Beth-eked of the Shepherds, [13]Jehu met relatives of King Ahaziah of Judah and said, "Who are you?" They answered, "We are kin of Ahaziah; we have come down to visit the royal princes and the sons of the queen mother." [14]He said, "Take them alive." They took them alive, and slaughtered them at the pit of Beth-eked, forty-two in all; he spared none of them.

15 When he left there, he met Jehonadab son of Rechab coming to meet him; he greeted him, and said to him, "Is your heart as true to mine as mine is to yours?" Jehonadab answered, "It is." Jehu said, "If it is, give me your hand." So he gave him his hand. Jehu took him up with him into the chariot. [16]He said, "Come with me, and see my zeal for the LORD." So he had him ride in his chariot. [17]When he came to Samaria, he killed all who were left to Ahab in Samaria, until he had wiped them out, according to the word of the LORD that he spoke to Elijah.[25]

18 Then Jehu assembled all the people and said to them, "Ahab offered Baal small service; but Jehu will offer much more. [19]Now therefore summon to me all

---

23. Dietrich attributed 9:36b-37 to his DtrN, tentatively.

24. The reference to Elijah as "his servant" suggests dtr provenance. In this case, the Dtr offers an overview from Samuel (cf. 1 Sam 3:19) to Elijah, in which the undoing of the house of Ahab is the doing of YHWH. For much the same sentiment expressed in v. 10a, but with variations of formulation, cf. Josh 21:45 and 1 Sam 3:19.

25. There is no pointer to dtr formulation in v. 17b (see the note on 2 Kgs 1:17 above).

Main pre-DH:	Other pre-DH:	HKL: + single	**Josianic DH:**
Prophetic Record and PR Extension	single sideline	underline	**from the Dtr**

the prophets of Baal, all his worshipers, and all his priests; let none be missing, for I have a great sacrifice to offer to Baal; whoever is missing shall not live." But Jehu was acting with cunning in order to destroy the worshipers of Baal. *²⁰Jehu decreed, "Sanctify a solemn assembly for Baal." So they proclaimed it. ²¹Jehu sent word throughout all Israel; all the worshipers of Baal came, so that there was no one left who did not come. They entered the temple of Baal, until the temple of Baal was filled from wall to wall. ²²He said to the keeper of the wardrobe, "Bring out the vestments for all the worshipers of Baal." So he brought out the vestments for them. ²³Then Jehu entered the temple of Baal with Jehonadab son of Rechab; he said to the worshipers of Baal, "Search and see that there is no worshiper of the LORD here among you, but only worshipers of Baal." ²⁴Then they proceeded to offer sacrifices and burnt offerings.*

Now Jehu had stationed eighty men outside, saying, "Whoever allows any of those to escape whom I deliver into your hands shall forfeit his life." ²⁵As soon as he had finished presenting the burnt offering, Jehu said to the guards and to the officers, "Come in and kill them; let no one escape." So they put them to the sword. The guards and the officers threw them out, and then went into the citadel of the temple of Baal. ²⁶They brought out the pillar that was in the temple of Baal, and burned it. ²⁷Then they demolished the pillar of Baal, and destroyed the temple of Baal, and made it a latrine to this day.

28 Thus Jehu wiped out Baal from Israel.²⁶
²⁹But Jehu did not turn aside from the sins of Jeroboam son of Nebat, which he caused Israel to commit.²⁷

---

26. The PR ends here with the extirpation of Baal worship from Israel.

27. Here begins the so-called "extension" of the PR. It extends from after Jehu until the end of the northern kingdom (Hoshea), and its identification is based on the particular pattern recurring within

—the golden calves that were in Bethel and in Dan.²⁸

³⁰The LORD said to Jehu, "Because you have done well in carrying out what I consider right, and in accordance with all that was in

---

the judgment formulas in the DH (see Campbell, *Of Prophets and Kings*, 139-68, following on from H. Weippert). The accusation of not turning aside from (not departing from) the sins of Jeroboam is central to this pattern identified in these judgment formulas (see 2 Kgs 10:29; 13:2, 11; 14:24; 15:9, 18, 24, 28). Campbell terms this "pattern A" (see Introduction and Tables). It cannot be accounted for by random distribution; it is used exclusively for the northern kings from Jehu to Pekah, a series ending with Hoshea. The text attributed to this extension is set in italics.

The focus of this PR Extension is on the sin of Jeroboam; Jehu and his successors did not "depart" from it. The PR culminated in Jehu's coup and the purge of Baal worship from Israel. Subsequent reflection on the experience of the northern kingdom forced a shift of focus back to its founder, Jeroboam, and a theological emphasis on his sin. This sin is seen as a pervasive and corrosive element in the society of northern Israel. Its identification is not simple. For the PR and its extension, the sin may have included the indiscriminate ordination of priests, eroding the religious fabric of society (cf. Hos 4:4-10); but this sin was focused on the house of Jeroboam (1 Kgs 13:34). The text associated with the establishment of the golden calves is surprisingly muted, but seems to convey some sense of national sin (see 1 Kgs 12:30 and the discussion there). For the Josianic and later DH, the golden calves came to symbolize apostasy, expressed by the rejection of the exclusive worship of YHWH in Jerusalem (cf. 1 Kgs 12:26-30, 31-33; 13:33b-34; and for later dtr, 1 Kgs 14:9bα).

28. The reference to the golden calves is in apposition to the immediately preceding pronoun in Hebrew, itself referring to the sins of Jeroboam. For the sins of Jeroboam, see the preceding note. The

---

After the Dtr:	DH	*Revision:*	*Revision:*	Other:
indented and sans serif font	Extension	*royal focus*	*national focus*	double sideline

my heart have dealt with the house of Ahab, your sons of the fourth generation shall sit on the throne of Israel." [31]But Jehu was not careful to follow the law of the LORD the God of Israel with all his heart; he did not turn from the sins of Jeroboam, which he caused Israel to commit.[29]

32 In those days the LORD began to trim off parts of Israel. Hazael defeated them throughout the territory of Israel: [33]from the Jordan eastward, all the land of Gilead, the Gadites, the Reubenites, and the Manassites, from Aroer, which is by the Wadi Arnon, that is, Gilead and Bashan. **[34]Now the rest of the acts of Jehu, all that he did, and all his power, are they not written in the Book of the Annals of the Kings of Israel?** *[35]So Jehu slept with his ancestors, and they buried him in Samaria. His son Jehoahaz succeeded him.* **[36]The time that Jehu reigned over Israel in Samaria was twenty-eight years.** [30]

---

reference here recalls the nature of Jeroboam's action. At the earliest, it reflects the ideology of the Dtr; it may derive from later generations.

29. **Text signals** in 2 Kgs 10:30-31. (i) The introduction, in which God speaks directly to the king, is unique for a prophecy in the DH. (ii) Jehu's dynasty is not described as a "house" but as "your sons." (iii) The combination of "to do well" and "to do the right" is not found elsewhere in the DH—or in the Hebrew Scriptures. (iv) The fulfillment notice in 2 Kgs 15:12 is outside the regnal framework and formulated differently from the Dtr's fulfillment notices. (v) Terminology such as "doing right" in God's eyes and what was "in my heart" has echoes of dtr language. (vi) The accusation in the first part of v. 31 is clearly concerned with the law (v. 31a); the second part resumes the thread of v. 29.

Text-history approach. Dynasties are important in the DH. Omri's ran for four kings and three generations. Jehu's ran for four generations. An explanation is needed: why four and why only four? V. 30 offers such an explanation. The text signals make dtr attribution unlikely; hence the double sideline. The condemnation of Jehu, especially if associated with the golden calves, needed to be balanced by the tradition that Jehu did God's bidding through Elisha and the history that he founded a four-generation dynasty. The prophets claimed that Jehu indeed did God's bidding but it was in relation to the elimination of Ahab's dynasty. Note the language of vv. 30-31; v. 30 relates to God's will ("in my heart") and v. 31a to Jehu's actions ("his heart"). V. 31b is a resumptive repetition, picking up the thread of v. 29.

Present-text potential. The condemnation in v. 29a situates Jehu in the broad sweep of the text that

11 Now when Athaliah, Ahaziah's mother, saw that her son was dead, she set about to destroy all the royal family. [2]But Jehosheba, King Joram's daughter, Ahaziah's sister, took Joash son of

---

reaches back to the sins of Jeroboam, whether the indiscriminate consecration of priests or the apostasy associated with the golden calves or some combination. The promise of a dynasty reflects the prophetic commission to eliminate the house of Ahab. The text presents Jehu as an ambivalent figure: obedient to the prophetic commission; unwilling to depart from or reform the political necessities of his kingdom.

Dietrich attributed 10:17 to his DtrP and 10:10, 30-31a to his DtrN.

30. Verses 32-33 could be omitted from a minimal text of the PR Extension and regarded as a later addition. They make good sense, however, as the beginning of an increasingly negative trajectory. They are not incompatible with our observations on the text history in Deuteronomy and Joshua with regard to details of the east-of-Jordan tribes; there may in fact be a causal connection, following this "trimming off."

It may be noted here that the synchronistic chronology, its associated formulas, and the references to the Book of the Annals of the Kings of Israel, as well as similar chronological observations, all derive from the Dtr. The Extension continues in 13:2.

| Main pre-DH: *Prophetic Record and PR Extension* | Other pre-DH: single sideline | HKL: + single underline | **Josianic DH: from the Dtr** |

Ahaziah, and stole him away from among the king's children who were about to be killed; she put him and his nurse in a bedroom. Thus she hid him from Athaliah, so that he was not killed; [3]he remained with her six years, hidden in the house of the Lord, while Athaliah reigned over the land.[31]

4 But in the seventh year Jehoiada summoned the captains of the Carites and of the guards and had them come to him in the house of the Lord. He made a covenant with them and put them under oath in the house of the Lord; then he showed them the king's son. [5]He commanded them, "This is what you are to do: one-third of you, those who go off duty on the sabbath and guard the king's house [6](another third being at the gate Sur and a third at the gate behind the

31The story of Athaliah's coup and its reversal is of sufficient substance and interest to have circulated independently. It involves the survival of the Davidic dynasty, the fall of Athaliah, daughter of Ahab and Jezebel, the death of Mattan, priest of Baal, and the emergence of Jehoash as king, instructed by the priest Jehoiada. A variety of influences is visible in the chapter and its literary unity has been debated (for the discussion, see O'Brien, *Deuteronomistic History Hypothesis*, 218, n. 164).

In the present text, this Athaliah story is a balance to the story of Jehu's revolt. By contrast with Jehu's bloodbath, Jehoiada's counter-coup in the south is achieved with a minimum of violence—with Athaliah's execution outside the temple, an appropriate renewal of the people's commitment to yhwh, the demolition of Baal's temple and the execution of his priest (and this in Jerusalem!), and the enthronement of the king in his palace.

Queen Athaliah ruled over Judah in Jerusalem for six years or more (cf. 11:3). Recognition of royalty in scripture is uneven. Abimelech gets it from no one; Ishbaal gets it from the Dtr but no one else (2 Sam 2:10a); Athaliah gets it neither from the Dtr nor from most scholarship.

guards), shall guard the palace; [7]and your two divisions that come on duty in force on the sabbath and guard the house of the Lord [8]shall surround the king, each with weapons in hand; and whoever approaches the ranks is to be killed. Be with the king in his comings and goings."

9 The captains did according to all that the priest Jehoiada commanded; each brought his men who were to go off duty on the sabbath, with those who were to come on duty on the sabbath, and came to the priest Jehoiada. [10]The priest delivered to the captains the spears and shields that had been King David's, which were in the house of the Lord; [11]the guards stood, every man with his weapons in his hand, from the south side of the house to the north side of the house, around the altar and the house, to guard the king on every side. [12]Then he brought out the king's son, put the crown on him, and gave him the covenant; they proclaimed him king, and anointed him; they clapped their hands and shouted, "Long live the king!"

13 When Athaliah heard the noise of the guard and of the people, she went into the house of the Lord to the people; [14]when she looked, there was the king standing by the pillar, according to custom, with the captains and the trumpeters beside the king, and all the people of the land rejoicing and blowing trumpets. Athaliah tore her clothes and cried, "Treason! Treason!" [15]Then the priest Jehoiada commanded the captains who were set over the army, "Bring her out between the ranks, and kill with the sword anyone who follows her." For the priest said, "Let her not be killed in the house of the Lord." [16]So they laid hands on her; she went through the horses' entrance to the king's house, and there she was put to death.

17 Jehoiada made a covenant between the Lord and the king and people, that they should be the Lord's people; also between the king and

| After the Dtr: indented and sans serif font | DH Extension | **Revision: royal focus** | Revision: national focus | Other: double sideline |

the people. [18]Then all the people of the land went to the house of Baal, and tore it down; his altars and his images they broke in pieces, and they killed Mattan, the priest of Baal, before the altars. The priest posted guards over the house of the LORD. [19]He took the captains, the Carites, the guards, and all the people of the land; then they brought the king down from the house of the LORD, marching through the gate of the guards to the king's house. He took his seat on the throne of the kings. [20]So all the people of the land rejoiced; and the city was quiet after Athaliah had been killed with the sword at the king's house.

21 Jehoash was seven years old when he began to reign.

12 In the seventh year of Jehu, Jehoash began to reign; he reigned forty years in Jerusalem. His mother's name was Zibiah of Beer-sheba.

[2]Jehoash did what was right in the sight of the LORD all his days, because the priest Jehoiada instructed him. [3]Nevertheless the high places were not taken away; the people continued to sacrifice and make offerings on the high places.[32]

4 Jehoash said to the priests, "All the money offered as sacred donations that is brought into the house of the LORD, the money for which each person is assessed—the money from the assessment of persons—and the money from the voluntary offerings brought into the house of the LORD, [5]let the priests receive from each of the donors; and let them repair the house wherever any need of repairs is discovered." [6]But by the twenty-third year of King Jehoash the priests had made no repairs on the house. [7]Therefore King Jehoash summoned the priest Jehoiada with the other priests and said to them, "Why are you not repairing the house? Now therefore do not accept any more money from your donors but hand it over for the repair of the house." [8]So the priests agreed that they would neither accept more money from the people nor repair the house.[33]

---

32. Two elements point to the standard form of what we are calling the HKL: approval of the king and reserve about the continued use of the high places. The occurrence here is a return to the standard form of this judgment, after the variations involving Jehoram and Ahaziah, both of whom had married into the house of Ahab (2 Kgs 8:18, 27). Jehoram's death is reported in 2 Kgs 8:24. If Ahaziah's death and his succession by Jehoash featured in the HKL, the former has been replaced by the story of Jehu's coup and the latter by the story of Athaliah. For discussion of the HKL, see the Introduction and the note on 1 Kgs 22:43-44; this information will not need to be repeated with subsequent occurrences.

---

33. The question has been raised whether vv. 4-16 (NRSV; Heb., vv. 5-17) are pre- or post-exilic in provenance—in the latter case, modeled on 2 Kgs 22:3-10. Temple repairs may be presumed to have happened often; we have only these two texts on the subject. Reference to the high priest, if original, would favor a post-exilic origin; with the possible exception of 2 Kgs 12:10 (under Jehoash) and 2 Kgs 22:4, 8; 23:4 (under Josiah), the title is not found before the exile. On the other hand, the king's secretary in v. 10 is preceded by a singular verb; those that follow are plural. We favor a pre-exilic origin for the passage (for discussion of the details, see O'Brien, *Deuteronomistic History Hypothesis*, 241-43). In particular here, we may note that Jehoiada, the central priestly figure, is not referred to as the high priest and that it is difficult to account for the later creation of such a story associated with the otherwise almost neglected figure of King Jehoash.

Our conclusion, mirrored in the text, is that the adjective "high" (*gādôl*) has been inserted to qualify the

---

Main pre-DH:	Other pre-DH:	HKL: + single	**Josianic DH:**
Prophetic Record and PR Extension	single sideline	underline	**from the Dtr**

9 Then the priest Jehoiada took a chest, made a hole in its lid, and set it beside the altar on the right side as one entered the house of the LORD; the priests who guarded the threshold put in it all the money that was brought into the house of the LORD. [10]Whenever they saw that there was a great deal of money in the chest, the king's secretary and the [high] priest went up, counted the money that was found in the house of the LORD, and tied it up in bags. [11]They would give the money that was weighed out into the hands of the workers who had the oversight of the house of the LORD; then they paid it out to the carpenters and the builders who worked on the house of the LORD, [12]to the masons and the stonecutters, as well as to buy timber and quarried stone for making repairs on the house of the LORD, as well as for any outlay for repairs of the house. [13]But for the house of the LORD no basins of silver, snuffers, bowls, trumpets, or any vessels of gold, or of silver, were made from the money that was brought into the house of the LORD, [14]for that was given to the workers who were repairing the house of the LORD with it. [15]They did not ask an accounting from those into whose hand they delivered the money to pay out to the workers, for they dealt honestly. [16]The money from the guilt offerings and the money from the sin offerings was not brought into the house of the LORD; it belonged to the priests.

17 At that time King Hazael of Aram went up, fought against Gath, and took it. But when Hazael set his face to go up against Jerusalem, [18]King Jehoash of Judah took all the votive gifts that Jehoshaphat, Jehoram, and Ahaziah, his ancestors, the kings of Judah, had dedicated, as well as his

priest here and also in 2 Kgs 22:4, 8; 23:4. Hence "the [high] priest."

own votive gifts, all the gold that was found in the treasuries of the house of the LORD and of the king's house, and sent these to King Hazael of Aram. Then Hazael withdrew from Jerusalem.[34]

19 Now the rest of the acts of Joash, and all that he did, are they not written in the Book of the Annals of the Kings of Judah? [20]His servants arose, devised a conspiracy, and killed Joash in the house of Millo, on the way that goes down to Silla. [21]It was Jozacar son of Shimeath and Jehozabad son of Shomer, his servants, who struck him down, so that he died. He was buried with his ancestors in the city of David; then his son Amaziah succeeded him.[35]

13 In the twenty-third year of King Joash son of Ahaziah of Judah, Jehoahaz son of Jehu began to reign over Israel in Samaria; he reigned seventeen years. *[2]He did what was evil in the sight of the LORD, and followed the sins of Jeroboam son of Nebat, which he caused Israel to sin; he did not depart from them.*[36]

[3]The anger of the LORD was kindled against Israel, so that he gave them repeatedly into the hand of King Hazael of Aram, then into

34. The ransacking of the temple by threatened kings of Judah has been noted on four occasions, of which this is the second. It is attributed to the royal focus within the dtr revision process (see above, on 1 Kgs 15:22).

35. These verses are attributed to the HKL. The HKL almost invariably has at least four elements: accession, judgment, death, and succession for each king of Judah. Here we have the assassination of Joash and the succession of his son Amaziah. Amaziah, too, will be assassinated and succeeded by Azariah (2 Kgs 14:19-21).

36. Resumption of the Extension from 10:35.

| After the Dtr: indented and sans serif font | DH Extension | **Revision: royal focus** | Revision: national focus | Other: double sideline |

the hand of Ben-hadad son of Hazael. ⁴But Jehoahaz entreated the LORD, and the LORD heeded him; for he saw the oppression of Israel, how the king of Aram oppressed them. ⁵Therefore the LORD gave Israel a savior, so that they escaped from the hand of the Arameans; and the people of Israel lived in their homes as formerly. ⁶Nevertheless they did not depart from the sins of the house of Jeroboam, which he caused Israel to sin, but walked in them; the sacred pole also remained in Samaria.³⁷

⁷*So Jehoahaz was left with an army of not more than fifty horsemen, ten chariots and ten thousand footmen; for the king of Aram had destroyed them and made them like the dust at threshing.* **⁸Now the rest of the acts of Jehoahaz and all that he did, including his might, are they not written in the Book of the Annals of the Kings of Israel?** ⁹*So Jehoahaz slept with his ancestors, and they buried him in Samaria; then his son Joash succeeded him.*³⁸

---

37. **Text signals** in 13:3-6. (i) In v. 3, the focus is on Israel, whereas in v. 2 it is on Jehoahaz. (ii) A reflection is evident of the framework and theology of Judges 3–9, but with significant differences. What is common: doing of evil (here in v. 2); God's anger; God's punishment through oppressors; cry to the LORD; giving of a savior; deliverance. The differences are noteworthy. In Judges, the evil is Israel's; here, it is Jehoahaz's (in v. 2). In Judges, Israel cried ($\sqrt{Z'Q}$) to the LORD; here, Jehoahaz entreated ($\sqrt{HLH}$) YHWH; both the subjects and the verbs are different. In Judges, a savior is "raised up"; here, the savior is "given." There is no mention of "rest" or of fidelity for the savior's generation. (iii) Israel ("they") is accused of the sins of the house of Jeroboam; normally, this accusation is made against the king. (iv) In v. 2, Jehoahaz did what was evil in the sight of the LORD; in v. 4, Jehoahaz entreated the LORD; this is the Judges sequence, from impious and unpunished to punished and pious. (v) The deliverance (v. 5) does not sit well with the military impoverishment of Jehoahaz (v. 7)—despite v. 6.

Text-history approach. The shift of emphasis from king to people, the echo of the pattern of the Judges (nowhere else in the DH account of kings), the absence of legal language, and the various differences noted suggest a post-dtr attribution.

Present-text potential. An understanding here needs to go back to 2 Kgs 10:32 where "the LORD began to trim off parts of Israel." Much of the northeast is noted in 10:33. The diminishment of

Jehoahaz's army at the hands of the Syrians is noted in 13:7. These verses, 13:3-6, express faith that God's deliverance under the Judges was still available to Israel; they squandered it by not departing from the sins of the house of Jeroboam.

38. **Text signals** for 13:7—14:16. This passage is problematic in the extreme, for some difficult and for others disordered. We will offer two possibilities for interpretation that we believe reasonable; we will not be rash enough to make any definitive claim. Not all possibilities will be developed.

Before anything else, the signals in the text need careful attention. The major signal is that the formulas for the end of Joash's reign (13:12-13) recur in 14:15-16, but this is not the only matter demanding attention. In our treatment, the **text signals** for 13:7–14:16 will be listed here. The **present-text potential** will also be discussed here. The aspect of **text-history approach** will be treated in separate notes: see on 13:12-13, 13:14-25 (for the Elisha traditions), 13:23, 14:5-7, and 14:8-14 (for the civil war tradition).

The **text signals**. (i) 13:12 is virtually identical with 14:15. (ii) 13:13 is identical in content with 14:16. (iii) Joash of Israel is dead and succeeded by Jeroboam II in 13:13 while in 13:14 he is alive and well and visiting the dying Elisha. (iv) In 13:7, Israel is militarily powerless, thanks to the Syrians; in the next generation, Israel is defeating the Syrians (13:25). (v). In 13:7, Israel is militarily powerless; in 14:8-14, Israel overwhelms Judah which has been powerful enough to defeat Edom. (vi) 13:14-21 contains a tradition

---

Main pre-DH:	Other pre-DH:	HKL: + single	**Josianic DH:**
Prophetic Record and PR Extension	single sideline	underline	**from the Dtr**

10 In the thirty-seventh year of King Joash of Judah, Jehoash son of Jehoahaz began to reign over Israel in Samaria; he reigned sixteen years. *¹¹He also did what was evil in the sight of the LORD; he did not depart from all the sins of Jeroboam son of Nebat, which he caused Israel to sin, but he walked in them.³⁹*

¹²Now the rest of the acts of Joash, and all that he did, as well as the might with which he fought against King Amaziah of Judah,

---

about Elisha which is isolated in text and time—Elisha was last active in 9:1-3 and three or four generations of kings have passed since Elisha's service began in the time of Elijah and Ahab. (vii) Civil war between Israel and Judah and the sacking of Jerusalem and pillaging of its temple by Israel (14:8-14) are matters for national shame. (viii) The Elisha tradition explains the renewed military power of Israel (13:14-25); this renewal is in proximity to the report of civil war, with its plundering of Jerusalem and God's temple there (14:8-14). (ix) 13:22 reports that Hazael "oppressed Israel all the days of Jehoahaz," while 13:9 reported the death of Jehoahaz. (x) 13:24-25 deal with Joash (Jehoash) strongly reflecting the Elisha story. (xi) Marked chronological discrepancies exist in association with this material (cf. 12:1 and 13:10; 13:1 and 14:23). So far, no satisfactory solution to these discrepancies has emerged (cf. T. R. Hobbs, *2 Kings*, 184-85). (xii) While 13:25 is evidently the fulfillment of Elisha's prophecy, there is no notice to that effect.

The Lucianic text of the LXX has certain differences. For example, the offending 13:12-13 is found after 13:25; 13:23 is found after 13:7. Fundamentally the Lucianic moves, while interesting, do not resolve the basic issues.

Present-text potential of 13:7–14:16. Several options are available to the reader of the present text. One is to consider it as disordered and beyond meaningful recovery; the duplication of the regnal formulas is not susceptible of intelligent interpretation. Alternatively, the closure of the reign of Joash (13:12-13) creates a certain distance between the negative of v. 11 and the positive of v. 14; it also places the prophetic story outside the regnal framework and so highlights the autonomous role of Elisha. In this second option, the prophetic traditions are viewed on their own; they are not associated with the civil war traditions to come. A third option does associate these prophetic

traditions with the civil war, recognizing that Israel's military recovery was a prerequisite for its victory in the war, which had so sacrilegious an outcome. In this case, the repetition of the regnal formulas (13:12-13 and 14:15-16) allows the prophetic and civil war traditions to be bracketed out, if so desired. Such a repetition, not necessarily with the same function, is found in Josh 24:28-31 and Judg 2:6-9. There the repetition frames variant traditions of the Israelites' occupation of Canaan; here the repetition may create a variant option for telling the nation's story.

The Elisha story attributes the restoration of northern Israel's military strength and its international fortunes to the power of the dying prophet. Joash, practically bereft of horsemen and chariots (cf. 13:7), addresses Elisha with his own words to Elijah, "My father, my father! The chariots of Israel and its horsemen!" (see 13:14 and 2:12; cf. also 6:17). The prophet promises victory, but limited. In this context, the burial story (13:20-21) symbolizes the new life Israel has received from contact with Elisha. With his burial, the limits may now not be lifted.

Verses 22-25 encapsulate the outcome of this experience. They look to the past under Jehoahaz, with the impact of Syrian oppression mitigated by God's compassion (vv. 22-23), and to the present context of Jehoash, with victory achieved three times (vv. 24-25).

Amaziah of Judah and his reign are introduced in 14:1-7. The civil war he precipitated, with its sacrilegious consequences, is reported in vv. 8-14. It is possible to see an association between the military restoration, enabled by Elisha, and the defeat of Judah, inflicted by Jehoash.

With 14:15-16, the text returns to the ordinary sequence of Israelite kings.

39. The Extension continues in 14:16.

| After the Dtr: indented and sans serif font | DH Extension | **Revision:** **royal focus** | *Revision:* *national focus* | Other: double sideline |

are they not written in the Book of the Annals of the Kings of Israel? [13]So Joash slept with his ancestors, and Jeroboam sat upon his throne; Joash was buried in Samaria with the kings of Israel.[40]

14 Now when Elisha had fallen sick with the illness of which he was to die, King Joash of Israel went down to him, and wept before him, crying, "My father, my father! The chariots of Israel and its horsemen!" [15]Elisha said to him, "Take a bow and arrows"; so he took a bow and arrows. [16]Then he said to the king of Israel, "Draw the bow"; and he drew it. Elisha laid his hands on the king's hands. [17]Then he said, "Open the window eastward"; and he opened it. Elisha said, "Shoot"; and he shot. Then he said, "The LORD's arrow of victory, the arrow of victory over Aram! For you shall fight the

Arameans in Aphek until you have made an end of them." [18]And he said *(Heb.; NRSV, He contin-ued)*, "Take the arrows"; and he took them. He said to the king of Israel, "Strike the ground with them"; he struck three times, and stopped. [19]Then the man of God was angry with him, and said, "You should have struck five or six times; then you would have struck down Aram until you had made an end of it, but now you will strike down Aram only three times."

20 So Elisha died, and they buried him. Now bands of Moabites used to invade the land in the spring of the year. [21]As a man was being buried, a marauding band was seen and the man was thrown into the grave of Elisha; as soon as the man touched the bones of Elisha, he came to life and stood on his feet.

22 Now King Hazael of Aram oppressed Israel all the days of Jehoahaz.

[23]But the LORD was gracious to them and had compassion on them; he turned toward them, because of his covenant with Abraham, Isaac, and Jacob, and would not destroy them; nor has he banished them from his presence until now.[41]

24 When King Hazael of Aram died, his son Ben-hadad succeeded him. [25]Then Jehoash son

---

40. **Text-history approach.** 13:12-13 is considered secondary to the Josianic DH, because the standard formulation for regnal formulas is found in 14:15-16 (a combination of the Josianic Dtr [v. 15] and the PR Extension [v. 16]). The formulation here is marginally but significantly different. In any view, 13:12-13 constitutes a problem. It is not explained by chance displacement; the text is not the same as 14:15-16. From one aspect, following vv. 10-11, it is without question in the right place; from another aspect, with vv. 14ff., it is without question in the wrong place. It is an enigma, still to be unraveled (see above, on 13:7—14:16).

One option derives vv. 12-13 from a focus on 13:14-25. The insertion separates vv. 11 and 14; it shifts the focus to the separate tradition of the prophet and the fulfillment of his word. Another option derives vv. 12-13 from a focus on the association of 13:14-25 with 14:8-14, found shocking. The insertion allows a reader to stop at 13:13, bypass the following episodes, and resume with 14:17. A further option dismisses the text as disordered. In these verses, nothing points to identifiable dtr revision.

41. **Text-history approach** to 13:23. As has been noted for 1 Kgs 19:10, 14, the term "covenant" in the DH is usually later than the Josianic Dtr; the conjunction of Abraham, Isaac, and Jacob is unlikely to be earlier than the Dtr (cf. Deut 1:8; 6:10; 9:5, 27; 29:13; 30:20; 34:4; however, see 1 Kgs 18:36). The verse claims to account for the survival of Israel under Jehoahaz, neither destroyed nor exiled in the oppression by Hazael. The appeal to the covenant with the ancestors is a quite different theology from 13:3-6, modeled on the Judges. The "until now" at the end of the verse could refer to the exile of either 722 or 586.

Dietrich attributed 13:4-6, 23 to his DtrN.

Main pre-DH:	Other pre-DH:	HKL: + single	**Josianic DH:**
Prophetic Record and PR Extension	single sideline	underline	**from the Dtr**

of Jehoahaz took again from Ben-hadad son of Hazael the towns that he had taken from his father Jehoahaz in war. Three times Joash defeated him and recovered the towns of Israel.[42]

14 **In the second year of King Joash son of Joahaz of Israel, King Amaziah son of Joash of Judah, began to reign. ²He was twenty-five years old when he began to reign, and he reigned twenty-nine years in Jerusalem. His mother's name was Jehoaddin of Jerusalem.** ³He did what was right in the sight of the LORD, yet not like his ancestor David; in all things he did as his father Joash had done. ⁴But the high places were not removed; the people still sacrificed and made offerings on the high places. ⁵As soon as the royal power was firmly in his hand he killed his servants who had murdered his father the king.[43]

⁶But he did not put to death the children of the murderers; according to what is written in the book of the law of Moses, where the LORD commanded, "The parents shall not be put to death for the children, or the children be put to death for the parents; but all shall be put to death for their own sins."[44]

7 He killed ten thousand Edomites in the Valley of Salt and took Sela by storm; he called it Jokthe-el, which is its name to this day.

8 Then Amaziah sent messengers to King Jehoash son of Jehoahaz, son of Jehu, of Israel, saying, "Come, let us look one another in the face." ⁹King Jehoash of Israel sent word to King Amaziah of Judah, "A thornbush on Lebanon sent to a cedar on Lebanon, saying, 'Give your daughter to my son for a wife'; but a wild animal of Lebanon passed by and trampled down the thornbush. ¹⁰You have indeed defeated Edom, and your heart has lifted you up. Be content with your glory, and stay at home; for why should you provoke trouble so that you fall, you and Judah with you?"

---

42. **Text-history approach.** The attribution of 13:14-25 (apart from 13:23) must be regarded as uncertain. There is evident celebration of Israel's recovery, from weakness (Jehoahaz under Hazael, 13:7) to strength (Jehoash over Ben-hadad, 13:25), thanks to Elisha. Yet the story is not triumphant: Jehoash is victorious, but only three times; without a prophet, Israel's success is limited. There is conflict with 13:4-5. Here, however, in vv. 14-25*, we have a prophetic story; there, in 13:3-6, we have material modeled on the deliverance in Judges.

The text juxtaposes the negative judgment on Joash in v. 11 with his positive portrayal in v. 14. The juxtaposition was acceptable to someone. For the Josianic Dtr, v. 11's condemnation was related to worship outside Jerusalem; the Dtr may also have been aware of the increasing ambivalence of the prophetic story beyond v. 14.

The verses can be treated as a unit, despite possible differences of origin (note, for example, 13:18-19 and 13:20-21; also the spelling of Joash/Jehoash in vv. 14 and 25a and b). Vv. 22, 24-25 give an almost annalistic summary of the situation. The reversal of fortune is attributed to Elisha in vv. 14-21.

43. The qualified judgment formula and the complaint about high places is standard for the HKL. V. 5 is best associated with the HKL, given its close association with Amaziah's accession. The conspiracy against his father, Joash of Judah, and his assassination were attributed to the HKL in 12:20-21.

44. The Dtr's concerns are with the fate of kings and dynasties rather than individual retribution; quotations from the dtn law are rare in the DH (here, Deut 24:16; cf. 1 Kgs 11:2). The term "the book of the law" is predominantly late (see the note on 2 Kgs 22:10).

After the Dtr: indented and sans serif font	DH Extension	**Revision: royal focus**	*Revision: national focus*	Other: double sideline

11 But Amaziah would not listen. So King Jehoash of Israel went up; he and King Amaziah of Judah faced one another in battle at Beth-shemesh, which belongs to Judah. 12Judah was defeated by Israel; everyone fled home. 13King Jehoash of Israel captured King Amaziah of Judah son of Jehoash, son of Ahaziah, at Beth-shemesh; he came to Jerusalem, and broke down the wall of Jerusalem from the Ephraim Gate to the Corner Gate, a distance of four hundred cubits. 14He seized all the gold and silver, and all the vessels that were found in the house of the LORD and in the treasuries of the king's house, as well as hostages; then he returned to Samaria.[45]

15 Now the rest of the acts that Jehoash did, his might, and how he fought with King Amaziah of Judah, are they not written in the Book of the Annals of the Kings of Israel? *16Jehoash slept with his ancestors, and was buried in Samaria with the kings of Israel; then his son Jeroboam succeeded him.*

17 King Amaziah son of Joash of Judah lived fifteen years after the death of King Jehoash son of Jehoahaz of Israel. **18Now the rest of the deeds of Amaziah, are they not written in the Book of the Annals of the Kings of Judah?** 19They made a conspiracy against him in Jerusalem, and he fled to Lachish. But they sent after him to Lachish, and killed him there. 20They brought him on horses; he was buried in Jerusalem with his ancestors in the city of David. 21All the people of Judah took Azariah, who was sixteen years old, and made him king to succeed his father Amaziah.

22He rebuilt Elath and restored it to Judah, after the king (*Heb.; NRSV, King Amaziah*) slept with his ancestors.[46]

---

45. **Text-history approach.** We have attributed 14:8-14 to the royal focus within the dtr revision, well aware that such a tradition is extremely difficult to situate. References to civil war between Israel and Judah are not infrequent (e.g., 2 Sam 3:1; 1 Kgs 14:30; 15:6, 7, 16, 32). However this tradition is about more than civil war. Jehoash demolishes the invulnerability of Jerusalem and takes money, hostages, and "all the vessels that were found in the house of the LORD" (14:14). Kings of Judah have taken money from the temple treasury (cf. 1 Kgs 15:16-22; 2 Kgs 12:17-18; 16:5-9; 18:14-16 and the note on the first of these texts). This is different. This concerns the temple vessels (cf. 1 Kgs 7:15-50; 2 Kgs 25:13-17). Apart from this story, in the entire DH only one person pillages the temple vessels and that is Nebuchadnezzar of Babylon. In 2 Chron 28:24, Ahaz is reported to have cut in pieces the vessels of God's house. What is reported here of Jehoash is without parallel: an Israelite pillaged the vessels of the Jerusalem temple. It is sacrilege. It is desecration.

It may not have been reported by the Josianic Dtr; neither was the case of Ahaz. Given the portrayal of stubborn folly for Amaziah and the shameful action of Jehoash, it is possible that the passage was inserted by the royal focus within the dtr revision, reflecting its hostility to the kings. It appears to have been originally a northern tradition, blaming Judah for the initiative and stupid stubbornness.

46. A note concerning the rebuilding and restoration of Elath. A secondary attribution is suggested by the reference to an anonymous king (despite the NRSV) who died peacefully ("slept with his ancestors"). According to the text above, Amaziah was killed at Lachish; B. Alfrink suggests the possibility that v. 22 referred to the king of Edom ("L'Expression," 106–18, esp. p. 112). The verse stands after the final report for Amaziah (14:18-21) and before the initial report for Azariah (15:1-4).

Main pre-DH:	Other pre-DH:	HKL: + single	**Josianic DH:**
Prophetic Record and PR Extension	single sideline	underline	**from the Dtr**

23 In the fifteenth year of King Amaziah son of Joash of Judah, King Jeroboam son of Joash of Israel began to reign in Samaria; he reigned forty-one years. *24He did what was evil in the sight of the LORD; he did not depart from all the sins of Jeroboam son of Nebat, which he caused Israel to sin.*

> 25He restored the border of Israel from Lebo-hamath as far as the Sea of the Arabah, according to the word of the LORD, the God of Israel, which he spoke by his servant Jonah son of Amittai, the prophet, who was from Gath-hepher.47 26For the LORD saw that the distress of Israel was very bitter; there was no one left, bond or free, and no one to help Israel. 27But the LORD had not said that he would blot out the name of Israel from under heaven, so he saved them by the hand of Jeroboam son of Joash.48

28 Now the rest of the acts of Jeroboam, and all that he did, and his might, how he fought, and how he recovered for Israel Damascus and Hamath, which had belonged to Judah, are they not written in the Book of the Annals of the Kings of Israel? *29Jeroboam slept with his ancestors, the kings of Israel; his son Zechariah succeeded him.*

---

47. There is no prophecy corresponding to this notice of fulfillment. Otherwise, it is similar to others from the Dtr. Dietrich attributed the insertion of 14:25 to his DtrP.

48. Not necessarily separate from v. 25, vv. 26-27 draws on the theology of 13:3-6 (i.e., God's mercy to his afflicted people and deliverance of them by a savior). In contrast to 13:3-6, the savior is here explicitly identified as Jeroboam II. The theology is scarcely that of the Dtr; the language of God's blotting out the name of Israel is unique.

Dietrich attributed 14:15-16, 26-27 to his DtrN.

15 In the twenty-seventh year of King Jeroboam of Israel King Azariah son of Amaziah of Judah began to reign. **2He was sixteen years old when he began to reign, and he reigned fifty-two years in Jerusalem. His mother's name was Jecoliah of Jerusalem.**

3He did what was right in the sight of the LORD, just as his father Amaziah had done. 4Nevertheless the high places were not taken away; the people still sacrificed and made offerings on the high places. 5The LORD struck the king, so that he was leprous to the day of his death, and lived in a separate house. Jotham the king's son was in charge of the palace, governing the people of the land.49 **6Now the rest of the acts of Azariah, and all that he did, are they not written in the Book of the Annals of the Kings of Judah?** 7Azariah slept with his ancestors; they buried him with his ancestors in the city of David; his son Jotham succeeded him.

8 In the thirty-eighth year of King Azariah of Judah, Zechariah son of Jeroboam reigned over Israel in Samaria six months. *9He did what was evil in the sight of the LORD, as his ancestors had done. He did not depart from the sins of Jeroboam son of Nebat, which he caused Israel to sin. 10Shallum son of Jabesh conspired against him, and struck him down in public and killed him, and reigned in place of him.* **11Now the rest of the deeds of Zechariah are written in the Book of the Annals of the Kings of Israel.**

> 12This was the promise of the LORD that he gave to Jehu, "Your sons shall sit on the throne of Israel to the fourth generation." And so it happened.50

---

49. 15:5 is best associated with the HKL, given its close association with Azariah's death and the succession (for similar associations, cf. 12:20-21; 14:5).

50. 15:12 draws attention to God's promise, given in 2 Kgs 10:30. In our judgment, this promise did not

---

After the Dtr: indented and sans serif font	**Revision:** **royal focus**	Revision: national focus	Other: double sideline

13 Shallum son of Jabesh began to reign in the thirty-ninth year of King Uzziah of Judah; he reigned one month in Samaria. *14Then Menahem son of Gadi came up from Tirzah and came to Samaria; he struck down Shallum son of Jabesh in Samaria and killed him; he reigned in place of him.* **15Now the rest of the deeds of Shallum, including the conspiracy that he made, are written in the Book of the Annals of the Kings of Israel.** *16At that time Menahem sacked Tiphsah, all who were in it and its territory from Tirzah on; because they did not open it to him, he sacked it. He ripped open all the pregnant women in it.[51]*

17 In the thirty-ninth year of King Azariah of Judah, Menahem son of Gadi began to reign over Israel; he reigned ten years in Samaria. *18He did what was evil in the sight of the LORD; he did not depart all his days from any of the sins of Jeroboam son of Nebat, which he caused Israel to sin. 19King Pul of Assyria came against the land; Menahem gave Pul a thousand talents of silver, so that he might help him confirm his hold on the royal power. 20Menahem exacted the money from Israel, that is, from all the wealthy, fifty shekels of silver from each one, to give to the king of Assyria. So the king of Assyria turned back, and did*

not stay there in the land. **21Now the rest of the deeds of Menahem, and all that he did, are they not written in the Book of the Annals of the Kings of Israel?** *22Menahem slept with his ancestors, and his son Pekahiah succeeded him.*

23 In the fiftieth year of King Azariah of Judah, Pekahiah son of Menahem began to reign over Israel in Samaria; he reigned two years. *24He did what was evil in the sight of the LORD; he did not turn away from the sins of Jeroboam son of Nebat, which he caused Israel to sin. 25Pekah son of Remaliah, his captain, conspired against him with fifty of the Gileadites, and attacked him in Samaria, in the citadel of the palace along with Argob and Arieh; he killed him, and reigned in place of him.* **26Now the rest of the deeds of Pekahiah, and all that he did, are written in the Book of the Annals of the Kings of Israel.**

27 In the fifty-second year of King Azariah of Judah, Pekah son of Remaliah began to reign over Israel in Samaria; he reigned twenty years. *28He did what was evil in the sight of the LORD; he did not depart from the sins of Jeroboam son of Nebat, which he caused Israel to sin.*

29 In the days of King Pekah of Israel, King Tiglath-pileser of Assyria came and captured Ijon, Abel-beth-maacah, Janoah, Kedesh, Hazor, Gilead, and Galilee, all the land of Naphtali; and he carried the people captive to Assyria. 30Then Hoshea son of Elah made a conspiracy against Pekah son of Remaliah, attacked him, and killed him; he reigned in place of him, **in the twentieth year of Jotham son of Uzziah.** **31Now the rest of the acts of Pekah, and all that he did, are written in the Book of the Annals of the Kings of Israel.[52]**

32 In the second year of King Pekah son of Remaliah of Israel, King Jotham son of Uzziah of Judah began to reign. **33He was**

---

derive from dtr editing. The fulfillment notice is outside the regnal framework and formulated differently from the Dtr's notices.

Dietrich attributed 15:12 to his DtrN.

51. Views differ on the event referred to in v. 16. The identification of Tiphsah is uncertain (cf. Jones, *Kings*, 2.523-24). If the understanding "its territory from Tirzah on" (v. 16) is accepted, a correlation with the coup of v. 14 is appropriate; Menahem sacked the territory on his way to Samaria where he killed Shallum. The dtr formula recognizes this, concluding the account of Shallum in v. 15 and opening the account of Menahem in v. 17.

---

52. The Extension continues in 17:2.

Main pre-DH:	Other pre-DH:	HKL: + single	**Josianic DH:**
Prophetic Record and PR Extension	single sideline	underline	**from the Dtr**

twenty-five years old when he began to reign and reigned sixteen years in Jerusalem. His mother's name was Jerusha daughter of Zadok.

³⁴He did what was right in the sight of the LORD, just as his father Uzziah had done. ³⁵Nevertheless the high places were not removed; the people still sacrificed and made offerings on the high places.

He built the upper gate of the house of the LORD. ³⁶Now the rest of the acts of Jotham, and all that he did, are they not written in the Book of the Annals of the Kings of Judah?[53]

³⁷In those days the LORD began to send King Rezin of Aram and Pekah son of Remaliah against Judah. ³⁸Jotham slept with his ancestors, and was buried with his ancestors in the city of David, his ancestor; his son Ahaz succeeded him.[54]

16 In the seventeenth year of Pekah son of Remaliah, King Ahaz son of Jotham of Judah began to reign. ²Ahaz was twenty years old when he began to reign; he reigned sixteen years in Jerusalem.

He did not do what was right in the sight of the LORD his God, as his ancestor David had done, ³but he walked in the way of the kings of Israel.

He even made his son pass through fire, according to the abominable practices of the nations whom the LORD drove out before the people of Israel. ⁴He sacrificed and made offerings on the high places, on the hills, and under every green tree.[55]

5 Then King Rezin of Aram and King Pekah son of Remaliah of Israel came up to wage war on Jerusalem; they besieged Ahaz but could not conquer him. ⁶At that time the king of Edom recovered Elath for Edom, and drove the Judeans from Elath; and the Edomites came to Elath, where they live to this day. ⁷Ahaz sent messengers to King Tiglath-pileser of Assyria, saying, "I am your servant and your son. Come up, and rescue me from the hand of the king of Aram and from the hand of the king of Israel, who are attacking me." ⁸Ahaz also took the silver and gold found in the house of the LORD and in the treasures of the king's house, and sent a present to the king of Assyria. ⁹The king of Assyria

---

53. The reference to building "the upper gate of the house of the LORD" in v. 35b could belong in the HKL or be the work of the Dtr. Within the HKL, it would be expected between the present vv. 34 and 35. For the Dtr, as part of the activity of Jotham, it would appropriately precede the closure of his reign in v. 36. Attribution to the Dtr is marginally more likely.

54. In 2 Kgs 10:32, it was noted that God sent foreign powers against northern Israel; here the same process is set in train for Judah (cf. 2 Kgs 16:5; Isa 7:1). In 2 Kgs 10:32, the text was attributed to the extension of the PR; here, it is most appropriately attributed to the HKL.

55. The evident hostility to the king, over and above that of the HKL, suggests attribution to the royal focus within the dtr process of revision. This is supported by the occurrences for passage through fire (cf. 2 Kgs 17:17; 21:6; 23:10); these are later than the Dtr. The "abominations of the nations" is not earlier than the Dtr, more probably later (cf. Deut 18:9; 1 Kgs 14:24; 2 Kgs 21:2). V. 4 transfers to the king (Ahaz) the accusation normally (in the HKL) made against the people. The reference to the hills and green tree is a simpler formulation than in other contexts (cf. 1 Kgs 14:23 and Holladay, "On Every High Hill," 176); it could belong within the royal focus of the dtr revision. It is also possible that this phrase and the "abominations of the nations" could derive from later contexts, sharpening the accusations. Equally, the rest might possibly be attributed to the HKL, directly indicting the last king before Hezekiah's reform.

After the Dtr: indented and sans serif font	DH Extension	**Revision: royal focus**	*Revision: national focus*	Other: double sideline

listened to him; <u>the king of Assyria marched up against Damascus, and took it, carrying its people captive to Kir; then he killed Rezin</u>.[56]

10 When King Ahaz went to Damascus to meet King Tiglath-pileser of Assyria, he saw the altar that was at Damascus. King Ahaz sent to the priest Uriah a model of the altar, and its pattern, exact in all its details. [11]The priest Uriah built the altar; in accordance with all that King Ahaz had sent from Damascus, just so did the priest Uriah build it, before King Ahaz arrived from Damascus. [12]When the king came from Damascus, the king viewed the altar. Then the king drew near to the altar, went up on it, [13]and offered his burnt offering and his grain offering, poured his drink offering, and dashed the blood of his offerings of well-being against the altar. [14]The bronze altar that was before the LORD he removed from the front of the house, from the place between his altar and the house of the LORD, and put it on the north side of his altar. [15]King Ahaz commanded the priest Uriah, saying, "Upon the great altar offer the morning burnt offering, and the evening grain offering, and the king's burnt offering, and his grain offering, with the burnt offering of all the people of the land, their grain offering, and their drink offering; then dash against it all the blood of the burnt offering, and all the blood of the sacrifice; but the bronze altar shall be for me to inquire by." [16]The priest Uriah did everything that King Ahaz commanded.

17 Then King Ahaz cut off the frames of the stands, and removed the laver from them; he removed the sea from the bronze oxen that were under it, and put it on a pediment of stone. [18]The covered portal for use on the sabbath that had been built inside the palace, and the outer entrance for the king he removed from the house of the LORD. He did this because of the king of Assyria.[57]

---

56. Verses 5-9 are uncertain with regard to their derivation. They can scarcely be treated in isolation from the similar passages 1 Kgs 15:16-22; 2 Kgs 12:17-18; 18:14-16. As noted above (cf. note on 1 Kgs 15:22), three of these are attributed to the royal focus within the dtr revision, with this passage on Ahaz attributed to the HKL. The justification for this exception is threefold: (i) its anticipation in 15:37; (ii) the negative judgment on Ahaz in the HKL (16:2b-3a), esp. v. 3a for a king who was not married into the family of Ahab (as Joram and Ahaziah were); (iii) Tiglath-pileser's march on Damascus (v. 9) provides a convenient attachment for vv. 10-19. For these reasons, we have here gone beyond the minimal position for the HKL represented elsewhere in this book. The uncertainty involved in these attributions needs to be emphasized.

57. **Text signals.** Three elements suggest that vv. 10-18 do not belong with vv. 5-9. (i) The content is different; vv. 5-9 concern the rescue of Ahaz as vassal, while vv. 10-18 are focused exclusively on temple furniture and practice. (ii) The title "King Ahaz" is used throughout vv. 10-18. (iii) The usage at the end of v. 18 with reference to the king of Assyria generally denotes fear, not present in vv. 5-9.

Text-history approach. There is no characteristically dtr language in vv. 10-18. While the dtr use of titles fluctuates (e.g., 2 Kgs 8:25-26, 28-29), the sustained use of the title in vv. 10-18 is unusual. The term used for "pattern" is late; the coupling of "model" and "pattern" occurs only here. Priestly interest is suggested by the emphasis on instructions complied with in the construction and on the central role of the priest Uriah. There is little evidence to compel a division between pre-dtr and post-dtr material. A later date for the whole is likely.

| Main pre-DH: *Prophetic Record and PR Extension* | Other pre-DH: single sideline | HKL: + single underline | **Josianic DH: from the Dtr** |

19Now the rest of the acts of Ahaz that he did, are they not written in the Book of the Annals of the Kings of Judah?

20Ahaz slept with his ancestors, and was buried with his ancestors in the city of David; his son Hezekiah succeeded him.

17 In the twelfth year of King Ahaz of Judah, Hoshea son of Elah began to reign in Samaria over Israel; he reigned nine years.
*2He did what was evil in the sight of the LORD, yet not like the kings of Israel who were before him. 3King Shalmaneser of Assyria came up against him; Hoshea became his vassal, and paid him tribute. 4But the king of Assyria found treachery in Hoshea; for he had sent messengers to King So of Egypt, and offered no tribute to the king of Assyria, as he had done year by year; therefore the king of Assyria confined him and imprisoned him.*58

5 Then the king of Assyria invaded all the land and came to Samaria; for three years he besieged it. 6In the ninth year of Hoshea the king of Assyria captured Samaria; he carried the Israelites away to

Assyria. *He placed them in Halah, on the Habor, the river of Gozan, and in the cities of the Medes.*59

7 This occurred because the people of Israel had sinned against the LORD their God, who had brought them up out of the land of Egypt from under the hand of Pharaoh king of Egypt. They had worshiped other gods 8and walked in the customs of the nations whom the LORD drove out before the people of Israel, and in the customs that the kings of Israel had introduced. 9The people of Israel secretly did things that were not right against the LORD their God. They built for themselves high places at all their towns, from watchtower to fortified city; 10they set up for themselves pillars and sacred poles on every high hill and under every green tree; 11there they made offerings on all the high places, as the nations did whom the LORD carried away before them. They did wicked things, provoking the LORD to anger; 12they served idols, of which the LORD had said to them, "You shall not do this." 13Yet the LORD warned Israel and Judah by every prophet and every seer, saying, "Turn from your evil ways and keep my commandments and my statutes, in accordance with all the law that I commanded your ancestors and that I sent to you by my servants the prophets." 14They would not listen but were stubborn, as their ancestors had been, who did not believe in the LORD their God. 15They despised his statutes, and his covenant that he made with their ancestors, and the warnings that he gave them. They went after false idols and became false; they followed the

---

The insertion of this tradition here may reflect the behavior of Jeroboam at Bethel (cf. 1 Kgs 12:33); the king who determined the fate of the northern kingdom is to some degree mirrored in Judah by the last king before Hezekiah and his reform. Echoes of royal concern for the temple in 2 Kings 12 may be alleged on the more positive side. Certainty is out of reach.

Present-text potential. The judgment on Ahaz is negative: "he walked in the way of the kings of Israel." His behavior intensifies this. His politics have him turn not to the God of Israel but to Tiglath-pileser. His orders bring the temple under Assyrian influence and royal domination.

58. The continuation of the Extension from 15:30a. No notice is given of Hoshea's death; the use of his reign as a chronological reference continues in v. 6.

---

59. The Extension continues in 17:21 and concludes with 17:23b.

After the Dtr: indented and sans serif font	DH Extension	**Revision: royal focus**	Revision: national focus	Other: double sideline

nations that were around them, concerning whom the LORD had commanded them that they should not do as they did. [16]*They rejected all the commandments of the LORD their God and made for themselves cast images of two calves; they made a sacred pole, worshiped all the host of heaven, and served Baal.* [17]*They made their sons and their daughters pass through fire; they used divination and augury; and they sold themselves to do evil in the sight of the LORD, provoking him to anger.* [18]*Therefore the LORD was very angry with Israel and removed them out of his sight; none was left but the tribe of Judah alone.*

19 Judah also did not keep the commandments of the LORD their God but walked in the customs that Israel had introduced.

20 The LORD rejected all the descendants of Israel; he punished them and gave them into the hand of plunderers, until he had banished them from his presence.[60]

21 For Israel broke away from the house of David, and (NJPSV, correctly; NRSV, When he had torn Israel from the house of David,) *they made Jeroboam son of Nebat king. Jeroboam drove Israel from following the LORD and made them commit great sin.* [22]*The people of Israel continued in all the sins that Jeroboam committed; they did not depart from them* [23]*until the LORD removed Israel out of his sight,* **as he had foretold through all his servants the prophets.** *So Israel was exiled from their own land to Assyria until this day.*[61]

---

60. **Text signals** for vv. 7-20. (i) The focus is primarily on the people rather than their kings and the trajectory from exodus to exile, without reference to the sin of Jeroboam. (ii) While the reference is to northern Israel and the context relates to northern Israel, the reality is that this is not exclusively the case. The crimes, the misdemeanors, the apostasy, the sins listed range more widely than northern Israel alone; at times they relate exclusively to Judah. While the fate described pertains only to the north (vv. 1-6), the catalog of sins is taken from accusations made earlier in the history against both Israel and Judah. For example, only Judah is accused of setting up pillars and asherim on the high places and burning incense there (1 Kgs 14:23; 22:43; 2 Kgs 12:4 [NRSV, 12:3]; 14:4; 15:4, 35a); only Davidic kings and Judah are accused of worshiping the host of heaven, of passing children

through fire, and of using divination and sorcery (2 Kgs 16:3; 21:6; 23:10). (iii) Judah is explicitly named in vv. 13, 18b, and 19. (iv) The role of the prophet in vv. 13-14 is that of preacher of the law. (v) The passage contains law-oriented language (esp. vv. 13 and 15). (vi) After the exile of northern Israel (v. 18a), the failure of Judah is also noted (v. 19). (vii) After the comment on Judah in v. 19, making explicit what an attentive ear will have heard earlier in the passage, v. 20's "all the descendants of Israel" is best understood as denoting the entity that includes the people of both Israel and Judah. The phrase "descendants of Israel" (*zera' yiśrā'ēl*) is relatively rare and difficult to date (cf. 2 Kgs 17:20; Isa 45:25; Jer 23:8; 31:36, 37; Ezek 44:22; Ps 22:24; Neh 9:2; and 1 Chron 16:13).

Text-history approach. All the text signals noted point to attribution within the national focus of the dtr revision. The focus is on the people, not the kings. The failure of both Israel and Judah is taken for granted. The national focus's concern with observance of the law is expressed in both the role attributed to the prophet and the presence of legalistic language. It would be possible to attribute v. 19 to a second hand and v. 20 to a third, but it is unnecessary. Judah has been latent in this text from its beginning with v. 7. Drawing the text together, v. 20 provides an appropriate conclusion to this review.

Present-text potential. See below, on v. 23.

61. **Text signals** for vv. 21-23. (i) Within the initial clause of v. 21, there is no explicit mention of YHWH as

---

Main pre-DH:	Other pre-DH:	HKL: + single	**Josianic DH:**
Prophetic Record and PR Extension	single sideline	underline	**from the Dtr**

24 The king of Assyria brought people from Babylon, Cuthah, Avva, Hamath, and Sepharvaim, and placed them in the cities of Samaria in place of the people of Israel; they took possession of Samaria, and settled in its cities. ²⁵When they first settled there, they did not worship the LORD; therefore the LORD sent lions among them, which killed some of them. ²⁶So the king of Assyria was told, "The nations that you have carried away and placed in the cities of Samaria do not know the law of the god of the land; therefore he has sent lions among them; they are killing them, because they do not know the law of the god of the land." ²⁷Then the king of Assyria commanded, "Send there one of the priests whom you carried away from there; let him go and live there, and teach them the law of the god of the land." ²⁸So one of the priests whom they had carried away from Samaria came and lived in Bethel; he taught them how they should worship the LORD.⁶²

---

subject, the usual indicator of the direct object is absent, and there is no reference to the kingdom as what is torn away (cf. M. Brettler, "2 Kings XVII 7-23," esp. p. 278; see also NJPSV and *Nueva Biblia Española*, and Jones, "denotes a new beginning," *Kings*, 2.543). Elsewhere, in this connection, the kingdom as the object that is torn away is explicitly mentioned (e.g., 1 Sam 15:28; 28:17; 1 Kgs 11:11, 12, 13, 31; 14:8). It is worth comparing 1 Kgs 14:8 with 2 Kgs 17:21. (ii) In v. 21, the accusation that Jeroboam made Israel commit great sin reflects the element in Pattern A, "which he caused Israel to sin." (iii) In v. 22, the accusation that "the people of Israel continued in all the sins that Jeroboam committed; they did not depart from them" reflects the element in Pattern A, "he did not depart from (all) the sins of Jeroboam." (iv) In v. 23, the reference to "all his servants the prophets" is a characteristic of dtr ideology.

Text-history approach. The signals suggest that vv. 21-23 are best attributed to the conclusion of the PR Extension, that took the line of northern kings from the end of the PR (with Jehu) down to the end of the northern kingdom (with Hoshea). This extension is determined by the presence of Pattern A for the royal judgment formulas. The shift from the singular for each king to the plural for the people is what would be expected for the context, a collective conclusion.

In v. 23, the dtr citing of the prophets is an appropriate insistence on the dtr schema of prophecy and fulfillment. The little tag, "until this day," could have been original or added at almost any time (cf. Childs, "Study of the Formula," esp. pp. 289-90).

Present-text potential. The text as a whole (vv. 7-23) deals with the fate of the people of Israel as a whole. Its vision includes the exodus (v. 7) and both peoples (v. 13) and the exile of the north (vv. 18, 20, 23). Vv. 7-20 function both as an accusation against northern and southern Israel and as a defense of God. As accusation, the verses claim that the people abandoned all that was proper to them; they went after falsity and became false (v. 15). As defense of God, the text points to God's sending of the prophets and their appeal to the law.

In a growth-of-text perspective, vv. 7-20 unfold the earlier tradition of vv. 21-23. In a present-text perspective, vv. 21-23 narrow the focus of vv. 7-20, bringing the broader picture back to the context of the northern exile. This allows for modulation into the situation in Israel after the exile of the northerners (i.e., vv. 24-41).

Here, with the fall of the northern kingdom of Israel, the PR Extension ends. Dietrich attributed 17:21-23 to his DtrP and 17:12-19 to his DtrN.

62. **Verses 24-41.** From the outset, it may be helpful to indicate the problematic and difficult nature of this passage. It opens with a relatively straightforward account of the experience of the people who had been forcibly relocated into the newly formed Assyrian provinces of the former northern Israel. This con-

---

| After the Dtr: indented and sans serif font | DH Extension | **Revision: royal focus** | *Revision: national focus* | Other: double sideline |

> 29 But every nation still made gods of its own and put them in the high-place house *(Heb.; NRSV, shrines of the high places)* that the people of Samaria had

> made, every nation in the cities in which they lived; [30]the people of Babylon made Succoth-benoth, the people of Cuth made Nergal, the people of Hamath made

cludes with a statement that the priest sent them taught them "how they should worship the LORD" (v. 28). This view is then modified by a passage insisting on the dualism of their worship: "they worshiped the LORD but also served their own gods" (vv. 29-33, cf. esp. v. 33). Next, a strong protest is voiced against this dualism being accepted as worship of YHWH (vv. 34-40). V. 41 is ambivalent; it either reasserts the views of vv. 29-33 or reverses them in the light of vv. 34-40 (see below).

Certain aspects are surprising. First, the dualistic solution adopted would have been unacceptable to a dtr theologian. In vv. 24-33, it is treated as acceptable; it solves the lion problem. Second, the failure to centralize, implicit in worship at the high places, is not condemned in vv. 24-33, in contrast to vv. 7-23. In the circumstances, it would have been absurd; but dtr theologians never extended such leniency to Jeroboam and the north. Third, dtr influence is felt; dtr language is mimicked without being replicated—is aped but is absent. Against this background, we are in a position to examine the passage more closely.

Text signals in vv. 24-41. (i) The particular usage of participles here is typical of late biblical Hebrew, influenced by Aramaic (cf. P. Joüon, *Grammaire de l'hébreu biblique*, §121 g; in detail, J. MacDonald, "The Structure of II Kings XVII," 29–41). (ii) The participial phrase for a believer ("revered the LORD," "feared the LORD," "worshiped the LORD") occurs four times here (vv. 32, 33, 34, 41); in the rest of the DH, there are three occurrences (1 Kgs 18:3, 12; 2 Kgs 4:1). It is notable that all three are to be found in prophetic stories. (iii) The lions featured as signs of divine displeasure in vv. 24-28 are reminiscent of the lion in 1 Kgs 13:25-28 and 20:36 and the bears in 2 Kgs 2:24. Again, these are found in prophetic stories; the imagery is more characteristic of prophecy than of the Dtr (cf. Hos 5:14; 13:7-8; Jer 4:7; 5:6; Lam 3:10).

(iv) The designation "high-place house" (vv. 29, 32) is not found within the texts attributed to the Josianic DH. Interestingly, apart from the HKL, the high places in themselves are not a major dtr concern before Manasseh's reversal of his father's reforms. For the Dtr, centralization is key; the high places are its antithesis. (v) In vv. 24-41, the issue of centralization is not raised explicitly. (vi) The term *mišpāṭ* for "law," "manner," or "custom" occurs six times outside the occurrences here. While this context requires it, it is remarkably rare (cf. 1 Kgs 18:28; 2 Kgs 11:14). (vii) The assertion in v. 34b, "they do not worship the LORD" contradicts v. 33 (cf. later v. 41a). (viii) Vv. 34 and 41b both note contemporary practice, with v. 41b invoking at least three generations.

Other signals are significant for vv. 34-41. (i) There is a density of repetition in these verses that is unusual; the prohibition against the worship of other gods is repeated three times (vv. 35, 37, 38). V. 38, in particular, is a first-person resumption of the preceding. (ii) The designation of the people of Israel as "children of Jacob" is rare. The nine references in Genesis are to the sons of the patriarch; the references in 1 Chron 16:13 and Ps 105:6 are from the same song; beyond these, there are only Mal 3:6; Ps 77:15; our text; and 1 Kgs 18:31—again a prophetic story. Note that the "children of Jacob" designates northern and southern Israel, while vv. 24-33 concern only the north. (iii) There are three occurrences of sequences of four commands or prohibitions defining worshipers of YHWH (vv. 34, 35, and 37); these three with their constituent elements have no parallel elsewhere. (iv) The stereotyped reference to God's action in the exodus is here "with great power and with an outstretched arm" (cf. Deut 9:29; and referring to creation, Jer 27:5 and 32:17) and not the commoner dtr version "with a mighty hand and an outstretched arm" (Deut 4:34; 5:15; 7:19; 11:2; 26:8; Ps 136:12; cf. 1 Kgs

Main pre-DH:	Other pre-DH:	HKL: + single	**Josianic DH:**
Prophetic Record and PR Extension	single sideline	underline	**from the Dtr**

Ashima; [31]the Avvites made Nibhaz and Tartak; the Sepharvites burned their children in the fire to Adrammelech and Anammelech, the gods of Sepharvaim. [32]They also wor-

shiped the LORD and appointed from among themselves all sorts of people as high-place priests (*Heb.; NRSV, priests of the high places*), who sacrificed for them in the high-

---

8:42; 2 Chron 6:32; also solely in a context of power and wrath, Ezek 20:33, 34). (v) V. 41 covers much the same ground as vv. 33-34. (vi) 3rd person report dominates vv. 34 and 40-41; 2nd person address dominates vv. 35-39.

Text-history approach. These signals indicate that vv. 24-41 constitute an unusual text that is unlikely to warrant dtr attribution. Vv. 34-40 assert the demand for exclusive worship, but without explicit claim for centralization and without dtr characteristics of language. The passage does not fit well with dtr concerns. The Josianic Dtr would appropriately have stopped with 17:23. His interest was in the fulfillment of prophecy: It has happened; move on to Hezekiah. The associations with prophetic traditions—the lion and bears, the echoes of 1 Kgs 18:3, 12, 28, 31; also 2 Kgs 4:1—all raise questions about the provenance of this material. Some annalistic material has been claimed here; it may well have formed part of the raw material, but it has been thoroughly blended into the final product (e.g., v. 24 supplies the subject for v. 25).

Assigning a date to such a passage, or its components, is difficult and unhelpful. Much of the content could be relatively early. Indications among the text signals (e.g., use of participial forms) suggest that the composition could be relatively late. This is reflected in our use of the double sideline.

The passage expresses conflicting views. It exposes a problem, reports a solution (effectively syncretism—a version of what we might call the "Naaman option," cf. 2 Kgs 5:18), expresses a protest against the solution, and finally revisits the solution (v. 41). It is important to realize that vv. 35-40 describe the situation of the children of Jacob, the people of Israel; v. 40 refers to Israel. Nelson's interpretation of v. 40 has to be right in seeing that "both Israel and these imported foreigners committed the

same crime, trying to 'fear the Lord' while worshiping other gods" (*Kings*, 232).

Verse 41 has often been seen as a resumptive repetition of vv. 33-34. The move from "their gods" (v. 33) to the "carved images" of v. 41 calls for caution. This and other shifts in language leave the issue of origin open. The emphasis on three generations (v. 41b) does not determine the date of the passage. It is probable that v. 34 in its entirety belongs with what follows (so Gray, *Kings*, 655); it is certainly possible. In this case, it is equally possible that v. 41 closes the passage that began with v. 34 (against Gray, *Kings*, 656; Jones, *Kings*, 2.556). The expression of v. 34a is mirrored chiastically in Hebrew by v. 41b; the content of v. 33 is revisited in v. 41a. If v. 34a belongs with what follows, the concern for the contemporary scene, "this day," is restricted to this one passage, vv. 34-41.

Three options are open. First, v. 41 followed immediately on vv. 24-33, affirming the dual worship. Because of the repetition, we judge this improbable. Second, v. 41 belonged with vv. 34-40, declaring the dual worship unacceptable in the light of the repeated affirmation of exclusive worship, required by the law in vv. 34-39. In this scenario, v. 40 declares the failure of Israel and v. 41 declares the failure of the foreigners. Third, v. 41 is a later addition, reaffirming the position of v. 33 over against the exclusivity of vv. 34-40.

Present-text potential. It is possible to understand vv. 24-41 as a neutral statement of the political situation after the exile of the northerners (vv. 24-33), followed by a protest about this sort of behavior. As such, the passage is little more than a historical note with a contrasting theological observation.

Alternatively, vv. 24-41 can be understood as a subtle but striking subversion of the entire dtr theology, followed by a strong but also subtle rebuttal of the subversion. First the subversion. Dtr theology, expressed in vv. 7-23, attributed the downfall of northern

---

| After the Dtr: indented and sans serif font | DH Extension | **Revision: royal focus** | Revision: national focus | Other: double sideline |

place house *(Heb.; NRSV, shrines of the high places)*. [33]So they worshiped the LORD but also served their own gods, after the manner of the nations from among whom they had been carried away.[63]

[34]To this day they continue to practice their former customs. They do not worship the LORD and they do not follow the statutes or the ordinances or the law or the com-

mandment that the LORD commanded the children of Jacob, whom he named Israel. [35]The LORD had made a covenant with them and commanded them, "You shall not worship other gods or bow yourselves to them or serve them or sacrifice to them, [36]but you shall worship the LORD, who brought you out of the land of Egypt with great power and with an outstretched arm; you shall bow yourselves to him, and to him you shall sacrifice. [37]The statutes and the ordinances and the law and the commandment that he wrote for you, you shall always be careful to observe. You shall not worship other gods; [38]you shall not forget the covenant that I have made with you. You shall not worship other gods, [39]but you shall worship the LORD your God; he will deliver you out of the hand of all your enemies." [40]They would not listen, however, but they continued to practice their former custom.

41 So these nations worshiped the LORD, but also served their carved images; to this day their children and their children's children continue to do as their ancestors did.

Israel to the failure to worship YHWH exclusively. Vv. 24-33 subvert this view by pointing to a more inclusive theology, the successful worship of both YHWH and their national gods by the relocated people in the north. Success can be claimed; there is no further mention of the problem with lions. There is even good precedent for such inclusive theology; we have referred to the "Naaman option" in 2 Kgs 5:18.

Against this subversion, vv. 34-41 are a strong reassertion of dtr theology, by someone who has imbibed dtr ideology but has not scripted dtr documents. The exacting dtr style is not reproduced. The text points to the descendants of Jacob, the people of north and south. It emphasizes YHWH's covenant with them (v. 35); Deut 29:1 allows the possibility that the 1st person form in v. 38 reflects Moses, the covenantal intermediary, thus lightening the repetition in v. 39 (cf. v. 36). The overwhelming emphasis is on not worshiping other gods (vv. 35, 37, 38). The children of Jacob did not listen (v. 40); the relocated peoples were no better (v. 41). Both attempted the "Naaman option" of inclusive (syncretistic) worship. The verdict on both has been expressed in v. 34b: "they do not worship the LORD" (borne out for Israel by v. 40).

Finally, it is possible to read v. 41 as a reaffirmation of the position taken in vv. 24-33, despite the protest of vv. 34-40.

63. The paragraphing at this point follows the Hebrew text in BHS and JPSV against the NRSV. The relevant pages are missing from the Aleppo codex; the unmarked gaps of BHS paragraphing are not represented in the Leningrad codex (nor, in this instance at least, in the NJPSV).

18 In the third year of King Hoshea son of Elah of Israel, Hezekiah son of King Ahaz of Judah began to reign. ²He was twenty-five years old when he began to reign; he reigned twenty-nine years in Jerusalem. His mother's name was Abi daughter of Zechariah.

³He did what was right in the sight of the LORD, just as his ancestor David had done. ⁴He removed the high places, broke down the pillars, and cut down the sacred pole. He broke in pieces the bronze serpent that Moses had made, for until those days the people of Israel had made offerings to it; it was called Nehushtan. ⁵He trusted in the LORD the God of Israel; so that

---

Main pre-DH:	Other pre-DH:	HKL: + single	**Josianic DH:**
Prophetic Record and PR Extension	single sideline	underline	**from the Dtr**

there was no one like him among all the kings of Judah after him.[64]

|| or among those who were before him[65]

[6]*For he held fast to the L*ORD*; he did not depart from following him but kept the commandments that the L*ORD *commanded Moses.*[66]

[7]The LORD was with him; wherever he went, he prospered. He rebelled against the king of Assyria and would not serve him. [8]He attacked the Philistines as far as Gaza and its territory, from watchtower to fortified city.[67]

9 In the fourth year of King Hezekiah, which was the seventh year of King Hoshea son of Elah of Israel, King Shalmaneser of Assyria came up against Samaria, besieged it, [10]and at the end of three years, took it. In the sixth year of Hezekiah, which was the ninth year of King Hoshea of Israel, Samaria was taken. [11]The king of Assyria carried the Israelites away to Assyria, settled them in

Halah, on the Habor, the river of Gozan, and in the cities of the Medes.[68]

[12]*because they did not obey the voice of the* LORD *their God but transgressed his covenant—all that Moses the servant of the* LORD *had commanded; they neither listened nor obeyed.*[69]

13 In the fourteenth year of King Hezekiah, King Sennacherib of Assyria came up against all the fortified cities of Judah and captured them.[70]

[14]*King Hezekiah of Judah sent to the king of Assyria at Lachish, saying, "I have done wrong; withdraw from me; whatever you impose on me I will bear." The king of Assyria demanded of King Hezekiah of Judah three hundred talents of silver and thirty talents of gold.* [15]*Hezekiah gave him all the silver that was found in the house of the* LORD

---

64. From the HKL. The references to the kings "after him" has caused surprise. Its contradiction of the judgment on Josiah (23:25) is widely noted. It is troublesome and no satisfactory solution has been proposed; it would appear to antedate Josiah. Within the conclusion to the HKL, it is not inappropriate.

65"Those who were before him" is even more problematic than the kings "after him." Again, no satisfactory solution is offering. At best, it can be said that the phrase expresses exaggerated enthusiasm for Hezekiah, coupled with apparent oversight of David, the exemplary ancestor (v. 3). It is cognate with 23:25—and just as difficult.

66. The language of "holding fast to" tends to be secondary dtr (cf. Deut 4:4; 10:20; 11:22; 13:4; 30:20; Josh 22:5; 23:8). The emphasis on fidelity to the commandments suggests the national focus of the dtr revision.

67. End of the HKL.

68. Verses 9-11 allow the Josianic Dtr to correlate the reign of Hezekiah with the fall of the north. The primary synchronism is in v. 9, with a development in v. 10. The historical information is taken from the PR in 17:5-6 (cf. Jones, *Kings*, 2.560, 563).

69. The language of obedience to the law suggests attribution to the national focus of the dtr revision. The designation of Moses as "servant of the LORD" supports this attribution.

Dietrich attributed 18:6-7a, 12 to his DtrN.

70. The chronological difficulties associated with this verse are legendary (see commentaries etc. for suggested coregencies and emendations). Our attribution of the verse to the Josianic Dtr—along with 18:1-2, 9-10—assumes that the Dtr did not have access to the Assyrian records as we have now, relatively recently. 18:2 speaks of a twenty-nine-year reign and 20:6 speaks of a fifteen-year extension; the Dtr's conclusion could well have been that the illness and extension occurred in Hezekiah's fourteenth year (cf. M. Cogan and H. Tadmor, *II Kings*, 228).

| After the Dtr:
indented and sans serif font | DH
Extension | **Revision:**
royal focus | Revision:
national focus | Other:
double sideline |

and in the treasuries of the king's house. [16]At that time Hezekiah stripped the gold from the doors of the temple of the LORD, and from the doorposts that King Hezekiah of Judah had overlaid and gave it to the king of Assyria.[71]

[17]The king of Assyria sent the Tartan, the Rabsaris, and the Rabshakeh with a great army from Lachish to King Hezekiah at Jerusalem. They went up and came to Jerusalem. When they arrived, they came and stood by the conduit of the upper pool, which is on the highway to the Fuller's Field. [18]When they called for the king, there came out to them Eliakim son of Hilkiah, who was in charge of the palace, and Shebnah the secretary, and Joah son of Asaph, the recorder.[72]

19 The Rabshakeh said to them, "Say to Hezekiah: Thus says the great king, the king of Assyria: On what do you base this confidence of yours? [20]Do you think that mere words are strategy and power for war? On whom do you now rely, that you have rebelled against me? [21]See, you are relying now on Egypt, that broken reed of a staff, which will pierce the hand of anyone who leans on it. Such is Pharaoh king of Egypt to all who rely on him. [22]But if you say to me, 'We rely on the LORD our God,' is it not he whose high places and altars Hezekiah has removed, saying to Judah and to Jerusalem, 'You shall worship before this altar in Jerusalem'? [23]Come now, make a wager with my master the king of Assyria: I will give you two thousand horses, if you are able on your part to set riders on them. [24]How then can you repulse a single captain among the least of my master's servants, when you rely on Egypt for chariots and for horsemen? [25]Moreover, is it without the LORD that I have come up against this place to destroy it? The LORD said to me, Go up against this land, and destroy it."

---

71. Two options for the attribution of this and three similar texts are discussed at 1 Kgs 15:22. It is appropriate for the royal focus of the dtr revision to emphasize traditions that highlight flaws in the behavior of these otherwise favorably viewed kings. 18:14-16 points to a tradition preserving an alternative to the traditional view of Hezekiah as trusting in God and being delivered from the Assyrians. It is closer to the picture of Hezekiah in 20:12-19 (see below).

72. The classical analysis of the following Isaiah material (18:17—19:37) has stood the test of time. There are two (legendary) accounts with a prayer and response. There is general agreement that none of this material was composed in dtr circles. The two accounts very probably derive from Hezekian or at least pre-dtr circles. There is growing acceptance of considerable literary activity associated with Hezekiah, perhaps stimulated by the fall of the north and the near escape of Jerusalem. In this book, we have identified the HKL as part of this activity. We believe it prudent not to try shaping these potentially Hezekian traditions into a more identifiable form.

They constitute traditional material available to the Josianic Dtr. Of the Isaiah legends, the first account (18:17–19:9a and 19:36-37 [B1]) is enclosed within a single-line box for ease of identification; the second (19:9b-15a, 20, 32, 34-35 [B2]) is marked by a single sideline. For access to the issues and text signals, see B. S. Childs, *Isaiah and the Assyrian Crisis* and R. E. Clements, *Deliverance of Jerusalem*, and commentaries on Second Kings or Isaiah.

For a discussion of the **present-text potential**, see below on 19:37. Dietrich attributed the insertion of 18:17–20:19 to his DtrP.

Main pre-DH:	Other pre-DH:	HKL: + single	**Josianic DH:**
Prophetic Record and PR Extension	single sideline	underline	**from the Dtr**

26 Then Eliakim son of Hilkiah, and Shebnah, and Joah said to the Rabshakeh, "Please speak to your servants in the Aramaic language, for we understand it; do not speak to us in the language of Judah within the hearing of the people who are on the wall." 27But the Rabshakeh said to them, "Has my master sent me to speak these words to your master and to you, and not to the people sitting on the wall, who are doomed with you to eat their own dung and to drink their own urine?"

28 Then the Rabshakeh stood and called out in a loud voice in the language of Judah, "Hear the word of the great king, the king of Assyria! 29Thus says the king: 'Do not let Hezekiah deceive you, for he will not be able to deliver you out of my hand. 30Do not let Hezekiah make you rely on the LORD by saying, The LORD will surely deliver us, and this city will not be given into the hand of the king of Assyria.' 31Do not listen to Hezekiah; for thus says the king of Assyria: 'Make your peace with me and come out to me; then every one of you will eat from your own vine and your own fig tree, and drink water from your own cistern, 32until I come and take you away to a land like your own land, a land of grain and wine, a land of bread and vineyards, a land of olive oil and honey, that you may live and not die. Do not listen to Hezekiah when he misleads you by saying, The LORD will deliver us. 33Has any of the gods of the nations ever delivered its land out of the hand of the king of Assyria? 34Where are the gods of Hamath and Arpad? Where are the gods of Sepharvaim, Hena, and Ivvah? Have they delivered Samaria out of my hand? 35Who among all the gods of the countries have delivered their countries out of my hand, that the LORD should deliver Jerusalem out of my hand?' "

36 But the people were silent and answered him not a word, for the king's command was, "Do not answer him." 37Then Eliakim son of Hilkiah, who was in charge of the palace, and Shebna the secretary, and Joah son of Asaph, the recorder, came to Hezekiah with their clothes torn and told him the words of the Rabshakeh.

19 When King Hezekiah heard it, he tore his clothes, covered himself with sackcloth, and went into the house of the LORD. 2And he sent Eliakim, who was in charge of the palace, and Shebna the secretary, and the senior priests, covered with sackcloth, to the prophet Isaiah son of Amoz.

3They said to him, "Thus says Hezekiah, This day is a day of distress, of rebuke, and of disgrace; children have come to the birth, and there is no strength to bring them forth. 4It may be that the LORD your God heard all the words of the Rabshakeh, whom his master the king of Assyria has sent to mock the living God, and will rebuke the words that the LORD your God has heard; therefore lift up your prayer for the remnant that is left."[73]

---

73. The clash with v. 5 is obvious. A response from Isaiah requires vv. 6-7. Vv. 3-4 evoke the mockery of v. 16 and request a prayer for the remnant, echoing the later situation represented by vv. 29-31. Isaiah's prophecy in vv. 6-7 addresses the contemporary danger.

| After the Dtr: indented and sans serif font | DH Extension | *Revision: royal focus* | *Revision: national focus* | Other: double sideline |

⁵When the servants of King Hezekiah came to Isaiah, ⁶Isaiah said to them, "Say to your master, 'Thus says the LORD: Do not be afraid because of the words that you have heard, with which the servants of the king of Assyria have reviled me. ⁷I myself will put a spirit in him, so that he shall hear a rumor and return to his own land; I will cause him to fall by the sword in his own land.' "

8 The Rabshakeh returned, and found the king of Assyria fighting against Libnah; for he had heard that the king had left Lachish. ⁹When the king heard concerning King Tirhakah of Ethiopia, "See, he has set out to fight against you,"

¹⁶Incline your ear, O LORD, and hear; open your eyes, O LORD, and see; hear the words of Sennacherib, which he has sent to mock the living God. ¹⁷Truly, O LORD, the kings of Assyria have laid waste the nations and their lands, ¹⁸and have hurled their gods into the fire, though they were no gods but the work of human hands—wood and stone—and so they were destroyed. ¹⁹So now, O LORD our God, save us, I pray you, from his hand, so that all the kingdoms of the earth may know that you, O LORD, are God alone."[74]

20 Then Isaiah son of Amoz sent to Hezekiah, saying, "Thus says the LORD, the God of Israel:[75]

He sent messengers again to Hezekiah, saying, ¹⁰"Thus shall you speak to King Hezekiah of Judah: Do not let your God on whom you rely deceive you by promising that Jerusalem will not be given into the hand of the king of Assyria. ¹¹See, you have heard what the kings of Assyria have done to all lands, destroying them utterly. Shall you be delivered? ¹²Have the gods of the nations delivered them, the nations that my predecessors destroyed, Gozan, Haran, Rezeph, and the people of Eden who were in Telassar? ¹³Where is the king of Hamath, the king of Arpad, the king of the city of Sepharvaim, the king of Hena, or the king of Ivvah?"

14 Hezekiah received the letter from the hand of the messengers and read it; then Hezekiah went up to the house of the LORD and spread it before the LORD.

¹⁵And Hezekiah prayed before the LORD, and said: "O LORD the God of Israel, who are enthroned above the cherubim, you are God, you alone, of all the kingdoms of the earth; you have made heaven and earth.

---

74. Verses 15-19 constitute a prayer of Hezekiah's to which vv. 20b-28 (29-31) constitute a reply. Clearly, a variety of traditions circulated, celebrating and making capital out of this deliverance of Jerusalem. Here, Gray remarks: "The theme is no longer simply the earnest prayer of the prophet or king for the relief of Jerusalem, but rather the vindication of the Assyrian affronts" (*Kings*, 667). This material (vv. 15-19 and 20b-28 [29-31]) is clearly different from the other two accounts, and quite probably later. Note, for example, the theme of mocking (√ḤRP), found in 1–2 Kings only here at 19:4, 16, 22, 23.

75. As should be clear, at least three literary pieces have crystallized around the traditions associated with faith in the deliverance of Jerusalem from Sennacherib. All three are built around an impact on the king (crisis) and the prophetic response and outcome (crisis resolution). This allows for their combination in quasi-concentric form, indicated in our formatting by the single-line box (outside), the single sideline (middle), and the double sideline (center). The first two are probably pre-dtr; the third (the double sideline) is probably post-dtr. In combining these, it is possible that some of the introductions have been altered, moved, or otherwise separated from their

---

| Main pre-DH: | Other pre-DH: | HKL: + single | **Josianic DH:** |
| *Prophetic Record and PR Extension* | single sideline | underline | **from the Dtr** |

I have heard your prayer to me about King
    Sennacherib of Assyria.
²¹This is the word that the LORD has spoken
    concerning him:
She despises you, she scorns you—
    virgin daughter Zion;
she tosses her head—behind your back,
    daughter Jerusalem.

²²Whom have you mocked and reviled?
    Against whom have you raised your
      voice
and haughtily lifted your eyes?
    Against the Holy One of Israel!
²³By your messengers you have mocked
    the LORD,
    and you have said, 'With my many
      chariots
I have gone up the heights of the
    mountains,
    to the far recesses of Lebanon;
I felled its tallest cedars,
    its choicest cypresses;
I entered its farthest retreat,
    its densest forest.
²⁴I dug wells
    and drank foreign waters,
I dried up with the sole of my foot
    all the streams of Egypt.'

²⁵Have you not heard
    that I determined it long ago?
I planned from days of old
    what now I bring to pass,

that you should make fortified cities
    crash into heaps of ruins,
²⁶while their inhabitants, shorn of strength,
    are dismayed and confounded;
they have become like plants of the field
    and like tender grass,
like grass on the housetops,
    blighted before it is grown.

²⁷"But I know your rising and your sitting,
    your going out and coming in,
    and your raging against me.
²⁸Because you have raged against me
    and your arrogance has come to my ears,
I will put my hook in your nose
    and my bit in your mouth;
I will turn you back on the way
    by which you came.

    ²⁹"And this shall be the sign for you: This year you shall eat what grows of itself, and in the second year what springs from that; then in the third year sow, reap, plant vineyards, and eat their fruit. ³⁰The surviving remnant of the house of Judah shall again take root downward, and bear fruit upward; ³¹for from Jerusalem a remnant shall go out, and from Mount Zion a band of survivors. The zeal of the LORD of hosts will do this.[76]

    32 "Therefore thus says the LORD concerning the king of Assyria: He shall not come into this city, shoot an arrow there, come before it with a shield, or cast up a siege ramp against it. ³³By the way that he came, by the same he shall

---

original context (cf. LXX). As a result, our present formatting assumes that v. 20a originally introduced vv. 32-33 and owes its present position to the introduction of vv. 20b-28 (29-31). Naturally, there are other possibilities.

76. Verses 29-31 are distinguished from the preceding by their address to Hezekiah and not Sennacherib. There is a proverbial flavor to v. 29. A check of the language suggests that it is too idiosyncratic to be easily characterized.

After the Dtr: indented and sans serif font	DH Extension	**Revision: royal focus**	*Revision: national focus*	Other: double sideline

return; he shall not come into this city, says the LORD."

> [34]For I will defend this city to save it, for my own sake and for the sake of my servant David.[77]

35 That very night the angel of the LORD set out and struck down one hundred eighty-five thousand in the camp of the Assyrians; when morning dawned, they were all dead bodies.

> [36]And King Sennacherib of Assyria set out, and went off, and returned home; *(Heb.; NRSV, Then King Sennacherib of Assyria left, went home,)* and lived at Nineveh. [37]As he was worshiping in the house of his god Nisroch, his sons Adrammelech and Sharezer killed him with the sword, and they escaped into the land of Ararat. His son Esar-haddon succeeded him.[78]

---

77. 19:34 is practically identical with 20:6b. 19:34 comes after the "says the LORD" of v. 33, normally the ending of prophecy, and it lies outside the chiastic inclusion (Hebrew) made by "he shall not come into this city" in vv. 32a and 33b. 20:6b is fully acceptable as a statement of motivation, but it does repeat the assurance of deliverance; it is possibly dispensable, but not necessarily. The textual differences with Isa 38:5-6 are noteworthy. Dating is difficult: "my servant David" occurs over a wide range chronologically; "for my own sake" is found beyond this material only in Isa 43:25 and 48:11. Such faith can be expressed after as well as before a disaster. The upshot for us is to treat both 19:34 and 20:6b with some caution.

78. **Present-text potential** of 18:17—19:37. After the favorable report of Hezekiah's reform (18:1-5), this material indulges Hezekiah's reputation as one of the great kings of ancient Israel. He encounters the greatest threat to Jerusalem before the exile and meets it with trust in God and God's prophet.

20 In those days Hezekiah became sick and was at the point of death. The prophet Isaiah son of Amoz came to him, and said to him, "Thus says the LORD: Set your house in order, for you shall die; you shall not recover." [2]Then Hezekiah turned his face to the wall and prayed to the

---

The text presents a fourfold structure: i) a threat from the Assyrians; ii) Hezekiah's recourse to God; iii) a prophecy from Isaiah; iv) realization of the prophecy. This structure is found in the dtr presentation of the two other great kings of ancient Israel, David and Josiah. Its elements are: (i) a critical event in the king's reign; (ii) consultation of a prophet; (iii) a favorable prophecy; (iv) fulfillment of the prophecy. It is worth noting that this emphasis of the Josianic DH is preserved in the combination of the present text.

The Assyrian invasion is Hezekiah's critical event. The Rabshakeh delivers two speeches: one to Hezekiah (18:19-25) and the other to the citizens of Jerusalem (vv. 28-35), both calculated to undermine the trust in God of Hezekiah and the people. Hezekiah first turns to the prophet. Isaiah's "Thus says the LORD" in 19:6 corresponds to the Rabshakeh's "Thus says the great king, the king of Assyria" in 18:19. Isaiah's prophecy is unequivocally favorable. God will deliver Hezekiah, through means that are the staple of politics—rumor and revolt.

Despite this, the text reports an intensified assault on Hezekiah's trust in God, by means of a letter directly from the king of Assyria. With the army in place and the threat mounting, Hezekiah is portrayed turning directly to God in prayer at the temple. God's response comes through the prophet Isaiah, asserting the power of God over the mocking Sennacherib and assuring Hezekiah. The prophetic response culminates in an assurance of the total failure of the siege. The outcome is narrated: the death of the army, the departure of Sennacherib, his death, and the succession of Esar-haddon.

19:35 effectively fulfills 19:32; with the Assyrian army destroyed, there can be no attack on Jerusalem. The fulfillment of 19:33 is left unspecified; v. 36 notes

---

Main pre-DH:	Other pre-DH:	HKL: + single	**Josianic DH:**
Prophetic Record and PR Extension	single sideline	underline	**from the Dtr**

LORD: [3]"Remember now, O LORD, I implore you, how I have walked before you in faithfulness with a whole heart, and have done what is good in your sight." Hezekiah wept bitterly. [4]Before Isaiah had gone out of the middle court, the word of the LORD came to him: [5]"Turn back, and say to Hezekiah prince of my people, Thus says the LORD, the God of your ancestor David: I have heard your prayer, I have seen your tears; indeed, I will heal you; on the third day you shall go up to the house of the LORD. [6]I will add fifteen years to your life. I will deliver you and this city out of the hand of the king of Assyria."[79]

Sennacherib's return, but "the way" is not mentioned. 19:36-37 fulfill 19:7. In the present text, there is no mention of the prophesied rumor (v. 7); the news of Tirhakah's expedition provokes intensified pressure on Hezekiah and not a return home by Sennacherib. It should be avowed that the junction of the two accounts in v. 9 is not wholly satisfactory (cf. Jones, *Kings*, 2.575-76). In all of this, the clarifying role of the storyteller would need to be considerable.

79. In 20:1-11, King Hezekiah is clearly portrayed favorably. Over against the word of the prophet (20:1b), the piety of the king prevails and his plea is heard by YHWH (vv. 2-6a). Vv. 7-11 may be seen as achieving a balance, with emphasis on the prophetic power both to heal (v. 7) and to elicit a sign from God (vv. 8-11; for details of the sign, see Jones, *Kings*, 2.588-89).

The portrayal of Hezekiah, as a king whose prayer is heard and whose request for a sign is granted, is coherent with the favorable presentation of Hezekiah in the Josianic DH. Careful analysis reveals no characteristic dtr language. A pre-dtr origin is probable. It is possible that vv. 1-6a and vv. 8-11 were originally independent traditions.

Despite its position after the deliverance of Jerusalem, the text situates this episode before that event. This is achieved exclusively by the last clause of v. 6a ("I will deliver . . . king of Assyria"). Earlier in this

I will defend this city for my own sake and for my servant David's sake.[80]
[7]Then Isaiah said, "Bring a lump of figs. Let them take it and apply it to the boil, so that he may recover."

8 Hezekiah said to Isaiah, "What shall be the sign that the LORD will heal me, and that I shall go up to the house of the LORD on the third day?" [9]Isaiah said, "This is the sign to you from the LORD, that the LORD will do the thing that he has promised: the shadow has now advanced ten intervals; shall it retreat ten intervals?" [10]Hezekiah answered, "It is normal for the shadow to lengthen ten intervals; rather let the shadow retreat ten intervals." [11]The prophet Isaiah cried to the LORD; and he brought the shadow back the ten intervals, by which the sun had declined on the dial of Ahaz.

12 At that time King Merodach-baladan son of Baladan of Babylon sent envoys with letters and a present to Hezekiah, for he had heard that Hezekiah had been sick. [13]Hezekiah welcomed them; he showed them all his treasure house, the silver, the gold, the spices, the precious oil, his armory, all that was found in his storehouses; there was nothing in his house or in all his realm that Hezekiah did not show them. [14]Then the prophet Isaiah came to King Hezekiah, and said to him, "What did these men say? From where

passage there is no mention of an Assyrian threat. It is possible that this association with Jerusalem's deliverance was made in conjunction with the combining of traditions to form vv. 1-11. From a present text point of view, the passage can be read either as a flashback or, given its position, as a promise of protection in any future crisis.

80. See the discussion on 19:34.

| After the Dtr: indented and sans serif font | DH Extension | *Revision: royal focus* | *Revision: national focus* | Other: double sideline |

did they come to you?" Hezekiah answered, "They have come from a far country, from Babylon." [15]He said, "What have they seen in your house?" Hezekiah answered, "They have seen all that is in my house; there is nothing in my storehouses that I did not show them."[81]

[16] Then Isaiah said to Hezekiah, "Hear the word of the LORD: [17]Days are coming when all that is in your house, and that which your ancestors have stored up until this day, shall be carried to Babylon; nothing shall be left, says the LORD. [18]Some of your own sons who are born to you shall be taken away; they shall be eunuchs in the palace of the king of Babylon." [19]Then Hezekiah said to Isaiah, "The word of the LORD that you have spoken is good." For he thought, "Why not, if there will be peace and security in my days?"

20 The rest of the deeds of Hezekiah, all his power, how he made the pool and the conduit and brought water into the city, are they not written in the Book of the Annals of the Kings of Judah? [21]Hezekiah slept with his ancestors; and his son Manasseh succeeded him.

21 **Manasseh was twelve years old when he began to reign; he reigned fifty-five years in Jerusalem. His mother's name was Hephzibah. [2]He did what was evil in the sight of the LORD.**[82]

following the abominable practices of the nations that the LORD drove out before the people of Israel

---

81. In 20:12-19, the portrayal of Hezekiah is negative; his conduct meets an unfavorable response from the prophet (vv. 16-18). Vv. 13-15 situate the passage in time before 18:14-16; it is clear that Hezekiah showed the envoys a well-stocked treasure house. The stripping of the treasury (18:14-16) is in line with similar passages (i.e., 1 Kgs 15:18; 2 Kgs 12:18; 14:14; cf. 2 Kgs 16:8). The hostility toward the king suggests attribution to the royal focus of the dtr revision. The prophetic allusion to the Babylonian exile (vv. 17-18) may explain the passage's position here at the end of Hezekiah's reign rather than earlier in the story.

Dietrich attributed the insertion of 18:17—20:19 to his DtrP.

82. **Text signals** in 21:1-18. For vv. 10-14, see below. (i) The dtr formulas for the accession and judgment of the king extend through vv. 1-7. There is a strong sense in these verses that basic accusations have been sharpened by later additions. Pointers to this are both linguistic and stylistic. Precise identification of the base and the expansions is difficult and dubious. In what follows, we will list the linguistic signals first and then the stylistic. In the text itself, the formatting adopted is tentative in the extreme, more illustrative than demonstrative, as the discussion will show. (ii) The linguistic features are: "abominable practices of the nations" (cf. 1 Kgs 14:24; 2 Kgs 16:3); "host of heaven" (cf. Deut 4:19; 17:3; 1 Kgs 22:19; 2 Kgs 17:16; 2 Kgs 23:4, 5), where the particular emphasis on worship and service seems to be later; "pass through fire" (cf. 2 Kgs 16:3; 17:17; 23:10); "soothsaying and augury" and mediums and wizards (cf. Deut 18:9-10; 2 Kgs 23:24); "provoking to anger" (cf. 2 Kgs 23:19, the only other case where the infinitive is found alone without an object). (iii) The stylistic features are: doublets of the host of heaven (vv. 3, 5) and God's name at Jerusalem (vv. 4, 7); use of a nonnarrative verbal form (vv. 4, 6).

Text-history approach. Verses 2b and 6 are relatively clear as later expansions, whereas in vv. 3-5 the later material is not so easily identified. However, vv. 3b-4 anticipate both vv. 5 and 7. Any accusation of Manasseh after v. 7 would be anticlimactic. V. 3b specifies worship and service; v. 4 highlights the out-

---

³For he rebuilt the high places that his father Hezekiah had destroyed; he erected altars for Baal, made a sacred pole, as King Ahab of Israel had done.

> *worshiped all the host of heaven, and served them. ⁴He built altars in the house of the LORD, of which the LORD had said, "In Jerusalem I will put my name."*

⁵He built altars for all the host of heaven in the two courts of the house of the LORD.

> *⁶He made his son pass through fire; he practiced soothsaying and augury, and dealt with mediums and with wizards. He did much evil in the sight of the LORD, provoking him to anger.*

⁷The carved image of Asherah that he had made he set in the house of which the LORD said to David and to his son Solomon, "In this house, and in Jerusalem, which I have chosen out of all the tribes of Israel, I will put my name forever.

> *⁸I will not cause the feet of Israel to wander any more out of the land that I gave to their ancestors, if only they will be careful to do according to all that I have commanded*

them, and according to all the law that my servant Moses commanded them." ⁹But they did not listen; Manasseh misled them to do more evil than the nations had done that the LORD destroyed before the people of Israel.[83]

10 The LORD said by his servants the prophets, ¹¹"Because King Manasseh of Judah has committed these abominations, has done things more wicked than all that the Amorites did, who were before him, and has caused Judah also to sin with his idols; ¹²therefore thus says the LORD, the God of Israel, I am bringing upon Jerusalem and Judah such evil that the ears of everyone who hears of it will tingle. ¹³I will stretch over Jerusalem the measuring line for Samaria, and the plummet for the house of Ahab; I will wipe Jerusalem as

---

rage of building altars to the host of heaven in the temple where YHWH's name has been put.

Present-text potential. After the lengthy presentation of the exemplary reforming king, Hezekiah (with the exception of 2 Kgs 18:14-16; 20:12-19), the text introduces his son, Manasseh, who undid his father's reforms and introduced evils of his own. He is the first king of Judah to desecrate YHWH's temple by building blasphemous altars there (vv. 3-5) and introducing the cult symbol of a rival deity (v. 7). For further details, see below on vv. 10-14.

For a comprehensive study of Manasseh and his context, see P. S. F. Van Keulan, *Manasseh*.

---

83. In vv. 8-9 and v. 15, we have the dtr revision's national focus reworking and refining the comments on Manasseh made by both the Josianic Dtr and, in vv. 10-14, the revision's royal focus. V. 8 shifts the focus abruptly from Manasseh's desecration of the temple to the theme of exile from the land, a shift from the king to the people. There is a law-oriented implication that breach of the Mosaic law leads to exile. The text rejects the prospect of any further exile, but this is subject to Israel's obedience (cf. Deut 4:25-31 and 30:1-10—both dtr revision, national focus). V. 9 continues the emphasis on the people. Surprisingly, the simple "they did not listen" is in the DH a late usage (cf. Josh 5:6; Judg 2:17, 20; 2 Kgs 17:14, 40; 18:12; 22:13). Picking up on vv. 10-14, v. 9 places a focus on the people whom Manasseh led astray. Manasseh's evil is the core of the dtr revision's royal focus (vv. 10-14), with its consequences for the people (vv. 12-14). V. 15 picks up on these people and emphasizes their responsibility in characteristic language (cf. note on 1 Kgs 16:1-4).

After the Dtr: indented and sans serif font	DH Extension	**Revision: royal focus**	Revision: national focus	Other: double sideline

*one wipes a dish, wiping it and turning it upside down. ¹⁴I will cast off the remnant of my heritage, and give them into the hand of their enemies; they shall become a prey and a spoil to all their enemies."*⁸⁴

---

84. **Text signals** in vv. 10-14. (i) The reference to "his servants the prophets" reflects 2 Kgs 17:23, and signals that what Jeroboam did to Israel there, Manasseh is doing to Judah here. The fulfillment is noted in 24:2-3. (ii) "Abominations/abominable practices" (v. 11) is a term characteristic of later revision (cf. v. 2b above). (iii) "Idols" (*gilulîm*) is equally a later characteristic (cf. Deut 29:17 [Heb, v. 16]; 1 Kgs 15:12; 21:26; 2 Kgs 17:12; 23:24). (iv) The metaphors in vv. 12-13 are so idiosyncratic that comparisons are not helpful. "Two ears" (Heb.) is found in 1 Sam 3:11; "tingling ears" is found in Jer 19:3. That is all; it is not enough for conclusions. (v) The accusations are leveled against Manasseh; he is the only king of Judah so accused, paralleling Jeroboam for the north—although the explicit reference is to the "house of Ahab" (v. 13).

Text-history approach. The perspective voiced here of the exile of Judah places this passage outside the context of the Josianic Dtr. It intensifies the Dtr's negative portrayal of Manasseh. The language used, the heightened emphasis on Manasseh, and the similarity with the expansions in vv. 1-7 point to the royal focus within the dtr revision process.

The royal focus of the revision here draws two parallels in its accusation of Manasseh. First, there is Jeroboam; only he and Manasseh are accused of causing their people to sin. Second, there is the house of Ahab; here it is drawn on to depict the punishment rather than the sin. It is noteworthy that the elimination of the house of Ahab coincides with the end of the PR; the fall of Samaria coincides with the end of the PR Extension.

Present-text potential. The basic contribution of vv. 10-14 is their identification of Manasseh as having the same responsibility for Judah that Jeroboam had

---

¹⁵because they have done what is evil in my sight and have provoked me to anger, since the day their ancestors came out of Egypt, even to this day.

16 Moreover Manasseh shed very much innocent blood, until he had filled Jerusalem from one end to another, besides the sin that he caused Judah to sin so that they did what was evil in the sight of the LORD.⁸⁵

17 Now the rest of the acts of Manasseh, all that he did, and the sin that he committed, are they not written in the Book of the Annals of the Kings of Judah? ¹⁸Manasseh slept with his ancestors, and was buried in the garden of his house, in the garden of Uzza. His son Amon succeeded him.

19 Amon was twenty-two years old when he began to reign; he reigned two years in Jerusalem. His mother's name was Meshullemeth daughter of Haruz of Jotbah. ²⁰He did what was evil in the sight of the LORD, as his father Manasseh had done.

²¹He walked in all the way in which his father walked, served the idols that his father served, and worshiped them;

---

for Israel—he caused them to sin. Note how this is reiterated in v. 16.

Manasseh is accused of bringing about the downfall of Judah; this fall will involve both the city of Jerusalem and the dynasty of David. Samaria points to the city; Ahab's house may evoke the dynasty.

85. Going beyond the cultic accusations above, v. 16 accuses Manasseh of killing, the shedding of innocent blood—an issue of social justice. Manasseh is the only king of Judah so accused. Reference to "innocent blood" is widespread, some twenty occurrences; it is worth noting that five of these are in Deuteronomy and six in Jeremiah (cf. also 2 Kgs 24:4). The introductory word of the verse, here translated "moreover," at 24:4 "and also" (both *wĕgam* in Hebrew), often signals a later addition.

22_he abandoned the Lord, the God of his ancestors, and did not walk in the way of the Lord._[86]

23The servants of Amon conspired against him, and killed the king in his house. 24But the people of the land killed all those who had conspired against King Amon, and the people of the land made his son Josiah king in place of him.[87]

25Now the rest of the acts of Amon that he did, are they not written in the Book of the Annals of the Kings of Judah? 26He was buried in his tomb in the garden of Uzza; then his son Josiah succeeded him.[88]

22 Josiah was eight years old when he began to reign; he reigned thirty-one years in Jerusalem. His mother's name was Jedidah daughter of Adaiah of Bozkath. 2He did what was right in the sight of the Lord, and walked in all the way of his father David; he did not turn aside to the right or to the left.[89]

3 In the eighteenth year of King Josiah, the king sent Shaphan son of Azaliah, son of Meshullam, the secretary, to the house of the Lord, saying, 4"Go up to the [high] priest Hilkiah, and have him count the entire sum of the money that has been brought into the house of the Lord, which the keepers of the threshold have collected from the people; 5let it be given into the hand of the workers who have the oversight of the house of the Lord; let them give it to the workers who are at the house of the Lord, repairing the house, 6that is, to the carpenters, to the builders, to the masons; and let them use it to buy timber and quarried stone to repair the house. 7But no accounting shall be asked from them for the money that is delivered into their hand, for they deal honestly."

8 The [high] priest Hilkiah said to Shaphan the secretary, "I have found the book of the law in the house of the Lord." When Hilkiah gave the book to Shaphan, he read it. 9Then Shaphan the secretary came to the king, and reported to the king, "Your servants have emptied out the money that was found in the house, and have delivered it into the hand of the workers who have oversight of the house of the Lord." 10Shaphan the secretary informed the king, "The priest Hilkiah has given me a book." Shaphan then read it aloud to the king.[90]

11 When the king heard the words of the book of the law, he tore his clothes. 12Then

---

86. Verses 21-22 are highly pleonastic in relation to the judgment formulas of the Josianic Dtr (cf. 1 Kgs 3:3; 15:26, 34; 16:26; 2 Kgs 22:2). "Idols" has been noted above as a mark of later editing; the verb "to abandon" is equally late (cf. Judg 2:12-13). Attribution to the royal focus within the dtr revision reflects the similar hostility shown Manasseh in the revision's royal focus above.

87. For Noth, 21:23-24 is from the Chronicles of the Kings of Judah (*DH*, 105).

88. Dietrich attributed 21:10-14 to his DtrP and 21:4, 6, 7b-9, 15-16 to his DtrN.

89. In 22:1, the thirty-one year reign is clearly a later precision in the Josianic DH. In v. 2, the last clause is possibly, but not necessarily, an addition from the national focus of the dtr revision.

90. Verses 3-10 combine repairs to the temple with discovery of a book, believed to be the dtn lawcode. The sequence is not impossible: vv. 3-7, repairs to the temple (cf. discussion at 2 Kgs 12:8); v. 8, discovery of a book; v. 9, report to the king on the repairs; v. 10, report to the king on the discovery. Whatever of the pre-dtr raw materials, the finished product here can be attributed to the Josianic Dtr. For the square brackets we have used with "the [high] priest," see the discussion at 2 Kgs 12:8.

The term "book of the law" is found in passages that are secondary in the DH (Deut 28:61; 29:20;

After the Dtr: indented and sans serif font	DH Extension	**Revision:** **royal focus**	Revision: national focus	Other: double sideline

the king commanded the priest Hilkiah, Ahikam son of Shaphan, Achbor son of Micaiah, Shaphan the secretary, and the king's servant Asaiah, saying, [13]"Go, inquire of the LORD for me, for the people, and for all Judah, concerning the words of this book that has been found."

> for great is the wrath of the LORD that is kindled against us, because our ancestors did not obey the words of this book, to do according to all that is written concerning us.[91]

14 So the priest Hilkiah, Ahikam, Achbor, Shaphan, and Asaiah went to the prophetess Huldah the wife of Shallum son of Tikvah, son of Harhas, keeper of the wardrobe; she

resided in Jerusalem in the Second Quarter, where they consulted her. [15]She declared to them,[92]

30:10; 31:26; Josh 1:8; 8:31, 34; 23:6; 24:26; 2 Kgs 14:6. If the two occurrences here (vv. 8 and 11) are also considered secondary—which is possible—there is no stimulus or trigger for the consultation of Huldah, her prophecy, and in fact Josiah's reform. In our judgment, the references in 22:8, 11 are most appropriately attributed to the Josianic Dtr.

It is important to keep in mind that 2 Chronicles 34–35 presents a different view of Josiah's reform and reign. The issues are thoroughly discussed by Jones, who opts for the sequence of events as in Chronicles (*Kings*, 2.602-6). Our concern here is not to reconstruct the history but to unfold and understand the text of Kings. While the two cannot be wholly dissociated, for us the unfolding of Kings is primary. For the literature, see Knoppers (*Two Nations*, 2.125-69).

91. The kindling of YHWH's wrath is a combination of verb and noun that is found only here and in v. 17; v. 17 has strong links to the national focus of the dtr revision. The linguistic usage of our ancestors not obeying (literally: hearing) is also rare; the terms are found in the secondary Judg 2:17 and Jer 34:14.

92. This passage dealing with Josiah's consultation of Huldah about the book of the law is the subject of much debate. Uncertainty is the order of the day. At stake is how much, if any, of Huldah's original prophecy remains. As our formatting shows, we distribute the text across the Josianic Dtr, the royal focus of the revision process, and the revision's national focus. What is involved in this process is the replacement of text rather than its editing (for other examples, see: 1 Kgs 3:4-15; 5:1-12; 11:26-40). In our understanding, this is unusual. Each aspect of the text will need careful scrutiny. Initially, an overall view will be helpful.

Text signals in 22:15-20. For clarity, it may help to group the signals in the text around the levels just mentioned: the Josianic Dtr, the royal focus of the dtr revision, and the national focus.

At the level of the Josianic Dtr: (i) Huldah's prophecy is addressed to "the man who sent you" (v. 15)—unusual if the king's involvement had been told her. (ii) V. 18's "that you have heard" accurately reflects vv. 10-11; v. 16's "that the king of Judah has read" does not. (iii) The implementation of the reform in chap. 23 requires the authentication of the book by Huldah as the word of YHWH. This aspect is valid at all levels. At the level of the Josianic DH, the signals allow for the possibility that Huldah's response was restricted to this endorsement of the words of the book. This was the response taken "back to the king" (v. 20).

At the level of the royal focus of the dtr revision. Josiah's unexpected death at Megiddo posed a problem; in dtr terms, death as the reward for an obedient reformer could have seemed scandalous. (i) God's words "against this place, and against its inhabitants" (v. 19) are threats in the newly discovered book read to the king (differently in v. 16). (ii) Even before the prophecy, Josiah's response is given in brief: "he tore his clothes" when he heard the words of the book (v. 11). (iii) The prophecy goes beyond this to add peni-

| Main pre-DH: | Other pre-DH: | HKL: + single | **Josianic DH:** |
| *Prophetic Record and PR Extension* | single sideline | underline | **from the Dtr** |

tence, humility, and tears (v 19). (iv) The text has Josiah gathered to his ancestors and, somewhat repetitively, gathered to his grave in peace. First, any reference to Josiah's death in a response emerging from an inquiry about the book is odd. Second, any report of Josiah's violent death after the reform is odd. The death of one's king in battle is normally a disaster. Third, the phrasing is odd. Apart from this occasion, to be gathered to one's ancestors is used only once (Judg 2:10). "Be gathered to your grave": first, the usage is unique; second, the repetition of "gather" stands out but emphasizes the difference between the death and the burial. The death is YHWH's doing ("I will gather you"); the burial is the people's ("you shall be gathered"). "In peace" is used three times with regard to death (Gen 15:15; 1 Kgs 2:6; Jer 34:4-5); only in this case does it occur with regard to burial. All of this corresponds appropriately to Josiah's death in battle at Megiddo and burial in peace in Jerusalem (cf. Dietrich, *Prophetie und Geschichte*, 58; M. Rose wriggles, "Bemerkungen zum historischen Fundament," 50-63, esp. p. 59). Burial in peace is to be contrasted with the shame of unburied bones (cf. 1 Sam 31:13; 2 Sam 21:12-14; 1 Kgs 14:11; 16:4; 21:24; 2 Kgs 9:34-37; 23:14-16; Jer 8:1-2; 25:33; Ezek 29:5).

At the level of the national focus of the dtr revision. (i) V. 16 foretells the disaster threatened in "the words of the book." (ii) V. 17 spells out the justification for this disaster, in terms characteristic of the national focus within the dtr revision; it is directed against the people, not the king. (iii) V. 18, by contrast, implies favor for the king of Judah "who sent you to inquire of the LORD." (iv) V. 16 has the king read the book, whereas v. 10 has Shaphan read it to him.

Text-history approach. The situation of the text of 22:11-20 may seem complex; in reality, it is not. As with Genesis 1 and 2, any confusion arises from the fact that the chronologically later text comes earlier in the passage. Reconstruction needs to work from evidence and eschew flights of fancy. What is said here will be minimal.

The carrying out of the Josianic reform as reported in chap. 23 implies as a minimal response from

Huldah: obey, it is of God. The death of Josiah, following this response and the reform, opens the way to the possibility for a scandalous interpretation: through the book and the prophetess, Josiah was lured to his doom. The claim might be expected from Josiah's enemies: the reform was never God's will; Josiah's death is proof. While such a conclusion may be possible, another is virtually inescapable: the deconstruction of the dtr theology of reward and punishment.

In vv. 19-20a, the text provides a different interpretation of Josiah's death. Josiah might implement reform; Judah would not reap its fruit. The damage inflicted by Manasseh had become irreparable. Josiah's death and burial before the disaster was a reward for his reforming attempts. His eyes were spared the sight of the failure of his reform and the disaster involved for Judah. Careful examination of the elements of this passage reveal it as remarkably idiosyncratic. For example: "this place and its inhabitants" is not dtr, but it is found at Jer 19:12; "humble oneself before YHWH" and "penitent heart" are not dtr, nor Jeremiah either; "desolation and curse" are not dtr; they are found in Jeremiah, but in series of three or four. Instead, there are reflections of earlier texts: Ahab for humbling (1 Kgs 21:29), Hezekiah for weeping (2 Kgs 20:3), and Josiah here for tearing of clothes (22:11).

Attribution is difficult. There is reference in v. 20 to the coming disaster; reasons are not given for it. Reasons are supplied by vv. 16-17, but in language characteristic of the national focus of the dtr revision. The disaster is inevitable in the light of 21:10-14 and reaffirmed by 23:26-27, both texts attributed to the royal focus of the revision. Focus on the disaster links all three. So too does the attitude toward the king's responsibility for the disaster: accusing Manasseh, sparing Josiah. Economy of hypothesis suggests attribution of vv. 19-20a to the royal focus of the revision process. Certainty is out of place.

Verses 16-18a move the focus from royal responsibility—the sins of Manasseh—to the responsibility of the people, "on this place and on its inhabitants" (v. 16). The responsibility is itemized in v. 17, in language characteristic of the national focus of the dtr revision (abandoning YHWH, offerings to other gods, provoca-

After the Dtr: indented and sans serif font	DH Extension	**Revision: royal focus**	Revision: national focus	Other: double sideline

‖ Thus says the Lord, the God of Israel[93]
"Tell the man who sent you to me:
>   [16]*Thus says the Lord, I will indeed bring disaster on this place and on its inhabitants—*

all the words of the book that the king of Judah has read. [17]Because they have abandoned me and have made offerings to other gods, so that they have provoked me to anger with all the work of their hands, therefore my wrath will be kindled against this place, and it will not be quenched. [18]But as to the king of Judah, who sent you to inquire of the Lord, thus shall you say to him

Thus says the Lord, the God of Israel: (Heb., nil; nrsv, Regarding) **the words that you have heard**[94]
>   **[19]*because your heart was penitent, and you humbled yourself before the Lord, when you heard how I spoke against this place, and against its inhabitants, that they should become a desolation and a curse, and because you have torn your clothes and wept before me, I also have heard you, says the Lord. [20]Therefore, I will gather you to your ancestors, and you shall be gathered to your grave in peace; your eyes shall not see all the disaster that I will bring on this place."***

tion to anger). The language ($ḥēmâ$ with $yāṣat$) of kindling yhwh's wrath occurs only in this context (2 Kgs 22:13, 17).

It is important to bear in mind that the presumed original text and the process of revision are addressing different situations. In the original text, what is believed to have been the dtn lawcode was read to the king (22:10-11). Judging from 2 Kings 23, to provoke Josiah's reaction the equivalent of Deuteronomy 12 (cult places) and Deuteronomy 16 (Passover) would have sufficed. Hearing God's law that was so obviously neglected would be adequate justification for a pious king to tear his clothes. The revision was dealing with the DH in near-to-final form; revisers would have had in view much of the curse material in Deuteronomy 28. Bringing disaster (v. 16) and becoming a desolation and a curse (v. 19) are not surprising.

Present-text potential in 22:15-20. The text portrays the right response of a king to the word of God and the fearful effect of deeply entrenched evil (in equivalent terms: false values) in a people. The story of the discovery of the book is not about its origins (fraud or fortune) but about a king's reaction to the word of God. The royal response is repentance and action. A hint of what is to come is given in the comment that "our ancestors did not obey the words of this book" (v. 13). Huldah's prophetic response begins with what is undeniably true and will be borne out in events: the people have abandoned God and God's anger will not be quenched (v. 17; in equivalent terms: the entrenched values of the people are not easily altered). The text addresses Josiah's repentance (torn clothing) and the death that will spare him the agony to come. The narrative then proceeds to the reform.

93. The reason for not giving this introduction to Huldah, but attributing it to a later hand (and so the double sideline) is that the "me" of "the man who sent

you to me" becomes God; tolerable for a redactor, less likely for an author. The effect of its placement is to characterize all that follows as God's message to Josiah.

94. The attribution of the introduction here to the original saying follows the observation on v. 15. The second phrase is not in accord with v. 16 (heard vs. read); it is in accord with v. 11 and v. 19a (heard and heard). It could be attributed to either the original (as here) or to the royal focus within the dtr revision, but it must be admitted that the present Hebrew phrase is unintelligibly unattached. The nrsv's "regarding" is more than adequate; it can be achieved by a simple emendation (cf. E. Nicholson, "II Kings XXII 18."

Main pre-DH:	Other pre-DH:	HKL: + single	**Josianic DH:**
Prophetic Record and PR Extension	single sideline	underline	**from the Dtr**

They took the message back to the king.[95]

23 **Then the king directed that all the elders of Judah and Jerusalem should be gathered to him.** [2]**The king went up to the house of the LORD, and all the people of Judah, and** (Heb.) **all the inhabitants of Jerusalem went with him** (Hebrew order), and (Heb.) **the priests, and** (Heb.) **the prophets, and all the people, both small and great; he read in their hearing all the words of the book of the covenant that had been found in the house of the LORD.** [3]**The king stood by the pillar and made a covenant before the LORD, to follow the LORD** *and to keep* (Heb.; NRSV, *keeping*) *his commandments, his decrees, and his statutes,* **with all his heart and all his soul, to perform the words of this covenant that were written in this book. All the people joined in the covenant.**[96]

---

95. Dietrich attributed 22:16-17, 18-20 to his DtrP and 22:17aβ, 19b (or to a later gloss, cf. p. 38) to his DtrN.

96. In v. 2a, it is likely that the three specific groups are an addition, expanding the more general "people of Judah" and "inhabitants of Jerusalem." The NRSV makes a unified text look plausible; the Heb. makes it highly unlikely. The NRSV's "and with him went" renders a Heb. "with him" (*'itô*) located after "all the inhabitants of Jerusalem." The addition makes the Heb. sentence ungainly, but it is our assumption that editors wanted their work to be, as a rule, recognizably separate from the traditions they interpreted. Such ungainliness was acceptable.

In the Heb. of v. 3a, the "keeping his commandments, his decrees, and his statutes" is either a second element of the covenant or a proleptic unfolding of what is meant by "the words of this covenant" that are to be performed. The sentence has three infinitives—to follow, to keep, to perform. Of these, only "to keep" is preceded by "and"—a possible indication of

4 The king commanded the [high] priest Hilkiah, the priests of the second order, and the guardians of the threshold, to bring out of the temple of the LORD all the vessels made for Baal, for Asherah, and for all the host of heaven; he burned them outside Jerusalem in the fields of the Kidron.[97]

---

an insertion. An addition from the national focus within the dtr revision is likely, but not certain.

97. **Text signals** in 23:4-14. The analysis of these verses is highly controverted. There has been debate whether a pre-dtr source for the report existed; and, if so, then over its extent and over the issue of later expansions within it. Agreement has been minimal (for details, see O'Brien, *Deuteronomistic History Hypothesis*, 251-52). In our judgment, the bulk of these verses can be distributed between the Josianic DH and the royal focus of the dtr revision. Beyond this lies uncertainty.

(i) Cleansed from the temple were cult objects for Baal, Asherah, and all the host of heaven, included by the Josianic Dtr under the sins of Manasseh (2 Kgs 21:3, 5, 7). (ii) Carrying ashes to Bethel relates to issues of the north. (iii) The initial verb in v. 5 is a non-narrative form (*wĕqāṭal*), not infrequently associated with additions (cf. vv. 8b, 10, 14 below). (iv) The phrase "the kings of Judah," as subject of a generalized accusation, occurs in vv. 5, 11 and 12, and nowhere else in the DH; the alleged crimes are not reported in the DH. As a category, the kings of Judah attract Jeremianic interest (Jer 1:18; 8:1; 19:3, 13; 20:5; 44:9). (v) The sun, the moon, and the host of heaven occur together only in Deut 17:3b (late) and Jer 8:2; "the constellations" occurs only here. (vi) In v. 8b, the unidentified "the city" occurs twice and nowhere else in vv. 4-14. (vii) Passage through fire is referred to in v. 10, a verse beginning with a non-narrative verb form. This "passage through fire" is elsewhere associated with the royal focus of the dtr revision (2 Kgs 16:3; 17:17; 21:6; cf. also Deut 18:10). (viii) The horses here and the chariots of the sun as cult objects associated with the Jerusalem temple are unknown (v. 11), as are the altars on the roof (v. 12); for Manasseh's

| After the Dtr: indented and sans serif font | DH Extension | *Revision: royal focus* | *Revision: national focus* | Other: double sideline |

and carried their ashes to Bethel. ⁵He deposed the idolatrous priests, whom the kings of Judah had ordained to make offerings in the high places at the cities of Judah and around Jerusalem; those also who made offerings to Baal, to the sun, the moon, the constellations, and all the host of the heavens. ⁶He brought out the image of Asherah from the house of the LORD, outside Jerusalem, to the Wadi Kidron, burned it at the Wadi Kidron, beat it to dust and threw the dust of it upon the graves of the common people. ⁷He broke down the houses of the male temple prostitutes that were in the house of the LORD, where the women did weaving for Asherah. ⁸He brought all the priests out of the towns of Judah, and defiled the high places where the priests had made offerings, from Geba to Beer-sheba.

|| he broke down the high places of the gates that were at the entrance of the gate of Joshua the governor of the city, which were on the left at the gate of the city.⁹⁸

⁹The priests of the high places, however, did not come up to the altar of the LORD in Jerusalem, but ate unleavened bread among their kindred.

¹⁰He defiled Topheth, which is in the valley of Ben-hinnom, so that no one would make a son or a daughter pass through fire as an offering to Molech. ¹¹He removed the horses that the kings of Judah had dedicated to the sun, at the entrance to the house of the LORD, by the chamber of the eunuch Nathan-melech, which was in the precincts; then he burned the chariots of the sun with fire. ¹²The altars on the roof of the upper chamber of Ahaz which the kings of Judah had made, and the altars that Manasseh had made in the two courts of the house of the LORD, he pulled down from there and broke in pieces, and threw the rubble into the Wadi Kidron.

---

altars, see 2 Kgs 21:5 (Josianic Dtr). (ix) Vv. 13-14 introduce a concern for high places in a sequence concerned with altars (cf. v. 12 2x; v. 15). (x) V. 13 appears to be a conflation of traditions from 1 Kgs 11:5 and 7, generalizing the accusation of building high places as well as qualifying all three as abominations.

Text-history approach in 23:4-14. Attribution to the Josianic Dtr is appropriate for the basic material of vv. 4, 6-8a, and 9. The primary concern is with the temple in Jerusalem; it is purified of cult materials and special attention is given to the image of Asherah. Still in Jerusalem, the male temple prostitutes are dealt with (cf. 1 Kgs 14:24; 15:12; 22:46 [Heb., v. 47]; Job 36:14). The attention then moves outside Jerusalem, to the priests of the high places of Judah.

There are clear pointers to the presence of the royal focus of the dtr revision. For the carrying of ashes to Bethel (in v. 4b), there is the association with Bethel in vv. 15-20. For v. 5, see text signals (iii), (iv), and (v). For vv. 10-12, see text signals (iv), (vii) and (viii). Within this material, there may be passages attributable to the Josianic Dtr (e.g., Manasseh's altars). The possibility is unquestionable; any attribution would be uncertain.

For vv. 8b and 13-14, see the relevant notes below.

Present-text potential of 23:4-14. There is an all-embracing presentation of the reforming measures required before Josiah's celebration of the Passover. The text unfolds in a repeated pattern, moving three times from temple to high places (temple: vv. 4, 6-7, 11-12; high places: vv. 5, 8-10, 13-14).

---

98. This is an odd little text which could be associated with a specific situation at Beer-sheba (cf. Y. Yadin, "Beer-sheba: The High Place Destroyed by King Josiah."

---

¹³The king defiled the high places that were east of Jerusalem, to the south of the Mount of Destruction, which King Solomon of Israel had built for Astarte the abomination of the Sidonians, for Chemosh the abomination of Moab, and for Milcom the abomination of the Ammonites. ¹⁴He broke the pillars in pieces, cut down the sacred poles, and covered the sites with human bones.⁹⁹

15 Moreover, the altar at Bethel, the high place erected by Jeroboam son of Nebat, who caused Israel to sin—he pulled down that altar along with the high place. He burned the high place, crushing it to dust; he also burned the sacred pole. ¹⁶As Josiah turned, he saw the tombs there on the mount; and he sent and took the bones out of the tombs, and burned them on the altar, and defiled it, according to the word of the LORD that the man of God proclaimed, when Jeroboam stood by the altar at the festival; he turned and looked up at the tomb of the man of God who had predicted these things. ¹⁷Then he said, "What is that monument that I see?" The people of the city told him, "It is the tomb of the man of God who came from Judah and predicted these things that you have done against the altar at Bethel." ¹⁸He said, "Let him rest; let no one move his

*bones." So they let his bones alone, with the bones of the prophet who came out of Samaria. ¹⁹Moreover, Josiah removed all the shrines of the high places that were in the towns of Samaria, which kings of Israel had made, provoking the LORD to anger; he did to them just as he had done at Bethel. ²⁰He slaughtered on the altars all the priests of the high places who were there, and burned human bones on them. Then he returned to Jerusalem.*¹⁰⁰

21 The king commanded all the people, "Keep the passover to the LORD your God as prescribed in this book of the covenant." ²²No such passover had been kept since the days of the judges who judged Israel, or during all the days of the kings of Israel or of the kings of Judah; ²³but in the eighteenth year of King Josiah this passover was kept to the LORD in Jerusalem.¹⁰¹

---

99. The verses fill a gap in Josiah's reform measures, eliminating the cultic installations built in Jerusalem by Solomon. The sequence without vv. 13-14 is concerned principally with altars (vv. 12a and 15; see above, text signal #ix). Assuming a conflation from 1 Kgs 11:5 and 7 (text signal #x), the verses are probably later than the national focus of the dtr revision.

100. In vv. 15-20, an account of the fulfillment of the prophecy concerning Josiah (1 Kgs 13:2) is sandwiched between two elements of an account claiming Josiah's reform of the north, at Bethel itself (v. 15) and in the towns of Samaria (vv. 19-20). V. 19 reflects the prophecy in 1 Kgs 13:32; v. 20, similarly, reflects 13:2. As we have suggested, 1 Kings 13 may be seen as a contribution inserted into the DH by the dtr revision's royal focus (for details, see the note on 1 Kgs 13:2). It is appropriate here to attribute vv. 15-20 to this same focus of revision. Both v. 15 and v. 19 begin with "Moreover" (*wĕgam*), a pointer to the possibility of an addition.

Along the lines of the pattern occurring in vv. 4-14, Jeroboam's central cultic establishment is dealt with first (vv. 15-18), followed by the country installations in vv. 19-20.

101. In our judgment, this is the culmination of the report of Josiah's reform; with v. 25a, the Josianic

---

| After the Dtr: indented and sans serif font | DH Extension | **Revision: royal focus** | Revision: national focus | Other: double sideline |

24 Moreover Josiah put away the mediums, wizards, teraphim, idols, and all the abominations that were seen in the land of Judah and in Jerusalem, so that he established the words of the law that were written in the book that the priest Hilkiah had found in the house of the LORD.[102]

25Before him there was no king like him, who turned to the LORD with all his heart, with all his soul, and with all his might, according to all the law of Moses.[103]

nor did any like him arise after him[104]

26 Still the LORD did not turn from the fierceness of his great wrath, by

which his anger was kindled against Judah, because of all the provocations with which Manasseh had provoked him. 27The LORD said, "I will remove Judah also out of my sight, as I have removed Israel; and I will reject this city that I have chosen, Jerusalem, and the house of which I said, My name shall be there."[105]

DH comes to an end. The insistence on the eighteenth year here (cf. 22:3) emphasizes the prompt royal compliance with the discovery of God's law. The emphasis of the text is not necessarily in conflict with the reality of events, especially if restricted to the texts identified here as Josianic. For the chronological issues, see O'Brien, *Deuteronomistic History Hypothesis*, 266.

102. The focus of the list here is likely to be late: e.g., mediums (2 Kgs 21:6); wizards (2 Kgs 21:6); teraphim (Judg 17:5; 18:14, 17, 18, 20); idols (Deut 29:17 [Heb., v. 16]; 1 Kgs 15:12; 21:26; 2 Kgs 17:12; 21:11, 21); abominations, plural (Deut 29:17 [Heb., v. 16]). Its focus is on the law found by Hilkiah; no particular attribution is indicated.

103. The account of Josiah's reign ends on a positive note, as it began in 22:2. The echo of 2 Kgs 18:5, despite the reverse order, associates the two great reforming kings. The allusion to Deut 6:5 is evident. With the citation of the "Shema," the beginning of the DH is evoked positively; with the achievement of the reform, the Josianic DH ends on the equally positive note of Josiah, who embodied this central core of Israel's faith. It is important to realize that this supreme accolade, associated with the reform and the Passover, belongs more than a decade before Josiah's death (i.e., c. 622–609 B.C.E.). The Josianic DH ends here.

104. Given the failure of Josiah's four successors to maintain his reform, the final comment is not surpris-

ing. Attribution to the royal focus within the dtr revision is reasonable; the emphasis is on the kings.

105. Verses 26-27 reaffirms the condemnation of Manasseh made in 2 Kgs 21:10-14 and, like it, can be attributed to the royal focus of the dtr revision. The reaffirmation does not repeat the imagery (21:12-13). As in 21:4, it discreetly drops the "forever" of 21:7.

Dietrich attributed 23:26-27 to his DtrN.

Looking back over chaps. 22–23 from this vantage point, the text holds together the tension of the reform undertaken by Josiah and the people (23:3) and the magnitude of Manasseh's evil that here attracts YHWH's ongoing anger. The passage offers an occasion for reflection on the intersection of a present-text approach with a growth-of-text approach. For a growth-of-text approach, the royal focus within the dtr revision here, coming after the failures in 23:31–25:30, can attribute the ineffectual outcome of the reform to the deep-seated evil of Manasseh. For a present-text approach, the impact of Manasseh's evil does not come from subsequent reflection but is stated as the attitude of God prior to the disasters to come and, in fact, their cause. In either approach, the text here prepares us for the extension of the DH to come.

There is a temptation for moderns to see in the enduring evil of Manasseh the statement that his policies over a long reign became deeply engrained in the people. It is noteworthy that the text does not actually make that move at this point. As in vv. 26-27, the blame is laid upon Manasseh. A hint may be given in 2 Kgs 21:20-21, where Amon's evil is directly correlated with that of his father. In the national focus within the dtr revision process, the shift of responsi-

Main pre-DH: *Prophetic Record and PR Extension*	Other pre-DH: single sideline	HKL: + single underline	**Josianic DH: from the Dtr**

28 Now the rest of the acts of Josiah, and all that he did, are they not written in the Book of the Annals of the Kings of Judah? [29]In his days Pharaoh Neco king of Egypt went up to the king of Assyria to the river Euphrates. King Josiah went to meet him; but when Pharaoh Neco met him at Megiddo, he killed him. [30]His servants carried him dead in a chariot from Megiddo, brought him to Jerusalem, and buried him in his own tomb. The people of the land took Jehoahaz son of Josiah, anointed him, and made him king in place of his father.[106]

31 Jehoahaz was twenty-three years old when he began to reign; he reigned three months in Jerusalem. His mother's name was Hamutal daughter of Jeremiah of

bility from king to people is comprehensive. However, in its final statement, within Huldah's prophecy (2 Kgs 22:16-17), Manasseh is not mentioned.

106. What we refer to as the "DH Extension" takes the DH on from Josiah's reform to the end of the monarchy in Judah. In our understanding, the Josianic DH ended with 2 Kgs 23:25a. The extension continues the story through the last four kings. The royal focus within the dtr revision found an explanation of the dtr reform's failure in the infidelity of the kings. Its groundwork was laid in 1 Samuel; its culmination was with Jeroboam I (for the north) and Manasseh (for the south). The national focus, on the other hand, included the people in this responsibility, with a far-reaching reworking of the DH. The evidence for the DH Extension is discussed below.

Text signals. for 23:28—25:30. (i) The judgment formulas for the kings (2 Kgs 23:32, 37; 24:9, 19) constitute a pattern distinct from the others (Pattern D in our Tables, and for Weippert Schema III, see note on 23:37 below; see also G. Vanoni, "2 Kön 23, 25–25,30," in *Das Deuteronomium*, 357-62). (ii) These judgment formulas evince a high degree of regularity, but with some variation in their reference to the royal predecessors. 23:32 and 37 refer to "his ancestors"; 24:9 has "his father" in the singular; 24:19 simply has "Jehoiakim." (iii) This variation has a regularity of its own. For the third and fourth kings, one ancestor functions as model—Jehoiakim, who is father of

Jehoiachin (24:9) and, according to the MT, is half-brother of Zedekiah (24:19; cf. 23:31 and 24:18 together with 23:34 and 36). For the first and second of these kings (Jehoahaz and Jehoiakim), the negative judgment involves a plural reference to "his ancestors," instead of the exclusively singular references to "his father" occurring in preceding judgment formulas. The plural reference discreetly avoids comparison with their father, Josiah. (iv) The four judgment formulas are terse, tightly focused, and with minimal theological unfolding. The rich diversity of preceding formulas must be analyzed with care. As presented above, the formulas from Jehu to Hoshea derive from the extension of the PR, not from the Dtr; the formulas from Jeroboam I to Joram, in our judgment, derive from the Dtr, but they refer exclusively to northern kings; the formulas from Rehoboam to Hezekiah derive from what we have called the HKL. As presented here, three judgment formulas for kings of Judah come directly from the Josianic Dtr: for Manasseh, Amon, and Josiah. Even so, the difference from the four formulas here is marked. Manasseh comes under the formulaic condemnation: "he did what was evil in the sight of the LORD" (21:2a); details are then provided (high places, altars, a pole, and an image; cf. vv. 3*, 5, 7). Amon comes under the formulaic condemnation, with explicit reference to his father Manasseh (21:20). After the formulaic condemnations, the first two judgment formulas here refer back generally to "his ancestors"; no details are given, no cultic abuses specified. Neither the crimes of the northern kings (or their southern counterparts, Abijam, Jehoram, Ahaziah, Ahaz, Manasseh, and Amon) nor the high places (for the favored southern kings of the HKL) are mentioned. For the third and fourth formulas, the reference is to Jehoiakim (either "his father" or by name); no specifics are mentioned.

Text-history approach. The text signals discussed point to a continuation of Israel's story after Josiah's

After the Dtr: indented and sans serif font	DH Extension	**Revision: royal focus**	Revision: national focus	Other: double sideline

Libnah. [32]He did what was evil in the sight of the LORD, just as his ancestors had done. [33]Pharaoh Neco confined him at Riblah in the land of Hamath, so that he might not

reign in Jerusalem, and imposed tribute on the land of one hundred talents of silver and a talent of gold. [34]Pharaoh Neco made Eliakim son of Josiah king in place of his father Josiah, and changed his name to Jehoiakim. But he took Jehoahaz away; he came to Egypt, and died there. [35]Jehoiakim gave the silver and the gold to Pharaoh, but

---

death, featuring judgment formulas for the four kings concerned that are notably different from what preceded them in the books of Kings. The narrative associated with these kings we term the DH Extension. It is important to insist that the term "extension" has no chronological significance; the narrative could have been composed at any time in Israel's subsequent history. The establishment of Jehoahaz on the throne is closely associated with the report of the death and burial of his father Josiah (23:28-30). It seems appropriate, therefore, to begin the extension at 23:28. This implies an understanding of the Josianic DH as a document supporting Josiah's reform and completed during his lifetime.

We have attributed 2 Kgs 23:26-27 to the royal focus within the dtr revision, given its association with 2 Kgs 21:10-14. It deals with the fate of Judah, caused by the provocation of Manasseh. It is theological reflection rather than historical extension. The reform of Josiah is followed by the rejection of Judah because of the sin of Manasseh. The comment belongs with the report of Josiah's reform rather than with the DH Extension.

An appropriate identity for "the people of the land" is controverted. Their active role in the DH is restricted to 2 Kgs 11:14-20 and 21:24; 23:30 (in 2 Kgs 14:21, King Azariah is installed by "all the people of Judah"). Here, "the people of the land" install Josiah as king (21:24, after killing Amon's conspirators), install his son Jehoahaz as king (23:30), and are taxed by Neco's appointee, Jehoiakim (23:35). They figure in other roles (cf. 2 Kgs 24:14 [cf. 25:12]; 25:3, 19). The diversity suggests caution.

The text from 23:28–25:30 is not unified. While its bulk is constituted by the Extension, additions or theological reflections have been made at certain points—and will be dealt with below. Overall, the Extension takes the narrative from Josiah's end to

Judah's "exile out of its land" (25:21). Structured by the four judgment formulas, the text moves from domination by Egypt to domination by Babylon—ultimately to deportation, destruction, and exile.

Present-text potential of 23:28–25:30. The text presents a narrative of the last four kings of Judah, the devastation wrought by Babylon, the appointment of Gedaliah as governor at Mizpah (not in Jerusalem), and the favor shown to the exiled former king of Judah, Jehoiachin, in Babylon. Theological comment is found at strategic points. The troubles of Jehoiakim are correlated with the sins of Manasseh (24:2-3), "according to the word of YHWH" (v. 2). Similarly, the first ransacking of Jerusalem by Nebuchadnezzar is characterized as foretold by YHWH (v. 13). Immediately before the final destruction of Jerusalem and the downfall of the Judah, the theological claim is made that the fate of city and people results from YHWH's anger against them (v. 20).

Following the final statement of Judah's exile (25:21), two passages seem to reflect on concrete detail but may in symbol extend far further. Gedaliah's appointment as governor signals the end of the monarchy. His acceptance of foreign rule signals the end of Judah's independence. His murder, by a member of the Judah's royal family, is a rejection of enslavement to the foreigner. The flight of "all the people" to Egypt is ironically a return to the symbols of enslavement and a reversal of Israel's exodus. Jehoiachin remains in Babylon in ambivalence, in a situation evoking the end of Saul's family (cf. Mephibosheth, 2 Samuel 9). The two passages leave two questions unanswered. Is it ended for the nation of Judah? Is it ended for the dynasty of David?

Main pre-DH:	Other pre-DH:	HKL: + single	**Josianic DH:**
Prophetic Record and PR Extension	single sideline	underline	**from the Dtr**

he taxed the land in order to meet Pharaoh's demand for money. He exacted the silver and the gold from the people of the land, from all according to their assessment, to give it to Pharaoh Neco.

36 Jehoiakim was twenty-five years old when he began to reign; he reigned eleven years in Jerusalem. His mother's name was Zebidah daughter of Pedaiah of Rumah. [37]He did what was evil in the sight of the LORD, just as *(NRSV, all; a translational error)* his ancestors had done.[107]

24 In his days King Nebuchadnezzar of Babylon came up; Jehoiakim became his servant for three years; then he turned and rebelled against him.

[2]The LORD sent against him bands of the Chaldeans, bands of the Arameans, bands of the Moabites, and bands of the Ammonites; he sent them against Judah to destroy it, according to the word of the LORD that he spoke by his servants the prophets. [3]Surely this came upon Judah at the command of the LORD, to remove them out of his sight, for the sins of Manasseh, for all that he had committed. [4]and also for the innocent blood that he had shed; for he

filled Jerusalem with innocent blood, and the LORD was not willing to pardon.[108]
[5]Now the rest of the deeds of Jehoiakim, and all that he did, are they not written in the Book of the Annals of the Kings of

---

108. **Text signals** in 24:2-4. There is no question that these verses are difficult. The following signals need careful attention and are susceptible of more than one interpretation. (i) The transition from the rebellion that ends v. 1 to the end of the reign that begins v. 5 is abrupt. A reaction by Nebuchadnezzar would be expected (cf. 24:20b—25:2). (ii) LXX has "And he sent" in place of the MT "The LORD sent"; the LXX subject is clearly Nebuchadnezzar. (iii) Apart from this instance, in 1-2 Kings the term "band" (gĕdûd) occurs almost exclusively in traditions associated with the prophet Elisha (i.e., 2 Kgs 5:2; 6:23; 13:20, 21; cf. also 1 Kgs 11:24, absent from LXX). (iv) The reference to God's utterance "by his servants the prophets" recalls 2 Kgs 21:10 (elsewhere only 2 Kgs 17:13, 23; in 2 Kgs 9:7 it is a matter of avenging their blood). (v) The reference to Manasseh recalls 2 Kgs 21:10-14. (vi) 2 Kgs 21:11 speaks of Manasseh's "abominations" and that he caused Judah to sin with his idols. Here, it is simply the "sins of Manasseh," without reference either to Judah or the idols. Note that in 23:26 a different terminology is used, "because of all the provocations with which Manasseh had provoked him." (vii) The reference to the shedding of innocent blood recalls 2 Kgs 21:16. It goes beyond 21:16 with the idea of God's unwillingness to pardon (cf. 23:26; 24:20).

Text-history approach. Two understandings of the composition here are possible. Our formatting with the double sideline does not exclude the alternative to be discussed below. In favor of the double sideline are the following: (i) The assumption of vv. 2-4 as an addition indicates a sensitivity to the lack of reaction to Jehoiakim's rebellion. Here the reaction is YHWH's. (ii) The language of "band" does not suggest any dtr revision; as a group of four, the raiders are unknown elsewhere (cf. as pairs, Jer 35:11; Zeph

---

107. The error here is surprising and significant. In all four cases in Hebrew, the phrasing is identical, all that the ancestors did. "All his ancestors" here wrongly includes David, Hezekiah, and Josiah. The accuracy of the RSV is worth reproducing:

23:32   according to all that his fathers had done
23:37   according to all that his fathers had done
24:9   according to all that his father had done
24:19   according to all that Jehoiakim had done

These four occurrences constitute Weippert's Schema III ("Beurteilungen," 333-34).

After the Dtr: indented and sans serif font	DH Extension	*Revision:* ***royal focus***	*Revision:* *national focus*	Other: double sideline

Judah? [6]So Jehoiakim slept with his ancestors; then his son Jehoiachin succeeded him. [7]The king of Egypt did not come again out of his land, for the king of Babylon had taken over all that belonged to the king of Egypt from the Wadi of Egypt to the River Euphrates.

[8] Jehoiachin was eighteen years old when he began to reign; he reigned three months in Jerusalem. His mother's name was Nehushta daughter of Elnathan of Jerusalem. [9]He did what was evil in the sight of the LORD, just as his father had done.

[10] At that time the servants of King Nebuchadnezzar of Babylon came up to Jerusalem, and the city was besieged. [11]King Nebuchadnezzar of Babylon came to the city, while his servants were besieging it; [12]King Jehoiachin of Judah gave himself up to the king of Babylon, himself, his mother, his servants, his officers, and his palace officials. The king of Babylon took him prisoner in the eighth year of his reign.

[13] He carried off all the treasures of the house of the LORD, and the treasures of the king's house; he cut in pieces all the vessels of gold in the temple of the LORD, which King Solomon of Israel had made, all this as the LORD had foretold. [14]He carried away all Jerusalem, all the officials, all the warriors, ten thousand captives, all the artisans and the smiths; no one remained, except the poorest people of the land.[109]
[15]He carried away Jehoiachin to Babylon; the king's mother, the king's wives, his officials, and the elite of the land, he took into captivity from Jerusalem to Babylon. [16]The king of Babylon brought captive to Babylon all the men of valor, seven thousand, the artisans and the smiths, one thousand, all of them strong and fit for war. [17]The king of Babylon made Mattaniah, Jehoiachin's

---

2:8-9). (iii) Under the rubric "his servants the prophets," a present utterance is intended, not past oracles as in 2 Kgs 17:13, 23; a fulfillment notice is not required, but could be supplied by a later hand. (iv) The minor variations on 2 Kgs 21:10-14 could suggest later reflection on this Manasseh text. (v) With regard to the shedding of innocent blood, 2 Kgs 21:16 is treated as double sideline, and v. 4 goes beyond it in relation to God's unwillingness to pardon.

In favor of an alternative understanding are the following. (i) If the LXX is followed ("And he sent"), the reaction is Nebuchadnezzar's and any abruptness is eased. The first part of v. 2 would then belong with the DH Extension in v. 1. (ii) The reference to God's utterance "by his servants the prophets" can be regarded as a fulfillment notice for 21:10-14. As such, it can be attributed to the royal focus of the dtr revision. It may begin either with "according to the word of YHWH" (v. 2b) or with the earlier "he sent them against Judah" (noting the repetition of "sent" and assuming that the revision understood Nebuchadnezzar as God's instrument). (iii) Vv. 3-4 are attributed to an unidentifiable source (double sideline), as in the first alternative.

Present-text potential. The present text makes clear that the fate of Judah has begun to unfold and that this is a result of the evil of Manasseh. For the wider context, see above on 23:30.

Dietrich attributed 24:2 to his DtrP and 24:3-4 to his DtrN.

---

109. With the reference to YHWH's word at the end of v. 13, vv. 13-14 may be a fulfillment notice for 2 Kgs 20:16-18. It is to be noted that they present what might be deemed an alternative view to vv. 15-16. While the interest in fulfillment might suggest attribution to the royal focus of the dtr revision, the double sideline (unidentifiable) may be the more prudent course.

Main pre-DH:	Other pre-DH:	HKL: + single	**Josianic DH:**
Prophetic Record and PR Extension	single sideline	underline	**from the Dtr**

uncle, king in his place, and changed his name to Zedekiah.

18 Zedekiah was twenty-one years old when he began to reign; he reigned eleven years in Jerusalem. His mother's name was Hamutal daughter of Jeremiah of Libnah. [19]He did what was evil in the sight of the LORD, just as Jehoiakim had done.

[20]Indeed, Jerusalem and Judah so angered the LORD that he expelled them from his presence.[110]

Zedekiah rebelled against the king of Babylon.

25 And in the ninth year of his reign, in the tenth month, on the tenth day of the month, King Nebuchadnezzar of Babylon came with all his army against Jerusalem, and laid siege to it; they built siegeworks against it all around. [2]So the city was besieged until the eleventh year of King Zedekiah. [3]On the ninth day of the fourth month the famine became so severe in the city that there was no food for the people of the land. [4]Then a breach was made in the city wall; the king with all the soldiers fled by night by the way of the gate between the two walls, by the king's garden, though the Chaldeans were all around the city. They went in the direction of the Arabah. [5]But the army of the Chaldeans pursued the king, and overtook him in the plains of Jericho; all his army was scattered, deserting him. [6]Then they captured the king and brought him up to the king of Babylon at Riblah, who passed sentence on him. [7]They slaughtered the sons of Zedekiah

before his eyes, then put out the eyes of Zedekiah; they bound him in fetters and took him to Babylon.

8 In the fifth month, on the seventh day of the month—which was the nineteenth year of King Nebuchadnezzar, king of Babylon—Nebuzaradan, the captain of the bodyguard, a servant of the king of Babylon, came to Jerusalem. [9]He burned the house of the LORD, the king's house, and all the houses of Jerusalem; every great house he burned down. [10]All the army of the Chaldeans who were with the captain of the guard broke down the walls around Jerusalem. [11]Nebuzaradan the captain of the guard carried into exile the rest of the people who were left in the city and the deserters who had defected to the king of Babylon—all the rest of the population. [12]But the captain of the guard left some of the poorest people of the land to be vinedressers and tillers of the soil.

13 The bronze pillars that were in the house of the LORD, as well as the stands and the bronze sea that were in the house of the LORD, the Chaldeans broke in pieces, and carried the bronze to Babylon. [14]They took away the pots, the shovels, the snuffers, the dishes for incense, and all the bronze vessels used in the temple service, [15]as well as the firepans and the basins. What was made of gold the captain of the guard took away for the gold, and what was made of silver, for the silver. [16]As for the two pillars, the one sea, and the stands, which Solomon had made for the house of the LORD, the bronze of all these vessels was beyond weighing. [17]The height of the one pillar was eighteen cubits, and on it was a bronze capital; the height of the capital was three cubits; latticework and pomegran-

---

110. See 2 Kgs 13:3, 23; 17:20. In the light of these texts, more precise attribution would be unwise.
Dietrich attributed 24:20a to his DtrN.

| After the Dtr: indented and sans serif font | DH Extension | **Revision: royal focus** | *Revision: national focus* | Other: double sideline |

ates, all of bronze, were on the capital all around. The second pillar had the same, with the latticework.

18 The captain of the guard took the chief priest Seraiah, the second priest Zephaniah, and the three guardians of the threshold; [19]from the city he took an officer who had been in command of the soldiers, and five men of the king's council who were found in the city; the secretary who was the commander of the army who mustered the people of the land; and sixty men of the people of the land who were found in the city. [20]Nebuzaradan the captain of the guard took them, and brought them to the king of Babylon at Riblah. [21]The king of Babylon struck them down and put them to death at Riblah in the land of Hamath. So Judah went into exile out of its land.[111]

22 He appointed Gedaliah son of Ahikam son of Shaphan as governor over the people who remained in the land of Judah, whom King Nebuchadnezzar of Babylon had left. [23]Now when all the captains of the forces and their men heard that the king of Babylon had appointed Gedaliah as governor, they came with their men to Gedaliah at Mizpah, namely, Ishmael son of Nethaniah, Johanan son of Kareah, Seraiah son of Tanhumeth the Netophathite, and Jaazaniah son of the Maacathite. [24]Gedaliah swore to them and their men, saying, "Do not be afraid because of the Chaldean officials; live in the land, serve the king of Babylon, and it shall be well with you." [25]But in the seventh

month, Ishmael son of Nethaniah son of Elishama, of the royal family, came with ten men; they struck down Gedaliah so that he died, along with the Judeans and Chaldeans who were with him at Mizpah. [26]Then all the people, high and low and the captains of the forces set out and went to Egypt; for they were afraid of the Chaldeans.[112]

27 In the thirty-seventh year of the exile of King Jehoiachin of Judah, in the twelfth month, on the twenty-seventh day of the month, King Evil-merodach of Babylon, in the year that he began to reign, released King Jehoiachin of Judah from prison; [28]he spoke kindly to him, and gave him a seat above the other seats of the kings who were with him in Babylon. [29]So Jehoiachin put aside his prison clothes. Every day of his life he dined regularly in the king's presence. [30]For his allowance, a regular allowance was given him by the king, a portion every day, as long as he lived.[113]

---

112. Verses 22-26 are widely regarded as derived from Jer 40:7—41:18. On the other hand, the account in Jeremiah of the sack of Jerusalem (Jer 39:1-10) is derived from 2 Kgs 25:1-21. This tends to confirm the ending of the extension in 25:21. For discussion and literature, see O'Brien, *Deuteronomistic History Hypothesis*, 271.

113. By contrast with the preceding, the Jeremiah treatment of this episode (Jer 52:31-34) is regarded as derived from these verses in Kings (25:27-30). Its position at the end of the book of Jeremiah, separated from Jer 39:1-10, supports its attribution here as an addition. For reflections on the present text, see the note on 2 Kgs 23:30. Both vv. 29 and 30 use the phrase "all the days of his life"; as for Hoshea (17:4), no mention is explicitly made of Jehoiachin's death.

Dietrich attributed 25:22-30 to his DtrN.

---

111. With this verse and this appropriate statement, the DH Extension comes to an end. This judgment is confirmed by the discussion of the two passages that follow. See below.

Main pre-DH:	Other pre-DH:	HKL: + single	**Josianic DH:**
Prophetic Record and PR Extension	single sideline	underline	**from the Dtr**

Bibliography of Works Cited

Albertz, Rainer. "Le Milieu des Deutéronomistes."
Pp. 377-407 in *Israël construit son histoire: L'historiographie deutéronomiste à la lumière des recherches
récentes*. Edited by A. de Pury et al. MDB 34.
Geneva: Labor et Fides, 1996.

Alfrink, Bern. "L'Expression שָׁכַב עִם אֲבוֹתָיו." *OTS* 2
(1943) 106-18.

Alt, Albrecht. "Das System der Stammesgrenzen im
Buche Josua." 1927. Pp. 193-202 in *Kleine
Schriften zur Geschichte des Volkes Israel*, Vol. 1.
Munich: Beck, 1953.

———. "Judas Gaue unter Josia." 1925. Pp. 276-88 in
Kleine Schriften zur Geschichte des Volkes Israel,
Vol. 2. Munich: Beck, 1953.

———. "Menschen Ohne Namen." 1950. Pp. 198-
213 in *Kleine Schriften zur Geschichte des Volkes
Israel*, Vol. 3. Munich: Beck, 1959.

Amit, Yairah. *The Book of Judges: The Art of Editing*.
BibInt Series 38. Leiden: Brill, 1999 (Hebrew
original, 1992).

Auld, A. Graeme. *Joshua, Moses and the Land: Tetra-
teuch-Pentateuch-Hexateuch in a Generation Since
1938*. Edinburgh: T. & T. Clark, 1980.

———. *Kings Without Privilege: David and Moses in the
Story of the Bible's Kings*. Edinburgh: T. & T. Clark,
1994.

Barrick, W. Boyd. "On the Meaning of בֵּית־הַ/בָּמוֹת and
בָּתֵּי־הַבָּמוֹת and the Composition of the Kings History." *JBL* 115 (1996) 621-42.

Barthélemy, Dominique. *Critique textuelle de l'Ancien
Testament 1*. OBO 50/1. Fribourg, Suisse: Éditions
universitaires, 1982.

Begg, Christopher T. "The Literary Criticism of Deut
4,1-40. Contributions to a Continuing Discussion." *ETL* 66 (1980) 10-55.

Boecker, Hans Jochen. *Die Beurteilung der Anfänge des
Königtums in den deuteronomistischen Abschnitten des
I. Samuelbuches: Ein Beitrag zum Problem des
"deuteronomistischen Geschichtswerks."* WMANT
31. Neukirchen-Vluyn: Neukirchener, 1969.

Boomershine, Thomas E. "Jesus of Nazareth and the
Watershed of Ancient Orality and Literacy."
Semeia 65 (1994) 7-36.

Brettler, Marc. "Ideology, History and Theology in 2
Kings XVII 7-23." *VT* 39 (1989) 268-82.

Campbell, Antony F. *The Ark Narrative (1 Sam 4–6;
2 Sam 6): A Form-critical and Traditio-historical
Study*. SBLDS 16. Missoula: Scholars Press,
1975.

———. "Psalm 78: A Contribution to the Theology
of Tenth Century Israel." *CBQ* 41 (1979) 51-79.

———. "Yahweh and the Ark: A Case Study in Narrative." *JBL* 98 (1979) 31-43.

———. "From Philistine to Throne." *AusBR* 34
(1986) 35-41.

———. *Of Prophets and Kings: A Late Ninth-Century
Document (1 Samuel 1—2 Kings 10)*. CBQMS 17.
Washington, D.C.: Catholic Biblical Association
of America, 1986.

———. *The Study Companion to Old Testament Literature: An Approach to the Writings of Pre-Exilic and
Exilic Israel*. OTS 2. Collegeville, Minn.: Liturgical Press, 1989/1992.

———. "Structure Analysis and the Art of Exegesis (1
Samuel 16:14–18:30)." Pp. 76-103 in *Problems in
Biblical Theology: Essays in Honor of Rolf Knierim*.
Edited by Henry T. C. Sun et al. Grand Rapids:
Eerdmans, 1997.

———. "Martin Noth and the Deuteronomistic History." Pp. 31-62 in *The History of Israel's Traditions:*

The Heritage of Martin Noth. Edited by S. L. McKenzie and M. P. Graham. JSOTSup 182. Sheffield: Sheffield Academic Press, 1994.

———. *1 Samuel.* FOTL 7. Grand Rapids: Eerdmans, forthcoming.

Campbell, Antony F. and Mark A. O'Brien. *Sources of the Pentateuch: Texts, Introductions, Annotations.* Minneapolis: Fortress Press, 1993.

———. "1–2 Samuel." Pp. 572-607 in *The International Bible Commentary.* Edited by W. R. Farmer et al. Collegeville, Minn.: Liturgical Press, 1998.

Childs, Brevard S. "A Study of the Formula 'Until This Day'." *JBL* 82 (1963) 279-92.

———. *Isaiah and the Assyrian Crisis.* SBT 2/3. London: SCM, 1967.

———. *Exodus.* OTL. Philadelphia: Westminster, 1974.

Clements, Ronald E. *Isaiah and the Deliverance of Jerusalem. A Study of the Interpretation of Prophecy in the Old Testament.* JSOTSup 13. Sheffield: JSOT Press, 1980.

Clendinnen, Inga. *Reading the Holocaust.* Melbourne: Text Publishing, 1998.

Cogan, Mordechai and Hayim Tadmor. *II Kings.* AB 11. Garden City, N.Y.: Doubleday, 1988.

Cross, Frank M. "The Structure of the Deuteronomic History." Pp. 9-24 in *Perspectives in Jewish Learning.* Annual of the College of Jewish Studies 3. Chicago: College of Jewish Studies, 1968.

———. "The Themes of the Book of Kings and the Structure of the Deuteronomistic History." Pp. 274-89 in *Canaanite Myth and Hebrew Epic: Essays in the History of the Religion of Israel.* Cambridge: Harvard University Press, 1973.

Dietrich, Walter. *Prophetie und Geschichte: Eine redaktionsgeschichtliche Untersuchung zum deuteronomistischen Geschichtswerk.* FRLANT 108. Göttingen: Vandenhoeck & Ruprecht, 1972.

———. *David, Saul und die Propheten: Das Verhältnis von Religion und Politik nach den prophetischen Überlieferungen vom frühesten Königtum in Israel.* BWANT 122. Stuttgart: Kohlhammer, 1987.

———. *Die frühe Königszeit in Israel: 10. Jahrhundert v. Chr.* Biblische Enzyklopädie 3. Stuttgart: Kohlhammer, 1997.

Dietrich, Walter and Thomas Naumann. *Die Samuelbücher.* ErFor 287. Darmstadt: Wissenschaftliche Buchgesellschaft, 1995.

Driver, Samuel R. *Notes on the Hebrew Text and the Topography of the Books of Samuel.* 2nd ed. Oxford: Clarendon, 1913.

Farmer, William R. et al. (eds.). *The International Bible Commentary: A Catholic and Ecumenical Commentary for the Twenty-First Century.* Collegeville, Minn.: Liturgical Press, 1998.

Fritz, Volkmar. *Das Buch Josua.* HAT I/7. Tübingen: Mohr, 1994.

Gordon, Cyrus H. *The Common Background of Greek and Hebrew Civilizations.* New York: Norton, 1965.

Gray, John. *I & II Kings.* OTL. 2nd ed. Philadelphia: Westminster, 1964.

Handy, Lowell K. (ed.) *The Age of Solomon: Scholarship at the Turn of the Millennium.* Studies in the History and Culture of the Ancient Near East 9. Leiden: Brill, 1997.

Halpern, Baruch and David S. Vanderhooft. "The Editions of Kings in the 7th-6th Centuries B.C.E." *HUCA* 62 (1991) 179-244.

Hanson, Paul D. "The Song of Heshbon and David's *Nîr.*" *HTR* 61 (1968) 304-16.

Hentschel, Georg. *Die Elijaerzählungen: Zum Verhältnis von historischem Geschehen und geschichtlicher Erfahrung.* ETS 33. Leipzig: St. Benno, 1977.

Hertzberg, Hans Wilhelm. *I & II Samuel.* OTL. Trans. J. S. Bowden. Philadelphia: Westminister, 1964.

Hobbs, T. R. *2 Kings.* WBC 13. Waco, Tex.: Word Books, 1985.

Hoffmann, Hans-Detlef. *Reform und Reformen.* ATANT 66. Zürich: Theologischer Verlag, 1980.

Holladay, William L. "On Every High Hill and Under Every Green Tree." *VT* 11 (1961) 170-76.

Hughes, Robert. *The Fatal Shore: A History of the Transportation of Convicts to Australia, 1787-1868.* London: Collins Harvill, 1987.

Ishida, Tomoo. *The Royal Dynasties in Ancient Israel: A Study on the Formation and Development of Royal-Dynastic Ideology.* BZAW 142. Berlin: de Gruyter, 1977.

Jones, Gwilym H. *1 and 2 Kings.* 2 vols.: *1 Kings 1–16:34* and *1 Kings 17:1—2 Kings 25:30.* NCB. Grand Rapids: Eerdmans, 1984.

Joüon, Paul. *Grammaire de l'hébreu biblique.* Rome: Pontifical Biblical Institute, 1923.

Kallai, Zecharia. *Historical Geography of the Bible: The Tribal Territories of Israel.* Jerusalem: Magnes, 1986.

Klein, Ralph W. *1 Samuel.* WBC 10. Waco, Tex.: Word Books, 1983.

Kloppenborg, John S. "Joshua 22: The Priestly Editing of an Ancient Tradition." *Bib* 62 (1981) 347-71.

Knoppers, Gary N. *Two Nations Under God: The Deuteronomistic History of Solomon and the Dual Monarchies.* 2 vols. HSM 52-53. Atlanta: Scholars Press, 1993-94.

L'Hour, Jean. "L'Alliance de Sichem." *RB* 69 (1962) 5-36; 161-84; 350-68.

Langer, Lawrence. *Versions of Survival: The Holocaust and the Human Spirit.* SUNY Series in Modern Jewish Literature and Culture. Albany: State University of New York Press, 1982.

Lohfink, Norbert. *Das Hauptgebot: Eine Untersuchung literarischer Einleitungsfragen zu Dtn 5–11.* AnBib 20. Rome: Pontifical Biblical Institute, 1963.

———. *Rückblick im Zorn auf den Staat: Vorlesungen zu ausgewählten Schlüsseltexten der Bücher Samuel und Könige.* Frankfurt a.M.: Hochschule Sankt Georgen, 1984.

———. "Gab es eine deuteronomistische Bewegung?" Pp. 313-82 in *Jeremia und die "deuteronomistische Bewegung."* Edited by Walter Groß. BBB 98. Weinheim: Beltz Athenäum, 1995.

Long, Burke O. *1-2 Kings, with an Introduction to Historical Literature.* FOTL 9-10. Grand Rapids: Eerdmans, 1984-91.

McCarter, P. Kyle Jr., *I-II Samuel.* AB 8-9. Garden City, N.Y.: Doubleday, 1980-84.

McCarthy, Dennis J. *Treaty and Covenant: A Study in Form in the Ancient Oriental Documents and in the Old Testament.* AnBib 21A. New edition completely rewritten. Rome: Biblical Institute, 1978.

MacDonald, John. "The Structure of II Kings XVII." *Glasgow University Oriental Society Transactions* 23 (1969-70) 29-41.

McKenzie, John L. *Dictionary of the Bible.* New York: Macmillan, 1965.

McKenzie, Steven L. *The Trouble with Kings: The Composition of the Book of Kings in the Deuteronomistic History.* VTSup 42. Leiden: Brill, 1991.

———. "The Books of Kings in the Deuteronomistic History." Pp. 281-307 in *The History of Israel's Traditions: The Heritage of Martin Noth.* Edited by S. L. McKenzie and M. P. Graham. JSOTSup 182. Sheffield: Sheffield Academic Press, 1994.

McKenzie, Steven L. and M. Patrick Graham (eds.). *The History of Israel's Traditions: The Heritage of Martin Noth.* JSOTSup 182. Sheffield: Sheffield Academic Press, 1994.

Mayes, A. D. H. *Deuteronomy.* NCB. London: Oliphants, 1979.

———. *The Story of Israel between Settlement and Exile: A Redactional Study of the Deuteronomistic History.* London: SCM, 1983.

Minette de Tillesse, Gaëtan. "Sections 'tu' et sections 'vous' dans le Deutéronome." *VT* 12 (1962) 29-87.

Na'aman, Nadav. *Borders and Districts in Biblical Historiography: Seven Studies in Biblical Geographical Lists.* Jerusalem Biblical Studies 4. Jerusalem: Simor, 1986.

Nelson, Richard D. *The Double Redaction of the Deuteronomistic History.* JSOTSup 18. Sheffield: JSOT Press, 1981.

———. "Josiah in the Book of Joshua." *JBL* 100 (1981) 531-40.

———. *First and Second Kings.* Interpretation. Louisville: John Knox, 1987.

———. *Joshua.* OTL. Louisville: Westminster John Knox, 1997.

Nicholson, Ernest W. "II Kings XXII 18—A Simple Restoration." *Hermathena* 97 (1963) 96-98.

Niditch, Susan. *Oral World and Written Word: Ancient Israelite Literature.* Library of Ancient Israel. Louisville: Westminster John Knox, 1996.

Nielsen, Eduard. *Deuteronomium.* HAT 1/6. Tübingen: Mohr, 1995.

Noth, Martin. *The Deuteronomistic History.* JSOTSup 15. 2nd ed. Sheffield: JSOT Press, 1981/1991. German original, 1943.

―――. *Das Buch Josua*. HAT 7. 2nd ed. Tübingen: Mohr, 1953.

―――. *Könige*. 1. Teilband. *I Könige 1-16*. BKAT 9/1. Neukirchen-Vluyn: Neukirchener Verlag, 1968/1983.

Nueva Biblia Española. Translation under the direction of Luis Alonso Schökel and Juan Mateos. Madrid: Ediciones Cristianad, 1975.

O'Brien, Mark A. *The Deuteronomistic History Hypothesis: A Reassessment*. OBO 92. Freiburg, Schweiz: Universitätsverlag, 1989.

O'Brien, Mark A. and Antony F. Campbell. "1–2 Kings." Pp. 608-43 in *The International Bible Commentary*. Edited by W. R. Farmer et al. Collegeville, Minn.: Liturgical Press, 1998.

Okure, Teresa. "John." Pp. 1438-1505 in *The International Bible Commentary*. Edited by W. R. Farmer et al. Collegeville, Minn.: Liturgical Press, 1998.

Polzin, Robert. *Moses and the Deuteronomist. A Literary Study of the Deuteronomic History*. Part One. New York: Seabury, 1980.

―――. *Samuel and the Deuteronomist. A Literary Study of the Deuteronomic History*. Part Two. San Francisco: Harper & Row, 1989.

―――. *David and the Deuteronomist. A Literary Study of the Deuteronomic History*. Part Three. Bloomington: Indiana University Press, 1993.

Preuss, Horst Dietrich. *Deuteronomium*. ErFor 164. Darmstadt: Wissenschaftliche Buchgesellschaft, 1982.

Provan, Iain W. *Hezekiah and the Books of Kings. A Contribution to the Debate about the Composition of the Deuteronomistic History*. BZAW 172. Berlin: de Gruyter, 1988.

Rad, Gerhard von. *Old Testament Theology*. 2 vols. Trans. D. M. G. Stalker. Edinburgh: Oliver and Boyd, 1962-65.

Rendtorff, Rolf. "Beobachtungen zur altisraelitischen Geschichtsschreibung anhand der Geschichte vom Aufstieg Davids." Pp. 428-39 in *Probleme biblischer Theologie: Gerhard von Rad zum 70. Geburtstag*. Edited by H. W. Wolff. Munich: Kaiser, 1971.

Richter, Wolfgang. *Die Bearbeitungen des "Retterbuches" in der deuteronomischen Epoche*. BBB 21. Bonn: Peter Hanstein, 1964.

―――. *Traditionsgeschichtliche Untersuchungen zum Richterbuch*. BBB 18. 2nd ed. Bonn: Peter Hanstein, 1966.

―――. "Die Überlieferungen um Jephtah. Ri 10, 17-12, 6." *Bib* 47 (1966) 485-556.

Rose, Martin. "Bemerkungen zum historischen Fundament des Josia-Bildes in II Reg 22f." *ZAW* 89 (1977) 50-63.

Rost, Leonhard. *The Succession to the Throne of David*. Trans. M. D. Rutter and D. M. Gunn. Historic Texts and Interpreters in Biblical Scholarship 1. Sheffield: Almond, 1982. German original, 1926.

Sauer, Georg. "Die chronologischen Angaben in den Büchern Deut. bis 2. Kön." *ThZ* 24 (1968) 1-14.

Schama, Simon. *Citizens: A Chronicle of the French Revolution*. New York: Knopf, 1989.

Schlauri, Ignaz, "Wolfgang Richters Beitrag zur Redaktionsgeschichte des Richterbuches." *Bib* 54 (1973) 367-403.

Schmidt, Ludwig. *Menschlicher Erfolg und Jahwes Initiative*. WMANT 38. Neukirchen-Vluyn: Neukirchener Verlag, 1970.

Schmitt, Hans-Christoph. *Elisa. Traditionsgeschichtliche Untersuchungen zur vorklassischen nordisraelitischen Prophetie*. Gütersloh: Mohn, 1972.

Scott, R. B. Y. "Solomon and the Beginnings of Wisdom in Israel." Pp. 262-79 in *Wisdom in Israel and in the Ancient Near East*. Edited by M. Noth and D. W. Thomas. VTSup 3. Leiden: Brill, 1955.

Seiler, Stefan. *Die Geschichte von der Thronfolge Davids (2 Sam 9–20; 1 Kön 1–2): Untersuchung zur Literarkritik und Tendenz*. BZAW 267. Berlin: de Gruyter, 1998.

Smend, Rudolf. "Das Gesetz und die Völker: Ein Beitrag zur deuteronomistischen Redaktionsgeschichte." Pp. 494-509 in *Probleme biblischer Theologie: Gerhard von Rad zum 70. Geburtstag*. Edited by H. W. Wolff. Munich: Kaiser, 1971.

―――. *Die Entstehung des Alten Testaments*. Theologische Wissenschaft: Sammelwerk für Studium und Beruf 1. 2nd ed. Stuttgart: Kohlhammer, 1981.

Soggin, J. Alberto. *Joshua*. Trans. R. A. Wilson. OTL. Philadelphia: Westminster, 1972.

―――. "Compulsory Labor under David and Solomon." Pp. 259-67 in *Studies in the Period of*

David and Solomon and Other Essays. Edited by T. Ishida. Winona Lake, Ind.: Eisenbrauns, 1982.

Stähli, Hans-Peter. *Knabe-Jüngling-Knecht*. BBET 7. Frankfurt a.M.: Peter Lang, 1978.

Steck, Odil Hannes. *Überlieferung und Zeitgeschichte in den Elia-Erzählungen*. WMANT 26. Neukirchen-Vluyn: Neukirchener Verlag, 1968.

Stoebe, Hans Joachim. *Das erste Buch Samuelis*. KAT 8/1. Gütersloh: Mohn, 1973.

Svensson, Jan. *Towns and Toponyms in the Old Testament: with Special Emphasis on Joshua 14–21*. ConBOT 38. Stockholm: Almqvist & Wiksell, 1994.

Talstra, E. *Solomon's Prayer: Synchrony and Diachrony in the Composition of I Kings 8, 14-61*. CBET 3. Kampen: Kok Pharos, 1993.

Tosato, Angelo. "La colpa di Saul (1 Sam 15, 22-23)." *Bib* 59 (1978) 351-59.

Tov, Emanuel. *Textual Criticism of the Hebrew Bible*. Minneapolis: Fortress Press, 1992.

Trebolle Barrera, Julio C. *Salomón y Jeroboán. Historia de la recensión y redacción de 1 Reyes 2–12, 14*. Jerusalem-Valencia: Casa de Santiago, 1980.

Tsevat, Matitiahu. "Interpretation of I Sam. 2:27-36: The Narrative of KARETH." *HUCA* 32 (1961) 191-216.

Tuchman, Barbara. *The Proud Tower: A Portrait of the World Before the War, 1890–1914*. Papermac; London: Macmillan, 1997; original publication, 1966.

Van Keulan, Percy S. F. *Manasseh Through the Eyes of the Deuteronomist: The Manasseh Account (2 Kings 21:1-18) and the Final Chapters of the Deuteronomistic History*. OTS 38. Leiden: Brill, 1996.

Van Seters, John. "Histories and Historians of the Ancient Near East: The Israelites." *Or* 50 (1981) 137-85.

———. *In Search of History: Historiography in the Ancient World and the Origins of Biblical Historiography*. New Haven: Yale University Press, 1983.

———. "Joshua's Campaign of Canaan and Near Eastern Historiography." *SJOT* 4.2 (1990) 1-12.

———. "Solomon's Temple: Fact and Ideology in Biblical and Near Eastern Historiography." *CBQ* 59 (1997) 45-57.

Vanoni, Gottfried. "Beobachtungen zur deuteronomistischen Terminologie in 2 Kön 23,25–25,30." Pp. 357-62 in *Das Deuteronomium: Entstehung, Gestalt und Botschaft*. Edited by N. Lohfink. BETL 68. Leuven: Leuven University Press, 1985.

Veijola, Timo. *Das Königtum in der Beurteilung der deuteronomistischen Historiographie. Eine redaktionsgeschichtliche Untersuchung*. AASF B 198. Helsinki: Suomalainen Tiedeakatemia, 1977.

———. *Die ewige Dynastie. David und die Entstehung seiner Dynastie nach der deuteronomistischen Darstellung*. AASF B 193. Helsinki: Suomalainen Tiedeakatemia, 1975.

———. "Bundestheologische Redaktion im Deuteronomium." Pp. 242-76 in *Das Deuteronomium und seine Querbeziehungen*. Edited by T. Veijola. SFEG 62. Helsinki: Finnische Exegetische Gesellschaft, 1996.

Vogt, Ernst. "Die Erzählung vom Jordanübergang, Josue 3–4." *Bib* 46 (1965) 125-48.

Walsh, Jerome T. *1 Kings*. Berit Olam: Studies in Hebrew Narrative & Poetry. A Michael Glazier Book. Collegeville, Minn.: Liturgical Press, 1996.

Weinfeld, Moshe. *Deuteronomy and the Deuteronomic School*. Oxford: Clarendon, 1972.

Weippert, Helga. "Die 'deuteronomistischen' Beurteilungen der Könige von Israel und Juda und das Problem der Redaktion der Königsbücher." *Bib* 53 (1972) 301-39.

White, Marsha C. *The Elijah Legends and Jehu's Coup*. Brown Judaic Studies 311. Atlanta: Scholars Press, 1997.

Wolff, Hans Walter. "The Kerygma of the Deuteronomic Historical Work." Pp. 83-100 in *The Vitality of Old Testament Traditions*. W. Brueggemann and H. W. Wolff. 2nd ed. Atlanta: John Knox, 1982.

Würthwein. Ernst. *Die Bücher der Könige*. 2 vols.: *1. Kön. 1–16* and *1. Kön. 17—2. Kön. 25*. ATD 11/1-2. Göttingen: Vandenhoeck & Ruprecht, 1977-84.

Yadin, Yigael. "Beer-sheba: The High Place Destroyed by King Josiah." *BASOR* 222 (1976) 5-17.

Patterns and Judges

Dtr (i)	Othniel	Ehud	Deborah	Gideon	Dtr (ii)	Jephthah	Samson	Samuel
Evil: apostasy 2:11	Evil: apostasy 3:7	Evil again: unspecified 3:12a	Evil again: unspecified 4:1a	Evil: unspecified 6:1a	*After Abimelech Tola delivers* Evil again: apostasy 10:1, 6		Evil again: unspecified 13:1a	Apostasy 7:3-4
Anger: kindled 2:14aα	Anger: kindled 3:8aα				Anger: kindled 10:7a			
Oppressed: given to plunderers; sold to enemies 2:14aβb	Oppressed: sold to Cushan-rish. 8 yrs 3:8aβb	Oppressed: strengthened Eglon against 18 yrs 3:12b-14	Oppressed: sold to Jabin 20 yrs 4:2, 3b	Oppressed: given to hand of Midian 7 yrs 6:1b	Oppressed: sold to Philistines Ammonites 18 yrs 10:7b-8	*[11:12-28 is separate; for Noth, it may be post-Dtr]*	Oppressed: given to Philistines 40 yrs 13:1b	
Distressed 2:15				Impoverished 6:6a	Distressed 10:9b			
(God moved to pity by their groaning) 2:18	People cried out 3:9aα	People cried out 3:15aα	People cried out 4:3a	People cried out 6:6b	People cried out confess sin of apostasy 10:10			People fasted confess sin Samuel cried out 7:5-6, 8-9
Raised judges: deliver from plunderers 2:16	Raised deliverer spirit came judged fought 3:9aβb-10	Raised deliverer 3:15aβ	(prophet) (judged) 4:4	(deliver) (spirit came) (deliver) 6:14, 15, 34, 36	*10:11-16 Oppress—12a Cry—12b Deliver—12b*	(spirit came) 11:29a	He will begin to deliver Spirit began to stir 13:5, 25	God thundered Philistines confused and routed Israel pursues 7:10-11
God with judge God delivered them 2:18	God gave CR into his hand Hand prevailed 3:10	Moab subdued under hand of Israel 3:30a	God subdued Jabin under hand of Israel 4:23-24	Midian subdued before Israel 8:28a	*Apostasy—13a Not deliver—13b etc—14*	Ammonites subdued before Israel 11:33b		Philistines subdued 7:13a
All the days of the judge 2:18	Rest/quiet: 40 yrs 3:11a	Rest/quiet: 80 yrs 3:30b	Rest/quiet: 40 yrs 5:31b	Rest/quiet: 40 yrs 8:28b	*Sinned—15a Rescue—15b Reform—16a Compas-sion—16b*	Jephthah died was buried 12:7b	He judged Israel 20 yrs 15:20; 16:31	All the days of Samuel 7:13b
Judge dead: people relapse 2:19	Othniel died (Relapse— 3:12a etc) 3:11b	Shamgar: delivered (Ehud died) 3:31 (4:1b)		Gideon died was buried people relapse 8:32-33				Samuel judged Israel all his life Sons unjust 7:15-17; 8:1-3

12 Aug 95/28 Sep 99

JUDGMENT FORMULAS: PATTERN A
for the second set of northern kings
from Jehu (midway) to Hoshea (end)

Jehu   (2 Kgs 10:29)

Yet   the sins of Jeroboam the son of Nebat
                                                                  which he made Israel to sin

Jehu **did not depart from**   after them.

Jehoahaz   (2 Kgs 13:2)
And he did what was **evil** in the sight of YHWH
                  and he walked after   the sins of Jeroboam the son of Nebat
                                                                  which he made Israel to sin

he **did not depart from**   it.

Jehoash   (2 Kgs 13:11)
And he did what was **evil** in the sight of YHWH
              he **did not depart from**   all   the sins of Jeroboam the son of Nebat
                                                                  which he made Israel to sin

but he walked in it.

Jeroboam   (2 Kgs 14:24)
And he did what was **evil** in the sight of YHWH
              he **did not depart from**   all   the sins of Jeroboam the son of Nebat
                                                                  which he made Israel to sin.

Zechariah   (2 Kgs 15:9)
And he did what was **evil** in the sight of YHWH
          as his fathers had done;
              he **did not depart from**   the sins of Jeroboam the son of Nebat
                                                                  which he made Israel to sin.

Menahem   (2 Kgs 15:18)
And he did what was **evil** in the sight of YHWH
              he **did not depart from**   [all]*   the sins of Jeroboam the son of Nebat
                                                                  which he made Israel to sin,   all his days.

* MT: *mēʾal*; NRSV, "any of"

Pekahiah   (2 Kgs 15:24)
And he did what was **evil** in the sight of YHWH
              he **did not depart from**   the sins of Jeroboam the son of Nebat
                                                                  which he made Israel to sin.

Pekah   (2 Kgs 15:28)
And he did what was **evil** in the sight of YHWH
              he **did not depart from**   the sins of Jeroboam the son of Nebat
                                                                  which he made Israel to sin.

Hoshea   (2 Kgs 17:2)
And he did what was **evil** in the sight of YHWH
          yet not as the kings of Israel who were before him.

JUDGMENT FORMULAS: PATTERN B
southern kings from Rehoboam to Hezekiah

Judah (Rehoboam)   (1 Kgs 14:22a, 23a)
And Judah   did what was **evil**   in the sight of YHWH
for they also built for themselves **high places**,   and pillars and Asherim.

Abijam   (1 Kgs 15:3a)
And he WALKED in   all the SINS which   HIS FATHER   committed before him.

Asa   (1 Kgs 15:11-12a, 14a)
And Asa   did what was **right**   in the sight of YHWH
as David   HIS FATHER   had done.
He put away the male cult prostitutes out of the land.
But the **high places**   were not taken away.

Jehoshaphat   (1 Kgs 22:43a, 44)
And he WALKED in   all the WAY of Asa   HIS FATHER;   he did not depart from it.
Yet the **high places**   were not taken away.
and the people still sacrificed and burned incense on the high places.

Jehoram   (2 Kgs 8:18)
And he WALKED in   the WAY of the   KINGS OF ISRAEL,
as the house of Ahab had done   for the daughter of Ahab was his wife.
And he   did what was **evil**   in the sight of YHWH

Ahaziah   (2 Kgs 8:27)
And he WALKED in   the WAY of the   house of Ahab,
and   did what was **evil**   in the sight of YHWH
as the house of Ahab had done   for he was son-in-law to the house of Ahab.

Jehoash   (2 Kgs 12:3-4)
And Jehoash   did what was **right**   in the sight of YHWH, all his days,
because Jehoiada the priest instructed him.
Yet the **high places**   were not taken away.
and the people still sacrificed and burned incense on the high places.

Amaziah   (2 Kgs 14:3-4)
And he   did what was **right**   in the sight of YHWH,
yet not like David   HIS FATHER;
he did in all things as Joash   HIS FATHER   had done
Yet the **high places**   were not taken away.
and the people still sacrificed and burned incense on the high places.

Azariah   (2 Kgs 15:3-4)
And he   did what was **right**   in the sight of YHWH,
according to all that Amaziah   HIS FATHER   had done
Yet the **high places**   were not taken away.
and the people still sacrificed and burned incense on the high places.

Jotham   (2 Kgs 15:34-35a)
And he   did what was **right**   in the sight of YHWH,
according to all that Uzziah   HIS FATHER   had done
Yet the **high places**   were not taken away.
and the people still sacrificed and burned incense on the high places.

Ahaz   (2 Kgs 16:2b-3a)

And he   did not do what was **right**   in the sight of YHWH, his God,

as DAVID   HIS FATHER   had done.

But he WALKED in   the WAY of the   KINGS OF ISRAEL,

Hezekiah   (2 Kgs 18:3-5)

And he   did what was **right**   in the sight of YHWH,

according to all that DAVID   HIS FATHER   had done.

He removed the **high places**,   and broke the pillars, and cut down the Asherah.

And he broke in pieces the bronze serpent that Moses had made,

for until those days the people of Israel had burned incense to it; it was called Nehushtan.

He trusted in YHWH, the God of Israel;

and there was none like him among all the kings of Judah after him [nor who were before him].

JUDGMENT FORMULAS: PATTERN C

for the first set of northern kings
from Jeroboam (start) to Joram (midway)

Israel (Jeroboam)   (1 Kgs 14:15-16)

. . . because they made their Asherim
provoking YHWH   to anger.

And he will give Israel up   for   the **sins**   of **Jeroboam**   which he sinned and
                                                            which he made Israel to sin.

Nadab   (1 Kgs 15:26)
And he   did what was **evil**   in the sight of YHWH
                           and WALKED   in the **way**   of his **father**   and in his sin
                                                                    which he made Israel to sin.

          (1 Kgs 15:30)

*for   the **sins**   of **Jeroboam**   which he sinned and
                                                            which he made Israel to sin,*

*and because of the anger to which he
provoked YHWH, the God of Israel.*

Baasha   (1 Kgs 15:34)
And he   did what was **evil**   in the sight of YHWH
                           and WALKED   in the **way**   of **Jeroboam**   and in his sin
                                                                    which he made Israel to sin.

Elah   *(1 Kgs 16:13)*

*. . . for all   the **sins**   of **Baasha**   which he sinned and
                           the **sins**   of **Elah** his **son**   which he sinned and
                                                                    which they made Israel to sin,*
provoking YHWH, the God of Israel.   to anger by their idols.

Zimri   *(1 Kgs 16:19)*

*. . . and for   his **sins**   which he sinned,*
doing what was **evil**   *in the sight of YHWH*
                           *WALKING   in the **way**   of **Jeroboam**   and in his sin which he committed
                                                                    making Israel to sin.*

Omri   (1 Kgs 16:25-26)
And Omri   did what was **evil**   in the sight of YHWH
                   and did more evil than all who were before him;
                                   and he WALKED   in the **way**   of **Jeroboam**   the son of Nebat   and in his sin
                                                                    which he made Israel to sin,
                           provoking YHWH, the God of Israel,   to anger by their idols.

Ahab   (1 Kgs 16:30-33)
And Ahab the son of Omri
                   did what was **evil**   in the sight of YHWH
                           more than all that were before him; and as if it had been a light thing for him
                                   to WALK   in the **sins**   of **Jeroboam**   the son of Nebat   (vv. 31b-33a)
                           and Ahab continued   to **provoke** YHWH, the God of Israel,   to anger
                   more than all that were before him.

Ahaziah   (1 Kgs 22:53-54)

And he   did what was **evil**   in the sight of YHWH

      and he WALKED   in the **way**   of his **father**

      and   in the **way**   of his **mother**

      and   in the **way**   of **Jeroboam**   the son of Nebat

                                    who made Israel to sin.

He served Baal and worshiped him,

      and **provoked** YHWH, the God of Israel,   to anger

      in every way that   his **father**   had done.

Joram   (2 Kgs 3:2-3)

And he   did what was **evil**   in the sight of YHWH

                          yet not like   his **father**   and his **mother**.

    But he put away the pillar of Baal which   his **father**   had made.

                yet   to the **sins**   of **Jeroboam**   the son of Nebat he clung,

                      which he made Israel to sin   he did not depart from it.

JUDGMENT FORMULAS
OVERVIEW of PATTERNS A, B, C

for
NORTHERN ISRAEL

Names of Kings	#1	#2	#3	#4	#5	#6	#7	#8	#9	#10
PATTERN C										
Israel/Jeroboam		J	x	x				x	x	
Nadab	x-e	J	x x	x		x-w		x x	x	
Baasha	x-e	J	x			x-w		x		
Elah			x	x				xx	x	
Zimri	x-e	J	x	x		x-w		xx+		
Omri	x-e	JbN	x			x-w	x-c	x	x	
Ahab	x-e	JbN		x		x-s	xx-cc		x	
Ahaziah	x-e	JbN	x			xxx-w			x	
Joram	x-e	JbN	x	x	x		xx-ab			
PATTERN A										
Jehu		JbN	x	x	x					
Jehoahaz	x-e	JbN	x	x	x	(x)				
Jehoash	x-e	JbN	x	x	x					
Jeroboam	x-e	JbN	x	x	x					
Zechariah	x-e	JbN	x	x	x		x-a			
Shallum	nil									
Menahem	x-e	JbN	x	x	x					
Pekahiah	x-e	JbN	x	x	x					
Pekah	x-e	JbN	x	x	x					
Hoshea	x-e						x-b			

for
JUDAH

Names of Kings	#1	#2	#3	#4	#5	#6	#7	#8	#9	#10
PATTERN B										
Judah/Rehoboam	x-e									
Abijam						x-s				
Asa	x-r						x-a1			x-0.5
Jehoshaphat	x-(r)				x	x-w				x
Jehoram	x-e					x-w	x-b			
Ahaziah	x-e					x-w	x-b			
Jehoash	x-r									x
Amaziah	x-r						xx-a1a			x
Azariah	x-r						x-a			x
Jotham	x-r						x-a			x
Ahaz	x-(e)					x-w	x-a1			
Hezekiah	x-r						x-a1			

The listed elements

Element #1 e/r	he did what was evil/right in the sight of YHWH	
Element #2	Jeroboam/Jeroboam ben Nebat	Element #6 w/s he walked in the way of/the sins of X
Element #3	which he made Israel to sin	Element #7 comparison: types a, a1, b, and c
Element #4	plain reference to: the sins of X	Element #8 which he sinned OR and in his sin
Element #5	he did not depart from	Element #9 to provoke to anger
		Element #10 the high places were not taken away

Comparison types (#7):   a = with father(s);   a1 = with David his father;   b = with some other(s);   c = of degree (more/less than)

JUDGMENT FORMULAS: PATTERN B/C
southern kings
from Manasseh to Josiah

Manasseh   (2 Kgs 21:2-6)
And he   did what was **evil**   in the sight of YHWH
               according to the abominable practices of the nations whom YHWH drove out before the people of Israel.
And he rebuilt the **high places** which Hezekiah HIS FATHER   had destroyed;
               and he erected altars for Baal, and made an Asherah as Ahab KING OF ISRAEL had done,
               and worshiped all the host of heaven and served them.
               And he built altars in the house of YHWH, of which YHWH had said, "In Jerusalem will I put my name."
               And he built altars for all the host of heaven in the two courts of the house of YHWH.
He did much **evil**   in the sight of YHWH
                    provoking him   to anger.   (vv. 7-9)

Amon   (2 Kgs 21:20-22)
And he   did what was **evil**   in the sight of YHWH
                         according to all that Manasseh   HIS FATHER   had done
               And he WALKED in   all the WAY in which   HIS FATHER   walked
                         and served the idols that   HIS FATHER   served, and worshiped them.
               He forsook YHWH, the God of   HIS FATHERS,
               and did not WALK in   the WAY of YHWH

Josiah   (2 Kgs 22:2; 23:25)
And he   did what was **right**   in the sight of YHWH,
                    and WALKED in   all the WAY of David   HIS FATHER;   and he did not turn aside
                                                                              to the right hand or to the left
Before him there was no king like him, who turned to YHWH
               with all his heart and with all his soul and with all his might,
               according to all the law of Moses;
               nor did any like him arise after him.

JUDGMENT FORMULAS: PATTERN D
the four southern kings
after Josiah

Jehoahaz   (2 Kgs 23:32—son of Josiah; three-month reign)
And he did what was evil in the sight of YHWH
according to all that his *fathers* had done.

Jehoiakim   (2 Kgs 23:37—son of Josiah; eleven-year reign)
And he did what was evil in the sight of YHWH
according to all that his *fathers* had done.

Jehoiachin   (2 Kgs 24:9—son of Jehoiakim; three-month reign)
And he did what was evil in the sight of YHWH
according to all that his *father* had done.

Zedekiah   (2 Kgs 24:19—uncle of Jehoiachin,
                              brother of Jehoahaz,
                              son of Josiah; eleven-year reign)
And he did what was evil in the sight of YHWH
according to all that *Jehoiakim* had done.

Index of Biblical References

All citations follow the numbering of the NRSV.